CANADA
Our Century, Our Story

John Fielding
Faculty of Education
Queen's University, Kingston

Rosemary Evans
Branksome Hall
Toronto

Jan Haskings-Winner
Toronto DSB

Robert Mewhinney
Toronto DSB

Tracey Robertson
Toronto CDSB

Gord Sly
Limestone DSB

Jim Terry
Lambton Kent DSB

NELSON
THOMSON LEARNING

Australia • Canada • Mexico • Singapore • Spain • United Kingdom • United States

Canada: Our Century, Our Story
by John Fielding, Rosemary Evans

Director of Publishing:
David Steele

Publisher:
Carol Stokes

Executive Editor:
Jessica Pegis

Managing Editor:
Norma Kennedy

Project Editor:
Glen Herbert

Senior Development Editor:
Dayne Ogilvie

Contributing Writers:
Martha Ayim, Phil Hall, Su Mei Ku, David MacDonald, Todd Mercer, Dayne Ogilvie, Denyse O'Leary, Gillian Scobie, Neil Santin

Development Editors:
Su Mei Ku, David MacDonald, Todd Mercer, Denyse O'Leary, Stephen Sanborn, Gillian Scobie, Susan McNish

Art Direction:
Suzanne Peden

Cover Design:
Peter Papayanakis

Interior Design:
Suzanne Peden, Julie Greener, Katherine Strain

Layout and Composition:
Marnie Benedict, Susan Calverley, Zenaida Diores, Erich Falkenberg, Anne Goodes, Linda O'Neill, Peter Papayanakis, Ken Phipps, Katherine Strain

Illustrations:
Andrew Breithaupt, Steven Corrigan, Deborah Crowle, Nicolas Debon, John Fraser, Norman Lanting, Henry Van Der Linde

Production Coordinator:
Julie Preston

Permissions:
Vicki Gould, Karen Taylor

Printer:
Transcontinental Printing Inc.

COPYRIGHT © 2001 by Nelson Thomson Learning, a division of Thomson Canada Limited. Nelson Thomson Learning is a registered trademark used herein under license.

Printed and bound in Canada
1 2 3 4 04 03 02 01

For more information contact Nelson Thomson Learning, 1120 Birchmount Road, Scarborough, Ontario, M1K 5G4. Or you can visit our internet site at http://www.nelson.com

ALL RIGHTS RESERVED. No part of this work covered by the copyright hereon may be reproduced, transcribed, or used in any form or by any means—graphic, electronic, or mechanical, including photocopying, recording, taping, web distribution or information storage and retrieval systems—without the written permission of the publisher.

For permission to use material from this text or product, contact us by
Tel 1-800-730-2214
Fax 1-800-730-2215
www.thomsonrights.com

Canadian Cataloguing in Publication Data

Fielding, John (John F.)
   Nelson history 10

For use in grade 10 in Ontario.
ISBN 0-17-620001-0

1. Canada – History – 20th century – Juvenile literature. I. Evans, Rosemary, 1951- . II. Title.

FC600.F53 2000
971.06   C00-930136-4
F1034.2. F53 2000

TABLE OF CONTENTS

Acknowledgements	vi
Historical Inquiry Model	viii
The Government of Canada	ix
Prime Ministers of Canada	ix

Unit One
Canada Comes of Age 1891–1928

Chapter 1 A New Century	**4**
Farewell to a Founder	6
The Laurier Years	8
An Economy on the Move	18
Chapter 2 Canada and the British Empire	**28**
Part of the British Empire	30
Troubles with the Neighbour	33
Women: The Struggle for Rights	37
Arts and Leisure in Canada	42
Chapter 3 Canada and World War I	**52**
The Causes of World War I	54
Life in the Trenches	62
The War at Home	66
The Conscription Crisis	69
The War at Sea and in the Air	71
The War Unfolds	72
The Paris Peace Settlement	77
Chapter 4 The Roaring Life in Canada	**84**
Political Change After WW I	88
Changing Social Attitudes	94
Prosperity in the 1920s	102
An Outpouring of Canadian Culture	106

Unit Two
Depression and War 1929–1945

Chapter 5 The Great Depression	**118**
Black Tuesday: The 1929 Stock Market Crash	120
The Government Responds	124
Conditions of the Unemployed Across the Nation	127
Bennett's New Deal	132
Voices of Regional Discontent	135
Culture and the Arts: Escape from Harsh Reality	141
Chapter 6 Towards Autonomy and War	**148**
Towards Autonomy	150
International Developments After World War I	154
The Road to War	164

Chapter 7 Canada and World War II — 172
To War Again? — 174
Hitler Engages the West — 175
A Mouse Comes to the Aid of an Elephant — 176
Canadians Go into Combat — 179
The Call for More Personnel — 184
Canadian Economic and Social Conditions — 188
The Plan to End the War: Operation Overlord — 190
The End of the War — 196
The Holocaust — 198

Unit Three
**A North American Nation
1945-1967**

Chapter 8 Canada, a North American Nation — 208
The Postwar Boom — 210
The Labour Movement — 216
They Came … and They Shopped — 218
American Culture in Canada — 221
Promoting Canadian Cultural Identity — 222
Women in Postwar Canada: A Difficult Transition — 227
The Native Peoples — 230

Chapter 9 Politics in Canada — 234
Newfoundland Enters Confederation — 236
The Liberals Control Canadian Politics — 238
The Emergence of the Welfare State — 240
The Diefenbaker Years — 243
The Liberals Return — 245
Canada on Stage — 250

Chapter 10 Canada and the World — 256
A World Divided — 258
The Cold War — 260
Defences and Insecurities — 263
Canada Enters the Atomic Age — 267
The Race for Space — 268
Nuclear Weapons: A Balance of Terror — 269
Canada and the United Nations — 273
Canada, a Middle Power — 274

Unit Four
**Changing Times
1967-1983**

Chapter 11 Living in Trudeau's Canada — 284
Pierre Trudeau and the "Just Society" — 286
Culture and Counterculture — 291
The Women's Movement — 298
The Native Peoples — 302
Trudeau's Last Term — 307

Chapter 12 The Question of Quebec — 310
Competing Visions of Canada — 312
The Parti Québécois: A Democratic Option — 315
Legislating to Protect French — 318
Language Politics and Francophones Outside Quebec — 322
The Constitution Versus the Referendum — 323
The New Constitution — 328

Chapter 13   The Economy, the West, and the United States — 336
World Economic Change and Canada — 338
Economic Choices with a Price Tag — 339
Canada During the Oil Crisis — 343
US Investment and Canadian Independence — 347
Canada Versus Alberta: Western Alienation — 352
Foreign Policy and the US — 356

Unit Five
**Into a New Century
1984-1999**

Chapter 14   1984: A New Direction — 364
A New Prime Minister — 366
Era of the Charter — 378
Arts and Culture — 385

Chapter 15   Unfinished Business — 394
Federalism Under Fire — 396
The Native Peoples' Push for Justice — 403
Canada's Environmental Issues — 411
Winds of Change in Canadian Politics — 414

Chapter 16   Global Forces — 422
A Turning Point: The Chernobyl Nuclear Accident — 424
War and Peacekeeping — 426
Environmentalism: A Global Concern — 434
Human Rights: Canada's Policy Abroad — 436
The Global Economy — 440
The Force of Technology in Globalization — 446
Shaping Policies in the Global Village — 448

Chapter 17   What History Teaches — 452
Bookends to the Century: Wilfrid Laurier and Jean Chrétien — 454
What is "Canadian"? — 457
The Women's Movement — 460
Technology and Progress — 462
Look Back — 463

Glossary — 464
Index — 467
Credits — 472

ACKNOWLEDGEMENTS

To Dianne, my friend and partner of 36 years, and to Jennifer and Brendan, our children whom we love so very much, thank you.

Thank you to all Grade 10 teachers of Canadian history who have the daunting task and wonderful opportunity to turn students on to history, especially the history of this incredible country.

To Canadians of the past, both famous and everyday, who contributed to the creating and building of Canada through your decisions, sweat, blood, persistence, parenting, and citizenship. As I heard someone once say about the Fathers of Confederation, "You build better than you know." I would say the same about many Canadians.

A special thank you to Jessica Pegis for inviting me to work with her and the Nelson Thomson team on this project. And thanks to Publisher Carol Stokes and Director of Publishing David Steele. Your supportive presence was noteworthy. I appreciate your confidence in me and your expression of continued encouragement. Thanks to this project, I have also had the privilege to work with teachers in the implementation of the new Canadian History in the Twentieth Century courses.

Thank you to Rosemary Evans, whose work I have admired for many years, for agreeing to be co-senior author. It has been a pleasure. Thank you to my colleagues, the teachers who contributed to the writing of *Canada: Our Century, Our Story*. This is part of your story now. And thank you to those who reviewed this book, not only for your critical observations and suggestions but also for your positive comments and encouragement. We listened carefully to you. Thank you to all the editors who worked with our team of writers for polishing and shining our work in order to make this textbook read well and look great.

Finally, a thank you to Mark Cressman, James Reeve, Deborah Millard, Patricia Willis, Teresa Tamburro, Barbara Vogt, Sharon Lee, Dallas Trottier, and all the sales staff and marketing staff who helped me through the many workshop presentations. You are the greatest.

John Fielding
Kingston, Ontario

Advisory Panel

George Adams,
Dufferin–Peel CDSB

Tony Coccimiglio,
Dufferin–Peel CDSB

Tom Goodman,
Lakehead DSB

Natasia Kotsovolos,
Upper Canada DSB

Joe Tersigni,
Wellington CDSB

Mike Clare,
York Region DSB

Tom Conklin,
Ottawa–Carleton CDSB

Sandra Fryer,
Peel DSB

Lela Lilko,
Peel DSB

George Wrobel,
Toronto CDSB

Reviewers

Laina Andrews,
Kawartha Pine Ridge DSB

Bill Brown,
Durham DSB

James Cocchetto,
York Region CDSB

Vince Dannetta,
York Region DSB

Halton Doyle,
Ottawa–Carleton CDSB

Dave Isherwood,
Lakehead DSB

Peter Kehoe,
Ottawa–Carleton CDSB

Ken Manderville,
Hastings and Prince Edward DSB

Marian B. Moon,
Hastings and Prince Edward DSB

Tina Noel,
Renfrew County CDSB

Joe Sheik,
Thames Valley DSB

Steven Sliwa,
Renfrew County DSB

Sandy Viik,
Lakehead DSB

Stephen Bloom,
York Region DSB

James H. Carter,
Lakehead DSB

Paulette Courchene,
Ottawa–Carleton DSB

Sandy Dobec,
Ottawa–Carleton CDSB

Marianne Froehlich,
Durham DSB

Jane Isherwood,
Durham DSB

Hugh MacPherson,
Durham DSB

Chuck McWhirter,
Hastings and Prince Edward DSB

John Murphy,
Ottawa–Carleton DSB

Scott Reaney,
Upper Canada DSB

Gary Simons,
Upper Canada DSB

Carmen Spiteri-Johnson,
York Region DSB

Eero Vuorinen,
Lakehead DSB

Historical Inquiry Model

Focus on an issue, event, individual

- Begin to formulate questions to guide your initial research
- Who? What? Where? When? Why?

Survey to discover sources of information available on your topic

- Start with your textbook
- Use encyclopedias and other texts
- Move from general sources to more specific sources that focus on the topic

Formulate a research or thesis question to guide your research

- Thesis or research questions may vary from descriptive (What?) to analytical (Why?) to evaluative (To what extent? Which explanation best explains?)
- You may need to rework your thesis question as you learn more

Research to answer your question

- Locate a variety of information sources
- Determine the relevance and reliability of the information you obtain
- Look for different perspectives or points of view
- Be aware of bias
- Decide how you will record the information
  - identify main ideas and supporting details
  - differentiate facts from opinions
- Record the sources of your information for use in a bibliography and relevant page numbers for use in footnotes or endnotes

Organize your information to answer your question

- Classify and catagorize the information you have collected
- Look for relationships
- Use charts and graphic organizers

Determine the answer to your question

- Synthesize and evaluate your findings
- Formulate a thesis statement that succinctly answers your questions
- Be sure that your thesis statement really answers your question
- Determine the arguments and supporting evidence that will help you elaborate on or defend your answer

Decide how you will communicate your findings

- Consider the purpose of your research and your audience
- You might consider
  - an essay
  - an oral presentation
  - a web page
  - a debate
  - a role-play

The Government of Canada

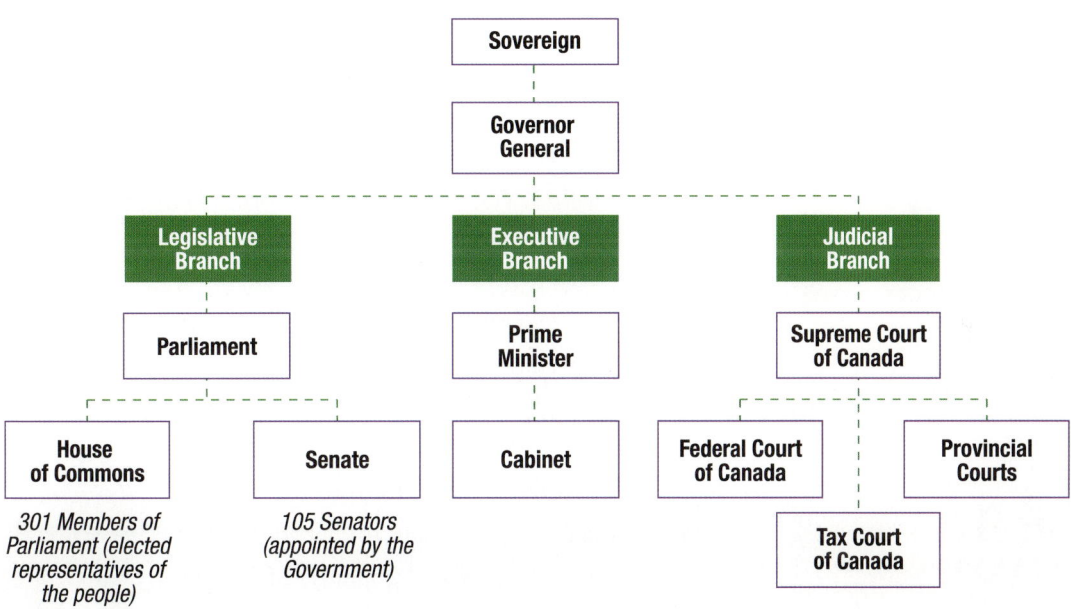

Prime Ministers of Canada

Dates	Prime Minister	Dates	Prime Minister
July 1867–November 1873	**Sir John A. Macdonald**	August 1930–October 1935	**R. B. Bennett**
November 1873–October 1878	**Sir Alexander Mackenzie**	October 1935–November 1948	**William Lyon Mackenzie King**
October 1878–June 1891	**Sir John A. Macdonald**	November 1948–June 1957	**Louis St. Laurent**
June 1891–November 1892	**Sir John J. C. Abbott**	June 1957–April 1963	**John Diefenbaker**
December 1892–December 1894	**Sir John S. Thompson**	April 1963–April 1968	**Lester B. Pearson**
December 1894–April 1896	**Sir Mackenzie Bowell**	April 1968–June 1979	**Pierre Elliott Trudeau**
May 1896–October 1896	**Sir Charles Tupper**	June 1979–March 1980	**Joe Clark**
July 1896–October 1911	**Sir Wilfrid Laurier**	March 1980–June 1984	**Pierre Elliott Trudeau**
October 1911–July 1920	**Sir Robert Borden**	June 1984–September 1984	**John Turner**
July 1920–December 1921	**Arthur Meighen**	September 1984–June 1993	**Brian Mulroney**
December 1921–June 1926	**William Lyon Mackenzie King**	June 1993–October 1993	**Kim Campbell**
June 1926–September 1926	**Arthur Meighen**	October 1993–	**Jean Chrétien**
September 1926–August 1930	**William Lyon Mackenzie King**		

Unit 1

Canada Comes of Age

1891–1928

As the 1800s gave way to the 1900s, Canada underwent dramatic changes. The first 30 years of the new century brought in a growing population of immigrants, spectacular technological advancements in transportation and communcation, and giant political and legal gains for women. Planes, trains, and automobiles constantly evolved, and created an increasingly mobile population. The telephone alone opened up the world for everyone.

But times were also hard for many people, with poverty, political upheavals, prohibition, and repressive policies and attitudes towards minority groups. Political unrest in Europe involved Britain and, by association, Canada when it boiled over into World War I. After proving themselves a worthy force during the War, Canadians were ready to "let loose" and enjoy a more prosperous economy during the Roaring Twenties.

After WW I, Canada took steps to assert its independence from Britain, and to stabilize a positive relationship with the United States. It was an ongoing struggle, but Canadians established their own unique identity.

The start of the century was bumpy but progressive. Canada matured, with renewed national and international strength and stability.

Prime Ministers	Dates of Office
Sir John J. C. Abbott	1891–1892
Sir John S. Thompson	1892–1894
Sir Mackenzie Bowell	1894–1896
Sir Charles Tupper	1896
Sir Wilfrid Laurier	1896–1911
Sir Robert Borden	1911–1920
Arthur Meighen	1920–1921; 1926
William Lyon Mackenzie King	1921–1926; 1926–1930

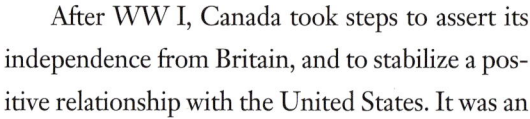

Anticipation Guide

In this unit, you will:

- learn about patterns and problems of immigration
- summarize the main events of John A. Macdonald's life
- explore the rocky beginnings of organized labour groups
- investigate both sides of the Alaska Boundary Dispute
- identify examples of technological developments that affected Canadians' daily lives
- identify specific "firsts" for women in many areas
- discover the contributions of Canadians to the sports world
- explore how conscription divided Canada
- research the causes of World War I and Canada's initial involvement
- explore Canada's and individuals' contributions to WW I and to its victories
- identify symptoms of Canada's changing relationships with Britain and the United States
- explore the link between artistic endeavours and the Canadian identity
- examine the ongoing struggles and achievements of aboriginal Canadians

1950 1960 1970 1980 1990 2000 2010

1 A New Century

Focus Questions

Economic Conditions and Structures
What policies adopted at the turn of the century by the Laurier government encouraged the changes and subsequent prosperity of this era?

Demographic Patterns
Who did not share in the progress and prosperity of the era? Why and how were they excluded?

How were some people encouraged to immigrate to Canada, and some discouraged from immigrating?

Scientific and Technological Impact
What inventions and technological advancements at this time significantly changed people's lives?

At the turn of the twentieth century, Canadians were in an optimistic mood. Liberal leader Wilfrid Laurier, who became prime minister in 1896, promised that "the twentieth century shall be the century of Canada." Laurier's government pursued an ambitious agenda—promoting Canadian industry, building more railways, and, above all, opening the West to immigration from Europe.

The arrival of half a million Europeans who spoke neither English nor French started Canada towards multiculturalism. But in Laurier's time, multiculturalism did not mean equality or equal opportunity. British immigrants were preferred, and non-Europeans, such as Chinese or Sikhs, were discouraged or forbidden. The huge waves of immigration also threatened the very survival of the Native peoples. The federal government's response was to enact many laws and policies to make them give up their land and culture and assimilate into the mainstream.

Many Canadians enjoyed an improved standard of living during this period because of the new railways, the harnessing of electric power, and new inventions such as the telephone. However, in a society without income tax, social security, or collective bargaining, the gap between rich and poor widened steadily. Some Canadians found life terribly hard, and began to seek relief through protests or strikes. As the century unfolded, these and other issues would be debated, but not always resolved.

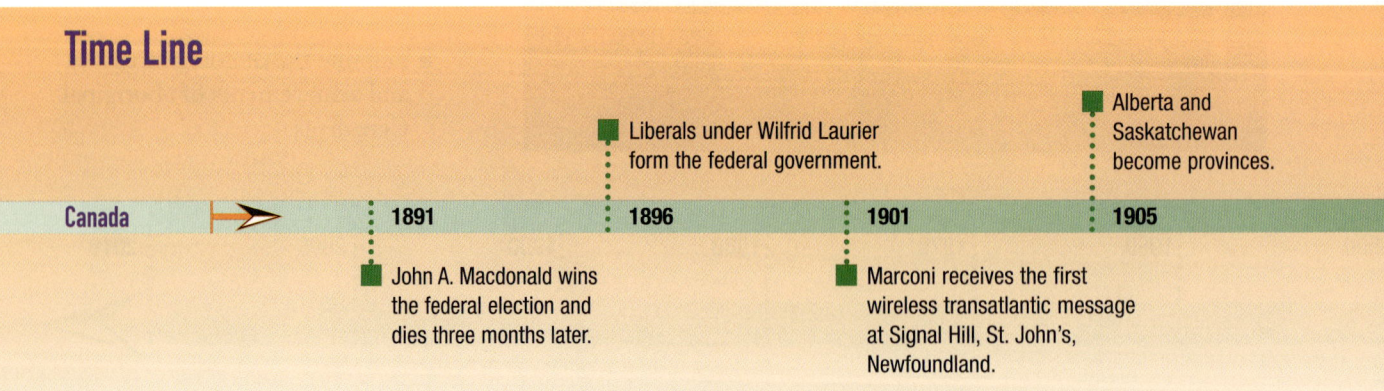

Time Line

Canada

- **1891** — John A. Macdonald wins the federal election and dies three months later.
- **1896** — Liberals under Wilfrid Laurier form the federal government.
- **1901** — Marconi receives the first wireless transatlantic message at Signal Hill, St. John's, Newfoundland.
- **1905** — Alberta and Saskatchewan become provinces.

Perspectives

This photograph was taken on June 5, 1901 and shows Torontonians celebrating a victory during the Boer War. It tells us a lot about the times and the people. Try to place yourself in the picture. What would surprise you the most and make you feel different, or possibly uncomfortable? Step into the picture and recreate the conversations people might be having about Canada—the economy, work, politics, fashion, sports, leisure, the electric streetcars, the cluttered streetscape, the bicycle traffic, the British Empire. What might they say about being Canadian? (Note the flags people are carrying.) How would these conversations be different for a business person, a worker, a recent immigrant, or perhaps a Franco-Ontarian? How would these conversations be different for a boy or a girl, or a rich person or poor person?

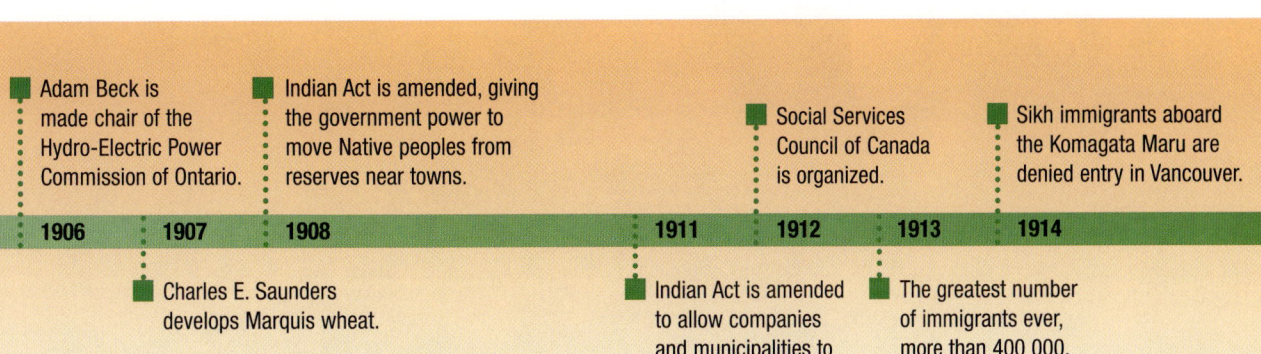

- **1906**: Adam Beck is made chair of the Hydro-Electric Power Commission of Ontario.
- **1907**: Charles E. Saunders develops Marquis wheat.
- **1908**: Indian Act is amended, giving the government power to move Native peoples from reserves near towns.
- **1911**: Indian Act is amended to allow companies and municipalities to expropriate portions of Native reserves.
- **1912**: Social Services Council of Canada is organized.
- **1913**: The greatest number of immigrants ever, more than 400 000, arrive in Canada.
- **1914**: Sikh immigrants aboard the Komagata Maru are denied entry in Vancouver.

FAREWELL TO A FOUNDER

When Patrick J. "Paddy" McFall climbed into the engineer's seat of the black-and-purple draped railway engine on June 10, 1891, he probably knew he was part of history. As McFall released the throttle, the train carrying the body of Sir John A. Macdonald solemnly eased its way out of the crowded Smiths Falls station. All along the route to Kingston, people gathered at every station platform and on roadsides near the tracks. Even lone figures in the field stopped their work to pay their respects to the man, the politician, and the leader who had done more than any other to create the Dominion of Canada.

John A. Macdonald was returning to the city where his family had first arrived in Canada from Scotland in 1819, when he was just four years old. Macdonald was a successful student and apprenticed in a law office. Even without going to university, he soon developed a reputation as a fine lawyer. By age 19, he was involved in local Kingston politics and, in 1844, he was elected to the legislative assembly of the province of Ontario. In 1854, Macdonald was instrumental in creating the Conservative Party. As leader of the government of Upper Canada, he also learned how to work collaboratively with his French-Canadian colleagues, especially his friend George-Étienne Cartier.

Although he initially opposed the idea of Confederation, Macdonald soon became its staunchest advocate. He worked hard at the Charlottetown and Quebec conferences to ensure that Canada would have a strong federal government. As the master lawyer, he drafted two-thirds of the provisions of the British North America Act, Canada's first constitution. On July 1, 1867, the Dominion of Canada was born, and John A. Macdonald was its first prime minister.

The years between 1867 and 1891 held tragedy, scandal, and triumph for Macdonald. In 1873, news leaked out that Macdonald's government had accepted money from US backers of the CPR. The so-called "Pacific Scandal" tainted Macdonald's reputation and

Data File

Sir John A. Macdonald's face is as familiar as the ten-dollar bill. Ironically, Macdonald had recurring financial problems in his personal life and once had to declare bankruptcy.

forced him to resign. In the ensuing election, Alexander Mackenzie and the Liberals triumphed. Undaunted, Macdonald won the 1878 federal election, campaigning on his new National Policy. He won every election after that.

Macdonald never got the chance to retire, although he had often thought about it. At the age of 76 he campaigned hard in the 1891 election, using the slogan "The Old Flag, The Old Policy, The Old Leader." Macdonald won the campaign, but it left him exhausted. He died three months later. Sir John A. Macdonald left an extraordinary legacy. He could truly take credit for the three policies that launched Canada as a nation: Confederation, and the expansion of the number of provinces to include Manitoba (1870), British Columbia (1871), and Prince Edward Island (1873); the building of the first Canadian transcontinental railway (the Canadian Pacific Railway); and, finally, the National Policy.

At the funeral, fellow Conservatives would have remembered the crowds months earlier that had shouted "You'll never die, John A." And they may have wished it were true. For without an obvious successor of Macdonald's stature, there was concern about the very survival of the young Dominion of Canada.

Between 1891 and 1896, four Conservative prime ministers tried to fill Macdonald's shoes. A feeble cabinet chose 70-year-old Sir John Abbott of Montreal from the Senate because he was "not particularly obnoxious to anybody." Fed up with politics, Abbott resigned in 1892. The next prime minister was Sir John Thompson from Halifax, Canada's first Catholic leader. Thompson was only 47, and a decent and honourable leader with the potential for greatness. Unfortunately, he died of a heart attack at Windsor Castle after being honoured by Queen Victoria in 1894. Senator Mackenzie Bowell, an honest but indecisive Orangeman from Belleville, Ontario, became the next prime minister. The Conservative Party ousted him after less than two years. Sir Charles Tupper, known by many as the bullying "War Horse of the Cumberland," became prime minister in 1896. He led the Conservatives into the election of 1896, and defeat.

Paddy McFall, the railway engineer from Ireland, saw many politicians come and go, including Wilfrid Laurier, the prime minister at the turn of the century. But like Laurier, who viewed Canada's future with glowing optimism, McFall's rugged Irish faith allowed him to see the silver lining behind even the darkest cloud.

Up Close

1. As you read pages 6 and 7, list the major events in Macdonald's life. Use your list to create a time line.

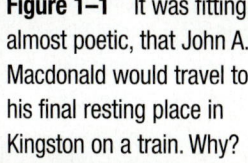

Figure 1–1 It was fitting, almost poetic, that John A. Macdonald would travel to his final resting place in Kingston on a train. Why?

THE LAURIER YEARS

The year 1896 marked a turning point in Canada's history. Laurier and the Liberals gained power, ending years of Conservative rule. Laurier made an elegant prime minister, and was Canada's first charismatic leader. Born in the village of St. Lin, just outside Montreal, Laurier had parents who wanted him to learn English. He put himself through law school by working in a Montreal law office, and entered the House of Commons in 1874. Laurier went on to dominate Liberal politics in Quebec by demonstrating qualities that would mark his leadership following the 1896 election. Faced with sharp divisions of opinion, Laurier avoided confrontation, favouring the "sunny way" of compromise and fairness. His ability to persuade through oratory is illustrated by this speech, given in 1904, with its famous reference to "the century of Canada":

> ... Let me tell you, my fellow countrymen, that the twentieth century shall be the century of Canada and of Canadian development. For the next 75 years, nay for the next 100 years, Canada shall be the star towards which all men who love progress and freedom shall come. To those, sir, who have life before them, let my prayer be this: Remember from this day forth, never to look simply at the horizon as it may be limited by the limits of the Province, but look abroad over all the continent ... and let your motto be: 'Canada first, Canada last, and Canada always.'

Up Close

2. Laurier's quote suggests that he was a fervent Canadian nationalist. Reread the quote and write a definition of the term "nationalist."

Data File

The Métis leader Louis Riel (1844–1885) is considered to be the founder of Manitoba. Riel's drive helped Manitoba join Confederation in 1870 on its own terms, with protection of English- and French-language rights, and education rights for Protestants and Catholics.

Laurier selected the ablest cabinet Canada had ever seen, including three former Liberal premiers. His most strategic move was to appoint Clifford Sifton Minister of the Interior. Sifton's first challenge was to convince Manitoba premier Thomas Greenway to budge on the Manitoba Schools Question. Greenway's government had passed legislation in 1890 that eliminated bilingualism and the separate school system. This had been guaranteed by the Manitoba Act of 1870. By 1896, the situation had become a national crisis, as it placed language, religious, and minority rights in doubt. Laurier came under attack for his indecision. In 1897, Sifton convinced Greenway to alter the legislation. Now Manitoba's minorities could go to school in their own language if they could form classes of ten or more students. Religious instruction would be optional and come at the end of the day. For some Catholics, the settlement was unacceptable. But most Roman Catholic Church leaders took some pleasure in dealing with a French-Canadian and Catholic prime minister. The settlement reduced tensions, but it was still only a compromise. The damage done to English-French relations remained a permanent grievance for French-Canadian nationalists.

Policies for Prosperity

More than most countries, Canada needed foreign investment and foreign markets for its products. In 1896, world economic prospects were flourishing and Canada was on the verge of a boom. The time was ripe for the three developments that would make Macdonald's National Policy succeed. First, Laurier abandoned his campaign for free trade with the US and left the Conservative's

tariffs in place. These placed high tariffs on US and British imports, which protected Canadian manufacturers by giving their products a lower price in the Canadian market. Secondly, Laurier encouraged the building of more railways to promote east-west trade and Western settlement. Finally, as Minister of the Interior, Sifton launched aggressive campaigns to attract an unprecedented number of immigrants. This would create both a massive new workforce and a market for Canadian goods.

Laurier's policies worked because circumstances were right. In 1896, the United States closed its public land to settlement. Overnight the Canadian prairies became the "Last Best West." Given the opportunity, settlers now would choose Canada rather than the United States, including many American settlers. Gold pouring out of South Africa and then the Klondike Gold Rush sent prices for food and other natural products climbing, while shipping prices stayed low. These conditions were ideal for resource-rich Canada, and they created a world market for our products, especially wheat.

Canada was a rich nation in terms of **gross national product** and **per capita income**. It was listed eighth in the world table of industrial development. Compared with most other countries, Canada was highly industrialized and progressive. But there were weaknesses in the economy as well. Canada's dependence on foreign investment and export markets meant that world economic conditions—both good and bad—would determine its rate of growth. Canada's geography was vast, so transportation—mainly railways—had to be expanded and made more efficient. Canada was rich in resources, but these also needed to be developed. The most pressing need, however, was to recruit a labour force.

Up Close

3. As you reread this section, use jot notes to describe Laurier's three "policies for prosperity."

Time to People the Country

The new era was right for the peopling of the country, especially the West. Laurier's prediction that the twentieth century would be "the century of Canada" would not come true without immigrants to settle the land and work on the farms and in the forests, mines, factories, offices, and stores.

Between 1896 and 1914, more than 3 million immigrants came to Canada. More than 1 million settled in the Canadian Prairie. Most people who came spoke English, including more than a million from Britain and about 784 000 from the US. Another 500 000 came from the Ukraine, Germany, Austria, Hungary, Scandinavia, Russia, and Poland. This marked the first time that a large number of non-British and non-French settlers had come to Canada. It changed Canada forever and started the country on the road to multiculturalism.

Figure 1–2 This typical Canadian advertisement gave a very positive impression of life on the farm.

Figure 1–3 Clifford Sifton took to the road, enlisting Canadian farmers in his campaign to attract new immigrants.

The job of enticing immigrants to Canada fell into the energetic hands of Clifford Sifton, the Minister of the Interior. Not content to wait for people to discover Canada, Sifton took Canada to them. He sent bales of pamphlets, piles of posters, and hundreds of speakers armed with magic lantern slides to Britain, the US, and many countries in Europe.

Sifton enlisted editors and farm leaders to join guided tours. Lush prairie produce was sent to win prizes at international agricultural shows. He sent colonization agents to the ports of Europe, where immigrants would set sail to America. He was bluntly indifferent to the old immigration policies that favoured British and English-speaking immigrants. "I think that a stalwart peasant in a sheepskin coat, born on the soil, whose forefathers have been farmers for ten generations, with a stout wife and half-dozen children is good quality," he proclaimed. Sifton's mission was to sell Canada, and he and his agents did not work alone. The railways and shipping companies eagerly offered assisted passage and bonuses to agents and settlers.

WHITE PINE PICTURES

On pages 10 to 16, the stories of the Shumiatchers, Lem Wong, Martha Black, and Bagga Singh have been adapted from *A Scattering of Seeds*. This book is based on a documentary film series about Canada's immigrants, produced by White Pine Pictures. Excerpts from these films are available for viewing in class.

Who Came and Why

It was official government policy to promote immigration, but previous generations of immigrants did not welcome newcomers to Canada. Established immigrants were hostile, often on the grounds that new immigrants were taking away jobs or working too cheaply. The reality was just the opposite. Immigrants expanded markets, provided a workforce, and created jobs.

In addition, Canada's immigration policy was not truly open. The government viewed British immigrants as the most desirable settlers, and it tolerated other ethnic groups because it needed cheap labour. Despite the barriers and hardships, millions of people did come, and they came from many countries for many reasons. Each of them has a place in history and a story that is personal and unique.

The Shumiatchers Came When the Shumiatchers arrived in Alberta in 1909, about 90 000 Jewish immigrants were already living in Canada. The largest communities were in Montreal, Toronto, and Winnipeg. Judah and Chasia Shumiatcher and their eleven children had been born in Russia, but were prisoners in their own country. For generations, Jewish communities in Russia had suffered under the repressive **tsars**. Judah had heard about free land for immigrants in the Canadian West and decided the family would go to Calgary, where a friend had settled.

Historical Inquiry: Analysing/Evaluating Information

Historian at Work

History, Whose History?

Like most people, you probably accept the history you read as fact—a true representation of what happened in the past. However, history is not just a series of facts; it is also a story. The version of history you read about in this text might not be accepted by everyone who reads it.

Modern historians try to be objective about historical facts. Most of them don't deliberately lie about what took place. So why are there so many versions of the same events? One reason is that historical facts are often hard to pin down, even though historians do painstaking research and care deeply about what is true and what is not. Moreover, history and historians themselves are products of a time and culture. History takes a certain form because it mirrors what the historian and the wider world accept as important or good, and what they regard as unimportant or bad. This is what is called **bias**.

Sometimes groups of people are omitted from history, or terribly misrepresented. In our own country, history books published before 1960 bothered very little with the history of women. They often stereotyped the Native peoples as savage and virtually ignored the history of Black and Asian Canadians. You may wonder why students and teachers living in the 1940s or 1950s never noticed this bias. The reason is that Canadian society by and large accepted this world view. People tend to notice these things only when they're left out of the story.

Some historians think that it's important for a country to have a national story—one that is accepted by everyone—because it can build a sense of national identity. In his book *Canada, the Foundations of its Future*, writer Stephen Leacock said he was writing "the story of the making of Canada…to show the foundations of our present national life…"

The drawback to a national story is that it may not be everyone's story. This is especially true in a country like Canada, with its many groups of people and points of view. Some historians think that these differences should be the basis of the story of Canada. Michael Ignatieff, for example, describes history as

Figure 1–4 Historian Michael Ignatieff

> …the story of our arguments: French versus English, native-born versus new arrivals, rich versus poor, race versus race, religion versus religion. It is also the story of how we managed to resolve them, how we created a way of agreeing to disagree.

In spite of these debates, and perhaps because of them, historians take ever greater care to write history which can stand the test of time, and be meaningful to all readers of the story of human progress.

Activities

1. Have you ever told a story about a past event or incident that you observed, then discovered that others had a different version of the same event? Outline reasons that might explain why different people might have different accounts of the past.

2. Stephen Leacock wrote during World War II. Read his quote carefully. What might be his bias?

3. Reread Michael Ignatieff's quote. State in your own words what he feels is the purpose of studying history.

Figure 1–5 The Calgary Stampede is an annual event that still captures the spirit of Canada's West.

Up Close

4. Choose one of the immigrants whose stories you are reading on these pages. In the role of that person, write two diary entries—one written just before leaving your home country for Canada, and another written soon after you arrive in Canada.

They arrived in Alberta and received a quarter section of land outside Calgary. Although the Shumiatchers, now the Smiths, were experienced farmers, they were drawn to the growing city of Calgary. Judah had carried a Torah scroll, the first of its kind in the city, all the way from Russia. He became the shamas, or sextant, for the synagogue. The Hebrew Free School opened in 1912, and Judah became one of its first instructors, teaching Hebrew. Soon all the Shumiatchers were in Calgary and the family prospered. They mastered English and quickly adapted to the ways of a cowboy town. Indeed, it was Calgary's cowboy identity that brought them success. Morris converted an establishment that cleaned and blocked hats into a hat manufacturer and retailer. He made "Smithbuilt" hats, eventually producing the famous white cowboy hat that has become synonymous with Calgary and its Stampede.

Lem Wong Came Lem Wong was sent to Canada in 1897 by his mother just as British Columbia was trying to close its doors to Chinese immigrants. His uncle already lived in Vancouver, and paid his $50 **head tax**. For the past 50 years, the Chinese had been crossing the Pacific to come to *gum sahn hak* (the Golden Mountain) to make their fortunes and return to China. They came to build railways, to find gold in the Cariboo, and to work hard. What Lem Wong didn't know was that about 1500 Chinese had died laying the tracks for the railway and that Chinese were paid only half the wages of White workers.

After only five months in Vancouver, Lem Wong hopped a freight train. He travelled across Canada, finding small jobs in many towns before stopping in Sydney, Cape Breton. Here he often worked 14-hour days scrubbing clothes, six or seven days a week. He slept under the counter of the shop—or on the ironing board. Often he was called humiliating names, but Lem Wong didn't fight back. Instead, he studied his customers. He remembered their names. He asked them questions about their homes; sometimes they asked him questions about his. Lem's curiosity got the best of his customers and they grew to like him.

After five hard years saving his money, Lem Wong returned to China to find a wife. But when he tried to bring Toye back to Canada in 1903, the head tax had been raised to $500 (comparable to $10 000 today). He learned of other immigration policies that had been put in place to stem the flow of Chinese wives. He now had to be a merchant—restaurants and laundries didn't count. Lem Wong returned to Canada alone, leaving his wife to give birth to his son in China. He moved to London, Ontario and succeeded with a fruit-and-vegetable shop. In 1912, he finally brought his wife and their nine-year-old son Victor to Canada.

Figure 1–6 Members of Calgary's Chinese community meet with city officials on October 13, 1910. During the building of the railway, Calgary's Chinatown was forced to relocate.

Despite discrimination and humiliating government policies, Chinese Canadians spread out from British Columbia all across the country, opening laundries and restaurants. Lem Wong opened Wong's Cafe in London. His friendly manner made customers feel welcome and his business grew, as did his family. His eight children, all with English names, grew up in the shadow of the cafe. In 1947 the Chinese Immigration Act was repealed and the vote was finally extended to Asian Canadians. Lem and Toye Wong's legacy to their chosen country was their children: three doctors, a professor of chemistry, a draftsperson, and a lawyer.

Many Ukrainians Came On September 7, 1891, Vasyl Eleniak and Ivan Pylyiw disembarked in Montreal and soon travelled west. They were the first Ukrainian farmers to immigrate to Canada and they wrote back to their relatives and friends in Ukraine with encouraging reports on farming in Canada. With the active support of the Canadian government, especially after 1896, Ukrainian farmers were recruited to immigrate to Canada West. Between 1891 and 1914, more than 150 000 settled on the prairies between Winnipeg and Edmonton. They claimed their land and cleared it under very difficult conditions. Often their first home would be a soddie, a shelter made of sod. To make ends meet, the men often had to find work in mining, the forests, the factories, or building railways. The women would be left to run the farm and raise the children.

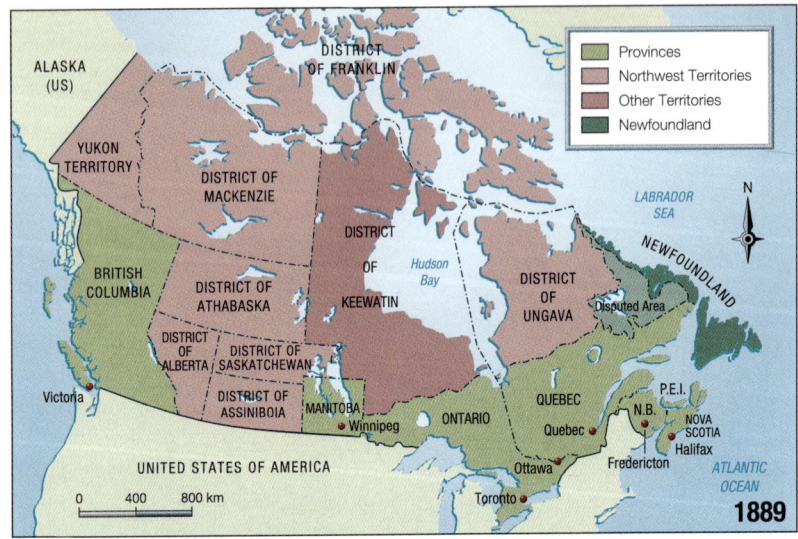

Figure 1–7 The map of Canada was being redrawn at the turn of the century.

Martha Black, an American, Came Martha Purdy Black came to the West from Chicago in 1898, the same year that the Yukon was named a territory. She came to retrieve a fortune in gold from the Klondike. She stayed and became the "First Lady of the Yukon" when her husband, George, was named commissioner of the Yukon Territory in 1912.

Martha Black was not typical of the 740 000 Americans, many of them returning Canadians, who immigrated to Canada between 1890 and 1914. Most American immigrants were farmers who wanted the free or cheap land in the Canadian West, which was opening up with the building of even more railways by the Laurier government.

It was Black's spirit of adventure that lured her from Chicago's high society and onto the track of the Klondike Gold Rush in 1898. Unlike most of the more than 30 000 gold rush stampeders who travelled to the Yukon, Black did not leave as abruptly as she came. She did leave at one point, but her privileged life in Chicago now seemed stifling. She felt trapped. She returned to the Yukon, and stayed to invent a new life for herself as a successful sawmill owner and business person. In 1935 her husband, George Black, became too ill to defend his seat in the House of Commons. At the age of 70, Martha Black ran in his place and became the second woman ever to be elected to Canada's parliament.

Bagga Singh Almost Didn't Come Most Canadians caught their first glimpse of Sikhs in 1902, when a military contingent crossed Canada on its way to England and the coronation of King Edward VII. Canadians were astonished by their appearance and military professionalism. These Sikhs returned to India with stories of a wonderful land waiting to be settled by British subjects such as themselves. More than 5000 South Asians, 90 percent of them Sikhs, came to British Columbia before Asian immigration was banned in 1908.

Change and Continuity: Demographic Patterns

Flashpoint

Entry Barred: The Komagata Maru

The *Komagata Maru* had been at sea for seven weeks when it arrived at Victoria's quarantine station on May 21, 1914. There were 376 passengers on board, including two women and three children.

Gurdit Singh, a businessman, had hired the steamer to carry Sikh immigrants on a direct passage from India to Canada. This had become a requirement after the Canadian government amended the Immigration Act in 1906 in an effort to stop Asian immigration. Two days later the ship pulled into Vancouver, but the Canadian government denied it entry. The Sikh passengers became prisoners on the ship and were even forbidden to make contact with Vancouver's Sikh community.

But word did reach Vancouver's Sikh community, which launched a court challenge. More than a month passed. With supplies of food and water blockaded, conditions on board became critical. Immigration officials then served passengers deportation papers and ordered the captain to leave the harbour. The Sikhs who controlled the ship refused, however, and the standoff became an international incident.

Finally, on July 23, the *HMCS Rainbow* escorted the *Komagata Maru* out of Vancouver's harbour. Canada's navy consisted of only two ships. In other words, the government deployed half of its navy to prevent Sikhs, who were also British subjects, from landing in Canada. The government had proved its point: East Indians were not welcome in Canada, and it would break its own laws to keep them out. Not until 1947 would Sikhs be granted full citizenship and the right to vote.

Discrimination against Sikhs did not end with the *Komagata Maru* incident. In 1991, controversy erupted when a Sikh RCMP officer demanded the right to wear his turban—a Sikh religious custom—rather than the regular Mountie hat. The RCMP eventually allowed it, and constable Baltej Singh Dhillon graduated with his classmates.

In December 1999, 29-year-old Pardeep Singh Nagra was prevented from competing in the Canadian Boxing Championship at Campbell River, BC because of his beard, which he wears for religious reasons. Boxing officials ruled that beards are forbidden by international regulations and pose a potential danger. Nagra had worn a net over his beard when he won the Ontario light flyweight championship earlier in 1999, but this didn't satisfy the national boxing officials. Nagra filed a human rights complaint and an Ontario court affirmed his right to compete in the championship.

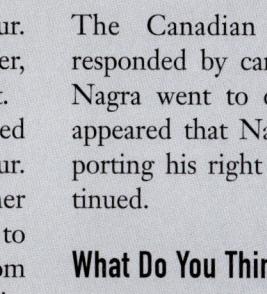

Figure 1–8   Pardeep Singh Nagra

The Canadian Amateur Boxing Association responded by cancelling the light-flyweight class. Nagra went to court again. In January 2000, it appeared that Nagra had won a court order supporting his right to fight, but the legal fight continued.

What Do You Think?

1. Why would the Canadian government have forbidden the Sikhs on board the *Komagata Maru* to talk to other members of the Sikh community in Vancouver? What would happen today?

A New Century

Bagga Singh was lured away from his family, children, and wife in India by stories of opportunities in BC. In 1913, he snuck into Canada via the US. Vancouver was hostile to foreigners, but cheap labour was in short supply. Bagga found work in a sawmill and lived in the cramped quarters of a bunkhouse. British Columbia was producing 60 percent of Canada's sawn lumber, and Sikhs working in those mills were helping to house the growing, prosperous nation. Ironically, Sikhs usually lived in ghettos that moved from job to job. Singh saved every cent he could and sent it home to India. The Sikhs lived a supportive, communal life that was virtually without women—only nine Sikh women were allowed into Canada between 1904 and 1920. And Sikhs could not vote, enter the professions, or get government contracts

Bagga Singh spent 17 lonely years working in BC's sawmills before he was finally allowed to bring his wife and children to Canada. Today, three generations later, Sikh communities in BC prize education and have moved steadily towards affluence. However, it may take many more generations before the discrimination they have endured comes to an end.

Up Close

5. Using the photo and caption for information, draw up a list of pros and cons for a British woman who is trying to decide whether or not to immigrate to Canada to work for Penman's in the early 1900s.

About A Million British Came: Some Were Children The total number of British immigrants, including English, Scottish, Irish, and Welsh, during this period was about 1 million. Of this number, 77 000 were boys and girls known as "home children." They were sent to work on farms and in Canadian homes by British **philanthropic organizations** such as the Barnardo and Annie MacPherson homes. Leslie Henry Baden Powell Fielding, a 12-year-old with a long, important-sounding name, was abandoned by his mother on December 28, 1912 in the Hackney workhouse in London, England. He was persuaded to go to Canada

Figure 1–9 Many British women came to Canada to work in the textile industry. In the early 1900s, the Canadian Manufacturers' Association helped the Penman Company representatives recruit experienced "women textile workers" in Britain. Penman's was Canada's largest knit-goods manufacturer, and it could not find enough skilled workers. Penman's offered the women wages that were 50 percent higher than what they could get in Britain. Still, women workers in Canada earned only half the salary of men.

with stories of "cowboys and Indians." When he arrived in August 1913, Fielding's new life would have little to do with adventure or fun. He spent his first few months in Canada living with the farm animals in a barn.

On Christmas Day, neighbours saw a light burning in the barn and thought this was unusual, since the farmer was away. They decided to investigate and found a very cold, frightened young boy inside. The Peppers took Fielding into their home, where he was treated decently until he was old enough to leave.

Canada today is a country of more than 30 million people. Clearly, decisions made by politicians like Laurier and Sifton created the foundations for Canada to grow and develop at the turn of the twentieth century. But we can also see how it was the difficult, risky decisions made by millions of individual immigrants that built on these foundations and created the country we now inhabit.

Immigration and Canada's Native Peoples

For the Laurier government, immigration was the key to growth and prosperity. For Native peoples, it was just the opposite. Native leaders knew that their old way of life was passing. They feared for their cultures and the lives of their children. As immigrants invaded western Canada, disease, malnutrition, and low morale continued to take their toll: the very survival of Canada's First Nations was in doubt.

Settlers and the Canadian government tended to see the Native peoples as obstacles to progress. First Nations were pressured to move to reserves and to sign treaties giving up their claim to their traditional land. The Klondike Gold Rush was the catalyst in 1899 for Treaty 8, one of the largest concessions of land in Canadian history. In many cases, Native leaders actually asked to negotiate treaties, but government leaders would arrive with the terms already drawn up. Worse, they did not write down conditions that the Native peoples believed had been agreed to orally.

Figure 1–10 A family waits during the signing of Treaty 8.

Native peoples and their cultures were seen as inferior, or "savage." Most officials of the Department of Indian Affairs believed that the "solution" was to **assimilate** Native peoples within the dominant Canadian—or British—way of life. In 1883, the federal government introduced its first White-run boarding schools. Native children were forced to speak English and give up all traces of their cultures. By 1900, there were 64 **residential schools**. In the decades ahead, thousands of Native children would be physically, emotionally, and sexually abused in these institutions.

As the century progressed, the Canadian government continued to **marginalize** the Native peoples. Frank Oliver, Minister of the Interior and Indian Affairs, amended the Indian Act in 1908 so that aboriginal peoples could be removed from reserves near towns with more than 8000 residents. In 1911, he passed a further amendment that allowed municipalities and companies to expropriate portions of reserves for roads, railways, or other public purposes. Under this law, the Blackfoot were forced to sell half of their reserve for about $1 million. In British Columbia, the Laurier government faced challenges to its policies. In 1907, the Nisga'a First Nation formed a committee to claim **title** to their ancestral lands. They said that they had signed no treaties, had never been conquered, and that the concept of reserves did not apply to them. In 1913, the Nisga'a took their case to the British Privy Council in London. The Nisga'a would pursue their case for the rest of the century, and it would lead to historic changes in the relationship between Native peoples and Canadian governments.

Even faced with such overwhelming prejudice, Native peoples adapted to change and industrialization. Many Ojibwa and Swampy Cree near Lake Manitoba found employment in fishing, lumbering, and gypsum mining. Others worked as hunting and fishing guides. Iroquois from the Kahnawake Reserve, near Montreal, developed a reputation as the best high steel men in the construction industry in Ontario and New York. In the Maritimes, Mi'Kmaq worked in the coal mines, on railroads, and in ironworks. In Saskatchewan, Native farmers on the Assiniboine Reserve produced successful harvests of wheat, barley, oats, and vegetables. The Cowichan and Fraser River Valley people raised livestock, cereals, and market produce. On the West Coast, aboriginal men and women found work in canneries, commercial fishing, lumber mills, and mines. Tragically, the Native peoples' historic contributions and achievements were undervalued and overshadowed by the growing and ambitious immigrant population.

AN ECONOMY ON THE MOVE

As the Laurier era began, Canada's economy was changing as dramatically as its population. And there were growing pains. One of the most pressing problems was **regional disparity** in the rates of industrial development. Ontario was growing at far above the national average, while Quebec remained steady. The Maritimes were falling further and further behind, while the West was just becoming a major economic player. This regional disparity was reflected in migration, where the US had played a large role.

The Dominion Land Act of 1872 granted a free quarter section to settlers who cleared a portion of the land and built a home within three years. Even so, most immigrants chose the United States over Canada. Even many Canadians left for US frontier lands, industrial jobs, and a milder climate. As a result, Canada's population grew slowly. In Atlantic Canada, close family ties and geographical proximity had long made New England a place to find work. When the Maritime shipbuilding industry collapsed in the 1880s, for example, shipbuilders found carpentry jobs in the growing US cities, rather than in other parts of

---

Up Close

6. Create a chart to summarize how Native peoples across Canada adapted to the economic changes occurring in the country during the Laurier era. Use as headings the major regions of the country: Atlantic Canada, Central Canada, The Prairies, Western Canada.

Up Close

7. Before reading this section, write down what you think is meant by "regional disparity." Revise your explanation when you have read the section. Compare "before and after" notes with a classmate.

Canada. In an even larger migration, more than 700 000 Quebeckers left Canada for the mill towns of New England.

As you learned earlier, the US closed its frontier lands to settlers in 1896, the year of the Laurier election. This had an enormous impact. It not only increased immigration to Canada (see the table in Figure 1–11), it also changed migration patterns within Canada. Between 1881 and 1911, for example, many Quebeckers crossed the border into northern and eastern Ontario to find work in farming, mining, lumber, and the growing federal government. The number of Franco-Ontarians jumped from 102 743 to 202 442. This brought their numbers to 10 percent of the provincial population. And many of the people who moved to Canada's West were Canadians from other parts of Canada; the US was no longer a choice. Ontario, by far, provided the largest number of settlers to the West from within Canada.

| Canada's Population (in thousands), 1861-1921 ||||||
Year	Natural Increase*	Immigration	Emigration	Net Migration	Population
1861					3230
1861-71	610	260	410	-150	3689
1871-81	690	350	404	-54	4325
1881-91	654	680	826	-146	4833
1891-01	668	250	380	-130	5371
1901-11	1025	1550	740	810	7207
1911-21	1270	1400	1089	311	8788

*Natural Increase is the number of births minus the number of deaths.

Figure 1–11 This table provides population information over a 60-year period. In what periods did more people emigrate from Canada than immigrate to it? What possible reasons would account for this?

Railways and Beyond

At the turn of the century, Canada's rapid growth was straining existing transportation systems. Railways were seen as the solution. They were needed to move people to the land and to move resources and products to Canadian markets and ports, where they could be shipped to Britain and Europe. It seemed obvious that one transcontinental rail line was not enough. *The Manitoba Free Press* declared "We want all the railways we can get." Farmers, promoters, contractors, and most politicians agreed.

Every little community vied to be on the rail line. It was their link to a prosperous future. If Sir John A. Macdonald could boast of building the CPR, then Laurier and the Liberals would do better. Laurier proposed two transcontinental lines and unveiled more and more railway plans. Most Canadians agreed, re-electing him in 1904.

Up Close

8. As you read to page 21, note the following names: The Temiskaming and Northern Ontario Railway; Francis Clergue, Adam Beck; Massey-Harris; The Ford Motor Company; Guglielmo Marconi. Then write one sentence for each one, explaining how each contributed to Canada's industrial development.

Figure 1-12 This painting of the silver mine at Cobalt, *A Northern Silver Mine,* was painted by Franklin Carmichael, of the Group of Seven. The Cobalt silver mine was the site of the first mining strike in Ontario history in 1907.

Not only were there more railways, but services improved. By 1900, a six-day trip across the country was possible. Standard gauge rails, better bridges, more powerful locomotives, specialized cars—box, pullman, and refrigerator—brought railways into the golden age of freight and passenger service. Sometimes railway building also created unexpected and surprising benefits. During the building of the Temiskaming and Northern Ontario Railway, in 1903, the richest silver deposit in the world was uncovered at Cobalt. It set off a mining bonanza in Northern Ontario.

Railway building and industrial development also led to political scandals. In the 1890s, US business promoter Francis Clergue convinced Ontario politicians to finance his plans for an industrial complex in Sault Ste. Marie. It included mines, forestry, steel and power companies, and a railway. Eventually, Clergue's grand scheme employed 7000 people. Clergue's financing was disastrous, and collapsed in 1903. The Ontario Liberal government had to foot the bills to keep the dream of the "New Ontario" of the north alive. Algoma Steel Inc. survived, and remains a major employer in the region. In Ottawa, Conservative leader Robert Borden attacked Laurier's railway-building schemes. These left the government responsible for nine-tenths of the cost of building the Grand Trunk Railway, while guaranteeing a profit to its largely British investors. Many Canadians were outraged, but Laurier responded that anyone with a "stout Canadian heart" would welcome the scheme.

If railways were the key to prosperity, then electricity—especially hydroelectricity—promised to end the darkness and isolation of the Canadian winter. The potential of electric power was so great that a movement for **public ownership** developed. In Ontario, it was led by Adam Beck, and supported by municipal politicians, businesspeople, labour, and churches. Beck campaigned to ensure that hydroelectric resources would belong to the community, and not become a business **monopoly**. The Ontario government appointed Beck to head an inquiry in 1905, and by 1910 the Hydro-Electric Power Commission of Ontario was founded. It was the first provincially owned electric utility in Canada.

More Industrialization, More Inventions

Between 1850 and 1900, Canada experienced the first phase of its industrial revolution, with expansion in the manufacture of consumer goods such as textiles, clothing, footwear, cigars, and rope. After 1900, heavy industry grew rapidly.

Canadian factories sprang up, turning out rails and railway stock, farm equipment, carriages, furniture, and household appliances. Most "industrial establishments," as defined by the government, were small operations. Of the 75 968 on record, 64 842 had fewer than five employees around the turn of the century. They included 419 printing companies, 349 carriage makers, and 1097 fish canneries.

There were also some very large and very successful businesses. Massey-Harris, founded in 1891, became the largest company in Canada, accounting for 15 percent of the total manufactured exports in 1911. It was the largest manufacturer of farm equipment in the British Empire. Canadians also enthusiastically embraced the automobile. A branch plant of the US Ford Motor Company opened in Windsor, Ontario in 1904, soon followed by General Motors and Chrysler. By 1920, no fewer than 39 Canadian and 8 US companies were building cars in Ontario alone.

Canada played a major role in inventions that were changing the world, especially in telecommunications. Alexander Graham Bell's experiments led to the invention of the telephone between 1874 and 1876. In 1902, Bell and the Canadian government provided Guglielmo Marconi with money to build a station at Glace Bay, NS to regularly transmit messages between Canada and England. By 1906, Marconi had achieved radio transmission of voice, rather than Morse code. The radio, often called the "Marconi," became a common household appliance and led to massive social changes. Bell also worked to develop the airplane with Canadian colleagues J. A. D. McCurdy and F. W. Baldwin in Nova Scotia. In 1909, McCurdy piloted the Silver Dart in the first airplane flight in Canada.

McCurdy and Baldwin remained in Canada, but some Canadian inventors moved to the US to gain fame and fortune. Bell moved to Boston and then Washington. Reginald Fessenden, whose discoveries made radio possible, left Canada to work for US laboratories and universities. Some inventors did stay, however. Ontario-born Thomas Ahern (1855–1938) patented 11 electrical devices, including a flat iron, the electric stove, water heater, snow-sweeper to clear tram-tracks, and an electric automobile in 1899. He died in relative obscurity.

Heritage Minute

The date is December 12, 1901, the place, Signal Hill, St. John's, Newfoundland. Guglielmo Marconi has just received the first wireless transatlantic message—three dots of Morse code. He has proven that radio waves can carry sound, and he will become an international hero. Marconi's experiments will lay the foundations for the age of radio and the modern era of telecommunications. In 1909, he will be awarded the Nobel Prize for physics.

Farming Still Led the Way

As the twentieth century began, urban growth and industrialization were transforming Canada. The majority of Canadians, however, still lived in rural areas. The most spectacular success story of the new century was the wheat boom in the prairies. The big breakthrough came in 1907, when Charles Edward Saunders developed Marquis wheat, a heartier, faster maturing variety that quickly replaced Red Fife. Saunders worked at Ottawa's Central Experimental

Farms, which had been created by the federal government in 1886. Because Marquis wheat was hardy, it could be grown farther north, and this vastly increased the amount of land that could be farmed. Between 1901 and 1913, prairie wheat production skyrocketed from 56 million to 224 million bushels—or from 14 percent to 42 percent of Canada's total exports.

Other factors contributed to the prairie success story: the great number of immigrant settlers tilling the soil; the chill steel plough, which could break up prairie sod; and gas-driven tractors, although they were too costly for most farmers until the 1920s. Another technological breakthrough was the steam thresher. Although these machines were expensive, they could process more wheat in a day than a farmer could in one year. In addition, transportation costs were lower thanks to a new network of rail lines that made shipping produce more efficient.

Rich and Poor: The Gap Widens

As the new century began, the world seemed full of endless possibilities, and many people believed that great fortunes were just waiting to be made. In 1909, *The Canadian Courier*, Canada's first news magazine, captured this widespread sense of optimism:

> Canada is a perpetual Christmas Tree with a present for every son of the house ... We are adventurers living the thrilling life of discovery, of daring, of chance and of conquest. Barefooted boys become millionaires in palaces. In the knapsack of every Canadian schoolboy there is—not a marshal's baton—but a millionaire's bank book.

Up Close

9. Summarize the evidence to support the contention that "Government seemed to favour the rich and powerful" over workers and the poor.

One such schoolboy was Max Aitken. Born in 1879 to a Scottish-Presbyterian minister, Aitken was raised in poor, rural New Brunswick. He became a millionaire before he was 30. Aitken made friends easily, including such influential people as R. B. Bennett, a future prime minister of Canada (1930-1935). By 1906, Aitken was operating out of Montreal, Canada's financial heart. In 1909 he merged 13 cement companies into Canada Cement and earned $1.5 million. He made almost as much again creating the Steel Company of Canada. Aitken moved to Britain and became a **press baron**, a politician, and, eventually, Lord Beaverbrook. Later in life, he donated millions of dollars to the University of New Brunswick, the cities of Fredericton and Saint John, and the Miramichi Valley. While widely admired, Aitken's tactics and intrigues horrified others. One Labour prime minister of Britain described Aitken as "the only evil man I ever met."

Wealthy and powerful people—especially self-made millionaires—were more often seen as heroes. Their success stories kept people's dreams alive, and they were seen to be making Canada prosperous. Some millionaires also felt a sense of civic responsibility. Clifford Sifton, a millionaire as well as a politician, worked for environmental improvements. He opposed power exports to the US, and raised public awareness and concern about industrial pollution, drainage, forest fires, and migratory birds. He also promoted town planning.

Historical Inquiry: Analysing/Evaluating Information

Primary Source
Reading Photographs

When historians write stories of the past, they rely on many sources. Primary sources are a key way to identify, research, and understand these stories. They are links to the past that come to us directly, without any intervention. There are two basic forms of primary sources: written and visual. Written primary sources include court documents, diaries, books, laws, oral reports and newspaper reports. Visual primary sources include paintings, drawings, posters, cartoons, and photographs.

A photograph usually doesn't lie: We see what we see. But we do not always see the whole truth. We can describe what we see in a photograph, but we also often make inferences. We make judgements to complete the "story" of the picture. When historians use a photograph as a primary source, they must ask important questions.

Study Figure 1–13. What is it? It is a picture of Doukhobor women pulling a plough. But why are the women pulling, not the men, or animals? Is this a normal situation? Did the women volunteer to do this, or were they forced? What do you infer from this situation, without having more information? Do you infer that Doukhobor women were treated cruelly? What is the "whole truth" of this photograph? How can we know it?

Historical records tell as that 7500 Doukhobors immigrated to Canada from Russia in 1899. They came to escape religious and ethnic persecution by the tsar and received 400 000 acres (about 162 000 hectares) of unbroken land near Yorkton, Saskatchewan. As strict pacifists, the Doukhobors refused to swear allegiance to Queen Victoria. They

Figure 1–13 Doukhobor women pulling a plough

believed their only allegiance was to God, and they lived communally, refusing to register their land claims. In daily life, there was no compulsion to work; everyone worked because he or she felt they should.

So why are the women pulling the plough? The Doukhobors had no farm animals during their first spring, so they hitched themselves to the plough. The men, except for a few, were away, working on railway construction to earn money for the community. Many Canadians saw this picture at the turn of the century, however, and drew negative conclusions about the Doukhobors.

What Do You Think?

1. Select another photograph from the text: for example, Figure 1–14 on page 24. Describe what you see. What inferences can you make? Formulate three or four important questions that will help guide further understanding of the photograph. For more information on formulating questions, see page 113.

Figure 1–14 Clifford Sifton and his wife at their Toronto estate in 1925

The harsh reality in Canadian society, however, was the wide gap between rich and poor. Everyday life for most Canadians was hard. Most work was physical, dreary, and seemingly endless: dawn to dusk for all on the farm; nine or ten hours in factories or shops, six days a week, with maybe half a day off for picnicking in the summers. Not even a free quarter section of land in the West was guaranteed to save you. The failure rate among Western homesteaders was about 40 percent.

Government seemed to favour the rich and powerful. It helped financiers in their railway-building and industrial schemes, and there was no capital gains tax or income tax to rein in the wealthy. On the other hand, there was no unemployment insurance for workers who lost their jobs, no workers' compensation for those injured, and no government health care to pay doctors and hospital fees. And for the elderly, there was no government pension. If you were unemployed, too old to work, or disabled in any way, you had to turn to family, friends, churches, or fraternal societies. These policies seem cruel today but the Laurier government was simply operating as all governments had up to that time.

After paying the rent, working Canadians had little money left for food and clothing. Malnutrition and terrible housing conditions were common in Canada's growing cities and produced high death rates, especially among infants. In one working-class ward in Montreal in 1895, the annual death rate was 35 per 1000, compared to less than 13 per 1000 in the better area of the city. Infant mortality rates in larger Canadian cities were little different from those in the poorest areas of the developing world.

The Struggle for Working People

Despite all the signs of prosperity, most Canadians worked long hours for small incomes. Working conditions in factories, offices, and mines were crowded, dirty, and dangerous. Workers tried to organize, but the trade union movement grew slowly. The government did not recognize the right of workers to collective bargaining, and it frowned on unions. The flood of immigrants into Canada had also created a new pool of labour that was easily exploited. Immigrants were hired for the toughest jobs at the lowest possible wages, and they endured working conditions that established Canadians would not tolerate.

The effort to organize workers was led by the Trades and Labour Congress of Canada (TLC), which succeeded the earlier Canadian Labour Union in 1886. The TLC attempted to persuade government of the need for labour reform and better working conditions. In 1894, the Conservative government did establish Labour Day as a statutory holiday. At their meeting in Winnipeg in 1898, the TLC adopted 16 points as their principles. These included many progressive ideas: free compulsory education; an eight-hour working day; a minimum living wage; public ownership of all franchises such as railways, telegraphs, water works, and lighting; abolition of all labour by children under 14 years of age; and compulsory arbitration of labour disputes. In 1913, the TLC added equal suffrage for men and women to their platform.

Strikes were frequent, with more than 1000 labour disputes between 1901 and 1911. And they could turn violent. In London, Ontario, the Amalgamated Association of Street Railway Employees went on strike in 1898. The public generally supported the workers, and the company surrendered. A year later, however, the US owners of the streetcar system fired all union members and reneged on its promises. A second strike broke out, with Londoners again supporting the strikers. This time violence erupted, with thousands of people smashing cars, beating strike breakers, and defying police. The mayor read the riot act and called in the militia to clear the streets. The strike was broken.

More radical unions emerged. The Western Federation of Miners, and later the International Workers of the World, called the "Wobblies," tried to organize all workers based on industries. They even tried to organize migrant workers in the construction, logging, and mining camps. But they had little success. Distance, small numbers, and internal conflicts—more than any lack of belief in the need for labour to organize—prevented the trade union movement from becoming a national force.

To gain workers' votes, however, Laurier created a small Department of Labour in 1900. He hired William Lyon Mackenzie King, a young graduate student and future prime minister, to be in charge. In 1908, King was elected to parliament, and was appointed Minister of a full-fledged Department of Labour. Despite these signs of progress, however, business and government refused to concede that labour unions had the right to exist, or that workers had the right to bargain collectively to improve their lives.

Up Close

10. In the role of a labour union leader within the TLC, list reforms you want the government to adopt. Present your list in a form relevant to the times, for example, a newspaper, a poster or notice, a speech.

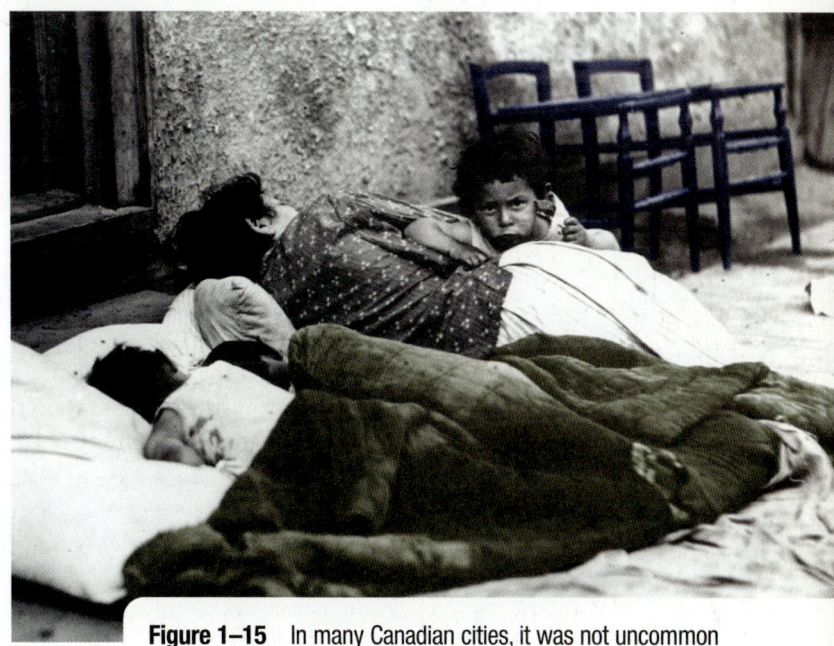

Figure 1–15 In many Canadian cities, it was not uncommon to see entire families living on the streets. This photograph was taken in Toronto circa 1907.

CONCLUSION

During the first part of the twentieth century, Canadians hoped that growing prosperity would solve the serious social problems created by regional disparity and the growing income gap between rich and poor. Many also saw assimilation to British culture as the only answer for the dispossessed Native peoples and Canada's new immigrants. But, of course, French Canadians did not see becoming more British as a solution. They were proud of their language and culture, and committed to protecting them. The Native peoples and newcomers to Canada would later openly rebel against assimilation. However, during this period they had little opportunity for a show of strength. Meanwhile, Canada was experiencing a weakening of its relationship with Britain and a strengthening of its relationship with the United States. Most significant of all, Canada was beginning—through its painters, writers, and athletes—to forge an identity of its own. You will explore these developments in more detail in the next chapters of this unit.

CHAPTER ACTIVITIES

Check Your Understanding

1. a) Why were immigrants considered necessary to Canada's prosperity?

   b) What convinced them to come?

2. Copy the following chart into your notebook. After reading the stories of the immigrants listed, identify the "push" factors that encouraged them to leave their old country and the "pull" factors that brought them to Canada.

Immigrant	Country of Origin	"Push" Factor	"Pull" Factor
The Shumiatchers			
Lem Wong			
Martha Black			
Leslie Fielding			

3. Provide examples of three developments other than immigration that brought Canada prosperity in the early 1900s.

Develop Your Thinking

4. Research John A. Macdonald's life and career and, in a biography-style report, indicate whether or not he should be seen as a great man or as the right person at the right time. Fully explain your perspective.

5. Create three questions that you would ask each of the following people if you were able to interview them: Sir John A. Macdonald; Sir Wilfrid Laurier; Clifford Sifton. Choose one of the characters and communicate what you believe their responses would be.

Express Yourself

6. Create a poster or pamphlet that would have attracted immigrants to the Canadian West from Eastern Europe.

7. Choose one side of the following statement—for or against—and list evidence supporting your perspective. Be prepared to debate your view with a classmate.

    "Advances in both farming and industry ensured that Canadians were experiencing a 'Golden Age' in the early 1900s"

Apply Your Learning

8. Many historians have compared the computer revolution of the past few decades with the industrial revolution of the early 1900s. Develop a list of categories to compare and contrast the two time periods and then complete a list of the characteristics in each category. Which revolution has had the greater impact on life in Canada? Explain your answer.

Extend Your Learning Using the Internet

9. Use Internet resources to research Laurier's "Last Best West" advertising campaign which succeeded in attracting large numbers of immigrants to the Canadian prairies in the late 1800s and early 1900s. What was the purpose of the campaign? Who was the target audience? What groups were not targeted in the campaign? Who was excluded from Canada in the early decades of the century?

10. Compare the immigration patterns in the last years of the twentieth century with those of the first two decades. Brainstorm how and why Canadian immigration policies are different now from what they were then.

2

Canada and the British Empire

Focus Questions

Canada's International Status and Foreign Policy
How did the Boer War, the Naval Services Act, and the reciprocity agreement divide Canadians?

Social and Political Movements
At the turn of the century, what rights and reforms did women fight for? What challenges did they face?

Canadian Identity
Who are some of the best-known Canadian writers and artists of the era? How did their works make a statement about the nature and identity of Canada?

What were the favourite sports and pastimes of Canadians at the turn of the century? Who were some of the participants who made names for themselves?

As Canada entered the twentieth century, its relationship with Britain became a source of both pride and conflict. While many English Canadians felt loyal to the British Empire, French Canadians wanted their government to act independently. The Boer War would bring these differences to a head and the Laurier government would struggle to keep the country united.

To the south, Canada's US neighbour was growing stronger and more powerful. This would affect Canada's relationship with the US, and its relationship to Britain as well. In a dispute over the boundary between Alaska and Canada, Canada would feel betrayed by Britain. Still, Laurier, aware of the mushrooming US market for Canadian goods, would campaign for a free-trade agreement with the US.

Industrialization was changing the world of work, and more people were moving to the cities. As the labour market expanded, women were drawn to new work opportunities that took them outside the home. Traditional roles were being challenged, and the fight for women's rights began in earnest.

Admidst all the social upheaval, a new Canadian identity was emerging. Canadian painters and writers were challenging traditional ideas of art, while Canadian athletes, including the celebrated Tom Longboat, were redefining amateur and professional sports. These achievements not only helped to foster a Canadian outlook, they were also a growing source of national pride.

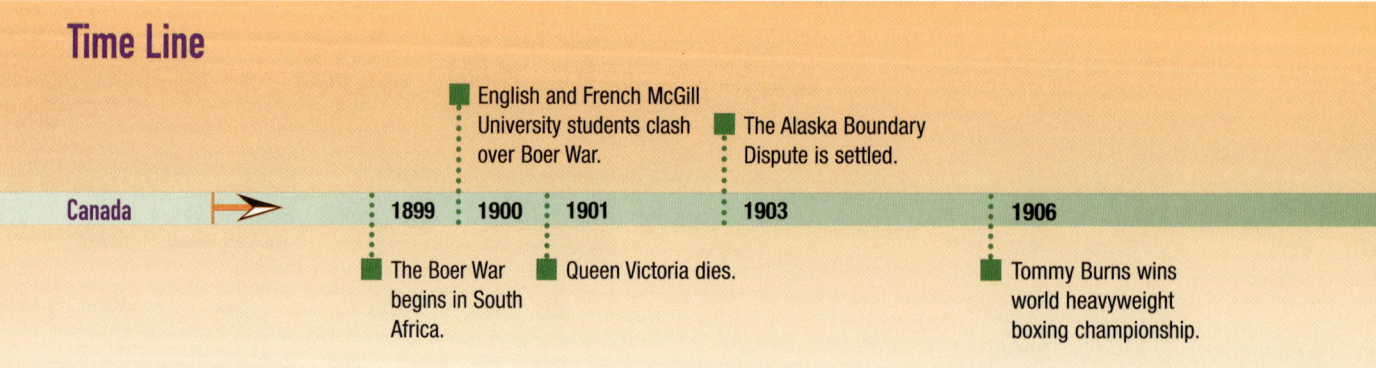

Time Line

Canada

- 1899 — The Boer War begins in South Africa.
- 1900 — English and French McGill University students clash over Boer War.
- 1901 — Queen Victoria dies.
- 1903 — The Alaska Boundary Dispute is settled.
- 1906 — Tommy Burns wins world heavyweight boxing championship.

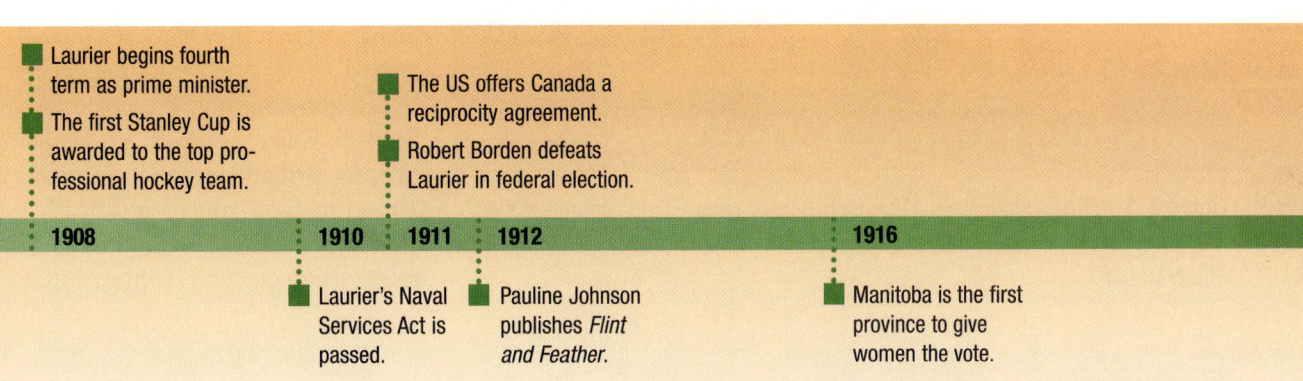

Perspectives

Prime Minister Wilfrid Laurier holds onto his hat as he campaigns in the 1911 federal election in Simcoe, Ontario. Look closely at this photo. In your opinion, does the car play a large or a small role? How would cars and roads affect a candidate's ability to campaign? Does the poster "Our Chieftain" look like one you would see today? Step into the picture as an English Canadian and then as a French Canadian. Describe your responses to the flags and symbols that you see.

- Laurier begins fourth term as prime minister.
- The first Stanley Cup is awarded to the top professional hockey team.
- The US offers Canada a reciprocity agreement.
- Robert Borden defeats Laurier in federal election.

1908   **1910**   **1911**   **1912**   **1916**

- Laurier's Naval Services Act is passed.
- Pauline Johnson publishes *Flint and Feather*.
- Manitoba is the first province to give women the vote.

PART OF THE BRITISH EMPIRE

The children would often start their chant as they tumbled out of school into the spring sun.

> On the twenty-fourth of May
> It's the Queen's birthday
> And if we don't get a holiday
> We will all run away!

The queen, of course, was Queen Victoria. Each twenty-fourth of May, Canadians everywhere—except those in Quebec—held a public holiday to celebrate her long, glorious reign as Queen and Empress of the British Empire. Canada's strong ties to Britain were part of daily school life. At the front of classrooms hung a portrait of Queen Victoria (replaced by a portrait of King Edward VII when Victoria died in 1901). Britain's flag, the Union Jack, flew from school flagpoles. Each morning, children sang "God Save the Queen." World maps showed many countries marked in red to indicate that they were part of the British Empire, the largest empire the world had ever seen. Students felt pride when they learned that Canada was the biggest country in the Empire. But was Canada really a country? Or was it really only a colony?

Today the word "imperialism" conjures up images of exploitation and domination of the weak by the strong. At the turn of the century, however, English-Canadians were proud to be a part of the British Empire. French-Canadian Prime Minister Laurier was drawn to British ideals of liberty and justice, and to British parliamentary traditions. He even became "Sir" Wilfrid Laurier, after being knighted by the Queen at the 1897 Colonial Conference, which celebrated Queen Victoria's Diamond Jubilee.

Data File

The Monday on or before May 24 is a public holiday in English Canada. It is still often referred to as "Victoria Day."

The Dominion Divided

French Canadians were happy that Britain had given the Dominion of Canada the right to self-government, and that they had been guaranteed language, religious, and legal rights. But they did not share English Canada's pride in being tied to Britain and the Empire. Emotionally and politically, French Canadians were proud of their language and culture, and

Figure 2–1 Alberta students in a one-room school, circa 1910. A portrait of King Edward VII hangs beside the flags. Teachers taught students to express loyalty to the British Empire.

they were committed to protecting them. However, events such as the Manitoba and Saskatchewan Rebellions, the hanging of Louis Riel, and the Manitoba Schools Question, had left many French Canadians feeling betrayed by English Canada.

Laurier realized that the differences between English Canada and French Canada were the major threat to the new Dominion. In a letter to a friend, he wrote:

> My object is to consolidate Confederation, and to bring our people, long estranged from each other, gradually to become a nation. This is the supreme issue. Everything else is subordinate to that idea.

The Boer War

Nothing exposed the differences between English Canada and French Canada more dramatically than reactions to the Boer War. In 1899, Britain became embroiled in a conflict with **Afrikaner** settlers in South Africa. Britain called for, and expected, Canadian troops to help them win the war. In English Canada, imperialist feelings ran high, and there was strong support to send troops to defend the British Empire. Although Laurier believed the war was just, he was equally certain that it was not important to Canada's defence. In other words, Canada should not send troops. Almost all of Laurier's Quebec supporters strongly agreed. Most English Canadians were outraged: Britain needed help, and Canada should be there.

In the end, Laurier compromised. Canada would recruit, equip, and transport 1000 volunteers to South Africa, but Britain would have to pay them. Henri Bourassa, Laurier's Quebec protégé, believed that this would be just the first of many imperial wars in which Britain would call for Canadian troops. He, and his more extreme nationalist colleagues, quit the Liberal Party in disgust.

Bourassa's resignation complicated life for Laurier, whose political power rested on maintaining a delicate balance of support from both Quebec and English Canada. Quebec's position, represented by Bourassa, was to stay clear of British imperial ambitions and wars. In contrast, English Canadians believed it was in Canada's best interest to stand behind the British Empire. Besides, many English Canadians "felt British," and were eager to participate in imperial affairs.

Before the Boer War ended, 8300 Canadian volunteers had gone to South Africa. Four Canadians were awarded the **Victoria Cross**. One man, Private R. R. Thompson of the Royal Canadian Regiment, was decorated with the Queen's Scarf, an honour so rare that only four men had ever received it. Although the Empire had won, the war had been neither glorious nor glamorous. Imperial forces had suffered humiliating defeats. Of the Canadian troops, 89 soldiers were killed in combat, and 252 were wounded. Most of the Canadian casualties, however, were not the result of heroic battles for Queen and Empire; 135 Canadian soldiers died as a result of accidents or from diseases that ravaged the military camps.

Up Close

1. For both the Boer War and the Naval Crisis, describe: a) the issue involved; b) the point of view of English Canadians; c) the point of view of French Canadians; d) Laurier's compromise; e) the reaction of English Canadians; f) the reaction of French Canadians.

Figure 2–2 Minnie Affleck was one of four nurses who went with Canada's first contingent of troops to South Africa in 1899. In 1901, the Canadian Army Nursing Service was formally recognized as part of the Canadian Army. Nurses were the first women to officially serve in the army.

McGill Students Went on a Rampage

Tensions between French and English Canadians over the Boer War were especially bitter in Montreal. On March 5, 1900 they erupted when anglophone McGill University students attacked the offices of two French-language newspapers. Looking for more trouble, the students marched on Université Laval (now the Université de Montréal). The next day, francophone Laval students staged a peaceful counter-demonstration and were attacked by a crowd of English-speaking students and townspeople. The police had to disperse the mob with water hoses and call in the militia to preserve public order.

Data File

In 1906, Britain launched the *HMS Dreadnought*, a fast, "all-big-gun" cruiser that could catch and destroy any armoured cruiser. Germany responded by producing its own big battleships. This sparked an arms race between the two countries that would lead to World War I.

The Naval Crisis

In the years after the Boer War, Laurier skillfully avoided involving Canada in the wars and defence of the British Empire. He tried to keep Canada independent of Britain's imperial policies. By the time Laurier won the 1908 federal election, his fourth victory in a row, tension was growing between Great Britain and Germany. Germany's fast-growing navy was challenging Britain's control of the seas. Most Canadians recognized that Canada benefited from the British defence system. The debate was whether Canada should contribute to the Empire's defence or create its own armed forces.

In 1909, tensions between Great Britain and Germany reached a crisis and Laurier was forced to take action. By May 1910, the Laurier government passed the Naval Service Act in the midst of furious parliamentary debate. It created a small Canadian navy that, in times of crisis, could become part of the imperial navy. This was another Laurier compromise, but it satisfied no one.

In Quebec, Henri Bourassa opposed Laurier's naval bill. He argued that it would commit Canadian ships and men to every imperial conflict and would surely lead to **conscription**. Bourassa established a newspaper, *Le Devoir*, to defeat Laurier's plans. In English Canada, Laurier's navy was denounced as "too little, too late." After the government purchased two used British light cruisers, the Royal Canadian Navy was mocked as a "tin pot navy."

The naval issue destroyed Laurier's support in Quebec and led to his defeat in the 1911 election. In 1913, Robert Borden, Laurier's successor as prime minister, introduced a naval bill that contributed $35 million to Britain for the construction of three dreadnoughts. The naval debate would soon be overshadowed by the outbreak of World War I, which you will read about in Chapter 3.

Questions about the size and purpose of our military forces would continue to divide Canadians for the rest of the century, as you will read in later chapters. During both World Wars, Canada's armed forces would expand immensely. Canada would make great military contributions in times of international crisis. After World War II, Canada would join defence organizations such as NATO and NORAD (see Chapter 10). It would make major commitments to United Nations peacekeeping missions. Yet the size of Canada's military would shrink, decade after decade. Again, debates would erupt. How could Canada claim independence if it relied on another superpower for its defence? In the last half of the twentieth century, that power would be the United States, not Britain.

Figure 2–3 This cartoon from the January 1910 issue of Calgary's *The Eye Opener* was captioned: "Dangerous: Watch us crowd the big fellows." How does the cartoonist portray Laurier's proposed navy?

TROUBLES WITH THE NEIGHBOUR

In a 1904 speech in Ottawa, Laurier predicted that the twentieth century would belong to Canada—not the United States. Earlier, however, the US had demonstrated its growing military strength by winning control of Cuba and the Philippines from Spain in the Spanish American War of 1898. Canadians were feeling threatened by their increasingly powerful neighbour to the south.

Britain was also keenly aware of growing US power, and it was determined to stay on good terms with the Americans. There were two reasons for this. The growing arms race between Britain and Germany was heating up, and Germany was competing with Britain for colonies. In case of a major war, Britain was eager to keep the US as a potential ally. As a result, Britain's influence in Canada's relations with the United States became a very complicated affair.

The Alaska Boundary Dispute

At the turn of the century, a number of territorial issues led to conflicts between Canada and the US. The most controversial dispute was over the boundary between Alaska and Canadian territory. The US purchase of Alaska from Russia in 1867 included a "panhandle" of coastal land that ran south to Portland Inlet. The agreement, however, did not specify the boundaries of the Alaskan panhandle. The US interpreted the boundary as extending further inland than did Canada and Britain.

For years, the issue was ignored, but in 1898 the three governments agreed that a joint high commission would settle the dispute. Negotiations soon collapsed. Talks started again because the Yukon Gold Rush and all its riches made the question urgent. Canadians did not want to have to cross US territory to get to the Yukon gold fields.

Up Close

2. Create headlines for a Canadian newspaper and for an American newspaper announcing either the resumed negotiations about the Alaska Boundary Dispute, or the decision of the tribunal.

Images
Symbols of a Nation

Figure 2–4 Canada's first postage stamp, 1851

At the turn of the century, when school children rose to sing the national anthem, they sang "God Save the King" and faced the **Red Ensign** or the **Union Jack**. In the early 1900s, Canada had few national symbols. There was the beaver, and the maple leaf, of course. The beaver had been the mainstay of the fur trade, and was first used as a symbol in the 1600s. Canada's first postage stamp, issued in 1851, featured the beaver, which is still seen on the Canadian nickel. As a symbol, the beaver came to represent hard work and perseverance.

From as early as 1700, the maple leaf has been a symbol of the land we now call Canada, perhaps because maple trees were common along the St. Lawrence River. Alexander Muir's song, "The Maple Leaf Forever," composed in 1867, was the closest Canada got to a national anthem for many years. After the current national flag was introduced in 1965, the maple leaf became Canada's most instantly recognizable symbol around the world (see Chapter 9, pages 250, 252).

As the century unfolded, the distinctive red uniform of the Royal Canadian Mounted Police (or the Royal North-West Mounted Police, as they were known until 1920), would become another Canadian symbol. Early Hollywood depictions of Canada often featured diligent RCMP officers who always "got their man." The RCMP hat and red tunic became a symbol of Canada at home and abroad. In the 1990s a storm of controversy swept Canada when Disney paid for the rights to the RCMP logo. After a few years—and little profit in licensing fees—Disney let the agreement lapse.

English and French Canadians have not always agreed on Canada's symbols. "The Maple Leaf Forever," for example, opened with these words:

Communities: Canadian Identity

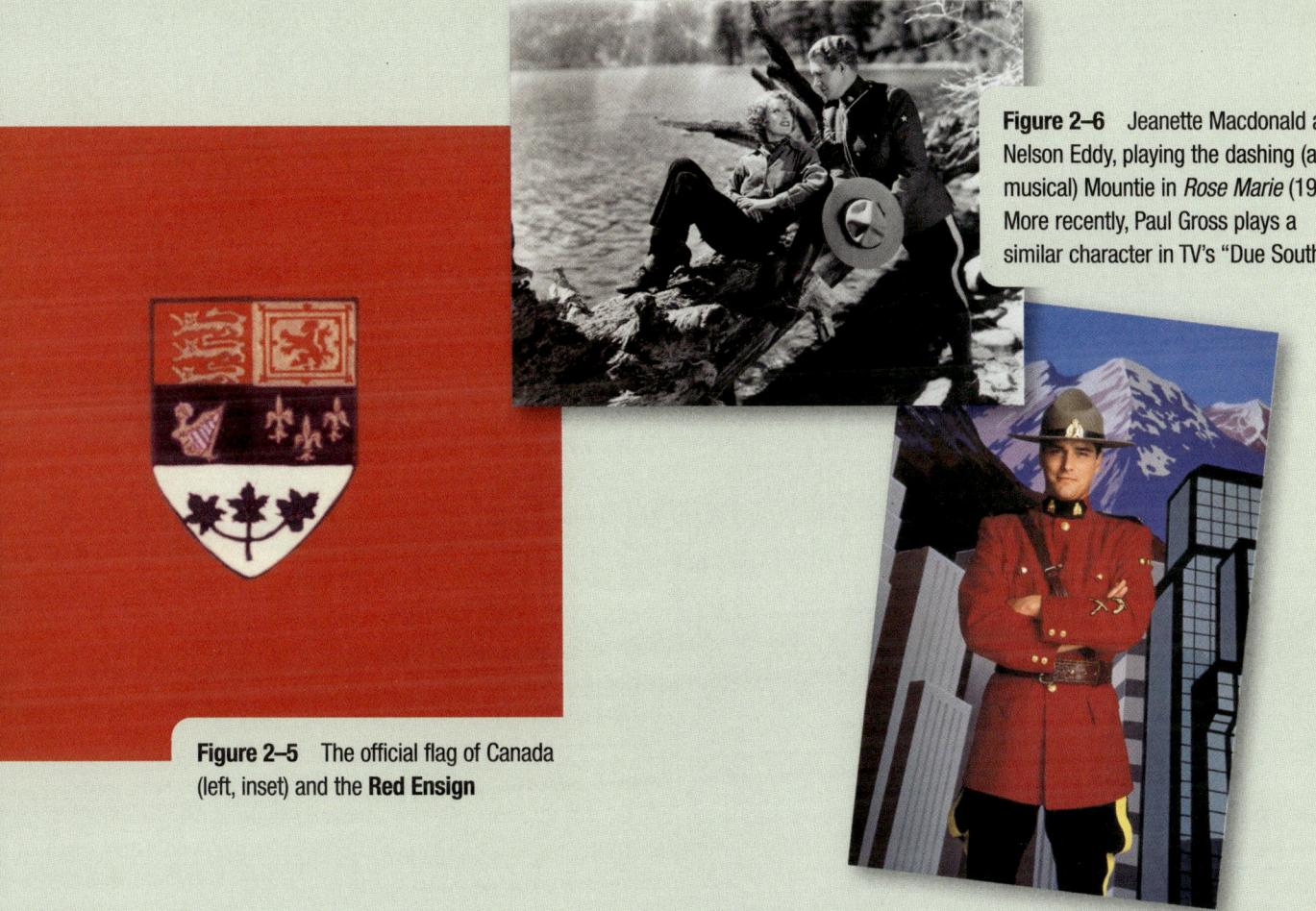

Figure 2–5 The official flag of Canada (left, inset) and the **Red Ensign**

Figure 2–6 Jeanette Macdonald and Nelson Eddy, playing the dashing (and musical) Mountie in *Rose Marie* (1936). More recently, Paul Gross plays a similar character in TV's "Due South."

In days of yore, from Britain's shore,
Wolfe, the dauntless hero came,
And planted firm Old England's flag,
On Canada's fair domain!
Here may it wave our boast, our pride,
And joined in love together,
The Thistle, Shamrock, Rose entwine,
The Maple Leaf forever!

Needless to say, the song was never as popular in French Canada as it was in English Canada. In 1880, Calixa Lavallée composed the music for "O Canada," with French lyrics by Adolphe-Basile Routhier. When it premiered at the St. Jean Baptiste Society's celebration that same year, it met with thunderous applause. French Canadians quickly adopted it as their national anthem. English Canadians, however, still favoured "The Maple Leaf Forever," even after Robert Weir's English version of "O Canada" gained some official acceptance in 1908. Today, with updated lyrics, "O Canada" is the nation's official anthem.

What Do You Think?

1. Do national symbols inspire patriotism or are they the result of patriotic feelings?
2. Are the national symbols discussed here still relevant today? Explain your answer.
3. How are national symbols meaningful to Canadians both inside and outside Canada?
4. What are some "unofficial" symbols of Canada that have meaning to you?

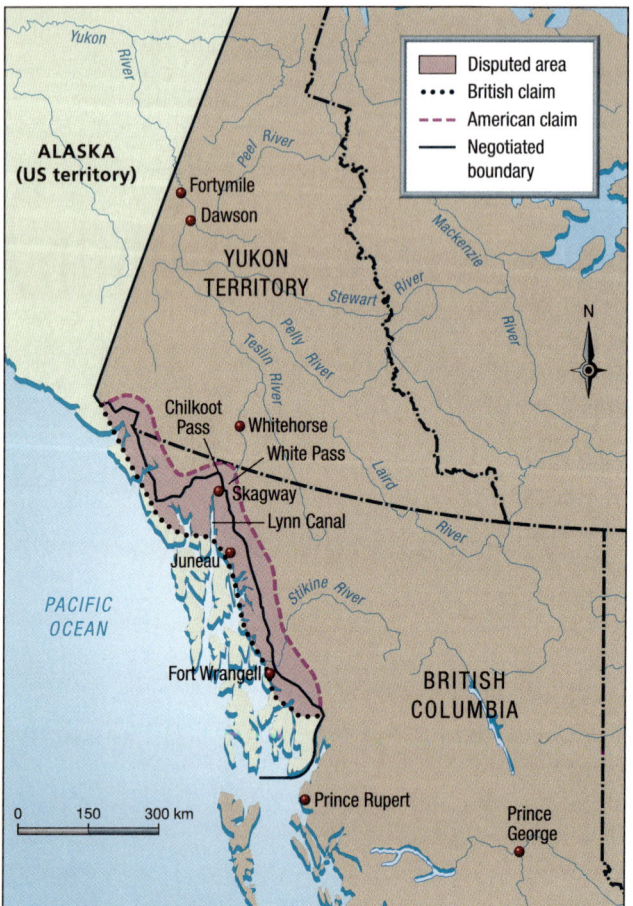

Figure 2–7 This map shows the area in question during the Alaska Boundary Dispute.

The British suggested an arbitration panel. After vocal debates, a six-member tribunal was finally established. It consisted of three American, two Canadian, and one British member. Laurier was determined to take a hard-line position, but circumstances turned against him.

The US wanted British support to build the Panama Canal. Laurier believed that this could be used to win concessions in the Alaska Boundary Dispute. But in 1901, the British sided with the Americans on the Panama Canal issue. Britain was still entangled in the Boer War, and it was eager to stay on good terms with the United States.

Another circumstance worked against Canada. In 1901, US President William McKinley was assassinated. Teddy Roosevelt, a blustering US nationalist, became president and sent 800 troops to Alaska. His message was clear: the US could use its military power to resolve the dispute. Roosevelt instructed the US members of the arbitration panel—who were supposed to be impartial—to make no compromise in defending the US claim.

Finally, in 1903, the tribunal ruled in favour of the US. The British member supported the US. The frustrated Canadian members refused to sign, and left for Ottawa. The treaty, however, was finalized. The Americans had won, with British support. The Alaska boundary negotiations and outcome stirred strong feelings across Canada. Nationalism was in the air, combined with anti-American sentiments and resentment of Britain's lack of support. Despite Canadian anger over the Alaska Boundary Dispute, by 1911 Canada and the US had successfully negotiated no fewer than eight treaties and agreements, removing many irritants between the two countries.

US Money: Opportunity or Threat?

American investment was playing an increasingly important role in Canada's economic development at the beginning of the century. British investment in Canada was still three times that of the US, but American investment was quickly increasing. By 1911, 60 percent of Canada's imports came from the US, although Britain remained Canada's biggest export market. Laurier and the Liberals looked towards the burgeoning US markets and saw opportunity, not a threat.

In 1910, Laurier's finance minister, W.S. Fielding, returned from Washington with an offer for a **reciprocity** (free-trade) agreement. The US was willing to permit free trade in natural resources, while allowing Canada to keep

Up Close

3. Make a chart showing who disagreed with Laurier's policy of reciprocity with the US and why, and who supported him and why.

its tariffs on most manufactured goods. This seemed to be a glittering prize for Laurier's 15-year-old government, which badly needed a boost.

At first, the Conservative Opposition was stunned. Within weeks, however, they discovered that free trade was unpopular in industrialized Ontario. Within a month, eighteen prominent Toronto businessmen—some of them Liberals—came out against reciprocity. Even Sir Clifford Sifton, who as interior minister had played a role in Laurier's early success, came out against reciprocity. Sifton argued that reciprocity with the US would mean that Canada was turning its back on Britain. Most English Canadians agreed. To settle the issue, Laurier called a general election.

During the election campaign, Bourassa attacked Laurier in Quebec for passing the Naval Services Act of 1910, and for serving the British Empire. In Ontario, Laurier was under attack for not supporting the British Empire, and for the reciprocity agreement. Laurier knew he was trapped:

Figure 2–8 Laurier thought his 1911 election tour would be triumphant. Instead, at stops such as this one in Mission City, BC, he was greeted with petitions and complaints.

> I am branded in Quebec as a traitor to the French and in Ontario as a traitor to the English … In Quebec I am attacked as an imperialist, and in Ontario as an anti-imperialist.

Farmers in western Canada did support Laurier's reciprocity agreement. They had always believed that Macdonald's national policy of protective tariffs benefited eastern industrialists at the expense of the West. Still, in September 1911, Laurier was ousted, and Canadians elected Conservative Robert Borden as their new prime minister.

WOMEN: THE STRUGGLE FOR RIGHTS

By 1900 Canada's industrialization was speeding up. There were more factories, more railways, more mines. There was a demand for an army of service workers from clerks, cleaners, cooks, and secretaries, to managers, bankers, lawyers, engineers, and civil servants.

Industrialization changed the labour market, and with it the lives of women. Earlier, few occupations had been available to women. Most working women had been employed as domestic servants. By increasing the demand for workers, industrialization created more options for women. Greater numbers of women entered the work force.

Figure 2–9 This 1904 group portrait of Vancouver Royal Bank employees shows Jeanie Moore, one of the first women employed by the bank. Banks tended to hire women for less visible roles such as clerks and stenographers.

In 1901, one in six Canadian workers was a woman. Women accounted for 25 percent of all manufacturing and mechanical workers. With more alternatives, Canadian-born women became less interested in the low wages of domestic service. Domestic positions were now filled by immigrants, or by young women who left farms for the attractions of the city. The work of Canadian farm women was not calculated in any statistics. Yet aside from performing all the domestic work, they made vital contributions to running the farm. They looked after daily chores such as milking cows and feeding animals. During the harvest, their work load increased because they cooked and baked for all the harvest teams.

Data File

In 1891, women accounted for 14.3 percent of clerical workers in Canada. By 1921, that figure had increased to 41.8 percent.

Women Who Worked for Change

As more women entered professional life, men gradually accepted them in the workplace. Discrimination against female employees became less obvious, but it did not disappear. Many of the early advocates of women's rights were educated, professional women. While many women continued to fight for the right to vote, social reform moved to the forefront in the 1890s. Social issues such as temperance and prohibition, public health, and education became of greater concern to women activists than obtaining the right to vote.

The National Council of Women of Canada, founded in 1893, focused on the needs of women and children. In 1897, Adelaide Hunter-Hoodless started the first Women's Institute, in Stoney Creek, Ontario. The Institute promoted social reform in Canada's rural communities and encouraged better education to prepare women for motherhood and homemaking. By 1913, there were Women's Institutes in every province of Canada. The movement quickly spread to other countries and eventually became the largest women's organization in the world.

The Woman's Christian Temperance Union (WCTU), founded in 1874, campaigned for the prohibition of alcohol. By 1900, the WCTU had 10 000 members and influence far beyond its numbers. The Canadian Suffrage Association and the WCTU later joined forces to bring about social reform by focusing on obtaining political rights for women. In a speech delivered in 1914, the WCTU president explained her view of the connection between prohibition and women's right to vote:

> During all the time since ever liquor was introduced women have ever and always been its chief sufferers. Its sword has pierced her very soul; she has again and again seen the lord of her life, her husband, transformed into a veritable beast through its malignant spell; and if there be one thing harder than this I think it must be for a mother to see the idols of her soul, her own children, dragged down to the nethermost depths because of it … Is it any wonder, then, that the WCTU ardently desires the enfranchisement of women: Why? Not from such low aims as to add a little paltry power to their positions; ah, not so, but because we realize that the ballot in the hands of the women must mean eventually the outlawry of the liquor traffic.

The WCTU fight for prohibition appealed mostly to the middle-class and to Protestants. It found little support in Quebec and among Catholics, or with the urban working-class and recent immigrants. Many workers saw prohibition as an attempt to outlaw one of the few pleasures they had in their hard, impoverished lives.

Figure 2–10 Adelaide Hunter-Hoodless was one of the founding members of the National Council of Women. After her son died from drinking impure milk, she formed the first Women's Institute and went on to be instrumental in establishing the Victorian Order of Nurses and the Canadian YWCA.

A Mother and Daughter Became Doctors Between 1880 and 1920, Canadian women achieved some notable firsts in their professions. In 1883, Ontario-born Augusta Stowe-Gullen became the first woman to obtain a medical degree in Canada. Her mother, Dr. Emily Stowe, had been the first Canadian woman ever to practise medicine in Canada, but she had been forced to obtain her medical degree in the United States when no Canadian medical school would accept her. Both Stowe and Stowe-Gullen served as presidents of the Dominion Women's Enfranchisement Association.

Cora Hind Became a Journalist Western Canada's first female journalist, Cora Hind, could not get a job with the *Free Press* when she arrived in Winnipeg in 1882. She found work as a secretary and stenographer, but continued to write and submit articles on agriculture to the newspaper. Finally, in 1901, the *Free Press* hired her as its agricultural editor. In 1904 she became president of the Canadian Women's Press Club. Hind was active in the causes of women's suffrage and the WCTU.

Emily Murphy Studied the Law Emily Murphy, author of the popular Janey Canuck books, was a self-taught legal expert. Her appointments in 1916 as police magistrate for Edmonton and then Alberta made her the first woman magistrate in the British Empire. On her first day as magistrate, a lawyer challenged Murphy's right to sit on the bench. Under British law, he said, a woman was not considered to be "a person." This inspired Murphy to begin a long battle to have women declared legal "persons." Louise McKinney, who was active in the WCTU, joined Murphy in this battle. In 1917, McKinney was elected as an MLA (Members of Legislative Assembly) in Alberta, making her one of the first women elected to a legislature in the British Empire.

Other women were also demanding change. Flora MacDonald Denison, for example, was a Toronto businesswoman and journalist who served as president of the Canadian Suffrage Association. From 1909 to 1913, she wrote a regular column, which some suffragists considered far too radical. In Montreal, Marie Gérin-Lajoie worked as an author and educator to improve women's lives. What prompted her to become involved was discovering—in her father's law books—how unequally women were treated in the justice system. In 1907 she helped to establish the Fédération Nationale St-Jean-Baptiste, an organization for francophone women who were members of charitable and professional organizations.

> **Up Close**
>
> 4. Canadian women achieved many "firsts" during this period. Provide at least four examples.

The Incredible Nellie McClung

Perhaps the most dynamic leader in the struggle for women's suffrage was Nellie McClung. Born in Ontario in 1873, her family moved to Manitoba when she was six. McClung started school at 10. By the time she was 16, she was ready to begin her career as a teacher. McClung was not only a teacher to her students, she was a seamstress, barber, and football referee. She also saw first-hand the devastating effects of alcoholism and poverty on her students, which inspired her to become a social reformer.

McClung became an active member of the WCTU and campaigned for prohibition. By 1896, she had married and quit teaching. In her activism, she began to see that women needed to have a direct voice in government. They needed the right to vote and run for office. For McClung, religion, temperance, and political rights for women became intertwined:

> ... if women ever get into politics there will be a cleaning out of pigeon holes and forgotten corners, on which the dust of years has fallen, and the sound of the political carpet-beater will be heard in the land.

Encouraged by her mother, Annie, McClung turned her hand to writing. In 1908, she published *Sowing Seeds In Danny*, a comic novel about life in a rural town in the West. It became an instant hit, selling 100 000 copies. McClung earned $25 000 in royalties—a fortune in those days. McClung kept publishing and gave many readings in Canada, the US, and Britain. She became an international celebrity and used her popularity to push for women's suffrage, prohibition, factory safety, and the right of widows to inherit a share of their husbands' property. She became a driving force behind the Political Equality League, an organization seeking to improve working conditions for women.

> **Up Close**
>
> 5. Write a "wish list" of all the changes Nellie McClung wanted to see occur in Canadian society.

Historical Inquiry: Analysing Information

Primary Source

At Least Two Petticoats

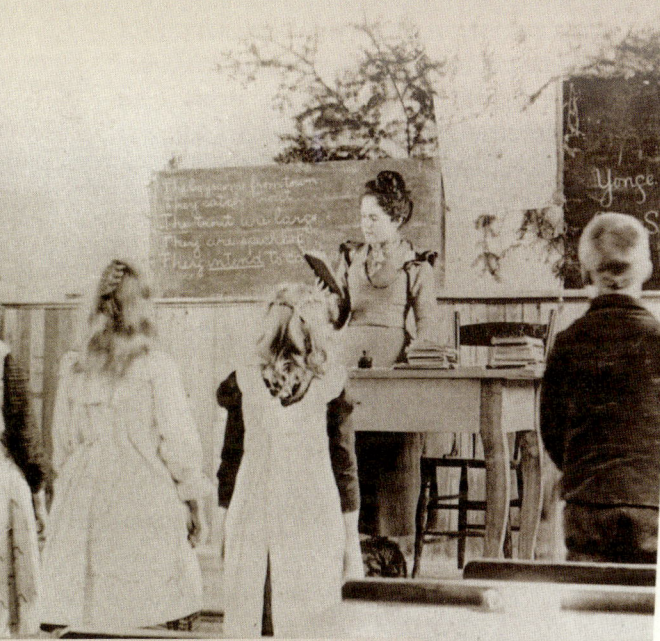

Figure 2–11 A schoolteacher at the turn of the century

> **Rules for Women Teachers (circa 1900)**
>
> 1. You will not marry during the term of your contract.
> 2. You are not to keep company with men.
> 3. You must be home between the hours of 8 p.m. and 6 a.m., unless attending a school function.
> 4. You may not loiter downtown in ice cream stores.
> 5. You may not travel beyond the city limits, unless you have permission of the chairman of the board.
> 6. You may not ride in a carriage or automobile with any man unless he is your father or brother.
> 7. You may not smoke cigarettes.
> 8. You may not dress in bright colors.
> 9. You may under no circumstances dye your hair.
> 10. You must wear at least two petticoats.
> 11. Your dresses must not be any shorter than two inches above the ankle.
> 12. To keep the school room neat and clean, you must: sweep the floor at least once daily; scrub the floor at least once a week with hot soapy water; clean the blackboards at least once a day; and start the fire at 7 a.m. so the room will be warm by 8 a.m.

In the Victorian era, social behaviour was rigidly defined. The way you dressed and spoke, where you were seen, whom you were seen with—all of these reflected a person's moral character. Breaking these rules of social conduct could have serious consequences on your work life and social position. For women in particular, these rules were especially narrow. Generally, women were assumed to be subservient to men. Ideally, they would make good wives and mothers.

By the turn of the century, however, more and more women were entering the workforce. Most nurses and teachers were women. Still, working women fell outside the norm and were often viewed with some suspicion. They were very closely watched. Women who taught school had to follow rules that covered far more than the classroom.

What Do You Think?

1. Why would a special set of rules be written for women teachers? What do these rules reveal about society's view of women at the turn of the century?
2. In which of today's occupations are people held to a different standard of behaviour than other members of society? What are the expectations for each?
3. How do the rules relating to personal appearance in the document above compare with those in today's schools?

Canada and the British Empire

Figure 2–12 A cartoon depicting one reaction to women wanting the vote

> Why is [there] not a woman factory inspector in this city, where there are so many more women employees than men? Why are women's petitions so regularly and systematically ignored? Why are women not given equal pay for equal work? Why are women debarred from taking up Homesteads? Why are women, physically weaker than men, further handicapped in the race of life by political nonentity? Why are women on election day classed with idiots, lunatics, and criminals? These are some of the questions women are asking in this Province and the wise politician is the one who listens.
>
> -Nellie McClung

ARTS AND LEISURE IN CANADA

In the early years of the 1900s, working-class people did not have a lot of leisure time. Women raised their families without any modern conveniences, so household duties took much longer than they do today. For many working men and women, it was common to work 60 to 80 hours a week. Leisure might consist of a Sunday afternoon, which in summer could mean a picnic or a trip on the new, electric railway.

More people were moving to the large cities, and the working class was growing. As more people learned to read, new kinds of newspapers appeared that were meant to appeal to working people. They cost less than more established newspapers and featured more photographs and cartoons, while emphasizing local news and classified ads. By 1913, the number of daily newspapers in Canada reached an all-time high of 138. Competition was fierce, however, and many newspapers went out of business or merged with competitors. Magazines, such as *Saturday Night*, *Busy Man's Magazine* (later *Maclean's*), and *Canadian Magazine*, tended to be more popular with the middle class.

Canadians with more literary interests were discovering Canadian writers whose works are now considered classics of Canadian literature. Robert Service had emigrated from Scotland in 1894. As a bank employee, he worked throughout BC before being stationed at Whitehorse and Dawson City. His first collection of poetry, *Sounds of a Sourdough*, was published in 1907. Service became famous as "the poet of the Yukon."

Lucy Maud Montgomery grew up in Prince Edward Island, which provided the setting for her first novel, *Anne of Green Gables*. The book, published in 1908, was an instant international bestseller and its main character continues to be famous all over the world. The story and its sequels tapped into the real-life aspirations of young women in the industrial age. Montgomery captured their yearning to leave the rural environment, attend university, and pursue a career. Many critics

Up Close

6. In what ways was Anne of Green Gables an appropriate character to represent the Laurier era?

Citizenship: Individual Canadians

Flashpoint

Turning the Tables on the Men

Figure 2–13 Nellie McClung (right) welcomes the English suffragette Emmeline Pankhurst to Winnipeg.

Nellie McClung and other suffragists had to be inventive to reach their goals. Many Canadians—male and female—were certain that equality for women would mean the breakdown of the family. Granting women the right to vote was particularly controversial. In Manitoba, suffragists were making no progress with Conservative Premier Rodmond Roblin. They tried to convince him that if women could vote, it would end many of the abuses women suffered in the workplace. Roblin simply replied that "nice women" did not want the vote.

To pressure Roblin, the Political Equality League decided to stage a Mock Parliament. They would turn the tables on male politicians by staging a debate in which men would petition female politicians for male suffrage. The women would respond by using the same arguments that male politicians had been using against female suffrage for years. Nellie McClung would star as the premier.

The Winnipeg theatre was packed on opening night on January 28, 1914. On stage, a group of men presented their case for male suffrage. McClung rose to speak. She complimented the men on their outfits, then began her attack. "Nice men do not want the vote," she told the men. "Another trouble is that if men start to vote they will vote too much. Politics unsettles men, and unsettled men mean unsettled bills—broken furniture, broken vows, and—divorce ..." The audience roared with laughter.

The Mock Parliament got a rave review in the *Manitoba Free Press* and ran to full houses for another two nights. It created a stir in the newspapers, and was said to have "shamed the premier." Public support for the League's cause grew tremendously. In the 1915 provincial election, Roblin's Conservative government went down to defeat. In January 1916, Manitoba became the first province to grant women the right to vote and hold public office. Saskatchewan and Alberta followed later the same year.

What Do You Think?

1. For years women had been lobbying for women's suffrage. Why then would the Mock Parliament manage to "shame" the premier?

2. McClung was known for her use of humour. Why might humour have been an effective technique to use in the political argument over suffrage?

3. What are some other arguments McClung might have used in her speech during the Mock Parliament? Write your own version of such a speech.

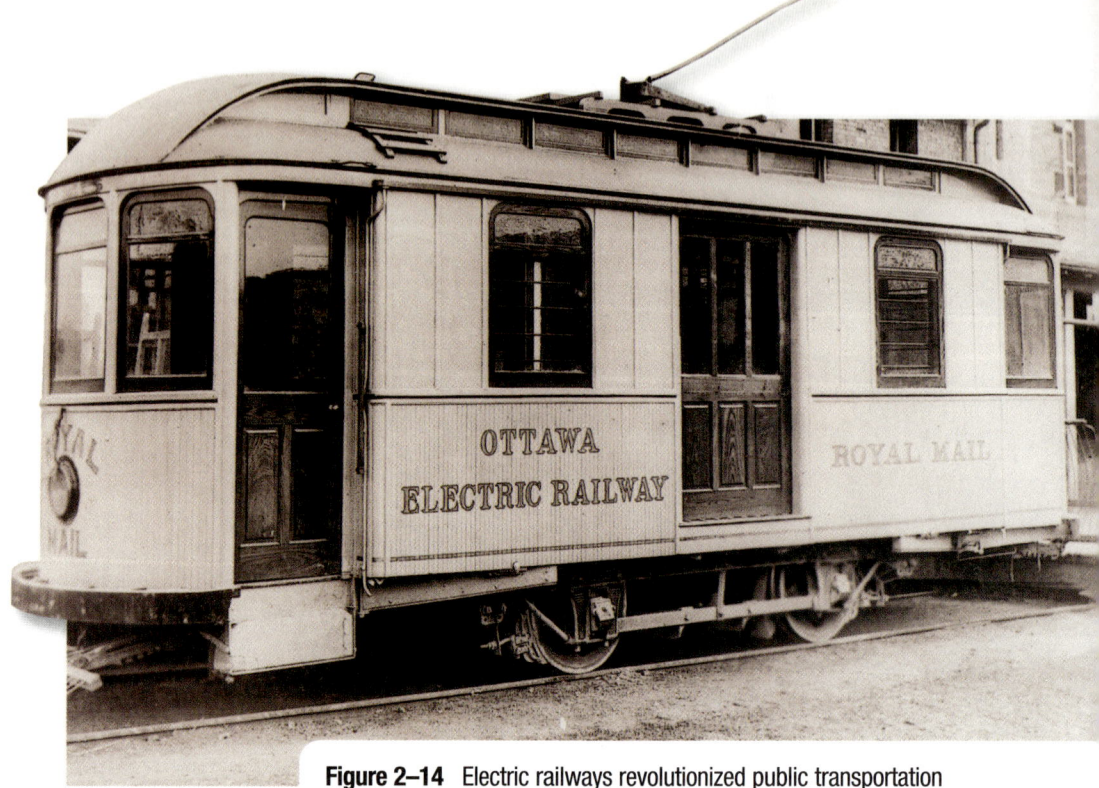

Figure 2–14 Electric railways revolutionized public transportation in cities.

have seen Anne as a character who captured the universal need to escape restrictive conventions and drudgery of life through the use of the imagination.

Stephen Leacock used wit and irony to poke fun at business practices and ethics of the time. His books *Sunshine Sketches of a Little Town* (1912) and *Arcadian Adventures of the Idle Rich* (1914) were read by millions of people around the world, in many languages. You will read more about Leacock in Chapter 4.

Popular Performances

Live performances were very popular in Canada in the early twentieth century. These included dramas, musicals, vaudeville, singing, dancing, literary readings, and storytelling. By 1907, Toronto, Montreal, Vancouver, and Winnipeg had large theatres that seated more than 1000 people. Smaller cities and towns often had an "Opera House" for presenting theatrical productions, both amateur and professional. Many British and US performers and repertory companies regularly toured Canada.

One of the most popular writer/performers of the time was Pauline Johnson, who later took the aboriginal name Tekahionwake. The daughter of a Mohawk chief and an Englishwoman, she grew up on the Six Nations reserve near Brantford, Ontario. Many of her poems, such as "The Song My Paddle Sings," are celebrations of her aboriginal heritage. In the 1890s, Johnson began a series of speaking tours across Canada, the United States, and England. She often dressed as an Aboriginal princess for dramatic readings and acted as an unofficial

Up Close

7. Create a poster advertising an upcoming speaking engagement by Pauline Johnson in your neighbourhood.

cultural ambassador. In Canada, she travelled to remote areas seldom visited by performers. *Flint and Feather*, her best known collection of poems, was published in 1912, the year before she died.

Painting: A Canadian Style?

In the world of art, some Canadian painters were beginning to develop reputations for having a distinctive "Canadian style." Quebec artist Ozias Leduc spent much of his career producing paintings and decorative murals for churches. But he is also known for his still-life paintings and for landscapes depicting the area around St-Hilaire, Quebec, where he was born in 1864. Leduc pursued his own artistic vision and was not greatly influenced by popular artistic styles and trends of the time. His landscape paintings are considered to be his finest works.

James Wilson Morrice, born in Montreal in 1865, was one of the first Canadian painters to paint in the modernist style. He was also one of the first to find recognition abroad, although he remained little known in Canada until after his death in 1924. Morrice's paintings of winter and Quebec City, such as *The Ferry, Quebec City*, and *The Ice Bridge*, are distinctively Canadian, with their cold light and stark forms.

Unlike Morrice, Ontario painter Homer Watson achieved national success during his lifetime. Many of his paintings show an idealized view of rural life, with fields of grain and grazing cattle. Much of Watson's art reflected a basic theme of the Canadian experience: the pioneer's struggle to make a living from the rugged land. This kind of art was much more popular at the turn of the century, and it may account for Watson's success.

In the decade before World War I, a group of painters who would later form the Group of Seven befriended one another in Toronto. At the time, all but one had to make a living as commercial artists. In British Columbia, Emily Carr spent much of her life struggling to make a living from her art. Her paintings of the rugged BC landscape—particularly the Native totem poles, artifacts, and villages of the Northwest Coast— brought her only modest financial success much later in life. Carr and the Group of Seven would change the face of Canadian art in the years ahead. You will learn more about them in Chapter 4.

Figure 2–15 *Neige Dorée* by Ozias Leduc. Warm colours and soft light characterized many of Leduc's landscape paintings.

Figure 2–16 While many Canadian painters focused on natural landscapes, Robert. F. Gagen's painting of Toronto, *Temples of Commerce*, shows a modern, industrialized cityscape.

Most people at the turn-of-the-century could not afford to buy art, but folk art and handicrafts were part of their everyday lives. They produced handicrafts that were often practical, as well as bringing colour and beauty to their surroundings. Knitting, quilting, and embroidery were very popular. Collages of shells and paper were carefully crafted. Barns, taverns—even horse-drawn delivery wagons—were frequently painted with elaborate and colourful designs and images.

Canadian Sports

Canadians loved outdoor activities of all kinds at the turn of the century, and they enjoyed a variety of sports in all seasons. Snow-shoeing, tobogganing, sleighing, rowing, and canoeing were especially popular among people who couldn't afford a lot of equipment. Wealthier Canadians were fond of tennis, badminton, cricket, golf, and curling. Most of these sports required a membership in clubs, and were too expensive and time-consuming for the average Canadian.

Bicycling was another popular sporting activity. In the days before automobiles, the modern safety bicycle had created a social revolution. With new, air-filled tires, it was comfortable, cheaper and cleaner than a horse, and could be

> **Up Close**
>
> 8. Before reading the section on Canadian Sports, make a list of sports you think would have been popular with Canadians around the turn of the century. When you've finished reading, revise your list.

managed easily by anyone. First produced in the 1880s, the safety bicycle remained virtually unchanged until the 1950s.

In 1909, Thomas Ryan invented five-pin bowling. Patrons at his ten-pin bowling club in Toronto found the ball too heavy and the game too strenuous, so Ryan set out to make it more accessible. He reduced the number of pins to five and made the ball lighter, and the sport quickly grew in popularity. Today, five-pin bowling remains a popular participant sport in Canada.

Team sports such as baseball, rugby, football, and lacrosse—which was considered Canada's national game—were popular forms of recreation and entertainment. With improvements to ice skates, however, hockey became the fastest-growing sport. By 1900, it had replaced lacrosse as Canada's national game for many people. In 1893, Governor General Lord Stanley had donated a cup to be awarded to the best Canadian hockey team. In 1908, the Stanley Cup became an award for the top professional team, and the Allen and Memorial cups were presented to the best senior and junior amateur hockey teams. Nine years later, the National Hockey League was established.

Some Canadians Became Sports Legends

In the late 1800s and early 1900s, Canada produced some athletes whose names would become legends in Canada and around the world. Toronto's Ned Hanlan was the world's champion sculler between 1880 and 1884. A colourful showman and brilliant rower, Hanlan developed a reputation that drew huge crowds. Victories in the United States and Britain brought him international fame.

Figure 2–17 Bicycles became so popular that they changed women's fashion. Corsets, bustles, and other constricting garments for women were on their way out.

Distance runner Tom Longboat became Canada's first national sports hero of the twentieth century. Born on the Six Nations reserve in Ontario, he was the most talented long-distance runner of his day. He broke many world records and won the Boston Marathon in 1907, when he was only 19. Two years later, he won the World's Professional Marathon Championship. Longboat was so fast that people said he "showered and ate before the other runners finished."

Tommy Burns, from Hanover, Ontario, was relatively small for a heavyweight boxer, but he managed to win the world heavyweight boxing championship in 1906.

Up Close

9. Using the names and information on these pages about Canadian Sports Legends, create a quiz to challenge your classmates. For a format, you might choose multiple-choice, True/False, or game cards.

Heritage Minute

Most team sports, such as hockey, lacrosse, and baseball, evolved over time. But in 1891, Dr. James Naismith, from Almonte, Ontario, did something remarkable. He invented a new sport. Naismith found himself teaching a bored and rebellious gym class in Massachusetts. He quickly devised his 13 rules for basketball and nailed two peach baskets to the gym balconies. Naismith had invented a game that stressed skill over strength, speed, and power. Today, basketball is one of the most popular games in the world. It can be played in $500 spring-loaded running shoes, or in wheelchairs.

After working briefly as a lumberjack in New England, strongman Louis Cyr returned to his native Quebec to become a policeman. There was no organized sport of weightlifting in the late 1800s, so competitions took the form of challenge matches. These events drew huge crowds, and Cyr became famous. He was never defeated. He even won a horse from the British Marquis of Queensbury after betting that he could hold two horses to a standstill—one tied to each arm. In 1895 Cyr accomplished the remarkable feat of lifting, on his back, a platform that held 18 men. Total weight: 1967 kilograms. At the turn of the century, Cyr toured the world as a circus performer and celebrity.

Less well known than Cyr, but equally fascinating, were golfer George S. Lyon and rodeo-rider Tom Three Persons. Lyon was 46 when he won Olympic gold in 1904, after only eight years of playing the game. A well-rounded athlete, he had earlier set Canadian records in the pole vault and cricket, and was also active in baseball, rugby, soccer, curling, and lawn bowling. Three Persons was the only Canadian to make it to the finals of the world saddle-bronc riding competition at the 1912 Calgary Stampede. He drew Cyclone, the toughest horse on the circuit, and somehow managed not to get thrown. Three Person's victory made him a hero, and he was later inducted into the Canadian Rodeo Hall of Fame.

Figure 2–18 Distance runner Tom Longboat (on the right) served as a dispatch runner during World War I.

Historical Inquiry: Investigating Historical Topics

Historian at Work

The Historian's Vocabulary

Like other professionals, historians use a specialized vocabulary—words and phrases that help them organize their thoughts and describe their activities. Since historians are interested in learning about events that have already happened, much of their professional language has to do with time. In fact, the work of historians is to try to build a **time line** of the past, sometimes called a **chronology**. By studying the order and consequences of events over long periods of time, historians can chart, describe, analyse, and present the changes, growth, successes, and failures of humanity.

To do this, they use different kinds of **evidence**. Sometimes evidence comes from those who saw or heard about an event, often in the form of **eyewitness accounts**. Sometimes evidence is found in documents such as letters and memoranda. These are called primary sources. You have encountered examples of **primary sources** in this book. Historians usually work with primary sources, but sometimes turn to indirect accounts, called **secondary sources**. A history text is an example of a secondary source, as it is composed of researched information. Both primary and secondary sources must be tested for **validity**. To be valid, a piece of evidence must be strongly supported and defensible.

Reliability of evidence is also important. Historians must determine if the evidence—and/or the source—is trustworthy and appropriate. Suppose an historian found a letter written in 1867, which described the writer's views on what Prime Minister John A. Macdonald was thinking. As an historical document, the letter would be valid, but it wouldn't provide evidence about what Macdonald was actually thinking, it would not be reliable. Historians want to be sure the evidence they use is strong and true, and comes from trustworthy sources. Evidence has to be both reliable and valid to be useful.

Figure 2–19 Is this certificate a primary or secondary source?

Historians use evidence to build an **historical narrative**, sometimes called an **historical account**. A narrative is the historian's description of what happened, as reconstructed from the evidence. The narrative identifies causes and effects, among other things, and describes events. Since historians are people who are products of their own time, and because evidence is open to interpretation, historical accounts can never be truly objective or scientific.

To give structure to their historical accounts, historians divide the past into segments—periods or **eras**. Historians can identify eras because they can look back, searching for major themes, ideas, and changes. This process of dividing the past into eras is part of building a chronology for the past.

Activity

1. Build an illustrated chronology of your life, from birth to your present age. Select only the most important events. Divide your life into segments or periods, and identify each one.

CONCLUSION

Responding to Britain's concerns and problems was costly for Canada, not only in money but in national unity. Francophone Quebec was unwilling to support Britain in the Boer War, or to provide navies or troops for Britain's other conflicts. But Britain itself was more concerned with keeping the United States happy than with worrying about Canada's problems. Therefore, Britain did not support Canada in the critical Alaska Boundary Dispute. Laurier and his Liberal government may have felt betrayed by Britain, but they were also eyeing the huge American market as a source of business and financial capital. When Laurier was increasingly unable to please most of the many factions that sprang up around these political and economic issues, he was defeated in 1911.

Meanwhile, Canadian society was continuing to change in important ways. Industrialization meant that many more professions were created, as well as many more social problems. Women began to take part in the professions and to help deal with the problems. When women were refused entry to schools of law, medicine, and journalism, they insisted on their right to participate. To deal with social problems, they organized groups such as the Women's Christian Temperance Union. At the same time, the Canadian identity became stronger through the efforts of authors, artists, and sports figures who excelled at their craft.

While Canadians across the country struggled to establish economic and political standards that all could live with, circumstances in Europe were about to boil over into "the war to end all wars." Canada was about to respond to the call of World War I.

CHAPTER ACTIVITIES

Check Your Understanding

1. List some of the main reasons Laurier lost the election of 1911.
2. Why did women see themselves as leaders of the Prohibition movement?
3. What is the relationship between industrialization and the development of leisure time?

Develop Your Thinking

4. Assume the identity of a student from Université Laval and write a letter dated March 6, 1900—the day after the riot—protesting the actions of the rioters to the McGill University student newspaper.

5. The early 1900s is seen as a key time in the development of a unique Canadian identity. Assume you are a writer for a European travel magazine, visiting Canada at that time. You are assigned the task of describing Canadian culture. Write an article for the people in your homeland.

Express Yourself

6. The English language newspaper *The Montreal Star* was known for its rabid Imperialism. As the editor of the paper, write an open letter to all Canadians encouraging them to volunteer for military service in South Africa.

7. Create a political cartoon focusing on Laurier's handling of the Navel Crisis that might have appeared in *Le Devoir* on the eve of the election of 1911.

8. The quotation that appears on page 37 is part of a speech that Laurier wrote in an effort to get re-elected. Following this quotation, he said, "I am neither, I am a Canadian." Finish his election speech for him by identifying at least three supporting arguments for this statement. Present your speech to the class.

9. Investigate and explore several examples of Canadian art from the turn of the 19th century. Sketch or paint your own artwork reflecting the themes that were common to Canadian paintings at the time.

Apply Your Learning

10. Since 1989, Canada has had a reciprocity or "Free Trade" agreement with the United States. Investigate the political situation that existed at that time and create a chart comparing it to Laurier's experiences in 1911.

11. Choose one of the sports heroes mentioned in the text and research their popularity and status. Prepare a report that concludes by comparing the status and role of sports figures at the end of the nineteenth century with their role today.

Extend Your Learning Using the Internet

12. Research the extent of the British Empire in the early 1900s. Create a global map to illustrate how political and economic interests will likely cause challenges to Canada's relationship with Britain and the US during the century.

13. Using Internet archival sources and current data, create a comparison chart of the economic status of Canadian women at the beginning and the end of the century. What advances have women gained? What remains to be done?

3
Canada and World War I

Focus Questions

Canada's Participation in War, Peace, and Security

What were the causes of World War I? How and why did Canada get involved?

What part did women and people of various ethnocultural backgrounds play in the war effort, both at home and overseas?

How did Canada's military forces contribute to the Allied victories?

Changing Role of Government

How could the government justify actions such as conscription, rationing, and operating internment camps during the war?

World War I presented Canada with the greatest challenge it had ever faced. Going to war would involve every Canadian, regardless of race, gender, or ethnic background. It would change the entire country. Before the war, the federal government intervened very little in the lives of ordinary Canadians. Directing and paying for the war effort would change this. After 1914, the government would be much more involved in its citizens' lives. It would pass legislation that marked certain immigrants as "enemy aliens," and it would intern thousands of them during the war. It would make "war loans," and Canadians would invest billions of dollars in their government and the war effort. It would introduce income tax for the first time.

Canada was a nation of fewer than 8 million people during World War I. Yet more than 600 000 men and thousands of women would enlist. This extremely high rate of participation had a profound impact on the entire nation. Women would join the workforce by the thousands, producing millions of artillery shells and making vital contributions to the war effort. Canadian farmers would push production beyond previous limits in order to supply the Allied troops with bread and foodstuffs. At the beginning of the war, Canada was still seen simply as a colony of the British Empire. It was automatically at war when Britain declared war on Germany. By the end of the war, Canada had become more independent, both in spirit and in its actions on the world stage.

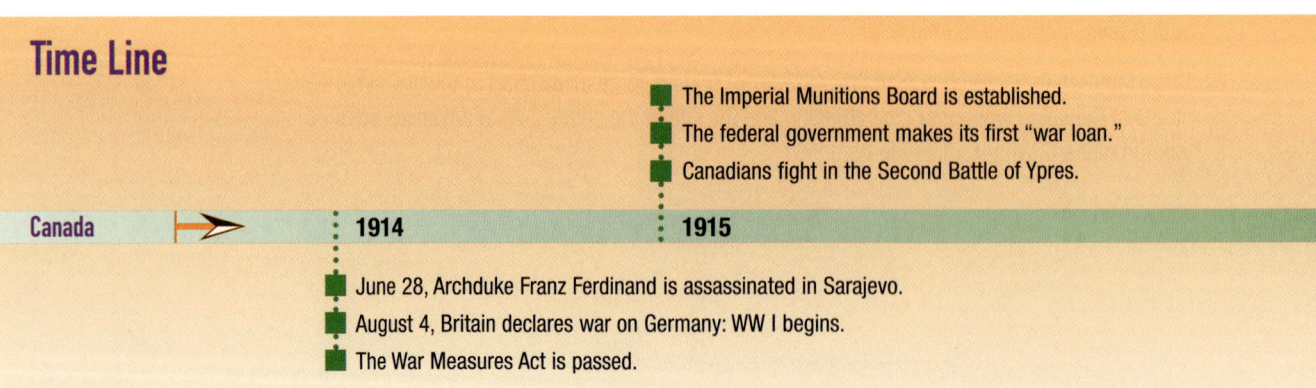

Time Line

1915
- The Imperial Munitions Board is established.
- The federal government makes its first "war loan."
- Canadians fight in the Second Battle of Ypres.

Canada → **1914**
- June 28, Archduke Franz Ferdinand is assassinated in Sarajevo.
- August 4, Britain declares war on Germany: WW I begins.
- The War Measures Act is passed.

Perspectives

It is August 1914 and Britain has declared war on Germany. Tens of thousands of Canadian men and teenagers are rushing to recruitment tents, like the people photographed here. They are eager to fight and defend "freedom." Step into the picture and create conversations that the youngest boy might have with the boy behind him, or the young man to his right, or the men holding onto the fence. Is his father here? Who might that be? What might he say to his son? Step into the picture again, but this time you know what lies ahead, that the war will be long and that millions will die. What will you say to all of these men?

- Black Canadians are allowed to enlist.
- Canadians fight at the Battle of the Somme—24 000 are killed or wounded.

1916

- April, the Canadian Corps captures Vimy Ridge.
- August, the Military Service Act is passed.
- December 17, Borden wins the federal election.

1917

- Canadian women win the right to vote in federal elections.
- The Canadian Corps spearheads the final Allied offensive.
- November 11, 11 a.m., the armistice ends World War I.

1918

THE CAUSES OF WORLD WAR I

Many factors led to the outbreak of World War I. For one thing, the last major war—one involving all European nations—had ended in 1815. Europeans had no memory of what a major war was like. By 1914, Europeans had become increasingly militaristic. Nations competed to have the strongest military forces (see Chapter 1, "The Naval Crisis") and maintained large armies. Conscription was common, and most European men had had some military experience. The majority of Europeans also felt that war was a good way to settle international disputes and to reduce tensions. Most wars in the nineteenth century had been short.

Europe had also split into two alliance systems. Britain, France, and Russia formed the "Triple Entente" (or "the Allies"), while Germany, Italy, and the Austro-Hungarian Empire formed the "Triple Alliance" (or "the Central Powers"). While it seemed this arrangement might deter war, it actually meant that an attack against one alliance nation would be treated as an attack against all members.

Nationalism had also swept Europe, and most nations believed their way of life was superior to others. Most European nations also felt they had legitimate grievances against other nations, and that it was their right to promote their international ambitions at the expense of other nations. Between the late 1890s and 1914, crises erupted between the nations of Europe's alliances. Each time, a major war loomed, but each time it was averted. Nonetheless, tensions continued to build. Today, most historians believe that a major war was inevitable.

On June 28, 1914, the two gunshots that would trigger World War I rang out in Sarajevo, the capital of Bosnia (then part of the Austro-Hungarian Empire). As Archduke Franz Ferdinand, heir to the Austro-Hungarian throne, and his wife Sophia rode in an open car, a group of Serbian terrorists waited for them. One of them, 19-year-old Gavrillo Princip, made his way to the car and fired two bullets. Ferdinand and Sophia were killed.

Serbia was a small nation, and Serbian nationalists had been demanding control of Bosnia. Austria blamed Serbia for the killings, and presented it with demands. Russia, Serbia's ally, objected. Serbia rejected one of the demands, and Austria declared war in late July. Within a week, the two alliances were at war. When Britain declared war on Germany on August 4, 1914, Canada was also automatically at war.

Canadians Respond To The Call

Canada was prospering when Conservative Robert Borden won the election of 1911. By 1914, however, Canada's economy was struggling, and thousands of Canadians could not find work. One reason for the downturn was that the growing tensions in Europe had slowed investment in Canada and trade. The outbreak of World War I seemed, somehow, to be a relief. The response of Canadians was unprecedented. On the night of Britain's declaration of war, thou-

---

Data File

Medical Checklist, 1917

To serve in World War I, Canadian recruits had to have a medical examination. Here are a few items from the medical examiners' checklist.

- sufficiently intelligent
- speech is without impediment
- chest is capacious
- free and perfect motion of all joints
- between the ages of 18 and 45
- at least 5 feet for infantry; 5' 4" for artillery corps
- one or two toes may be missing as long as big toes are intact

Communities: War, Peace, and Security

Foundations

War and Remembrance: We Shall Not Sleep

You have probably seen war movies and visited war memorials and monuments. You probably also know that each year November 11 is observed as "Remembrance Day," or "Armistice Day." In Canada and Britain it is also called "Poppy Day." You may have worn a poppy, and stood for a moment's silence in class at 11 a.m. What you may not know is exactly how these customs came about.

In this chapter you will look at the battles of World War I and learn of the devastating toll they took on millions and millions of people around the world. You will also learn of the valour and courage of many thousands of Canadian soldiers. Young Canadian soldiers fought many battles in the fields of Flanders. During one such a battle, at Ypres, a Canadian medical officer, John McCrae, scribbled a poem that would immortalize the war and transform the poppy into a symbol of remembrance.

Figure 3–1 Remembrance Day. This British Airways flight attendant observes a moment's silence on November 11, 1999 at the Eaton Centre in Toronto. She was upset that many people simply continued shopping as the clock struck 11 a.m.

In Flanders Fields

In Flanders fields the poppies blow
Between the crosses, row on row,
    That mark our place; and in the sky
    The larks, still bravely singing, fly
Scarce heard amid the guns below.

We are the Dead. Short days ago
We lived, felt dawn, saw sunset glow,
Loved, and were loved, and now we lie
    In Flanders fields.

Take up our quarrel with the foe:
    To you from failing hands we throw
    The torch; be yours to hold it high.
If ye break faith with us who die
We shall not sleep, though poppies grow
    In Flanders fields.

What Do You Think?

1. In Britain, controversy broke out when some people began to wear white poppies instead of the traditional red poppies. These people oppose war, but wish to pay their respects to those who are buried at Flanders. Why do you think it created a controversy?

2. In the 1990s, Dan Murphy had a poppy painted on his motorcycle before leaving on a cross-Canada adventure. Why is it important for him and all of us to think about those who fought in wars for Canada before we were born?

3. Think of some new ways to honour the spirit of Remembrance Day that have personal significance for you.

Canada and World War I

Figure 3–2 Is there something odd about this picture? The father, Reg Heath, seems not to be part of the photograph. After the second time he was wounded and then sent back to the trenches, he had his picture taken. He sent it back to Canada with instructions to insert it into a family photograph. Reg was sure that he would die in the war, and he wanted his family to remember him.

Figure 3–3 The lion, symbol of the British Empire, calls out for help. Many Canadians, especially those born in Britain, answered the call.

sands of Canadians cheered in the streets. Canada was about to be thrust into a war that none of them could ever have imagined.

English Canada rushes to war

Colonel Sam Hughes, Canada's Minister of Militia, boasted of the 100 000 men who quickly volunteered to enlist. Two-thirds of the first wave of volunteers, in fact, were British. Of the 470 000 soldiers who served overseas with the Canadian Expeditionary Force during the war, 53 percent were born outside Canada. Most of these were born in Great Britain and made up 25.3 percent, or 118 910 soldiers, of the total force.

Reginald and Hester Heath's story is a piece of that picture. Born in England, they immigrated to Canada in 1913 with their three young daughters. Reg found work as a farm labourer, and Hester took in laundry. Times were hard, however, and they missed their families in England. For Reg, the declaration of war was a chance to see England again and to receive regular pay. Besides, everyone was sure it would be over by Christmas.

After the early enthusiasm, and when casualty figures became public, enlistment fell significantly, including among those of British heritage.

French Canadians hesitate

Sir Wilfrid Laurier, Opposition leader and former prime minister, responded "ready, aye, ready" to Britain's call. But he hardly spoke for all French Canadians. Henri Bourassa, a nationalist and consistent opponent of the war and conscription, probably spoke for more French Canadians: "English-speaking Canadians enlist in much smaller numbers than the newcomers from England, because they are more Canadian; French Canadians enlist less than English Canadians because they are totally and exclusively Canadian. To claim that their abstention is due to the 'baneful' influence of the Nationalists is pure nonsense."

However, about 35 000 French Canadians did serve in Canada's armed forces. Thousands of Quebecers died on the battlefields of France and Belgium. Others were taken prisoner, gassed, or suffered other casualties. Many were disabled for life. French-Canadian civilians endured rationing, and large numbers of women worked in factories to produce munitions.

The Native peoples respond During the early days of the war, the Borden government discouraged aboriginal Canadians from enlisting. When the initial flood of volunteers slowed to a trickle after 1915, however, the government changed its policy. Now Canada's Native peoples were encouraged to volunteer. By the end of WW I, one in three able-bodied First Nations men had enlisted.

Figure 3–4 This poster tried to recruit French Canadians by reminding them of former war heroes. It had little success.

Some First Nations responded with extraordinary enthusiasm. The Algonquin of Gold Lake, Ontario sent all but three of their able-bodied young men. Roughly half of eligible Mi'kmaq and Maliseet of New Brunswick and Nova Scotia enlisted. And with British Columbia's Head of the Lake People, every single male between the ages of 20 and 35 volunteered.

World War I's **trench warfare**, chlorine gas, and machine guns massacred a generation of young Canadian men. Among them were at least 300 aboriginal soldiers. Others died of illness, particularly tuberculosis, which thrived in the damp trenches. Countless aboriginal soldiers returned home infected with this often-fatal disease. During the war, aboriginal soldiers won medals in practically every major land battle. The Native peoples also supported the war effort at home, donating money and goods to relief and patriotic funds, and investing in **victory bonds**. First Nations women, like other Canadian women, formed patriotic leagues, Red Cross Societies, and other charity groups, and collected clothes, money, and food to ship overseas.

Black Canadians: Not Wanted In 1914, Canada was in many ways a racist society, officially and unofficially—as was the rest of the world. Most people had little understanding of prejudice, stereotyping, discrimination, and racism, despite the abolition of slavery in the nineteenth century. For Black Canadians, the first battle of WW I was for the right to enlist. Despite their record of fighting to defend Canada in the War of 1812 and during the

Figure 3–5 William Semia, a member of the Cat Lake Band in northern Ontario, spoke no English or French when he joined the 52nd Battalion. He learned to speak English from an aboriginal volunteer and used it later to drill platoons.

Upper Canada Rebellion, Black Canadians were rejected at recruiting stations. Finally in 1916, the No. 2 Construction Battalion, the first and only Black battalion in Canadian history, was formed. It was led by White officers, and the 1049 men were allowed to do manual labour: logging, milling, shipping, and trench digging. Black men throughout the country immediately volunteered. Nova Scotia alone provided over 300 recruits.

Each individual had his own reasons for joining. Nova Scotian William F. Guy explained his this way:

> My friend Herby Burchell and I travelled by horse and team from Clementsport to Annapolis Royal, and we were both accepted. We knew what we had to do … We were fighting … for our parents and for our people to have a country to live in. I never expected to come back.

Captain Reverend Dr. William Andrew White was the son of ex-slaves. He came to Nova Scotia from Virginia in 1900 to study theology at Acadia University. He was Acadia's first Black student. White was ordained a minister in 1906. When WW I broke out, White enlisted in No. 2 Construction Battalion and became the only Black chaplain and the only Black officer in the Canadian Army.

Japanese Canadians are rejected Even though Japanese Canadians could not vote, hold political office, or be involved in professions such as law, pharmacy, and the civil service, many young Japanese Canadian men wanted to volunteer.

In December 1915, Mankichi Omura read in a Japanese-language newspaper that the Canadian Japanese Association was calling for volunteers to serve in the Canadian Army. By fighting for their new country, Japanese immigrants would show their loyalty. Mankichi knew what he had to do. He joined 200 Japanese volunteers as they paraded down Powell Street in Vancouver, and the Canadian Japanese Association wired Ottawa that the volunteers were ready. The government reply was a blow. It said the Japanese had peculiar customs, a strange language, and a different appearance. They would not make good Canadian citizens. The volunteers disbanded and Mankichi returned to the Skeena River for another season of fishing.

Some time later, while painting his boat, Mankichi saw one of the volunteers from Vancouver come running down the gangplank in a Canadian Army uniform. With him was a young officer. "Oi," he yelled at Mankichi. "We can get in. Pack your things and let's go to Alberta!"

Mankichi joined with 55 other Japanese young men, all from British Columbia, and enlisted in the 175th Overseas Battalion in Medicine Hat,

Figure 3–6 Two Canadian soldiers rest while loading ammunition.

Up Close

1. Make jot notes about how each of these groups responded to the call to war and how they were treated: English Canadians, French Canadians, Native peoples, Black Canadians, Japanese Canadians, Ukrainian Canadians, German Canadians.

Alberta. By the end of the war, of these 56 Japanese soldiers, 20 were killed and 23 wounded. In total, of 196 Japanese volunteers, 54 were killed and 93 wounded. Only 59 returned home safely.

Ukrainian Canadians enlist even though they are "enemy aliens" Shortly after the war broke out in 1914, the Borden government passed the War Measures Act. This gave the government extraordinary powers. During a state of war, Cabinet could pass legislation without debate in the House of Commons or approval from the Senate. The government could also take over areas of provincial jurisdiction and control any social and economic activities deemed essential to the war effort. The Act also defined immigrants from Germany or Austria-Hungary as "enemy aliens." These people could be arrested, without any charges being laid, and detained indefinitely.

Figure 3–7 Sergeant Masumi Mitsui was awarded the Military Medal for bravery at the Battle of Hill 70 in 1917. Here he is seen (second from left) with other wounded Canadian soldiers at a casualty clearing station.

About 171 000 Ukrainian immigrants were living in Canada, mostly on the Prairies. Since many had come from the Austro-Hungarian provinces of Galicia and Bukovina, their citizenship could be identified as Austrian. Under the War Measures Act, 8579 "enemy aliens" were imprisoned, including about 5000 Ukrainians. Another 80 000 Ukrainians were classified as "enemy aliens" and had to report regularly to police and carry identification cards.

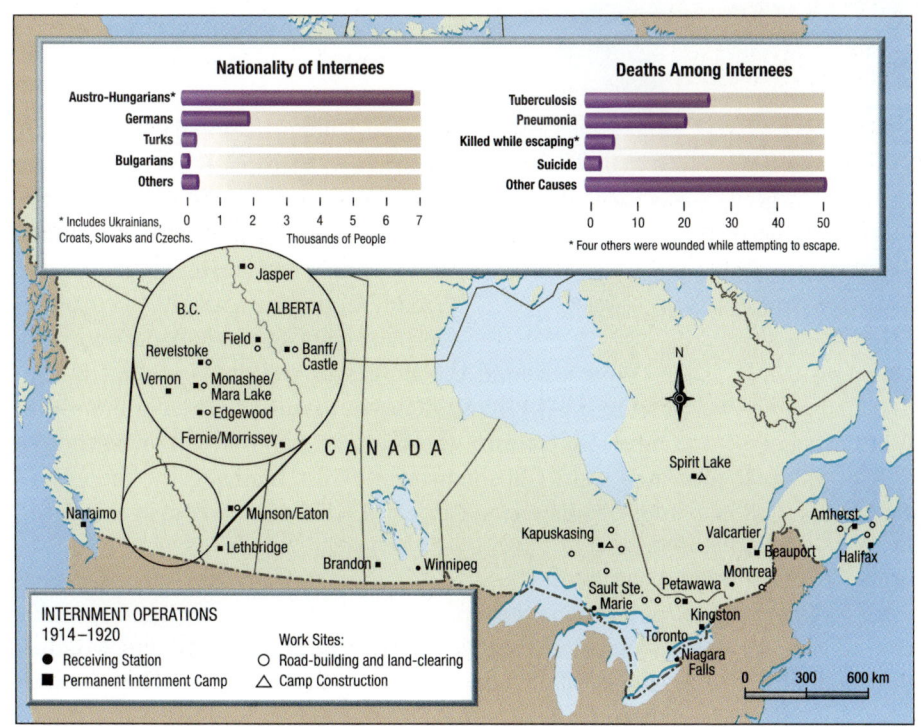

Figure 3–8 Ukrainian internment camps, 1914–1920

Canada and World War I **59**

Imprisoned Ukrainians were sent to internment camps in Quebec, Alberta, and British Columbia. They were obliged to construct the camps, build roads, cut wood, clear land, and build railways. Harsh working and living conditions and enforced confinement took their toll—107 Ukrainian internees died. For many, the experience destroyed the hopes they had when they arrived in Canada. Despite this, about 10 000 Ukrainians enlisted. Some said they were Polish or Russian in order to be accepted. Many felt that they were not appreciated, as one recalls:

> Look here! Our boys respond to the call of this country and enlist. But do the English respect them? No, not at all. They point to them with their fingers and say, 'Look, there is a Galician in the uniform of a British soldier,' and then laugh at them.

Figure 3–9 This is the interior of the Kaiserhoff Hotel in Victoria, BC, after it was trashed by angry anti-German citizens in 1915. Even though thousands of Canadian soldiers were being killed in the trenches, do you believe these people were justified?

German Canadians are feared By 1914, there were more than 400 000 German Canadians. They formed Canada's third largest ethnic group, after the British and French. Many could trace their roots to Loyalists who had migrated from the US in the 1780s. Untold thousands of German Canadians enlisted and fought bravely. Yet it was not a good time to have a German name. Bitter feelings against German Canadians increased as war casualties mounted, and many people justified their hostility as patriotism.

In two cities with substantial German Canadian populations (Berlin, Ontario and Victoria, BC) tensions were particularly high. The use of the German language was officially banned from schools and universities. And the Canadian government ordered German-language newspapers to print in English only. Riots broke out, and the homes of well-known citizens with German names were attacked. At Ottawa's Chateau Laurier Hotel, waiters with German names were fired. In Toronto, the German Club closed, even though 900 of its 1000 members were Canadian-born. Most dramatically, the city of Berlin changed its name to Kitchener, after Lord Kitchener, a British war hero.

Some Canadians oppose the war Pressure to support Canada's war effort was intense. Everywhere, posters and newspapers encouraged young men to enlist and all citizens to buy victory bonds. Churches, the Red Cross, and women's organizations did everything from buying machine guns to pinning white feathers (a symbol of cowardice) on healthy young civilian men. Yet, by 1917, the number of volunteers was seriously lagging as casualties increased. As you will read later in this chapter, Borden finally introduced conscription as a way to solve the problem of reinforcements, even though he had stated this would never happen.

For many French Canadians, the idea of conscription was an outrage. When it became law, most French Canadians feared it would destroy Canada. Borden's about-face shook their trust in public servants and the federal government. Opposition to the war was often portrayed as unpatriotic, even treasonous, but opponents to conscription and the war were patriotic, and their reasoning was clear-sighted.

Opposition to the war was not limited to French Canada, but was spread across the country. Prominent women's rights leaders, such as Flora McDonald Denison and Nellie McClung, wrote books condemning the militarism of the male-dominated government and all forms of war. Many Methodist ministers who had served as chaplains on the front lines returned to Canada convinced that the war was, in fact, evil. They would go on to push for political change in Canada.

On the Prairies, many farmers did not want to see men taken from the important job of producing food. Anna Smokorowsky, born in Manitoba in 1902 of parents recently emigrated from Ukraine, spoke for many when she told the story of her neighbour's son:

Figure 3–10 Pacifism remains a deeply held belief for many Canadians. These Quakers are protesting in front of the Peace Tower in Ottawa in 1998, just before the bombing of Iraq.

> This boy was out bindering, like doing harvest. ... and the RCMP came and took him right off that binder, and left the binder and the horses in the bush there. When the father came, the binder was empty, he didn't know what happened till a week or a few weeks later. That was bad because the farmers, the older people, felt that they should have their sons to look after this harvest that they were growing. ... But the townspeople supported conscription, although I remember this Mrs. Newton saying that she didn't want her boy to go. She said that it was somebody else's war, that it wasn't a war to defend Canada. It was defending some other land that this boy didn't know about.

Up Close

2. Write a sentence to explain why each of the following opposed the war:
   a) French Canadians
   b) Nellie McClung
   c) Methodist ministers
   d) Prairie farmers
   e) Quakers, Hutterites, Mennonites, Doukhobors

For other Canadians, pacifism was a fundamental religious belief. These included Quakers, Mennonites, Hutterites, and Doukhobors. They had been guaranteed the right to live according to their beliefs when they immigrated to Canada. And they made up the largest number of conscientious objectors during both world wars. Bishop David Toews of Saskatchewan revealed the Mennonites' deep commitment to peace in this statement:

> We do not require anyone to shed his blood for us. We would rather die ourselves or languish in prison or leave our homes and settle again in some wilderness as our forebears have done, than to require sacrifice of any kind by anyone on our behalf.

LIFE IN THE TRENCHES

The German invasion of France was fought to a standstill in December 1914, and the German and Allied armies literally had to dig in for winter. Soon a ragged line of trenches cut across Europe—from the English Channel into Belgium and across France. The war would not be quick and glorious. World War I introduced trench warfare, and as the war wore on, life in the trenches became horrific. Most people in Canada had no idea of actual conditions. The Canadian government, and the media, presented war reports that were told in heroic terms—this would increase public support of the war. Later, veterans told a different story.

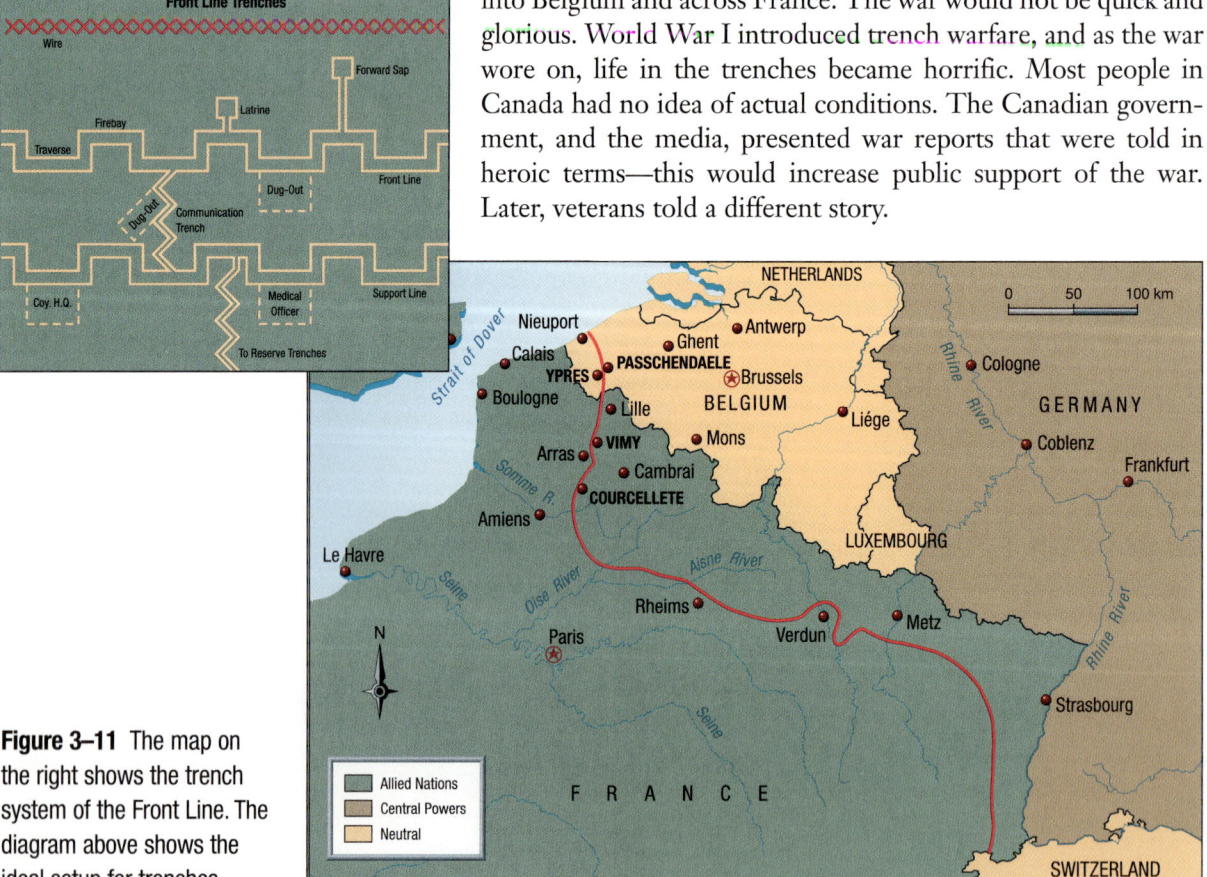

Figure 3–11 The map on the right shows the trench system of the Front Line. The diagram above shows the ideal setup for trenches.

62 Chapter 3

Greg Clark, an infantryman, won the Military Cross at Vimy Ridge:

Trenches is too romantic a name. These were ditches, common, ordinary ditches. As time went by they became filthy. We had no garbage disposal, no sewage disposal. You would dig a little trench off the main trench, dig a deep hole, and that was your latrine. You threw everything you didn't want out over the parapet ... And if you stood ever at a place, where ... you could look at the trenches, you saw this sort of strange line of garbage heap wandering up hill and down dale as far as the eye could see, and in that setting men lived as if it were the way men should live, year after year.

Corporal Craigie Mackie served with the 2nd Gordon Highlanders during WW I. Like all troops in the trenches, he endured the cold and the lack of food and water: "We just got biscuits, bully beef, jam, pork 'n beans and, towards the finish, lots of butter. We could always chew the biscuits so we never got hungry." Fresh vegetables and fruit were unheard of. Water was often carried in cans that were tainted with gas. Outside, in the shell holes, water was undrinkable because of the bodies and blood: "Water was a terrible thing." Mackie had joined up with seven of his friends: "[we] had grown up together, went to school together, played soccer together, joined the army together and only two of us came out alive."

Up Close

3. Create a mind map that records what life was like in the trenches.

Figure 3–12 What does the photograph on the left indicate about living conditions in the trenches? What awaited soldiers in **no man's land** (right), the area just outside the trenches?

By the outbreak of WW I, Max Aitken had become a British MP. During the war, he represented the Canadian government at the front:

The men in the firing and supporting trenches exchange places every 48 hours. After a four days spell they all retire for four days rest, fresh troops taking their places as they move out. At the end of their four days rest they return again to the trenches. All relieving movements are carried out in the dark to avoid the enemy's rifle fire.

Canada and World War I

Images
Will R. Bird: An Ordinary Soldier

Figure 3–13 Between October 26 and November 7, 1917, more than 15 000 Canadian soldiers were killed or wounded in the Battle of Passchendaele. They won the battle, and nine Victoria Crosses.

Will R. Bird, from Amherst, Nova Scotia, was 24 when WW I broke out. He tried to enlist three times, but each time was rejected because of bad teeth. Steve, his younger brother, enlisted in 1914 and was killed in action in 1915. On his fourth attempt at enlistment, Will R. Bird was accepted. He arrived in England in October 1916 and was in the trenches by December.

As a corporal in the 42nd Battalion, the Royal Black Watch of Canada, Bird fought in France until the Armistice in November 1918. Fifty years later, he wrote a memoir, *Ghosts Have Warm Hands*. Many people consider it one of the most moving accounts of war ever written by an ordinary soldier. Because it is vivid and detailed, it also gives historians insights into the experiences of the Canadians who fought in the trenches. In the excerpts that follow, Bird describes an experience he had one night shortly after the Battle of Vimy Ridge. Bird and two companions found a dugout in which to sleep, and covered themselves with a groundsheet:

> The groundsheet pegged over our heads was pulled free and fell on my face, rousing me. Then a firm warm hand seized one of mine and pulled me up to a sitting position. It was very early, as first sunshine was glittering on the dew-wet grass. I was annoyed … I tried to pull free. But the grip held. I was face to face with my brother, Steve, who had been killed in '15! Steve grinned as he released my hands, then put his warm hand

over my mouth as I started to shout my happiness. "Get your gear," he said softly.

As I grabbed it he turned and started walking away rapidly. It was hard to keep up with him. Then I noticed he had a soft cap on, and no gas mask or equipment. Somehow he knew where the 42nd was, and our "D" Company, but how in the world did he know where I was sleeping? At that moment, my equipment … slipped off and fell to the ground before I could catch it. As I stooped and retrieved it Steve went into a passageway in the ruins and I ran to catch him.

Bird searches the ruins of the village of Petit Vimy looking for his brother, then dozes off. He is found later by men in his unit, who tell him that his dugout was hit by German shells. His two friends are dead.

Later, Bird and his battalion are involved in the Canadian attack on Passchendaele, during the Third Battle of Ypres. In the destroyed landscape, fighting is extremely dangerous. McIntyre, an officer in Bird's unit, decides to capture a German **pillbox**:

'How far is it to the pillbox?' I asked. McIntyre said it was about 150 yards. Clark (another officer) said it was twice as far, and to the right of the road. McIntyre said he was wrong. He had seen the map. It was to the left of the road. Never through the war was I more sickened and discouraged than at that moment. … None knew what defences the German had or his strength. The place after dark was a swampy wilderness without anything to use as a guide. Half the men had never been in an attack, and that included the officers. Furthermore … I discovered that Clark had also had too much rum.

The company of 25 splits into four groups. Two go up one side of the road, and two on the other. McIntyre leads one group, with Will behind, and Clark leads the other:

There was quite a drop of bank on our left. McIntyre did not look left or right but kept scrambling along as fast as possible. I peered over the bank from time to time and suddenly saw three or four Germans raise their heads … I seized McIntyre's foot to signal him. He yanked it away and spoke angrily. The Germans fired instantly … I threw my grenades over the bank. Both exploded as they went down, and the Hun stopped shooting at once. McIntyre had never stopped and was now quite a distance ahead. I left the group and ran to catch up with McIntyre. Machine guns opened up on all sides. The night was in an uproar. There was a flaming white-hot instant—and oblivion!

When I recovered consciousness … all around us was a clamour of machine guns, bombs and rifles. I heard McIntyre shouting 'Five rounds rapid!' Then his voice shut off abruptly. At that moment, Clark appeared … trying to run and reeling all over the place. 'Come on!' he shouted. 'Let's give them hell!' His shout ended and he pitched into the mud ahead of us. He was dead when we tried to raise him. … McIntyre was lying to our left, shot through the stomach, and dying, unconscious.

Bird and the surviving men try to retreat, but more men are killed by German fire. In the morning, Bird and two other soldiers make it back the trench:

We huddled there until noon, then I roused up and peered over the side of our refuge. A few yards away were three green-scummed pools. White chalky hands reached out of one, and from the farther one a knee stuck up above the filthy water.

What Do You Think?

1. Draw, sketch, or paint an image to go with Will Bird's memory of his dead brother saving his life.

2. If you could sit down with Will Bird, what would you talk about? Write some questions you would like to ask him.

3. Look up another first-person account of a war experience to read. How do such writings affect how you think about war, and history in general?

THE WAR AT HOME

As Minister of Militia, Sam Hughes handled supplies for Canadian troops. Hughes liked to be in charge, and he liked dealing with friends. Contracts were awarded to his buddies, resulting in slipshod, sometimes dangerous, goods. In one case, 2 million boots were shipped overseas, where it was discovered they had cardboard soles. The troops nicknamed Hughes "Sir Sam Shoes." In 1915, Prime Minister Borden took control of supplies away from Hughes and set up a War Purchasing Commission.

Hughes also helped set up a Shell Committee, composed of prominent industrialists. By the beginning of 1915, it had won $170 million in contracts from the British Army. Again, there were quality problems. Some of the shells exploded prematurely, killing gun crews. By the end of 1915, only $5.5 million worth of shells had been produced. Borden stepped in again and established the Imperial Munitions Board (IMB) in December 1915. The IMB, which was tied to the British government, was placed under the control of Joseph Flavelle, a prominent Ontario bacon producer and loyal Conservative Party member. Flavelle acted like a dictator. He broke labour strikes, revoked contracts if shoddy goods were produced, and stifled any complaints by using the provisions of the War Measures Act.

Financing the War

WW I was the costliest conflict the world had ever known to that time. On average, the war cost Canada more than $1 million a day. Because federal expenditures (money spent) far exceeded revenues (money brought in), the government resorted to three methods to raise money. The first was to borrow by selling government bonds to investors (the government still raises extra revenues this way). The first such "war loan" in 1915 raised more than $179 million, and promised large and small investors a return of 5 percent. The government had expected to raise only $50 million. Two similar loans followed in 1916 and 1917, bringing in $460 million.

Between 1917 and 1919, the finance minister offered another kind of war loan, called "victory bonds." These were offered to the general public at a return of 5.5 percent. More than 3 million Canadians bought victory bonds, raising $1738 million. Again, the response far exceeded government expectations. It was a stunning display of confidence and determination by Canadians. Together, the six war loans raised $2377 million.

Figure 3–14 This poster warned people against stockpiling food during wartime shortages.

In 1917, the government came up with its third source of revenue: a direct tax, the first of its kind in Canada. The Income War Tax collected 3 percent of the gross earnings of a family that earned more than $3000 a year, and from individuals who earned more than $1500 per year. At the time, the average family income was less than $800 a year. Only 31 130 Canadians paid the income tax, and Canadians were assured that income tax would end with the war.

Women Contribute to the War Effort

By 1917, more than 600 Canadian factories were producing $2 million worth of munitions and war goods a day. To keep production going, Flavelle hired 30 000 women to work in precision jobs in various munitions factories. Many labour unions protested the hiring of women, but the needs of the Imperial Munitions Board won out. The IMB was crucial to Allied arms production, and eventually helped win the War. The IMB not only changed the makeup of the workforce, it created a new industrial base that would later spur economic growth in Canada during the 1920s (see Chapter 4). Finally, the IMB also manufactured airplanes and trained more than 3300 pilots for duty in the Royal Air Force.

More than 2400 Canadian women enlisted as nurses. They served in Canadian and British **field hospitals**, or in convalescent hospitals in Britain. Of these, 18 were killed when enemy shells exploded in the field hospitals. In the field, nurses constantly dealt with suffering and death. During WW I, the Germans used **chlorine gas** as a chemical weapon, which led to thousands of cases of "gas gangrene." Soldiers' bodies would swell to twice their normal size and they would die in agony. Nurse Elizabeth Paynter served in a field hospital during the Battle of the Somme and recalled a harrowing night after a young New Zealand soldier died of a hemorrhage.

> The same night another patient died, and another still was very low, while there were at least four other delirious head cases [soldiers with head wounds], who seemed to take turns pulling off their dressings or getting out of bed. We also had a number of gas gangrene cases, and these are quite a worry, as the infection travels so fast, and last, but not least, the hemorrhages, which so often occur in the dead of night when the lights are dim. Here is where my flashlight served me in good stead and I then blessed old Waldron for insisting on us buying them in Kingston, where we were outfitted.

Another 1000 Canadian women served in the Royal Flying Corps and the Royal Air Force, mostly as drivers of vehicles. Other Canadian women made their way to Europe to serve as volunteers with the British Red Cross.

Countless thousands of Canadian women worked in victory-bond drives, and another 6000 worked in the Canadian civil service. Many more spent their free time knitting garments for the troops. This was absolutely vital. The only way combat soldiers could avoid trench foot—which was caused by standing ankle- or knee-deep in muddy water and could lead to complications and amputations—was to have regular changes of dry socks. The bitter winters of Northern France

Up Close

4. Before reading this section, brainstorm a list of ways you think women contributed to the war effort, both overseas and at home. After reading, revise your list to match what you read.

Figure 3–15 WW I changed the social roles of thousands of women. At left, Canadian women inspect shell fuses in a munitions factory in 1917. On the right, Grace MacPherson from Vancouver drives an ambulance with the Volunteer Aid Detachment of the British Red Cross.

also required gloves and scarves to keep out the cold. These women's efforts saved the lives and health of thousands of grateful Canadian soldiers on the Western Front.

Women work through "rugged" times In the final years of the war, prices increased rapidly. This is known as "inflation," and it caused hardship across Canada. Wages did not increase enough to keep up with inflation and working women were paid less than men to begin with. Women whose husbands were fighting in the war received a fixed income, which did not increase during the war.

Frank Bell lived in Montreal during the war and later described one woman's experience:

> This woman I boarded with in Montreal had two young girls. Her husband was overseas for four years, and she certainly never went out anywhere. They led a pretty lonely life. She wasn't even allowed a telephone. She got $20 a month from her husband's pay (soldiers were paid $1.10 per day during the war) and she got $20 a month from the (Canadian) Patriotic Fund. But this wasn't a gift; it was charity ... administered by a group of rich men's wives, and if they found that a woman was running around, or that she was living beyond her means (they thought), or something, they would cut her off.

In Toronto, Mrs. Doris Rosenburg had to be thrifty to get by: "It was very rugged, because—you know, inflation—everything became expensive." Eggs were so expensive that she would go down to the St. Lawrence Farmers Market and stand by the chicken coops. Whenever a chicken laid an egg, she would grab it and then haggle with the dealer for a lower price. She bargained with all the farmers this way.

Data File

Many German prisoners of war were transported to Canada on troopships returning from Britain. They were then sent to prisoner-of-war camps, most of which were in the Prairies. By 1916, many of these men were being put to work to help harvest wheat.

THE CONSCRIPTION CRISIS

In 1917, a crisis threatened to cripple Canada's war effort. Enlistment was shrinking, and more and more Canadian soldiers were being killed and wounded. It was estimated that Canada needed 100 000 reinforcements to fulfill its commitments at the front. At the same time, the British Army was relying increasingly on both Canadian and Australian soldiers to carry the fighting—these troops were highly skilled and captured their objectives.

While in England in 1917, Borden had visited wounded Canadian soldiers in the convalescent hospitals. They were being patched up and rushed back to the front, because there simply were not enough reinforcements. He returned to Canada convinced of the need for drastic action. On May 18, 1917 he made a stunning speech in the House of Commons:

> All citizens are liable to military service for the defence of their country, and I conceive that the battle for Canadian liberty and autonomy is being fought today on the plains of France and Belgium. The time has come when the authority of the state should be invoked to provide reinforcements necessary to maintain the gallant men at the front.

In other words, it was time for conscription. Sir Wilfrid Laurier, leader of the Opposition and former prime minister, was strongly opposed. He knew conscription would completely alienate Quebec and he feared it would tear Canada apart:

> The law of the land declares that no man in Canada shall be subjected to compulsory military service except to repel invasions or for the defence of Canada.

Borden, however, did not back down. Reaction across the country was swift. Anti-conscription riots broke out in Montreal, and unions threatened to strike. Regardless, Borden introduced the Military Service Act in June. In August, it was passed. All men between the ages of 19 and 45 would have to enlist. The issue was so explosive, however, that conscription did not immediately take effect. Borden formed a Union Government, composed of Conservatives and pro-conscription Liberals, and called an election for December 17, 1917. It was the only way to find out if the country supported conscription.

In 1917, Borden's government also quickly passed the Wartime Elections Act. This extended the federal vote to women for the first time, but only to nurses at the front and to the wives, sisters, and mothers of soldiers. They were sure to support conscription—and Borden. (In 1918, the federal vote was extended to all Canadian women.) The Military Voters Act was also passed, allowing soldiers at the front to cast their votes (soldiers voted 90 percent in favour of Borden, and conscription). Borden's Union Government won the election, but the country was indeed split. Borden had overwhelming support in

Enlistment/Casualty Rate, 1917		
Month	**Enlistments**	**Casualties**
January	9 194	4 396
February	6 809	1 250
March	6 640	6 161
April	5 530	13 477
May	6 407	13 457
June	6 348	7 931
July	3 882	7 906
August	3 117	13 232
September	3 588	10 990
October	4 884	5 929
November	4 019	30 741
December	3 921	7 476
Total	**64 339**	**122 946**

Figure 3–16 Canada's enlistments and casualties in 1917. How do you explain the difference in the totals?

Up Close

5. Make a chart showing the pros and cons of conscription. Include names of people and groups on each side.

Figure 3–17 These injured WW I veterans are sitting on a bench in Toronto during the 1917 conscription crisis. Look at the graffiti. Do you think these veterans supported conscription? Explain.

Ontario, BC, and the Maritimes. But almost all Quebec seats went to the Liberals, who opposed conscription. The West was divided. Many farmers did not want to lose vital workers to the army and risk losing their crops.

The anger that marked the election spilled over as conscription went into effect. In the spring of 1918, anti-conscription riots broke out in Quebec City. When the federal government sent in police, more violence broke out. In the end, four people were killed. Conscription also proved to be ineffective. More than 400 000 men were conscripted, but the vast majority appealed to be exempted. Others simply did not show up at recruitment offices. By war's end, only 24 000 conscripts served at the front.

By early 1918, fewer than 15 000 trained men were available as trained reinforcements in France and Britain. Further, the French Army was no longer capable of launching any sort of major offensive. The Americans had declared war on Germany in April 1917. By early 1918, they were landing 200 000 troops in France each month. The US troops, however, were not ready for combat. It was unlikely that the US would be able to mount significant attacks until 1919. There was a strong feeling that the war would be decided before then—but no one was sure which side would win.

Figure 3–18 As the war progressed and farm workers became scarce, the government encouraged boys aged 15 to 19 to become "Soldiers of the Soil." Participants received an official uniform and a medal in recognition of their service. Why would the Montreal Shirt Company (which produced and distributed this poster) be willing to advertise this program?

THE WAR AT SEA AND IN THE AIR

As World War I began, the war at sea developed as few had expected. The great naval fleets of Germany and Britain clashed only once, in 1916, off the coast of Denmark. After that, neither country would risk losing their fleet in a major battle. Instead, both navies set up blockades to destroy shipments of troops, goods, and supplies bound for the "enemy." The British navy laid sea mines to choke off all supplies bound for Germany. And the Germans introduced a deadly new weapon, the submarine, or "U-boat" to enforce their blockade of Britain. From 1915 onwards, German submarines targeted and sank thousands of ships sailing from North America to Britain. In this kind of war, it wasn't only soldiers who suffered, but civilians as well. **Rationing** became necessary.

By 1917, Britain's blockade of Germany had taken its toll on war supplies, food, and medical equipment. Now desperate, the Germans began unrestricted submarine warfare. Even ocean liners carrying passengers became targets. The sinking of the *Lusitania* led the US to declare war on Germany on April 6, 1917. Canadians played an indirect role in the war at sea, but Canadian shipyards built ships for the convoys and submarine patrol. And thousands of Canadians joined the British navy or served on merchant ships.

At the outset of the war, airplanes were still new. Sam Hughes dismissed them as "an invention of the devil." At first, airplanes were used only to scout enemy troops and artillery. Eventually, technological improvements allowed them to be used on bombing missions. More than 20 000 Canadians served with the Royal Flying Corps and other branches of the British flying services, such as the Royal Naval Air Service. They served as spotters and pilots of fighters and heavy bombers.

The most celebrated flyers of the war were the fighter aces. Among the top 21 aces from all over the British Empire, no fewer than ten were Canadian, and of the top ten aces from every country on both sides in the war, four were Canadian. (To qualify as an ace, a pilot had to down five enemy aircraft.) Lieutenant-Colonel Billy Bishop, the first Canadian airman to win the Victoria Cross, was ranked third among all aces, with 72 victories.

Heritage Minute

Just before the federal election of 1917, catastrophe struck Halifax, Nova Scotia. On December 6, the *Mont Blanc*, a French steamer carrying 2400 tonnes of explosives, collided with another ship. Within minutes the *Mont Blanc* exploded, killing 1600 people, injuring 9000 and destroying much of Halifax. It was the largest man-made explosion in history and would remain so until the atomic bombing of Hiroshima.

Figure 3–19 Billy Bishop, Canada's top flying ace of WW I, became a hero across Canada and around the world. Bishop and fellow ace Raymond Collinshaw would help to organize the Royal Canadian Air Force in 1918.

THE WAR UNFOLDS

Up Close

6. For each battle described on pages 72 to 76, create a newspaper headline which might have appeared in a Canadian newspaper reporting on the war.

It was in the trenches of the Western Front that Canada made its major contribution in WW I. In a series of battles that stretched from 1915 to the last day of the war, Canadian soldiers fought valiantly and with increasing skill and determination. In the early years of the war, the Canadian government and Canadian officers had little say in how Canadian troops were used. They were simply deployed by British high command, and ordered by British officers. Through the course of the war, that would change. While Canada would never have a direct say in the overall strategy of the war, Canadian officers would gain more and more authority of Canadian troops, and a Canadian officer would finally command the Canadian Corps.

Second Battle of Ypres: April 1915

Soldiers in the Canadian Expeditionary Force saw their first major action in the Second Battle of Ypres. During November 1914, the British had held the town of Ypres and the surrounding countryside. As a result, the British line bulged into the German line in what is called a "salient." Two Allied brigades, one Canadian, one French, were holding the line just north of Ypres, near the town of St. Julien. On April 22, 1915, at 5 p.m., the Germans released a nightmarish weapon: chlorine gas.

The French troops were hit hardest. Choking and dying, they fled towards Ypres. The Canadians were left to close the gap as the Germans attacked from behind the cloud of gas. For five days, Canadian and British troops fought desperately to halt the German advance. They were pushed back about 3 kilometres, but stopped the German advance. Of 59 000 Allied casualties, 6000 were Canadians. Canadian Colonel Arthur Currie showed outstanding leadership and personal courage during the battle, and would quickly rise through the military ranks.

The Second Battle of Ypres exposed how the war would play out on the Western Front. One side would attack and make minor gains, then the other side would increase its defence. Thousands upon thousands of soldiers would be killed and wounded as the battles continued. WW I would be long and lethal.

The Battle of the Somme: July to November 1916

The Battle of the Somme was the major British offensive of 1916. General Douglas Haig, commander of the British Army in France, wanted it to serve two purposes. First, he intended to draw away German troops to help the French Army, which was fighting a major battle at Verdun. Second, Haig hoped to break through the German line.

Haig assembled a large number of heavy guns and bombarded the German trenches non-stop for two weeks leading up to the battle. He believed the shelling would destroy the German trenches and troops and obliterate the barbed wire in no man's land. Then British troops could quickly occupy the German positions.

On July 1, 1916, the shelling stopped at dawn. Three hours later, the British rose from their trenches and started across no man's land, each man carrying 30 kilograms of equipment. But the barbed wire was intact, and the German troops, sheltered in deep **bunkers**, had survived. The British were slaughtered. They suffered 60 000 casualties that day alone. Haig, however, continued the attack for the rest of the summer. The British suffered appalling casualties.

In August, the Canadian Corps, now composed of four **divisions** (a total of 80 000 men), was sent to the Somme. Between September and October, all four divisions were added to the British offensive. Shelling and the autumn rains turned the battlefield into a wasteland of mud and rotting bodies. Still, the attacks continued. The Canadians fought valiantly, but the Germans defended their positions. Finally, the Battle of the Somme ended in early November. The British had gained, perhaps, 6 kilometres. Total British casualties numbered over 623 000, and 24 000 of the killed and wounded were Canadians.

The Battle of the Somme came to symbolize the futility of WW I. An attack that should have been called off after the first day continued at a horrible human cost. The Germans lost some 420 000 men, but were not defeated. The Canadian Corps had learned some lessons, however, and they would be applied in 1917 at the Battle of Vimy Ridge. British general Julian Byng, the British aristocrat and officer appointed to command the Canadian Corps, worked closely with Canadian subordinates. Together they realized that for any attack to work, it would have to be carefully planned and executed.

Hill 70: August 1917

After the success at Vimy Ridge (see Flashpoint, pages 74–75), the Canadians were instructed to capture Hill 70, to the northeast of Vimy Ridge. General Currie once more made careful preparations before attacking the German line. As at Vimy, the Canadians advanced under a **creeping barrage**. On August 15, the Canadians captured their objectives, taking Hill 70 and holding it during fierce German counterattacks. The battle cost Canada just under 6 000 casualties. Unfortunately, the next battle would be the worst that the Canadian Corps would face in the war.

The Third Battle of Ypres: July–November 1917

After the Battle of the Somme, British general Haig decided that an offensive in Flanders could win the war for the British. The plan was to attack from the Ypres salient, punch a hole in the German line, and then force the Germans up to the Channel coast, some 30 kilometres away. As at the Somme, Haig's plan had little to do with the actual battle.

Up Close

7. Choose one of these major battles of the war and summarize, in point form, the main elements.

Flashpoint

The Battle of Vimy Ridge: April 9–12, 1917

The Battle of Vimy Ridge marked the turning point for Canada in WW I. For the first time, all four divisions of the Canadian Corps would be fighting together as a single unit. For the Corps, and for Canada, the battle would be a test of courage, purpose, and skill. It would also give the soldiers of the Canadian Corps something they had never had—a sense of nationhood. Mankichi Omura, the Japanese volunteer from British Columbia, said that when he heard he would be fighting at Vimy Ridge, he felt proud, and like a true Canadian for the first time.

Preparations for the attack were extensive, and inclusive. As Captain Ian Sinclair of the 13th Battalion, 5th Royal Highlander, later recalled:

> There had never in history been such detailed planning and spreading of information. Everybody down to the lowest private knew exactly what the plan was from beginning to end. In our **billet** we had stone floors on which we spread out our maps. Every trench and fine detail was marked … The maps were distributed all through the battalion …

General Byng and Arthur Currie, who now commanded the 1st Canadian Division, left nothing to chance. By 1917, airplanes had become increasingly important in the war. Aerial photographs were taken of the German lines and defences, and detailed models were built. Captain Walter Moorhouse, of the 4th Canadian Mounted Rifles, later recalled:

> Every effort was concentrated on the coming attack on Vimy Ridge. Technicians made plaster models of the Ridge to scale, with Hun positions, trenches and deep dugouts accurately marked, and every officer and man was given the opportunity to study them.

Finally, the attack was launched on Easter Sunday morning, April 9, 1917, during a blinding snowstorm. After a short artillery barrage, the Canadians attacked the German lines. Waves of Canadian soldiers continued the assault, but this time they were protected by a creeping barrage of artillery fire. This new strategy took the Germans completely by surprise. Within hours, thousands of German soldiers were in retreat and the Canadians captured key objectives. The strategy was so effective that the British Army adopted it in 1918, and it made a major contribution to the Allied victory.

The Canadian artillery barrage was so thorough, however, that it destroyed the terrain of the Ridge. It was almost impossible for the Canadians to move their heavy guns forward to shell the retreating Germans. As Bombadier James F. Johnson, 5th Canadian Mounted Rifles recalled:

> … the 4th Division on our left [at the "pimple"] was having a bad time and meeting tough opposition, suffering heavy casualties. One battalion lost 60 percent of its men, another battalion lost every officer. The 1st, 2nd and 3rd Divisions could not move forward to their second objectives until the 4th Division had reached their first one.

After the early gains, the Corps was broken down into very small components. Each platoon was given specific objectives, and every soldier was briefed. For example, if an officer or sergeant were killed or wounded, any soldier in the attacking group would take over to achieve the objective.

For four days, the assault on Vimy Ridge continued. Finally, on the fourth day, the Canadian Corps broke through and took the "Ridge." It was something the British and French armies had failed to achieve in three years of fighting. As H. F. Mills recalled later:

Communities: War, Peace, and Security

I never felt like a Canadian until Vimy. After that I was Canadian all the way. We had a feeling that we could not lose, and if the other Allies packed it up we could do the whole job ourselves.

In terms of the entire war, the victory was a small event. Little ground was captured, and no great strategic advantage was gained. But through careful planning and a successful attack, the Canadian Corps had proven itself to be the equal of any military force. In June, the Canadian Corps would be placed under the command of a Canadian: Arthur Currie.

What Do You Think?

1. Re-examine this feature. Provide reasons why the Canadians were successful in capturing Vimy Ridge.

2. If the Battle of Vimy Ridge was not significant in terms of the entire course of the war, why was it so important for Canadians?

3. After the Ridge was captured, the Germans were in head-long retreat in front of the 1st and 2nd Canadian Divisions. Why were these divisions unable to make use of their advantage?

4. Examine the map in Figure 3–21. For each Canadian brigade involved, indicate how far it travelled in the course of the battle. Suggest reasons why the 3rd and 4th Brigades gained less ground than the 1st and 2nd Brigades.

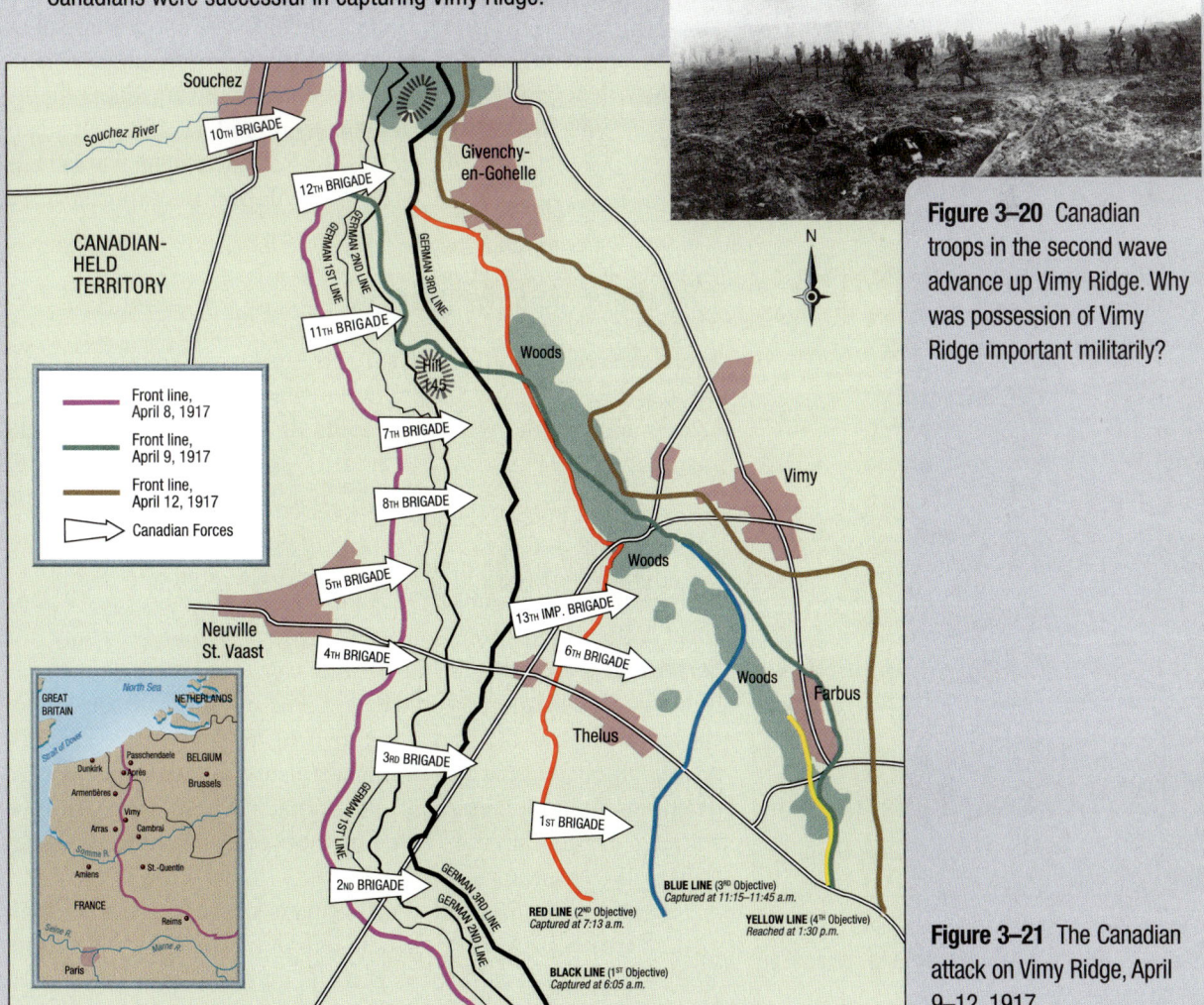

Figure 3–20 Canadian troops in the second wave advance up Vimy Ridge. Why was possession of Vimy Ridge important militarily?

Figure 3–21 The Canadian attack on Vimy Ridge, April 9–12, 1917

Data File

Canadian troops captured the Belgian town of Mons on the night of November 10/11, 1918. It had been the site of the very first battle between German and British forces in August 1914.

From July to October, 1917, the British slowly pushed back the Germans, perhaps 6 kilometres. But fighting became more difficult with each attack. The terrain of Flanders is low-lying, flat, and naturally swampy. Over the previous centuries, farmers had constructed a system of dikes to make this productive farmland. British shelling, however, destroyed the drainage system. With the heavy rains of autumn, the area had reverted to swamp. Huge shell craters dotted the landscape, and the mud was thick and heavy. It could take eight to ten men to bring out one casualty. Often, wounded men would drown in the ooze of the battlefield.

In October, Haig turned to the Canadian Corps to carry on the offensive. The objective: the small Belgian village of Passchendaele. Currie and his officers applied the same careful preparation that had worked at Vimy Ridge and Hill 70. Unfortunately, the mud was so deep and thick that it was almost impossible to find stable ground on which to place the guns. Without these, advancing troops would not have the protection of the creeping barrage. With backbreaking effort, guns were moved forward.

On October 26, 1917, the 3rd and 4th Divisions of the Canadian Corps attacked. They made little progress in the quicksand-like mud, and casualties were heavy. In early November, the 1st and 2nd Divisions were sent in to replace the decimated 3rd and 4th Divisions. On November 10, the Canadians finally captured Passchendaele. The British lost 330 000 men, and 15 600 Canadians were killed in the last two weeks of the battle. As for Passchendaele, it was little more than a pile of bricks in a sea of mud, and a position of little importance.

1918 and Canada's 100 Days

From March until June 1918, the Germans mounted a final offensive to drive a wedge between the British and the French armies and win the war. They could do this because Russia had surrendered in January 1918, after the revolution of 1917. Nearly 600 000 German troops could now be moved to the Western Front.

The Germans had two other reasons to act. As you learned earlier, the US had joined the Allies in late 1917. By late 1918 or early 1919, huge numbers of US troops would be ready for combat. If Germany did not win the war before then, the sheer number of US troops would guarantee an Allied victory. Also, the British naval blockade of Germany was, after three years, having an effect. German troops were suffering from a shortage of rations, and the German civilian population was, quite simply, starving. If the Germans failed in their offensive of early 1918, they would lose the war.

In the early months, the Germans drove the French and British armies back more than 48 kilometres. But the Allied line held. On August 8, 1918, the British launched a major offensive

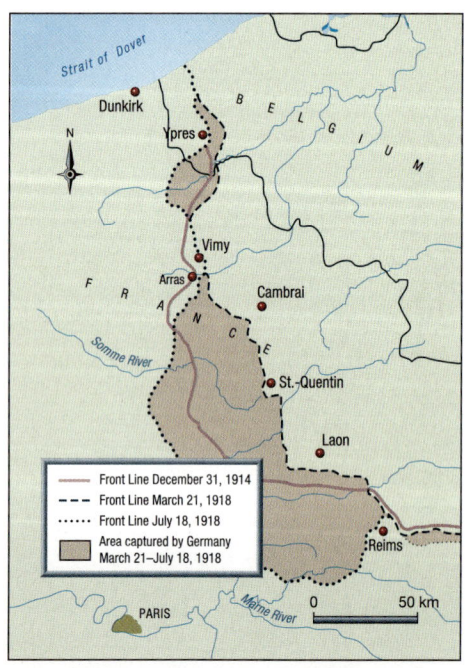

Figure 3–22 German spring offensive, 1918. How close did the Germans come to splitting the Allied forces?

at Amiens—and it was spearheaded by the Canadian and Australian divisions. In one day, they gained almost 13 kilometres. Von Ludendorff, commander of the German Army, quickly realized the Germans could not win. For this reason, August 8, 1918, is referred to as "The Black Day of the German Army." For the Canadian Corps, the battles from this day to November 11, 1918 became known as "Canada's 100 Days."

At the end of August, the Canadians were again in action, attacking German positions in the area of the Somme battles of two years earlier. The Germans fought hard, and the attack stopped when the Canadians reached the Canal du Nord in early September. The Canadians were then given the mission to cross the canal, which was very heavily defended. General Currie, however, noted that a narrow part of the canal was still dry. In a dawn attack on September 27, the Canadians crossed the canal and pushed the Germans out of their last strongly defended position, the Hindenberg Line.

In early October, in heavy fighting, the Canadians captured the important French town of Cambrai. The entire German front began to collapse. All along the Western Front, the Allies pursued the retreating Germans. And it was the Canadians who spearheaded the British advance. In early November, with rebellions breaking out in Germany and the Allies storming towards its borders, the German government asked for an **armistice**. On November 11, 1918, at 11 a.m., the armistice was agreed to, and World War I came to an end.

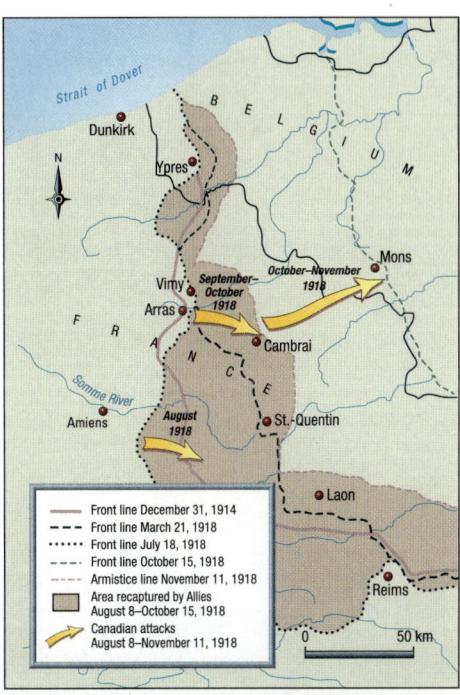

Figure 3–23 Allied advances, August–November 1918

THE PARIS PEACE SETTLEMENT

The armistice of November 11, 1918 ended the battles of WW I, but it was really only a cease-fire. War could break out again without a satisfactory peace settlement. The armistice imposed extremely hard terms on the Germans. The Allies felt that Germany must be placed in a position that would make it impossible for it to resume war. According to the terms of the armistice, Germany had to
- immediately evacuate all territories captured during the war and surrender all its overseas colonies
- withdraw all troops 10 kilometres east of the Rhine River and leave behind all artillery, machine guns, trucks, and other equipment
- surrender its navy and all merchant ships
- compensate the Allies for war damages
- surrender most of its **railway rolling stock** and locomotives to France and Belgium.

Data File

World War I was fought over incredibly small distances. Until 1918, the Front Line never moved more than ten kilometres as a result of an offensive. Yet World War I destroyed a generation of young men. The horrors of this war were so unthinkable that it became known as "the war to end all wars."

Primary Source

War Art: Insights and Information

Figure 3–24 *The Second Battle of Ypres*, 1915, by Richard Jack. This painting portrays war from a nineteenth-century perspective. An officer rallies his troops to plug the gap in the line, and stop the German advance. There is a lot of action in the painting, but the officer is the heroic focal point.

During World War I, the War Art Program was established by the Canadian War Records Office, under the direction of Max Aitken (now Lord Beaverbrook). Its purpose was to create visual records of the war. Through the Program, many Canadian and British artists created paintings and drawings of the war, often under fire. Today these works are housed at the Canadian War Museum in Ottawa.

War art is very useful to the historian because artists provide visual insights that are quite different from photographs or motion pictures. By its very nature, art is subjective, and the feelings and attitudes of the artists come through their work. There are three types of war art, and each provides different kinds of information.

Art for Patriotism Some war art is designed to promote support for soldiers fighting for their country. This type of art is usually painted quite realistically, but often lacks accuracy. Because of this, historians view such art as a reflection of attitudes of the time, not as a precise depiction.

Art as Documentation This kind of art is extremely valuable to historians. All photographs of WW I are in black and white. For this reason alone, this type of art is important because it provides a record of the colours of the war. As well, photographers were often restricted as to what they could photograph, and their images were sometimes censored. This was

Historical Inquiry: Analysing/Evaluating Information

Figure 3-25 *For What?*, F. H. Varley, 1917. This painting shows us the cost of the war, as members of a burial party go about their work during the Third Battle of Ypres. Besides having strong emotional content, the painting captures the destructiveness of the battle, as well as the colours of the battlefield. Varley would later become a member of the Group of Seven and one of Canada's most important painters.

not the case with war artists. Their images are often the only record available of certain events.

Art as Social Commentary War artists who worked in the front lines generally came to oppose war. Many produced art that reflects this attitude. Their feelings were shared by many ordinary soldiers, and so this type of art also tells their story. Other painters depicted factories and scenes relating to the war efforts in Canada.

Figure 3-26 *The Conquerors*, Eric Kennington, 1918. This painting is interesting for a number of reasons. The painter captures the nature of the war very subjectively, and the painting of this Canadian Highland battalion is rich in detail. Look especially at the faces of the soldiers. The artist's intention is to show that some of the conquerors are dead. How does he do that?

What Do You Think?

1. Imagine that you are a WW I veteran looking at *The Second Battle of Ypres*. With a partner, discuss what is "wrong" about this picture. What are your feelings about it? What feelings might a civilian get from looking at the same picture?

2. What sort of message is Varley attempting to convey in his painting, *For What?* Compare it to photographs of battles and the trenches in this chapter. How does this painting enhance your appreciation for those photographs?

3. Examine *The Conquerors*. What does the ethnic composition of the batallion say about the Canadian Army or about Canada? Look closely at the soldiers' expressions and write a description of what they have come through, and what they are facing.

Canada and World War I

In addition, the Allied blockade of Germany was to continue until a peace treaty was signed. As a result, hundreds of thousands of German civilians—including women and children—starved to death during the winter of 1918-1919. German resentment towards the Allies would become deep-rooted.

The Treaty of Versailles and Its Terms

In early 1919, Allied delegates met at the Paris Peace Conference to draft a treaty that would formally end the war. At first, Canada was simply part of the British delegation. Prime Minister Borden, however, insisted that Canada's war efforts entitled it to be represented as a separate nation, with the right to vote. The US was strongly opposed. It feared that if Canada were given the right to vote, so would other dominions of the British Commonwealth. Britain would then have too much power. In the end, there was a compromise. Canada sent a separate delegation, independent of Britain, but it had no vote.

At Versailles, just outside Paris, the US, France, and Britain drafted the Treaty of Versailles. The Canadian delegation said the terms were too hard on Germany, but it had no influence. According to the Treaty of Versailles, Germany had to accept the terms of the armistice and also

- evacuate the Rhineland (Germany west of the Rhine River)
- demilitarize the Rhineland and allow it to be occupied by Allied troops
- reduce its army to 100 000 men and abolish conscription
- abandon its air force
- cease building submarines and tanks
- reduce its navy to six battleships (all built before 1905)
- admit responsibility for causing the war (known as the "war guilt clause")
- pay damages (reparations) to the Allies in the amount of $30 billion.

German delegates to the Paris Peace Conference were not allowed to attend the negotiation meetings. If they did not sign, however, the war would resume. Under protest, Germany signed the Treaty of Versailles on June 23, 1919. Germans called the Treaty of Versailles the **diktat**.

> This is not a peace treaty—it is an armistice of 20 years.
>
> –Marshall Foch, 1919

Canadians, by and large, were content with the Treaty of Versailles, primarily because Canada did not wish to be drawn into European affairs. While it could not vote, Canada did sign the Treaty of Versailles as a separate nation. It also became a member of the League of Nations, a new organization that would try to promote international cooperation. Canada had entered World War I as a colony in the shadow. Through four years of bloodshed and the efforts of millions of Canadians, it had emerged on the threshold of full nationhood.

Up Close

8. In your own words, write an explanation of Marshall Foch's comment. What exactly is he referring to?

Historical Inquiry: Analysing Information

Historian at Work

Using Graphic Organizers

It's easier to organize information when you have a purpose in mind. Think about the ways in which you could use the information in *Canada: Our Century, Our Story*. Perhaps you want to

- understand the chronology of a period or issue
- make notes from the text for further study
- brainstorm all your ideas about a topic
- compare people or events

How can you best record and organize information for each of these purposes?

Understanding Chronology

Time lines are an easy way to see chronology at a glance. Draw a horizontal line across the page or a vertical line down the page. At each end of the time line, enter the start and end dates, for example, 1920 and 1929. Next, create equal sections along your line and mark these off. Then plot the events you wish to record.

Note-taking

Note-taking is useful for many purposes, including studying and further research. Notes can help you identify the main ideas in your textbook, as well as the supporting details. As you read, notice that main ideas are usually presented first, followed by the supporting details. In note-taking, record the main idea first, then jot down some of the details. For example:

> At the <u>outset of the war, airplanes were still new.</u> Sam Hughes dismissed them as "an invention of the devil." At first, airplanes were <u>used</u> only <u>to scout enemy troops and artillery.</u> Eventually, technological improvements allowed them to be <u>used on bombing missions.</u>

(main idea — underlined first sentence; supporting details — other underlined phrases)

Brainstorming

When you brainstorm, your thinking should flow in all possible directions. For this purpose, a mind map can be useful. A mind map begins with a word or topic in the centre of the page and then branches out into subsets of topics or ideas. Your teacher can provide you with a sample mind map.

Comparing

When you want to compare events, people, or ideas, a comparison chart is a useful way to organize your information. A simple comparison chart lists the two items being compared in a horizontal bar across the top. The points of comparison are usually listed in a vertical column to the left:

	WW I: War in the Air	WW I: War at Sea
Goals		
Technology		
Personnel		

Activities

1. Refer to the section in Chapter 2 on women's struggle for rights (pages 37–40).
   a) Create a time line from 1900–1920. Select information from this section to show some of the milestones in women's history during this period.
   b) Reread the section on page 40, "The Incredible Nellie McClung." Identify main ideas presented in each paragraph, as well as the key supporting details.

2. Create a comparison chart and use it to compare the backgrounds and experiences of some early immigrants to Canada (refer to Chapter 1, "Who Came and Why" on pages 10–17).

Canada and World War I

CONCLUSION

Canada entered World War I with great enthusiasm, despite the fact that the war was a conflict between European powers. For those Canadians with emotional ties to Britain, the declaration of war was a matter of simple loyalty. For those Canadians who were not British in origin, it was a chance to prove their loyalty. But the prolonged, enormous suffering and huge losses of the war affected Canada in a number of important ways. Canadians were proud of how well their soldiers performed under desperate conditions. But they also began to wonder whether independence from Britain would not be the best policy in the long run. On the basis of its considerable war effort, Canada insisted on a seat at the Paris Peace Treaty (even though it did not have a vote). Later, it insisted on membership in the League of Nations.

World War I brought about some changes in Canadian life that were fundamental and enduring. Women, who had staffed the factories while the men were overseas, received the right to vote. The federal government also introduced income tax as a "temporary measure" that has yet to be withdrawn. At the time, the extra revenue gave the federal government power to help shape the lives of citizens by funding social programs and preventing extreme poverty, a power that would become quite important later in the century.

CHAPTER ACTIVITIES

Check Your Understanding

1. Write definitions for "imperialism" and "nationalism." Then check your definitions against a dictionary's.

2. Using jot notes you may have made for Up Close #1 (page 58), create a comparison organizer to demonstrate how the war affected Canadians from various ethnocultural groups, both at home and overseas.

Develop Your Thinking

3. By the end of WW I, Canada had "emerged on the threshold of full nationhood." In a report, indicate what you think are the most important people and events of the war which led to a stronger sense of nationhood.

4. In many ways, Sam Hughes failed to act in the best interests of the overseas troops he was shipping supplies to. Should he have been removed from his position as Minister of the Militia? Use specific evidence when building your case.

Express Yourself

5. Choose one of the people mentioned in this chapter and write the script for a televised Heritage Minute detailing the importance of their role in the war effort. Indicate the kinds of photographs, music, and dramatic elements you would use to illustrate their story.

6. In the role of a soldier or a nurse at the Front Line, write a letter home describing your experiences in the course of a single day. Before you write, consider that some people at the Front chose to adjust their stories so as not to alarm their friends and family back home. Decide how truthfully you will relate your experiences of war.

7. Design a propaganda poster encouraging Canadians at home to do one of the following:
   - buy Victory Bonds or other war loans
   - act responsibly when rationing supplies and food
   - recycle materials, such as metal and rubber, which are essential to the war effort

Apply Your Learning

8. Compare and contrast the events leading up to WW I with more recent military aggressions. How are current hostilities similar to, or different from, the events that resulted in the assassination of Archduke Franz Ferdinand? Evaluate why current conflicts are less likely to result in world war.

9. Canadians such as Mankichi Omura and Dr. William Andrew White were eager to join the war effort and were frustrated by the obstacles presented to them. Would Canadians today be as willing to fight for their country? How have attitudes to war changed since WW I? Provide evidence from history, as well as your own experience, to give support to your perspective.

Extend Your Learning Using the Internet

10. How did World War I contribute to changes in Canadian attitudes towards the labour movement and equality for women? Draw your conclusions from Internet sources that contain accounts of the personal experiences of soldiers and nurses on the battlefield, and of Canadians on the home front.

11. How did Canada's military respond to the enlistment of different groups of Canadians? Compare the policies of today's military. What degree of equality has been gained? What still needs to be done?

4

The Roaring Life in Canada

Focus Questions

Individual Canadians and Canadian Identity
What political changes ushered in the 1920s? Who were the two leading politicians of the era? How and why were they in conflict?

Demographic Patterns
What developments during this time further undermined the lives of Aboriginal people?

Scientific and Technological Impact
What technological developments hurried Canada towards becoming a consumer society?

Canadian Identity
How was Canada's identity clarified and enhanced through the arts and sports in the 1920s?

During World War I, a number of social issues were ignored or suppressed, particularly farm issues and labour strife over working conditions. But after the war, a short recession and the many returning veterans who needed jobs intensified the conflicts. One result was the rise of new regional parties, ending the old two-party system. Another was new immigration policies. The government continued to show its preference for White, English-speaking Britons and Americans. But it also signed the Railway Agreement, by which railway companies could recruit immigrants as cheap labour. Another outcome of the war was the fact that the crisis over conscription gave a big boost to Quebec nationalism during the postwar period.

While a distinctly Canadian culture was developing in arts and sports, the new technology of radio increased the threat of cultural domination by the US. But the radio also expanded horizons. It brought issues such as prohibition, jazz, and women's rights into many homes. For many, growing urbanism coincided with growing prosperity, and the beginnings of a consumer society. For the Native peoples, however, the 1920s were a time of great upheaval. During this period, the Canadian government forged ahead with its plan to place Native children in residential schools far away from home—a decision that would haunt them later in the century.

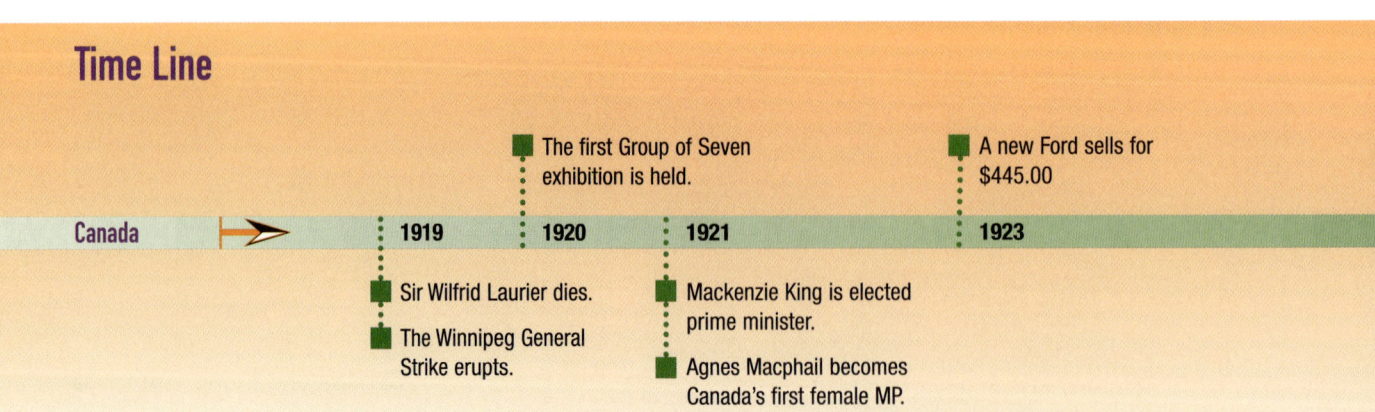

Time Line

Canada

- **1919** — Sir Wilfrid Laurier dies. The Winnipeg General Strike erupts.
- **1920** — The first Group of Seven exhibition is held.
- **1921** — Mackenzie King is elected prime minister. Agnes Macphail becomes Canada's first female MP.
- **1923** — A new Ford sells for $445.00

Perspectives

The Roaring Twenties was an age of new styles and new attitudes: Flappers exposed their legs, and jazz was the new music. But with the new trends and tastes came a testing of established social boundaries. In this photograph, a group of flappers and musicians participate in a Charleston dance competition in January 1926. If you were there, what kind of music would you be hearing? What other sounds might there be? What would you like to ask any of the participants? What do you think some people may have found objectionable about this group?

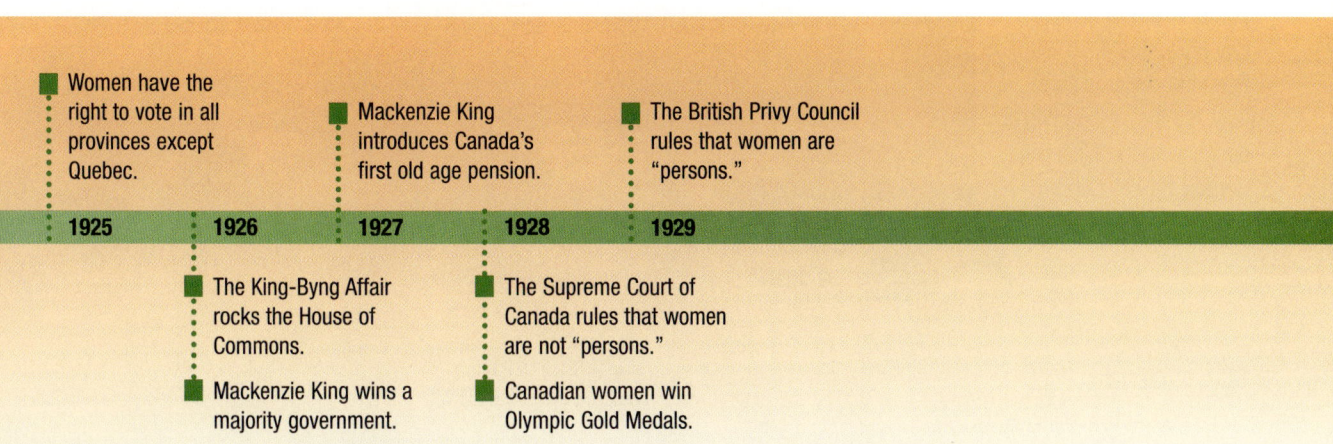

- Women have the right to vote in all provinces except Quebec. **1925**
- The King-Byng Affair rocks the House of Commons. **1926**
- Mackenzie King wins a majority government.
- Mackenzie King introduces Canada's first old age pension. **1927**
- The Supreme Court of Canada rules that women are not "persons." **1928**
- Canadian women win Olympic Gold Medals.
- The British Privy Council rules that women are "persons." **1929**

Flashpoint

The Winnipeg General Strike

World War I was over, but by 1919 relations between Canadian workers and employers were becoming explosive. Unions had grown stronger during the war, and they wanted to keep and expand their power. Wages and working conditions had improved little, if at all, since the turn of the century.

In March 1919, western labour leaders met at the Western Labour Conference in Calgary. Some delegates proclaimed **solidarity** with revolutionaries in Russia and Germany and broke off from the more conservative, Ontario-centred Trades and Labour Congress. The leaders proposed One Big Union, a plan to organize all working men and women. In the following months, a referendum was held to ask union members if they supported the idea.

In an unrelated labour dispute, the Winnipeg Trades and Labour Council (WTLC) had reached a standoff with management. The WTLC wanted better pay and working conditions for its members in the metal and building trades. Management refused to recognize the WTLC, or its right to bargain collectively for workers. On May 15, 1919, the Council called for a general strike.

Within days, more than 30 000 unionized and non-unionized workers walked off the job. They included postal workers, firefighters, police, telephone operators, waiters, and factory workers. Trains stopped running, shops closed. Winnipeg ground to a halt. As the strike continued—it would last six weeks—it won support from people across the city and across Canada. Eventually, sympathy strikes spread from Nova Scotia to British Columbia.

Winnipeg's most powerful industrialists, bankers, and politicians quickly formed the Citizens' Committee of 1000. They refused to meet with WTLC leaders and denounced the strike as the work of communist "enemy aliens." They used the local press to get their message out. The *Winnipeg*

Figure 4–1 World War I veterans wave placards during a rally at Winnipeg City Hall, June 4, 1919. Read the placards carefully. Are they supporting or denouncing the Winnipeg General Strike? Explain your response.

Citizenship: Social and Political Movements

Tribune declared that "Winnipeg was now under the Soviet system of government." As the strike wore on, it became international news. The *New York Times* ran feature editorials, including one that called the strike "an attempt at revolution."

In Ottawa, Prime Minister Robert Borden feared the conflict would grip the nation. He sent federal representatives to Winnipeg, led by Arthur Meighen, minister of the interior. Meighen immediately supported the Committee of 1000 and refused to meet with strikers. He advised the government to order federal employees to go back to work or lose their jobs. The government amended the Immigration Act so that any immigrant, including British-born, could be deported more easily. Then the Criminal Code definition of **sedition** was broadened to give police sweeping new powers of arrest.

On June 17, ten strike leaders (eight of them British-born) and two leaders of the One Big Union were arrested and denied bail. Four days later, on June 21, a crowd—including women and children—gathered peacefully on Winnipeg's Main Street to protest the arrests. Members of the Royal North-West Mounted Police rode into the group, swinging baseball bats. When strikers started hurling stones, the police opened fire—with real bullets. One man was killed and 30 injured in what is now known as "Bloody Saturday."

For the next five days, government militia patrolled Winnipeg streets riding in cars with mounted machine guns. The cars had been donated by some of Winnipeg's wealthiest citizens. After six weeks of tension, and finally bloodshed, the WTLC called off the strike. On June 26, it was all over.

No enemy aliens were ever discovered or deported. But seven of the arrested leaders were convicted of conspiracy and received sentences of from six months to two years. Even while jailed, they continued their activism for workers' rights. Arthur Meighen never apologized for the government's hard-line approach, but Prime Minister Borden promised a Royal Commission would study labour conditions. The WTLC, too, took a different approach: the next battles for better wages and working conditions would be fought in the political arena, not on the streets.

The Winnipeg General Strike, however, was a terrible defeat for organized labour. It would take 30 years before the federal government recognized unions and the right to collective bargaining. But one person arrested was J. S. Woodsworth, a **pacifist** and former Methodist minister. His crime had been to write editorials supporting the strike. In 1921, Woodsworth was elected to parliament. He remained an immensely popular Winnipeg MP for the next 21 years. He would grill Meighen in the House of Commons. In 1927, he would pressure Mackenzie King to introduce Canada's first old age pension. By 1932, Woodsworth would help found the Co-operative Commonwealth Federation, which would later become the New Democratic Party.

What Do You Think?

1. Was it a "fair fight" between the WTLC and its opponents? What strengths did each side have—and use?

2. With what you know about working conditions at this time, do you feel the workers were justified in going on strike? Explain.

Figure 4–2 A streetcar is tipped over by strikers and their supporters in Winnipeg in June 1919. Look at their grooming and clothing. Compare it to Figure 4–1. Do they differ? Do the people in this group look like an angry mob to you? Do they look like "enemy aliens"? Explain.

The Roaring Life in Canada

POLITICAL CHANGE AFTER WW I

During and just following World War I, Conservative Prime Minister Robert Borden did more than any other prime minister to make Canada independent of Britain. In 1917, however, his government had also introduced the Military Service Bill. This was drafted by Arthur Meighen, one of Borden's most able ministers. As you learned in Chapter 3, conscription tore Canada—and its traditional political parties—apart.

To win the 1917 federal election, one of the most vicious in Canadian history, Borden campaigned under the banner of the Union Government. This was a coalition of pro-conscription Liberals and Conservatives. Borden won the election and quickly passed the Military Service Act. As conscription went into force, however, violent riots broke out in Quebec. Western farmers, who had been promised an exemption, felt betrayed when fathers and sons were conscripted in 1918.

Organized labour had clashed often with the Borden government during World War I. In the final war years, strikes and labour disruptions closed down munitions plants and coal mines. After the war, labour conflicts erupted. The economy, which had been operating at full capacity, plunged into a **recession**. Prices and unemployment soared. Returning veterans could not find work, let alone claim the financial help Borden had promised.

By 1919, it was clear that peace had brought neither prosperity nor reconciliation. Canada remained deeply and bitterly divided. It was also clear that political power was passing into new hands. Liberal leader Wilfrid Laurier died in February 1919. In the same year, William Lyon Mackenzie King became the new leader of the Liberal Party. In December 1919, Borden was so exhausted that his doctor ordered him to resign. In July 1920, he stepped down. Arthur Meighen became his successor and Canada's ninth prime minister.

Two Politicians Who Dominated the Twenties

Up Close

1. Create character sketches for Mackenzie King and Arthur Meighen.

William Lyon Mackenzie King and Arthur Meighen were classmates at the University of Toronto, and they were both first elected to parliament in 1908. The only other thing they had in common was that they loathed one another.

King came from a prominent Ontario family and saw himself following in the footsteps of the politician he most admired—Laurier. King was a conciliator, someone who could bring warring parties together. Like Laurier, he knew that maintaining support in Quebec was vitally important, not only to hold onto power, but also to keep Canada united. As an internationally recognized labour expert, he shared Laurier's vision of a society that would balance the needs of workers and business.

> … the most contemptible charlatan ever to darken the annals of Canadian politics …
>
> —Arthur Meighen, describing Mackenzie King

Meighen came from a modest, rural Ontario background. He became a schoolteacher, but was so strict and harsh that his teaching days were short-lived. Through talent and hard work, he became a successful small-town lawyer in Manitoba. In 1908, he ran for the Conservatives and was elected to parliament. His combative, brilliant debating style created many enemies, but caught the eye of Borden. Over the years, Canadians came to admire Meighen's dedication and sharp mind, but they also considered him cold and arrogant.

> … sarcastic, vitriolic, and the meanest type of politician …
>
> Mackenzie King, describing Arthur Meighen

Elections and Scandal in the 1920s

As the leader of a party that had made unpopular decisions during World War I, Meighen faced an uphill battle in the election of 1921. He had helped to draft the Military Service Act, but made no efforts to heal wounds in Quebec or the West over conscription. He had authored the War Measures Act, which allowed Cabinet to govern by **decree** when it felt there was a threat of "war, invasion, or insurrection, real or apprehended." As justice minister, he had used the Act to stifle anti-war protests. Again, he conceded nothing to critics during the campaign. As far as he was concerned, he was, simply, right.

In 1919, Meighen had crushed the Winnipeg General Strike. Again, he had no apologies, no second thoughts. His view was that workers and the unions were wrong—law and order had to be maintained. By 1920, however, the recession hit with full force. Ever uncompromising, Meighen was now pitted against a wide range of groups, including workers, farmers, immigrants, and Quebecers.

Figure 4–3 This 1921 cartoon portrays Meighen's campaign style. What aspects of Meighen's personality does the cartoonist emphasize? How is the audience reacting?

In 1920, another federal party entered Canadian politics: the Progressive Party. It was composed of organized Ontario and prairie farmers and Liberals who had broken with their party over high tariffs. During the 1921 election, the Progressives campaigned for free trade, nationalization of key industries, and direct democracy—which would use **referenda** to decide important political questions.

In the 1921 election, Meighen's Conservatives won only 50 seats. The Progressives won 65, and King's Liberals won 116, the slimmest majority. Mackenzie King was now prime minister, and he would remain so for 22 of the next 27 years.

Figure 4-4 Mackenzie King makes a campaign speech through the new medium of radio.

It was natural that Canadians would compare Mackenzie King to his grandfather, the great Upper Canadian rebel, William Lyon Mackenzie. But King's route to political success would be as a mediator. King had the reputation of being a social reformer. He was known to believe in policies such as workers' compensation and unemployment insurance, which were radical by standards of the time. Yet he was also a **pragmatist**; he would do whatever necessary to stay in power.

In his first years as prime minister, King was often vague. Meighen attacked him again and again for being without principles. King often walked a political tightrope, trying to be responsive to different groups. He lowered tariffs enough to keep the support of Progressives, but not enough to anger industrialists. In British Columbia and industrialized Ontario, he favoured protectionism. In the Prairies and rural Ontario, he supported free trade. In front of Quebecers, he criticized British imperialism and conscription, which he had opposed. He made promises, such as creating an old age pension, which he postponed.

In the election of 1925, King was sure he would win another majority. He was wrong. Meighen's Conservatives won 116 seats to the Liberals 99, and King lost in his own riding. Both Meighen and King, who won a seat in a by-election, fought for the backing of the 24 Progressives. The Progressives saw the Liberals as the lesser of two evils, and supported them. King had a minority government, but the coalition did not last.

The King-Byng Affair By 1924, prohibition in Canada was a lost cause, but it was still the law in the US. In 1926, a Conservative charged the Liberals, including the customs minister, of taking bribes from **rumrunners**, who were smuggling alcohol into the US. King denied the charges and was unapologetic, but the pure-minded Progressives had had enough. By withdrawing their support for the Liberals, they would cause King to lose his coalition government. King went to the governor general, Viscount Byng of Vimy, with a request to dissolve

Parliament and call an election, hoping to strengthen the Liberal party's standing. Byng refused, saying that Meighen must have the chance to form the government with the Progressives.

King resigned and stirred up a public uproar: A British-appointed governor general had rejected the request of Canada's elected prime minister! It was unconstitutional. Within days, Meighen's government was defeated. Now Byng had to dissolve parliament and call an election. To this day, political analysts still debate the constitutional issues surrounding the King-Byng Affair. Most argue that Byng was behaving responsibly and that King was exploiting the situation for political gains.

In the 1926 election, King promised to loosen Canada's ties to Britain and won a majority government. Meighen was defeated in his own riding. Disgusted, he quit politics and resigned as leader of the Conservative Party. The election also signalled the collapse of the Progressive Party.

> **Up Close**
>
> 2. Recount the events of the King-Byng affair in point form, in chronological order.

Regional Developments

During the Winnipeg General Strike, some of the strongest protests had come from World War I veterans. Some supported the Citizens' Committee of 1000, but many others supported the strike. Across Canada, veterans were looking for jobs and demanding better wages and working conditions. They wanted health care and government compensation for service during the war. Their old jobs had disappeared or been filled by women and immigrants, who worked for lower wages. Veteran demands became a national issue.

Many veterans did not return to the farms. Europe had opened their eyes, and they were drawn to seek work and an urban lifestyle in Canada's growing cities. Many other Canadians were also moving to the city. By the end of the 1920s, for the first time, more Canadians would live in cities than in rural areas. Canada was changing from a rural, or agrarian, nation into an urbanized, modern one. Farmers felt even more alienated from the federal Liberals and Conservatives, who seemed to cater to central industrial and business interests. The decade became a hotbed of regional complaint and disparity.

Farmers demanded that high tariffs, which had protected Canadian industry during World War I, be lowered. They also wanted the federal government to lower freight rates. That way their products could be shipped more cheaply to compete in international markets. Ottawa did not seem to be listening. Regional farmers' parties emerged—such as the United Farmers of Ontario (UFO) and the Progressive Party movement in the West. As you read earlier, the Progressive Party became a national party in 1920 and played a key role in federal politics until 1926. Even though Progressive power declined, the days of Canada's two-party federal system were over. Throughout the decade, powerful regional parties, movements, and speakers would emerge.

> **Up Close**
>
> 3. As you read pages 91 to 94, make jot notes under these headings: UFO, Progressive Party, Maritime Rights, *L'Action Francaise*, UFA.

The Maritimes During the postwar recession, the Maritime Rights movement became this region's strongest voice of protest against federal policies. During the 1920s, the Maritime economy suffered one setback after another. Coal mining

The Roaring Life in Canada **91**

Figure 4–5 Strikes gripped the coal mining and steel industries in the 1920s. These two photos show miners and company guards during the 1925 strike at the Bootleg Coal Pits in Cape Breton, Nova Scotia.

had boomed during the war, but newly developed energy resources—such as oil and hydroelectricity—destroyed the market for Maritime coal. The Canadian National Railway takeover of the Intercolonial Railway, approved by the federal Conservatives in 1919, resulted in huge freight rate increases for Maritime industry. These factors, and the high tariffs that protected central Canada's manufacturers and industries, led to an economic depression in the Maritimes. Thousands of Maritimers had to seek work in the US and across Canada.

The Maritimes Rights movement never became a political party, but it did pressure federal parties. It supported Mackenzie King's Liberals in the 1921 federal election. When King failed to address Maritime grievances, Maritime voters turfed out federal Liberals in the 1925 elections. In 1926, King appointed a Royal Commission. It upheld the claims of the Maritime Rights movement and even recommended federal subsidies to support Maritime economic development. King, however, only implemented reforms that were politically expedient for his party. The Maritime economy would endure hardships throughout the 1920s. These would only worsen in the 1930s.

Quebec The conscription crisis of World War I had driven a wedge between Quebec and the rest of Canada. In its wake, Roman Catholic priest and historian Lionel-Adolphe Groulx became a leader of Quebec nationalism. During the 1920s, his publication, *L'Action Française*, promoted a national vision of a Quebec that would follow the moral values of Roman Catholicism and the virtues of rural life. Groulx portrayed the modern industrialization and urbanization in English Canada as a threat to Quebec society. And the history that Groulx was writing portrayed Confederation as a disaster for Quebec. Today, many historians believe that Groulx laid the foundations for the separatist movement.

Henri Bourassa, the other prominent Quebec leader, provided a counterpoint to Groulx. Bourassa also promoted an **insular** form of Quebec nationalism, but he saw Confederation as good for Quebec. Unlike Groulx, Bourassa was often actively involved in an existing Canadian federal party, the Liberal Party.

In Quebec provincial politics, Liberal Louis-Alexandre Taschereau held power from 1920 until 1936. Unlike Groulx and Bourassa, Taschereau did everything in his power to modernize Quebec's economy, workforce, educational system, and social policies. He actively sought foreign investment and saw no need to insulate Quebec from outside forces. During the 1920s, he was successful: foreign investment poured into Quebec.

Up Close

4. Make a chart to compare the policies of Lionel-Adolphe Groulx and Henri Bourassa.

Ontario Farmers' movements and parties expanded in almost every province during the postwar decade. Most wanted reforms that would put more money into the hands of farmers, but demands differed from region to region. In Ontario, rapid urbanization led to the founding of United Farmers of Ontario (UFO) in 1914. The UFO placed a high value on rural life and wanted political assurances that it would continue. By 1919, the UFO had become a political party, winning a large number of seats in the provincial election.

As with the national Progressive Party and other provincial farmers' movements, UFO members disagreed on goals. Some wanted to use the UFO election victory to promote the agrarian way of life. Others, including UFO Premier E. C. Drury, wanted a more balanced government for all Ontarians, regardless of where they lived.

Figure 4–6 In 1921, Agnes Macphail was the first woman ever elected to the House of Commons. She was a member of the Progressive Party, which was affiliated with the United Farmers of Ontario. She would remain a federal MP for the next 19 years.

While in power, the UFO supported prohibition and refused to limit the teaching of French in Ontario schools. Both proved to be unpopular with voters. In the 1923 election, Conservative Howard Ferguson triumphed. He allowed alcohol to be bought and sold in Ontario, but under heavy taxes and provincial control. Ferguson pushed for increasing urbanization and industrialization—and he kept power until 1930. Ontario's experiment with the UFO was over.

The Prairies During the 1920s, farmers' parties and movements grew on the prairies. Although they were also plagued by disunity, they had a common enemy: the central Canadian railroads, banks, and industrialists. The strongest of these groups was the United Farmers of Alberta (UFA), which was headed by Henry Wise Wood from 1916 to 1930.

Wood at first believed that farmers should avoid forming political parties. Instead, he believed that economic interest groups, such as farmers, should cooperate with other groups to achieve their goals. With government reform as their platform, however, the UFA won the provincial election of 1921. It held power until 1935. Wood did not become premier, but chose to remain behind the scenes as president and "philosopher" of the UFA.

The UFA party eventually disintegrated as Mackenzie King's Liberal policies lured many Progressives into the Liberal fold. Wood's leadership of the UFA, however, led to the creation of the Alberta Wheat Pool. This placed control of the sale of Alberta's wheat in the hands of the farmers who grew it. Wood did not achieve his goal of group government, but his theories broke the hold of the two traditional parties on prairie politics for good.

British Columbia British Columbia's politics differed from other western provinces in the 1920s. For one thing, BC's agricultural industry was quite small. Forestry, shipbuilding, and mining were far more important. This may explain why third parties could not gain a foothold in provincial politics.

With the completion of the Panama Canal, shipping and exports became more important to BC's economy in the 1920s. Still, the BC economy struggled after World War I and into the 1920s. Under Liberal Premier John Oliver (1918-1927), fruit-growing was encouraged in the Okanagan Valley. His government also pressured the federal government to reform freight rates and railway policies. Eventually, freight rates were reduced and Vancouver was linked by rail to the northern interior of BC.

CHANGING SOCIAL ATTITUDES

The 1920s were years of contrasts, conflict, and change. In the burgeoning cities, members of the Woman's Christian Temperance Union would be lobbying to ban gambling, drinking, theatre attendance, and public dancing, while down the street, young people would be drinking and dancing to the wild new sounds of jazz.

After the postwar recession, Canada's economy appeared to boom. New inventions and new forms of popular entertainment swept the country. They challenged old values and led to bold—often

Figure 4–7 With her short hair and skirt, her scandalous bare legs, and her handy flask of alcohol, this **flapper** embodied the freewheeling defiance of the Roaring Twenties.

defiant—attitudes and outlooks. Under the glitter and glamour of the "Roaring Twenties," however, old social problems remained unsolved. The gap between rich and poor did not narrow. Immigration increased, provoking a backlash and a challenge to Canada's sense of tolerance and national identity. Women won the right to vote and hold public office, but then they had to go to Britain to demand legal recognition as "persons." And although they were far removed from mainstream life, Canada's Native peoples continued to be pressured to assimilate.

Prohibition and After

As you learned in Chapter 2, the US and Canadian temperance movements sprang up in the late nineteenth century. In both countries, they had remarkable success. Between 1915 and 1917, every province except Quebec outlawed the sale and consumption of alcohol. In 1918, Prime Minister Borden incorporated prohibition into Canada's war effort. Distillers' and brewers' ingredients were needed to feed the troops.

> I wish somehow that we could prohibit the use of alcohol and merely drink beer and gin as we used to.
>
> –Stephen Leacock, *Frenzied Fiction*

Figure 4–8 The aftermath of a police raid on a "blind pig" (an illegal distillery) in Elk Lake, Ontario, in the late 1920s

In the US, prohibition was federal law from 1920 to 1933. In Canada, however, the so-called "noble experiment" sputtered out. Quebec never enforced prohibition, and most provincial governments gave up on total prohibition by the early to mid-1920s. Prohibition was unpopular with voters; besides, governments could raise money by controlling and taxing the sale of liquor.

Prohibition did reduce alcohol consumption, by about 80 percent. It also inspired a wave of crime that created tensions between Canada and the US. Prohibition laws were hard to enforce. Many people were prepared to break them, either because they liked to drink or because they could get rich selling alcohol illegally. And the ingredients and technology for brewing and distilling were easy to come by.

Samuel Bronfman expanded the family business One of the most remarkable Canadian risk-takers of the prohibition era was a man named Samuel Bronfman. Bronfman was born while his family was en route to Saskatchewan in 1889, having emigrated from Russia. His family established a successful prairie hotel business and Sam capitalized on its success when he founded the Canada Pure Drug Company of Yorkton, Saskatchewan in 1919. Canadian laws allowed his company to import unlimited amounts of liquor from Europe, for "medicinal purposes."

Up Close

5. Write a eulogy for Samuel Bronfman, describing his life and contributions to Canadian industry and economy.

The Fate of Prohibition in Canada	
Province/Territory	Year Prohibition Ended
Quebec	1919
British Columbia Yukon	1920
Manitoba	1923
Alberta Saskatchewan	1924
Newfoundland	1925
Ontario New Brunswick	1927
Nova Scotia	1930
Prince Edward Island	1948

Figure 4–9 The fate of prohibition in Canada

This liquor was then distributed to company warehouses along the Canadian side of the border. From there, liquor was quietly smuggled into the US.

Between 1919 and 1933, the Bronfmans earned and invested their way into millions of dollars in profits. When the US repealed prohibition in 1933, the Bronfman empire was poised to make their liquor business strictly legitimate. By the mid-1960s their company, Seagram, had sales exceeding $1 billion. Since then, the Bronfman empire has diversified into such ventures as sports teams, charitable and heritage foundations, real estate, forestry, and banking. In 2000, they held the **controlling interest** in MCA-UA, one of the world's largest entertainment multinationals.

Canadians turned a blind eye to the liquor being smuggled from Canada into the US. In Canada, it wasn't, technically, breaking the law. Canadian schooners sailed the waters of the US East Coast from the Gulf of Mexico to Maine transporting massive quantities of liquor. Dozens of US Coast Guard gunboats were posted along the Atlantic and Pacific coasts. Illegal drinking establishments, called "speakeasies," lined the Canadian side of the border. And Canadian border towns often erupted in violence.

Flappers and All That Jazz

Up Close

6. Create a newspaper ad that a US radio station might have placed in a Canadian newspaper to entice Canadian listeners.

As liquor was flowing from Canada into the US, newly licensed US radio stations were beaming the latest American music north into Canada. In 1919, radio pioneer Guglielmo Marconi had established the first radio station in the world, XWA in Montreal. But it was American entrepreneurs who saw the commercial possibilities of the new medium. Soon US radio stations were broadcasting the most up-to-date music, fashion, and cultural trends into Canada.

Jazz was the hot new music that defined the Roaring Twenties. Created by African-American musicians in Louisiana, jazz had its roots in ragtime and vaudeville. It swept like wildfire into the expanding urban centres of the northern US and into the growing Canadian cities along the US border. By the 1920s, jazz radio broadcasts and gramophone recordings were immensely popular. The hottest ticket in town would be a live performance by a local jazz band. In Montreal, people could take in the Westmount Jazz Band, in Winnipeg, the Elk's Band or the Winnipeg Jazz Babies.

The dance crazes of the new music roared into Canada from the US: the Charleston, the Black Bottom, and the Lindy were some of the most popular. This freewheeling American music, dance and attitude were embodied in the flapper. Flappers were fashionable young women who defied the old conventions of proper "feminine" behaviour. They scandalized the public by abandoning the padded clothes of the Victorian era. At nightclubs, they would dance the newest dance crazes in beaded dresses that went only to the knee. And they didn't always wear stockings. Flappers also cut their hair into "boyish" bobs, smoked in public, drank alcohol, and drove their own cars.

Figure 4–10 Winnipeg's Elk's Band, shown here in 1922, was a popular jazz band that played nightclubs across Canada.

Immigration: Backlash and Necessity

By 1919, more than 20 percent of Canada's population was composed of immigrants. During the postwar recession, however, jobs were scarce, and a backlash spread against immigrants and federal immigration policy. With the Immigration Act of 1919, the government reaffirmed its preferred list of immigrant nationalities. White, English-speaking Britons and Americans topped the list, followed by northern Europeans. Lower down the list were people from eastern and central Europe. At the bottom of the list were Asians, Blacks, Gypsies, and Jews.

The Act classified any immigrants who had "peculiar customs, habits, modes of living and methods of holding property" as undesirable. According to the Act, such people would not be "readily assimilated" into Canadian society. In Quebec, French Canadians feared the Act would increase the number of English-speaking Canadians and threaten Quebec's culture. When the economy boomed after the postwar recession, industrialists complained as well—they needed immigrant labourers.

The president of the Canadian Pacific Railroad (CPR) objected to government limits because he wanted cheap immigrant labour to build and maintain the railway. The government eased restrictions and passed the 1925 Railway

| Immigration to Canada, 1919-1929 ||
Year	Immigrants Arriving in Canada
1919	107 698
1920	128 824
1921	91 728
1922	64 224
1923	113 729
1924	124 164
1925	84 907
1926	135 982
1927	158 886
1928	166 783
1929	164 993

Figure 4–11 Immigration to Canada, 1919-1929

Agreement. This allowed the CPR and Canadian National Railways (CNR) to recruit immigrants themselves. And railway recruiters drew many more immigrants from the non-preferred nations than from Britain, the US, or northern Europe. One-hundred-and-sixty-five thousand Hungarians, Czechs, Slovaks, and Ukrainians and twenty thousand Mennonites came to Canada in the following years. Labour unions, religious organizations, and farmers protested, but the government renewed the agreement in 1928.

More than 1 300 000 immigrants came to Canada between 1919 and 1929, but Canada's doors were not wide open. In 1923, the government banned Chinese immigrants, and limited Japanese immigration to 150 a year. The government also ordered immigration officials to turn back all Black Americans, on the basis that they were unsuited to Canada's cold, harsh climate.

Many immigrants found work in road-building, mining, and pulp and paper mills in remote regions. Many others, including 20 000 Jews, gravitated to manufacturing jobs—building cars and the new appliances—in the industrialized cities. Recent immigrants often lived in neighbourhoods with others of their national or cultural heritage. Canada's major cities became much more culturally diverse. The same neighbourhoods, however, were easy targets for extremist anti-immigration groups such as the Ku Klux Klan. The Klan opposed immigration of non-English-speaking, non-Protestant, non-White peoples. They targeted Japanese immigrants in the West, in particular, and had some influence in limiting immigration. By the close of the decade, the economy would collapse and the doors to immigration would virtually slam shut.

Figure 4–12 These immigrants, leaving Scotland for Alberta, were at the top of the Canadian government's preferred list.

Residential Schools and Native Resistance

During most of the nineteenth century and up to the mid-twentieth century, the Canadian government's aboriginal policy had two contradictory goals. It attempted to "protect" Native peoples from White society, but it intended to assimilate them at the same time. Soon after Confederation, Prime Minister John A. Macdonald told parliament that the government's goal was "to do away with the tribal system and assimilate the Indian people in all respects with the inhabitants of the Dominion, as speedily as they are fit to change."

One way the government did this was to exclude Native peoples from having a say in their own affairs. Any existing powers of Native self-government were not recognized, but centralized within the federal government. The federal government also outlawed expressions of Native culture. For example, the **potlatch** was banned between 1884 and 1951. As well, during the early part of the twentieth century, aboriginal people were forbidden from appearing in their traditional dress or performing traditional dances at fairs and stampedes.

Treaties obligated the federal government to provide and maintain schools on reserves, but these proved to be expensive. As you learned in Chapter 1, the government began building residential schools in 1883, which were run by churches. This cut costs. By 1923, there were 72 such schools, and by 1931 there were 80. By 1920, legislation made school attendance compulsory for Native children between the ages of 7 and 15. As well, Native children could be committed to boarding schools and kept there until the age of 18.

Policymakers saw the residential schools as the ideal way to prepare Native children for assimilation. For one thing, they completely removed them from their communities. "The more remote from the Institution and distant from each other are the points from which the pupils are collected, the better chance for their success," wrote one official. Once inside a residential school, children had little or no contact with their families. Officials feared students would "revert" to Native ways if they returned to the reserves.

Most residential schools prohibited children from speaking their Native languages. Frequently, students who broke the rule were severely punished. Students were also forced to wear uniforms. Traditional aboriginal dress was seen to be "uncivilized" and a dangerous expression of individuality. Native parents were also not allowed to contribute to the content of studies, or to have any control over the way schools were run.

Until 1930, the curriculum was largely religious instruction and moral education promoting the values of White society. The remaining schooling was practical. Boys were taught carpentry, farming, black-smithing, and shoemaking. For girls, studies included sewing, shirt-making, knitting, cooking, laundering, and ironing. One educational authority concluded that a residential school student would be lucky to reach the academic equivalent of grade five by the time he or she was 18. More damaging still, when students left the schools they were not accepted in Canadian towns and cities. And they were no longer at home in their own communities.

Figure 4–13 Kanadian Knights of the Ku Klux Klan stand outside their office in Vancouver. The Klan started as a white supremacist group in the US but spread to Canada in the 1920s. They were considered extremists, objecting to any non-White, non-English-speaking peoples.

Up Close

7. List some of the supposed benefits of residential schools. Beside each, write an argument against it.

The residential schools became notoriously under-funded. Government and church officials raised concerns about the quality of diet, sanitation, and health care, but the federal government did not increase funding. Discipline in the schools was also criticized. In 1921 an incident was reported at one school in which boys were strapped and then chained to benches. Duncan Campbell Scott, who directed the administration of Indian Affairs from 1913 to 1932, wrote a directive forbidding such practices. It had little impact. Residential schools were not only far removed from Native communities, but from mainstream society as well. They were worlds unto themselves.

Native leaders, however, did not let federal policies go unchallenged. Frederick Ogilvie Loft, a Mohawk chief from Ontario, returned home after serving in WW I. He tried to get politicians in Ottawa and London to do something about the conditions facing Canada's Native peoples. When those governments did not respond, Loft helped found the League of Indians in 1920. This was a national organization that pushed for the right of Native peoples to vote, without losing their Indian **status**. During the 1920s, other Native groups emerged in other parts of Canada, even though the federal government banned political organizations among Native groups.

Figure 4–14 Quewich (left) is the father of the children seen in their crisp residential school uniforms. This kind of photograph was used to promote residential schools. What message would it send to White Canadians? To Canada's Native peoples?

Getting the Vote and Winning Office

The women's rights movement merged with the spirit of reform in the 1920s. For more than 50 years, women's groups and individual Canadian women had spearheaded movements for temperance, educational and social reform, and for farmer and labour rights. During WW I, more Canadian women had also worked outside the home, contributing enormously to Canada's wartime effort. Once the veterans returned, many of these women were not prepared to give up their newfound independence.

Many of the outspoken leaders you read about in Chapter 2 continued to push for women's equality in the 1920s. As you learned in that chapter's Flashpoint, Nellie McClung and the Political Equality League "shamed" the premier of Manitoba into extending the vote to women in 1916. With the exception of Quebec, all other provinces would follow by 1925 (see Figure 4–16). Within the same time frame, women also won the right to run for elected office.

The **enfranchisement** of women on the federal level was a different kind of story. When Arthur Meighen drafted The Wartime Elections Act in 1917, he granted the vote to women whose husbands or relatives were serving or had served in the armed forces. At the same time, he took away the vote from "enemy alien" immigrants. These calculated political moves paid off for Borden, who won the 1917 election and introduced conscription. After many attacks in the House of Commons, Borden extended the vote to all Canadian women on May 24, 1918.

Emily Murphy becomes a "person" As you read in Chapter 2, Emily Murphy was appointed an Alberta police magistrate in 1916 and was soon challenged by male lawyers. As a woman, they asserted, Murphy was not a "person" under British law. She was not entitled to hold an **appointed** office. With the support of Alberta MLA Louise McKinney, Murphy vowed to have the law overturned.

Following World War I, women across Canada, particularly in the West, were outraged when the federal government failed to appoint even one female Senator. Murphy's campaign gained momentum. Henrietta Muir Edwards, co-founder of The National Council of Women, and Irene Parlby and Nellie McClung—newly elected Members of the Legislative Assembly of Alberta—threw their support behind Murphy. They became known as the "Famous Five." By 1928, they had pushed the "Persons Case" all the way to the Supreme Court of Canada.

Murphy argued that women were "qualified persons" and must be entitled to hold appointed public office. The Supreme Court of Canada disagreed, unanimously. Under the BNA, it ruled, women were not considered to be persons in the traditional office-holding sense. The highest court of appeal, however, was the British Privy Council in London. And in 1929, the Famous Five took their case there to be heard. The Privy Council agreed with Murphy and ruled that not only were women persons under the Constitution, but that to exclude women from appointed public office was "a relic of days more barbarous than ours."

Figure 4–15 Senator Cairine Wilson (back row, right), Nellie McClung (front row, right), and Prime Minister Mackenzie King unveil a tablet honouring the women who won the Persons Case.

Women's Enfranchisement in Canada

- **1916** Manitoba, Alberta, and Saskatchewan
- **1917** British Columbia and Ontario
- **1918** Nova Scotia and the federal government
- **1919** New Brunswick
- **1922** Prince Edward Island
- **1925** Newfoundland (not yet part of Canada)
- **1940** Quebec
- **1960** First Nations men and women, federal vote

Figure 4–16

On February 20, 1930, Prime Minister Mackenzie King appointed Cairine Wilson, a loyal Liberal supporter, as Canada's first female Senator. Nineteen years later, she would be Canada's first female delegate to the United Nations.

PROSPERITY IN THE 1920s

During the war, Canada's resource industries and manufacturing operated at full capacity. Many manufacturers, such as the Massey-Harris Company, even suspended normal production to contribute to the war effort. Canada, for example, produced more shells than any other Allied nation. The wartime boom meant that Canada's cities grew. For the first time, Toronto rivalled Montreal in size and economic importance. In the West, Winnipeg had grown to become Canada's third largest city. In the war years, Canadian farmers had also prospered, providing food for countries whose own agricultural industries were devastated by war.

The Twenties, however, started with an economic whimper. As the nations of the world returned to peacetime production, Canadian goods faced stronger competition. Farmers, manufacturers, and industrialists did their best to adapt, and called on the federal government for help. As you have already learned, the government's responses rarely pleased everyone. But by 1923 it looked as though better times had arrived, and the Roaring Twenties could begin.

From the Farms to the Cities

Three factors helped to shape Canada and its economy in the 1920s. Two of these—tariffs and freight rates—were determined by the federal government. The third, increasing mechanization, was a product of technology. All three helped push Canadians towards the cities.

Tariffs affected everyone. To protect Canada's manufacturing and industrial base—overwhelmingly located in central Canada—the federal government imposed protective tariffs on imported goods. This meant, for example, that US-made farm machinery would be taxed so that it was more expensive than Canadian-made farm machinery. This made manufacturers happy, but it infuriated farmers. Unfortunately, the US did the same thing, and Canadian goods suffered in the US market. Not only were farmers affected, but also workers in the resource industries—such as miners and pulp and paper workers. Throughout the 1920s, tariff **protectionism** would have serious consequences in Canada and around the world.

Figure 4–17 Massey-Harris resumed production of farm equipment after WW I.

The Canadian government also increased freight rates under pressure from the railroads, which were run from Toronto and Montreal. In the West and in the Maritimes, this meant much higher shipping costs. Again, it was good for the railroads, but costly to farmers, coal miners, fishers, forestry workers, and factory workers in other regions of Canada. These industries suffered, and many people who could not find work gravitated towards Canada's largest cities.

Western farmers were particularly vulnerable to world economic conditions. Between 1918 and 1921 they saw the world price of wheat plummet from $2.45 to $.80 a bushel. Other nations of the world were now producing bumper crops of wheat. To survive, farmers had to lower their costs of production. By the mid-1920s, Canadian farmers were abandoning the horse for the new tractors, threshing machines, and combines. This mechanization meant they could harvest crops more quickly, with fewer farm workers. And with less farm labour needed, more people from rural areas went to the cities to find work.

Cities such as Toronto teemed with newcomers. By the mid-1920s, Toronto's population exceeded half a million people. With the growing cities came new challenges and greater economic activity. Municipal governments had to supply residents with water, electricity, sewage systems, and public transit. Houses, office buildings, and roads had to be built. The list went on and on. More than ever, cities were the engines driving Canada's economy.

Up Close

8. Write a paragraph describing what you know about tariffs and their effect on the economy of the time.

Bush Pilots and the North

Canada's booming cities were hungry for something that rural areas had: raw materials and resources. By the end of the war, most of southern Canada was linked, if not by road, then by rail. But the North and its rich resources were inaccessible. Wartime breakthroughs in transportation technology helped change the situation in the 1920s.

Canada's aircraft industry was still in its infancy. But in late 1917, Fairchild Aerial Surveys of Canada had become the first Canadian company to fly in winter. This was key to opening the North for mineral exploration and development. Canada's aircraft industry tackled the problems of northern flight and adapted its planes. Because much of the North was heavily forested, the most open areas were lakes or large rivers. By 1926, the industry was modifying planes so that they could land not just on the ground, but on water or snow as well.

Former Royal Air Force pilots were eager to put their skills to

Figure 4–18 Bush pilots revolutionized transportation in the North.

The Roaring Life in Canada 103

profitable use as bush pilots. They began by flying forest-fire patrols from Lake of the Woods, in northern Ontario, to as far north as James Bay. By the mid-1920s, they were delivering mail and freight, transporting passengers, and conducting aerial surveys. They also flew supplies to workers in northern mines and mills. By the end of the 1920s, more than 250 bush planes were in service, three of them flown by men with names worthy of the jazz players of the era: Punch Dickens, Wop May, and Doc Oaks.

Don't Worry—Shop!

With the good times of the 1920s came the most astonishing number of consumer products Canadians had ever seen. During the "bubble" of prosperity from 1923 to 1929, many Canadians had full-time jobs and regular paycheques. And with the beginning of **mass media** came the beginnings of mass advertising. Canadians were bombarded with messages in flyers and catalogues, on billboards and product packaging, in newspapers and magazines, and on the radio. Canadians who could afford it—and even those who couldn't—did some serious shopping.

Figure 4–19 Halifax's Samuel Cunard founded a steamship company in 1839 that became the world's leading purveyor of luxury ocean cruises. By the 1920s, Cunard posters such as this one seduced the wealthy, and the not-so-wealthy, to spend money and time cruising the Atlantic in style.

The era marked the beginnings of a consumer society, and many factors contributed to this. Jobs seemed to be more secure than in earlier times. By modern standards, many of the jobs did not pay particularly well. But more Canadians than ever were earning more than they needed for the basics—food, clothing, and shelter. They had "disposable" income left over. In 1920, a worker such as a skilled carpenter could earn $.90 per hour over a 44-hour workweek. The take-home pay of $39.60 a week was a respectable sum. A seamstress working in Toronto in 1925 could take home about $12.50. Assembly-line workers were also making good livings. Also, housing was comparatively inexpensive. In many parts of the country, a family could rent a six-room house for about $20 a month. Seven thousand dollars would buy a four-bedroom brick home in Toronto. Food, too, was relatively cheap: a bushel of apples cost 27 cents, a litre of milk 4 cents, and a kilogram of sugar 18 cents.

Advertisers were able to make luxury items seem like necessities to hundreds of thousands of Canadians. Department stores such as the T. Eaton Company Limited offered an astounding range of household goods and appliances. They also offered monthly payments and lay-away plans. The Eaton's catalogue became a part of life in Canada's cities and farms. It featured many little miracles: an automatic washing machine for $98.00, or a hand-operated washing machine for $19.00. An electric iron was $3.50, an electric toaster $3.75. Part of the appeal of the appliances was that they saved people time in domestic tasks. Another result was that society's expectations for cleanliness went up.

The top item for consumers was the automobile. In 1923, a person could make monthly payments on a new Ford automobile priced at $445.00. Two years later, car prices had dropped somewhat, and a person could buy a Model T Ford, built in Windsor, for $424.00. For slightly more money, the car came with options: a spare tire, a speedometer, and lights. By 1928, shoppers might want to check out a Chevrolet or Pontiac that had been built in Regina. The dream car for many Canadians was the upscale General Motors McLaughlin Buick, built in Oshawa, Ontario, by Canadian tycoon Sam McLaughlin's company. As with household goods and appliances, the choices seemed limitless. By 1929, a large percentage of Canadian families owned a car. Over the course of the decade, car ownership had increased 300 percent.

Figure 4–20 By 1930, over a million automobiles were registered in Canada.

Once Canadians bought cars, they wanted to drive somewhere. The public demanded better roadways, and the government responded. By 1929, close to 600 000 kilometres of paved roads crisscrossed Canada, interwoven with nearly the same length of dirt and gravel roads. The family "Sunday drive" became a regular social event in Canadian life. Before the 1920s, only the very rich had been able to tour parts of Canada by rail. With the popularity of the car, that changed. The era marked the beginning of mass tourism in Canada. Niagara Falls, in particular, became a major tourist destination for car owners.

Perhaps even more popular than the car was the radio. The entire family would huddle around a huge radio set made of tubes and burnished wood. They would listen in hushed excitement as their favourite weekly shows of music,

The Roaring Life in Canada

Figure 4–21 A family's radio, such as the one in this Eaton's Catalogue, became a status symbol. The larger and more elaborate it was, the better.

comedy, soap opera, education, news, preaching, poetry—even ventriloquism—wafted through the room and into their imaginations.

As you read earlier, US entrepreneurs quickly saw radio stations as a way to make money on advertising. The few radio stations in Canada could hardly compete, and their programming was less popular than that of the US stations. As more and more Canadians tuned into US stations, Canadian radio stations often became US **affiliates**. Many Canadians, and certainly the Canadian government, saw this as an American cultural invasion.

AN OUTPOURING OF CANADIAN CULTURE

During World War I, Canadians had begun to feel enormous pride in their country. Hard-won military victories such as Vimy Ridge had revealed to the world, and to Canadians themselves, that Canada was a force to be reckoned with. In the blood-soaked trenches of Europe and in the war efforts at home, Canadians had shown great courage. Following the war, national pride spread into all areas of Canadian culture, from fine art, popular culture, and literature, to professional and amateur sports. In the 1920s, no person or group more embodied this growing sense of a national identity—and of Canada, the land—than the Group of Seven.

The Group of Seven emerged from a circle of friends who worked primarily as commercial artists in Toronto. At the centre was Tom Thomson, an artist who loved the outdoors and painted the rugged landscapes of the Canadian Shield with bold brush strokes and colours. Thomson drowned mysteriously while canoeing in Algonquin Park in 1917, but his pioneering vision continued to fire the imaginations of his fellow artists. They rejected the naturalistic pastoral landscapes and still lifes that were fashionable at the time, and envisioned canvases of Canadian landscapes that would be as rugged and imposing as the country itself. In 1920, they formed the Group of Seven and set out to transform Canadian art by the sheer passion of their convictions.

At first, most critics mocked the Group's work. Hector Charlesworth, a prominent art critic, ridiculed their "crudity in colour and brushwork." But before the end of the decade, their work was accepted—even embraced—by the public and critics alike. The Group of Seven also influenced other Canadian

Up Close

9. As you read pages 106 to 112, make notes about these people: the Group of Seven, Emily Carr, Stephen Leacock, Mazo de la Roche, Foster Hewitt, Ethel Catherwood, Bobbie Rosenfeld, Dr. James Naismith, Mary Pickford.

artists of the time. One such artist was Emily Carr. After meeting the Group in Toronto in 1927, she returned to her painting in British Columbia with renewed passion and purpose.

Humour and Heartbreak

Stephen Leacock was perhaps the major figure in Canadian arts and letters in the 1920s. He was also a man of contradictions. His close friends and students knew him as chair of McGill University's department of economics and political science. The public knew him as the most popular humorist in the English-speaking world. Leacock was born in England in 1869, but was raised on a farm in Ontario. His masterpiece, *Sunshine Sketches of a Little Town*, is a satire set in the fictional rural Ontario town of Mariposa. It was based on Orillia, where Leacock spent his summers. Leacock's portrait of Mariposa, and of its citizens' fumbling efforts to deal with a changing world, was sometimes cutting, but written with warmth and affection. The book focused entirely on Canadian characters and concerns, yet it was a hit around the world.

Another Canadian author achieved world fame in the 1920s, but with writing that was more serious in tone than Leacock's. In 1927, Mazo de la Roche published the dramatic novel *Jalna*, about a family named Whiteoaks. It won international acclaim and de la Roche went on to write a series of novels and plays based on this family, its heartbreaks, and its home, Jalna. Again, a Canadian writer achieved international fame, using specifically Canadian locations, characters, and themes. Her novels sold more than 9 million copies in English and foreign-language editions, and were made into films and plays for radio and the stage.

Figure 4–22 The Group of 11? Six of the Group of Seven at Toronto's Arts and Letters Club in 1921. From the right: J.E.H MacDonald, Arthur Lismer, Franz Johnston, art critic Barker Fairley, Lawren Harris, A.Y. Jackson, and F.H. Varley. Absent is Franklin Carmichael. Tom Thomson is also often included in the Group. Before it disbanded in 1931, the Group expanded to include A. J. Casson, Edwin Holgate, and L. L. Fitzgerald.

Figure 4–23 Stephen Leacock's influence on Canadian writing has continued through the Leacock Medal for Humour. Since 1947, it has been awarded to writers such as Robertson Davies, W. O. Mitchell, Bill Richardson, and Mordecai Richler.

The Roaring Life in Canada

Images

Emily Carr: A Vision in the Wilderness

Figure 4–24 *Heina.* Emily Carr's 1928 painting shows her ongoing connection to aboriginal culture. Eventually, under Harris's influence, Carr would create more abstract paintings of the BC interior.

Emily Carr was born to British parents in Victoria, BC, in 1871, and raised in a traditional home. From an early age, however, she had an instinctive love of art and writing. She soon developed a deep interest in the history of her province, particularly its aboriginal cultures, and a strong connection to the landscapes of the BC interior. Carr created many majestic paintings of Native totems and communities in the years leading up to World War I. However, she could not find buyers for her paintings. After 1913, she built and ran a boarding house in Victoria and taught art to children to make ends meet. She was discouraged in her art, and produced few paintings.

In 1927, Carr participated in an exhibition of West Coast art at the National Gallery in Ottawa. During her trip east, she met the Group of Seven. Her long period of artistic isolation was over. Here were artists like herself, painters trying to capture the essence of Canada. "You are one of us," Lawren Harris said to her. And Carr had nothing but lavish praise for Harris and the Group.

Although Carr was 57 at the time, the event marked a new start for her career. Their love of the drama, isolation, and immensity of the Canadian wilderness—whether in BC, northern Ontario, Quebec, or the Maritimes—had

Communities: Canadian Identity

Figure 4–25 Lawren Harris's 1924 oil painting *Pic Island* shows the powerful impact of the northern Ontario landscape. Harris was moving towards a more abstract painting style, which influenced Emily Carr and other Canadian painters of the time.

bonded Carr and the Group. In the years following their meeting, Carr journeyed into the BC interior to create some of her best-known works. In 1937 and 1938, she had major shows in Toronto and Vancouver. When Carr became too ill to travel on painting expeditions, she turned to writing. In 1941, she published *Klee Wyck*, for which she won a Governor General's Award. In the decades after her death, Carr's writings and journals were published to great acclaim and growing public interest. Today, Emily Carr's reputation as a pioneering figure in Canadian culture continues to grow.

What Do You Think?

1. Painters such as Lawren Harris and Emily Carr are celebrated, in part, because they worked to create a vision of Canada that was unique and independent of British or American influence. Compare the two paintings reproduced here. What vision of Canada do they present? Do they continue to provide an accurate representation of Canada?

2. Examine Carr's *Heina*. What aspects of Haida culture does it convey? How might a member of that culture relate to this painting?

3. The 1920s marked a time in Canadian history when more people were migrating to the cities. However, the Group of Seven used natural landscape as representative of Canada. How does this contrast between the landscape and urban life complicate the Canadian identity?

The Roaring Life in Canada

Data File

The sailing ship that has been on the back of the Canadian dime since 1937 is the schooner the *Bluenose*. Launched as a fishing and racing ship in Lunenburg, Nova Scotia in 1921, the *Bluenose* immediately began winning races and did so for the next two decades. It ended its days as a cargo ship and was wrecked off Haiti in 1946—an inglorious end for Canada's most celebrated ship.

A Golden Age of Sports

The 1920s certainly roared in Canadian sports. Hockey was central to the era and many of the most famous names in the sport were active in this decade. In 1923, Foster Hewitt used a telephone to do possibly the first-ever radio broadcast of a hockey game. Soon Hewitt's voice, and the phrase he used repeatedly—"He shoots! He scores!"—would be familiar to hockey fans across North America. The National Hockey League, formed in Montreal in 1917 with four Canadian teams, expanded in 1924 to include its first US club, the Boston Bruins. By 1926, the NHL had ten teams, six of them American. Hockey may have been Canada's favourite game, but as a professional sport it needed a broader base than Canada in order to be profitable for club owners.

At the 1928 Olympic Games in Amsterdam, Canada once more proved itself on the world stage. Percy Williams of Vancouver won two gold medals, in the 100-metre and 200-metre sprints. James Ball of Manitoba won two medals—a silver in the 400-metre and a bronze in the 1600-metre relay. But Canadian women made the biggest splash of all. It was the first time that women had been allowed to compete in track and field at the Olympics, and the Canadian women's team stole the show.

Ethel Catherwood, known as "Saskatoon Lily," had already broken the world record for the high jump when she won gold at the Olympics. She became an

Figure 4–26 Canada's 1928 gold medal women's relay team was composed of, left to right, Jane Bell, Myrtle Cook, Ethel Smith, and Bobbie Rosenfeld.

international sensation. Her teammate, Bobbie Rosenfeld, won a silver in the 100-metre and a gold in the women's 4x100 metre relay, and just missed winning another medal in the 800-metres. Also at the Amsterdam Olympics were the Edmonton Grads, Canada's championship women's basketball team, which won virtually every championship from 1915 until they disbanded in 1940. Dr. James Naismith, the Canadian who invented basketball, called them "the greatest basketball team that ever stepped out on a floor."

The triumph of these women in international sports inspired women around the world, but Canadian women in particular. It proved, however, to be a fleeting moment in the progress women were making towards equal opportunities in sports. By the 1930s, medical and educational experts—almost exclusively male—were again arguing that it was unhealthy for women to compete and exert themselves physically.

> **The solemn periodic manifestation of male sport based on internationalism, on loyalty as a means, on arts as a background and the applause of women as a recompense.**
>
> —Baron Pierre de Coubertin, founder of the modern Olympic Games, describing his vision of the Games in the late 1890s

Figure 4–27 Bobbie Rosenfeld, pictured here in 1925, won many more trophies in track and field, including silver and gold at the 1928 Olympics. In 1950, Canadian sportswriters voted her Canada's Female Athlete of the Half Century.

Fears of US Cultural Domination

Between 1919 and 1929, Canadian culture flourished. But Canada was also experiencing ever-increasing influence from its southern neighbour, the US. With the mass popularity of radio and motion pictures, Canada was flooded with US radio programs and films. Canada had pioneered in radio. In fact, the first radio programs in North America were broadcast in 1919, from station XWA in Montreal. In 1922, 10 000 Canadians owned a radio set. By 1928, the number had climbed to approximately 400 000.

In 1923, the Canadian National Railway established a radio network that stretched from New Brunswick to British Columbia, broadcasting musical concerts, drama, comedy, and educational programs. But by the end of the decade, the fledgling network could provide only three hours of programming a week. By

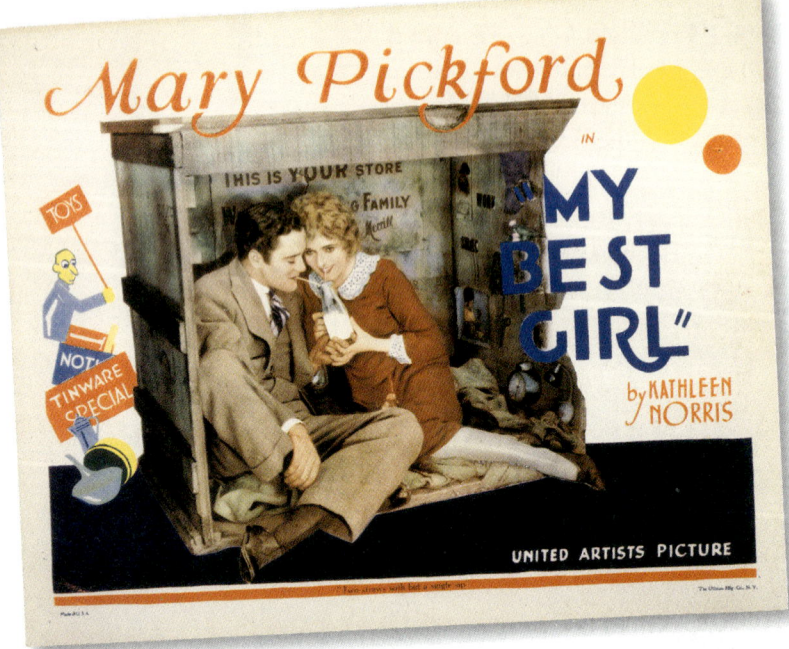

Figure 4–28 Mary Pickford has been called the "first movie star." Pickford portrayed an ideal of American sweetness and innocence, yet she was a Canadian.

that time, powerful, well-financed US radio stations were crowding the airwaves. At the end of the decade, 80 percent of the radio programs Canadians were listening to were American. The Canadian government grew concerned. In 1928, it appointed a royal commission to study the state of Canadian broadcasting. Eventually, the Aird Commission's report would lead to the formation of the Canadian Radio Broadcasting Commission in 1932.

The same trend was happening with motion pictures. Movies were being made in Canada, but not as many as were being produced in the US. Hollywood was already the movie capital of the world. As a result, Canadians were lining up for movies that were based on American life. Few in Hollywood cared to mention that "America's Sweetheart," Mary Pickford, was actually Gladys Smith from Toronto. Other Canadians conquered Hollywood as well. Perhaps the most popular silent slapstick comedies of all time were produced by Mack Sennett, who was born Michael Sinnott in Richmond, Quebec. As you will read in Chapter 14, Canadians continued to make a huge mark in Hollywood comedies in the decades ahead. Jack Warner, one of the founders of the powerful Warner Brothers studio in Hollywood, was born in London, Ontario. And legendary Louis B. Mayer, of MGM, was raised in Saint John, New Brunswick.

In the early years of these two new mass media, several patterns had emerged. In radio, the Canadian government took action to ensure a Canadian presence, for fears of US dominance. In the film industry, Canadian talent went to find opportunities in the US. If they achieved major success in the US, the rest of the world would view them as Americans, and their Canadian origins would be all but forgotten. In the years ahead, with the emergence of other new media, these patterns would repeat themselves again and again.

Heritage Minute

In 1899, Alfred Fitzpatrick founded the Reading Camp Association. Volunteers went into labour camps around the country to teach reading to those outside of the school system. Now called Frontier College, the program was awarded the UNESCO award for literacy in 1979. Today, graduates of Frontier College work with many immigrants and refugees who are starting a new life in Canada.

Historical Inquiry: Investigating Historical Topics

Historian at Work

Asking the Right Questions

One of the best ways historians have to investigate a time period or event is to interview "eyewitnesses to history." In this way, they learn how people felt, reacted, and coped with events and circumstances. Interviews can add missing pieces and details to the historical puzzle. They can add the human touch. Ordinary people are as valuable to historians as famous leaders, scientists, and celebrities. Family members such as parents and grandparents, for example, can be sources of historical information. Below are the stages of the interview process, along with types of questions.

Interview Preparation

- Do background research into the time period or event. This will allow the interview to focus on the subject's personal reactions and insights.
- Treat the interview subject with respect, and set the interview for a convenient time, time frame, and location.
- Agree on how the interview will be conducted: through written notes, audiotape, videotape, or a combination. Practise with the recording devices before conducting the interview.

Types of Questions

Factual Questions These ask for facts. For example, an interviewer might ask a woman who was a child in the late 1920s where she lived, where she went to school, and how many children were in her family.

Comparative Questions This kind of question compares different time periods, people, genders, points of view, and so on. For example, an interviewer could ask an elderly Japanese Canadian to compare life in the 1940s to life today.

Causal Questions These questions ask "why?" For example, "why did something happen."

An interview question with a person who left Canada for the United States could be "Why did you feel it was necessary to leave Canada?"

Speculative Questions These are opinion questions. For example, an interview question with a woman who grew up in the 1950s could be "Do you think that World War II had a positive or negative impact on you and other women of your generation?"

During the Interview

Be sure to be punctual and polite. Do everything possible to make the subject feel at ease--some memories may be painful. Listen carefully, and let answers go in unexpected directions. This may lead to rich information. Observe reactions. Body language, tone of voice, and emotion communicate as much as words. End the interview with an open-ended question, such as "Was there anything else you would like to add?" This may lead to more valuable information. And, of course, thank the person for their time.

After the Interview

Expand on your notes and material while the interview is still fresh in your mind. Send a thank-you note or a follow-up phone call to your subject, along with a final copy of the interview.

Activities

1. On your own or with a partner, prepare to interview a person or persons who lived in the 1920s. Perhaps arrange a visit with residents of a local retirement community.

CONCLUSION

Canada was taking shape during the postwar period as an independent and increasingly urban nation with its own culture. Many conflicts erupted, particularly on labour and immigration issues, and the changing role of women. King, who was a pragmatist, tended to give a little on each issue, to stay in power. However, the increasing prosperity of the period tended to soften social strife. While many of the controversies signalled important changes in society, they could hardly be compared to the deadly and horrifying conflict Canada had involved itself in during World War I. The key test of the new social attitudes and changes was what would happen if the prosperity suddenly vanished. You will learn about this in Chapter 5.

One outcome of Canada's new awareness of itself was an increase in cultural activity. Canadian writers, painters, and entertainers began to capture international attention for their distinctive styles. But the new Canadian cultural awareness did not include an appreciation for cultures other than the majority culture. For example, the impact of the decision to assimilate Native children to the majority culture in residential schools would be felt by Native peoples throughout the century.

CHAPTER ACTIVITIES

Check Your Understanding

1. Create a comparison chart to contrast the leadership styles of Mackenzie King and Arthur Meighan.

2. Create a time line to trace the events of the Person's Case.

Develop Your Thinking

3. Choose one of the people listed in the Up Close activity on page 106. Find out more about him/her and present your findings in a form of your choice.

4. How did flappers express the attitudes of the decade?

5. Interpret the long-term significance of the Winnipeg General Strike. Did it promote the development of labour unions or delay the progress of union organization? Write a report outlining your perspective. Use specific evidence to strengthen your case.

6. Some businesses begun at the time of prohibition are still operating today. How did the prohibition movement create opportunities for Canadian entrepreneurs?

■ Express Yourself

7. Create two posters promoting a showing of works by Emily Carr and the Group of Seven, one designed for an audience in the twenties and one for audiences today. Account for any differences between the two posters.

8. In the role of a sports journalist reporting on the 1928 Olympics, write a newspaper article noting the success of Bobby Rosenfeld and the women's relay team.

■ Apply Your Learning

9. Explore and interpret parallels between the Progressive Party (1921-1926) and the modern Reform Party (1993) as Western protest and opposition parties.

Extend Your Learning Using the Internet

10. In the early decades of the century, Native peoples in Canada tried unsuccessfully to form grassroots organizations to resist the government's policy of assimilation. Compare today's Native organizations with those of the past. Why have current organizations been more successful in achieving their goal of independence?

11. How did the works of Emily Carr and the Group of Seven contribute to a sense of Canadian identity? View works by these artists at Canadian virtual art galleries and select one work that exemplifies Canadian identity for you. In a brief oral presentation, explain the rationale for your choice.

Unit 2

Depression and War

1929–1945

For many people, the end of the 1920s marked the end of the good times. The stock market crash of 1929 ushered in the Great Depression, which gripped Canada and the world all through the 1930s. Although the good news was that the Depression would end, it took World War II to do it.

Throughout the Depression, thousands of unemployed Canadians suddenly needed public assistance just to survive. The 1930s gave birth to new political parties, which offered revolutionary solutions to the economic crisis.

The period was not all bleak. People still went to movies and listened to radio. In fact, radio grew so popular—especially US radio shows—that the CBC was created in the 1930s to broadcast made-in-Canada information and entertainment.

In 1931, Prime Minister King won his bid for autonomy, and Canada became an independent nation. But outside Canada, new political developments raised fears. Fascism took hold in Europe, and anti-Semitism was on the rise—in Canada, as well as in Europe. As the power of the Nazis grew, so did Hitler's plans to expand Germany. In the fall of 1939, Canada declared war. It fought alongside its allies until the war's end in 1945.

Prime Ministers	Dates of Office
Mackenzie King	1926–1930
R. B. Bennett	1930–1935
Mackenzie King	1935–1948

Anticipation Guide

In this unit, you will:

- examine events leading up to "Black Tuesday"
- explore the connection between the popularity of US entertainment and the creation of the CBC
- assess the ideas of the new political parties that emerged in the 1930s
- investigate what life was like for Canadians in the Great Depression
- create and use a time line of events showing Nazi persecution of the Jewish people from 1934 to 1939
- explore ways in which Canada helped—and failed to help—Jewish refugees
- explore the "cause and effect" relationship between the Treaty of Versailles and World War II
- debate whether or not the Battle of Dieppe was truly "a disaster"
- learn about the contributions of Canadians from many backgrounds to World War II

5 The Great Depression

Focus Questions

Social and Political Movements
What was the pattern of social and political reform during the 1930s?

Individual Canadians and Canadian Identity
How did average Canadians and their families get by during the Depression?

Economic conditions and social structures:
What factors caused and prolonged the Great Depression?

How did the economic realities of the 1920s and the 1930s compare? How were Canadians affected?

Canada had become a consumer society in the 1920s. But was the prosperity secure? Some signs of economic weakness had been ignored during the 1920s. When the crash came in 1929, Canada was highly vulnerable. Government policies that inflamed tariff wars and offered ineffective help to the unemployed only made things worse. Soon, millions were in serious need. On top of the economic collapse, the Prairies were afflicted by a devastating drought.

One important outcome was the rise of new political parties. Canadians increasingly looked to fresh, sometimes radical, political solutions to problems. New parties such as the Co-operative Commonwealth Federation, Social Credit, and the Union Nationale offered alternatives to traditional political thinking.

Canadian culture continued to develop during the 1930s, especially in the newer mediums of radio and movies. To some extent, Canadian popular culture became a means of escape from conditions that people could not change. The birth of the Dionne quintuplets in 1934 provided lots of diversion until the start of World War II. But this story was also about money. Amazingly, in such lean times, Canadians and other tourists poured $51 million into the Ontario economy by travelling to the quints' home in northern Ontario. Escapism did come at a price.

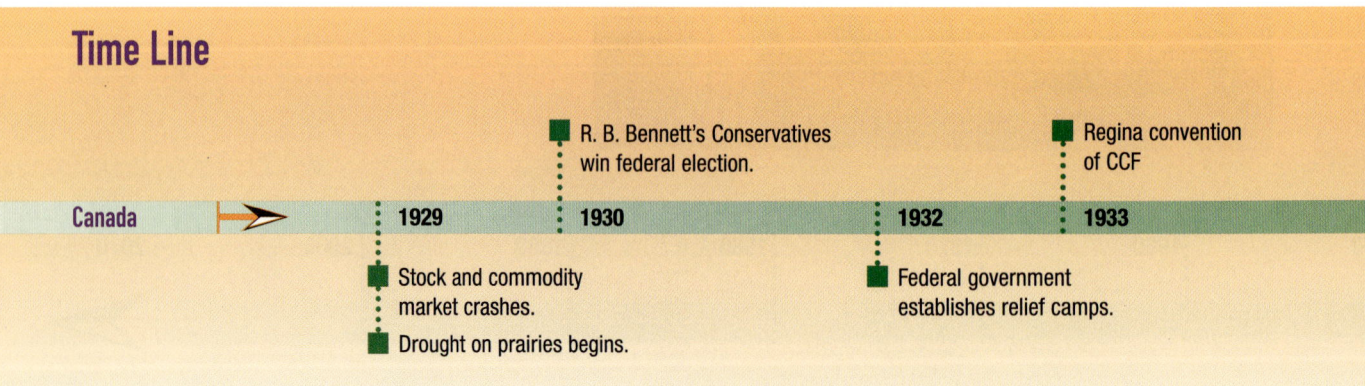

Time Line

Canada

- 1929: Stock and commodity market crashes. Drought on prairies begins.
- 1930: R. B. Bennett's Conservatives win federal election.
- 1932: Federal government establishes relief camps.
- 1933: Regina convention of CCF

Perspectives

This photograph of the Dionne quintuplets was taken in the late 1930s. The five identical sisters are dressed in matching coats and hats and are looking at a replica of a coach used for British coronations. Their family home in Corbeil, Ontario, is shown in the background. Does this photograph look like a picture from a family album? Why or why not? What aspects of the photograph guided your answer? What might be the purpose of such a picture?

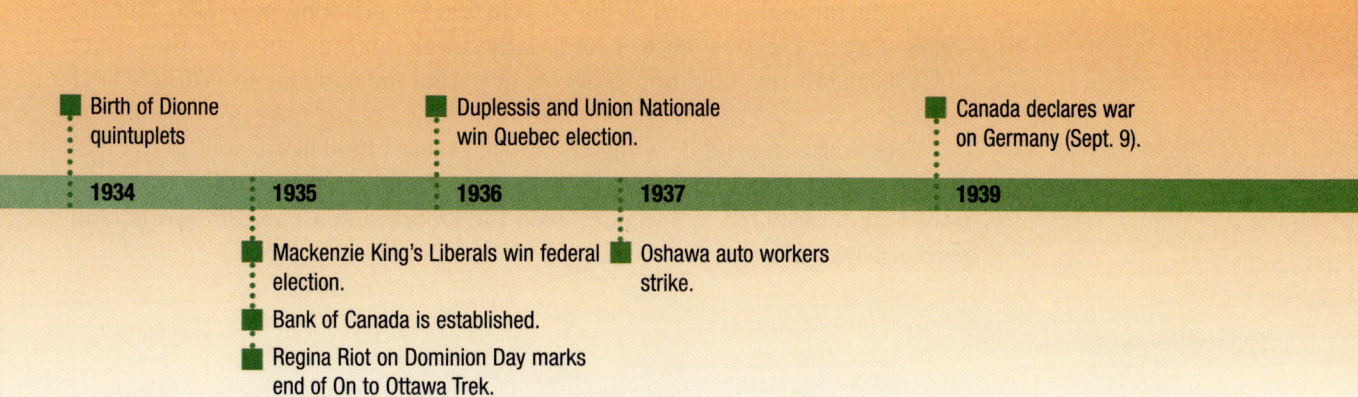

- Birth of Dionne quintuplets — 1934
- 1935 — Mackenzie King's Liberals win federal election. Bank of Canada is established. Regina Riot on Dominion Day marks end of On to Ottawa Trek.
- Duplessis and Union Nationale win Quebec election. — 1936
- 1937 — Oshawa auto workers strike.
- Canada declares war on Germany (Sept. 9). — 1939

BLACK TUESDAY: THE 1929 STOCK MARKET CRASH

Many people point to the stock market crash of 1929 as the cause of the Depression, but the crash was a symptom of a dangerous financial problem that had been building for years.

During the 1920s, Canada enjoyed a post-World War I economic boom known as "The Roaring '20s." This period of prosperity was actually shaky, however. It was built on easy **credit**, unrealistically high economic expectations, and the need to supply Europe with exports as it rebuilt after World War I. As early as 1928, disturbing economic indicators warned of a **financial downturn** in Canada; among these were declining wheat and newsprint prices, and an oversupply of most major export products.

"Black Tuesday"—October 29, 1929—signalled the end of the post-war prosperity. On this day, 16 million shares (portions of company ownership that people can buy and sell) were sold on the New York stock market. Soon, the value of stock market shares had decreased by $30 billion. Thousands of people lost their life savings.

There were stories of ruined bankers and investors jumping from New York skyscrapers. Many people believe that sensationalized media coverage worsened the impact of the crash. After reading such dire accounts, many people became fearful about the future and reluctant to spend. Without customers, stores and factories were soon closing all over North America.

Figure 5-1 The Canadian TV series "Wind at My Back" is set during the Depression. In the series, a mother is forced to leave her sons and find a job in the city.

The crippling blow to the American economic system had an impact on world economies: governments, industries, and banks stopped spending, investing, lending, and expanding. World trade sharply declined. The downward financial trend fed on itself and led to a long period of **economic stagnation**.

Still, many people assumed the crash was temporary. They felt it was just an adjustment to the normal business cycle (see Foundations, page 123). But the 1930s Great Depression was unusually bleak and drawn-out, the worst in Canada's history. It did not release its grip until the outbreak of World War II in 1939.

Economists are still debating about what caused the Depression. In the section that follows, you will read about some of the significant factors and conditions that contributed to and intensified the Depression around the world, and particularly in Canada.

Easy Credit

After World War I, companies in North America and Europe needed money to convert to peace-time production. They raised funds by going into debt, either by borrowing from banks, selling bonds, or by offering shares on stock markets.

Investors were optimistic about post-war growth, and their rush to buy shares drove up share prices. They were so confident that share prices would keep rising that they even borrowed money to purchase shares. As long as prices were going up, investors could sell their shares, repay lenders, and still make a profit. But if share prices decreased, lenders could immediately demand repayment of loans.

Companies and consumers had borrowed heavily to pay for high-priced items, such as production machinery or cars. So any reduction in sales or income made it difficult to keep up payments on borrowed money, and it meant that companies and people would stop buying goods. When Black Tuesday shook economic confidence, lenders began demanding that loans be repaid. People and institutions went broke, and investment stopped.

Lack of Financial Regulations

Easy borrowing was especially risky given that financial services companies in the US were largely unregulated by the government. Stock brokerages could easily lend money to investors for stock purchases. When the stock market crashed and individuals suddenly had to repay their loans, they had no money to use, since their investments were worthless. The crash drove many brokerages into bankruptcy.

Only between 5 and 10 percent of people had bought shares on the market, but when prices dropped, the consequences were widespread. Many American banks had purchased stock shares with depositors' money. When stock prices plunged, many Americans worried that banks had lost so much on the stock market that depositors might not be able to withdraw their money. People stampeded to take out their savings.

Ironically, the rush itself emptied bank cash reserves, bankrupting hundreds of American banks in the process. Canadian investors lost money on US and Canadian stock markets. Canadian banks, however, were better regulated, so few Canadian depositors lost their savings through bank failures.

The Vulnerable Canadian Economy

The Canadian economy was linked to the health of the American economy and depended on exports to the United States. With a severe economic slowdown, there were fewer orders for Canadian resources and products. Faced with declining consumer demand, American parent companies responded by cutting back or closing Canadian branches.

Up Close

1. On pages 120–121, find indications of people's emotions, for example, fearful, optimistic. For each one, note the causes for that emotion.

Up Close

2. Create a mind map to summarize the causes of the Depression.

Export Emphasis

During the early part of the century, the Canadian economy was geared to the export of minerals, lumber, newsprint, fish, and especially wheat. About 33 percent of Canada's gross national income came from exports, making Canada particularly vulnerable to changes in the world trade economy. Within three years of Black Tuesday, international trade had dropped by 50 percent, and massive unemployment had spread throughout Canada and the world.

Shrinking Demand for Canadian Exports

In the early Depression, world markets for Canadian grain, most notably wheat, decreased significantly. Meanwhile, other countries increased their wheat production. The Soviet Union, for example, resumed wheat exports in 1928, cutting into Canadian markets. At the same time, many European countries increased **tariffs** to protect their farmers. World wheat production had been at an all-time high in the 1920s, and there was a stockpile of some 7 million bushels of unsold wheat, with no buyers on the horizon.

Canadian wheat farmers were outraged to hear that other nations with a wheat surplus, such at the United States and Brazil, were burning their excess in order to create an artificial demand and restore the price per bushel. Instead of cutting back in production, Canadian wheat pools continued harvesting. As a result, there were huge supplies of wheat that traditional European and US markets could not absorb. This pattern of oversupply held for other major Canadian export products, such as newsprint and minerals, contributing to the glut in world markets.

Figure 5-2 Canadian wheat

International demand shrank and wheat prices collapsed, sinking from $1.03 per bushel in 1928 to just $0.29 by 1931. Since wheat was a key export of Manitoba, Alberta, and especially Saskatchewan, those provinces suffered badly. Farm income dropped from $363 million in 1929 to $10 728 000 in 1931. In 1937, there was virtually no wheat crop in Saskatchewan and roughly two-thirds of the province's rural population was forced to seek public assistance.

Trade Protectionism and Tariffs

Many countries dealt with the economic crisis by imposing **duties** on imports. This proved particularly catastrophic to a major exporting country such as Canada. The gigantic American market was soon closed off by punishing tariffs such as the 1930 Smoot-Hawley Tariff, which was designed to protect American agricultural producers from cheaper Canadian imports.

Economic Structures: Conditions

Foundations

The Business Cycle

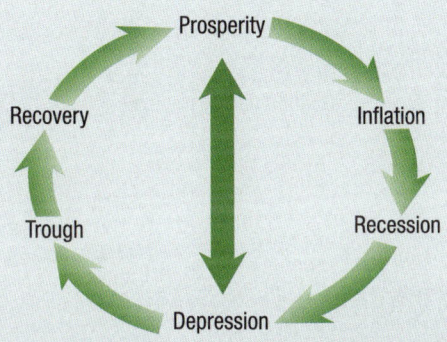

Figure 5-3 The Business Cycle

Economists define the business cycle as the fluctuation (change) in the level of economic activity that an economy goes through over time. The economy does not grow steadily, but shrinks and expands. The business cycle typically lasts from three and a half to seven years, and has four stages.

These are the four stages of business cycle:

1. Economic growth reaches its highest point at the *peak stage* of the business cycle. So many goods are sold that **inventories** begin to run out. There are not enough workers for the expanding factories, so workers can ask for higher pay. Higher wages, together with higher prices charged by manufacturers, increase **inflation**—widespread price increases in the economy. Interest rates rise along with prices, which makes consumers reluctant to borrow money to buy expensive items such as cars or houses. As the peak passes, consumers spend less, unsold products accumulate, and profits decline.

2. In the *recession stage* companies are faced with larger inventories and lower profits, and they reduce production. Sometimes they lay off workers. At the very least, they stop hiring, and stop expanding factories. Unemployed people cannot afford to spend much money. Those who do have jobs worry about losing them, and tend to save for the future. Less spending means fewer sales, further reductions in production, and more layoffs. Higher interest rates and weak demand discourage people from starting new businesses, and the number of bankruptcies increases. When a recession lasts a long time, or is especially severe, it is called a **depression**.

3. At the *trough stage*, declining sales and a surplus of workers mean that businesses cannot raise prices for goods. Also, workers cannot demand higher pay. As a result, prices stabilize, or even decrease, in a condition called **deflation**. Interest rates go down. As the low point of the recession passes, consumers who have saved money eventually begin to spend, since prices are low and borrowing is cheap.

4. When these consumers start spending again, the *recovery stage* has begun. Companies respond to increased sales and shrinking inventories by gradually increasing production. Unemployment is still high, so wages stay constant and inflation remains low. Factories do not immediately start expanding or hiring since there is still unused **production capacity**. The recovery stage lasts until the economic output of the peak of the previous expansion is reached. Growth above this point takes the business cycle into another expansion phase.

What Do You Think?

1. Where on the business cycle was the Canadian economy during the Great Depression? During the "Roaring Twenties"? Use information and ideas from the Foundations feature to explain your conclusions.

2. In what stage of the business cycle is the current year? Support your answer with real-life examples.

Data File

- By 1930 Canada had 13% unemployment. By 1933, this figure had climbed to over 26%. It fell back to 13% only when World War II broke out.
- Between 1929 and 1933, it is estimated that 1 in 5 Canadians became dependent upon government relief for survival.
- In Saskatchewan during the 1930s the total provincial income plummeted by 90% in two years, forcing 66% of the rural population onto welfare.

Decline in per capita income 1928 – 1933	
Canada	**48%**
Saskatchewan	72%
Alberta	61%
Manitoba	49%
British Columbia	47%
Ontario	44%
Quebec PEI New Brunswick Nova Scotia	Between 36-49%

Figure 5-4 This table shows how far Canadians' earnings fell between 1928 and 1933.

Up Close

3. Using a chart or Venn diagram, compare the political positions of Mackenzie King and R.B. Bennett in the election of 1930.

A very select few Canadians with fixed incomes or independent wealth found that their money had more buying power. For the majority of Canadians, however, the Depression meant great wage reductions and, all too often, unemployment. Many were unable to maintain even the basic necessities of life, and there were virtually no social assistance programs to help them.

> "These really are good times, but only a few know it."
> —US auto maker Henry Ford, March, 1931

THE GOVERNMENT RESPONDS

The 1930 election was fought between Liberal prime minister Mackenzie King and Conservative leader Richard Bedford (R.B.) Bennett. Bennett, originally from New Brunswick, had moved to Calgary as a young man, and he had become a millionaire through successful careers in law and business. He was a fiery speaker, sometimes called "Bonfire" Bennett for his rapid-fire speech. (A reporter once clocked him at 220 words per minute.) Bennett was a **capitalist** with conservative principles. He believed in law and order, a balanced budget, and a job for everyone. People liked Bennett's apparent enthusiasm in the face of hard times.

Prime Minister King seemed out of touch with the mood of Canadians. In spite of rising unemployment, he called an election for the fall of 1930. The campaign was one of the first to be fought over the issue of unemployment. Tariffs were a major issue as well. R. B. Bennett argued that higher tariffs were needed to preserve the Canadian market for Canadians until other countries, primarily the United States, lowered their own tariffs. Bennett felt he could use tariffs to "blast a way" for Canadian goods into world markets. This, he believed, would restore Canada's prosperity.

Unlike King, Bennett offered a solution to fix the mounting economic dilemma. Before the election, King had made a mistake that played into Bennett's hands. In the House of Commons, King said he would not give a "five-cent piece" to assist Tory provincial governments with the "alleged unemployment" problem. During the campaign, Bennett made him pay for his insensitive remark. At campaign appearances, King was often pelted with wooden nickels hurled by unemployed people.

To the surprise of many, Bennett's Conservatives swept the 1930 election. They won 137 seats, including an astounding 24 in Quebec, while King's Liberals took only 91. Bennett went on to govern Canada during the five worst years of the Depression. For King, the defeat was a blessing in disguise. He was now free to rebuke the government, but would not be responsible for handling the economic crisis.

Ineffective Economic Policies

During the first four years of his term, Bennett tried to restore prosperity with traditional economic policies. As a conservative, he detested spending money on large public works projects and relief payments. Bennett believed that a balanced budget would bring Canada out of the depths of the Depression. However, many economists think that the government goal of a balanced budget prolonged Canada's economic problems and the suffering of its people. Thinkers such as British economist John Maynard Keynes proposed that governments should spend their way out of a depression by increasing **deficits**.

Figure 5-5 R. B. Bennett with his sister

> I hope that in the future we shall be ready to spend on the enterprises of peace what the financial maxims of the past would only allow us to spend on the devastations of war.
>
> –Economist John Maynard Keynes, 1932

High Tariff Policy

In the 1930s, the US Congress raised the duty on US imports to the highest level in history. Bennett's response to these and other protective measures was to fulfill his election promise and raise Canada's tariffs. Such a move meant imposing tariffs on imported goods, which would protect Canadian manufacturers from external competition. Though the protective tariffs did help some central Canadian industries, it suffocated Canada's export trade. Bennett ignored the fact that the Canadian economy was tied to the international demand for Canada's primary resource exports, such as wheat, fish, forestry products, and minerals.

Imperial Preference

As early as 1930, Bennett strongly urged preferential tariffs for members of the British Commonwealth. In 1932, largely due to Bennett's urging, participants at the Imperial Economic Conference in Ottawa discussed these measures. It was agreed that within the Commonwealth a number of tariffs would be lowered in order to stimulate international trade. This step did increase Commonwealth trade, but not enough to make up for reduced trade with the United States. Later, the Americans fought back with their own tariffs against the trade wall. Bennett's

Up Close

4. Reread the quote from John Maynard Keynes. Rewrite it in your own words, and include yourself as the source.

imperial preference ignored the fact that Canada's largest trading partner was not the Commonwealth, but the United States.

Impact of Bennett's Protective Trade Polices

Protective tariffs were extremely harmful to the Canadian economy. Canadian exports dropped about 67 percent, from $1.4 billion in 1929 to $475 million in 1933. Many businesses went bankrupt, and corporations that had been financially secure were forced to restructure in order to survive. The annual deficit of the government-owned Canadian National Railways alone mounted to $60 000 000.

Responding to the Unemployment Crisis

Massive unemployment was a consequence of the severe economic downturn. By 1933, 826 000 people out of a population of 10 million were unemployed—and that doesn't include the out-of-work farmers and fishers, who were not counted in unemployment figures. Bennett had little choice but to increase federal payments to the provinces for unemployment relief. His government provided more than ten times the amount spent on relief in the previous decade. Still, municipal and provincial governments were left to pay for the social problems created by the economic collapse. In 1934 alone, municipal and provincial relief expenditures together rose to $97 million.

> I cannot make up my mind why this country between the lakes and the mountains should experience the Depression.
>
> –Prime Minister R. B. Bennett, 1931

Figure 5-6 The Sunstrum Relief Camp in Ontario

In 1932 the federal government established work camps throughout the country for single homeless men. It was believed that placing the unemployed in remote camps would ease the threat of trouble caused by thousands of young, unemployed men roaming Canada's streets. This stop-gap measure to deal with unemployment was highly unpopular. The camps primarily served to keep the unemployment problem out of sight.

Bennett's traditional methods for addressing the country's economic woes were not working. By 1934, there was growing unrest, the government's popularity was declining, and there was no end in sight to the Depression. Bennett became the butt of jokes. As the need for another election approached, R. B. Bennett realized that radically different economic and social measures were needed.

CONDITIONS OF THE UNEMPLOYED ACROSS THE NATION

The Impact of Unemployment

Within a year of the stock market crash, millions of formerly middle-class Canadians were out of work. Not once during the 1930s did the unemployment rate drop below 12 percent; in 1933 it peaked at 26.6 percent.

In the 1930s when people fell on hard economic times, there was no severance pay or unemployment insurance to fall back on. No protective social security measures existed, aside from a very modest old-age-pension scheme that had started in 1927. Many hospital beds were empty simply because people could not afford to get treatment.

The Great Depression affected virtually all aspects of the lives of most Canadians. Some individuals, families, occupational groups, and regions suffered more than others. Generally, young people, unskilled labourers, small-business people, and especially farmers bore the brunt of economic hardship. Imagine being a young person looking for work in 1936, when two-thirds of the young people entering the work force could not find steady employment.

Unskilled workers were particularly affected by massive unemployment. This was especially true for labourers who lived and worked in single-industry towns such as Windsor, Sudbury, and Oshawa in Ontario; and Sydney, Nova Scotia. A severe decline in the global use of metals had a particular impact on the industries of these communities.

Working women also suffered significant employment setbacks during the 1930s. It was socially unacceptable for a woman to take away a man's job. So,

Data File

Dark Depression Humour

Depression-era humour could be bitter, as reflected in these definitions coined during the government of Prime Minister R. B. Bennett (1930-35):

Bennett barnyard: an abandoned prairie farm

Bennett blanket: a newspaper

Bennett buggy: an engineless automobile drawn by a horse

Bennett coffee: roasted wheat

eggs Bennett: broiled chestnuts

Figure 5–7 In 1935, these young women participated in "Farm Girls Week" in Saskatoon, Saskatchewan. In the absence of other opportunities, community outreach often focused on traditional tasks for women. Women's attendance at university went down during this time, as did their employment rate.

frequently, school boards, professional organizations, governments, manufacturers, stores, and other major employers gave the very few jobs available to men. To survive, some women were forced to do domestic work for incredibly low wages; for example, in 1930 domestics earned about $300 a year.

Cutting Back—Drastically

At the onset of the Depression, automobiles commonly sold for between $500 and $1000. During the exuberant 1920s, cars were a symbol of freedom, success, and upward mobility. At that time, many Canadians could afford to buy an automobile on credit. However, when the Great Depression struck, purchases of new cars—and, for that matter, any other consumer goods bought on credit—stopped. All too frequently, cars, furniture, and appliances purchased on easy credit during the 1920s were repossessed in the 1930s.

The belt-tightening by no means applied only to luxury items; it also affected the necessities of life. Clothes were often mended and handed down rather than replaced. Fewer groceries were purchased. Farm and garden harvests were preserved for use over the uncertain months ahead.

Home and farm owners had a hard time paying their mortgages, bills, and property taxes. Likewise, utilities, home fuel companies, banks, municipalities, and

Figure 5–8 The elegant man in this ketchup advertisement is in sharp contrast to the out-of-work men beneath it. In the bleakest times, some people resorted to using ketchup to make soup.

landlords found it almost impossible to collect money owed to them. For property owners or renters who could not pay up, repossession or eviction was always a looming threat.

The Impact By Region

Not all areas of the country suffered equally. Canada's industrial heartland, southern Ontario and Quebec, had prospered during the booming 1920s. When the Depression hit, the region was less affected than other areas of the country. Protective tariffs erected by the federal government partially insulated Canadian industry located in central Canada.

As a rule, farm families in eastern and central Canada weathered the Great Depression better than families of the unemployed in urban centres or in western Canada. Eastern crops were more diversified than those in the Prairies, where wheat was a primary crop. Central Canadian mixed farms, then, could still grow enough to feed the family. Throughout Canada during the 1930s, farm incomes dropped below an average of $300 per year.

Drought, Dust, and Destruction In the 1920s, Saskatchewan was among the most prosperous farming communities in the world; in the 1930s, it was one of the poorest. The devastating decline was due to economic depression and the ravages of nature. An unprecedented prairie drought brought with it drifting soil, plagues of grasshoppers, plant rust, and ultimately crop failure.

The first sign of drought came in 1928, when the annual amount of precipitation was less than half of what it had been the previous year. 1929 was another dry year, removing vital subsoil moisture. From 1929, the drought continued on and off until 1937.

Agricultural experts say that during the 1930s 7.3 million hectares, or one-quarter of Canada's arable land, was affected by drought. A particularly afflicted area was the Palliser Triangle, which is roughly defined by lines joining Cartwright, Manitoba; Lloydminster, Saskatchewan; and Calgary, Alberta.

The Prairies have always been noted for their strong winds, but by spring of 1931, the winds were blowing up the loose, dry soil. The Prairie area most affected by these storms, including the Palliser Triangle, became known as the **dust bowl**.

Harsh prairie winds swept away fine topsoil from vast areas of cleared land, often taking newly planted seeds with it. The sky turned black with blowing topsoil; and dust and dirt penetrated houses and clothing and seared people's skin. With so much dirt blowing around, some farmers bitterly joked that if they threw

Figure 5–9 The Prairie winds sent so much soil into the air that the region became known as the Dust Bowl.

Up Close

5. Draw a map showing where the area called the Palliser Triangle was located. Write a caption for your map.

a gopher into the air, it would have dug itself a hole by the time it reached the ground.

So many millions of hectares of topsoil disappeared with the winds that one historical commentator said much of southern Saskatchewan ended up in the American Midwest. Many farmers harvested no crops at all, and the average grain yield plummeted to 2.7 bushels per acre.

When the winds did let up, the sun was often obscured by vast clouds of grasshoppers that swarmed over the land in search of grass or wheat to eat. The grasshopper problem was especially bad in 1937. One journalist described the insect invasion:

> **The grasshoppers came in clouds ... in concentrations never before experienced in Canada. Huge swarms appeared over Saskatoon and Regina in late July. They devoured everything in their paths as they ate their way out of sight ...**

There were no insect sprays at the time. Grasshopper populations are naturally kept under control when there is a cold, wet spring. But during the lingering 1930s drought, that was out of the question, so the growing grasshopper populations attacked the crops, leaving only worthless stalks.

On the farm, machinery and equipment were repaired rather than replaced, and horses were put back to work because it was cheaper to feed them than it was to buy oil and gasoline. It was almost as if the basic quality of life had reverted to conditions found hundreds of years earlier in Europe. Because there was a shortage of fruits and vegetables in many areas of the Prairies, reports of dietary-deficiency diseases, such as scurvy, were common.

As if these troubles were not enough for Prairie farmers, they also had to fight a fungus disease known as **rust**, which killed grain crops nearing maturity. The blight causes the maturing grain stalk to weaken and the seed head to fall from the stalk. In the face of such insurmountable odds, many Prairie farmers

Figure 5–10 A "Bennett buggy" was an automobile pulled by a horse—or by oxen.

loaded up their Bennett buggies, abandoned their farms, and moved their families elsewhere.

Was Relief in Sight?

Resourceful Canadians tried door-to-door selling—of insurance, vacuum cleaners, and other merchandise and services. When sales dropped off, some men resorted to panhandling.

Others tried to borrow money from family members, or ask for credit from the landlord or a local grocer. At some point, many people asked churches and charities for short-term help.

The need for relief during Depression was mind-boggling. By April 1, 1933, more than 1.4 million urban Canadian workers were collecting some form of municipal relief. Between 1931 and 1937, $813 million in relief money was distributed by various levels of government.

Figure 5-11 A destitute family in Saskatchewan

Public relief, called "the dole" or "pogey," was administered by the municipalities. It was never in cash, nor was it regular or enough to live on. The relief amounts varied markedly across the country. For example, the monthly relief rate for a family of five in Calgary was $60, while in Halifax it was $19. In 1932, a family of five living in Ontario needed at least $6 to $7 a week for food. In Toronto, where the rates were relatively high, the weekly relief food allowance for a family of seven was $6.93. Meanwhile, in rural areas of Quebec, a family of five received only $3.35 for food.

The unemployed not only had physical pangs of hunger to endure, there was also an assault on their dignity and pride. Many Canadians would have done virtually anything to avoid accepting public relief, because almost everything connected with the system was humiliating.

To qualify for relief, in most areas, a person had to have lived in one place for six months to a year. Such a requirement immediately disqualified the large number of unemployed men who travelled around the country looking for work.

Even if a person had lived in one area for the required time, relief assistance was not easy to obtain. In Ontario, for example, the following eligibility requirements were typical.

You must:
1. Prove that you are not able to support yourself and that no relative can help.
2. Be a man supporting a family.
3. Have been a resident of the municipality for at least one year before applying.
4. Turn in your liquor permit (prohibition was still in force).
5. Turn in your automobile licence plates and driver's licence.
6. Remove the telephone from your house.

7. Register at the unemployment office (to show your willingness to work).
8. Work on municipal projects from time to time.
9. Allow relief office investigators to come to your home to check on these rules.

The Canadian population became divided into those who were on relief and those who were not. Eventually those paying for relief through their taxes resented the payouts to others.

Figure 5–12   Riding the rails

"Riding the Rails"

Many men left their families and homes to try to find work in other regions of their province, or in the country. Often, these unemployed men rode the rods under railway boxcars, or rode in or on top of boxcars. The practice was known as riding the rails. Men from eastern Canada travelled west in the hope of finding steady employment. The Prairies, of course, produced few lasting job opportunities and many drifters continued their frustrating journey to British Columbia.

The soup kitchens, churches, charities, and municipal relief organizations of Vancouver, British Columbia could not handle the massive influx of the unemployed from other parts of the country. The provincial and municipal governments requested action from the federal government to remove the aimless men from their streets. The federal government's response, from 1932 to 1936, was relief camps.

Data File

In 1934, A. G. L. McNaughton, a Canadian Army general, was placed in charge of the relief camps. He boasted that the cost to the federal government per man per day in the relief camps was only $1.17.

BENNETT'S NEW DEAL

By 1935 it was obvious that the Depression was an economic problem that would not go away soon. If anything, the economy was getting worse, and there were widening divisions among regions within Canada. Bennett knew he needed to do something drastic to save the country and his political career, as an election was looming. Surprisingly, the strong-willed and confident Bennett began to doubt his own economic policies. The new measures Bennett proposed for Canada seemed at odds with everything he stood for as a capitalist and conservative who championed financial policies such as a balanced budget.

Historical Inquiry: Analysing/Evaluating Information

Primary Source
Life in the Relief Camps

During the height of the Depression, many unemployed men were sent to relief camps. The following is a first-hand account of what one 18-year-old saw, felt, and experienced in a relief camp. The passage comes from Barry Broadfoot's *Ten Lost Years*. Broadfoot compiled the oral history of people who lived through this bleak period.

> They'd march us out in the morning and we would be widening a trail or putting in a culvert or cutting and stacking wood for winter and every day there was a quota but after about an hour the guys would just sit down and wait for lunch and then sit around all afternoon snoozing ...
>
> They'd turned the running of these camps over to the Department of National Defence ... We were under K. R. and R. (King's Rules and Regulations) so we were under army law, so to speak, and they could pretty well do what they wanted. They couldn't keep you in camp if you didn't want to stay, but if they wanted to kick you out, then they could do that and in winter, 100 miles from nowhere and a supply truck coming in once or twice a week, that could be a real hardship ...
>
> We were paid 20 cents a day ... I've told this to people today and they always say, 'You mean twenty cents an hour, don't you?' and I'd say no, twenty ... cents a day. There was one guy in charge at that Hope camp who used to call us slaves. 'Okay, slaves, off your asses, we're going to cut trail today,' he'd say ...
>
> No, we never starved. The food was good. I mean good when it arrived but it was pretty awful when it hit our plates ... They [the cooks] could even foul up chocolate pudding and porridge. I knew guys from good homes, Dad gone broke, maybe, who would live on bread and butter and peanut butter and strawberry jam and prunes and canned milk and raw potatoes and oranges because they couldn't stand the sight of them big pots of greasy soup and watery stew.
>
> It was jail, you know. What else would you call it? All the fresh air and sunshine you could stand ... Just wind through the fir trees ... and guys lying around ... If you thought the army was bad, then you don't know about one of those camps.
>
> Nothing has ever been written about them because I think the government was too ashamed. Down the line the CCC [the Civilian Conservation Corps in the United States] did good work, so I've read, because they paid their guys and had decent leaders and discipline that made sense but you know what, I think down there a guy, well he didn't mind working in a camp. They had pride, they gave their guys pride. Parks built, dams built, roads a fellow could drive over years later and say to his wife, 'I helped build this road ... '
>
> But in Canada, not on your blinking life. It was 'get these dogs off the street before they offend people.'
>
> Everything about those camps was wrong, but the thing most wrong was they treated us like dirt. And we weren't. We were up against it, broke, tired, hungry, but we were farm boys who knew how to work ...

What Do You Think?

1. "Life in the Relief Camps" is an example of a primary source. Work with a partner and discuss the qualities of the passage that identify it as a primary source. Locate an example of a secondary source about Depression-era relief camps. Compare the two selections on the basis of tone, content, and impact on the reader.

Figure 5–13 Following the stock market crash, people in the US rushed to withdraw their savings from the banks.

American President Franklin Delano Roosevelt's New Deal Model

Bennett found new economic and social ideas in the programs of American President Franklin D. Roosevelt. When Roosevelt was elected president of the United States in 1932, he faced a nation crippled by the Depression. Americans were looking for a leader who could provide solutions. About 13 million Americans were unemployed, and Roosevelt confidently promised "action, and action now." To address his nation's economic ills, Roosevelt decided on a program that focused on three major areas: promoting recovery, providing relief to the needy, and reforming investment and banking regulations. Roosevelt's plan became known as the "New Deal."

As part of the New Deal, Roosevelt's government created hundreds of thousands of jobs in federal work projects. Farmers were paid for accepting government controls designed to cut down on crop surpluses, and the government made low-interest loans available to them. To increase public faith in banks, the government guaranteed bank deposits up to $5000.

In 1935, Roosevelt introduced unemployment insurance and old-age pensions, paid for by a national tax deducted directly from workers' wages. New laws ensured that workers earned at least an acceptable amount for their work (minimum wage) and that they weren't required to work an unreasonable number of hours per week.

On the international trade front, Roosevelt recognized that foreign trade was also extremely important to a healthy economy. He reduced tariffs on goods from other countries, which made possible the 1935 and 1938 trade agreements with Canada. The American people embraced Roosevelt and his promise of a New Deal. Canadians and their politicians, such as Bennett, took note of his success.

A Canadian Version of the New Deal

Faced with a very low public approval rating and the gathering momentum of new political parties, Bennett hoped the Canadian electorate would respond to a Canadian version of the New Deal.

Prime Minister Bennett surprised the Canadian people, the Opposition, and even his own Conservative Cabinet and colleagues by proposing radical economic and social reforms that borrowed heavily from Franklin D. Roosevelt's New Deal. On January 2, 1935, the Canadian prime minister began a series of

Roosevelt-style fireside chats (informal speeches aired on the radio) to people across the country, in which he outlined his bold program.

The revolutionary measures were needed, Bennett explained, because of the "crash and thunder of toppling capitalism." In a 1935 Speech from the Throne, Bennett's government stated, "You have been witnesses of grave defects and abuses in the capitalist system. Unemployment and want are proof of these. Great changes are taking place around us. New conditions prevail. These require modifications in the capitalist system to enable that system to more effectively serve the people."

These were strange words coming from a fervent capitalist and anti-communist. In effect, Bennett was calling for more direct federal government involvement in the Canadian economy. Bennett's sweeping changes included a more **progressive taxation** system, a maximum work week, a minimum wage, stronger regulations of working conditions, unemployment insurance, health and accident insurance, a revised old-age pension, agricultural support programs, and a grain board to regulate wheat prices.

Within weeks, Bennett's New Deal legislation was brought to the House of Commons in the most far-reaching reform package introduced by any Canadian government. Many of Bennett's own cabinet ministers opposed his economic and social policies, describing them as **communistic**. The prime minister's proposals met little opposition, since House members were already thinking about the fast-approaching election.

Canadians did not take to Bennett's New Deal as readily as Americans had to Roosevelt's program. The Liberals' election call in 1935 was "King or Chaos." On October 14, 1935, R. B. Bennett's government was swept from office. The election results were 171 Liberal, 39 Conservative, 17 Social Credit, 7 Co-Operative Commonwealth Federation (CCF), and one from the Reconstruction Party. Electoral patterns showed that voters had deserted Bennett and given their support to new parties such as the Social Credit and CCF. You will read more about these two parties in the next section. Almost all of Bennett's 1935 New Deal legislation was thrown out by the courts when judges decided that it went beyond the federal government's powers.

Up Close

6. Side-by-side in a chart, list some major points of both President Roosevelt's and Prime Minister Bennett's "New Deals."

"King or Chaos"

– 1935 Liberal election slogan

VOICES OF REGIONAL DISCONTENT

Voting patterns in the 1935 federal election reflected growing dissatisfaction with traditional political parties. These parties had failed to deal effectively with the economic and social problems of the Depression. As the Depression dragged on, regionally based movements, parties, and positions emerged that provided alternatives to conventional political views.

During the 1930s, people from all parts of the country clamoured for change and staged protest disturbances.

Up Close

7. As you read about each of these people, jot down notes about them and their politics: Thomas Pattullo, J. S. Woodsworth, Major C. H. Douglas, William Aberhart, Mitchell Hepburn, Maurice Duplessis.

British Columbia

In British Columbia, Thomas Pattullo, a reform-minded Liberal, was elected premier in 1933. Pattullo campaigned on a platform of "work and wages," and tried to implement New Deal policies in his province. He favoured provincial health insurance.

Once in power, Pattullo quickly realized that such programs depended on federal funds. In sharp contrast with Mackenzie King, Pattullo wanted to spend his way out of the Depression. The BC premier welcomed any examination of federal-provincial relations that would provide his government with more money and autonomy to institute needed reforms. Pattullo was largely unsuccessful in achieving his broader reform goals.

Co-operative Commonwealth Federation (CCF)

In 1932 the Co-operative Commonwealth Federation was founded in Calgary as a coalition of farmers, labour leaders, and university teachers. They wanted to create a political party that could accomplish the economic reforms they thought necessary to improve the lives of those most affected by the Great Depression. The first CCF leader, J. S. Woodsworth, was uniquely gifted in uniting the very different elements within the CCF.

The 1933 Regina Manifesto, which stated the CCF platform, was written by some of the party's more **left-wing** thinkers. The Manifesto called for the replacement of the capitalist system, and proposed a number of measures that would make governments better able to do social and economic planning.

Among the measures outlined was the **nationalization**, or public ownership, of leading industries and financial institutions. The proposed nationalization would also include public utilities and transportation companies, especially the Canadian Pacific Railway, which was important to prairie farmers who depended on the railway for transporting their wheat.

> In the old days we would send people from the cities to the country. If they went out today they would meet another army of unemployed coming back from the country to the city; that outlet is closed. What can these people do? They have been driven from our parks; they have been driven from our streets; they have been driven from our buildings, and in this city [Ottawa] they actually took refuge on the garbage heaps.
>
> —J. S. Woodsworth

The CCF supported the establishment of a welfare state with such protection as universal pensions, health and welfare insurance, a children's allowance, unemployment insurance, and workers' compensation.

Social Credit in Alberta

The Social Credit party of Alberta was at the opposite end of the political spectrum from the CCF. Like the CCF, it originated from people's frustration with the Depression and the way their government was dealing with the crisis.

Citizenship: Social and Political Movements

Flashpoint
The Regina Riot

The Regina Riot began in the work camps of British Columbia. Frustrated by relief camp conditions and the federal government's inability to provide real work and decent wages, protesters from the camps gathered in Vancouver to voice their concerns.

On June 3, about 1800 men, organized by the communist-sponsored Relief Project Workers' Union, set off on the "On to Ottawa Trek." Organizers planned to send thousands of unemployed men on an orderly march to present their grievances to the R. B. Bennett government in Ottawa.

Trekkers travelled atop railway freight cars and picked up other protesters along the way, making stops in Calgary, Medicine Hat, Swift Current, and Moose Jaw before arriving in Regina on June 14 with about 2000 men.

Prime Minister Bennett was intent on stopping the Trek, so he supported a railway order refusing access to the trains. The men were temporarily sheltered in the Regina Exhibition Grounds.

Bennett agreed to meet with a small group of leaders, who journeyed on to Ottawa. Talks soon broke down, and the delegation returned to Regina. Bennett gave the order to clear the demonstrators out of Regina.

On July 1, some movement leaders organized an open-air meeting in downtown Regina, where they would present their grievances to local citizens. Bennett decided to arrest the leaders.

Seeing their leaders arrested only fuelled the anger of the frustrated men. Soon they were shoving and throwing curses, stones, fists, and bottles. Police moved in, swinging clubs. For hours the conflict raged through Regina's Market Square. When the riot finally ended, one city detective was dead, scores of police and demonstrators were injured, and about 130 protesters had been arrested.

Figure 5–14 "On to Ottawa Trek"

Coming less than 20 years after the Russian Revolution, the Regina Riot played into fears that Canada was on the verge of revolution. Bennett was determined that law and order would be maintained at all costs.

Four days after the Regina Riot, the Saskatchewan provincial government assisted the marchers on their way, and most returned to Vancouver. A Royal commission concluded that the RCMP and the federal government were blameless in the incident, citing the real villain as the Communist influence among marchers.

What Do You Think?

1. Make a time line showing key events before, during, and after the Regina Riot. Use information from the Flashpoint feature and from secondary sources. In a small group, explain why you think particular events on your time line are significant.

The Great Depression

The Social Credit philosophy came from the ideas of Scottish engineer Major C. H. Douglas. Douglas felt that the hardship people felt under the capitalist system resulted from inefficiencies within the system. Very simply, Douglas argued that economic depressions were not the result of **overproduction** but of **underconsumption**. The problem could be addressed by giving citizens "social dividends," or credit. Such a measure would increase their purchasing power and lead to economic revival. These social credit notions were highly appealing to Alberta farmers, who generally ran their farm businesses using huge amounts of borrowed money.

Douglas's Social Credit thinking found a voice in William "Bible Bill" Aberhart, a Calgary schoolteacher and evangelist. Aberhart had been using radio to broadcast his fundamentalist Protestant programs. He soon realized that he could use radio technology to spread his political message too. Aberhart modified some of Douglas's ideas for Alberta and proposed giving $25 a month to each adult. The offer had high appeal in the Depression, when many people had nothing.

The Social Credit Party won the Alberta provincial election in 1935, taking 63 out of 70 legislature seats, and on September 3, 1935 Aberhart became the province's first Social Credit premier. It was about 18 months before Aberhart introduced his government's policies. However, much of the eventual legislation was disallowed by federal authorities or the courts because it overstepped provincial authority.

Like Pattullo in British Columbia, Aberhart had trouble putting his policies into action. He soon realized that Ottawa controlled the purse strings and was not easily persuaded to fund ideas that were so different from those of the federal government.

Ontario

Liberal Mitchell Hepburn was a farmer from St. Thomas, Ontario. He served two terms in Ottawa before carrying the province in the 1934 provincial election and becoming Ontario's first Liberal premier in 30 years.

Hepburn won the election by promising to provide greater government assistance and to fight for the "dispossessed." Early in his term, Hepburn's government passed the pro-labour Industrial Standards Act. However, Hepburn proved to be no great friend of labour, as he showed during the Oshawa Strike of 1937.

On April 23, 1937, 4000 workers went on strike at the General Motors plant in Oshawa. They wanted better wages and working conditions, a seniority system, and recognition of their union, the United Auto Workers, which was affiliated with the Committee for Industrial Organizations (CIO).

Figure 5–15 Oshawa strike of 1937. As the strike wore on, women replaced male picketers in front of the General Motors plant.

Historical Inquiry: Research

Historian at Work

Using Statistics

Decline in per capita income 1928 – 1933	
Canada	**48%**
Saskatchewan	72%
Alberta	61%
Manitoba	49%
British Columbia	47%
Ontario	44%
Quebec PEI New Brunswick Nova Scotia	Between 36-49%

Figure 5–16

Statistics help us quantify important aspects of our past. For example, we remember key athletic events in terms of statistics: the fastest 100-metre dash, the first four-minute mile; the most home runs in a single season.

To an historian, statistics are vital records of the past. For many years churches were the main keepers of records on people in each parish. They kept track of births, marriages, and deaths. Church records—and headstones in cemeteries—can also tell a story about major events, such as epidemics and wars. These stories are reflected in many deaths recorded in a short time.

Statistics record the movement of people. Those that show a large number of people moving into or out of at a certain place at a certain time arouse our curiosity. Beneath the numbers may be a story of people fleeing poverty or war, or people attracted to new opportunities. The immigration policies of Wilfrid Laurier and Clifford Sifton, which you read about in Chapter 1, are examples of policies that led to this type of movement. Figure 1–11 on page 19 illustrates the impact of these policies, showing a dramatic increase in Canada's population from 1901 to 1911.

Statistics can also tell a story of changing social patterns, such as increasing numbers of women entering the labour force, or high unemployment in tough economic times. They can measure a country's overall economic health, by means of Gross National Product (GNP) or Gross Domestic Product (GDP) figures. These figures are used to compare one country with another, or to trace the growth of a single country's economy over time.

The census is an important method of gathering information about people. Canada holds a major census every 10 years to make accurate "headcount" of the population. The information is broken down into many different categories, including age, gender, ethnic origin, occupation, income, and education. This information is important to policy-makers. For example, they can use it to decide where government grants are most needed, and to ensure that the boundaries of political ridings are fairly drawn.

Activities

1. Look carefully at the statistics in Figure 5–16 showing declines in per capita income between 1928 and 1933.
   a) Why were these specific years chosen?
   b) Which provinces suffered the greatest declines? Which ones suffered the least? What reasons can you suggest for this?

2. Census taking is a vital tool for governments—so much so that it is against the law to refuse participation. But some regard this as an infringement on their rights. Make a list of reasons why people might feel this way. Discuss your list with a partner, then write a paragraph summarizing your own position on census taking.

Premier Hepburn had become a friend of big business in Ontario, and together they were determined to keep the unions of out of the province.

In his efforts to put down the strike, Hepburn asked Mackenzie King to use the RCMP to disperse the protesters. King refused because the demonstration was a peaceful one. So Hepburn organized his own police force, dubbed "the sons of Mitch's." The police force was to be used to quash the strike and drive union organizers out of the province.

The Oshawa strike lasted two weeks. Afraid of losing out to market competition, General Motors compromised and agreed to many of the union's demands.

The strike victory was seen as a major breakthrough for unions in Canada. Encouraged by that labour triumph, the CIO began a major campaign, and within a year it had unionized thousands of Ontario workers.

While the CCF gained support in both central Canada and the West, it had little impact in Quebec and the Maritime provinces. Some of the more extreme measures suggested in the Regina Manifesto made it difficult for J. S. Woodsworth to convince the general population that his was a moderate reform party. Out of the CCF grew today's New Democratic Party.

Up Close

8. Create a comparison organizer to illustrate the differences between the CCF, the Social Credit, and the Union Nationale parties.

Quebec and the Union Nationale

The Union Nationale party was founded in 1935 largely, like the CCF and Social Credit parties, in response to the unemployment and severe economic hardships of the Depression. At the centre of the party was Maurice Duplessis, a Conservative leader who was a gifted organizer and speaker.

The Union Nationale was an alliance of former Conservatives, reform-minded former Liberals, and Quebec nationalists. Much of Duplessis's support came from rural and agricultural communities, medium-scale businesses, and unorganized labour; among his key supporters were francophone, Catholic Quebecers.

Even though the Union Nationale had been formed only two weeks before the 1935 election, it was defeated only narrowly in the provincial election. The following year, the Union Nationale won a landslide victory, ending 39 years of Liberal rule.

Once in power, Duplessis became a staunch defender of the Catholic faith and a bitter enemy of any real or perceived opponent. Like Mitchell Hepburn in Ontario, Duplessis was elected as a reformer, but after taking power, the new Quebec premier distanced himself from the reform elements of his party. Increasingly, Duplessis became a friend of big business—the very interests that had been his targets during the election campaign. In catering to the needs of American and foreign capitalists who wanted to invest in Quebec, he sometimes permitted them to exploit workers.

Duplessis was a firm leader, known as *le chef* (the chief) throughout his controversial political career. He was not afraid to come down hard on anyone who opposed him.

One example of Duplessis's harsh tactics is the Padlock Law, passed in 1936. The premier used this law to exploit anti-communist feelings in Quebec. The Padlock Law made it illegal for anyone to use any building to discuss communist ideas. The legislation allowed police to close buildings where such meetings were taking place. In practice, "communist" could be interpreted to mean anything that Duplessis decided was dangerous to him or his party.

CULTURE AND THE ARTS: ESCAPE FROM HARSH REALITY

Many Canadians were concerned about the influence of American radio in Canada. In 1930, Alan Plaunt and Graham Spry founded the Radio League to rally support for public broadcasting in Canada. The Bennett government passed legislation forming the Canadian Radio Broadcasting Commission in 1932. The first CRBC broadcast was at Christmas of 1932, when Canadians from coast to coast heard a message from the king.

In November of 1936, the government of Mackenzie King founded the Canadian Broadcasting Corporation. The new CBC was given two basic goals: develop a distinctly Canadian radio network, and regulate private broadcasters. Throughout its existence, the CBC has played an important role establishing a sense of unity throughout Canada.

Radio Comes of Age

During the 1930s, radio became more accessible than ever before. Listening to the radio provided a diversion that could be enjoyed by all Canadians—rich and poor. By 1929 radio brought programs into almost every Canadian home, and by 1940 CBC broadcasts reached approximately 90 percent of Canadians.

But even the formation of the CBC could do little to stop the radio-wave invasion by popular American programs. Many Canadians huddled around their radios listening to American comedies, dramas, sports, serials, and variety shows.

During the Depression, Canadians wanted to forget their troubles, and Americans provided them with the

Figure 5–17 The Dumbells were originally formed of soldiers in the Canadian army. This troupe entertained soldiers during WW I, and then went on to tour Canada, the US, and Britain until the mid-1930s. The Depression forced them to disband in 1933.

The Great Depression 141

Figure 5–18 "The Happy Gang" was one of the most popular shows on CBC when it began in the late 1930s.

escapist entertainment they desired. The testimony of one Canadian listener reveals how much most radio shows were separated from reality:

> Do you remember Jack Benny—his name always comes first because he really was good—and Fred Allen and Fibber McGee and Molly and Singing Sam and Amos and Andy and all those famous radio personalities we used to listen to as if our life depended on it? Do you recall any one of them, just once, ever mentioning the Depression, that times were tough, millions out of work, kids sleeping in ditches and barns? ... Kind of scary, isn't it? There were two worlds in those days, the real one and the fantasy world.

Even though many Canadian-produced radio programs copied formats of popular American shows, some were successful and uniquely Canadian. In 1931 the Maple Leaf Gardens' broadcast booth was completed, and listening to Foster Hewitt's radio play-by-play became a ritual for Canadian hockey fans.

Then, in 1937, a radio troupe called "The Happy Gang" served up breezy entertainment that included likeable characters, corny humour, and easy-listening music. The popular Canadian show ran on CBC through two decades.

Escape Into the Movies

In motion pictures, several significant technological developments occurred during the 1930s. Among these were the more standard use of sound and the advent of Technicolor in 1932, evident in *Gone With the Wind* and *The Wizard of Oz*, both released in 1939. Walt Disney produced the first full-length animated cartoon, *Snow White and the Seven Dwarfs*, in 1938.

Most movies produced during the era were purely escapist—romance, laughs, and the thrills and chills of westerns and horror movies. Almost all were Hollywood-made, showing simplistic values: virtue always won, crime didn't pay, sin was punished, and true love ended in marriage.

Canadians flocked to see Hollywood stars such as Bing Crosby, the Marx Brothers, W. C. Fields, and Clark Gable. Movie stars affected Canadians' lives. For example, shortly after Gable removed his shirt in the 1934 movie *It Happened One Night* to reveal that he wasn't wearing an undershirt, sales of men's undershirts across Canada dropped dramatically.

Canadians in Depression Hollywood

The best hope for any Canadian wanting work in the movie industry was to head south. And many did, starting a talent drain that has continued to the present. Montreal-born Norma Shearer won an Oscar for *The Divorcee* (1930), and Winnipeg-born Deanna Durbin became one of the most popular stars of the 1930s. Fay Wray was born in Medicine Hat, Alberta and received her big break playing the love interest of a giant ape in *King Kong* (1933).

During the 1930s, Canadians started seeing Hollywood-film images of their own country. The 1936 movie *Rose Marie* has American Nelson Eddy playing a sombre, singing Mountie, and his stiff portrayal contributed to many stereotypes about Canada.

The National Film Board of Canada Although Canada was not known for creating feature-length movies (yet), the period did set the stage for significant future film contributions. In 1939 the government of Mackenzie King founded the National Film Board of Canada. Shortly after the birth of the NFB, John Grierson, considered to be the father of the documentary, was appointed its first film commissioner, and played a significant role in the agency's development.

Data File
Two Canadians played American president Abraham Lincoln—Walter Huston and Raymond Massey.

Magazines and Music

During the 1930s in Canada, American magazines such as *Life* consistently outsold Canada's *Maclean's*, *Chatelaine*, *Canadian Home Journal*, and *Saturday Night*.

As it would later do in the 1990s, the government tried to control the flood of American publications into Canada. In 1931, Prime Minister R. B. Bennett imposed a content tax on incoming US magazines that had more than 20 percent advertising. The result was that 50 US magazines began printing in Canada. However, after the election of 1935, Prime Minister Mackenzie King removed the tax and the magazines immediately closed shop and resumed printing in the US.

Some of the most popular music of the day was the mellow, big-band sound popularized by such Americans as Jimmy Dorsey, Benny Goodman, and Artie Shaw, who often packed large halls in Montreal, Toronto, Vancouver, and Winnipeg. However, the CBC afforded Canadians like Mart Kenney and his band a coast-to-coast audience, and they became highly popular.

A well-known Canadian musician of the era was London, Ontario's Guy Lombardo. With his band, The Royal Canadians, he played "the sweetest music this side of heaven." Lombardo moved to the United States in 1923 and went on to become synonymous with New Year's celebrations for decades.

Heritage Minute

Superman, superhero and defender of "Truth, Justice, and the American Way," was created in 1931 by Toronto-born cartoonist Joe Shuster and his friend Jerry Seigal—when both were 17 years old. Action Comics introduced the character to the public in 1938, and he became the most famous comic-book hero ever.

Sports and Recreation

Many Canadians followed American sports on their radios, particularly baseball and the career of heavyweight boxer Joe Louis. But Canadian athletics also experienced a high point in the 1930s—described by the Hockey Hall of Fame as part of "the golden age of hockey." During the depths of the Great Depression, sport, particularly hockey, provided many Canadians with hope. In Toronto, a grand new shrine to the game, Maple Leaf Gardens, was opened during the 1931–32 season. The 1932 Toronto Maple Leafs were treated like royalty throughout Ontario after their Stanley Cup win.

But tragedy could touch even hockey. On December 12, 1933, a vicious check by Boston's Eddie Shore almost killed popular Leaf player Ace Bailey. In 1934, the first all-star game was held in Toronto as a benefit for Bailey, when the Maple Leafs played NHL all-stars from the rest of the league. Then, in 1937, hockey legend Howie Morenz of the Montreal Canadiens died as a result of injuries suffered during a game. He was mourned from coast to coast, and thousands paid their respects.

In women's athletics, Dorothy Walton won the 1939 All-England Badminton Championships. Another Canadian sports success story was the Edmonton Commercial Graduates, a women's basketball team. Between 1915 and 1940 the Edmonton Grads compiled an astounding 93 percent winning record and won the North American championships in 1934, 1935, and 1936.

Figure 5–19 Guy Lombardo and his Royal Canadians

From Literature to Pulp Press

A number of major Canadian authors became famous in the 1930s. Often their serious themes ran counter to the popular appetite for escapist entertainment. During the 1930s, prolific Canadian author Mazo de la Roche found wide popularity in publishing her continuing saga of the Whiteoaks of Jalna. Other authors included fiction writer Morley Callaghan, who published *They Shall Inherit the Earth* in 1935 and *More Joy in Heaven* in 1937, and poet E. J. Pratt, whose work *The Titanic* appeared in 1935. Due to devastating Depression-era economics, many Canadian publishers either reduced their output or trimmed their author lists.

Images
The Dionne Quintuplets

On May 28, 1934, five identical baby girls—Annette, Cecile, Emilie, Marie, and Yvonne—were born on a farm near Corbeil, Ontario to proud but poor parents, Oliva and Elzire Dionne.

The girls were medical marvels, as each day they lived they set new records for the survival of quintuplets. The story spread rapidly, and within days of their birth, the children became the world's most famous babies.

The Dionne quintuplets offered a good-news story with cheerful photos of happy babies and upbeat reports of their medical progress. The Dionne story provided some relief to Depression-weary Canadians.

International interest in the children soon grew. Magazine covers featured pictures of the quintuplets, radio stations reported on them, and millions around the world followed their story on newsreels that played before feature movies in theatres.

But there was a dark side to the Dionne quintuplets' story. Once the children were out of medical danger, there were countless opportunities for commercial endorsements. The Dionne family was poor and needed to provide for the new arrivals plus their six other children—so they listened. It is estimated that the quintuplets brought in more than $1 million, which was put into a trust fund for them. But this amount—huge at the time—was small in contrast with the tourist revenue the children attracted to the province and their area. In 1934, tourists spent about $51 million on their way to the quintuplets' home. Two years later, that figure doubled.

"Quintland," a guarded and fenced facility built near the Dionne farm, became the biggest Ontario tourist attraction ever. At one point it had 6000 visitors every day.

Figure 5–20 The surviving Dionne quintuplets—Annette, Cecile and Yvonne

With so much at stake, there was concern about the quintuplets' welfare and about how the money they were generating would be handled. In 1935, the Ontario government of Mitchell Hepburn passed the Dionne Quintuplets Act, which made the children wards of the province. Four guardians were appointed, and the Dionnes were no longer in charge of their own babies.

Eventually, Oliva Dionne fought a nine-year court battle to have his children returned to their own home.

The story did not end happily. The trust fund soon disappeared. Emilie died in 1954 and Marie in 1970. The surviving quintuplets moved to Montreal. They launched a lawsuit against the Ontario government, and in the 1990s they received a multi-million dollar settlement, with much of the money being donated to charities on their behalf.

What Do You Think?

1. Suppose you could interview one of the surviving quintuplets. What would you ask her? Why? Draft a list of at least ten questions and rank them in order of importance. Work with a partner and role-play the interview. Review the Historian at Work on crafting interview questions on page 113.

CONCLUSION

The experience of the Great Depression changed Canada in many important ways. Canadians began to see the weaknesses of systems and assumptions that they had long taken for granted. They abandoned the traditional two-party political system in favour of regional parties that represented beliefs and hopes not supported by the historic parties. This change would have important consequences for national unity. Many also realized that giving preference to the Commonwealth over the United States as trading partners had been an unprofitable economic decision. Mackenzie King would change that policy, with far-reaching consequences. However, as you will learn in Chapter 6, while Canada struggled with its own problems and decisions during the 1930s, the world outside was drifting towards another global armed conflict, one into which Canada would inevitably be drawn.

CHAPTER ACTIVITIES

Check Your Understanding

1. Discuss the causes of the Great Depression in Canada under the following headings:
   - The stock market crash
   - Over-dependence on the US as a trading partner
   - Availability of easy credit combined with a lack of financial regulations
   - The drought

2. Make a chart with the headings CCF and Social Credit. For each party
   - summarize the party platform
   - list several characteristics of people who would find the party's ideas appealing
   - explain the party's success in the 1935 federal election

Develop Your Thinking

3. To illustrate a contraction phase of the business cycle, create a "chain reaction" graphic showing the wide-ranging effects of a) falling wheat production and/or b) a decrease in automobile production.

4. Use the information in the Flashpoint feature and information from additional sources to learn more about the "On to Ottawa Trek." List the events leading up to the July 1 Regina Riot and have a debate about who was to blame for it.

Express Yourself

5. Prepare a two-minute radio advertisement to popularize the party platforms of either the Liberal or the Conservative parties for the 1930 federal election. Include in your ad a list of things your party will do if elected.

6. Pretend you are living in the midst of the Great Depression. Write a letter of protest to the prime minister from the point of view of one of the following:
   - a Saskatchewan wheat farmer
   - a single homeless male at a relief camp
   - a female worker in a textile sweatshop
   - an unemployed factory worker on public assistance

   You may choose to research examples of actual protest letters that were written to Prime Minister Bennett.

Apply Your Learning

7. "For King the 1930 election defeat was a blessing in disguise." Investigate examples of other Canadian prime ministers who have won two or more elections, and test the hypothesis that victory is often a result of being in power during the "good times."

8. Bennett worried about the "insidious American influence" of US radio, and he brought about the creation of the CBC. Analyse the CBC's early popularity and explain how it helped to end regional isolation and strengthen Canadian national unity. Then discuss what the modern role of CBC radio should be.

Extend Your Learning Using the Internet

9. Work in small groups and use Internet financial sources to investigate the economic factors that led to the 1929 Crash and the Great Depression that followed. Present your findings in a group panel discussion. Then discuss, as a class, the relationship among the factors.

10. a) With three other students, present a role play in which an unemployed Canadian of the 1930s challenges representatives from a labour union and from the federal and provincial governments to find a solution to the unemployment problem. Each member of your group should research his or her role and situation using Internet primary and secondary sources on the Great Depression.

    b) Write a paragraph explaining how the role plays helped you understand the historical situation and decisions made by the four participants.

6 Towards Autonomy and War

Focus Questions

External Forces Shaping Canada's Policies
In what ways did Canada's relationship with the United States change during the 1930s?

What significant historical events led to Canada's involvement in the war on Germany?

Canada's International Status and Foreign Policy
What steps did Canada take towards independence from Britain during this time?

Individual Canadians and Canadian Identity
How did Prime Minster Mackenzie King establish his "place in the history books" in the 1920s and 1930s?

In 1914, most Canadians viewed their country as part of the British Empire—they accepted the idea that what was good for Britain was good for Canada. By 1919 this outlook had changed. The heavy price paid to support Britain in the war led many Canadians to conclude that Britain's goals were not necessarily in Canada's best interests. Prime Minister King firmly believed that Canadians should decide whether or not to follow Britain's lead in international affairs.

The ability of a country to make its own decisions, free from outside influence, is called **autonomy**. During the 1920s and 1930s, many of the countries that formed the British Empire began to express the desire for greater autonomy. Canada was at the forefront of this movement, which resulted in the shift from a British Empire to a British Commonwealth of Nations. Within the Commonwealth, countries were free to make their own decisions about domestic and foreign policy.

Canadians wanted to avoid getting involved in another European conflict that had nothing to do with Canada. The effects of World War I had led to increasing tensions in Europe, and many Canadians—and many Americans too—wanted to stay neutral if another war erupted. Nevertheless, towards the end of the 1930s it was clear that both countries would have to play their part in a second global conflict.

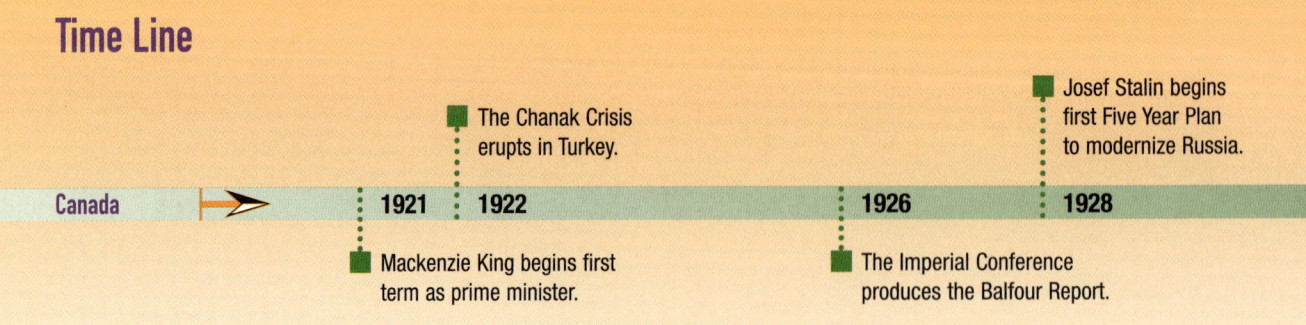

Time Line

Canada

1921 — Mackenzie King begins first term as prime minister.

1922 — The Chanak Crisis erupts in Turkey.

1926 — The Imperial Conference produces the Balfour Report.

1928 — Josef Stalin begins first Five Year Plan to modernize Russia.

Perspectives

The coronation of King George VI on May 12, 1936. The King, Queen Elizabeth, and their children Princess Elizabeth (left) and Margaret (right), greet the crowds of well-wishers gathered in London. Canadians, too, would be following the event with great interest. How might a French Canadian feel seeing this picture in the next day's newspaper? An English Canadian? How would you respond? Compare this picture with the one of Princess Diana in Chapter 16 (page 449). Do you think the idea of "royalty" has changed since the 1930s?

- Hitler becomes Chancellor of Germany.
  - 1933
- 1935
  - Mussolini invades Ethiopia.
- Hitler begins campaign of European aggression with the invasion of Austria.
  - 1938
- 1939
  - Canada declares war.
  - Canada turns away Jewish refugees aboard the *SS St. Louis*.

TOWARDS AUTONOMY

When Mackenzie King and the Liberals came to power in 1921, they had a lot of work to do. In Chapter 4, you read about how the Liberals worked to resolve the labour unrest that marked the start of the 1920s, and how they tried to mend the English and French divisions within their own party. But King also wanted to define Canada's role on the international stage. He was strongly opposed to an **imperial policy** that would force Canada to support the British in the event of a European conflict. After Canada's costly support of Britain in World War I, King felt he could not send troops to support Britain unless the Canadian people, through their representatives in Parliament, approved such an action.

It was a small crisis in another part of the world that tested his view. Chanak was a small Turkish seaport on the Dardanelles, a narrow strait that separates Europe from Asia. A 1920 peace treaty with Turkey allowed Britain to occupy territory along the Dardanelles. In 1922, Turkish nationalist forces moved in on the territory, trapping British troops at Chanak. For a time it appeared that Britain and Turkey might go to war. Then Britain fired off a telegram asking Canada to provide soldiers. The request was made public the following day, before King had received the message. Visiting Toronto at the time, King heard about the developing crisis from a reporter. In his diary, he wrote:

Figure 6–1 Modern-day Chanak, a seaport along the Dardanelles. A 1920 peace treaty allowed Britain to occupy some territory in Turkey. When Turkish nations tried to reclaim the area in 1922, Britain threatened war and expected Canada to help.

> I confess [the message] annoyed me. It is drafted designedly to play the imperial game, to test out centralization vs. autonomy as regards European wars ... I have thought out my plans ... No contingent will go without parliament being summoned in the first instance.

Most Canadians had no idea where Chanak was, and few wanted to send Canadian troops into a conflict that had nothing to do with Canada and its people. King told the British government that parliament would have to debate the issue before he would consider sending troops to Turkey. As it turned out, the situation at Chanak never did turn into a war. But King had sent the message that Britain could not take Canadian support for granted in conflicts not involving Canada. The stage was set for a decade of Canadian insistence on autonomy, much to the annoyance of the British government.

Canada Stands Firm

In 1923, Canada took a further step towards autonomy by signing a treaty with another nation—the United States. Canada had already negotiated treaties with other countries, but those treaties required British approval. The 1923 Canada-US treaty concerned halibut fishing rights in the North Pacific, a matter that did not concern Britain. The British government wanted its ambassador in Washington to sign the treaty, but King refused. The ambassador later received a telegram from King which noted that the treaty was "of concern solely to Canada and the United States" and that "signature on behalf of Canada by Mr. Lapointe [the Minister of Fisheries], who has full powers, should be sufficient."

Once the Halibut Treaty had received parliamentary approval, Canada did ask Britain to ratify the treaty. But the Canadian government had once again made clear its desire for autonomy.

In October and November of 1923, King represented Canada at an **imperial conference** in London which lasted six weeks. King's position was clear from the start: Canada and the other **dominions** were autonomous. That meant they were responsible for their own defence and foreign policies. King felt that the concerns of the British were not necessarily those of the dominions, and he believed that the British had no right to dictate foreign policy to them. In a speech to the imperial conference, King stated his position:

Up Close

1. As you read the following pages, make a list of the steps taken by King and others to establish Canada's independence. Use this information to create an autonomy time line, showing the steps towards Canadian autonomy.

Figure 6–2 Lord Curzon, the British foreign secretary in 1923, thought that Prime Minister King was "obstinate, tiresome and stupid" when it came to the autonomy issue.

> We believe that the decision of Great Britain on any important public issue, domestic or foreign, should be made by the people of Britain, their representatives in Parliament and the Government responsible to that Parliament. So the decision of Canada on any important issue, domestic or foreign, we believe should be made by the people of Canada, their representatives in Parliament and the Government responsible to that Parliament.

Lord Curzon, the British foreign secretary, found King and his views extremely irritating. Curzon and the British did not really want control over Canada's foreign policy, but they did want to be reassured that Canada would support any British action, as had been the case in 1914. In a letter written at the end of the 1923 Imperial Conference, Curzon expressed his opinion of King:

Towards Autonomy and War

The last two days have been a whirlwind of negotiations and trouble in order to get the Imperial Conference to agree to a report (written by myself) on Foreign Affairs. The obstacle has been Mackenzie King, the Canadian, who is both obstinate, tiresome and stupid, and is nervously afraid of being turned out of his own Parliament when he gets back …

The prime ministers of many of the dominions had come to the conference supporting the idea of a common imperial foreign policy. But King's views were influential and gained wider acceptance. The issue would not be resolved formally until the Imperial Conference of 1926.

Canada faced a similar challenge to autonomy in the League of Nations. Article 10 of the League Covenant stated that the members agreed to protect each other in the event of external aggression against any member. The League Council would decide on the appropriate action. King did not like the idea that the League could involve Canada in an international conflict. There was little chance that Canada itself would become involved in a conflict and require military support from the League. Why then, reasoned King, should Canada have to make the same military commitments as nations that were at much greater risk of aggression?

Canada supported a resolution that would amend Article 10 to give member nations more flexibility to decide on how each would contribute if another war broke out. The resolution was defeated in 1923. Canada's delegate to the League, Senator Raoul Dandurand, summed up Canada's reasons for supporting the amendment:

> The heavy sacrifice to which we agreed for the reestablishment of peace in Europe led us to reflect on what the future might hold in store.
>
> May I be permitted to add that in this association of mutual insurance against fire the risks assumed by the different states are not equal? We live in a fire-proof house, far from inflammable materials. A vast ocean separates us from Europe. Canada therefore believed it to be her duty to seek a precise interpretation of what appeared to her to be the indefinite obligations included in Article 10 of the Covenant.

Data File

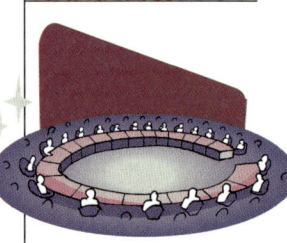

The League of Nations voted itself out of existence in 1946. Most of its property was transferred to the United Nations.

The Statute of Westminster In 1926, an imperial conference came to a decision about the relationship between Great Britain and the dominions. The conference produced the Balfour Report, which recognized the autonomy of the dominions, as well as the special ties that existed in the British Commonwealth of Nations. It was agreed that the dominions would be

> … autonomous communities within the British Empire, equal in status, in no way subordinate one to another in any aspect of their domestic or external affairs, though united by a common allegiance to the Crown, and freely associated as members of the British Commonwealth of Nations.

Up Close

2. Write in your own words what was agreed on in the Balfour Report.

Canada was now free to form its own foreign policy, and legislation no longer required approval from Britain. The Statute of Westminster, passed by the British Parliament in 1931, confirmed the independence of the British dominions within the British Commonwealth of Nations.

Closer Ties with the US

Canada now pursued closer ties with the United States. In 1927, King established the first Canadian foreign mission in Washington. He believed that expanding Canada's exports would help to solve the severe economic difficulties of the Depression. In the United States, President Franklin D. Roosevelt was also pushing for closer economic ties with Canada. In 1935, the two nations agreed on a trade treaty that lowered the American tariff on two-thirds of Canada's exports to the United States. Canada granted the United States **most-favoured-nation** status. This marked a significant change to the policy of economic **protectionism** that both nations had adopted at the beginning of the Depression. In 1938, the agreement was expanded to lower the tariffs on about 80 percent of Canada's exports to the United States. These agreements laid a foundation of cooperation between the two countries—cooperation that would become even more important during World War II.

Figure 6–3 Prime Minister Mackenzie King stands behind US President Franklin D. Roosevelt.

Import-Export Trade Between Canada and the United States		
Year	Imports from US (millions of $)	Exports to US (millions of $)
1938	414	270
1939	485	380
1940	711	442
1941	912	599
1942	1209	881
1943	1410	1147
1944	1435	1296
1945	1183	1193

Figure 6–4 Import-export trade between Canada and the United States grew steadily in the years following the 1938 trade agreement.

INTERNATIONAL DEVELOPMENTS AFTER WORLD WAR I

In the years leading up to World War II, most countries were preoccupied with severe economic crises at home. The government looked for solutions to sky-high unemployment and a tottering banking system. Josef Stalin's new Communist government was intent on building and modernizing the Soviet Union's economy. And in Europe, two new totalitarian regimes—Mussolini's Fascists in Italy and Hitler's Nazis in Germany—gained power with promises of relief and restoration.

The United States and Isolation

As you read in Chapter 5, the United States had been devastated by the Depression. Millions of Americans were unemployed and many had to turn to public soup kitchens to avoid starvation. When Franklin D. Roosevelt became president in 1932, his priority was to provide immediate relief to the American people, and to restore employment and confidence in the country's economic institutions. With his "New Deal," Roosevelt implemented government projects to create jobs, reformed banking and investment regulations, and established a social security program.

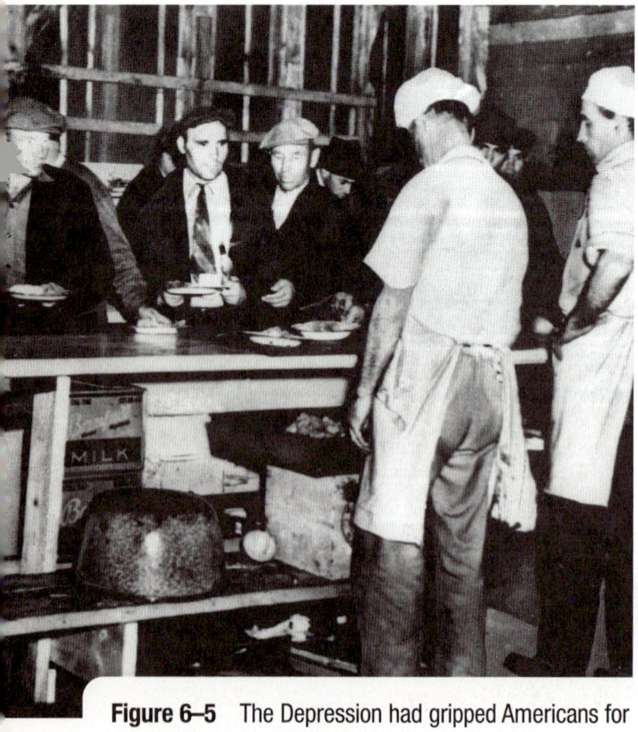

By the beginning of Roosevelt's second term in office, a new set of concerns had arisen. While, for the most part, Americans remained focused on the task of repairing the nation's economy, some were becoming aware of certain unsettling developments outside the US. Totalitarian regimes had emerged in Japan, Italy, and Germany, each with designs on expanding their own territories by means of military force. Those who noticed these developments and recognized the threat of another war made it clear that they did not want to become involved. Between 1935 and 1937, Roosevelt's government passed a series of **neutrality laws** to keep the US out of any new conflicts by forbidding trade with warring nations.

Japan was seen to pose the largest threat to US security. Even though the US had no intention or desire to engage in war, they did begin to rebuild the navy in 1934. When Japan invaded north China in 1937, Roosevelt did not proclaim neutrality, and the US was able to sell weapons to both sides. But when Roosevelt ventured to suggest that the US might get involved, saying that war was like a disease that peace-loving nations should quarantine, the people responded negatively and he withdrew the suggestion.

Figure 6–5 The Depression had gripped Americans for three years before Roosevelt became president.

The United States would continue to struggle with economic difficulties throughout the 1930s, but the Depression would finally end with the start of World War II. When the war broke out, Americans were torn between the desire to avoid involvement in the war, and the desire to come to the aid of the victims of Nazi aggression. At first, the US limited itself to assisting the Allied powers that did become directly involved. In 1939, the United States began to supply shells, guns, and planes to Britain and France. By the end of 1941, the United States itself would be at war.

The Rise of Russia

In 1917 Russia underwent enormous political and economic upheaval. A democratic revolution in March brought an end to tsarist rule of the Russian Empire, and the Bolshevik Revolution in November marked the start of Communist rule of the Soviet Union. However, the political changes did not go unchallenged, and a civil war raged on between the revolutionaries and their opponents for three years. By 1921 the Russian economy was in total collapse. Some economic recovery took place in the later 1920s, but the new Soviet Union was still far behind other industrial nations in terms of production.

After Lenin died in early 1924, there was a power struggle for leadership. By 1928, Josef Stalin had become leader of the Soviet Union. Stalin introduced the first of his Five Year Plans, a strategy to transform the Soviet Union into a powerful, modernized nation. Stalin introduced massive industrialization and collective ownership of agriculture. Small family farms were absorbed into enormous state-owned businesses, and men and women who had worked their own land now worked as farmers for the state. Many people objected and were forced at gunpoint to comply. By 1932, about half of the Soviet Union's farms were collectives. During the transition, the agriculture of the USSR virtually collapsed, and millions of peasants starved to death.

Up Close

3. What strategies did Stalin use to modernize Russian agriculture and industry as quickly as possible? List two positive and two negative results of this rapid change.

Figure 6–6 Turning the Soviet Union's farms into collectives was a disaster. Millions starved as a result.

To industrialize the economy, Stalin concentrated on heavy industry (factories producing goods needed by other factories and industries). The USSR claimed that its goals were achieved in all parts of the economy. Although this was not completely true, industrial production did rise. A second Five Year Plan (1933–1937), and a third (begun in 1938) completed the work of transforming the Soviet Union, which became an industrial power second only to the United States.

Figure 6–7 Josef Stalin became leader of the Soviet Union in 1928.

During the 1930s, Stalin began to fear that people were working to overthrow him. As a result, he began the Great Purge to rid Soviet society of "undesirable elements." Between 1934 and 1940, millions of Soviet citizens (including high-ranking Communists), diplomats, and generals, were convicted of crimes against the state in **show trials** in Moscow. Some were executed, but the vast majority—more than 10 million people—were sent to the prison camps of Siberia. Conditions in these camps were terrible, and most people did not survive. Stalin's brutal dictatorship led to the deaths of at least 20 million Soviet citizens.

Fascism in Italy

In Italy, the situation at the end of World War I led to a rise of extremism. The Italians, who had joined the Allies in 1915, felt they had been badly treated during the Paris Peace Conference. Lands occupied by Italians in Yugoslavia were not given to Italy, which caused resentment. Italy had also suffered heavy casualties in the war, and wartime inflation had reduced standards of living. The Italian parliament was split into many small factions, and effective government became impossible.

Benito Mussolini founded the Italian Fascist Party in 1919. By 1921, Mussolini and his supporters had become a powerful force in Italian politics. They attracted the attention of industrialists and other conservatives who believed that the Fascists could "clean up" Italy and then be removed from power. In October 1922, with yet another Italian government in disarray, Mussolini and his supporters began their "March on Rome." Their goal: to remove the government, by force if necessary. Frightened, the Italian king asked Mussolini to form a government.

Up Close

4. What was Mussolini's dream? Describe the steps Mussolini took towards his dream.

Over the next three years, Mussolini led a fascist **dictatorship** in Italy. His government forbade strikes, banned trade unions, and suppressed opposition parties. There was strict censorship, and the economy was divided into units or "corporations" to make government economic planning easier. With control of the country complete, Mussolini began to feel that he could achieve his dream of recreating a Roman Empire.

Hitler's Germany

The Treaty of Versailles had caused lasting resentment in Germany. It severely restricted the size of Germany's military forces, and permitted no air force at all. Germany was forced to give up much of its land, including coal fields that were important to German industry, and all of its colonies. The country was required to pay billions of dollars in reparations for damages caused by World War I. The War Guilt Clause stated that Germany had to accept sole responsibility for the war, even though it was clear that Germany was not the only country responsible.

As a result of the Treaty of Versailles the German economy suffered, especially its currency, the **mark**. Because the value of German goods fell after World War I, the mark rapidly lost its value compared to other currencies. By 1923, the situation was extreme. It was possible to join a line to buy butter at the price of 100 000 marks per pound and, on reaching the head of the line, find that the cost had risen to 500 000 marks. People went shopping with wheelbarrows filled with nearly worthless banknotes. In late 1923, a British tourist spent a week in Germany. Because the German currency was so weak, his vacation cost him about 25 cents!

Figure 6–8 Mussolini (front right) is seen here with Hitler (front left). Each of these fascist dictators used violence and propaganda to further their goals of building new empires.

Value of the German Mark in US Dollars, 1920–1923	
Month/Year	Number of German Marks Worth 1 US Dollar
1919	8
August 1920	2000
January 1923	50 000
July 1923	160 000
August 1923	1 100 000
November 1923	2 520 000 000 000

Figure 6-9 The value of the German mark fell drastically after World War I.

In early 1924, a new German currency, the rentenmark, was introduced. One rentenmark was equal to 1 trillion old marks. The Americans provided loans to the Germans so that reparation payments were guaranteed. Until the end of the 1920s, this system worked well.

Adolf Hitler rises to power The 1930s saw the rise of a political leader who would cast a dark shadow over history. Adolf Hitler was originally from Austria, where he had tried and failed to enter the Vienna Art College. He moved to Munich in 1913, served four years on the Western Front in World War I, and was awarded the Iron Cross for bravery. In 1919, he joined the National Socialist German Workers Party (the Nazi party), and soon became its leader. In 1923, he tried to overthrow the Bavarian state government, but the coup failed miserably. Hitler was sent to prison, where he wrote *Mein Kampf* (My Struggle), which set out his plans for restoring German greatness and dominating Europe. Between 1925 and 1929, Hitler tried to increase the Nazi party's strength and importance, but few listened to him.

Figure 6–10 This German woman is shown lighting her stove using worthless German marks in 1923. It was cheaper to start the fire using the paper money than it was to buy wood.

By 1933, worldwide unemployment was approaching 30 percent, and many people were deeply dissatisfied with traditional political parties. Of all the countries in Europe, Germany was the most severely affected. By 1931, unemployment had reached six million (33 percent of the work force), and many Germans looked to extremist parties for solutions. Hitler was able to capture support for his party by promising full employment for the German people. So desperate were people for work that few seriously questioned how he planned to achieve this.

In January 1933, Hitler manouvered himself into the position of Chancellor, a position equivalent to prime minister. He wasted no time in taking complete control of the government and transforming Germany into a Nazi state.

As Stalin and Mussolini had done before him, Hitler abolished strikes, unions, and political parties. All economic activity that, in Hitler's view, did not directly benefit the German state was forbidden. The government imposed censorship, and established youth organizations to teach young people the beliefs and values of the Nazi party. An important feature of the Nazi party was its belief in racial superiority. According to the Nazis, some races were better than others, and the **Aryan** (characterized as caucasian, especially Nordic, and non-Jewish) race was the best of all. Any problems the nation faced were blamed on the presence of non-Aryans in the country. The Nazis used this attitude to make scapegoats of certain groups, including the Jewish people.

A significant amount of **anti-Semitism** already existed in Germany, and this racial intolerance was fed by the myth of Aryan superiority. Under the Nazis, Jews were forbidden to participate in certain occupations and were no longer

Data File

During the Nazi persecution, more than 35 000 German Jews made their way to Shanghai, which was controlled by the Japanese at that time. Despite difficult conditions, they managed to survive the war there.

Historical Inquiry: Analysing Information

Historian at Work

Cause and Effect in History

Historians do more than just provide factual accounts of events. They also look for relationships between events. One way that events can be related is by "cause and effect." When one event causes or leads to another event, we say that there is a cause-and-effect relationship between the two events. For example:

Cause	Effect
The Treaty of Versailles forced Germany to make huge reparation payments.	The Germans did not have the money to make these payments, so they printed more money.

Here is how an effect might then become the cause of another event:

Cause	Effect
Germany printed more money.	A dramatic increase in the amount of money in circulation led to rapid inflation and devaluation of currency and economic stability.

Chains of cause-and-effect events can become quite long if events continue to become the causes of other events. It is much like a line of dominoes set up so that each domino will knock over the next.

Historians also refer to "short-term" and "long-term" consequences. An initial event (cause) can be related to its direct result (effect); but it can also be related indirectly to any number of other results (consequences). For example, one of the long-term consequences of the Treaty of Versailles was World War II. Some argue that if the terms of the treaty were not so harsh, Hitler might not have gained power in Germany. The economic terms of the treaty called for Germany to make vast reparation payments. The political terms of the treaty took away land and colonies that were important sources of income. In an attempt to keep up with reparation payments, Germany printed more money. This caused rapid inflation, which in turn left many Germans destitute. In hard economic times, people often look for a change in government to solve the economic problems. Germany's economic problems can be seen as one factor that aided Hitler in his rise to power.

Activities

1. Aside from huge reparation payments, what other terms of the Treaty of Versailles might have caused Germans to feel resentment towards the powers that negotiated the treaty? How might this resentment be one of the factors that led to war?

2. Read newspaper articles and editorials to find examples of cause-and-effect relationships between events. Use a flow chart to summarize the causes and effects.

3. Find cause-and-effect relationships between a series of events in your own life. The events might all take place in one day or over a longer period of time. Make a point-form list of the events in chronological order. Explain to a partner why you think a cause-and-effect relationship exists between each pair of events.

4. Historians often disagree over whether a cause-and-effect relationship exists between two events. Why might these arguments be difficult to resolve?

Towards Autonomy and War

Flashpoint

The Voyage of the SS St. Louis, 1939

In 1939, the Nazis were already beginning to deport German Jews to concentration camps. They would let them leave the country if they paid bribes, but widespread anti-Semitism meant that few had any place to go.

On May 13, 1939, some 1000 desperate refugees chartered the German ocean liner *SS St. Louis*, and sailed for Havana, Cuba. They hoped to enter as tourists and then immigrate to the United States. But the Cuban government feared a large influx of refugees, and would not let them land. Desperate relatives in motorboats bobbed near the anchored liner, shouting encouragement as they awaited the outcome of negotiations. On June 6, Cuba ended discussions and refused the passengers entry. They left Havana harbour, veering north to try Canada. To make sure that desperate passengers did not try to swim to the United States, an American gunboat shadowed the ship.

Influential Canadians begged Prime Minister King to accept the refugees. But King, who was touring Washington with the Royal Family, was per-

Figure 6–11 Passengers on the *SS St. Louis* await their fate in Havana.

suaded by his anti-Semitic bureaucrats to say no. The *SS St. Louis* sailed back to Europe, where passengers were eventually accepted. But, as many countries were overrun by the Nazis, the Jews were doomed.

Canada acted no differently from its allies in rejecting the *SS St. Louis* refugees. But Canada's overall record for helping Jewish refugees was much worse than theirs. From 1933 to 1945, the United States accepted more than 200 000 refugees. Britain accepted 70 000 people. Even impoverished Brazil accepted 27 000 refugees. But Canada accepted fewer than 5000. Canada even rejected gifted scientists, physicians, and entrepreneurs, claiming that they would not make good farmers. However, even when Jewish farmers with capital applied, they were rejected too. During the Depression, all immigration was curtailed. However, other Allies, who had similar prejudices and hardships, helped Jewish refugees much more than Canada did.

When faced with helping the refugees, King had two problems. Canada had an unusually high level of anti-Semitism, and it created a risk to national unity. American diplomats, who dealt with many anti-Semites at home, were surprised by how much anti-Semitism there was in English-speaking Canada. But King was especially worried about the national unity risk posed by anti-Semitism in Quebec. Many Quebecers opposed all immigration, but especially Jewish immigration. Most francophone media and many Quebec politicians spoke out strongly against it. King, who was committed—above all—to keeping Canada united, believed that Quebec would erupt violently if Jews were admitted. Also, he did not want to weaken the Quebec Liberal party, which had been defeated by the Union Nationale in 1936. Thus, immigration bureaucrats who kept Jewish refugees out were complying with Ottawa's unspoken wishes.

Historians have traced the fate of most *SS St. Louis* passengers. Of the 963 that Canada refused, probably 450 survived. The majority found a way into the United States. Only four were eventually accepted by Canada. Nearly half were murdered by the Nazis.

Figure 6–12 Two children stare out a porthole of the *St. Louis*.

Not all Canadians supported the federal government's policy of accepting anti-Semitism. Rev. Claris Silcox of the United Church toured Western Canada pleading on behalf of Jewish refugees. He attracted wide media support. But his efforts failed to change policy. And Mark Sorenson, a Canadian Pacific Railway immigration agent in Copenhagen who watched the Canadian government reject every Jewish application, had only one recourse: when he returned to Canada, he kept files of this "shameful chapter in the history of Canada" as evidence for later historians. He believed that "The day will come when the Ottawa Immigration Service shall be judged by [its] records."

What Do You Think?

1. Imagine you are a passenger on the *SS St. Louis*. In a letter, poem, or diary entry, express your feelings as you realize that you will not be allowed into Cuba.

2. Explain in your own words the "national unity risk" that King was worried about.

3. If you were a Canadian MP at the time, what arguments would you make in parliament to persuade the government to accept some of the refugees?

Jewish persecution under Nazi rule

1935 — The Nazis pass the Nuremberg Laws, which remove citizenship rights from the Jews and forbid marriage between Jews and non-Jews.

1936

1937

1938 — *Kristallnacht* ("the night of broken glass"). Gangs of Nazi youths roam Jewish neighbourhoods, breaking windows and destroying synagogues, shops and homes. Jewish students are expelled from German schools.

1939 — All Jews have to carry identification cards from this point on. Jewish businesses and valuables are taken by the Nazis. A curfew is imposed forbidding Jews to be out after dark.

1940 — First removal of Jews from selected areas of Germany

Figure 6–13 This photo shows how Hitler used children and teenagers at his massive rallies.

considered German citizens. In November 1938, hundreds of synagogues and Jewish businesses were looted and destroyed, and any Jew on the streets was in danger of being beaten to death. In every community signs began to appear that declared: "The Jew is our misfortune" or "Jews not wanted here." This was just the beginning of Hitler's plan for the Jews. In *Mein Kampf*, he had mentioned a "final solution" to what he called "the Jewish problem"—complete extermination of the Jews. The world would not comprehend the full horror of Hitler's treatment of the Jews until Allied forces liberated the first **concentration camps** near the end of the coming world war. You will read more about the **Holocaust** in Chapter 7.

Anti-Semitism in Canada In the 1930s, anti-Semitism was also common in Canada. These feelings were echoed by the government of Mackenzie King. King himself stated that Jewish refugees of "even the best type" would be damaging to Canadian society. He noted in his diary: "We must seek to keep Canada free from unrest and too great an intermixture of foreign strains of blood." Of the

800 000 Jewish refugees from Germany, Canada admitted fewer than 5000. King's deputy minister of immigration, Frederick Blair, was a confirmed anti-Semite who did his best to turn away Jewish refugees. "Pressure on the part of the Jewish people has never been greater than it is now and I am glad to say … that it has never been so well controlled. Fewer Jews are coming in than ever before," Blair said on one occasion. Even after World War II broke out and thousands of Canadian Jews volunteered for military service, the Canadian government maintained its policy of keeping Jewish refugees out of Canada. Fewer than 500 were admitted between 1939 and 1945.

Heritage Minute

Diplomat and war veteran Georges Vanier served as Canada's minister to France from 1939–43, and later as ambassador to France. Deeply moved by the plight of European war refugees, Vanier and his wife Pauline worked tirelessly to help them. They encouraged changes to Canadian immigration laws that prevented refugees, many of them Jews, from finding safety in Canada. But the Vaniers' pleas fell on deaf ears. After the war, Vanier expressed his deep feeling of shame that Canada had not done its part to aid those who would become victims of the Holocaust.

Figure 6–14 The issue of whether or not Canada should accept Jewish refugees who were fleeing Nazi persecution brought to the surface the anti-Semitic feelings of some Canadians. This sign was posted in St-Agathe, Quebec.

Figure 6–15 Unlike those who lived under the Nazi regime, people in Canada were free to protest against anti-Semitism. The photo shows a young woman protesting an anti-Semitic march in Toronto.

Up Close

5. Record in point form the "chess moves" around the world that were leading up to World War II.

THE ROAD TO WAR

The beginnings of World War II were like a chess game, with moves being played around the world. In Southeast Asia, Japan wanted to expand its empire, and decided to invade Manchuria, a region in northeastern China. Following this 1931 incident, China appealed to the League of Nations, which passed resolutions urging Japan to negotiate a peaceful settlement. But Japan's assault escalated with its large-scale invasion of China in 1937, and the League seemed powerless to respond.

In Italy, Mussolini continued to plan his new Roman Empire. He invaded the African nation of Ethiopia in 1935. Ethiopian emperor Haile Selassie protested to the League of Nations, which met in an emergency session to deal with the matter. Italy, a member of the League, was condemned for the act of aggression, and a committee of the League met to decide on sanctions that would forbid member nations to export certain goods to Italy.

During the crisis over Ethiopia, Canada was in the middle of a general election. Conservative leader R. B. Bennett, who was prime minister until Mackenzie King was returned to office in 1935, thought Canada should do something. W. A. Riddell, Canada's representative to the League of Nations, proposed that oil, coal, and steel exports to Italy be stopped. Without oil, he reasoned, Mussolini's army in Ethiopia would be forced to stop.

Sanctions against Italy were eventually approved by the League of Nations, but oil, coal, and steel were not on the list of forbidden exports. Because the League sanctions did not affect Italy's ability to maintain a military campaign, the Italians continued the war. Ethiopia fell to Italy in May, 1936. Once again, the League of Nations had failed to stop aggression.

Figure 6–16 Mackenzie King and W. A. Riddell

Hitler Begins to Attack

Between 1933 and 1935, Hitler began to re-arm the German military forces, and he created the Luftwaffe, the German air force. These actions violated the Treaty of Versailles. By 1935, the Luftwaffe had more airplanes than Britain. In early 1936, Hitler reoccupied the demilitarized Rhineland, again in violation of the Treaty of Versailles. The British government said that Hitler had a right to do so, and compared the action to "going into his own backyard." France was opposed to Hitler's move into the Rhineland, but was not willing to take military action on its own. The League of Nations discussed a resolution to condemn Hitler's actions, but nothing came of the discussion. Mackenzie King did not allow

Foundations

Types of Government

Figure 6–17 Alessandra Mussolini (Benito's granddaughter) was a minister in Italy's right-wing National Alliance party.

By the early 1900s there were several different types of government in Europe. There were democracies in Britain and France, fascist dictatorships in Italy and Germany, and the Soviet Union's communist regime. What is the difference between democratic and totalitarian governments, and between fascism and communism?

Democracy is a form of government in which citizens exercise the right to vote in order to make decisions about government actions and policies. In a true democracy all citizens have the right to vote. Most modern democracies, including Canada and the United States, are representative democracies in which citizens elect representatives to express their views. Most representative democracies have a constitution that limits the powers of the government and guarantees the individual rights of citizens.

Totalitarianism is a system in which the state controls all aspects of life in a country. There is only one official political party, which is controlled by a leader from whom all others take direction. Order is maintained by a secret police, which has the power to arrest, detain, torture, imprison, and execute anyone identified as an "enemy of the state." Often specific groups are targeted as scapegoats by the government. There is strict censorship; citizens see and hear only what the government allows. The government forbids all forms of public expression that are unacceptable to it, as well as labour disruptions, such as strikes.

Fascism is a form of totalitarianism. Fascism rejects the ideas of individual liberty and the equality of persons and races. Citizens have "collective rights" that are defined by the State and policed by the military. The leader of a fascist party demands unquestioning support by the citizens. To gain this support, the party promotes a "national myth," a story about the history and destiny of a country or people. Pageantry and symbolism play an important role in inspiring citizens to believe in the national myth. The word "fascism" was first used by Mussolini to describe the form of government he established in Italy in the 1920s. Hitler brought fascism to Germany in the 1930s.

Communism is similar to fascism in that both systems are often led by dictators, and citizens have few or no rights. However, under communism, citizens are supposed to share equally in the wealth of the state. Communism is meant to be a temporary state that exists until the workers become their own government and control their own destiny.

What Do You Think?

1. Do you think democratic countries should fight to help establish or preserve democracy in other countries? Explain your answer.

2. How might a national myth help to win support for fascism?

Canada to take part in the discussions, stating that "the attitude of the government is to do nothing itself."

By 1936, France and Britain realized that Hitler was preparing Germany for war, and both countries began to build up their armed forces. In March of 1938, German troops crossed the border into Austria. The following day, Hitler declared *Anschluss*, the political union of the two countries. This had been specifically prohibited by the Treaty of Versailles. Again, the British and French did not protest. Hitler by now concluded that any move to dominate Europe would not be opposed.

Hitler looked to Czechoslovakia for his next conquest and immediately started positioning troops along the country's western border. In the summer of 1938, Hitler demanded that Czechoslovakia turn over to Germany an area at the Czech–German border known as the Sudetenland. This area was populated by some 3.5 million German-speaking people whom Hitler wanted to include in the **Third Reich**. The mountainous Sudetenland area was part of Czechoslovakia's border defences; it also contained much of the country's industry. The French, the British, and the Soviets all warned Hitler not to attack. On May 22, Hitler said he had no plans for aggressive action against Czechoslovakia. On May 30 he informed his staff of his "unalterable decision to smash Czechoslovakia by military action in the near future."

Figure 6–18 The mass Nazi rallies at Nuremberg in the 1930s made no secret that Hitler was defying the Treaty of Versailles by building Germany's military strength. What effect might these rallies have had on the German people, who felt they had been humiliated by the treaty?

British Prime Minister Neville Chamberlain was appalled by the prospect of war. He thought war could be avoided by a policy of **appeasement**, which involves giving in to some of the demands of an aggressive nation in order to avoid war. Mackenzie King supported appeasement and travelled to London, Paris, and Berlin to promote a peaceful settlement to European conflict. After attending the 1937 coronation of King George VI, Mackenzie King went to Germany to meet with Hitler and communicate Canada's resolve to stand with Britain in the event of a war. King was impressed by Hitler, and thought him to be a capable leader who was unlikely to start a war.

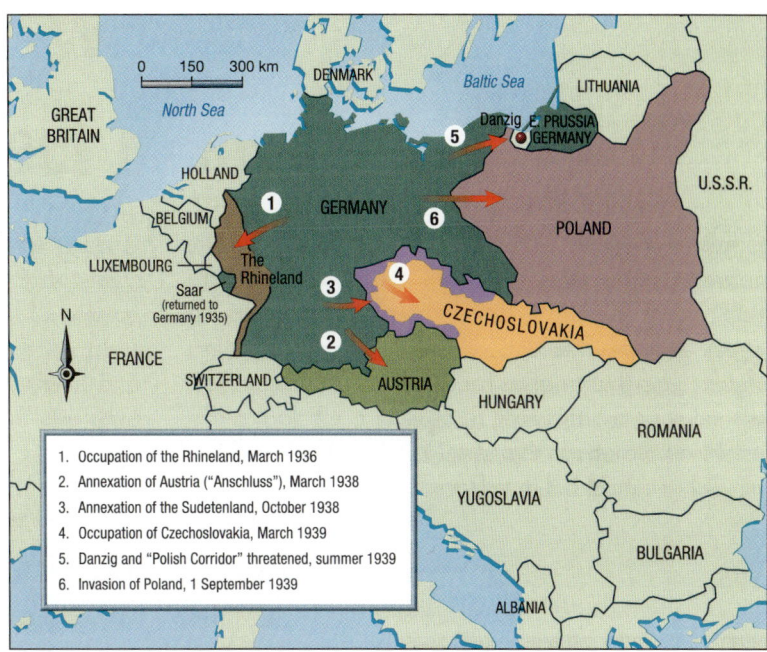

Figure 6-19 Sudetenland was on the Czech–German border.

Figure 6-20 Mackenzie King returned from Berlin with a favourable impression of Hitler and admiration for what Hitler had done for Germany. King's admiration would not last long.

At a four-power conference at Munich in October 1938, the British, French, Italians, and Germans agreed to let Germany have the Sudetenland. Czechoslovakia was not invited to the Munich Conference, nor were they consulted before the agreement was made. In a private meeting after the Conference, Hitler assured Chamberlain that he had "no more territorial demands in Europe." Chamberlain returned to Britain and proclaimed that the Munich agreement meant "peace for our time." Winston Churchill called the agreement "an unmitigated disaster."

Towards Autonomy and War

Figure 6–21 Leaders gathered at the Munich Conference, 1938.

Hitler was not satisfied with the Munich agreement. In March 1939, he annexed the rest of Czechoslovakia. Realizing that Hitler was not to be trusted, Chamberlain guaranteed British support to both Romania and Poland in case the Nazis invaded these countries. In the summer of 1939, Hitler demanded that the Poles surrender the city of Danzig as well as a corridor of land that would give Germany road and railway access to Danzig. The Poles refused. The British government warned Hitler not to invade Poland. In order to prevent any Soviet interference with his plans to attack Poland, Hitler negotiated the Nazi-Soviet non-aggression pact, the Molotov–Ribbentrop Treaty, in late August 1939. The two nations agreed not to attack each other, and to divide Poland between themselves.

On September 1, 1939, the Germans invaded Poland. Germany adopted a style of warfare known as **blitzkrieg** ("lightning war"), which involved attacking by surprise and pushing hard to achieve a quick victory. The Poles bravely fought back, but their army stood no chance against the Germans. The British had issued an ultimatum to the Germans to withdraw from Poland, but Hitler considered this a bluff and ignored it. On September 3, 1939, the British and French declared war on Germany. World War II had begun.

Canada Declares War

In 1914, Canada was automatically at war when Britain declared war on Germany. Between 1937 and 1939, Minister of Justice Ernest Lapointe expressed several times the legal position that a British declaration of war would involve Canada. Mackenzie King emphasized that, while Canada would be "at Britain's side" in the event of war, this would not necessarily mean that Canadians would be sent to fight on overseas battlefields.

A resolution declaring Canada's right to remain neutral was put forward in parliament, but King would not allow the issue to proceed to a vote because he feared it would divide the country. It was clear that Canada would support Britain in the war, but King was convinced that the people of Canada, through parliament, would have to formally approve a declaration of war. As a result, the House of Commons was recalled from its summer recess and the declaration of war was debated on September 8 and 9, 1939.

On September 10, 1939, Canada declared war on Germany. Over the next six years, Canada would be engaged in a war that would bring profound changes to both Canadian society and Canada's place in the world.

Data File

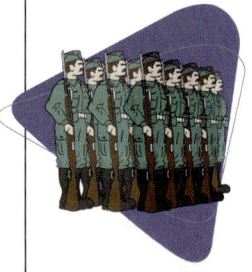

In 1938 the Czech armed forces were nearly as large as the forces of Germany, and were well armed with up-to-date equipment. With help from the British, it is likely that Hitler's army in Czechoslovakia would have been defeated.

Citizenship and Heritage: Individual Canadians

Images
J. S. Woodsworth

Figure 6–22 Woodsworth College of the University of Toronto was named in honour of J.S. Woodsworth.

When parliament debated the declaration of war in 1939, some MPs were not enthusiastic about the prospect. But only one MP stood up to oppose it—J. S. Woodsworth, leader of the Co-operative Commonwealth Federation (CCF).

A Methodist minister, Woodsworth had begun working with poverty-stricken immigrants in Winnipeg in 1904. This experience led him to question the structure of society in turn-of-the-century Canada. He saw that industrialization made only a few people very rich and had a heavy cost for the working class. He put forth the ideas of the "social gospel," a movement that promoted applying Christian ideals to address the problems of industrial society.

A strong pacifist, Woodsworth believed that war resulted from capitalist greed and competition between empire-building nations. In 1917 he was fired from his government job for opposing conscription and arguing that if men were to be conscripted, wealth should be conscripted, too. Woodsworth's public popularity increased when he was arrested for editorials he wrote in support of the Winnipeg General Strike. He helped to organize the Manitoba Independent Labour Party and was elected to the House of Commons in 1921.

Woodsworth's main goal was to create a reform movement of "Canadian Socialism," which he hoped would unite farmers and the urban working class. In 1933, he became the first president of the new CCF. One of the party's goals was to establish a welfare state that would include universal pensions, health and welfare insurance, children's allowances, unemployment insurance, and workers' compensation. Although the party was accused of communism and dangerous radicalism, the Liberals did eventually adopt some CCF policies.

When the prospect of a second world war loomed, Woodsworth saw that a growing number of CCF members believed that war was the only way to stop Hitler. In the parliamentary debate over the declaration of war, he stated:

> I would ask, did the last war settle anything? I venture to say that it settled nothing; and the next war into which we are asked to enter, however big and bloody it may be, is not going to settle anything either.

Woodsworth won his last election in 1940 and died in 1942, having gained a reputation as "the conscience of Canada."

What Do You Think?

1. Discuss Woodsworth's argument that "if men were to be conscripted, wealth should be conscripted too." Why do you think he lost his job for saying so?

CONCLUSION

Under Mackenzie King's leadership, Canada began to act as an independent nation making its own foreign policy decisions. During the Chanak crisis and as a member of the League of Nations, Canada demonstrated that it was anxious to avoid any further commitment to Britain or other European nations. King also believed that creating closer trade ties with the United States was a realistic economic decision for Canada. The two countries encouraged trade between themselves by significantly reducing protectionism—a decision that would have far-reaching effects.

But the world in which Canada was finding its way was a dangerous place. Germany, which deeply resented the harsh terms of the Treaty of Versailles, had fallen under the control of Adolf Hitler and the Nazis. Like the fascists who had seized power in Italy, the Nazis believed in war and violence to achieve their goals. Most nations, including Canada, accepted racism. But for the Nazis, racism was a central belief. Systematically, they set out to exterminate their own minorities, such as the Jews, and to attack other nations and take their land. The League of Nations, in which many had placed high hopes, was unable to stop fascist aggression. On September 10, 1939, after a short debate in the House of Commons, Canada was at war. The question was not whether to help Britain and its allies, but how. In a divided country, some difficult decisions would have to be made.

CHAPTER ACTIVITIES

Check Your Understanding

1. What factors most influenced Prime Minister King's decision to turn away the *SS St. Louis*? List three reasons in order of importance.

2. Create a chart using the headings below to trace the steps Canada took towards full autonomy.
   - The Chanak Crisis
   - The Halibut Treaty
   - The 1923 Imperial Conference
   - League of Nations Article 10
   - The Balfour Report

   For each step, identify Britain's expectations of Canada and King's position.

3. List reasons why the Treaty of Versailles would bring about resentment in Germany. Take into account:
   - territory lost to other countries as a result of the Treaty
   - the effect of payment of reparations for World War I on the German economy
   - the effect of the Treaty's disarmament terms on the morale of the German military

Develop Your Thinking

4. Refer to the statistics in Figure 6-4 and interpret the effects of Canada's entry into World War II while the US remained "neutral." Then look at the effects after 1941 when the US entered the war.

5. Define the concept of "Holocaust." Do careful research and prepare a detailed time line of events related to persecution of the Jews in Germany from 1934 until 1939. Refer to the time line on page 162 as a starting point.

Express Yourself

6. Imagine you are a newspaper correspondent filing stories on Canadian foreign policy after interviews with the Foreign Affairs Department. Write a brief dispatch on two of the following events:
   - Signing of the Treaty of Versailles, 1919
   - Failure of League of Nations to pass oil sanctions against Italy, 1935
   - King's visit with Hitler, 1937
   - The Munich Agreement, 1938
   - Canada's declaration of war against Germany on September 10, 1939

Apply Your Learning

7. a) Describe the relationships among countries of the British Commonwealth after 1931. Research which countries were members in 1931. Which were members in 1999?
   b) Hold a debate arguing for and against continuing as a member of the Commonwealth.

8. Research attitudes to accepting Jewish immigrants since the Holocaust. Why has the state of Israel survived?

Extend Your Learning Using the Internet

9. Create a computerized flow chart to demonstrate the evolution of Canada's autonomy from Britain and its growing dependence on the US during the period prior to World War II.

10. How did Canadian attitudes and government policies towards Jewish refugees reflect the anti-Semitism prevalent in the world during the 1930s and 1940s? What is Canada's official policy towards refugees today?

7
Canada and World War II

Focus Questions

External Forces Shaping Canada's Policies
What events, conditions, and social policies allowed the Holocaust to happen? What was Canada's role?

Canada's Participation in War, Peace, and Security
Militarily, economically, and individually, how did Canadians contribute to the Allied victory?

Economic Conditions and Structures
Why and how did the Canadian economy grow and diversify during World War II?

Changing Role of Government
In what ways did the war affect how the government treated Canadians?

Canada was anything but united on the question of going to war. Most Canadians feared another huge slaughter in a doomed effort to bring peace to Europe. Many were also sympathetic to fascist parties, who promised quick relief of social and economic woes. However, Canada, which had allowed its own military to rust away, agreed to supply Britain and help it train an Air Force.

The Nazi war machine was able to roll over unprepared countries. But things did not go so well for Germany during the war. Germany pounded Britain with aerial bombing, but Britain was unshaken. So Hitler decided to break the Molotov-Ribbentrop Pact and invade the Soviet Union instead. This proved to be a costly mistake. Meanwhile Japan drew the United States into the war on December 7, 1941, by bombing the US Pacific fleet. Canadians saw action first in Asia, and then in Europe. As more personnel were needed, Mackenzie King once again faced the controversial issue of conscription, which had proved so damaging to national unity during World War I. Canada played a significant role in the occupation of Italy, the invasion of Normandy on D-Day, and the liberation of the Netherlands and Belgium, but lost thousands of men in the liberation of France.

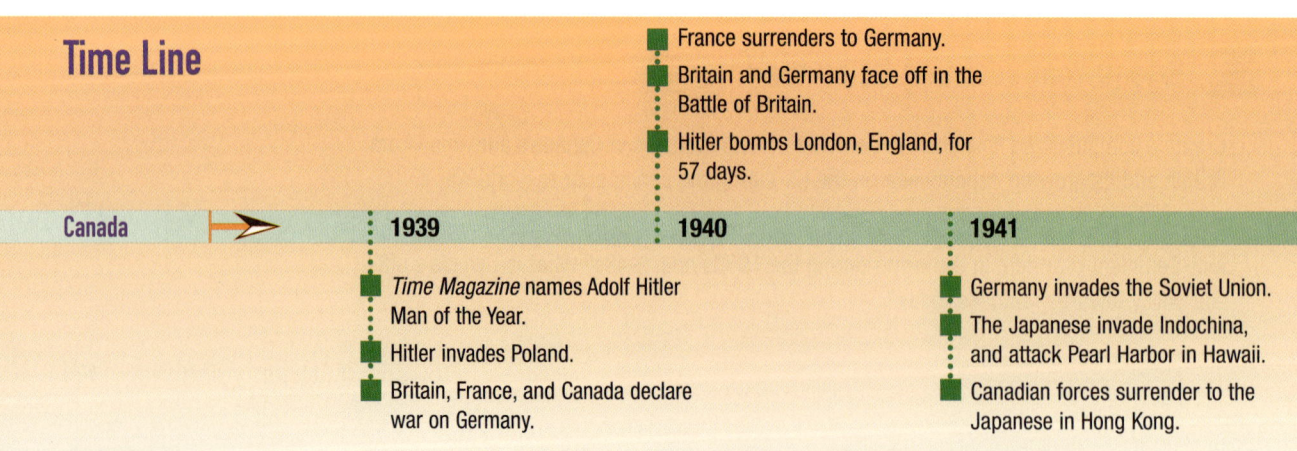

Time Line

Canada

1939
- *Time Magazine* names Adolf Hitler Man of the Year.
- Hitler invades Poland.
- Britain, France, and Canada declare war on Germany.

1940
- France surrenders to Germany.
- Britain and Germany face off in the Battle of Britain.
- Hitler bombs London, England, for 57 days.

1941
- Germany invades the Soviet Union.
- The Japanese invade Indochina, and attack Pearl Harbor in Hawaii.
- Canadian forces surrender to the Japanese in Hong Kong.

Perspectives

During World War II, a huge number of women entered the Canadian workforce. While many filled the positions left behind by men, 45 000 went overseas. This painting, *Maintenance Jobs in the Hangar*, by Paraskeva Clark, portrays the changing role of women. How does the painting capture the way women came to be viewed? How does it show the importance of women's new role? If you were a woman at the time of WW II, would you have wanted a job on the home front or overseas?

- Canadians raid the French port of Dieppe.
- Prime Minister King implements conscription in Canada.
- The Canadian government interns Japanese Canadians.
- The Allies land in Normandy—D-Day.
- Canadians enter the French town of Falaise and overrun the Germans.

1942   1943   1944   1945

- The Allies, including the First Canadian Division, land in Italy.
- The Allies invade Germany.
- Germany surrenders.
- The US drops 2 atomic bombs on Japan.

TO WAR AGAIN?

In January 1939, *Time Magazine* named Adolf Hitler the 1938 Man of the Year. The article concluded by noting that the Man of 1938 would probably "make 1939 a year to be remembered." These words would prove true. In 1939, the world went to war once again—this time to stop the advance of Nazi Germany. It would become the most destructive war in recorded history. On September 3, 1939, Britain and France declared war on Germany and its ally, Italy, after Hitler's forces invaded Poland. Canada declared war one week later. At this early stage of the war, Prime Minister King's vision of Canada's role was less as a supplier of combat troops and more a provider of munitions and training facilities.

Canadians felt they had paid too great a price fighting on foreign soil only two decades earlier in WW I. More than ever, there was a sense that Canada should stay out of foreign conflicts and concentrate on issues at home.

Unwilling to go to War

King also had to consider the views of the different cultures in Canada. In Quebec, there was little support for the war because Quebec had little loyalty to Britain. In fact, its relationship with Anglo-Canada was an ongoing source of discontent. Many Canadians of German and Italian descent felt a connection to their countries of origin, as did many British Canadians. This made their argument to stay out of the war as valid as British Canadians' argument to join it.

There were sympathizers for the Nazi and Fascist governments in both the Italian and German communities. Fascist groups were openly active in Saskatchewan, Manitoba, Ontario, and Quebec. Hitler and Italian leader Benito Mussolini were well aware of the social, political, and economic circumstances in Canada, and they knew that they could be exploited. Many historians believe that a good number of the Fascist sympathizers had been "planted" by the two European powers in order to create unrest in the Canadian political and social landscape.

But the support of fascist ideals went beyond national loyalties. Support came out of economic and social discontent as well. Canada, like most of the world, had suffered a deep depression in the 1930s. There was massive unemployment and economic hardship, and people were looking for someone or something to

Figure 7–1 Upon the occupation of Austria in 1938, some Austrians were quick to learn the Nazi salute. When the Germans invaded Poland the following year their reception would be less favourable. Within a week Canada would once again be at war in Europe.

blame. For some Canadians, such hardship made Hitler's anti-Semitic views less offensive. The Fascists' move to outlaw unions in Italy was also viewed favourably by many Canadians who were unnerved by the growing labour unrest in Canada. In Chapter 4, you read about how East Coast miners had protested the collapse of the Maritime coal industry, and how city workers in Winnipeg had clashed violently with police during the Winnipeg General Strike.

Unable to Go to War

There were other reasons why King did not want to commit troops immediately. In the years between the world wars, the Canadian armed forces were allowed to "rust away." Canada's small population made mounting a substantial military force difficult at the best of times. This was even more of a challenge under the economic conditions of the 1920s and 1930s. In 1938–39, the armed forces budget was only $35 million. The nation lacked both personnel and equipment to offer military support to Britain. The army had only 4000 troops, the navy had 3000 troops and about a dozen fighting ships, and the air force had only 1000 troops with, at most, 50 modern military planes. Although these numbers would change significantly by the end of the war, in 1939 Canada was a mouse in an elephant's game.

Heritage Minute

Although women were not especially welcome in the air force during World War II, Marion Orr didn't care. In 1941, she took flying lessons at her own expense and then went to England, where she joined the Air Transport Auxiliary ferry service. By 1944 she had flown 67 different types of planes and had more than 700 hours of flight-time. When the war was over Marion returned to Canada and started her own flying school.

HITLER ENGAGES THE WEST

Despite Canada's indecision, its assistance rapidly became critical. Before moving into Poland, Hitler had signed the Molotov-Ribbentrop Pact with the Soviet Union (see Chapter 6). The agreement ensured that neither country would launch military action against the other for at least ten years. This was most beneficial to Soviet leader Josef Stalin, because his army was a shambles and the agreement eliminated any immediate threat from Germany. But the pact went even further, granting the Soviet Union expanded territory in the Baltic region as a result of Germany's military activities. Not only did this mean that Hitler could move eastward without Soviet interference, but it also meant that he could turn his efforts westward without fear of what was going on behind him.

Germany Wins Round One

Even though France, Britain, and Canada had declared war in reaction to the invasion of Poland, little action was taken against Germany. These months of inaction are often referred to as "The Phoney War" since no armed conflict took

1. Summarize how Germany won "Round One" of the war.

place. This changed in the spring of 1940 when the German army turned westward. Without warning, the Germans invaded Denmark in April 1940, and then launched an invasion of Norway. It took the Germans less than two months to secure both of these countries. In doing so, they had also effectively isolated Sweden. Next, Germany launched its blitzkrieg against Holland, Luxembourg, Belgium, and France.

In World War I, Germany had invaded France from the north by first invading Belgium. Expecting a similar strategy, the best French troops and the entire British Army took up position in Belgium. Unfortunately, the Germans did not follow the same strategy. Instead, they moved on Sedan and then raced across northern France to the Channel coast, trapping the British and French soldiers. Facing intense pressure from all sides, the British were forced to evacuate their army via the port of Dunkirk. This dramatic rescue called on British ships of all descriptions. In all, 40 000 soldiers were successfully plucked to safety. The evacuation was so hasty, however, that much equipment was left behind. The French did not have a similar escape route, and over a million elite French soldiers were forced to surrender. The Germans quickly overran the rest of France, and on June 22, 1940, it surrendered. Britain was left to face the Germans alone.

A MOUSE COMES TO THE AID OF AN ELEPHANT

Britain refused to negotiate peace, so Hitler was forced to attack Britain head-on. This was not easy. The sea, which surrounds Britain like a giant moat, offered a major line of defence. In addition, Britain had a superb navy and air force. The Royal Air Force (RAF) not only protected the skies over Britain, but also protected the sea forces from aerial attacks. To reach Britain's shores Hitler would have to defeat the British navy—and come face to face with the RAF. To that end, much of the employment Hitler created in Germany during the 1930s was in building the Luftwaffe, the German air force. Between July and September 1940, the Battle of Britain raged.

Data File

The BCATP
Staff: 39 003
Graduates: 131 553
Total Cost: $1.6 billion

The British Commonwealth Air Training Plan (BCATP)

Considering the importance of air supremacy, pilot training and aircraft factories were critical. Although Canada lacked battle-ready troops and equipment, it was a safe haven for conducting training programs and producing munitions. In December 1939, the British Commonwealth Air Training Plan (BCATP) was established. Its purpose was to provide the locale, the aircraft, and the instructors to train Commonwealth air and ground crew, far from the dangers of the war in Europe. The entire country was divided into Training Command zones, although most training facilities were located on the Prairies and in Ontario.

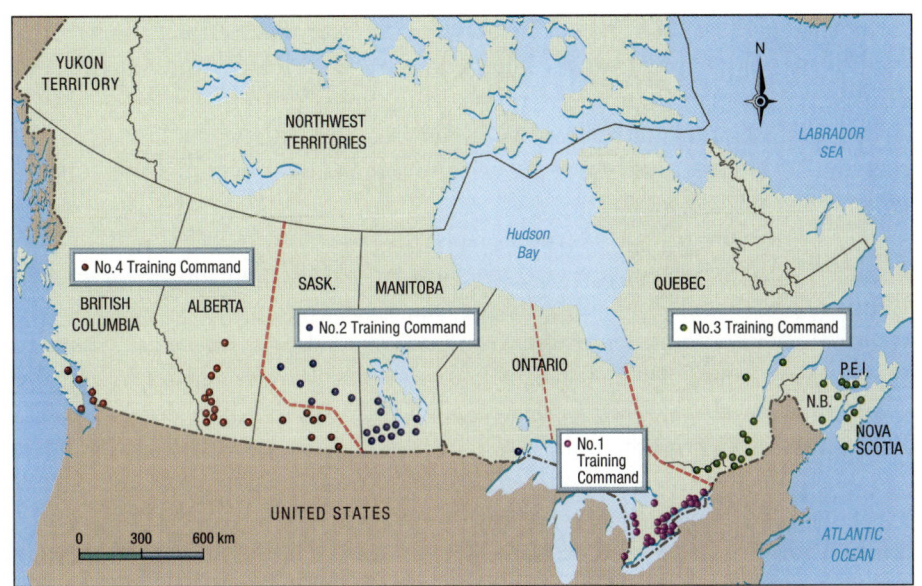

Figure 7–2 This map shows the Canadian stations in the British Commonwealth Air Training Plan.

The Battle of the Atlantic

Canada also provided supplies to Britain via the Atlantic Ocean. It was critical to the **Allies** (Canada, France, and Britain) that this supply line be kept open. It was equally important to Hitler that it be shut down. The result was the Battle of the Atlantic. Only six days after declaring war, Canada's first supply **convoy**

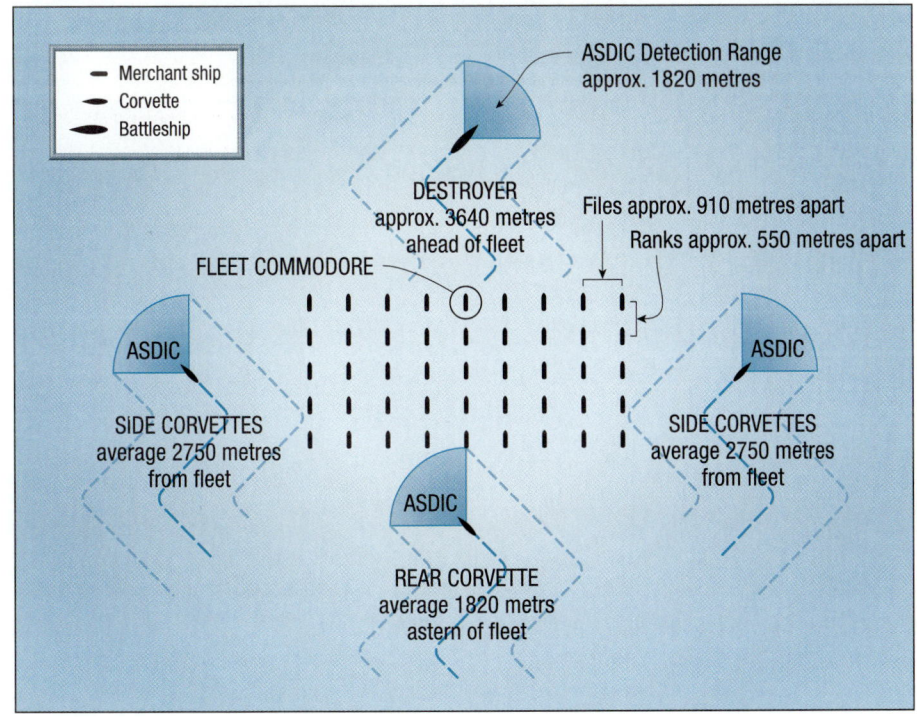

Figure 7–3 The convoy pattern: How the Canadian convoy was protected

Canada and World War II 177

set out from Halifax Harbour. Throughout the war the Germans launched a continuous campaign against these convoys, and losses were significant. However, Canadian shipyards reinforced the supply of ships at a rate that the British High Command referred to as "incredible." In fact, by late 1942 the skeleton naval force that began the war in Canada had grown to 16 000 members serving on 188 warships.

The Germans' primary weapon against the convoys was the **U-boat**, or submarine. At the height of the war, the German naval command had over 300 U-boats. They roamed the waters of the Atlantic in "wolf packs" of six to twenty vessels. Their stealth enabled them to go into waters dangerously close to enemy shores. Throughout 1942, German U-boats even roamed and terrorized the Gulf of St. Lawrence! They were a constant threat to the ships along Canada's East Coast throughout the war.

The Canadians used two lines of defence against the U-boats. The first was a new type of sea craft called a **corvette**. These boats could out-maneuvre a submarine, but they performed best in shallow waters. The second line of defence was provided by the Royal Canadian Air Force (RCAF). The RCAF was a highly effective force, but it lacked the long-range aircraft needed to fly protection over the heart of the Atlantic. The areas beyond the range of air support became known as the "Black Pit." Here, the U-boat reigned supreme. By the end of the war, more than 2000 vessels littered the sea bottom.

Up Close

2. Write a description of Canada's strategies of defence against the U-boats.

Figure 7–4 *Convoy Under Attack* by Tom Wood, 1943

Bombs Rain on London

Supplies delivered by Canada to Britain were very important in the first years of the war. Britain was under relentless attack from German air raids. Hitler launched a massive air campaign known as "the Blitz," which was meant to disable and demoralize the British. His powerful Luftwaffe pounded British factories and shipyards. On August 24, 1940, the war took a terrible turn when German bombers fell off course and accidentally bombed central London. British Prime Minister Winston Churchill was sure this was a deliberate attack on civilians. He responded by ordering three consecutive night-raids on Berlin.

Infuriated, Hitler unleashed a 57-day bombing campaign on London starting on September 7. On the worst of these nights, November 14, 1940, 449 German bombers dropped 1400 high explosive bombs and 100 000 incendiaries on Coventry. On that night alone 50 000 buildings were destroyed, 568 people were killed, and a thousand more were badly injured. The campaign was devastating, but it would have been even worse had it not been for the newly invented radar technology used by Britain. With no signs of the British weakening, Hitler turned his attention elsewhere.

Data File
During the eight-month Blitz, 18 000 tonnes of high explosives were dropped on British cities. A total of 18 629 men, 16 201 women, and 5028 children were killed. An additional 695 bodies could not even be identified.

Hitler Breaks the Molotov-Ribbentrop Pact

It had been only two years since Hitler had signed the ten-year non-aggression pact with the Soviet Union. But he had no intention of keeping his promise, which was no surprise to Stalin. In fact, Stalin may not have had any intention of keeping the agreement either. Both sides had used the agreement to buy time. Hitler needed the time to neutralize Western European powers, and Stalin needed the time to rebuild his army.

In June 1941, Germany began its invasion of the Soviet Union. Hitler was so confident of a quick campaign that he failed to provide winter clothing and equipment for his army. By December 1941, when the Soviets launched their counter-attack, the Germans were fighting both the Russians and their bitter climate. With their vast military, the Soviets forced the Germans away from Moscow. Hitler now had a major problem: he had not taken Britain or the Soviet Union. He now had a war on multiple fronts, something he had desperately tried to avoid. The Soviets spent the next two years slowly forcing the Germans back to their own borders, in one of the most savage battles in history.

Up Close
3. In the two sections on this page, there are references to two "errors" on the Germans' part. What are they and what were the consequences?

CANADIANS GO INTO COMBAT

Although Canadians were involved in the war, they had yet to engage in combat. The Americans, who had been assisting the British by providing munitions, were not yet willing to declare war against the Germans. They were concerned with the developments in Southeast Asia. As you read in Chapter 6, Japan had been looking to expand its empire and had already invaded China. Now it was eyeing the rest of Asia, hoping to gain control over vital raw materials. The Americans opposed this move, and when the Japanese took control of French Indochina in the summer of 1941, the US cut off oil supplies to Japan. Tensions were high and war seemed imminent.

To bolster morale in Asia—and possibly prevent war—Great Britain decided to reinforce Hong Kong. It asked Canada to lend two battalions for this purpose. This was a light, under-trained force, but it was believed that there was plenty of time to do further training. Unfortunately, just weeks later, on December 7, 1941, the Japanese launched a surprise attack against the US Pacific Fleet stationed at Pearl Harbor in Hawaii. The US responded by declaring war on Japan. At the same time, the Japanese attacked Northern Malaya, the Philippines, Guam, Wake Island, and Hong Kong. As a gesture of support for Japan, Hitler declared war on the United States. The war was now truly global. Japanese forces overran Hong Kong, and on Christmas Day 1941, the Canadian force surrendered. The Canadians suffered 286 casualties and another 266 were sent to Japanese concentration camps.

> **Up Close**
>
> 4. Create a graphic organizer to show the chain of events in the last half of 1941.

The Battle of Dieppe

The next year, Canadians raided the French port of Dieppe. They wanted to establish whether an attack from the sea was possible. The objective of the attack was simply to hold the town long enough to destroy its harbour installations and then withdraw. This raid tested new techniques and equipment in preparation for the eventual invasion of Europe. It was a training run of sorts, but it turned out to be a tragically costly lesson.

On August 19, 1942, the force of 6100 soldiers set out towards Dieppe. Roughly 5000 were Canadians. There were many unfortunate events that day, the first being a chance encounter with a small German convoy. The **expeditionary force** was able to repel the German attack, but the noise warned of the pending raid. This encounter also set back the timing of the attack. By the time the forces hit the beach they had lost their two main strategic advantages: surprise and darkness. In the light of dawn, Canadian soldiers stepped into a nightmare.

> We had no cover. We couldn't dig in the pebbles—it was like trying to make a hole in water… We had no protection. We were in a crossfire from the two high sides of the beach and a frontal fire which covered the whole beach. We were just pinned down. We couldn't walk back, we couldn't get forward, we couldn't go on the sides. We were dead, really, before dying.
>
> —Colonel Dollard Menard, Fusiliers de Mont Royal

Of 4963 Canadians who participated in the raid, 882 were killed, 587 were wounded, 1873 were taken prisoner, and only 2210 returned to England. In terms of a single day's loss, Dieppe was the deadliest battle in which the Canadians would participate.

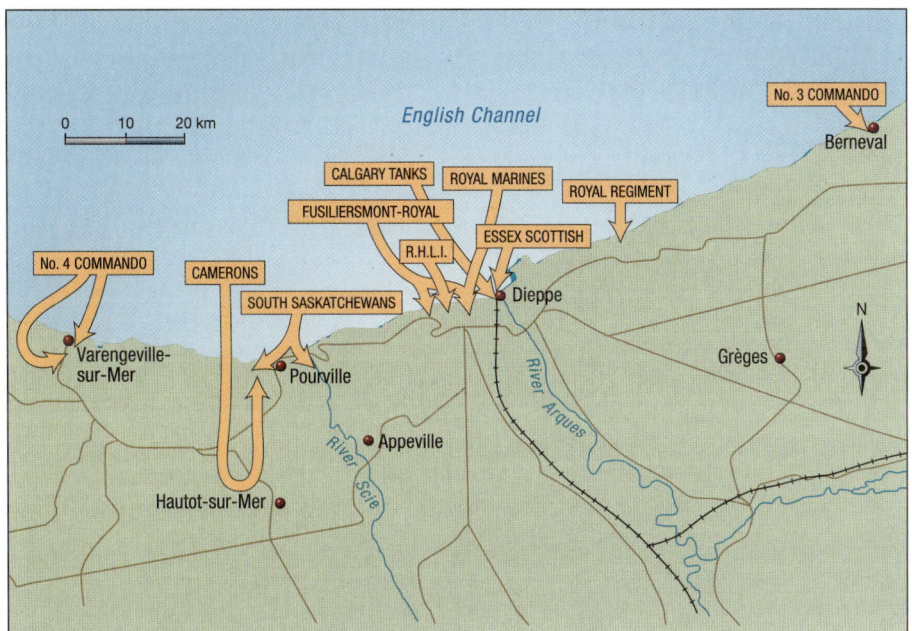

Figure 7–5 This map shows the various Canadian Forces and where they landed for the battle of Dieppe.

Was Dieppe a Total Failure? It is beyond question that the raid on Dieppe was a failure, but it did accomplish some objectives. In war there is a concept of **acceptable losses**. It suggests that a certain number of lives may reasonably be lost in the pursuit of long-term objectives. It is a difficult concept for most people to accept because it implies that there is a formula for calculating an acceptable loss of life. However, in these terms, Dieppe was not a complete failure.

The lessons learned at Dieppe were invaluable. Without these lessons, many more soldiers might have died in the invasion of Normandy in 1944. But there is some disagreement among historians as to the real priority at Dieppe. Some suggest that it was just what it appeared to be: a bungled operation. From this perspective, the architect of the raid, Lord Louis Mountbatten, was responsible for the slaughter of Canadian troops. Other historians suggest that the blame lay more with those Canadians and military leaders who wanted Canada to take a more active role.

Another theory states that it was Churchill who ordered the attack, and that he did so with full knowledge that it would fail! In the summer of 1942, the Soviet Union was protesting that the West was intentionally standing back while their two peacetime adversaries, Germany and the Soviet Union, pounded each other into oblivion. Stalin claimed that the West's inactivity was meant to weaken the German and Soviet states. Churchill somehow had to appease the Soviets while also showing that it was impossible to launch a successful attack at this time. A failed raid at Dieppe achieved both of these objectives.

Up Close

5. In a chart or other organizer, describe the two contrasting opinions about the battle at Dieppe.

Primary Source

War Propaganda Posters

During the 1920s and 1930s, Canadians were not very interested in events in Europe. Nor were they deeply committed to fighting another war in Europe. As a result, the Canadian government had to work hard to get Canadians involved in a total war effort.

Government agencies used every means of mass communication to spread wartime slogans. They urged Canadians to enlist, to get a job, to save and raise money, to salvage essential materials, and to distrust the enemy. The voice of actor Lorne Greene became known as "The Voice of Doom," and could be heard every day, announcing the events in Europe. Footage of the war ran before every feature film. Newspapers were filled with stories of war. One woman noted, "It was like in every city there was one big building full of people turning out propaganda."

A particularly successful propaganda tool was the poster campaign. To reach the general population, the messages were simple and direct, and designed to appeal to the emotions. The Canadian government employed graphic artists to produce posters in both English and French. Often the same images were used more than once, with the captions altered. The posters were displayed on billboards, in streetcars, in factories, and wherever large numbers of people would notice them.

There were two types of messages: positive and negative.

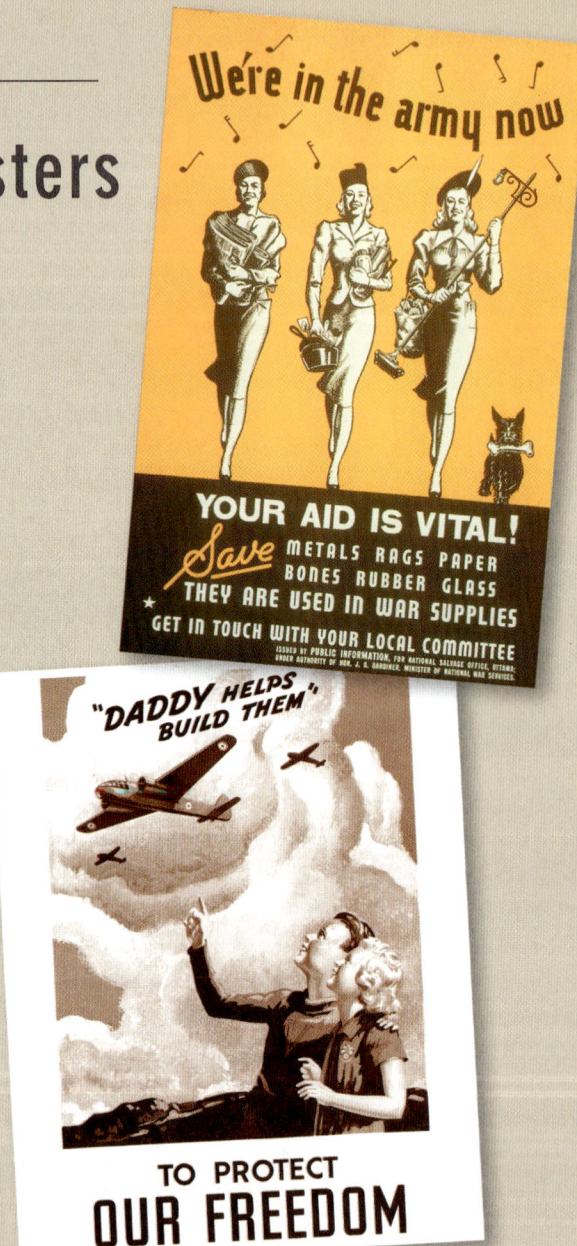

Figure 7–6 Two examples of positive propaganda posters

Positive Propaganda

Positive propaganda posters were designed to encourage readers to feel that they were part of a group that was doing beneficial things for the nation. The Nazis were masters of this type of propaganda; much of Hitler's success in Germany in the 1930s had to do with a vigorous campaign of positive propaganda.

Negative Propaganda

Negative propaganda posters played on people's fears. The enemy was portrayed as a threat to one's way of life. In World War II, Germans and the Japanese were often portrayed as monsters.

Historical Inquiry: Analysing/Evaluating Information

Altered Posters

In some cases, posters were altered as the war went on. Alex McLaren produced two versions of the poster below, one in 1941-42, the second in 1943.

What Do You Think?

1. Examine each of the posters on these pages and then answer the following questions:
   - What is the purpose of the poster?
   - Which section of the population is being targeted?
   - Is this effective propaganda? Explain your answer.

Figure 7–7 An example of a negative propaganda poster: Keep these hands off! Buy the new Victory Bonds.

Figure 7–8 As the war wore on, the image of the poster on the left was altered to the one on the right. Why do you think the image was modified?

Canada and World War II 183

Figure 7–9 *Dieppe Raid* by Charles Comfort, 1946

THE CALL FOR MORE PERSONNEL

From the start of the war, Mackenzie King was under increasing pressure to commit combat troops. The issue of conscription had been a sensitive issue during World War I, and King had come to power by opposing it. Now it looked as though he would have to go back on his word. In 1942, he held a **plebiscite** asking Canadians to release the government from its earlier promises to avoid conscription. Eighty percent of Canadians outside of Quebec voted "yes," while 72 percent inside Quebec voted "no." Many Canadians claimed that King's reluctance to implement conscription was placing domestic political concerns ahead of the war effort. In the end King did implement conscription, even though none of the conscripted soldiers ever saw action.

The Make-up of the Canadian Forces

The Native peoples go to war The Native peoples had been especially hard-hit by the Depression, and many regarded the war as a chance to escape severe poverty.

Up Close

6. As you read to page 186, jot down notes about how each of these groups responded to the call to war and the reaction to their responses:
Native Canadians,
French Canadians,
English Canadians,
Ukrainian Canadians,
Black Canadians,
Japanese Canadians.

As a result, a particularly large proportion of Native Canadians enlisted—about 6000 in all. Most served in the infantry, partly because that is where the highest numbers of soldiers were needed. But they had little choice in any case—non-Whites were barred from joining the air force and the navy until restrictions were lifted after the war was underway. Among the few who did eventually join the air force and the navy was Flying Officer William John Bolduc, an Ojibwa from Chapleau, Ontario. He was awarded the Distinguished Flying Cross for his performance as an air gunner in bombing attacks in 1943.

French Canadians answer the call Although opposed to conscription, French Canadians did answer the call to duty. In fact, French Canadians made up 19 percent of the Canadian military. In many ways, this is surprising. Beyond the cultural ties that hindered enlistment, the Canadian army was primarily an English organization. The language of work, including instruction, was English, and the vast majority of high-ranking officers in the military were English. Still, French Canadians were persuaded by posters that appealed to Roman Catholic values to join in the fight against Hitler.

Figure 7–10 Sargeant Mae Cunningham and her sister, Corporal Yvonne Cunningham, of Drumheller, Alberta. They served in the women's division of the RCAF for three years during the war.

English Canadians support Britain In 1939 about half of Canada's population was of British descent, and several campaigns encouraging Canadian support for the war made strong emotional appeals to British pride. In the spring of 1939, King George VI and Queen Elizabeth visited Canada, further cementing the emotional ties between Canada and Great Britain. Yet while many Canadians of English, Irish, Scottish, and Welsh descent did sign up to fight, they did so at about the same rate, and for the same reasons, as other groups.

Ukrainian Canadians show their loyalty The Canadian-Ukrainian community not only wanted to show their loyalty to Canada, they had national interests against Nazi Germany as well. They answered the call *en masse*. The Ukrainian National Federation (UNF) proposed to raise a 25 000-strong military unit to be known as the Ukrainian-Canadian Legion. Unfortunately, the Canadian government was not enthusiastic about the idea, and did not want private organizations recruiting soldiers. In the end, however, more than 35 000 Ukrainian-Canadian soldiers did enlist. And Ukrainian women supported the war effort by sending parcels to soldiers, raising money for the Red Cross, and working in the war industry.

Figure 7–11 The Ware brothers were among the youngest soldiers to serve in WW II.

Black Canadians are determined to enlist Black volunteers encountered many of the same prejudices they had experienced during WW I. In Dartmouth, Nova Scotia, Allan Bundy tried to enlist in the air force in 1939 and was rejected on racial grounds. He reapplied four years later and was accepted. As the war effort heated up, more Black volunteers were accepted. By the end of the war, several thousand Black recruits were serving in the army. While Black Canadians bravely fought and died alongside their peers, they were shown very little respect after the war. Veterans of colour were excluded from jobs and once again treated as second-class citizens. After the war, one woman recounted how her husband and another Black soldier—the only two Black men among a mostly White crowd—were picked out of a line-up for work, and were told to find work as porters.

Japanese Canadians fight and die for Canada Japanese Canadians fought and died for Canada, but they had to struggle for the right to join the Canadian army. Many Japanese Canadians who tried enlisting were turned away because they were seen as "enemies of the state." Canada and the Allied forces were at war with Japan, so Japanese Canadians, even those born in Canada, were under suspicion.

Figure 7–12 45 000 Canadian women volunteered in the war effort overseas.

> When the Japanese were in Hastings Park before they were all dispersed, the young fellows would come up to me and ask if I could arrange it so they could join the army. In labour battalions, anything, but just give them a chance to prove their patriotism ... I went to the authorities ... but it was impossible. I tried but I couldn't get anywhere. Turned down. Flatly. They weren't allowed. No hearing. Just out to the camps in the bush—and those young fellows would have made good soldiers.
>
> –*Six War Years*, page 112

Canadian women play a large role The women of Canada played a major role in WW II, both directly and on the home front. More than 45 000 women volunteered for active duty. These were non-combat roles, but they were critical nonetheless. Canadian women went to work as drivers of light vehicles, cooks, clerks, messengers, and canteen helpers. The fight for equality had a long way to

Citizenship and Heritage: Individual Identity

Images

A Voice for Women: Dorise Nielsen

Dorise Nielsen was an unusual woman. Elected to the House of Commons in 1940, she was the only sitting female Member of Parliament (MP). Even more unusual about her election victory was the fact that she was the first Communist MP, running under the United Progressive banner. Her affiliation with the Communist Party of Canada (CPC) was a closely guarded secret, since communism was illegal in Canada. The CPC was secretly founded in 1921 in a barn on the outskirts of Guelph, Ontario. Based on the teachings of Vladimir Lenin, the CPC saw itself as the voice of the oppressed—the working class.

For Nielsen, the working class represented an increasing number of women. As in World War I, women filled the gaps left by the men who went to war. While much of the female population stayed home to "continue raising their families, farming the land, and filling the jobs left unoccupied by servicemen," more than 45 000 women volunteered for military service.

But whether at home or overseas, women in the workforce were discriminated against. As Nielsen pointed out, "Not only do the women in armed services not receive equal pay for equal work, but all women in employment have suffered this liability ... Today women are performing over seventy percent of the operations necessary in the manufacture of machine guns. And more than eighty percent of those working in the instrument factories are women." Nielsen headed the cause of working women and demanded that the government recognize that women "have a place to fill in the years of peace, just as they had in the years of war." Further, Nielsen encouraged women to fight for their right to be recognized as men's equals in the workplace.

Figure 7–13 A woman assembles radio equipment in Montreal during WW II.

She said:

If women persist in working at low rates, they will help in establishing low rates for everybody ... Women must see that rates of pay are maintained for their own sake and for the sake of the men coming back and their families. Every woman now working should demand a rate of pay which would maintain her fully if she were working full time at it to earn her living.

Having experienced the Depression in Saskatchewan, Nielsen knew first-hand the sufferings of farming families. She believed that her mission was to represent the poor. Her public life gave her a forum to voice issues of the working class and the oppressed. Her affiliation with the Communist Party, however, soon became known and she came under scrutiny. In 1940, anti-war leaflets published by Nielsen were confiscated by the RCMP, and she came under attack in the House of Commons. She was subsequently defeated in the general election of 1945.

What Do You Think?

1. How did women change the labour force during the war?
2. How do Dorise Nielsen's comments apply to women workers today?

Data File

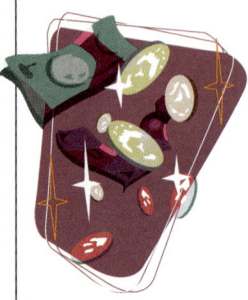

Does war pay? These figures—weekly wages during World War II — show that it did for women.

Live-in maid	$ 3.50
Eaton's order clerk	$12.00
War plant	$25.00

go, however. One of the initial calls for women workers was as laundresses. And even though women played a role equal to that of men, they were paid only two-thirds the wage. As the war went on, women were called on to provide support services in combat zones. As a result, 46 of them died for their country. Despite this, the women in the military suffered the disdain of many of their superiors and peers. As one woman recalled: "… the permanent force officers were just dreadful! They simply did not want women in the forces. They didn't belong, and that was that."

CANADIAN ECONOMIC AND SOCIAL CONDITIONS

The war was a mixed blessing for Canada. Even though economic activity was high, daily necessities were scarce. The focus was on munitions, and many of the **staple goods** that were produced were shipped overseas. Foods such as sugar and meat were **rationed**, and Canadians had to use ration books to obtain their share. The huge demand for munitions, however, created much-needed jobs. The high unemployment figures of the 1930s fell to under 2 percent in 1943. In practice, it became "illegal" to be out of work. Anyone without a job for longer than two weeks was required to report for suitable work. With the large number of men enlisting in the services, there were not enough workers to fill the jobs. Women entered the workforce in unprecedented numbers. This led to new roles for women in the workplace. Although certain jobs lasted only through the war years, popular ideas about what women could accomplish were changed forever.

The Canadian government took a fairly active role in the economy during WW II. Wages and prices were controlled to prevent excessive inflation, and workers were required to save money as a further inflation-fighting measure. During these years, federal spending rose from 3.4 percent of gross national product (GNP) in 1939, to 37.6 percent. To offset this spending, income taxes were increased, and Canadians were encouraged to buy Victory Bonds.

Racism at Home

Although some in the Italian and German communities were involved in pro-fascist activities, most were productive, loyal Canadians. Unfortunately, other Canadians failed to make this distinction. People were

Figure 7–14 Rationing was a fact of life for every Canadian.

caught in the frenzy of the war and were bombarded by war propaganda. As a result, German and Italian Canadians came under attack. These were often physical attacks. The discrimination came from the Canadian government as well. Hundreds of German and Italian Canadians were arrested and interned without any evidence of **subversive** activities. Their businesses and homes were sold off in the process. Even worse, thousands of them had their citizenship revoked, which immediately classified them as "enemy aliens."

Figure 7–15 Saying goodbye: Japanese Canadians say goodbye to family and friends as they are relocated to internment camps in interior British Columbia.

The Internment of Japanese Canadians Japanese Canadians suffered a similar fate. Even before the war, Japanese Canadians had been targets of anti-Asian rioting and were treated as second-class citizens. They were denied the right to vote, teach, or work in the civil service and other professions. The attack on Pearl Harbor created a wave of hysteria on the west coast of North America. It opened the floodgates of longstanding racial hostility. Japanese Canadians came under suspicion even though approximately 20 000 of them had been born in Canada. Despite reports from the RCMP that Japanese Canadians posed no threat, the government began to round up all Japanese Canadians in March 1942. They were placed in internment camps in the interior of British Columbia, in inadequate shelters. The men were put to work building roads in the interior and were paid 25 cents a day for their labour. Women, children, and the elderly were confined to the camps, where they remained until the end of the war.

Japanese Canadians were not only deprived of their liberty, but also had their property confiscated and sold at government auctions. Typically the price raised versus the actual value was about 5 cents on the dollar. Many Canadians took advantage of this and

Figure 7–16 The eating facility for Japanese Canadian women and children at the Hastings Park detention centre, Vancouver, 1942. Women and children were separated from the men, who were sent to work camps.

Canada and World War II **189**

Data File

Until 1988, the Canadian government did not apologize to those who had been interned during the war, nor offer financial compensation. Financial compensation was eventually worked out at $21 000 for each internee still living.

Figure 7–17 Confiscated Japanese Canadian vehicles at the Hastings Park detention centre, Vancouver, 1942

> There was a Japanese girl I went to school with in my class. You might call her my best friend… But the fact that her family was dispossessed, that they lost all they had, house and everything, when she and her family were scooped up, like almost in the night, that didn't really bother us at all. We never said anything about it—never questioned it at all. I never thought there was anything wrong about taking those thousands of people away and sticking them in camps in the bush… We just accepted it. It shows you what propaganda can do to you. The Japanese were our enemies—not our Japanese Canadians, but Japanese over the seas, in Japan—so our Japanese friends were bad. The point is, if authority did it, then it was right. It was a very disciplined time.
>
> –*Six War Years*, page 113

bought property that belonged to their neighbours and competitors. The Japanese Canadians saw almost none of the money raised from these sales. After the war they had no businesses or homes to return to. In late 1945 and 1946, more than half of the Japanese Canadians still in BC were forced to resettle in the Prairies or in Ontario. More than 6000 Japanese were forcibly sent to Japan. Many of these people had not seen their country of origin for decades. Others, born in Canada, felt no connection to Japan at all.

THE PLAN TO END THE WAR: OPERATION OVERLORD

The plan to end the war was code-named Operation Overlord. In 1944, the Allies decided that the conditions were right to prepare their invasion of Europe, but the plan had been in effect for some time. Normandy was chosen as the landing location as it offered the best odds for success. Still, the Allies needed to divert the German forces from this location. Consequently, Operation Overlord was made up of several smaller operations that distracted the Germans throughout the war, ensuring that the German force at Normandy was as light as possible.

Phase one began in 1941, when the British arrested as many German spies as they could identify in Britain. Once arrested, these spies were offered the option of being executed or turning over the details of their operation. They spent the rest of the war in jail while British intelligence officers assumed their identities. In their roles as "double-agents," British intelligence officers continued to feed accurate information to Berlin, but did so only on minor operations. The Germans grew to trust these sources since the information was always accurate. This enabled the British officers to feed misinformation to the Germans about the Allied invasion force. They told Berlin that the invasion force was much larger than it really was and that it was amassing on the southeastern coast of Britain in preparation for a landing at Calais.

The Germans could have easily uncovered this ruse if the Allies had not taken further steps. First, the Allies studied the radio patterns that take place in the area of a large military force and set up dummy transmissions to mimic this activity. It would appear to anyone monitoring the area as if there were a tremendous amount of activity. Second, the British and American movie industries helped create the appearance of a large military force. A fake army was constructed, complete with tanks, trucks, and buildings. From the ground, it was clear that the vehicles and structures were not real, but from the air, it looked as if a massive military force had been assembled. To ensure that this deception was not viewed from the ground, the entire southeastern coast was completely sealed off.

Up Close

7. Outline the elements of the Allies' ruse in Operation Overlord.

The Military Preparations: The Canadians in Italy

As had been the case from the beginning of the war, it was important that the Allied forces keep the **Axis** forces (Germany, Italy, and Japan) occupied on multiple **fronts**. The battle was still raging on the eastern front, and in 1943 the Allies pushed to open up a front in the south. On July 10, 1943, the First Canadian Division took part in the Allied landings in Sicily. Although Sicily was taken quite easily, 10 000 German troops escaped into the mainland. Despite Italy's surrender, the victory was rather empty since the mainland was now held by German troops.

This made a difficult offensive almost impossible. The mountainous terrain was not only tough to cross with a large force, it made defending a position much easier than advancing on it. It cost the German troops far fewer casualties than were suffered by the Allies. A further obstacle was the cold and wet Italian winter. In December 1943 the Canadians were assigned to take the town of Ortona, a key German stronghold. Two days after Christmas the town fell, but not before the First Canadian Division had lost 2339 soldiers. Another 16 000 had to be evacuated because of sickness and fatigue. Still, it was a major victory in a successful push towards Rome. Not only was the campaign in Italy successful in terms of land and troops captured, but it also pulled important German divisions away from the west coast of Europe.

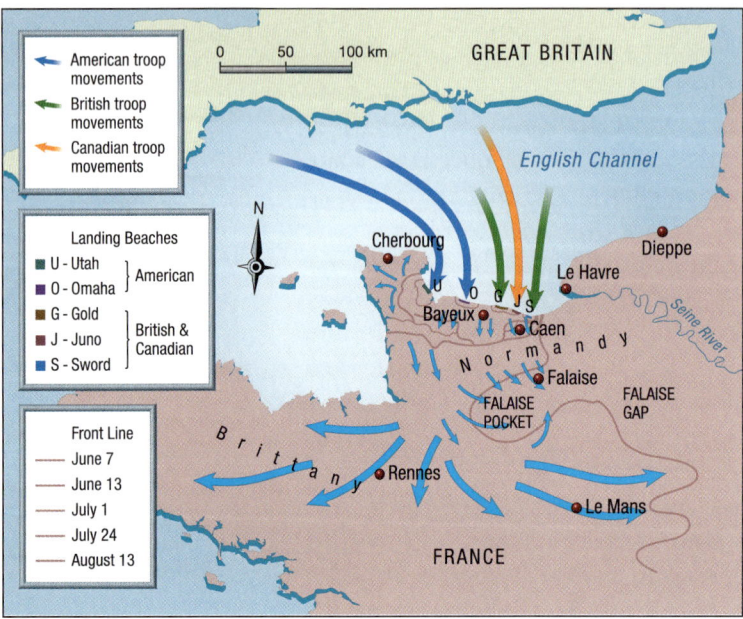

Figure 7–18 This map shows the Allied troops' landing sites, D-Day, 1944.

D-Day: The Normandy Invasion

The force assembled for the Normandy Invasion was a sight to behold. One sailor said that there were ships "as far as the eye could see!" It was the largest naval armada ever assembled. It was able to ferry upwards of one million ground troops within two or three weeks of the invasion. The success of the misinformation campaign was also apparent in the Germans' reaction to this force. As dawn broke on June 6, 1944, the German defence got a first glimpse of the Allied force. In response it made frantic calls to Berlin for reinforcements. However, the German command refused to move forces to the area, believing that this was just an attempt to divert them from their defence at Calais. This was no surprise to the Allies who, by this point in the war, had developed the world's first computer to break the Germans' "Enigma code," which had made German communications previously indecipherable.

The Canadian Third Division was responsible for landing at Juno Beach, between the British landings at Gold and Sword Beaches. The invading force was supported by a vast amount of artillery firepower provided by Allied ships. In addition, specialized landing craft had been equipped to fire rockets on the German defenders. Allied aircraft had also extensively bombed behind the German positions so that reinforcements could not get through. While facing heavier opposition on the beaches than expected, the Canadians managed to get through and move inland. They were the only Allied troops to reach their D-Day objectives.

Where	Size at a Glance	Comments
Air	6000 planes (3000 fighters)	Opposed by just 300 German planes
Sea	4000 ships of all sizes (battleships, cruisers, destroyers, troops transports, and landing crafts)	Crewed by 200 000 sailors. Canada provided 110 ships and 10 000 men.
Ground	107 000 soldiers with reserves in England of over 1 million	Canada contributed an infantry division and an armoured brigade to the invasion. Another infantry division and two armoured divisions were in reserve in England.

Figure 7–19 Statistics relating to Allied Forces on D-Day

The Push Eastward

The success at Normandy was the beginning of the end of the war in Europe. But for the Canadian troops, this was really the start of the war. Canadian forces had seen some action in Europe, but their involvement would now begin in earnest. With an Allied foothold established on the western mainland, the Germans were being squeezed on all sides.

As German reinforcements arrived, the Third Canadian Division faced one of the most skilled and fanatical German divisions—the 12th SS Panzer Division (*Hitler Jugend*). Much of this confrontation came at the town of Caen. It was supposed to be captured by British troops on D-Day but was not taken until July 9, 1944, after being flattened by one of the heaviest aerial bombardments of the war. Taking Caen cost the Canadians nearly 1200 men. Then, at the French town of Falaise in mid-August, 18 500 Canadian men were either killed, wounded, or missing. The Black Watch Regiment lost all but 15 of 500 men in a long, hopeless assault against a much larger German force. Despite this, the Canadians entered Falaise on August 16, inflicting many thousands of German losses in the process.

8. In point form, relate how and why D-Day was a victory for the Allies.

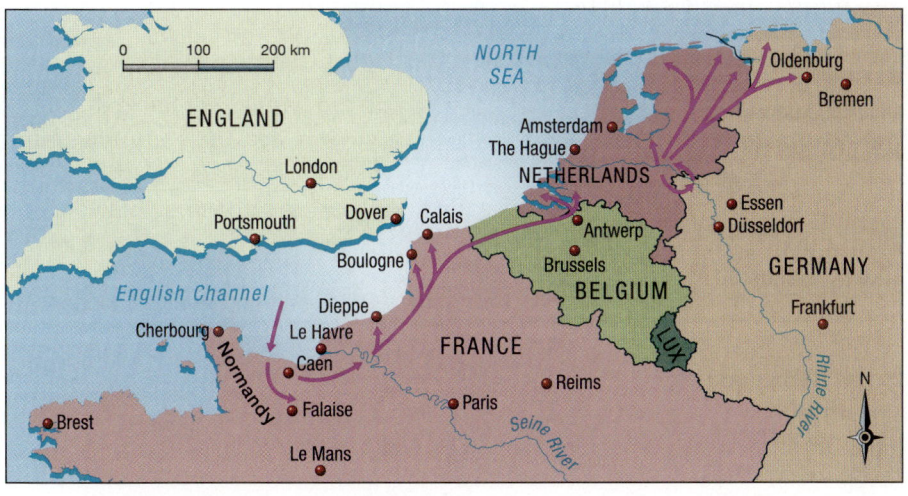

Figure 7–20 This map shows the movements of Canadian troops between 1944 and 1945, as they push the Germans back towards Germany.

The End of the War in Europe

With no more German troops in France, the Allies nearly reached Germany. It was early September 1944 and victory was all but certain. But with supply lines long and supplies dangerously low, the Allied armies were forced to stop their eastward march. The assault on Germany would not begin until February 1945, and Hitler used this time to bolster his forces. He extended the armed service to all males between 16 and 50 years of age, raising 750 000 troops and mobilizing 3000 additional tanks.

As the main Allied armies advanced into Germany, the Canadian troops were given the difficult task of liberating Belgium and Holland. The task was crucial, as the Dutch population had suffered severely in the last year of the war—many

Historian at Work

Using Historical Maps

Maps are as useful to historians as they are to geographers. They reflect changes in natural and cultural landscapes over time. The earliest maps were sketches drawn by explorers and travellers to describe to others where they have been, or to help people find their way to a destination. Historical maps can show many different kinds of changes—for example, changes in vegetation and land use, changes in political boundaries, the rise and fall of empires, the growth of religious and political ideas, and the routes of explorers.

This chapter contains several maps of sites that were important in World War II. They help us to understand the catastrophe at Dieppe and the scope of D-Day in Normandy by letting us see the landscape on which those battles took place.

Different scales of maps serve different purposes. Large-scale maps show a lot of detail on a small area. The scale of Figure 7–22 is larger than the scale of Figure 7–21. Figure 7–21 shows a large area but in much less detail. Note the scale on the upper left corner of each map. What information does it provide?

Map production has improved greatly over the years. While cartography (map making) is still an art, during the 1900s it drew more and more heavily on innovations in science and technology. The use of mathematics, aerial photographs, satellite imaging, and infrared sensing are all new ways to collect information, and they produce ever more precise maps. As a result of these new techniques, historians of the future will have much more accurate records than the ones we work with today.

Maps can illustrate a country's evolution. For example, look at Figure 1–7 on page 14. Here you can see the impact of changing political and economic conditions. In 1898, much of the north and west of Canada was sparsely populated and was governed from Ottawa; territories were divided into several districts. A population boom, resulting from the Klondike Gold Rush and Clifford Sifton's program to attract people to the Prairies, led to the creation of Alberta and Saskatchewan in 1905.

Maps can also show boundary disputes that have led to some major historical turning points. Figure 2–7 on page 36 illustrates the Alaska Boundary

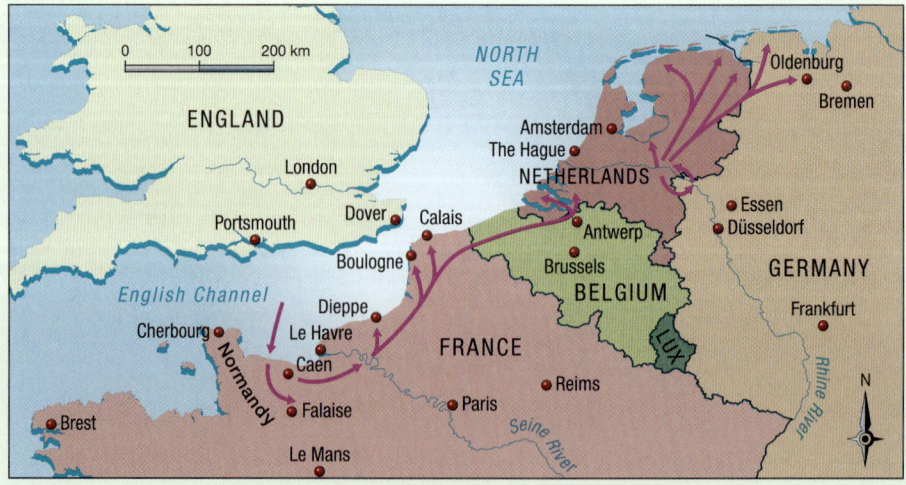

Figure 7–21 Canadian troop movements, 1944–1945. This is an example of a small-scale map.

194 Chapter 7

Historical Inquiry: Analysing/Evaluating Information

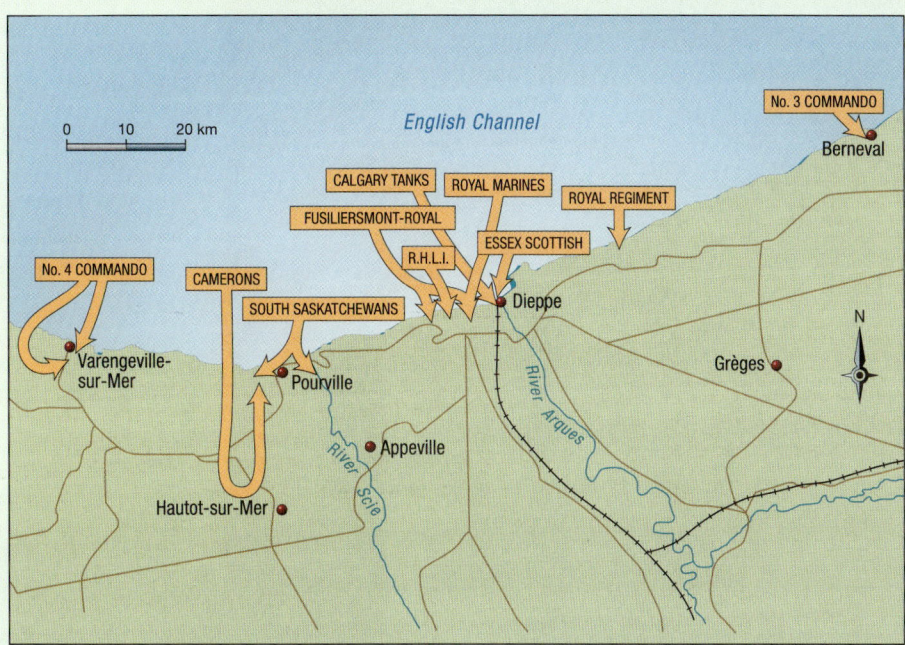

Figure 7–22 Canadian Forces at Dieppe. This is a larger-scale map than Figure 7–21.

Dispute. When a cash-strapped Russian tsar sold the Alaskan territory to the United States in 1867, it wasn't completely clear where the line should be drawn between Alaska and the northwest corner of British Columbia. No one was too concerned about it until gold was discovered in the Yukon at the end of the century. As you read in Chapter 2, the resulting dispute stirred up Canadians' resentment towards both the US and Britain.

An issue that resulted in much more disastrous consequences involved the redrawing of the boundaries of Eastern Europe at the end of World War I. US President Wilson believed the war was largely the result of so many different ethnic groups living under the rule of others in the Ottoman, Austro-Hungarian, and Russian empires. Following the war, the boundaries of much of Europe redrawn, and new states were created out of the old empires. While the effort was well-meant, it was far from perfect. Hitler seized Austria, the Sudetenland (and the rest of Czechoslovakia), and Poland because significant numbers of German people were behind the borders of these countries. A relatively short period of peace and stability came to an end with the outbreak of World War II.

ACTIVITIES

1. a) Look at Figure 7–22. Over what distance were most of the attacking forces concentrated? Why might this have been an advantage? How might it have been a disadvantage?

   b) Look at Figure 7–21. Over what distance were the forces spread out? Compare this with the map of the Dieppe Raid. Why would you not illustrate the Dieppe raid strategy on Figure 7–21?

2. While maps can give clues to historians, they cannot tell the whole story.

   a) Re-read the account of the Dieppe Raid in this chapter. What factors can you find that are not evident from the map which account for the failure?

   b) On page 181 it states that lessons learned from Dieppe helped make D-Day successful. List some of these lessons. Which ones showed that the Allied forces had applied lessons learned from Dieppe? Which of these relate to knowledge of geography?

Canada and World War II

were starving, and the Germans had flooded much of the country. More than 6300 Canadians were killed and wounded in this push, but by mid-April most German units had surrendered or were cut off. With this achieved, the Canadians turned their attention to helping the Dutch. It was an act that was never forgotten by the Dutch population.

The Great Land Grab

When the Allies reached the German border, a new issue emerged: With the Soviet forces pushing westward and the Canadian, American, and British forces pushing eastward, who would control the newly liberated countries? The East and West may have been allies in the war, but they were still adversaries in peacetime. With the end of the war in sight, their rivalry came to the forefront. Stalin used the delays on the western front to seize territory in Eastern Europe. These countries remained under Communist rule after the war. Ironically, one of these was Poland, whose independence had been a major reason for Britain to originally declare war. This "land grab" ended on May 8, 1945, when Germany officially surrendered. Any further geographical lines would be drawn up at the negotiating table.

Figure 7–23 Dutch children in the Netherlands celebrate after two Canadian Infantry Divisions liberated their city from German occupation.

THE END OF THE WAR

The war in the Pacific lasted a few months longer than the European war. The Americans had done most of the fighting against the Japanese, and it had taken them three years to bring their forces close enough to bomb Japan. The American military had already suffered about a million casualties, and they calculated that an invasion of Japan would cost at least a million more.

The Atomic Bomb

Throughout the 1930s, the idea of a new type of weapon had been circulating. It was the atomic bomb. In 1939, Albert Einstein wrote to President Franklin Roosevelt detailing this idea and its dangers. Fearing that the Germans were developing this weapon, the Americans assembled a group of prominent scientists at Los Alamos, New Mexico to begin its own work. The group carried out their work for three years, starting in August 1942. The highly secretive project was code-named "the Manhattan Project." It was a $2 billion gamble for the Americans, but on July 17, 1945, they tested the first successful atomic weapon. Reflecting upon the test, J. Robert Oppenheimer, the project's leader said, "I have become death, the shatterer of worlds." The scientists who worked on the project wrote a letter to Roosevelt pleading that their invention never be used.

Hiroshima and Nagasaki

The decision whether to drop an atomic bomb on Japan rested with the new US president, Harry S. Truman. Faced with a continuation of the war and the possibility of huge further casualties, he decided to try ending the war by dropping two bombs on Japanese cities. The first bomb, code-named "Little Boy" was detonated 500 metres above Hiroshima at 8:15 a.m. on August 6, 1945. It contained an explosive force equivalent to 20 000 tonnes of TNT—20 kilotons.

> The initial flash spawned a succession of calamities. First came heat. It lasted only an instant but was so intense that it melted roof tiles, fused the quartz crystals in granite blocks, charred the exposed sides of telephone poles for almost two miles, and incinerated nearby humans, so that nothing remained except their shadows, burned into asphalt pavements or stone walls. Bare skin burned up to two and a half miles away. After the heat came the blast, sweeping outward from the fireball with a force of a five hundred mile-an-hour wind. Only those objects that offered a minimum of surface resistance—handrails on bridges, pipes, utility poles—remained standing. Otherwise, in a giant circle more than two miles across, everything was reduced to rubble.
>
> –Eyewitness account in *The Making of the Atomic Bomb*, p. 714

Figure 7–24 A burnt-out schoolhouse in Nagasaki after detonation of the atomic bomb.

Eighty thousand people died instantly in the explosion and firestorm, and another 80 000 to 100 000 died later from the effects of burns and radiation. Three days later, a second bomb, code-named "Fat Man," was dropped on the city of Nagasaki. While no firestorm resulted, it instantly killed 40 000 people with another 60 000 dying from its effects. Over the next 50 years, the bombs' effects killed many more Japanese, usually from cancer. Until after the end of the war the Japanese were unaware of exactly what had transpired at Hiroshima and Nagasaki. In July 1945, some 80 000 Japanese civilians had been killed in fire-bombing raids on Tokyo; most Japanese thought that the atomic bombs were merely a new kind of incendiary bomb. Faced with continued American fire-bombing, the entry of the Soviets into the war, and the prospect of total devastation, Emperor Hirohito surrendered on August 15, 1945. World War II was over.

THE HOLOCAUST

The unspeakable horror of the Nazi regime was not fully understood until the Allies moved deeper into German territory. Hitler's vision was for the elimination or enslavement of all who were not part of his German "master race." The Nazis pursued Hitler's "Final Solution"—the elimination of all Jews in Europe—throughout the war. The Allied advance uncovered death camps, mass graves, burned bodies, and humans reduced to skeletal frames.

Between 1939 and the invasion of the Soviet Union in June 1941, Hitler tried to remove the Jews from the German consciousness. He segregated them in **ghettos** or sent them to **concentration camps**. With the German invasion of the Soviet Union, the vast Jewish population of western Russia fell under Nazi control. Hitler decided that the official extermination of Jews would now begin under the direction of Heinrich Himmler, the head of the Nazi elite forces (the **SS**). The Einsatzgruppen, consisting of German troops, auxiliary police, and volunteers from recently conquered territory, was formed to carry out the **genocide**. Their reward was a vast increase in pay as well as a share of the loot taken from their victims. The Einsatzgruppen went into Russia, and the killings began.

There were over 11 million Jews in Europe, so the Nazis sought an efficient means of extermination. Large numbers of Jews were put to work building roads in the east. They would work there until they either died or were unable to work. If they couldn't work, they were shipped to **extermination camps** such as the one at Auschwitz.

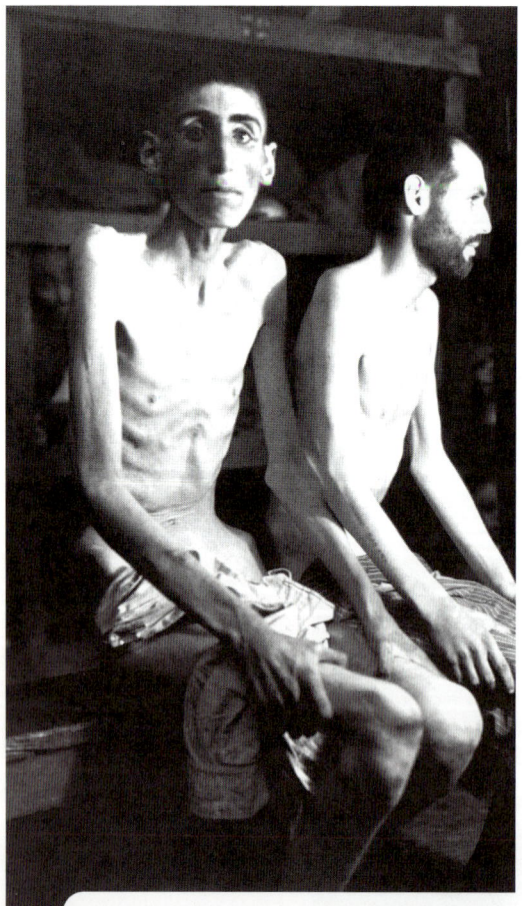

Figure 7–25 Allied forces discovered these and other prisoners in concentration camps, many of whom were starved and on the brink of death.

Figure 7–26 This famous photograph shows German storm troopers rounding up Jews in the Warsaw ghetto when residents attempted an uprising in 1943.

Opened in 1942, most of these camps used gas chambers, a terribly efficient killing tool. A few thousand people could be murdered in three to fifteen minutes. The bodies were then dragged out, stripped of everything, including their gold fillings and sometimes their hair, and then placed in the crematoria. Recent estimates indicate that between 1939 and 1945, of the 11 million Jews living in Europe, between 5.6 and 6.9 million were killed—around 64 percent of the entire population. Not all Jews were automatically sent to the gas chambers. Many were subjected to horrific "scientific" experiments carried out prior to their extermination.

Could the Holocaust Have Been Stopped?

While many people did shelter Jews at great risk to themselves, most people kept silent. Many Germans claimed that they knew nothing of the Holocaust, but this is difficult to believe. Although most death camps were located in occupied Poland, many existed in Germany as well. Jews on their way to the camps were transported in cattle cars by railway. And the burning of corpses is difficult to conceal—the smell of thousands of burning human bodies was unmistakable. It is more likely that people turned their backs out of self-preservation. Objecting would result in death. Those carrying out the actions also faced this dilemma. But in the Nuremberg trial on war crimes following the war, the defence of "following orders" was rejected.

Finally, Allied nations must be held partially accountable. Before the war, anti-Semitism was common throughout the world. Jews desperately trying to leave Germany in the 1930s often had nowhere to go. Even after the war began,

Data File

Few countries successfully resisted Hitler's Final Solution. But in 1943, the Danish King asked all citizens to wear the Star of David as a show of support. The Danes secretly moved all Danish Jews to neutral Sweden, allowing them to return to their homes after the war.

Canada and World War II **199**

and Hitler's "Final Solution" was known, there were still restrictions on the acceptance of Jews into Allied countries. Canada had restricted Jewish immigration since 1912.

There are people who deny that the Holocaust took place, even in the face of overwhelming graphic evidence. These views have been the subject of legal

Figure 7–27 Unspeakable crimes were committed in concentration camps. The barracks (inset, left) was where people slept in crowded conditions. The path leading to the gas chamber is shown (far right) and on the right (inset) are the ovens where the victims, after being gassed, were cremated.

cases in Canada. Canadians struggle with the value we place on free speech when it includes hate messages. We have chosen to limit this freedom and have objected to the messages of people such as Alberta schoolteacher Jim Keegstra and Nazi sympathizer Ernst Zündel. You will read more about their cases in Chapter 14.

It is still possible to visit the concentration camps built by the Nazis. Many people do so every year, to honour the victims of the Holocaust. It is always an emotional experience, even for those who have no personal connection to the event. Here is what one Canadian wrote after visiting Birkenau, the second camp built at Auschwitz:

> You can walk here for hours and not see anyone. There are no guards here, no uniformed personnel, no one to plan your tour. There is no admission charge, just a polite sign at the gate warning you that some of the buildings are collapsing and dangerous to walk in. The camp's centre road takes you further and further away from yourself, and closer to why you live and they don't. The grass has returned; so have the birds and the wildlife. But it is still the end of the world. When we had walked for more than two hours, we drove far away into the night, unable to speak, wondering why the sky brimmed with stars instead of tears.

Flashpoint

War Crime Trials: From Nuremberg to Kosovo

> The privilege of opening the first trial in history for crimes against the peace of the world imposes a great responsibility ... The crimes which we seek to condemn and punish have been so calculated, so malignant and so devastating that civilization cannot tolerate their being ignored, because it cannot survive their being repeated.
>
> –Justice Robert Jackson, October 20, 1945, Nuremberg, Germany

Figure 7–28 The courtroom heard about the atrocities of Hitler's Final Solution, including executions like this one in German-occupied Ukraine.

The Nuremberg Trial

In the first trial of its kind, 24 high-ranking German officials were each charged with one or more of the following:
- Count 1: Conspiracy to wage aggressive war
- Count 2: Crimes against peace
- Count 3: War crimes
- Count 4: Crimes against humanity

To the public, all the crimes were one and the same.

A year after the war, the world determined that "the men who had led Germany down her tragic road were going to pay the bills." Many people wanted swift judgment against them, but the International Military Tribunal (IMT) was intent on giving each defendant a fair trial. Unfortunately, some of the most guilty, including Hitler, who committed suicide when he knew he'd been defeated, could not be brought to trial. For the next nine months, prosecutors from the United States, Great Britain, France, and the Soviet Union presented their case.

During the trial, the world learned much about the horrors of death camps and the activities of Hitler's Thousand-Year Reich. Men, women, and children were experimented on, gassed, or shot to death in the extermination camps. One doctor who was involved in a gassing described it as "the most dreadful of horrors ... I could not imagine anything more disgusting and horrific." Another described how the prisoners were told they would be given a bath to disinfect them, and were then gassed in the cramped chambers. "They then started to cry out terribly for they knew what was happening to them ... After a few minutes there was silence. After some time had passed ... the gas chamber was opened. The dead lay ... all over the place. It was a dreadful sight."

Some of the defendants argued that they were not individually responsible for their acts; they were simply following orders. One key defendant, Hermann Göring, Hitler's right-hand man, said, "I was an officer, a soldier, and I was not concerned with whether I shared an opinion or not. I had merely to serve my country as a soldier." Another testified, "I only respected and acted according to the laws of my country." Still others argued that they "did not know in the crematoriums ... innocent human beings were being liquidated."

But in the end, none of the defendants' arguments could change the fact that the Holocaust had happened. The evidence against them was too powerful, and their crimes too horrific. On September 30 and October 1, 1946, verdicts and sentences were handed down: 12 defendants were sentenced to death, three were sentenced to life imprisonment, four were given prison sentences ranging from 10 to 20 years, and three were acquitted. The trial stood as a warning to all regimes that would persecute groups of people simply because they are different. In Europe and North America in particular, people began to recognize that this chapter in human history must never be repeated.

Post-Nuremberg War Trials

Nuremberg has been followed by numerous other trials of war criminals in other countries. Many people feel that Nuremberg never fulfilled its promise of a permanent international tribunal for war crimes. Various efforts were made in the latter half of the century, but all failed. Only in the 1990s, with the establishment of the United Nations' International Criminal Tribunal, did that promise begin to take form.

One of the International Criminal Tribunal's very first acts was in May 1999 when it indicted and issued arrest warrants for Yugoslav President Slobodan Milosevic, and four others. They were charged with crimes against humanity—specifically murder, deportation, and persecutions—and with violations of the laws and customs of war. It was the first time that an acting head of state was indicted for war crimes. Under Milosevic, Serbs carried out "ethnic cleansing," or more accurately, the murders of ethnic peoples, including Kosovars (see Chapter 16). It was the worst case of genocide in Europe since the extermination of Jews and other minority groups under Hitler.

Milosevic's **indictment** is significant because it shows that "no one, whether a head of state or private soldier, is immune from criminal responsibility for crimes against humanity and war crimes." His trial is of tremendous importance in bringing justice to all those who suffered under his regime. As United Nations General Secretary Kofi Annan has said, "There can be no global justice unless the worst of crimes—crimes against humanity—are subject to the law. In this age more than ever we recognize that the crime of genocide against one people truly is an assault on us all—a crime against humanity."

Figure 7–29 The defendants observe the gruesome evidence at the close of the trial. Many closed their eyes or turned away.

What Do You Think?

1. Some of the defendants at Nuremberg claimed that they were merely following orders and that they should not be individually held accountable. Do you agree? Why or why not? What would you have done under the circumstances? Explain.

2. The Holocaust is considered by many to be the most notable case of genocide ever recorded. In order to ensure that its effects are not forgotten, it is suggested that each class engage in some activity which directly addresses the Holocaust. Here are some suggestions:
   - Visit a local or nearby Holocaust centre.
   - Invite a Holocaust survivor to speak to your class.
   - As a class, participate in a Holocaust symposium in your area.

CONCLUSION

World War II was the most destructive war in human history. Both Allied and Axis powers suffered massive destruction and loss of life. Two of the casualties were Hitler and Mussolini. Hitler committed suicide, and Mussolini was shot during an escape attempt. But the discovery of the death camps of Europe and the aftermath of the atomic bomb in Japan also drove home to Canadians just how destructive racism and uncontrolled arms buildups could be. This would have far-reaching effects throughout the rest of the century. As Canadians became aware of the human costs of racism and armed confrontation, they began to challenge their acceptance much more vigorously.

Figure 7–30 Canadian fatalities in World War II

CHAPTER ACTIVITIES

■ Check Your Knowledge

1. In your own words, define and explain the following terms and phrases. Then create an activity—for example, a card game—challenging your classmates and family to match them up.
   - The Phoney War
   - Pearl Harbor
   - BCATP
   - CPC
   - The Manhattan Project
   - The London Blitz
   - RAF
   - The Black Pit
   - blitzkreig
   - propaganda
   - RCAF
   - Operation Overlord

2. What information does the soldier's quote on page 180 give that the text does not?

3. Create a time line that identifies significant historical events related to the Holocaust. Include the persecution of European Jews before the war (see Chapter 6) and events throughout the war.

■ Develop Your Thinking

4. Prepare the plan for the Dieppe Raid in a form that could be used by Canadian military leaders. Include the names of the regiments and troops involved, step-by-step moves assigned to each, dates and times, explanatory notes, and other information you think would be useful. Also create a map to illustrate the plan.

5. Create a Canadian character who lived in this era and prepare four to six interview questions to ask about his or her contributions to the war. Exchange questions with a partner, and write responses to each other's questions in the role of the interviewee. With your partner, prepare to present both interviews as a radio broadcast.

6. Imagine that you are a journalist. In dispatches for your newspaper, report on Canada's roles in at least three events that took place late in the war that led to the Allied victory.

■ Express Yourself

7. Write a letter to the Canadian government expressing your personal views of the treatment of Japanese-Canadians during the war. State what you think should be done in the way of compensation, and why. Then write the government's response in the form of a press release, defending the actions taken during wartime.

8. Research the involvement of Canadians in the development of the atomic bomb (the Manhattan Project). Then prepare a debate on the topic of whether or not dropping atomic bombs on Hiroshima and Nagasaki was justified.

■ Apply Your Learning

9. Research how Canadians responded to the revelations of the Holocaust and to the Nuremberg Trials.
   a) Find out to what extent Canada has helped to seek and try Nazi war criminals, and what agencies are still involved.
   b) Outline how memories of the Holocaust have been significant in shaping postwar Canadian policies towards refugees and human rights. Provide specific examples.

10. Interview at least one person whose family was directly affected by racist actions taken during World War II—Japanese-Canadian internment, concentration camps, immigration problems, loss of family members—and record their stories. Include the facts of the events as they are remembered, the emotions involved, the short- and long-term effects on the family. Write an analysis of the situation, including specific steps to create positive attitudes that would go towards preventing deep-seated racism.

Extend Your Learning Using the Internet

11. View Internet sites that contain first-hand accounts of German and Allied soldiers' experiences in World War II. Then write two radio news reports on one of the battles of the war; the reports should be from the vantage points of a Canadian and a German soldier.

12. Visit the Yad Vashem ("Everlasting Name") Internet virtual museum in Israel, and write a personal essay explaining how such Holocaust memorials help shape attitudes towards human rights.

Unit 3

A North American Nation

1945–1967

The years between 1945 and 1967 were prosperous ones for many Canadians. Technological innovations and the manufacturing power unleashed during World War II made Canada one of the richest nations in the world. People were eager to buy the latest gadgets and machines—radios, televisions, washing machines, cars, dishwashers—all new and improved and affordable to a large part of the population. New industries attracted skilled and educated workers from all over the world.

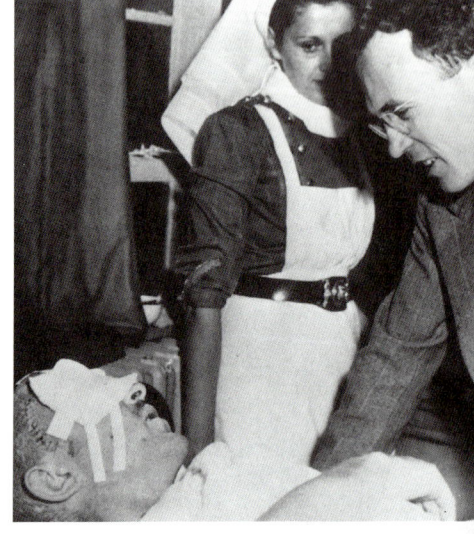

Because of this economic strength, Canada was able to play a bigger role internationally as a middle power when the United Nations was created. At the same time, Canada became more tied to the United States economically and culturally, and walked a fine line as the Cold War began.

Women and the Native peoples lobbied successfully for social change, and labour unions became stronger. Canada tested its new strength in the world, and established an international reputation as a voice of peace.

Prime Ministers	Dates of Office
William Lyon Mackenzie King	1945–1948
Louis St. Laurent	1948–1957
John Diefenbaker	1957–1963
Lester Pearson	1963–1968

1880 1890 1900 1910 1920 1930 1940

Anticipation Guide

In this unit, you will:

- learn how Canada became a major power after World War II
- examine the social culture of the 1950s and 1960s
- evaluate policies created to strengthen Canada's economy
- identify the accomplishments of prime ministers of this era
- find out about the Quiet Revolution
- summarize how new social policies evolved
- learn how the Native peoples organized political groups
- evaluate Canada's changing relationship with the US
- explain Canada's contributions to the United Nations
- explore women's changing status in Canadian society
- learn about Canada's changing relationship with Great Britain
- examine how immigrants contributed to Canada
- explore government efforts to shape a Canadian identity

8
Canada, a North American Nation

Focus Questions

Economic Conditions and Structures
How did the Canadian economy change as a result of the war? How did these developments affect Canadians' lives?

Social and Political Movements
What did the labour movement accomplish following the war? How were Canadians affected?

Canadian Identity
What culture-related councils and agencies did the government promote in this era? How did they contribute to a common Canadian identity?

Demographic Patterns
What strides did Native peoples make during this time in their efforts to be recognized politically?

After the hardships of the Depression and World War II, Canadians were anxious to get back to their dreams. Some dreams came at a price. Developing the economy, for example, required a huge investment of American capital. Many Canadians worried that Canada was becoming a "branch plant" economy, where the important decisions were made in the United States. Moreover, some parts of Canada were benefiting from the postwar economy, but others were not.

However, most Canadians were convinced that the future was bright. The labour movement made big gains after the legalization of collective bargaining in 1944. The standard of living went up, postwar Canadians had many children, and they spent a lot of money on them. Canadian culture also flourished, through the support and protection of government agencies.

Some Canadians faced difficult transitions after the war. Women, who had been given significant responsibilities in the war years, did not adapt easily to their traditional role, and they began to rethink their position in society. The Native peoples also began to organize politically, both to promote understanding of their culture and to fight stereotypes and prejudice. And in Quebec, the new postwar outlook meant throwing off the dominance of the English language—a goal that would have a profound effect on national unity.

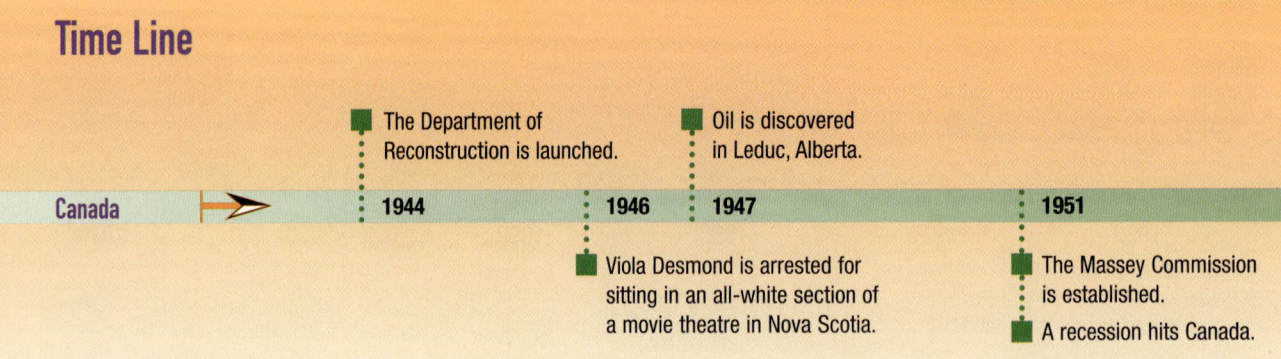

Perspectives

This 1956 *Maclean's* magazine cover illustrates the prosperous culture of the postwar boom. All the cars are big and new. What's going on in this scene? Why do you think everyone is so interested in this fender-bender? What might people be doing today? What was the painting saying to an audience in the 1950s?

- The CBC starts to compete with powerful American TV networks for Canadian viewers.

  1952

- The Trans-Canada Pipeline is completed.

  1958

- The St. Lawrence Seaway is opened by President Eisenhower and Queen Elizabeth.

  1959

- The Trans-Canada Highway opens

  1962

THE POSTWAR BOOM

In the years following World War II, Canadians believed there were no limits to growth. The signs were everywhere. In 1944, a new Department of Reconstruction began the transition from wartime manufacturing to peacetime industries under the leadership of C. D. Howe, "Minister of Everything." The energetic Howe immediately converted Canada to a free enterprise economy by minimizing government controls and encouraging investors with special tax breaks. All money was welcome, including capital from American investors.

Wartime technology spawned new industries and inventions, including electrical appliances for the home, plastics, and jet-engine airplanes. During the war, consumer spending was already on the rise, because more people had regular incomes and could buy the new cars and household gadgets that had been appearing since the 1920s. After 1945, **per capita incomes** would rise every year until the mid-1970s. Between 1945 and 1960, per capita incomes doubled. During the same period, the value of a typical family home rose from about $8000 to $16 300. Canadians thought the ride would last forever.

Figure 8–1 Only women and girls were interested in shopping for appliances, according to this McClary advertisement from the 1950s. The new postwar technology revolutionized homes, especially the kitchen.

New Resources, Big Projects

The economic boom gathered steam from new discoveries of natural resources—oil and natural gas in Alberta; iron ore in the North West Territories, Labrador and Quebec; copper in Ontario and British Columbia; zinc and nickel in Manitoba; and potash in Saskatchewan. When oil was discovered near Leduc, Alberta in 1947, it touched off a frenzy of oil and gas investment and development in the West. Howe quickly organized a Canadian-American consortium to build a pipeline that would transport the oil and gas to Ontario and Quebec markets, with a branch line to the United States. The election of another Liberal government in 1948, led by Louis St. Laurent, assured the success of the pipeline proposal. St. Laurent told Canadians that the pipeline would be the greatest transcontinental project since the building of the Canadian Pacific Railway.

American investment in Canada was definitely helping to fuel the postwar boom. Since the nineteenth century, American firms had opened **branch plants** in Canada to avoid high tariffs on imported products. Towards the end of the 1950s, **direct investment** was the main source of foreign **capital** in the Canadian economy. Americans owned more than three-quarters of Canadian mining, oil and manufacturing industries. Americans also owned a huge percentage of the

Up Close

1. List three ways that the US was a factor in Canada's postwar economic boom.

Economic Structures: Conditions and Structures

Images
C.D. Howe: Architect of Prosperity

C. D. Howe was the driving force behind the Canadian economy during World War II. Born in the United States in 1886, he was educated as an engineer at the Massachusetts Institute of Technology (MIT). He came to Canada in 1908 to teach at Dalhousie University, Halifax. During the 1930s Howe became a very successful businessman building grain elevators. Supporters persuaded him to run for a seat in the House of Commons in 1935 where his reputation landed him the job of Minister of Transport.

Howe's accomplishments in the early years were far-reaching. He was responsible for creating Trans-Canada Airlines, known today as Air Canada. Impatient with bureaucratic red tape and endless meetings, he mixed private and public monies to get things done, approaching everything in a no-nonsense, bossy manner. He was also a great promoter of Canada. Just before war broke out, Howe insisted that all the air forces in the British Empire train in Canada. He was on his way to Britain to finalize the details when his ship was torpedoed. The unsinkable Howe survived.

When World War II began, Howe moved quickly to bring the Canadian economy to war-readiness. The federal government established the War Supply Board with Howe at the helm. Almost overnight, Canadian factories were producing munitions, airplanes, ships and other war material. Unemployment was under 2 percent. Howe set out to hire the best industrial managers in the country at a salary of one dollar a year. These ambitious initiatives would transform Canada into a modern industrial nation by the end of the war.

Following the war, Howe headed the Department of Reconstruction and overhauled the economy for peacetime production. By 1948, Canada was ready for the biggest economic boom in its history. Howe's foresight and long-term planning led to the development of uranium and atomic

Figure 8–2 C. D. Howe boards one of Trans-Canada Airlines' first transcontinental flights. The airline would later become Air Canada. Howe was always ready to run one more megaproject. He is still famous for asking his critics: "What's a million?"

energy projects in Canada, as well as the St Lawrence Seaway, the Trans-Canada Highway, and the Trans-Canada Pipeline—long-discussed but never completed projects.

The Trans-Canada Pipeline would have a bittersweet ending for C. D. Howe. During the 1956 debate on the pipeline, Conservatives and labour organizations alike criticized him for accepting so much American money to fund the project. In 1957, St. Laurent's Liberals halted debate on the pipeline, effectively suppressing any criticism. Later that year, they were defeated in a general election.

What Do You Think?

1. C. D. Howe encouraged Americans to invest in Canada. In what ways might Canada be different if American capital had been refused?

2. Why do you think C. D. Howe was able to convince some of Canada's top business managers to work for only one dollar a year?

Data File
The Trans-Canada Highway, completed in 1965, is the longest national highway in the world.

electrical appliance industry that was revolutionizing North American homes. Frigidaire and General Electric (GE) were US brands, but they would soon become household names in Canada.

So much American involvement made a few Canadians nervous. In 1957, The Royal Commission on Canada's Economic Prospects asked whether Canada should be allowing the US to acquire so many of its natural resources, and to control so many of its industries. But the Commission's report on foreign ownership was largely ignored when it was released. Canadians were not yet ready to hear about the pitfalls of their newfound wealth.

The postwar boom made two transportation projects a reality: the Trans-Canada Highway and the St. Lawrence Seaway. Although Canadians had been pushing for a coast-to-coast highway since the early 1900s, the Trans-Canada Highway was only begun in 1950. When it opened in 1962, parts of it were still not paved. The 7821-kilometre highway and its accompanying network of roads made it easier to transport resources and products to markets, and gave Canadians a chance to drive from one end of the country to the other for the very first time.

The St. Lawrence Seaway was a Canadian-American project completed in 1959. This major water transportation system consisted of a system of locks and channels connecting the Great Lakes to the Atlantic Ocean. It provided access to the heart of North America for large lake freighters and ocean-going ships. The Seaway opened up the iron ore industry in northern Quebec and Labrador by providing easy transport to US and Canadian steel mills. Since construction of the Seaway meant that surrounding land had to be flooded, it also encouraged the development of hydroelectric power. This was not an altogether happy event. Whole communities had to be relocated to make room for the large reservoirs needed for the hydroelectric plants.

Figure 8–3 The Trans-Canada Highway is shown here heading through the Rocky Mountains.

The Towns Vanished For years after the St. Lawrence Seaway was completed, residents of Ingleside could still wander through their once cherished neighbourhood. Each year in the fall, when the water receded two or three metres, the ghostly remains of the old village of Aultsville would emerge from beneath the surface of the St. Lawrence River. Old cement porches and paved streets would reappear. You could even see the foundation of the old general store, where people had once sat around the pot-bellied stove and argued politics.

The Seaway destroyed, submerged, or relocated the histories of all the families who had lived along the 50-kilometre section of the St. Lawrence River between Iroquois and Cornwall. In all, 6500 people had to move. The job of relaying the news fell to Ontario Hydro, whose officials soon learned how unpopular the idea was with the locals. Some farmers angrily ordered surveyors and bulldozers off their land. One elderly woman even held up a gun to keep agents away.

Figure 8–4 This illustration shows the location of some of the locks en route from Hamilton to Montreal.

Figure 8–5 The 172-year-old Moulinette Anglican Church was saved when the seaway was built and moved to Upper Canada Village.

Canada, a North American Nation 213

Up Close

2. Outline the benefits of both the Trans-Canada Highway and the St. Lawrence Seaway. What was the downside of the construction of the Seaway?

The Canadian government could have **expropriated** the property, but it wanted to compensate owners fairly. Eventually, the homeowners gave in and took the cash. Ontario Hydro convinced many residents that they were part of a major historical event. A sign outside the community of Iroquois read: We Have to Go, but Watch Us Grow. Residents could build a new home or move their old home to one of the new planned towns. Graves of loved ones had to be dug up and moved to a new cemetery. It was painful, but better than leaving them behind.

When the relocation was completed, seven communities were **amalgamated** into the new towns of Long Sault and Ingleside and the restructured towns of Iroquois and Morrisburg. The villages of Mille Roches and Moulinette became Long Sault. Dickinson's Landing, Wales, Farran's Point, and Aultsville became the new town of Ingleside. Parts of Iroquois and Morrisburg were relocated north of the original town site. Churches, schools, and other buildings that were too large to be moved were bulldozed. The exception was the Moulinette Anglican Church, 127 years old in 1955. It is now located in Upper Canada Village.

Technology for all It seemed new technology was also changing the way everyone lived. In 1952, Thomas Eadie, president of the Bell Telephone Company of Canada, and Alphonse Ouimet, president of the Canadian Broadcasting Corporation (CBC), decided to build an all-Canadian system of microwave relay towers across the country. Now microwaves could be transmitted from coast to coast in a fraction of a second. As a result, live radio and television broadcasts became commonplace and the quality of long-distance telephone communication improved, and got cheaper. Around this time, electricity was introduced to rural Canadians, revolutionizing life on the farm. Widespread use of the self-propelled combine required fewer people for harvesting, and the new automatic milking machines let one farmer milk more cows than ever before. Farms got bigger, but there were fewer of them, especially in western Canada. Production was increasing but the labour force declined as machines replaced people in many of the production processes.

Figure 8–6 New inventions were created at a dizzying pace after the war, transforming everyone's lives. Here, Canada's first car radio-telephone.

Economic Structures: Conditions and Structures

Foundations

What is Regional Disparity?

Per Capita Income for the Provinces

	1944	1946	1950	1955	1959	1961	1962
Newfoundland			52	54	55	60	57
Prince Edward Island	53	58	56	55	62	62	63
Nova Scotia	79	86	75	73	75	77	75
New Brunswick	65	75	69	66	66	68	67
Quebec	80	82	85	85	85	88	87
Ontario	119	115	121	120	119	118	116
Manitoba	92	103	101	95	100	97	101
Saskatchewan	106	97	87	93	87	78	102
Alberta	97	108	103	103	104	107	102
British Columbia	111	114	123	122	118	116	113

Figure 8–7 Per capita income for the provinces expressed as a percentage of the Canadian average. This income includes all transfer payments from the provinces.

Regional disparity is defined as the economic inequality that exists in different parts of the country. Canada's base of economic power was firmly established in central Canada, and people living in this region always benefited from new industrial growth. They lived next door to the big centres of American industry, they had a large labour force, and they had access to capital funding.

American investment in Canada after World War II added a new twist. Now regional prosperity became dependent on the location of branch plants or raw materials. As a result, by 1950, 82 percent of all Canadian manufacturing was taking place in Ontario and Quebec. Immigration also contributed to regional disparity because immigrants provided skilled labour to industry. Since the federal government was giving 50 percent of its budget to **transfer payments** to the provinces, which included unemployment benefits, family allowances, and pensions, provinces with the biggest populations received the most money.

As Canada's economy became more industrialized, regional disparity became more acute. Many provinces lacked central Canada's advantages—proximity to the US, a large labour pool, and capital funding—and could not share in the prosperity. Saskatchewan's wheat and potash production depended on international demand, which varied a great deal from year to year. Alberta's dependence on the oil industry created a boom and bust economy. The Maritime fishing industry collapsed when the huge fishing trawlers came to the Grand Banks. Foreign trawlers equipped with freezers could catch and preserve a huge amount of cod on one trip. Many Maritimers were forced to abandon fishing and move to central Canada to find other employment.

Since Confederation, successive governments have introduced programs to reduce economic disparity, such as **equalization grants**. These grants were extended to provinces where per capita incomes were below average (see Figure 8–7). Despite these efforts, very little change has taken place over the years. The wealthier provinces often resent having to share the fruits of their production with other provinces, claiming that it slows their growth.

What Do You Think?

1. The federal government evens out economic disparity through equalization grants to the provinces. Can you think of a better way to promote more economic equality among the provinces? Describe your solution in a letter to the editor.

THE LABOUR MOVEMENT

The Canadian government finally legalized the **collective bargaining** process in 1944. This set the standard for labour-management relations following the war. Strong unions benefited both consumers and producers in the postwar boom period. It made economic sense for producers to pay fair wages to their workers because a consumer with more money could buy more goods. In this way, the labour movement helped to distribute purchasing power to many more Canadians, and contributed to the growth of a strong middle class.

During this period, the biggest unions were American-based. A powerful Canadian voice emerged with the formation of the Canadian Labour Congress in 1956. The CLC helped Canadian workers bargain in strength with huge multinational organizations. It also got involved in negotiations for fair wages and decent working conditions for its members. In 1961, it joined with the CCF (Co-operative Commonwealth Federation), a socialist political party, to form a new political party—the New Democratic Party (NDP). Over the years, the NDP has lobbied for strong social programs such as government-subsidized health insurance and daycare, and has spoken out against social inequality and discrimination in the work place.

In the late 1940s and early 1950s, there were nationwide strikes in many industries, including mining, steel, fishing, rubber, and textiles. These strikes let workers test their new collective bargaining rights. Even Eaton's had a strike—in 1951. If workers at the department store had been able to form a union, it would have been the largest union in Canada. In the end, Eaton's gave its employees wage increases and a pension plan, along with the message that getting involved with organized labour was not proper.

Up Close

3. List at least three ways in which the Canadian Labour Congress made a difference. Why was it important?

Figure 8–8 The NDP was a progressive new force in Canadian politics and supported by those left out of the new society.

Citizenship: Political Movements

Flashpoint
The Asbestos Strike of 1949

In February 1949, 2000 workers at the giant American-owned Johns-Manville asbestos plant in Asbestos, Quebec, walked off the job. They were protesting safety conditions and low wages. Asbestos is a dangerous material that can cause lung cancer. Yet the plant provided no protective equipment and paid workers a paltry 85 cents an hour.

The strike marked a turning point for a corrupt government that would hold power in Quebec for nearly 20 years. American branch plants had been lured to Quebec by Premier Maurice Duplessis, who assured US executives that he controlled the unions. Duplessis was a virtual dictator who had already refused to recognize workers' rights in other lengthy and violent strikes that had occurred in the rubber, textile, and woodworking industries two years earlier.

Immediately following the Johns-Manville strike, workers of three other asbestos producers in Quebec walked out in support—a total of 5000 workers. Duplessis immediately sent in police to break the strike. When some strikers were beaten and sent to jail, other workers responded by kidnapping and beating company officials and dynamiting company property. In early May, the company decided to break the strike for good. Police opened fire with machine guns and threw tear gas grenades.

In a direct challenge to the authority of Duplessis, the Catholic Church strongly supported the walkout. From his pulpit at Notre Dame Basilica, the Archbishop of Montreal, Monsignor Joseph Charbonneau, promised to support the strikers and their families. The bishops, along with university students from Montreal and Quebec City, collected and distributed food and supplies.

Journalists from inside and outside Quebec covered the strike in detail. Gerard Pelletier of *Le Devoir* and lawyer Pierre Trudeau were vocal in their support of the workers.

In the end, the striking workers achieved a raise of more than 10 cents an hour. But it was not a total

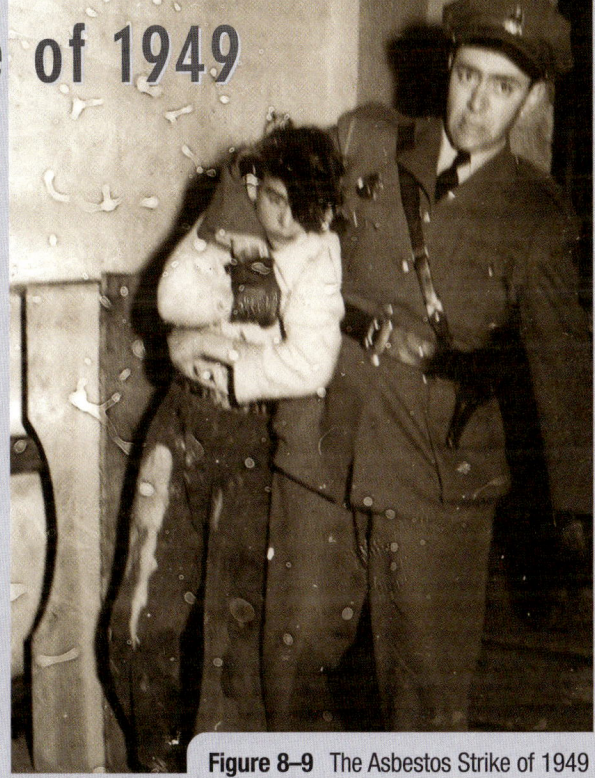

Figure 8–9 The Asbestos Strike of 1949

victory. Strikebreakers kept their jobs and at least 100 striking workers were never called back to work. Duplessis arranged to have Charbonneau dismissed.

The Asbestos strike revealed that significant changes were taking place in the social and political structure of Quebec society. A new spirit of nationalism was growing everywhere, and voices were being raised in opposition to foreign ownership. Of course, in Quebec, "foreign" meant English-Canadian as well as American. The strike helped to mark the end of almost 200 years of *la survivance* (survival after the Conquest) and the beginning of efforts to become *maîtres chez nous* (masters in our own house). The Quiet Revolution was underway.

What Do You Think?

1. Imagine you are a reporter covering the Asbestos strike. Develop questions to ask each of the following: Duplessis, Johns-Manville officials, a worker, a strikebreaker, Archbishop Charbonneau.

THEY CAME ... AND THEY SHOPPED

Data File
Pier 21 was recently restored after closing down in 1971.

For the first time in their history, many Canadians had money to spend. Almost immediately they started spending it on their children—and they had lots of them. By 1947, the Canadian population was increasing at a rate of 2 percent a year, a phenomenon that would be known as the Baby Boom.

Immigration was at its highest point since the turn of the century. In the ten years following the war, more than 1.5 million people came to Canada. They were refugees from war-torn Europe, war brides, and families fleeing from a revolution in Hungary. More than half were from the British Isles and western Europe, but immigrants from southern and eastern parts of Europe were also accepted in large numbers for the first time. Many immigrants were white-collar professionals or had skills in industry. These immigrants changed Canadian society in many ways—they brought their language, their customs, and their cultures.

Immigration to Canada by Region of Origin		
	1946-1957	1958-1967
Europe	1 467 212	944 080
United States	111 694	132 585
Asia	33 771	74 643
Central America and Caribbean	11 356	29 753
South America	11 829	20 346
Australia and Pacific	25 238	26 832
Africa	8 240	24 060
Total	1 669 340	1 252 299

Figure 8–10 This chart shows the changing pattern of immigration to Canada from 1946 to 1967.

They landed at Pier 21 Displaced persons, refugees, and immigrants who came to Canada from Europe after WW II arrived at Pier 21 in Halifax, Nova Scotia. Among those who came were Jewish men and women who had survived the Nazi concentration camps in Germany and Poland. By 1951, Pier 21 was arguably the busiest building in Canada. That year, almost 94 000 new Canadians passed through its doors. Some of the newcomers immediately boarded a train for the major cities, or for the West, where they planned to work as farmers. Others headed for the mines in northern Ontario. Sixteen-year-old Dorothy Van Helvert, a Dutch immigrant, lived in Pier 21 with her parents for six weeks because the family had no Canadian sponsors. Eventually the Van Helverts moved to St. Catharines. Van Helvert later told *The Globe and Mail* that, while not knowing English was difficult in the beginning, she "felt ... Canadian" and "didn't cling" to the old customs—a sentiment echoed by many immigrants during this time.

In 1947, the government passed the Canadian Citizenship Act. Canadians—those born in Canada as well as immigrants—were now defined as Canadian. Before this time, they had been defined as British subjects. Canadians could now also sponsor relatives living in their countries of origin to immigrate to Canada, something that had not been permitted before. With the exception of employment placement, immigrants received little help from the government when they

Up Close

4. Chart what you know about postwar immigrants, under headings such as: Who Came; Challenges; Contributions to Canadian Society.

arrived. The policy at the time was to let them adjust to Canadian society all on their own—no social assistance, no English-as-a-second-language classes, no job retraining. In addition, there was very little awareness of the needs of immigrants despite the huge influx. Immigrants themselves started creating an awareness of cultural identity, and began lobbying the government to end racial and ethnic discrimination. These initiatives eventually led to the more open immigration policy of the 1970s. You will read about this reform in more detail in Chapter 11.

Figure 8–11 Supermarkets were another symbol of the postwar prosperity.

More Homes, More Cars, More Everything

After the war, owning a home and car became a "must do." During the fifties, $60 billion worth of new Canadian housing went up, mostly on land around the cities—not just houses, but hospitals, schools, and libraries. Suburbia was the place to live, away from the noise, dirt, and congestion of downtown areas. The demand for housing was fueled by larger families and huge waves of immigration. Don Mills, located in northeast Toronto, became the first planned community in Canada in the 1950s. Within a few years there were twelve **suburban municipalities** in the area. The suburbs in turn created the need for a network of roads and freeways to connect them all—and cars.

The car was the most visible symbol of prosperity of the postwar period. Never had one product had such an impact on an economy. Never had the consumer had so much choice. Automobile manufacturers raced to produce the biggest, sleekest, fastest car with the best two-tone colour combinations, white-wall tires, rear fins, and power steering. The spin-offs of the automobile industry also fueled economic activity. Drive-in theatres, drive-in restaurants, motels, shopping centres, service stations, and suburban housing developments grew quickly.

Figure 8–12 "Fins" became popular in the 1950s—the bigger the better.

Canada, a North American Nation

Figure 8–13 Coffee cost 10 cents a cup in 1950.

The wonderful new buying power of most Canadians contributed significantly to the postwar boom. New products flooded the markets, including refrigerators, car radios, blenders, floor polishers, dishwashers, televisions, frozen foods, drip-dry shirts, power lawnmowers, and record players. Cashed-in war bonds—along with increased wages and benefits—pushed spending to new heights. Companies competed more intensely for the consumer dollar.

In the mid-1950s, there was a fierce department store battle between Eaton's and Simpson Sears. The T. Eaton Company and Robert Simpson Ltd. had been known to Canadian shoppers for years. In 1952 Simpson's became Eaton's first serious competition when it joined forces with Sears Roebuck of Chicago to create Simpson Sears. The merchandising war between these two giants found its way into nearly every home in Canada. The three most important books in most homes were the Bible and the two department store catalogues distributed twice a year.

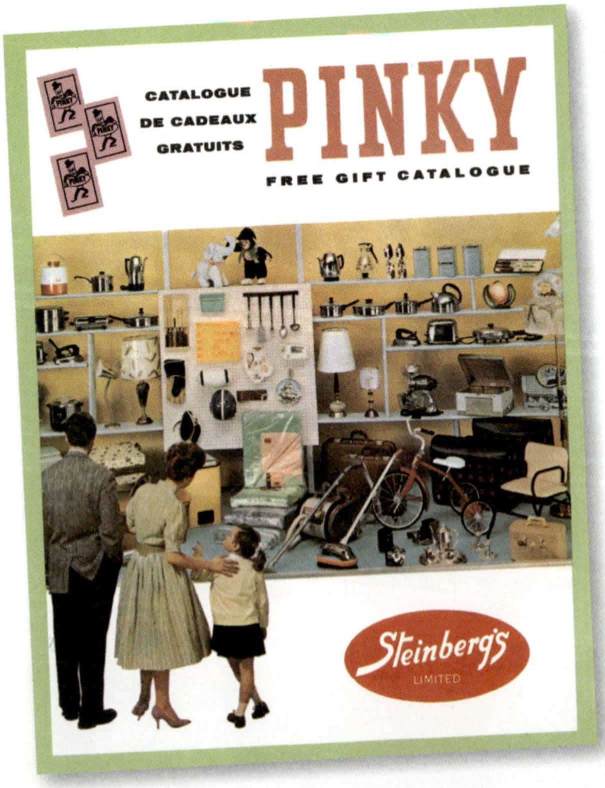

Simpson Sears revolutionized the department store market in strategic ways. Eaton's had traditionally closed at noon on Saturdays. Now Simpson Sears stayed open six days a week, introduced self-service counters, and gave its loyal customers credit cards. Because the new society used the car as the main means of transport, Simpson Sears capitalized on the trend by locating stores in the suburbs where there was lots of free parking. It also introduced huge two-level stores with escalators, making Eaton's elevators look almost old-fashioned.

Dark Clouds Ahead

The good times did not last forever. In 1957, a recession began that lasted until 1963. It occurred because the government tried to control **inflation** by restricting American investment and imports. Unemployment hit 6 percent, higher than it had been since 1940. The economy only recovered because the Canadian dollar, at 92.5 cents US, encouraged exports to the United States. Petroleum and natural gas exports to the United States also rose because

Figure 8–14 '50s shoppers gaze at the huge array of goods they could buy at this store.

American reserves were declining. By 1963, construction projects were booming again—new housing, shopping malls, especially around Toronto, new buildings for universities, such as York University in Toronto and Trent University in Peterborough, and cultural centres such as the National Arts Centre in Ottawa.

Another problem was looming, however. Industrial expansion was polluting the environment. Petroleum plants were dumping chemical wastes, paper mills were dumping poisonous mercury, and car exhaust was polluting the air. Yet no one seemed to be paying attention. In 1962, an American author, Rachel Carson, published *Silent Spring*. Carson's book shocked the world into realizing what unchecked new technology and unrestricted economic growth were doing to the planet. Her major concern was the effect of pesticides on farmers and households. American president John F. Kennedy was so impressed with the book that he set up a government panel to investigate its conclusions. In Chapter 11, you will read how environmental awareness continued to spread throughout Canada and the US in the late 1960s.

Up Close

5. Why do you think Rachel Carson's book, *Silent Spring*, "shocked the world" in 1962?

AMERICAN CULTURE IN CANADA

By and large, Canadian consumers were reaping the benefits of significant American investment in their economy. Consumption was about more than goods, however. It extended to culture—especially the American entertainment industry.

Technology played a major role in bringing more American culture into Canadian homes. When troops returned from overseas, radio was the biggest medium. People who once sat with ears glued to their radios for news of Canadian troops on the war fronts, now listened to dramas, soap operas, crime shows, situation comedies, and broadcasts of "big band" performances, nearly all of it American-produced, and containing American content and values. Since most Canadians lived along the southern edge of the country, within approximately 160 kilometres of the Canada-US border, their radios could pick up a steady stream of American programs, not to mention advertisements for US-made products.

Enter television, which would have a huge impact on popular culture and marketing during the postwar boom. Television had been introduced in the United States during the late 1940s. It gained a big following there, and caught on, more slowly, with Canadians. Still, many Canadians who lived near the border—within reception range of American stations—bought TV sets and started viewing American programming. As a result, they became familiar with American artists and performers.

Canadian television was born on September 8, 1952. As with the introduction of CBC Radio, the founding of CBC Television reflected the federal government's desire to counter American cultural influence by encouraging home-grown content. Television's popularity soared once it was introduced into

Up Close

6. Write a script for CBC's first broadcast on September 8, 1952, announcing the birth of Canadian television.

Canada, a North American Nation

Figure 8–15 Canadians loved TV, even if it wasn't always easy to get a picture in the early days.

Canada. Within two years of the launch of the CBC, Canadians had bought 1 million television sets. However, Canadians preferred to watch American shows, including "Our Miss Brooks," one of television's first situation comedies, and "The Ed Sullivan Show," a variety program.

The baby boomers were weaned on television shows such as "Davy Crockett," about an early American frontiersman. Wearing a Davy Crockett-style raccoon skin cap became a fad for Canadian youngsters. Some early CBC shows tried to imitate American television's successes, such as the Crockett show. However, when "Lord of the Wilderness," a show about the Canadian fur trader Pierre Radisson made its debut, it fizzled due to lack of interest.

PROMOTING CANADIAN CULTURAL IDENTITY

During the postwar period, Canada was undergoing a major transition in cultural affairs. Before World War II, Canadian culture was often looked upon as amateurish—something that was done on a volunteer basis. Following the war, Canadian society became more urbanized, professional, and multicultural. Pressure mounted across the country for an evaluation of the current and future prospects of Canada's culture.

In 1949, the federal government appointed Vincent Massey—Canada's governor general and an avid arts supporter—to head the Royal Commission inquiry into the state of culture in Canada. It was known as the Royal Commission on National Development in the Arts, Letters and Sciences, or the Massey-Levesque Commission. The co-chair was Henri Levesque. Released in 1951, the report was regarded by many as a great cultural landmark in Canadian history. Warning of the hazard of American cultural influence, Massey said: "We must not be blind to the very present danger of permanent dependence." The report showed that few artists could afford to live in Canada and work full-time at their craft. They either abandoned their dreams of artistic success or left Canada to live in another country.

The Massey-Levesque Commission strongly recommended increased support to preserve the unique character of Canadian broadcasting. As well, several measures were proposed to diminish American influence over Canadian cultural life. One of the report's most important recommendations was the creation of a Canada Council that would aid universities and fund creative and scientific efforts. The government was also asked to create a National Library of Canada.

In general, Canadians responded favourably to the Massey-Levesque Report. The reaction in Quebec, however, was mixed. While some Quebec thinkers

Up Close

7. Rewrite the quote by Vincent Massey in your own words. Then summarize the findings of the Massey-Levesque Commission. Do you agree or disagree with the recommendations of this report? Why or why not?

found the report encouraging, others saw it as a threat to Quebec's ability to create its own cultural programs and institutions. The culture-based disagreement helped to establish Quebec's first separatist party, L'Alliance laurentienne, which became the Parti Québécois in 1968.

Another significant event in Canadian cultural affairs during the post-war period was the Fowler Report. Robert Fowler was a Peterborough lawyer who led the Royal Commission on Broadcasting. This commission considered such problems as the financing of the Canadian broadcasting system and the role of private and public broadcasters. Fowler's report rejected the idea that the CBC should be responsible for Canadian content and that private broadcasters should be able to air whatever they wanted, including all-American programming. The report recommended cultural standards for private broadcasters, along with the creation of an independent regulatory agency to supervise broadcasting. This was the beginning of the Canadian Radio-Television Commission (CRTC), which still sets a standard for Canadian content for all broadcasters.

Home-Grown Cultural Successes

The Canada Council, formally established in 1957, would "foster and promote the study and enjoyment of, and the production of, works in the arts, humanities and social science in Canada." The Council helped to make the period from 1957 to the late 1960s one of the greatest periods in Canadian cultural history. These were the years when artists, writers, and musicians such as Jack Shadbolt, Harold Town, Farley Mowat, Glenn Gould, and many others were first receiving national and international attention.

Partly because of the support of the Canada Council, many significant cultural institutions began to flourish during the postwar boom. The Stratford Festival was born in 1951 when Tom Patterson, a local businessman, toyed with the idea of an annual drama festival. Patterson persuaded leading British director Tyrone Guthrie to become artistic director of a Shakespearean festival. The first Stratford Festival was held in 1953 with 1500 people seated in a modified circus tent. The festival went on to win international acclaim for its productions, and developed such fine Canadian actors as William Hutt, Martha Henry, Kate Reid, and Christopher Plummer.

In 1962, Brian Doherty, a lawyer and playwright, founded the Shaw Festival in Niagara-on-the-Lake, Ontario. As with the Stratford Festival, critics predicted the festival would last only a few years. Today, the Shaw Festival is still the only festival in the world dedicated to producing the plays of George Bernard Shaw.

Heritage Minute

As World War II was coming to an end, a Canadian hockey legend was born. During the 1944-45 hockey season, Maurice "Rocket" Richard of the Montreal Canadiens scored 50 goals in 50 games. It would be a triumphant record for hockey—and for Canada—for years to come. In 1952, Richard's tie-breaking goal against Boston won the Stanley Cup for Montreal. He retired in 1960, after setting even more records, and winning the adoration of fans.

Figure 8–16 Author and environmentalist Farley Mowat (right), along with Paul Watson, looks for seals in the Gulf of St. Lawrence to protect them from the seal hunt.

Historian at Work

Seeing History Through a Lens

Figure 8–17 Changing social values are explored in *Nobody Waved Goodbye*, produced by the National Film Board in 1964. Peter (Peter Kastner) finds the social values of his parents stifling. This film anticipates the social rebellion that would occur in the 1960s. The children born in the first wave of the baby boom started to question the materialism and conformity that marked the 1950s.

What can you learn about the postwar era by viewing movies made during the period or about the period?

Watching characters act out real-life events or observing the values and attitudes of the period makes history come alive. You have the opportunity to immerse yourself in the time, to understand the issues on an emotional level, and even to identify with people faced with issues and decisions not unlike your own.

If the film is historically accurate, you get to see how life was actually lived—what the clothing and furniture looked like, how people spoke to each other, how certain members of society were treated, what people wanted, and what they frowned upon.

Because movies provide an emotional connection to history, they often raise questions that are missed when reading a text.

When you're reading words in a text, you're absorbing information in a mainly intellectual way. When you're watching a movie, you're right in the middle of the action, and you're responding emotionally. The information may be the same but you're absorbing it in another setting.

What do movies actually tell you about history? Use the checklist on page 225 the next time you watch a movie to obtain information about an historical event or period.

Methods of Historical Inquiry: Research

Movie Checklist

- **Production date**

  Was the movie made during the period in which the events took place or much later? Films made during the period usually reflect the actual social values of that period. But films made at a later date, sometimes hundreds of years later, may reflect an understanding of events that is only possible by looking back on history.

- **Purpose**

  It's important to know who made the movie and why. Were the producers and directors interested in presenting an accurate and unbiased view of people and events? Or did they want to create a movie that reflected their own personal views about what happened? Does it seem that historical events were distorted to make the movie more entertaining for the audience?

- **Point of view**

  Some movies present events from the main character's perspective. If this is the case, consider whether other people might have a different view of the issues or events. For example, if the main character is from a privileged class, think about whether a person from the working class might view the issues or events differently.

- **Social make-up**

  What can you learn about Canadian society from the film? Is it inclusive of many culture groups? If not, why not? Could the film reflect local realities? Could it reflect discrimination in the entertainment industry? Which is it?

- **Values and behaviours**

  What can you learn about the values of people who lived at that time? Do the values of specific characters match the values of the society at large? Did different groups in the society hold different values? Did differences in values lead to conflicts?

- **Sets, props, and costumes**

  Historically accurate movies will show you how people dressed and furnished their homes. They may give you a good picture of specific environments, such as large cities, small towns, or the inside of factories.

- **Theme or message**

  A modern film might cater to contemporary values that weren't commonly held during the time period depicted. An historical film made during the period might provide a more accurate picture of the popular values of the time—or it might just present the values of the filmmaker.

What Do You Think?

1. Think about movies you've recently seen about life today. Did they give an accurate picture of the society in which you live? Did you identify with the values presented? Choose two movies and evaluate how well they depicted society as you view it. Consider trends, customs, language use, political and social attitudes, and clothing. Add any other markers of the time that you can think of.

2. Write a two-page outline for a movie about a typical day in your life. Try to make it reflect what your life is really like and how you see the society in which you live. When you've finished, read it over and imagine someone reading it 20 years in the future. What conclusions might they draw about you and your society? Would those conclusions be accurate? Now edit your outline to create a more accurate picture of your life and society for someone in the future.

During the early 1950s, the National Film Board changed significantly. With the National Film Act of 1950, the NFB was removed from direct government control with a mandate to "interpret Canada to Canadians and other nations." After the war, the NFB expanded its operations to include dramatic films and television productions, and won many prestigious awards, including Academy Awards for animation and short documentaries.

Canadian television also had some home-grown successes. CBC programs such as "Juliette" enjoyed high ratings. "Hockey Night in Canada," originally on radio, became an enormous television success. With his distinctive voice, play-by-play commentator Foster Hewitt broadcast the scintillating moves of such hockey legends as Maurice ("The Rocket") Richard, Frank Mahovolich, and Gordie Howe.

The Rise of Teen Culture

Canadian teenagers achieved new importance as a cultural group following the war. During World War II, young people were required to contribute to either family income or the war effort. However, after the war, teens had more leisure time and they could spend their money on themselves. Teens quickly became the target of advertisers.

What did teenagers buy? Often they followed their own new fads and fashions or openly rebelled against their parents' tastes. Taking a cue from the brooding character portrayed by American actor Marlon Brando in the 1953 movie *The Wild One*, some teenage males cultivated the "hood" look: black leather jackets with collars stuck up, leather boots, and a ducktail haircut (short on the top and long and greasy on the sides).

Figure 8–18 The prom was the highlight of the school year.

Other boys opted for the clean-cut look made popular by American singing star Pat Boone. Girls wore skirts to school, but jeans and pedal pushers were popular on the weekend. To school, girls wore sweaters (sometimes known as twin sets) or a white blouse, a pleated skirt, white bobby socks, and saddle shoes. The hairdo of choice was the pony tail.

On a typical Saturday night, 1950s teenagers would spend their time—and money—at a drive-in restaurant eating hamburgers and drinking pop. They might go to a movie at the local drive-in theatre, attend a "sock hop" dance at the high school, or cruise the town's "main drag" (main street) in their "souped-up" (rebuilt) used cars.

Around this time, dating revolved around "going steady." When teenagers went steady, they were faithful to one dating partner. A couple often spent much of their spare time together. Going steady served a strong need for security and conformity with the teenage peer group.

Up Close

8. In a chart, list the teenage slang from the 1950s mentioned in the text, and any contemporary equivalent for each term. Add other teen slang terms popular today.

Despite all the conformity, there was a strong streak of rebellion in teenage music. In fact, the 1950s gave birth to rock and roll. With their newfound purchasing power, Canadian teens bought millions of hits, recorded on 78, 45, and 33 1/3 rpm (revolutions per minute) vinyl disc records.

While the undisputed king of rock and roll during the mid- to late-1950s was American Elvis Presley, a number of Canadians made their mark on the teen music scene. Paul Anka from Ottawa, Ontario, became an international superstar with his 6-million-copy-selling-hit "Diana," a song he'd written for his babysitter.

Figure 8–19 Paul Anka composing at his home in Ottawa

WOMEN IN POSTWAR CANADA: A DIFFICULT TRANSITION

Canadian women had made vital contributions to the war effort between 1940 and 1945. Yet it was understood that women would be working only temporarily. During the war, there were incentives to go to work, such as government-sponsored day care. Ontario had 28 government-sponsored day nurseries; Quebec had five. By 1945 almost one third of all Canadian women were employed.

A Woman's Work

When the war ended, women were expected to give up their jobs to men and resume homemaking. The law required employers to reinstate veterans in their old jobs at their former rate of pay. By 1946, the rate of women's participation in the work force had dropped to Depression-era levels. Government incentives to working women, such as day care, were withdrawn. Women were encouraged to return to their "natural" role—as housewives and mothers. With the return to peace, there was renewed emphasis on family values. Some religious leaders and politicians went so far as to suggest that working women bred juvenile delinquents.

Figure 8–20 The image of the homemaker, dressed up to bake in her own kitchen, was promoted by advertisers in the 1950s. Visible minorities were rarely seen in such pictures.

Ironically, rapid economic growth in the 1950s provided more work opportunities for women. Even so, women who did work were expected to take jobs in narrowly defined "traditional" areas such as office or clerical work, sales, teaching, hospital service, and light industry. Women did suffer discrimination in these jobs. They often had to work longer hours than men, agree to unusual shifts, and put up with systemic pay and benefits discrimination.

Canada, a North American Nation

Data File

1965: % of jobs filled by women
- Doctors   7%
- Lawyers   3%
- Engineers 1%

Gains towards pay parity and equal rights with men were modest and long overdue. In 1948, women teachers in Toronto achieved pay equal to that of their male colleagues. In 1951, the Ontario government gave equal pay for equal work, but only in areas where women worked with men. Women won the right to serve on juries in Manitoba in 1952 and in New Brunswick in 1954.

Breakthroughs for Women

Despite the limitations imposed on women, there were many women who made significant breakthroughs. During the 1960s, lawyer Judy LaMarsh became a federal cabinet minister. As minister of national health and welfare, she was an architect of Canada's medicare system. Later, she served as secretary of state and implemented the Canada Pension Plan. Reformer and activist Thérèse Casgrain became the Quebec provincial leader of the CCF from 1951 to '57. In that role she helped mobilize opposition to Premier Duplessis. She founded the League for Human Rights in 1960, the Quebec branch of Voice of Women in 1961, and the Fédération des femmes du Quebec in 1966.

Figure 8–21 Kay Livingstone was the founding president of the Canadian Negro Women's Association in the 1950s.

Although social pressure discouraged many women from stepping outside their role in the home, some women were organizing. In the 1950s a number of women's groups formed the Congress of Canadian Women, which fought for women's equality. The Federated Women's Institutes of Canada established a national office in Ottawa in 1958. One of the aims of the organization was to develop informed citizens through the study of national and international issues, particularly those affecting women and children.

By the early 1960s, women began to protest pay inequity and barriers to the best jobs. In 1961, women who worked full-time and year-round earned 59 cents of every dollar earned by men in the same job categories. As late as the mid-1960s, women were underrepresented in professional and business careers. Women made up half the population and occupied fewer than 1 per cent of the top decision-making jobs in business, industry, or government.

Following a 1963 initiative by President John F. Kennedy's government to study the status of women in the United States, women's groups in Canada began to pressure the federal government to set up a royal commission. You will read more about this landmark event in the history of Canadian women in Chapter 11.

Up Close

9. Make a list of organized women's groups, showing what they fought for and why.

Citizenship and Heritage: Canadian Identity

Images
Carrie Best: Journalist and Activist

Carrie Best was part of the fourth generation of her family to be born and raised in Little Tracadie, Nova Scotia, near New Glasgow. Her mother, who ran a catering business—one of the few professions open to Black women in Nova Scotia in the early twentieth century—would tell her "The path to your destiny is hidden: you alone must find it."

In 1946, Best founded *The Clarion* because she wanted to write about the fact that, even after World War II, Nova Scotia was segregated. *The Clarion* (1946–1956), later called *The Negro Citizen*, was New Glasgow's Black weekly. It enabled Carrie Best to travel throughout Nova Scotia reporting on discrimination.

One of Best's top stories actually involved a close friend. Viola Desmond (1914–1965), a Black Nova Scotia businesswoman, operated a hairdressing salon in Halifax. She regularly toured Nova Scotia, promoting the line of cosmetics she had developed for Black women. In November 1946, when her 1940 Dodge faltered in New Glasgow, she decided to see a movie at the local Roseland Theatre while the car was being serviced. Desmond did not know that Blacks were forbidden to sit in the pit. They were forced to pay higher prices and sit in the balcony.

Even though Desmond offered to pay the difference, she was arrested for sitting in the pit, beaten, and thrown in jail overnight. She was later convicted of defrauding the province of one cent in amusement tax. After appeals sponsored by the Black community, the Nova Scotia Supreme Court upheld her conviction in March 1947. Only one judge pointed out the obvious—that the law against defrauding the province of tax money had been misused to discriminate against Desmond.

Maclean's and *Saturday Night* called for change. But perhaps the most significant media force against

Figure 8–22 Carrie Best championed the rights of Black people in Canada, and helped change laws that discriminated against Black Canadians.

racism at that time was actually Best's newspaper, *The Clarion*, which was now circulated nationally. Over many issues, Best headlined Desmond's doomed campaign for justice.

Best's editorials helped change anti-racism strategies in Canada. Many people began to realize that fighting individual cases, like Desmond's, was ineffective. Outlawing racial discrimination was the only solution.

After *The Clarion* ceased publication, Best wrote for a wider audience in the *Nova Scotia Gleaner* and the *Halifax Herald*. She was named an Officer of the Order of Canada in 1979.

What Do You Think?

1. Write the headlines for two newspapers about Viola Desmond's arrest. One should be for *The Clarion* and another should be for the New Glasgow newspaper.

Data File

Only in 1960 did the Native peoples win the right to vote in federal elections. To this day, many aboriginal peoples do not vote in Canadian elections, yet their participation in band elections is very high.

THE NATIVE PEOPLES

As you learned in Chapter 4, the goal of the Canadian government since the days of Confederation had been to assimilate all the Native peoples into Canadian society. The policy remained unchanged until about the mid-twentieth century. Even after World War II, the Canadian government continued to set policy that directly affected the Native peoples without considering the issues that were most important to them. In the 1950s, most Canadians had never heard the term "aboriginal land claim." Following World War II, the government streamlined the Indian Affairs department so it could better the conditions of reserve residents through improved education and social services. However, nothing was done to address broader issues of land and resources.

Getting Organized

The Native peoples had to overcome some major hurdles in their political organization. Before 1951, the Indian Act did not permit them to form political organizations or lobby groups. That year, a section of the Indian Act prohibiting the use of band funds to advance land claims was also dropped. Other important developments in the political mobilization of Native peoples resulted from a series of parliamentary inquiries that took place between 1946 and 1961. These inquiries spurred the formation of Native organizations. From 1959 to 1961, Native leaders appeared before Parliament in joint Senate-House of Commons hearings that were co-chaired by MP Noel Dorion and Senator James Gladstone.

At the 1959 to 1961 hearings, Native leaders made presentations on issues that were to become long-standing, such as Oka, in central Canada, and the rights of the Nisga'a in British Columbia. Conservative John Diefenbaker led the government of the day. Gladstone used his influence with the Conservatives, who had appointed him to the Senate, to lobby for changes recommended during the hearings. Largely as a result of Gladstone's efforts, the government drafted legislation creating a three-member Indian Claims Commission in 1962. Diefenbaker's government was eventually defeated, but in 1963 the new Liberal government of Lester Pearson brought forward similar legislation. Land claims were finally on the agenda.

Forming effective Native lobbying groups took time, and there were failures and successes. Soon after World War II, the First Nations attempted to form a national lobby group. The North American Indian Brotherhood was established in the late 1940s, but it was hindered by lack of national support and disbanded in the early 1950s.

Figure 8–23 James Gladstone was from the Blackfoot Nation. In 1958 he became Canada's first Native senator. He devoted most of his life to the betterment of Native peoples, fighting for treaty rights, better education, and the participation of Native peoples in administration of their own affairs.

In 1961, the National Indian Council was founded as an umbrella group to address the concerns of all the Native peoples, including the Métis. Its stated purpose was to promote "unity among all Indian people." The formation of the Council is a significant milestone in Native peoples' political history, because from this point on, First Nations of Canada has always had a national lobby group to represent them in Ottawa.

> **Up Close**
>
> 10. List the years and events relevant to Native peoples from pages 230 and 231. Use your list to create a time line.

Disturbing Stories about Residential Schools

During this period of political progress, most Native children still lived in residential schools. As you learned in Chapter 4, residential schools were part of an early government goal of Native assimilation. By the 1960s, some of the abuses at these schools had come to light. Children were often disciplined harshly and excessively—they were even punished for speaking their language of origin.

Stories of former residential school students also reveal how these schools failed in their purpose—to assimilate Native children. At the first Residential School Principals' Conference in 1965, "successful" former students were asked by the department of Indian affairs to offer their views on the schools. Two former students summarized the experience as "an insult to human dignity." Similarly, many educational and social welfare authorities who evaluated the schools' effectiveness produced damning reports. For example, a 1967 report by George Caldwell of the Canadian Welfare Council on nine Saskatchewan residential schools concluded that the education provided by the institutions not only left students ill-prepared for life and work in Canadian society, but also stranded between two cultures.

Changing Images

In the 1960s, the Native peoples started gaining the support and understanding of non-Native Canadian society. Traditionally, the entertainment industry had stereotyped the Native peoples as bad people. This stereotype began to break down as Native leaders became more well known. Dan George, for example, was the chief of a Squamish band in British Columbia from 1951 to 1963. He was a longshoreman, logger, writer, and is perhaps best remembered as a film actor. In film and television, such as CBC's 1961 series "Cariboo Country," Dan George portrayed a wise aboriginal elder. He also acted in the 1967 production *The Ecstasy of Rita Joe*, by George Ryga, a tragic story of Native characters facing the indifference of White society.

Figure 8–24 Chief Dan George helped improve the popular image of Native peoples through his film roles.

CONCLUSION

Between 1945 and 1967, most Canadians were grateful not to be at war, and were convinced that the society they had created was quite successful. But the new emphasis on individual rights had sown the seeds for many changes. In reality, not everyone was benefiting from the new prosperity and opportunities in Canada. Canadians who were old, sick, poor, or unemployed did not prosper—neither did some visible minorities. The Native peoples had just barely begun to organize politically and knew that much work lay ahead. They, together with Canadian women, began to insist on a better deal.

But what did a better deal consist of? Many of the policy decisions that were made during this period led into uncharted waters. You will read more about these developments in Unit 4.

CHAPTER ACTIVITIES

Check Your Understanding

1. The postwar prosperity was welcomed by most people, but not all. In chart form, list the benefits of the postwar boom and the concerns that emerged from each of those benefits.

Development	Benefit	Concern
American investment		
St. Lawrence Seaway		
Self-propelled combines		
Labour movement		
Industrial expansion		

2. List the main reasons for the prosperity of the 1950s and the main effects.

3. Chart a comparison of the efforts and successes of the women's movement and those of the Native peoples in the 1950s.

Develop Your Thinking

4. The introduction of television gave Canadians the opportunity to develop their own culture and to be exposed to US culture. Which effect was more dominant? Why? Use evidence from the text to support your answer.

5. Is there is a direct connection between the prosperity of the 1950s and the youth rebellion that exploded in the 1960s? Write both sides of a debate on this question.

6. Why was the labour movement so successful in the 1950s? Scan the text for the high and low points of the labour movement. Is there any connection between this success and economic prosperity of the period? Explain.

■ Express Yourself

7. Many new Canadians found it challenging to adjust to Canadian society in the 1950s. Nonetheless, many managed to cope and even thrive. Put yourself in the position of a German, Jewish, Italian, or Dutch immigrant and write two poems about the immigrant experience—one depicting the immigrant's first arrival to Pier 21. This poem could reflect emotions such as hope, fear, and a sense of isolation. Write the second poem as though it were several years later. Try to reflect the success or failure of the person's ability to adapt to Canadian society.

8. Write a radio play that reflects values of Canadian teenagers during the 1950s.

9. Create a poster or flyer advertising the inaugural season of either the Stratford Festival or the Shaw Festival.

10. Write a two-page memoir outlining the experience of a Native child in a residential school. Refer to Chapter 4 for additional ideas.

■ Apply Your Learning

11. The suburb of Don Mills was to be a planned community that reflected the prosperity of the 1950s. Investigate the proposal, planning, and implementation of this massive project. Write a report that evaluates the success of the project. Your report should state whether or not the community proposal achieved its desired goals.

12. Develop three questions to use to interview someone whose family came to Canada in the 1950s. Your questions should try to discover the obstacles they encountered, or any forms of discrimination they experienced. Try to ensure that your questions encourage more than a one-word response.

Extend Your Learning Using the Internet

13. Review the Foundations feature on regional disparity in this chapter. List the factors that contributed to regional disparity in Canadian per capita income during the 1940s, 1950s, and 1960s. Then, using current Statistics Canada data, compare past and present per capita income in Canadian regions. Hold a forum on the likely causes for the similarities and differences between the two sets of statistics.

14. During the decades following World War II, a healthy Canadian economy and US production caused a growth in Canadians' consumption of manufactured goods. How did US advertising help create this market? What effect did such advertising have on Canadian culture? Using Internet archival sources, prepare an illustrated report.

9
Politics in Canada

Focus Questions

Changing Role of Government
What were the steps and stages in the development of the "welfare state"?

Individual Canadians and Canadian Identity
What were Prime Minister John Diefenbaker's personal and political strengths and weaknesses?

Social and Political Movements
What role did the Quiet Revolution in Quebec play in the formation of separatist groups and parties?

Canadian Identity
How did Canada get a new flag? How does the flag contribute to a sense of Canadian unity?

In 1949, Newfoundland entered Confederation, and Canada's motto *A Mari Usque Ad Mare*— "From Sea to Sea"—finally became a reality. But the Canada that Newfoundland was joining was already becoming more decentralized. Although the Liberal Party dominated federal politics, many provinces were beginning to elect Conservative governments. The increasing number of social programs, such as universal health care, also encouraged decentralization. Under the BNA Act, the provinces were expected to operate these programs. To do the job properly, the provinces needed money from Ottawa, resulting in much provincial negotiation.

In 1958, the Conservatives swept to power under the leadership of John Diefenbaker. He became Canada's first Prairie-born prime minister. But it was a short-lived victory. The Liberals were back in power by 1963. By now, a new generation of Quebecers who had come of age were talking about the injustices to francophones. Some even talked seriously about separation from Canada. The Royal Commission in Bilingualism and Biculturalism, established by the Pearson government, warned that the alienation of French Canadians was the most serious crisis in Canada's history. Despite the national fanfare around a new flag, chosen in 1964, and a highly successful World's Fair in Montreal in 1967, the discontent simply would not go away.

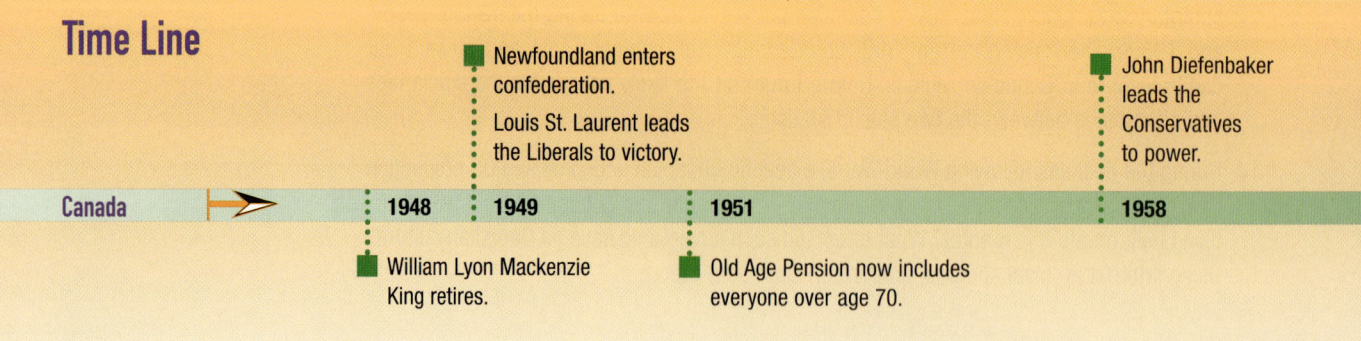

Time Line

Canada

- 1948: William Lyon Mackenzie King retires.
- 1949: Newfoundland enters confederation. Louis St. Laurent leads the Liberals to victory.
- 1951: Old Age Pension now includes everyone over age 70.
- 1958: John Diefenbaker leads the Conservatives to power.

Perspectives

John Diefenbaker looks on as Lester Pearson attempts to uncoil the cord of a translation earpiece. Neither leader spoke fluent French, and both failed to bring Quebec further into federal decision-making. Diefenbaker went so far as to criticize politicians before him for "coddling" French Canada. How might you react as a French Canadian upon seeing this photo? How might this image be symbolic for the political changes that occurred in the 1950s and 1960s?

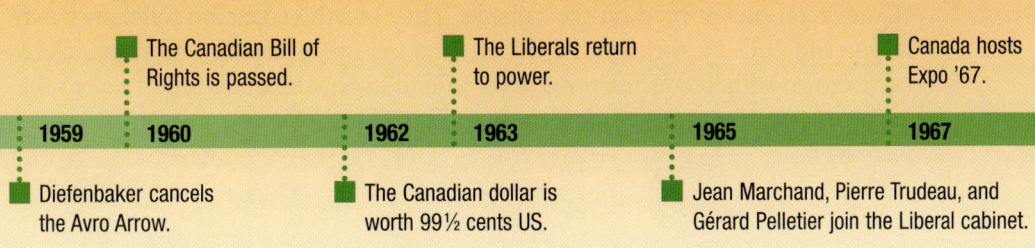

- 1959 — Diefenbaker cancels the Avro Arrow.
- 1960 — The Canadian Bill of Rights is passed.
- 1962 — The Canadian dollar is worth 99½ cents US.
- 1963 — The Liberals return to power.
- 1965 — Jean Marchand, Pierre Trudeau, and Gérard Pelletier join the Liberal cabinet.
- 1967 — Canada hosts Expo '67.

NEWFOUNDLAND ENTERS CONFEDERATION

On a map today, Newfoundland looks like a natural part of Canada. In fact, it was the last province to join Confederation. This final chapter of the Confederation story was not written until 82 years after Confederation passed in 1867.

Background To Union

From the earliest days, Canadians argued about whether Newfoundland should join Canada. In 1864, John A. Macdonald wanted Newfoundland in Confederation because of its strategic location: Newfoundland could help defend the colony of Canada against the United States. The American Civil War was coming to an end, and the northern states had defeated the southern states. During the war, Britain had supported the South. Would the victorious North retaliate against Britain by attacking British colonies? If so, the closest British colony was Canada. Obviously, a stronger union in Canada would be a good defence against such a threat.

In 1864, Newfoundland sent two delegates to the Quebec Conference where Confederation was finally achieved. However, these delegates—and Prime Minister Hoyes of Newfoundland—were unable to convince Newfoundlanders that union was in their best interests. The island's economy was based on fishing and sealing. Eighty percent of the population earned a living from the sea, and from trade with the West Indies and Britain. The people of Newfoundland were so convinced that their destiny lay with the Atlantic Ocean and Britain that they petitioned the British Government to protect the island's separateness and its role as a strategic outpost for Britain. They argued that Newfoundland had nothing in common with Upper or Lower Canada.

Figure 9–1 Throughout its history, Newfoundland's economy has depended on the sea. Newfoundland both resisted and welcomed Confederation based on its proximity to the Atlantic Ocean.

In the colony's 1869 election, the anti-Confederation forces won a major victory. In St. John's, merchants and fishers celebrated by making a large coffin with "Confederation" printed on the outside. They put the coffin on a horse-drawn wagon and pulled it through the city. A band followed, playing a death march. A large crowd gathered as the procession wound its way through the streets to the harbourfront, where an open grave lay waiting. The coffin was solemnly lowered into the hole.

Confederation was dead in Newfoundland. Or so it seemed.

There were later attempts to revive Confederation. Newfoundland has never been a wealthy province, but in 1885 it was in an especially severe economic slump. Export prices for salted cod had fallen drastically. The Newfoundland fishing industry was facing increased competition from European countries such as Norway, and from US fishers who came to its coastal waters. A very poor Newfoundland legislature approached Canada and asked for union. Prime Minister Mackenzie Bowell was not enthusiastic. If he gave special concessions to Newfoundland, the other provinces would expect similar deals. Confederation remained quietly in its grave for another few years.

The experience of the Great Depression and World War II encouraged Newfoundland to join Canada. During the Depression years (1929 to 1939), poverty struck Newfoundland once again, especially in the smaller coastal communities. World prices for fish and forest products had declined, eroding the region's economic base. Then during World War II, heavy Canadian and American defence spending at the military bases of Gander, Argentia, and Stephenville brought much-needed money to the island. Immediately following the war, officials met in St. John's to decide Newfoundland's future. That summer, a delegation travelled to Ottawa to broach the subject of joining Confederation yet again. But in Newfoundland itself, most people were wary of the idea.

A Mari Usque Ad Mare

The idea of Confederation had to be sold to the people of Newfoundland. Joey Smallwood, labour leader and broadcaster, made it his personal mission to promote union. In a seaplane equipped with a loudspeaker, he flew to remote fishing communities, "blasting" his case for union. Smallwood was either loved or despised for his campaign. There were many Newfoundlanders who thought he was betraying the British colony, but not a single person on the island could ignore the unfolding events.

The people of Newfoundland spoke in two referenda held in 1948. In the first referendum, the Confederation option lost. The second referendum barely put Confederation over the top—52 percent voted for union. In the end, it was Newfoundland's economic hardships that seemed to sway the vote. Newfoundland incomes were only one-third of the Canadian average, and belonging to Canada would provide much-needed assistance from Ottawa. Canada also welcomed Newfoundland, partly to counter a strong American presence that had developed there during the war.

On April 1, 1949, Newfoundland became Canada's tenth province. Canada really did stretch "from sea to sea." Now the challenge would be to hold it together.

Up Close

1. Show Newfoundland and Canada as two characters having a conversation about Newfoundland joining Confederation. Use speech balloons to show their dialogue.

Figure 9–2 Joey Smallwood takes the Confederation message to the people.

THE LIBERALS CONTROL CANADIAN POLITICS

Mackenzie King was still Canada's prime minister as Newfoundland took its final steps towards Confederation. When he retired in 1948, the Liberals continued to dominate Canadian politics. Especially after World War II, the Liberals seized and kept power by adapting to the needs of a rapidly changing Canadian society.

Home from the war in Europe, Canadians expected good paying jobs along with steady economic growth, and the Liberal government was well qualified to take on this task. Louis St. Laurent, an important corporate lawyer from Quebec, succeeded King as prime minister. His right-hand man was the go-getter C. D. Howe. As you read in Chapter 8, St. Laurent's government kept the wartime pace going. They developed Canada's natural resources to ensure strong industrial growth. Iron ore, oil and gas, transportation, and communications became major resources and industries in the early postwar years. As a result, during the 1950s, the federal government enjoyed strong centralized power.

Canadians in the early 1950s felt secure. They were more interested in their own well-being and livelihood, and less concerned about growing American control over the Canadian economy. Nationwide, the demand for social programs was not as vocal as it would become in the 1960s. By introducing some social programs, the Liberals would be able to reduce the influence of opposition parties on the Left, such as the Cooperative Commonwealth Federation (CCF) Party, which had also been campaigning for such programs in the West. The Liberals were fortunate to hold power during an economic boom, most of which was generated by their own policies. Like most governments in power during good economic times, the Liberals were popular, confident, and strong—perhaps too confident.

Data File

From 1900 to 1967, the Liberal Party held federal power for 47 of the 67 years.

Figure 9–3 Which aspects of C D Howe's personality are evident in this cartoon?

Cracks In The Armour

By the mid-1950s, cracks began to show in the Liberal armour. The Liberals had won huge majorities in 1949 and 1953. Sometimes governments with large majorities stop listening to the people who elected them. Many Canadians were now concerned about the increasing American dominance of the Canadian economy. The Liberals failed to notice this changing public mood.

The Trans-Canada Pipeline debate of 1956 highlighted this over-confidence. In parliament, the Liberals used "closure" to end the heated debate about the Trans-Canada Pipeline. In other words, they held enough seats—and had enough votes—to shut down opposing arguments when they needed to. But by using such power, they were misreading the changed mood of

Citizenship and Heritage: Individual Canadians

Images
The Legacy of Mackenzie King

Figure 9–4 Mackenzie King looks debonair at the Imperial Conference in Britain in 1926.

Canadians were silent as they filed past Mackenzie King's coffin on Parliament Hill in July 1950. King did not inspire affection easily, but he was one of Canada's shrewdest leaders. For three decades, Canadians respected him and depended on him. They knew he had helped win the war and had kept the country together, difficult tasks achieved with great skill.

In 1997, historians polled by *Maclean's* named Mackenzie King Canada's greatest prime minister. They were impressed by his political skills, his insistence on Canada's independence, his hand in creating Canada's social safety net, and his brilliant direction of Canada's war effort in World War II. One summed him up by saying, "King had a profound sense of his country's strengths and weaknesses."

King fulfilled Macdonald's dream of a nation from sea to sea when he joined Newfoundland to Canada. Like Macdonald, King knew the ruling party must also hold Quebec. In 1917, King stood by Sir Wilfrid Laurier in the fight against conscription, earning the loyalty of Quebecers. With that support, he won a great upset at the Liberal leadership convention in 1919.

When Quebec voted no to conscription in 1942, King changed the law so that the government would only use it to conscript soldiers for overseas service if necessary. When reinforcements were desperately needed in Europe in 1944, King did an about-face and agreed to conscription. Quoting one of Laurier's speeches on Canadian unity, King persuaded Quebec backbenchers to support him. Civil war could have erupted, but King managed to keep Canada strong and united.

Canada is an independent country with its own constitution today thanks to King. In Chapter 6, you read how King worked to achieve Canada's independence from Britain during the Chanak crisis. King had decided that Canada could think for itself. At the next two imperial conferences King ensured that Canada's autonomy became a reality.

King also envisioned a social welfare system that would help every Canadian in need. In 1927, his government enacted the first old age pension. By 1940, he had also pushed unemployment insurance into law. Public housing soon followed. King and his government levelled the playing field, so that everyone could share the country's wealth.

A country as diverse as Canada needs a strong central government and a pragmatist as prime minister. No one knew that better than Mackenzie King. No one accomplished more in his years in power.

What Do You Think?

1. Were the historians polled by *Maclean's* right or wrong when they named King as Canada's greatest prime minister? Give reasons for your answer.

2. List some of King's major accomplishments. What factors contributed to his longevity in office?

Data File

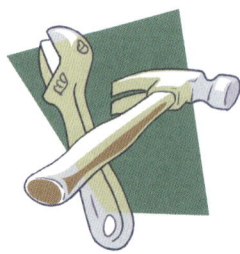

As industrialization drew more Canadians to cities for jobs, work accidents increased. The Workmen's Compensation Act of Ontario, passed in 1914, was the first modern social security program.

the Canadian people. Conservative governments were elected in Nova Scotia in 1956 and New Brunswick in 1952, and a Social Credit government was elected in British Columbia in 1952. Alberta had voted Social Credit since 1935. The nationwide Liberal stronghold was crumbling.

By the early 1960s, provincial involvement in federal politics was increasing. The provinces were talking about social programs, and the British North America Act clearly stated that such programs were to be run by the provinces. This meant that the provinces could exert power as never before. In addition, the death of Quebec premier Maurice Duplessis in 1959 liberated Quebec consciousness in a new way. Quebec now began a lengthy quest for its rightful place inside or outside Confederation. Political power was quickly becoming **decentralized**.

THE EMERGENCE OF THE WELFARE STATE

At the beginning of the century, Canadians believed that every person was responsible for his or her lot in life. People who had the misfortune to be old, handicapped, or poor were looked after—sometimes grudgingly—by the Church or by private agencies. Canadians' expectations of their government changed dramatically after the Depression and World War II. They saw that money could not be found to put people to work but could easily be found to finance the war. Depression-era programs to relieve poverty, such as military-style camps for the unemployed, struck many people as demeaning. During and after World War II, there was mounting pressure for the government to bring social policies out of the nineteenth century. People started to believe that society had a duty to the individual, and that people were not always to blame for their misfortunes. Business leaders were also in favour of government intervention because it could help stabilize the economy.

As with all revolutions, social security was many years in the making. As far back as 1919, Mackenzie King had promised industrial reform and social welfare. With the exception of a modest old age pension that was introduced in 1927 for those who could prove need, there was little progress. The Saskatchewan-based Cooperative Commonwealth Federation (CCF) was the first party in Canada to create a plan to make social security a reality. One of the goals of their *Regina Manifesto* of 1933 was the establishment of the welfare state, including a universal pension, and health and welfare insurance.

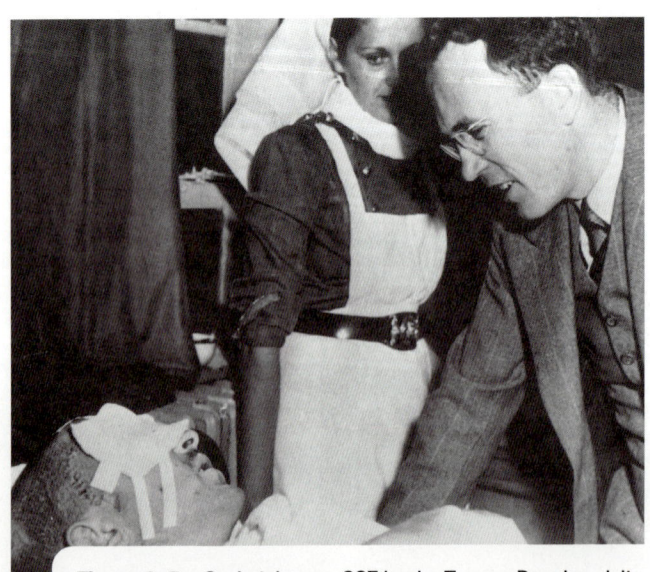

Figure 9–5 Saskatchewan CCF leader Tommy Douglas visits a Korean War vet. Canada went to war in Korea in 1950.

Political Structures: Changing Role of Government

Foundations

Beginnings of Medicare

Figure 9–6 Could an overburdened health care system result in a "two-tiered" approach?

Medicare is a system of medical health care that is administered and subsidized by the government. Since 1968, every citizen in Canada has had a right to health care. The social security this provides helps Canada maintain a more equitable standard of living. Better health also means improved education, as well as better housing and working conditons for everyone.

Medicare was first championed by the CCF in Saskatchewan. The idea gradually gained support until it was enacted in Ottawa.

In 1944, the CCF was elected in Saskatchewan, with T. C. (Tommy) Douglas as its leader. He was ready to fight for medicare. When the Medicare Act was passed in 1962, doctors in Saskatchewan went on strike for three weeks, arguing that the new program would turn them into civil servants. Tommy Douglas did not budge. Today he is known as "the father of medicare."

In 1964, the Hall Commission recommended that medical services be universal, so that health benefits would be available to everyone equally, and that quality care would not be based on the ability to pay. The commission also suggested that the cost of medicare be split between the federal and provincial governments.

To put these proposals into action, Judy LaMarsh, the Liberal Health and Welfare Minister, chaired a committee that suggested a Health Resources Fund of $500 million be established, and that medicare should be based on four basic principles:

- The plan would cover all medical treatments and a wide range of services.
- Every man, woman, and child would have equal access to medical care.
- People moving from one province to another would not lose their health benefits, and there would be no interruption of services.
- The plan would be administered by provincial governments.

Lester Pearson promised medicare during the 1963 election, but it wasn't until 1968—after all of the provinces had agreed on how to share the costs—that the National Medicare Plan was finally enacted.

Today, many of Canada's social welfare programs are under attack by governments that say they are too costly. There is even talk of moving back from a policy of equal and universal health care to a "two-tiered" system under which different people would qualify for different treatment. If Tommy Douglas were still around, he would not budge. But Canada without him may have to.

What Do You Think?

1. In Canada, everyone has a health card. Ask older family members if they remember what it was like before health cards and before medicare. Did anyone in your family not get the medical attention they needed? What differences can you list between then and now?

2. If you had been on Judy LaMarsh's committee, would you have added any principles, or changed the ones that were proposed? Suggest one or two you would add or change.

3. Newspapers today are full of attacks on Canada's "ailing" health care system. Is medicare really "ailing"? If so, why? What would you like to see happen?

In 1940, King's Liberals introduced unemployment insurance, Canada's first national social insurance program. Not long after, Leonard Marsh, a professor of economics at McGill University, recommended that Canada adopt a social security system to cover every Canadian. He said such a system should include health and income insurance, as well as old age pensions. He estimated that it would cost $900 million, and that the government should contribute $500 million, an amount that horrified business leaders. He also recommended that Canada use some of its new prosperity to invest in social insurance. This would allow people to keep buying goods and maintain economic stability if they lost their jobs.

The Marsh Report

The Marsh Report was the blueprint for the social system we have today, but Mackenzie King implemented just one of his recommendations—family allowances. He did so because he was afraid that the CCF was getting too much support across the country. King's move won the Liberals five more years in power. It also dealt a blow to the Opposition, especially the CCF, which had been calling for such programs for over a decade. Most of the other recommendations of the Marsh Report were eventually implemented over the next two decades.

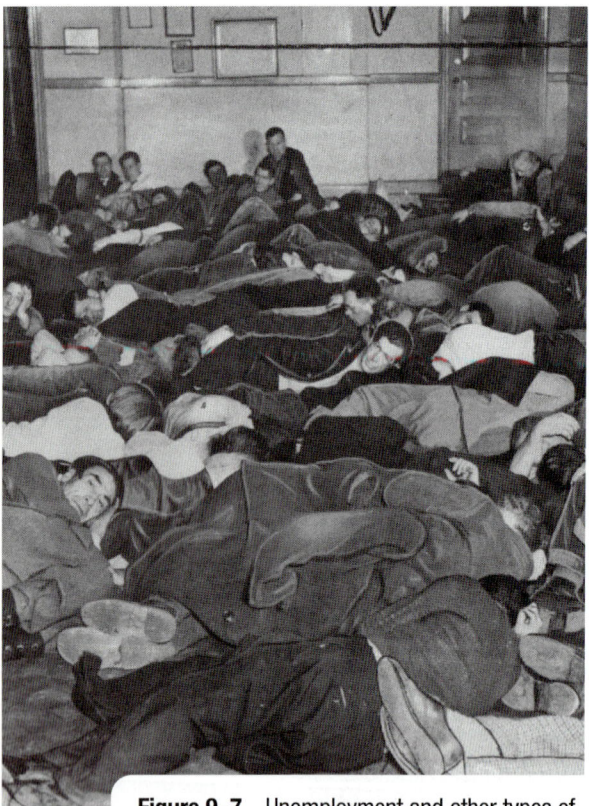

Figure 9–7 Unemployment and other types of social insurance were eagerly awaited by those who had fallen on hard times.

Additions to the welfare state were haphazard, and were more often the result of politics, not principles. Politicians quickly realized they could win votes with the promise of more social services. In 1951, the Old Age Pension was expanded to include all citizens over 70 who had been residents of Canada for ten years or more. In 1970, the age qualification dropped to 65. In addition, a new guaranteed income supplement helped retirees who had no other source of income. In 1965, the Canada Pension Plan was passed. Disability allowances and survivors' benefits were added, along with a supplement to the old age pension. One year later, the Canada Assistance Plan folded many of the existing programs into one comprehensive program. It included mothers' allowances, pensions for the blind and disabled, child welfare, and community development services.

All these new social programs required federal-provincial cooperation because the British North America Act had left control of most social security legislation in the hands of the provinces. The problem was, the programs were too expensive for the provinces to pay for on their own. The federal and provincial governments negotiated with each other to figure out how to share the responsibilities as well as the costs of many of the new social programs.

Access to universal health care was a hard-fought victory and took many years. When John Diefenbaker and the Conservatives came to power in 1958, they knew that Canadians were interested in government-sponsored health care insurance—free health care for everyone, rich or poor. Diefenbaker set up a Royal Commission to investigate the possibility of a national medicare program. The Conservatives were already out of office by the time the Commission made its recommendations: medical care should not depend on one's ability to pay, and everyone should have access to free medical services. These principles would become the cornerstone of Canada's health care system.

Up Close

2. Make a list of all the social benefits the governments (provincial and federal) provide that you can think of. Then reread the section on The Marsh Report and add any you have left out.

THE DIEFENBAKER YEARS

"My fellow Canadians," John Diefenbaker would shout as he began one of his campaign speeches, portraying himself as a man of the people. A forceful prairie presence, "Dief" had a legendary memory for names and faces. He was elected leader of the Conservative Party in 1956, and won the 1958 federal election by a huge majority. Television cameras adored Diefenbaker's wavy hair and big eyebrows. Cartoonists had a field day with his jowls and protruding teeth. As an opposition leader, his rhetoric was stinging and overbearing, especially during the pipeline debate of 1956. As a leader, he brought a vibrant, folksy brand of politics to Ottawa and the nation.

Diefenbaker, as his German name suggests, was the first prime minister of neither French nor English background. Born into an Ontario farming family, he moved with his parents to Saskatchewan as a child. Always attracted to public speaking, Diefenbaker entered law school and became a top criminal lawyer before running as a Conservative in the riding of Prince Albert. Once in power, Diefenbaker revolutionized parliament by bringing in a Chinese Member, a

Up Close

3. Create a character sketch of John Diefenbaker, including everything you know about him. Using your character sketch, write a character description of him in paragraph form.

Figure 9–8 Diefenbaker's fiery speeches won him elections, but he was brought down by his inconsistent decision-making.

Politics in Canada 243

Ukrainian Minister of Labour, and the first woman Cabinet minister, Ellen Fairclough. The Conservatives, for the first time since the days of Sir John A. Macdonald, had solid support from Quebec, with 61 percent of the francophone vote in 1958.

Diefenbaker's Accomplishments

A lifelong champion of human rights, Diefenbaker passed the Canadian Bill of Rights into law in 1960. This federal legislation helped to blaze the trail towards the 1982 Canadian Charter of Rights and Freedoms. The Bill of Rights
- recognized an individual's right to life, liberty, personal security, and enjoyment of property
- protected freedom of religion, speech, assembly and association, and the press
- guaranteed legal rights, such as the right to a lawyer and to a fair trial.

Diefenbaker also proclaimed a vision of Canada that included the Far North. He called this "the dream of opening Canada to its polar reaches." During his time in office, the government explored the Arctic region for oil and mineral deposits. However, despite the flow of cash, northern development under Diefenbaker resulted in just two new mines—a gold mine and a tungsten mine.

Diefenbaker's government poured money into the infrastructure of the North, building new roads, airports, and harbours in the Yukon and the Northwest Territories. The purpose of these projects was not necessarily to make life easier for northern communities, but to give the rest of Canada better access to the resources of the North.

Canadians expected Diefenbaker and his government to immediately take action against the economic recession of the late 1950s as well as rising unemployment. As you read in Chapter 8, a recession began in 1957, in part because the government tried to control inflation by restricting American investments and imports. Exports were also important to the economy and Canada lost its early postwar advantage as Europe and the US began offering stiff competition. Then interest rates were raised, which discouraged investment and spending. But Diefenbaker could not fix these woes. In addition, his habit of putting off decisions would soon make voters mistrustful. His other habit, of making decisions all by himself, soon began to annoy his colleagues in Cabinet.

In 1959, Diefenbaker made a strategic error by cancelling the Avro Arrow, a supersonic fighter plane that was the pride of Canadian industry and ingenuity. Diefenbaker was under pressure from the United

Figure 9–9 Nellie Cournoyea, Northwest Territories premier from 1991–1995, inherited the housing built by the Diefenbaker government. She charged that the program hadn't kept up with the needs of the northern aboriginal peoples.

States to acquire Bomarc missiles as part of the joint American-Canadian defence plan. As you will read in Chapter 10, the cancellation of the Arrow put 14 000 people out of work and caused some of Canada's top scientists and engineers to move to the United States. This decision contributed to Diefenbaker's declining popularity. As he continued to hold power, Diefenbaker became more egocentric, refusing to delegate responsibility or authority to his Cabinet.

Two years after the Conservatives' landslide victory, they were behind the Liberals in the polls. French Canadians were losing confidence in "the Chief" because no French Canadian had received a senior Cabinet post. The new NDP and Social Credit parties were gaining support, and the Liberals were regaining some of their former strength.

During the election campaign of May 1962, the International Monetary Fund forced Canada to reduce the value of its dollar to 92.5 cents American. This happened because investors lost confidence in the government and exchanged Canadian dollars for foreign currencies, which caused a **run** on the dollar. If the government had not **pegged** the dollar, it might have gone into freefall. As a result, the Canadian dollar jokingly became known as the "Diefenbuck." This foreign exchange crisis came at a bad time. In the June election that followed, the Conservatives managed to win only a minority government. The NDP and Social Credit parties made significant gains.

In the fall of 1962, the Cuban Missile Crisis flared, threatening nuclear war. When Russian missiles were discovered on the island of Cuba, a North American defence plan went on full alert. Canada had signed a defence agreement with the United States, so American President John F. Kennedy expected Canada to stand by, and possibly arm its missiles. But Diefenbaker hesitated, insisting that Canada had not been included in the decision-making process. Kennedy was outraged. Diefenbaker's stubborn refusal to meet Canada's commitments to NATO and NORAD eventually divided the Conservative Party. You will read more about this incident in Chapter 10.

In April 1963, a vote of non-confidence defeated the Diefenbaker minority Government. Canadians were going to the polls for the fourth time in six years.

Up Close

4. Using your own words, explain the meaning of the following, and how they are related to Diefenbaker: Avro Arrow, egocentric, Diefenbuck.

THE LIBERALS RETURN

When the Liberals returned to power in 1963 under the leadership of Lester Pearson, they were faced with the pressing question of Quebec. The death of Quebec premier Maurice Duplessis in 1959 had unleashed a huge amount of pent-up frustration in Quebec. Duplessis' grip on the province had begun to loosen after the Asbestos strike of 1949 revealed corruption in his government (see Chapter 8). His government was so corrupt that even the suppliers of paint for white lines on the highways paid bribes to him. However, he still wielded enough power to delay many needed reforms, especially in education and social services.

Most rural Quebecers were poor, and even in the cities, jobs were scarce. Average wages were well below those in other provinces. A younger generation of professors at the University of Montreal, led by Marcel Brunet, believed that modern French-Canadian society needed a strong industrial base. The notion of the rural Catholic society, so loved by Duplessis, seemed absurd in the mid-twentieth century. Besides, Quebec society was already changing. Between 1941 and 1961 Quebec's urban population doubled because of immigration. For the first time, a significant part of the population was neither French nor English.

In 1950, Pierre Trudeau, then a young lawyer, and Gérard Pelletier, a journalist, launched *Cité Libre*, a liberal magazine committed to individual freedom and democratic principles. The magazine attacked the Duplessis regime's corruption and noted that political and social power depended on economic power. While Trudeau and Pelletier believed in the federal system, other intellectuals were beginning to say that Quebec society must be distinctly French Canadian. They believed the provincial government was critical to the survival of the French in Quebec.

The Quiet Revolution

The 1960 election of a Liberal provincial government in Quebec, led by Jean Lesage, launched the Quiet Revolution. This was a program that modernized Quebec. Two major reforms symbolized this period. The 1963 Parent Report on Education recommended that only the province control education. The traditional educational system administered by the Church could not meet the needs of the baby boom generation. Separate

Figure 9–10 Lester Pearson flanked by Wayne (right) and Shuster

Figure 9–11 From birth to death, Quebec life is dominated by the Church in this whimsical painting. This idea changed dramatically following World War II.

Catholic and Protestant systems continued to operate but under the authority of a new Ministry of Education. The Parent Report succeeded in creating a modern system of education accessible to everyone.

Responsibility for welfare and health also shifted from the church to the state, tripling the provincial budget. At the same time the Lesage government nationalized the hydroelectric industry, removing smaller, private electrical companies from foreign hands. Power was vital to Quebec's future, and Hydro Quebec became a symbol of Quebec's economic liberation in the 1960s with the slogan *maîtres chez nous* ("masters in our own house"). Increasingly, the working language in Quebec was French. The reforms of the Quiet Revolution allowed Quebecers to see the extent of discrimination against French Canadians. A new middle class and new elites felt confident enough to challenge Quebec's position in Confederation. By 1961 three separatist groups had already formed. How would Ottawa handle Quebec's moves? Lesage was under no illusion that Ottawa would understand Quebec's needs.

The Federal Response

When the Quiet Revolution began, neither the federal government nor English-Canadians took much notice. Diefenbaker had always dismissed the rumblings from Quebec as the work of a few extremists. In March 1963, the first terrorist bomb exploded, the work of the FLQ (Front de Liberation du Quebéc), one of the first radical separatist groups. (You will read more about the FLQ in Chapter 12.) Following the bombing, the Liberals under Pearson immediately recognized they had a serious potential problem. The stirring in Quebec could not be ignored.

The Royal Commission on Bilingualism and Biculturalism

The Liberal government's next step was to establish the Royal Commission on Bilingualism and Biculturalism. The commission was made up of an equal number of French- and English-speaking members, as well as two members from other ethnic groups. Its mandate was to examine the state of French-English relations in Canada and to make recommendations. For four years the commission travelled across the country, listening to Canadians from all walks of life. Everywhere the commission went, it found a strong provincialism and regional self-interest. In Quebec the most outspoken people belonged to the radical separatist groups, the RIN (Rassemblement pour l'Independence Nationale) and the FLQ.

Because these findings were so grave, the commission issued an interim report in 1965. It characterized the conflict as a battle of two majorities, one from Canada and one from Quebec. The commission concluded that Canada was going through the most serious crisis in its history. It warned English Canadians to provide better guarantees for minorities and to stop acting as though Canada were a one-language country run by—and for—the English. It asked English Canadians to accept the French language and culture as part of Canada's culture and way of life, and to end prejudice and discrimination against the French. It

Up Close

5. What are your thoughts on why the modernization of Quebec was called "The Quiet Revolution"? Look for hints as you continue to read these sections.

Up Close

6. Summarize the findings of the Royal Commission on Bilingualism and Biculturalism in point form.

asked French Canadians to overcome their self-serving minority complex and accept that Canada's problems were their problems too.

The final report was postponed further until the end of Centennial year. Pearson did not want it to jeopardize the positive mood around Canada's birthday. The final report recommended that Canada should be a bilingual country, that English and French should be the official languages of parliament and the federal courts, and that government services should be provided in both languages anywhere in Canada. These recommendations were carried out in the Official Languages Act of 1969, introduced by the Trudeau government. The main beneficiaries of the Bi and Bi Report were francophones outside Quebec. Because the report had not dealt with constitutional questions, it could not alter Quebec's movement toward independence.

Up Close

7. As you read these two pages, note events from 1965 through 1968 that led to the creation of a legitimate separatist party.

Three Wise Men in Ottawa

By 1965, Quebec nationalism was growing and Quebecers who still believed in Canadian federalism were insisting that the Liberal government take more decisive action. Pearson realized he had to strengthen Quebec representation in the cabinet. He started courting Jean Marchand, whose influence as a labour leader in Quebec was legendary. Marchand agreed to join Pearson's cabinet only if Pierre Trudeau and Gérard Pelletier could come with him. Opposition Leader Diefenbaker dubbed them the "three wise men."

Marchand had some difficulty convincing the Liberals to include Trudeau and Pelletier because of their past anti-Liberal writings. In particular, the Quebec caucus of the Liberal Party questioned Trudeau's loyalty to the Liberal Party

Figure 9–12 Jean Marchand (left), Pierre Trudeau (centre) and Gérard Pelletier (right) got Quebec's demands heard in Ottawa, and not a moment too soon.

given his public praise of the New Democrats. But Marchand insisted that it was all or nothing, and seats were found for the trio in the 1965 federal election. These men gave the Pearson government a new credibility in Quebec—the Liberals went on to win 56 seats in Quebec in 1965. Trudeau's arrival in Ottawa led to his election as prime minister only three years later, and to a federal policy of resistance to Quebec's desire for autonomy.

While the federal government hoped that its initiatives would placate Quebec, these measures were not accepted without controversy. Instead of promoting unity, they sometimes opened old wounds in French-English relations in Canada. The western provinces resented the attention Quebec received, and the Maritimes resented the money it got. Quebecers themselves were divided on what they wanted, but the separatist movement continued to grow.

The Birth of Sovereignty Association

The name of René Lévesque is synonymous with the separatist movement in Quebec. Lévesque had worked as a war correspondent during World War II for the American Office of War Information rather than be associated with British officials. In the 1950s, he became the most popular TV personality in Quebec because of his ability to communicate complex issues and concepts to an audience. He entered politics after a strike at Radio Canada and became part of the Lesage Liberal Government in 1960. As Natural Resources Minister, Lévesque decided to nationalize Quebec's privately owned hydroelectric companies.

The Liberals were defeated in Quebec in 1966. A year later, Lévesque abandoned the Liberal Party and founded the Mouvement Souraineté-association (MSA). This was the first mainstream movement for separatism. A movement that had once been tainted with violence now had a new legitimacy. Lévesque galvanized separatist sentiment in Quebecers who had deplored the violence that radical separatist groups represented. These groups now disbanded, and some members joined the MSA. In 1968, it changed its name to the Parti Québécois, a party based on the platform of separatism.

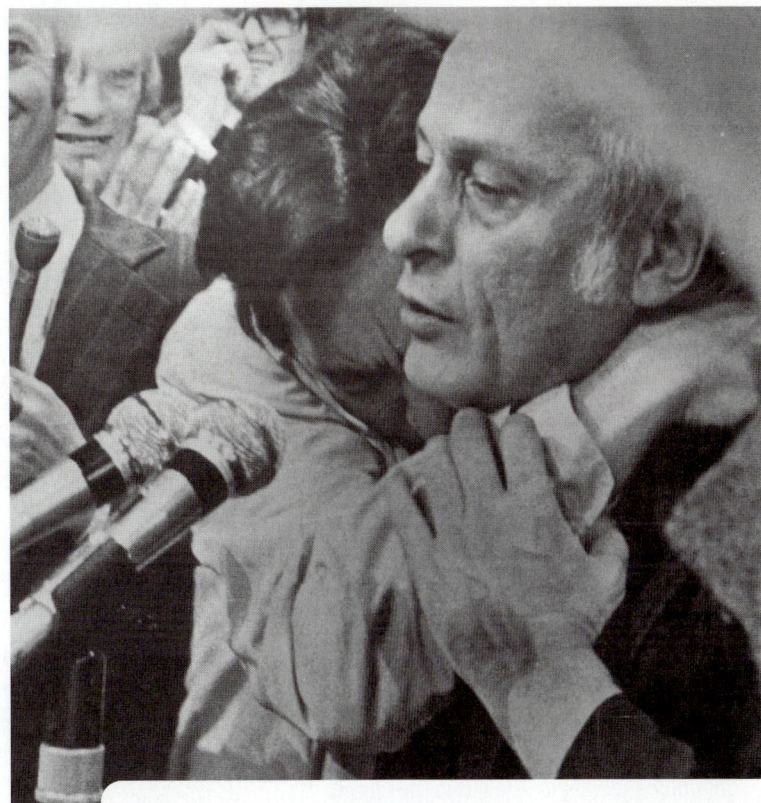

Figure 9–13 Camille Laurin cries on the shoulder of René Lévesque after a defeat of the Parti Québécois in 1973. After a few setbacks in the early seventies, the PQ would gain popular support and success in the 1976 provincial election.

CANADA ON STAGE

Canadians had been talking about having a flag of their own since Confederation in 1867. In 1892, the British Admiralty had allowed Canadian ships to fly the British flag, the Red Ensign, with the Canadian coat of arms added to its outer edge.

Prime Minister Mackenzie King ordered the Red Ensign to be flown from the top of the Parliament Buildings in 1924 as the unofficial Canadian flag. Then in 1925, King set up a parliamentary committee to design a new Canadian flag, but soon cancelled the committee because of strong opposition. He tried again in 1945, with the same result. Because they had fought under the British flag (old "Union Jack") in both world wars, many Canadians saw it as an emotional symbol of freedom. It wasn't until the 1962 and 1963 election campaigns that the possibility of a new Canadian flag was seriously considered again.

By 1964, Prime Minister Pearson was determined to carry through with this election promise. Because the Quiet Revolution was underway in Quebec, Pearson hoped that a new flag would foster Canadian unity. He was in favour of a flag with three red maple leaves at the centre of a white background, with blue bars at each end signifying "from sea to sea." He chose to unveil the new flag at an annual meeting of the Royal Canadian Legion—perhaps the toughest audience available.

When Pearson unfurled the new flag, one veteran shouted "You're selling Canada to the peasoupers"—a swipe at French Canadians. Because the old flag was British, many English Canadians felt that Pearson, by insisting on a new flag, was favouring French Canada too much. Many French Canadians saw the debate as a continuation of the old struggle between English Canadian nationalists and British imperialists. They did not want any remnant of the Union Jack on the flag, because they were eager to define themselves as separate from the English.

There was also some question about how important the debate actually was to Quebecers. Very few French Canadians were directly involved. Pierre Trudeau said, "Quebec doesn't give a tinker's damn about the new flag; it's a matter of complete indifference." But emotions were running high for other Canadians. At a Liberal Caucus meeting about the flag, J. R. Tucker, a member of parliament for Trinity-Conception, Newfoundland, got up in tears and recited 16 stanzas of a poem on the glories of the Union Jack. Premier Joey Smallwood of Newfoundland demanded that the Union Jack not be excluded. Jack Pickersgill, also from Newfoundland, supported Smallwood's demand by threatening to resign if some compromise could not be reached.

In the end, it was agreed that the Union Jack would be flown on particular occasions to symbolize Canada's membership in the British Commonwealth. John Diefenbaker was

Up Close

8. As you read about the ongoing flag debate, identify reasons why there was such an emotional response from many Canadians.

Heritage Minute

The House of Commons committee that chose the final flag design held 41 meetings and looked at 2000 designs—many submitted by Canadians from all walks of life. Committee members listened to the advice of experts and argued among themselves before they made their final choice.

Historical Inquiry: Investigating Historical Topics

Historian at Work

Developing a Thesis

A thesis is an author's opinion or conclusion on a specific topic. When writing an essay, it is important to decide what your thesis will be. Here are some steps that will help you to develop a thesis.

1. If you have not been given a specific essay topic, start by choosing an issue, event, person, or time period in which you are interested.
2. Brainstorm everything you already know about your topic. You might organize this information using the questions Who? What? When? Where? Why? and How? Then write down any questions you have. Is your topic associated with a specific controversy, an historical debate, or a question of interest? If so, investigate these areas in more detail.
3. Through research, find the answers to at least some of your questions, and find out other information about the topic. Jot down new questions for future reference.

Developing a Thesis Statement

4. Look over the information you have gathered and the questions you have written. Decide on the purpose of your essay. This is your thesis statement. It helps to "frame" your approach. Your thesis statement will appear in the introductory paragraph of your essay. It lets readers know the essay's subject (topic or main idea) and purpose (to inform readers or to persuade them to accept your viewpoint).

   For example, in the issue of Newfoundland joining Confederation, you could:
   - **State an opinion** Without Joey Smallwood, who promoted Confederation, it is unlikely that Newfoundland would have joined Canada.
   - **State a conclusion** In the long run, joining Canada assisted Newfoundland's economy.

Figure 9–14 Research can help you shape your thesis statement.

- **Answer an historical question or debate** Newfoundland joined Confederation because it had fallen on hard economic times, not because it cared about Canadian nationalism.

Make sure your thesis statement conveys your point of view. Don't just state the general topic. Be specific—avoid vague language. For example, don't say, "Confederation was good for the people of Newfoundland." Instead say, "By joining Confederation, Newfoundland received much-needed economic assistance."

As you write and do additional research, use your thesis statement to keep your efforts focused. Omit any information that is not directly related to your thesis.

Activity

1. Choose a topic from Chapter 9. Develop a thesis statement on that topic using the steps outlined above.

adamant in his opposition to a "two-flag" policy. He quipped to Jack Pickersgill: " ... two-flag Jack, one for show and one for Joe."

It was a long hot summer in 1964. Members of Parliament cancelled their summer vacations in order to continue the debate. Pearson was determined to see it through. Finally, in December 1964, the debate came to a dramatic end. On December 9, Leon Balcer, a Conservative Member of Parliament, invited the government to bring the debate to an end. The debate was transferred to an all-party committee of fifteen that would decide on a final design for the new flag. A vote was called. The vote was to take place at 1:00 p.m. on December 15. The Conservatives continued their delaying tactics. By 2:00 a.m., the vote was completed with 163 in favour and 78 against.

Canada had a new flag.

Canada's Party: Expo 67

Canadians began their centennial birthday year with mixed emotions. They enthusiastically anticipated the celebration, but were also worried about the future. Would Canada be able to stay unified for another 100 years? That year, Canada hosted a World's Fair, called Expo 67, in Montreal, Quebec.

The Fair attracted 50 million people from over sixty countries around the world. The normally reserved Canada staged a year-long, chest-pounding demonstration of pride. Even the new Canadian flag received universal acceptance as a proud symbol. The acclaimed Canadian film, *Labyrinth*, shown at Expo 67, seemed to suggest that Canada's future would be a journey through a labyrinth as well. Certainly Canada was facing many difficult challenges in 1967, so it was the perfect time for a party.

Figure 9–15 A protester holds one of the flag designs that didn't win.

Data File

The theme of Expo 67 was "Man and His World." Though sexist by today's standards, these words suggested an optimistic, forward-looking view in the late 1960s.

Figure 9–16 In 1967, Canada hosted a World's Fair, called Expo 67, in Montreal. Shown here, a futuristic apartment complex, called "Habitat," on display at the fair.

Communities: French-English Relations

Flashpoint

Charles de Gaulle's Visit to Quebec

By the time Expo 67 opened, many Canadians were hoping they could forget their differences and celebrate their unity. Many heads of state and dignitaries from around the world came to the fair, including Queen Elizabeth II.

Quebec also invited President Charles de Gaulle of France. He accepted, without consulting the Canadian government, as protocol required. Prime Minister Pearson was not pleased.

De Gaulle continued to violate protocol by going to Quebec first before visiting Ottawa. He flew to St. Pierre and Miquelon (island colonies of France off the coast of Newfoundland). From there he sailed on a French naval vessel to Wolfe's Cove below Quebec City. By snubbing Canada, de Gaulle seemed to be saying that he recognized Quebec as a quasi-sovereign state.

The motorcade that took de Gaulle from Quebec City to Montreal was a well-orchestrated show. Members of the separatist party Rassemblement pour l'independance Nationale (RIN) set up signs and cheering sections at strategic points along the way. Some of the placards that de Gaulle saw read "Québec Libre."

Later, at Montreal City Hall, a huge crowd booed during the singing of "O Canada." De Gaulle seized the moment and walked out onto the small balcony to make a short speech. To wild cheers, he said, "Vive Montréal, vive le Québec, vive le Québec libre, vive le Canada-Français, et vive la France." The last two pronouncements were drowned out by the deafening response from the crowd.

This was to become a defining moment in Canadian history. Many Canadians were stunned. Even René Lévesque could not believe his ears. Speculation mounted. Were de Gaulle's remarks intended as a rallying cry for Quebec independence, or had they been blurted out in the heat of the moment?

Figure 9–17 French premier Charles de Gaulle is trailed by reporters and security agents as he motors through Montreal.

The event certainly placed the federal government in an awkward diplomatic position. De Gaulle was scheduled to visit Ottawa before returning to France. How could the government deal with this situation without dividing the country even more? The situation was resolved by de Gaulle himself who cancelled the visit.

Mayor Jean Drapeau of Montreal calmed the situation somewhat by saying, "If we serve our country better as Canadians of French origin, so we serve France better and our humanity better … "

Daniel Johnson, the Union Nationale premier of Quebec, was more blunt. As de Gaulle was flying home, he quipped: "Well, de Gaulle is now up in the air, and so are we."

What Do You Think?

1. You are a journalist covering the visit of Charles de Gaulle to Canada in 1967. Record two or three snippets of conversations you overhear at the event. Remember that the event is taking place in Quebec. Which snippet makes the best quote? Why?

CONCLUSION

By the early 1960s, social justice had become an important issue in Canada. Concern about social justice had led to the Canadian Bill of Rights, which addressed discrimination, and the Royal Commission on Bilingualism and Biculturalism, which addressed the rights of francophones. As the role of government expanded to include social injustices and inequalities, provincial governments grew more powerful. Social issues were their responsibility under the BNA Act. This division of powers resulted in much greater decentralization, and created the possibility of new conflicts between the federal government and provincial governments in later years. You will learn more about these conflicts in Chapter 13.

The scene outside Canada presented a different, more dangerous, picture—a balance of nuclear terror between the western world and the eastern (communist) bloc. Canada's allies expected it to play a role in western defence strategies. But many Canadians opposed the idea of increasing the world's nuclear weapons arsenal, fearing that an arms buildup would make a nuclear war even more likely.

CHAPTER ACTIVITIES

Check Your Understanding

1. Joining Confederation was a controversial issue for Newfoundlanders. Briefly outline the arguments for and against joining. Why do you think the vote was so close?

2. Create a time line for the emergence of the welfare state in Canada. Begin in 1919 and end in 1965.

3. a) Name and explain three ways Prime Minister John Diefenbaker attempted to reflect the new realities of Canadian society.

    b) What factors contributed to the rapid decline in Diefenbaker's popularity?

Develop Your Thinking

4. Giving more power to the provinces has long been an issue for Canada. What possible danger does decentralization have for Canadian Confederation? What are the characteristics of Canada that make this decentralization an important issue? Explain your answer in a paragraph.

5. "The social welfare system in Canada developed as much out of political necessity as it did for genuine concern for the population." Support this statement by referring to specific events described in the text.

6. Why did the flag debate cause such furor in English Canada, but relatively little debate in French Canada?

▪ Express Yourself

7. As the creative minds behind a new marketing company in the 1950s, create a political television ad for the election of 1958. Choose either the Liberal or Conservative party as your client. Remember that this is a new way of advertising and that you want to prove its effectiveness to your client.

8. Look again at the painting of Quebec society that appears on page 246. Create a collage that incorporates images reflecting the new values and concerns of Quebec society.

9. Flags are symbolic representations of the values and realities of a country. Create a list of characteristics for an ideal new country. Now design a flag using symbols and colours that represent those values.

▪ Apply Your Learning

10. Examine the state of the Canadian social welfare system today. Prepare a report that explains to what degree the programs have changed. Discuss programs that have been expanded and those that have been scaled back. What are the reasons for these changes?

Extend Your Learning Using the Internet

11. Work with a partner to create a time line that shows changes in federal and provincial governments from 1945 to 1967. Use provincial Internet sites to collect your data. Then, look for patterns and trends in your time line. Draw inferences about political party changes that resulted from the conflicting agendas.

12. Using Internet sources, investigate how the rest of Canada dealt with issues in Quebec during the time of the Quiet Revolution. Draft and develop a thesis statement that presents your viewpoint on this historical question, and write an essay based on your thesis.

10
Canada and the World

Focus Questions

Canada's Participation in War, Peace, and Security
What roles did Canada play during the Cold War? Why did it adopt these roles?

Canada's International Status and Foreign Policy
How did Canada use its new status after WW II to help develop alliances and agreements for mutual defence and the promotion of peace?

External Forces Shaping Canada's Policies
What changes to its defence policy did Canada have to make as a result of the nuclear arms build-up?

Scientific and Technological Impact
How did the Cold War shape the space race, nuclear technology, and satellite communications in Canada?

In the aftermath of World War II, Canada realized that it could use its contribution to the war effort to advantage by playing a much larger role on the international stage. The world was changing quickly. A Cold War had developed between the two new superpowers—the United States and the Soviet Union. While it was better than outright conflict, it was still marked by animosity and mistrust. The new atomic weapons made the hostility all the more deadly. Canadian diplomats acted most effectively in international conflicts when they were not acting for a superpower, but for the resolution of the problem at hand.

When the United Nations (UN) was created in 1945, Canada was one of the founders. Canada also helped to found the North Atlantic Treaty Organization (NATO) and entered defence agreements with the Americans for protection against the Soviet Union. These agreements made Canada more dependent on the US. By the time the Vietnam War was raging in the 1960s, Canada had little influence on US policy. However, Canada did become well-known for sending peacekeepers around the world as part of its commitment to the UN.

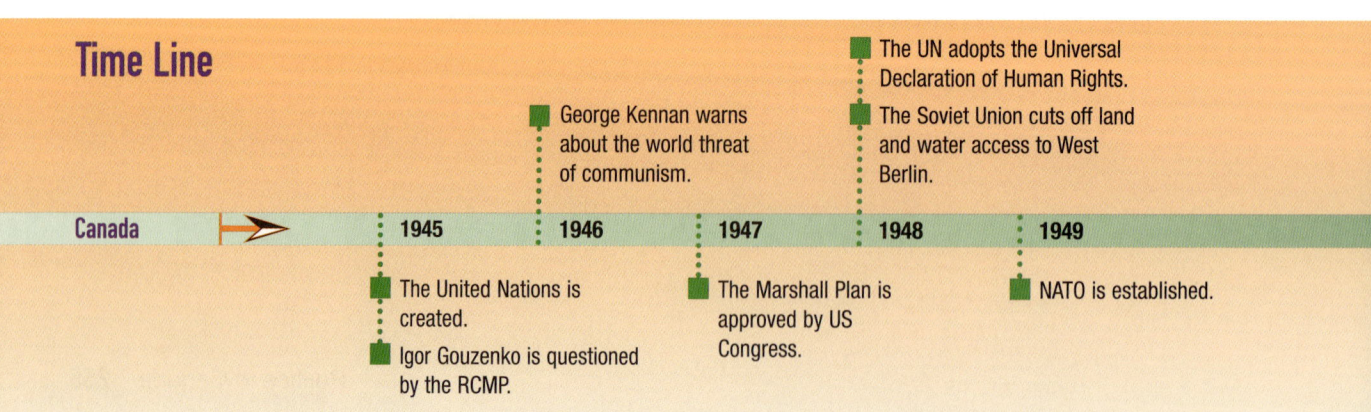

Time Line — Canada

- **1945**: The United Nations is created. Igor Gouzenko is questioned by the RCMP.
- **1946**: George Kennan warns about the world threat of communism.
- **1947**: The Marshall Plan is approved by US Congress.
- **1948**: The UN adopts the Universal Declaration of Human Rights. The Soviet Union cuts off land and water access to West Berlin.
- **1949**: NATO is established.

Perspectives

In 1964, Corporal Ernest Black of Sackville, New Brunswick, was a member of a UN peacekeeping mission in Cyprus, an island country in the Mediterranean. Canada participated in many such missions after WW II. In Cyprus, peacekeepers patrolled the line between Greeks and Turks, who were fighting for control of the region. Canadian forces proved to be highly popular with the Greek Cypriots, who were the larger group on the island. How does the picture convey this sentiment? What seems to be going on between Black and the other man?

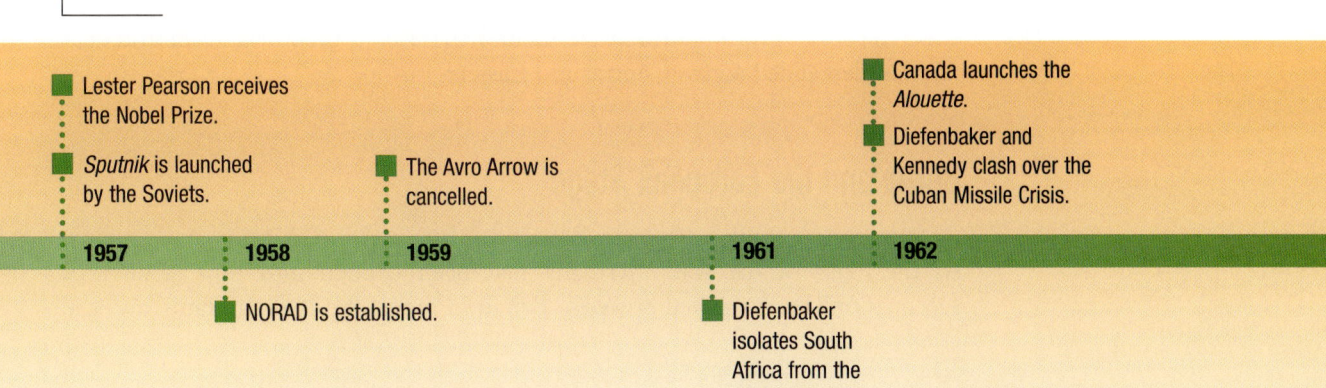

- Lester Pearson receives the Nobel Prize.
- *Sputnik* is launched by the Soviets.
- The Avro Arrow is cancelled.
- Canada launches the *Alouette*.
- Diefenbaker and Kennedy clash over the Cuban Missile Crisis.

1957 | 1958 | 1959 | 1961 | 1962

- NORAD is established.
- Diefenbaker isolates South Africa from the Commonwealth.

A WORLD DIVIDED

The Allied nations took away an important lesson from World War II: aggression between nations should be nipped in the bud.

When World War II ended, Soviet troops remained in many eastern European countries. An American foreign policy expert, George Kennan, noticed what appeared to be a rising threat. In 1946, he wrote that the Soviets wanted to replace western democracy with world communism. North Americans and people living in western Europe paid close attention to Kennan's views.

In 1948, the Soviets halted the democracy movement in Czechoslovakia. In 1953, they put down revolts against communist rule in East Germany. In 1956, they stopped the Hungarian revolution. Next, they installed communist governments in these countries to create a **buffer zone** between the Soviet Union and western European countries. These Moscow-controlled countries were called **satellites** of the Soviet Union. As well, there was a rise in the number of communist parties in many western European countries. In 1948, Canada's new prime minister, Louis St. Laurent, was one of the western leaders who feared Soviet expansion.

After World War II, the United States emerged as the richest and most powerful nation in the world. It soon became clear that the United States was the only world power capable of standing up to the Soviets. While the Soviet Union was setting up and supporting communist governments, the United States was helping to overthrow pro-communist governments. The postwar world became divided, or **polarized**, into countries aligned with or sympathetic to one of the two **superpowers**—the United States or the Soviet Union.

Soon after World War II, the Soviet Union tightened its control over eastern Europe, restricting travel into and out of the Soviet **bloc**. The geographical and political boundary between Soviet-controlled countries in eastern Europe and western Europe became known as the **Iron Curtain.** The term "Iron Curtain" came from a speech made by British leader Sir Winston Churchill in 1946, in which he said, "From Stettin in the Baltic to Trieste in the Adriatic, an iron curtain has descended across Central and Eastern Europe ... ."

Berlin and the European Stage

The mounting tension between East and West escalated in postwar Germany. At the close of the war, Germany had been divided into four "Zones of Occupation" by the Allied powers—Britain, France, the United States, and the

Figure 10–1 Europe after World War II

Up Close

1. List major events that increased polarization from the close of World War II through 1961. Use your list to create a time line.

Soviet Union. The German city of Berlin was situated about 150 kilometres inside the Soviet Zone.

In June 1948, the Soviets cut off all land and water access to West Berlin. They assumed that the tactic would starve West Berlin and eventually bring it under communist control. However, the United States maintained a round-the-clock airlift for ten months, bringing needed supplies to approximately 2 million West Berliners and thwarting the Soviet siege. At one point during the airlift, US supply planes were taking off every three minutes.

By May 1949, Soviet leader Joseph Stalin had curtailed the blockade. But it was only the first of many East-West confrontations during the tense postwar period known as "the Cold War." The Berlin Blockade set the tone for increased hostility between the USSR and the West. It also established that the Soviets did intend to dominate Europe.

In late 1961, the Soviets faced another crisis in East Germany. Berlin was still an open city, so skilled workers in East Germany started crossing into West Berlin. This happened so often that the East German economy was in danger of collapse. In August 1961, the Soviets responded to the problem by erecting the Berlin Wall. This action sealed off West Berlin from East Germans. Until it was demolished in 1989–1990, the Berlin Wall served as a barrier, and a symbol of East-West division.

Figure 10–2 The building of the Berlin wall

Countering Communism: The Marshall Plan

As a superpower and world leader, the United States had to fight the growth of communism in Europe. A major initiative in this area was the **Marshall Plan**, named after the American Secretary of State, George Marshall.

In June 1947, Marshall announced a massive program of direct aid to European nations. While the United States and its supporters wanted to help European nations recover and rebuild from the devastation of World War II, the US was also thinking of itself. Marshall thought that poor nations were the most likely to turn to communism. Thus, the United States wanted the European nations to develop strong economies as soon as possible. The 1948 Soviet invasion of Czechoslovakia ensured quick Congress approval for the foreign aid package the same year.

Canada joined the Marshall Plan and shipped $706 million worth of food, equipment, and raw materials to Europe. Between 1948 and 1953, Canada, the

> **Up Close**
>
> 2. Write a letter from a Canadian diplomat to a federal cabinet minister, recommending that Canada join the Marshall Plan. Refer to what you have learned so far in this chapter to support your arguments.

United States, and other nations that contributed to the recovery program sent $12.5 billion in economic aid to western Europe. This initiative produced an amazing economic recovery.

The Marshall plan was an example of a new American strategy in foreign policy, which became known as the Truman Doctrine, after American president Harry S. Truman. The Truman Doctrine called for **containment**, which means containing, or halting, the spread of communism in Europe and around the world.

THE COLD WAR

East-West relations were most tense between 1947 and 1953, the start of the period known as the Cold War. The term "Cold War" was first used in 1947 to describe the power struggle between the Soviet Union and the United States. A "cold" war is distinguished from a "hot" war in which there is outright fighting. The Cold War was a new type of world conflict. It was not fought primarily with military aggression but rather by using economic and political measures, as well as propaganda and **espionage**—using spies to obtain information.

The Cold War was an especially dangerous period in world affairs, characterized by mistrust on both sides. Often, leaders from both sides uttered threats and counter-threats. The consequences of these threats could have been earth-shattering. For example, during the early 1950s, United States Secretary of State John Foster Dulles made a reference to "massive nuclear retaliation to any Soviet advance," and Soviet leader Nikita Krushchev responded with similar threats of mass destruction.

Espionage in Canada: The Gouzenko Affair

The Cold War touched Canadian soil in the dramatic Gouzenko affair of 1945. The incident was a classic example of Cold War espionage.

On September 5, 1945, a Soviet **cipher** clerk left the Soviet Embassy in Ottawa, carrying over 100 top-secret documents, which showed that some Canadian officials were passing secret information to the Soviets. The clerk, Igor Gouzenko, claimed that the Soviets were gathering information about political activities, troop movements, and scientific developments—especially secrets related to building atomic bombs. Gouzenko also claimed the Soviets had established similar spy rings in Britain and the United States.

Gouzenko was questioned by the RCMP. Initially, Canadian authorities were skeptical of his story. After all, the Soviet Union had very recently been a wartime ally of Canada. But Gouzenko's story gained credibility when his apartment was ransacked while he was being questioned by Canadian police. It did seem as though the Soviets were trying to capture him and the secrets he carried.

> **Up Close**
>
> 3. Create a storyboard for a two-minute historical documentary on the Gouzenko affair.

The Secrets of Book Code

"Book code" is a secret code that is used to transmit messages. Throughout the Cold War, spies for both the Soviet Union and the United States were in constant communication with their governments. Because their information was carefully guarded, messages had to be passed in total secrecy. If the information fell into enemy hands, the balance of power could be tipped unfavourably.

Because book code is almost impossible to crack, spies could pass messages to their governments without fearing that messages would be intercepted. The code works like this:

Two parties who are passing information to each other agree to use one book as the basis for the code. It must be the very same book—even the same edition of the book. In advance, they agree that each letter of the message will be identified by a combination of numbers.

In our example, the first number refers to a book page. The second number is the text line number. The third number is the line letter number. A punctuation mark is counted as one letter, but spaces are not.

While both parties have to keep a copy of the code, it is worthless to someone who steals it unless he or she knows the book on which the code is based.

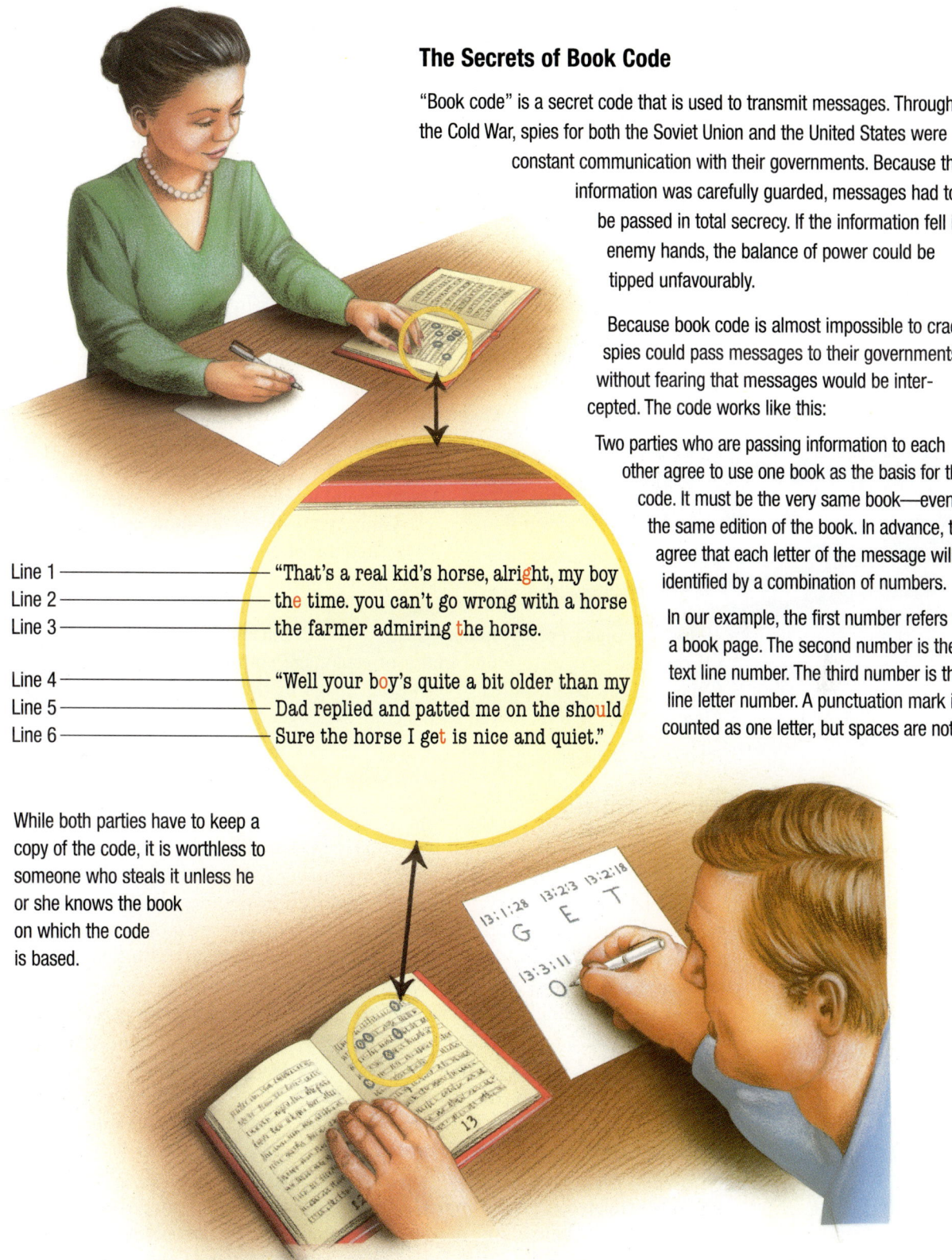

Figure 10–3 How cipher code works

Canada and the World **261**

Figure 10–4 Igor Gouzenko brought the reality of the Cold War to Canada.

On September 7, Gouzenko and his family were taken into protective custody. Prime Minister Mackenzie King alerted American President Harry Truman and British Prime Minister Clement Attlee to the affair because their countries' security was now at risk. The story soon made international headlines.

Canada's first reaction to Gouzenko's revelations of espionage was telling. Many people wanted to know why anyone would spy on Canada. Perhaps Canadians underestimated their growing importance on the international stage. Canada had contributed scientific expertise, as well as uranium, for the atomic bomb project. Canada also had close relations with the United States and Britain in many areas of research and intelligence.

Gouzenko's defection—and the documents he spirited out of the Soviet Embassy—produced proof that the USSR had been spying in Canada and was intent on developing an atomic bomb. In 1946, 12 people were arrested in connection with the incident and were later tried. Of these, several were found guilty of espionage and sent to prison. For many Canadians, an enduring early-television image of the Cold War period is Igor Gouzenko being interviewed with a cloth sack over his head to hide his identity.

The Korean War

In 1950, the Cold War turned hot. After 1945, the Soviet Union occupied the wealthy north part of Korea and the US controlled the south. When the superpowers left in 1949, they left behind two hostile regimes. In 1950, without warning, communist North Korea, using Soviet-made weapons, invaded and defeated South Korea. The US equipped the South Koreans with military supplies, and appealed to the UN Security Council to stop what they saw as communist aggression. The Council voted to send UN forces, including Canadians, to South Korea.

Canada said it was fighting for **collective security**, not for Korea itself, because it didn't want to identify too closely with the Americans' goal of defending the "free world." At first, Canada sent only three navy destroyers and an air-transport squadron. But the Americans pestered Canada to do more, and the public supported intervention. Prime Minister Louis St. Laurent had to rearm Canadian forces for combat. After three years of intense fighting, over 300 Canadians were killed, and more than 1000 were wounded. During this war, Canadians started to question American leadership, especially when US General MacArthur talked of expanding the Korean War into China, a possible recipe for World War III.

DEFENCES AND INSECURITIES

After World War II, Canada reduced the size of its military. However, with mounting Cold-War tension, it became obvious that the country had to increase its defence capabilities. In 1951, Defence Minister Brooke Claxton announced that the government would spend $5 billion over three years on building up the military. Such spending was unheard of for Canada in peacetime.

Many of the defence strategies Canada followed during the 1950s tied Canada closely to American defence policies. Although the two nations shared common security goals, the relationship between the United States and Canada over defence issues was sometimes strained. The tension was most obvious when John F. Kennedy was the president and John Diefenbaker was the prime minister.

Diefenbaker was always trying to establish Canadian independence in defence matters. During the early 1960s, his Conservative government resisted American pressure to arm Canadian forces with nuclear weapons and to keep nuclear weapons in Canada. Similarly, during the Cuban Missile Crisis, Diefenbaker annoyed Kennedy by not immediately putting Canada's military forces on full alert.

Often, Diefenbaker's defence policies were confusing. For instance, in 1962 he talked of equipping the Canadian military with the "necessary instruments" of war. This suggested that he was in favour of nuclear weapons. But he avoided any definite commitment to nuclear arms. Canada's defence policy was a big issue during the 1962 and 1963 election campaigns, and it contributed to Diefenbaker's defeat.

> **Up Close**
>
> 4. Before you read this section, write down your opinion on whether Canada should have refused to cooperate with US defence policies. After you have read it, list facts you did not know before. Do these facts change your opinion? How?

NATO

Canada's first-ever peacetime military alliance, the North Atlantic Treaty Organization (NATO), grew out of Cold War jitters. The idea for NATO was first advanced by a Canadian External Affairs official, Escott Reid. In 1947, Reid delivered a speech in which he urged "the peoples of the western world" to create an international security organization "with teeth." NATO, established on April 4, 1949, aimed to enable member nations to protect or defend each other against a possible Soviet attack. Each member nation agreed to contribute army, navy, and air force units to NATO defence.

Canada's major diplomatic goal was to persuade the United States to join NATO. As you read in Chapter 6, at various times the United States had assumed a position of **isolationism**. It wanted to focus on its own domestic affairs rather than deal with international responsibilities. The United States would be bound to take its place in the defence of western Europe if it were pressured to make a commitment to the NATO alliance.

Reid and others in External Affairs also saw the alliance as a way of moderating US influence over Canada's defence policies. Through their diplomatic work during World War II, he and his colleagues had learned that the United States and Britain always assumed the most powerful roles in defence planning.

> **Up Close**
>
> 5. Summarize Reid's arguments for forming NATO and persuading the US to join. Are there any disadvantages? Identify them.

Within an alliance of several nations, however, Canada could acquire greater influence over defence policy.

The NATO Treaty was a significant milestone in Canadian foreign affairs. It signalled an end to Canada's own prewar isolationism. The treaty also signalled Canada's emergence as a **middle power**, a strong ally of the US and Britain, extremely skillful in exerting influence in world affairs.

As a NATO member, Canada stationed troops abroad as part of a peacetime alliance. The Canadian NATO commitment included numerous Royal Canadian Air Force (RCAF) squadrons based in France and Belgium, in addition to the forces Canada had maintained in Germany since the early 1950s.

The Soviet Union denied that it was a threat to western Europe, insiting that Soviet forces were positioned in eastern Europe to protect the USSR from invasion. The Soviets responded to NATO by forming their own alliance, the Moscow-headquartered Warsaw Pact in 1955. This consisted of the Soviet Union and its satellites: Poland, Czechoslovakia, Hungary, East Germany, Romania, and Bulgaria.

NATO	
Founding Nations	**Joining Nations**
Canada	Turkey 1952
Luxembourg	Greece 1952
US	West Germany 1955
France	Spain 1982
Denmark	
Iceland	
Belgium	
Italy	
Great Britain	
Norway	
Holland	
Portugal	

Figure 10–5 It was Canada's idea to create NATO for mutual defence against the Soviet Union.

Defending North America

Defending North America from possible Soviet attack became a top military priority after World War II. Both the United States and Canada realized that the next war could be fought in North America. In a sneak attack, Soviet bombers would fly over the Arctic Ocean and Canada, so Canada's vast northern territory was of strategic importance to American and Canadian defence. It became clear that a continental approach to defence was required in which the United States and Canada cooperated closely.

Early Radar Warning During the 1950s, largely in response to East-West tensions in Europe, the United States and Canada built three lines of radar to provide an early warning of an attack. The first line, the Pinetree Line, had 33 radar stations and was completed in 1954 at a cost of $450 million. Of this, Canada contributed $150 million. The second line, the all-Canadian-financed Mid-Canada Line, included 98 radar stations and cost $250 million. It was completed in 1957. After pressure from the United States, construction began on the Distant Early Warning (DEW) Line, in 1954. The United States paid for the construction of the DEW Line, but Canadians, including many First Nations peoples, actually built it.

Advances in weapons technology soon made the early radar warning systems obsolete. Ground-based radar systems were unable to detect the approach of intercontinental or submarine-launched missiles or the low-flying cruise missiles developed later.

NORAD

Because of shared defence needs, the Americans began to pressure Canada to join them in a unified system of North American air defence. By the mid-1950s, Canadian authorities saw that safeguarding the country against possible Soviet attack meant joining with the more powerful United States. To achieve this goal, the United States and Canada created the North American Air Defence Agreement (NORAD). (In 1981, the name was changed to the North American Aerospace Defence Command to reflect the emphasis on defence against missiles.) NORAD integrated the air defence forces of the two countries under an American commander, with a Canadian second-in-command. NORAD headquarters were located in Colorado Springs, Colorado. From there, fighter planes could be dispatched over the Arctic to intercept attacking Soviet bombers.

Figure 10–6 NORAD's underground complex in North Bay, Ontario, also known as "the hole"

One of Diefenbaker's first acts as Canada's new prime minister in 1957 was to accept the terms of NORAD. However, because preparation was needed to integrate the American and Canadian air forces, the agreement was not signed until 1958. By signing the NORAD agreement, Diefenbaker put Canada under the American defence umbrella. This had some frightening implications. Canada became committed to joining wars it did not necessarily want to join. And since the North was so crucial to NORAD strategy, Canada, in effect, gave up sovereignty over vast tracts of its northern territory for defence purposes. Even though DEW Line installations were on Canadian soil, access to them was controlled by American authorities. When Canadian reporters wanted to visit a radar installation, they had to obtain clearance from the United States, and their news stories were censored by Americans.

Defence Equipment Agreements Canadians also relied on Americans for much of their defence equipment. In July 1958, Canada and the US signed a Defence Development and Production Sharing Agreement which closely tied the Canadian and American defence industries. When the Diefenbaker government cancelled the Avro Arrow in 1959 (see Flashpoint, p. 271), the defence technology that replaced it was largely American.

Data File

During the 1950s and 1960s, students held "Duck and Cover" drills in which they ducked under their desks and covered themselves to protect against the impact of bombs.

The Climate of Fear

For most Canadians after WW II, communism replaced fascism as the political nightmare. In 1949, the USSR acquired the atomic bomb. In the early 1950s, the threat of nuclear annihilation seemed very real to average Canadians.

North American paranoia about communism was evident in American Senator Joseph McCarthy's Senate subcommittee on "un-American activities," which hunted down real or imagined communists. This witchhunt ruined many peoples' careers. In Canada, basic civil rights were sometimes ignored so that suspected communists could be weeded out. For instance, in 1951 the Citizenship Act was changed to allow authorities to revoke the citizenship of naturalized Canadians who had been convicted of crimes involving "disaffection or disloyalty." The legislation was directed at communists.

Civil Defence Civil defence—preparation for a possible nuclear attack—became important across the country. In 1950, the federal government coordinated national civil defence planning and assisted provinces in setting up their own civil defence programs. In the event of attack, the CBC would become a 24-hour-a-day emergency survival network. Evacuation plans were prepared for major Canadian cities.

Fallout Shelter During the 1950s fallout shelters became something of a fad. These shelters were supposed to protect people in the event of a nuclear war. Some companies offered to build the underground shelters in backyards. Shelters that amounted to lengths of concrete pipe sold for about $700. The federal government took fallout shelters very seriously. It constructed large, fully equipped underground shelters to house high-level government officials in the event of a nuclear attack. Since they were initiated by John Diefenbaker's government, they were nicknamed "Diefenbunkers."

Figure 10–7 Complete with halls big enough for truck traffic, the biggest "Diefenbunker" remains one of the most vivid reminders of Canada's Cold War mentality. Begun in 1961, the bunker is a city underground from which political leaders could continue to govern the country—or what was left of it—after an all-out nuclear war. Four storeys high and constructed of poured concrete and steel, the bunker is hidden under a farmer's field in the Ottawa Valley. Within, living quarters and supplies were provided for 500 people who would live sealed underground for 30 days. The compound also housed everything deemed necessary to the survival of the country, including CBC Radio, to relay information about the nuclear attack and its aftermath, as well as a Bank of Canada vault. The facility was never used, and was turned into a museum after closing in 1994.

CANADA ENTERS THE ATOMIC AGE

While the nuclear age presented bleak scenarios of destruction, atomic energy also offered the prospect of exciting peacetime applications. For some, it became a source of national pride that, although Canada had the raw materials and scientific expertise to make atomic weapons, it chose to pursue the peaceful uses of nuclear energy.

Up Close

6. List, with a brief explanation, the peaceful uses of nuclear energy.

A Nuclear Research Leader

As early as 1944, Chalk River, Ontario, was the site of a heavy-water reactor to produce plutonium from uranium. By 1949, Canada was at the forefront of nuclear research, much of it done at Chalk River. From the single reactor of the early 1940s, Chalk River developed into a complex of five nuclear reactors owned by Atomic Energy of Canada Ltd. (AECL). The AECL, controlled by the federal government, was involved in heavy-water production and most applications of nuclear energy in Canada. The Chalk River research laboratory became a world-class science centre as well as one of two nuclear energy research centres in Canada. (The other was the Whitehall Nuclear Research Establishment north of Winnipeg, Manitoba.)

Nuclear Energy: Peaceful Power Source In the postwar period, nuclear power appeared to be the answer to Canada's energy needs. It was cheap, widely available because of Canada's abundant raw materials, and reliable. As Canada's manufacturing sector grew, nuclear power seemed to offer the inexpensive energy needed for continued industrial development.

Chalk River was also the site of Canada's first large research reactor, NRX, a 10-megawatt facility. The reactor began operating in 1947 and later helped Canadian nuclear scientists in the design and development of the CANDU reactor.

Canada's CANDU

Canada sells its famed CANDU nuclear reactors to countries around the world, helping these nations meet their energy needs. CANDU comes from combining "Canada" with two materials used in the nuclear-energy-generating process: deuterium and uranium. The CANDU nuclear reactor, designed and built in Canada, uses easily replaceable fuel bundles and a heavy-water cooling system. The CANDU reactor has significant advantages over other commercial nuclear reactors. It does not need to be shut down to replace its fuel source, and it produces a large amount of energy.

During the 1950s, Canada also drew scientific attention for its work in developing the "cobalt bomb," which used nuclear radiation in cancer therapy. Such inventions proved that radioactivity could have constructive as well as destructive uses.

Up Close

7. Given the risks, should Canada have developed nuclear energy? Write a paragraph giving your opinion, using information from this chapter.

THE RACE FOR SPACE

On October 4, 1957, the Soviet Union launched the world's first artificial satellite—*Sputnik I*. The launch was highly significant because it showed that the Soviets had developed the terrifying capability of delivering nuclear warheads anywhere in North America. This realization shocked Americans, as well as their close defence partner, Canada. The DEW Line's effectiveness in guarding against Soviet air attacks was immediately called into question, as the system had been designed to detect jets delivering nuclear warheads.

The race for space was now on.

American military analysts declared that there was a **missile gap**, because the United States did not have the Soviets' missile capability. The United States then speeded up development of its own missile technology. *Sputnik I* was followed 29 days later by another satellite, carrying a dog. This further shattered North Americans' image of their technology as superior. Washington State Senator Henry Jackson asked Americans to observe "a week of shame and anger."

Figure 10–8 Kennedy's promise came true when American astronauts landed on the moon on July 20, 1969. These stills show images from the televised broadcast relayed around the world.

With a heightened sense of inferiority, both the United States and Canada turned their attention inward. Many politicians and commentators directed blame at the "soft" North American educational systems for failing to prepare students adequately for technological challenges. In Canada, critics thought that schools did not produce enough engineers and scientists. As a result of the Sputnik launch, education for the baby boom became a major public priority, and funding increased significantly. Greater support for higher education also became widespread. US President John F. Kennedy set the "technology" tone for the 1960s when he promised that America would put "a man on the moon" by the end of the decade.

Canada's Satellite Program

Many of Canada's space achievements during the 1960s were the result of collaborating with the United States, specifically with the National Aeronautics and Space Administration (NASA). Canada signed an agreement with NASA to launch four Canadian satellites, beginning with *Alouette I* in 1962, followed by

Alouette II in 1965, *ISIS I* (International Satellites for Ionospheric Studies) in 1969, and *ISIS II* in 1971. Several other launch agreements with NASA followed.

The launch of *Alouette I* in September 1962 made Canada the third nation in space. The satellite was used to carry out experiments in the ionosphere (part of Earth's outer atmosphere that reflects radio waves and transmits them over a long distance). The mission was a significant technological success. Each succeeding Canadian satellite was more complex than the previous in design and measurement capabilities. By the time the ISIS satellites were launched, a major goal of Canada's satellite program, in addition to their scientific objectives, was to transfer the skills and knowledge developed by government scientists and technicians in space communications to private industry.

Canada's successful entry into space satellite technology aroused interest in using this technology for communications satellites. In 1967 the main objective of the Canadian satellite program shifted from scientific experimentation to applying satellite technology, particularly in the areas of domestic telecommunications and natural resource surveys.

The telecommunications application of satellite technology is well-suited to Canada because the country is so large and relatively sparsely populated. Such geographic and demographic realities make installing land-based communication systems, such as telephone lines, costly. In 1969 Telesat Canada was formed to provide domestic communication services by satellite throughout Canada.

Up Close

8. Summarize the reasons why satellite technology was especially useful to Canada.

NUCLEAR WEAPONS: A BALANCE OF TERROR

During the Cold War, the East and West eyed each other with suspicion. Each feared that the other intended to attack. These fears of a possible attack caused both sides to engage in an arms race. Canada and the United States spent vast sums on weapons and increased the size of their military forces. By 1952, Canada's defence spending had grown to ten times the amount spent just four years before.

When the Soviet Union tested its first atomic bomb in 1949, the United States lost its status as the world's only power with nuclear capabilities. The arms race now focused on nuclear weapons. Scientists in both countries tried to develop even more effective nuclear warheads. By 1957, both nations had a new weapon—the hydrogen bomb. This new bomb delivered an explosive power 1000 times greater than the atomic bomb the Americans had dropped on Hiroshima.

The arms race was also affected by the "race for space" between the United States and the Soviet Union. With the 1957 launch of *Sputnik I*, the Soviets demonstrated that they no longer needed to use aircraft to drop a nuclear bomb on the United States. The same type of rocket that sent *Sputnik* into space could carry a nuclear warhead over North America. Soon both countries had developed

Up Close

9. Do you think that a balance of terror made the world a safer place? Develop a slogan that expresses your view.

Intercontinental Ballistic Missiles (ICBMs) that could carry a hydrogen warhead across the Atlantic in less than half an hour.

As the US and the Soviet Union built more and more nuclear weapons, many people feared that the world was edging closer to the possibility of nuclear destruction. Each of the two nations had enough nuclear weapons to devastate the other many times over. **Fallout** from a nuclear attack could spread deadly radioactivity around the globe. But military strategists argued that the arms race actually helped to prevent a nuclear attack. They reasoned that if one side launched a nuclear attack, the other side would launch its own attack and both nations would be destroyed. As long as both sides had similar nuclear capabilities, neither would dare to attack the other. This theory was known as Mutual Assured Destruction (MAD). Those who opposed the arms race were not convinced that MAD made the world a safer place.

Figure 10–9 History or entertainment? In *Dr. Strangelove*, a movie produced in 1964, an American Air Force general is convinced that the Soviets are poisoning the US water supply. So the US decides to drop a bomb on the Soviet Union. However, the Soviets have developed a "doomsday machine" programmed to blow up the world if they are attacked. The film brilliantly captured the spirit of the Cold War—and the paradox of MAD.

Nuclear Weapons in Canada

In order to meet the commitments of the 1957 NORAD agreement, the Liberal government asked a Canadian company, A. V. Roe, to design a better fighter-bomber for the Air Force. The new CF-105 aircraft, known as the "Avro Arrow," was an impressive achievement, but the government decided it was far too expensive. Instead, Diefenbaker scrapped the Arrow and made an agreement with the US to deploy the American anti-aircraft missile. This was a much cheaper alternative to the Arrow, and the US had agreed to provide the missiles for free if Canada would build the installation sites. Because the missile could be fitted with a nuclear warhead, it would be a powerful weapon against Russian bombers. But the missile's nuclear warhead soon became a source of controversy.

Under American law, the US could not release atomic weapons to other countries. To go through with the deal, Canada would have to agree to accept American military staff to oversee the bombs, which would be under the control of the commander in chief of NORAD. It was not until 1960 that the general public learned that the missiles were intended to carry nuclear warheads. Many Canadians opposed the idea of nuclear weapons on Canadian soil.

Diefenbaker had great difficulty deciding whether to accept nuclear warheads for the missiles. He wanted a powerful nuclear weapon to ward off a pos-

Change and Continuity: Technological Impact

Flashpoint
The End of the Avro Arrow

Once the Soviet Union had the nuclear bomb, Canada felt it had to develop a highly effective air defence system. If the Soviets ever decided to launch a nuclear attack against the United States, Soviet bombers would have to fly through Canadian airspace to reach their target. The Liberal government asked the A. V. Roe Company of Malton, Ontario, to develop a new fighter jet—the Avro Arrow. The government was willing to buy up to 600 of the fighters at a cost of about $2 million each.

Early on, cost became an issue. Each aircraft came with expensive technology, and frequent changes in design delayed production and pushed the price even higher. When the Air Force cut its order to just 100 planes, efforts were made to find foreign buyers, but no foreign buyers were found. By 1957, the cost for each Arrow was estimated at between $6 million and $10 million.

The first prototype of the Avro Arrow was unveiled on October 4, 1957, the same day the Soviets sent the *Sputnik I* satellite into orbit. This Soviet achievement led many people to wonder if fighter jets like the Arrow would soon become obsolete. After all, the Soviet missile that launched *Sputnik* was powerful enough to send a nuclear warhead to North America.

In 1957, the Liberal government that had supported the Arrow project was defeated by Diefenbaker and the Conservatives. It was a time of deficits and unemployment. Diefenbaker wondered if Canada could afford such an expensive aircraft. New efforts to sell the Arrow to the United States failed. On February 20, 1959, Diefenbaker can-

Figure 10–10 The Avro Arrow marked the last time Canada had an independent technological breakthrough in military hardware.

celled the project. The A. V. Roe Company immediately fired 14 000 employees.

The decision to cancel the Avro Arrow was controversial. The Arrow had been an engineering achievement—at the time, some people considered it to be the most advanced aircraft in the world. After initial denials, the government admitted that it ordered all plans, prototypes, and photographs destroyed. Many of Canada's best scientists and engineers had been working on the project, and they were quickly recruited by NASA and other American organizations. Once again, Canada had to rely on the US for military aircraft, and Canadian defence dollars flowed into the US economy. But some argued that the Arrow was too expensive, not adequately tested, and would soon have been obsolete.

Activity

1. Create a public announcement for the Diefenbaker government on the cancellation of the Avro Arrow. Then create a dialogue between two laid-off employees who have just heard the announcement. Act out the dialogue with a partner for the class.

sible Soviet threat, but he didn't want the Americans to control weapons on Canadian soil. Pressure to make a decision increased once the first installation site in Canada was completed in February 1962. In January of the following year, Diefenbaker had still not decided. Liberal leader Lester Pearson claimed that the missiles were not effective weapons without the nuclear warheads. He asked the government to explain why it had accepted the missiles if it did not intend to make use of their nuclear capabilities. Diefenbaker replied that he would make a decision after the NATO allies met in May. Douglas Harkness, the Minister of Defence, resigned in exasperation and Diefenbaker's government was defeated in a non-confidence motion on February 5, 1963.

Up Close

10. Diefenbaker delayed a full alert during the Cuban Missile Crisis. List and briefly explain his reasons.

The Cuban Missile Crisis

The Cuban Missile Crisis began on October 22, 1962. US President John F. Kennedy had learned that the Soviet Union was building missile sites in Cuba that could launch a nuclear attack against the United States. Kennedy demanded that Nikita Krushchev, the Soviet leader, turn back the ships that were on their way to deliver missiles to Cuba. The US Navy formed a blockade around Cuba, and Kennedy threatened to take military action if Kruschev did not comply. For five days Krushchev refused to call back the ships. The world stood on the brink of nuclear war.

Kennedy requested that Canada immediately put its armed forces on military alert. Diefenbaker was outraged that Kennedy had not consulted him beforehand. He was afraid that a Canadian military alert would heighten tensions with the Soviet Union, and he also wanted to demonstrate Canadian independence from US foreign policy. Although the Canadian forces were quietly put on alert at the beginning of the crisis, formal authorization for the alert did not come until two days later. By delaying authorization, Diefenbaker believed he had taken a stand for Canadian independence. The crisis ended when Krushchev finally agreed to call back the ships. The Cuban Missile Crisis changed the opinions of many Canadians who had previously been against nuclear weapons in Canada.

Dates of Nuclear Test Explosions

Country	Atomic Bomb	Hydrogen
United States	1945	1952
Soviet Union	1949	1957
Britain	1952	1957
China	1954	1968
France	1960	1968

Figure 10–11 Nuclear explosion tests, 1945–1968

Proliferation and Protest

During the arms race, the United States and the Soviet Union built and stockpiled an increasing number of nuclear weapons. Both countries rushed to develop new types of these weapons and new systems for sending the weapons to a target. Soon there were enough nuclear weapons in existence to destroy the world many times over. This buildup of nuclear weapons is called **proliferation**.

Other countries began to develop and test their own nuclear weapons. During the 1950s and 1960s, Britain, France, and China tested both atomic bombs and hydrogen bombs. In 1963, the United States, the Soviet Union, and

Britain signed a nuclear-test ban treaty in Moscow. The treaty prohibited the testing of nuclear devices in the air, underwater, or in outer space. More than 100 countries later signed the treaty.

As the number of nuclear weapons increased, so did fears of a **nuclear holocaust.** The postwar peace movement in Canada now focused on "nuclear pacifism" and called for disarmament and an easing of Cold War tensions between East and West. The Canadian Peace Congress began a campaign to "Ban the Bomb" and urged Canadians to sign the Stockholm Appeal, an international petition that called for an end to nuclear weapons. In the early 1960s, the national volunteer organization Voice of Women (VOW) promoted peace and disarmament through educational programs, political lobbying, and conferences. As people learned more about the dangers of radioactive fallout from nuclear testing, public support for nuclear pacifism grew.

Figure 10–12 Many groups protested the presence of nuclear weapons in Canada. By the mid-1960s, the Vietnam War had become the major focus of the peace movement and public attention.

CANADA AND THE UNITED NATIONS

The United Nations was born in San Francisco in 1945. Fifty countries gathered to create a global organization that would keep world peace, defend human rights, and promote social, economic, and health developments around the world. That same year, the UN created the United Nations Educational, Scientific and Cultural Organization (UNESCO) to promote collaboration among nations through education, science, culture, and communication. Three years later, it created the World Health Organization (WHO) to promote health care around the world.

When the United Nations was founded, Mackenzie King was still Canada's prime minister. He wanted to make sure that Canada, along with other smaller nations, would not be forced into future wars by the so-called "Big Five"—the United States, the Soviet Union, Britain, France, and China. As a result, the UN charter stated that any country asked to supply troops or money to UN security operations had to be consulted first. In effect, Canada, along with Australia and other medium-sized countries, managed to stop the big powers from dominating the new organization. The UN became the forum for the next phase of Canada's growth as a nation—actively sharing in the responsibilities of a changing world.

Universal Declaration of Human Rights

The United Nations also recognized human rights as a matter of international law. This was a revolutionary idea. For the first time, all the peoples of the world had a charter that declared that they ought to have basic civil, economic, social, and political rights, regardless of the political system they lived under. The Universal Declaration of Human Rights was adopted by the UN in December 1948. John Humphrey, a professor of law at McGill University in Montreal, was one of the authors of the original draft of this document (see Images, page 277). The Declaration was the inspiration for Canada's Charter of Rights and Freedoms, which itself is now a model for other countries.

Figure 10–13 The General Assembly of the United Nations. Canada has played a key role since the UN began in 1945.

Data File
Although Canada contributes only about 3 percent of the total UN budget (which is based on the net national income) it has always been one of the top two providers of emergency and regular food aid to people facing starvation.

CANADA, A MIDDLE POWER

Canada's huge war effort had given it a voice as a middle power—not as big as the US or USSR, but too big to be overlooked. Both French and English Canadians believed that Canada should now play a larger role in world affairs. In the late 1950s, the Department of External Affairs, led by Lester "Mike" Pearson, drafted a new foreign policy that would give Ottawa more clout in the international arena—at the UN and through NATO. Diplomatic skill was a necessity, and able Canadian diplomats learned to keep their balance on the shifting political ground across the world. As a middle power, Canada was instrumental in finding compromises for conflicts that flared up after the war in newly independent countries in Asia and Africa. This was Canada's "golden age" of foreign policy.

Historical Inquiry: Research

Historian at Work

Building an Effective Argument

Figure 10–14 Arguing effectively can enhance your communication.

An argument is made up of two parts: a claim and an explanation. The claim is a viewpoint, opinion, or conclusion that someone wants you to accept. The explanation contains facts and logical reasons to persuade you to agree with the claim. Historians use arguments to state and discuss their interpretations of events in the past and to disprove the interpretations of other historians.

You probably use arguments every day. Whenever you disagree with someone and explain why you think your point of view is correct, you are presenting an argument. For example, imagine that you are asking your parents for permission to attend a concert with some friends, and the concert takes place on a school night.

Your claim: I should be allowed to go to the concert.

Your explanation:
1. The group performing is your favourite band.
2. You can pay for the ticket yourself.
3. You don't have any tests or exams the next day.

The explanation provides reasons that you hope will persuade your parents to accept your claim. The following quote is an example of an argument used by Canadian historian Desmond Morton.

> The Avro Arrow cancellation was the right choice ... The Arrow was born in strategic confusion, conceived by service commanders preoccupied with narrow interests, [and] fostered by politicians who felt no need to penetrate the hard core of defence issues.

Morton is summarizing his argument after a detailed discussion of the issue. To make an argument convincing, you need to explain how or why each of your reasons supports your claim.

How do you build an effective argument?

- **Step 1** Decide on your claim and then identify facts and reasons that support the claim.
- **Step 2** Anticipate criticisms of your argument and include in your explanation facts and reasons that defend your argument against these criticisms.
- **Step 3** Find out about different arguments that have been made on the topic. In your explanation, show why you don't agree with these arguments.
- **Step 4** Find the most effective way to present your argument. Here are some tips:
  - State your argument with confidence. Don't say, "I think this might have happened because …" Say, "This happened because …"
  - Be concise. Use as few words as necessary to make each point clear.
  - Decide on the best order in which to present your ideas.

Activities

1. What is the claim in the quote from Desmond Morton? How many reasons does he offer in his explanation? Do you find this argument convincing? Why or why not?

2. Look at the argument about going to a rock concert. What specific objections to the claim does the explanation anticipate?

3. Think of a claim you might make to a teacher or a parent. Develop an effective argument on the issue.

4. Develop an effective argument to support the following claim: The Avro Arrow should not have been cancelled.

Canada and the World

Canada and Britain

After the war, Britain was poor, and the US had the largest economy in the world. However, Canada did not want to be totally dependent on US trade. It wanted to restore its prewar balance of trade, with Britain and Europe on one side and the United States on the other. But by 1957, Britain accounted for only 9 percent of all Canadian trade, while the US accounted for 71 percent. American products were more dependable, more convenient, and cheaper than British products, and Canadians preferred them. Britain was simply not able to lead the world as it had in the past, and Canada had no choice but to become more economically dependent on the US. The Suez crisis showed that Canada understood how its loyalties had changed.

Figure 10–15 British and French aggression in the Suez opened the door for Canada's involvement as peacekeeper.

The Suez Crisis The high point of Canada's role as a middle power came when the Suez Crisis erupted in 1956. Gamel Abdel Nasser, the president of Egypt, wanted to create a pan-Arab state with Egypt in charge. He nationalized the Suez Canal so it would belong to Egypt. The canal was strategically important—it was the main waterway for shipping oil to Europe. Nasser's action enraged Britain and France, who had controlled the canal up to then. To protect their interests, they convinced Israel to attack Egypt. They then ordered Israel and Egypt to withdraw. Nasser refused.

Britain and France then bombed the Canal Zone, but they did not bargain for the consequences. The USSR condemned their aggression and threatened nuclear strikes against Paris and London. The US was angry because it hadn't been consulted. The Commonwealth was split, with the non-White countries supporting Nasser. Here Canada proved its mettle. Lester Pearson saw that Canada could not support Britain in this action. Ties of empire were not enough. It was more important to maintain the western alliance because any confrontation between the two new superpowers—the US and the USSR—could be deadly.

The conflict was about to escalate into a major war until Pearson went to the United Nations with a plan. He proposed defusing the situation by sending in a peacekeeping force run by member nations of the UN. The UN unanimously supported the idea. Within a couple of weeks, Canadian and other soldiers arrived. They stayed until 1967, when Nasser ordered them out and started the Arab-Israeli War. Pearson won the 1957 Nobel Peace Prize for his work.

Change and Continuity: International Status

Images
John Humphrey: Architect of Rights

The Universal Declaration of Human Rights is one of the United Nations' most important achievements. It has been called "one of the most influential documents of modern history." But when the Nobel Prize was awarded to recognize the achievement of the Declaration, John Humphrey, the Canadian responsible for the first draft, was passed over. Instead, a French diplomat was honoured as "Father of the Universal Declaration."

The Declaration states that everyone is born free and equal; has the right to be treated fairly and without discrimination; has civil and political rights; has the right to free choice of employment (as well as equal pay for equal work); and has the right to certain basic economic and social rights, including the right to housing, medical care, and social services.

Humphrey was born in New Brunswick and practised law in Quebec before joining the Faculty of Law at McGill University. In 1946, shortly after becoming dean of the faculty, he was appointed Director of Human Rights for the UN Secretariat. It was here that he drafted the Declaration, which speaks out against discrimination based on race, colour, sex, language, religion, and politics. Humphrey faced quite a challenge in his quest to get the UN to adopt the document, but he persevered and was eventually successful.

It is unclear how Humphrey's contributions to the Declaration disappeared from view when the Nobel Prize committee made its decision. Humphrey did not speak up to demand recognition for his efforts. Twenty years later, John Hobbins, associate director of libraries at McGill, discovered among Humphrey's papers the original draft of the declaration, in Humphrey's own handwriting. When word got out that Hobbins planned to publish an article about his discovery, proving that the French diplomat did not author the first draft, he received anonymous phone calls warning him that nothing could be proved if the papers were destroyed. Hobbins immediately stored them in a safe.

Figure 10–16 Canada Post stamp honouring Humphrey

Humphrey modestly commented that writing the draft was "just part of the job." When he was later honoured with a UN Human Rights Award, Humphrey explained, "To say I did the draft alone would be nonsense.... The final Declaration was the work of hundreds."

After retiring from the UN, Humphrey went back to teaching and continued his involvement in causes related to human rights. His many achievements include founding the Canadian Federation for Human Rights and the Canadian Society of Amnesty International. Humphrey was appointed an Officer of the Order of Canada in 1974.

What Do You Think?

1. Based on what you have learned in this chapter, can you think of reasons why Humphrey's contribution might have been overlooked? Explain.
2. Do you think Humphrey should have insisted on recognition? Why or why not?
3. Draft your own human rights charter for the students in your school. First, select categories of rights, then list specific rights under those categories. Think about all the situations you encounter at school to develop your categories.

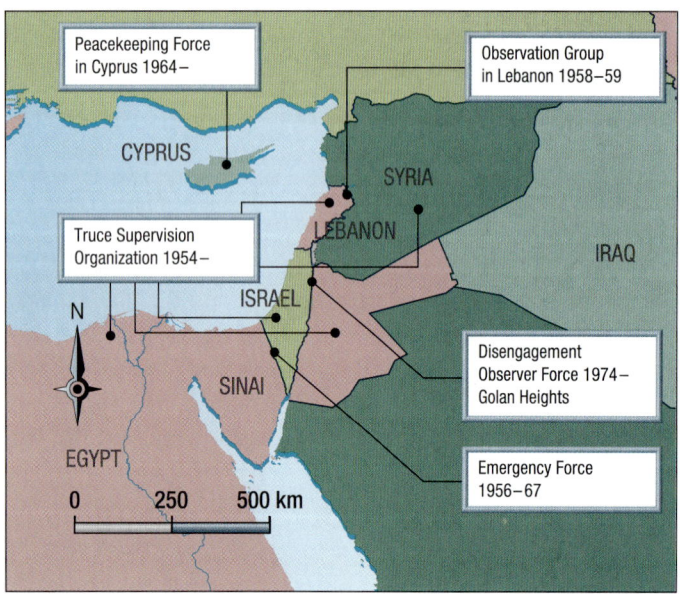

Figure 10–17 Canadian participation in peacekeeping operations in the Middle East to the mid-1970s

The Suez Crisis marked the first time Canada opposed the actions of its "mother countries," England and France. It also marked the start of Canada's involvement in UN peacekeeping missions—every one, right up to Kosovo in 1999. In the Middle East, Canadians served in hot spots such as Cyprus, Israel, Syria, Jordan, Egypt, and Lebanon. Peacekeepers were placed between hostile parties to supervise ceasefires and force withdrawals, and to bring calm to an area. The heyday of peacekeeping lasted until the mid-1960s, when some critics started to complain that peacekeeping did nothing to resolve tense situations. You will explore this issue in more detail in Chapter 16.

Canada and the Commonwealth

Since 1931, when the Statute of Westminster transformed the British Empire into many autonomous nations, Canada had been a leader of change in the Commonwealth. Until 1949, the "old" Commonwealth consisted of Britain, Canada, Australia, New Zealand, and South Africa. Mackenzie King and Louis St. Laurent welcomed non-White members. In 1947, St. Laurent encouraged India to remain in the Commonwealth when it became independent from Britain. Canada supported independence movements in Asia and Africa: Angola, Mozambique, Zimbabwe, and Namibia.

There were high hopes for a new kind of commonwealth—a multiracial group of countries making up a quarter of the world's population, who cooperated with each other. However, it was not to be. The size of the group, and racism in Rhodesia and South Africa, made consensus unlikely. Each country was moving in different directions because of the need to respond to the Cold War. In 1961, Diefenbaker played a key role in forcing South Africa out of the Commonwealth for its apartheid policy. But by then, the Commonwealth had slipped in importance as a force influencing world affairs.

Figure 10–18 Commonwealth leaders Winston Churchill and John Diefenbaker in London, England

Canada and the US

Because of the dominance of the United States, the Canadian government regarded it with caution. In an attempt to keep its political independence, Canada refused to join the Organization of American States, which brought the US together with countries in Central and South America. It refused to recognize communist China and it did not approve the American response in the Cuban Missile Crisis of 1962.

The reality of Canada's new relationship with the US became clear during the Vietnam War. North Vietnam had been taken over by Ho Chi Minh and his communist followers. At the time, western countries believed that if one country was taken over by communists, every other country in the area would be too. Canada worried that it would be forced into a war if the larger communist powers like China and the USSR got involved. This fear increased when the US intensified its bombing of North Vietnam in 1965. When Pearson dared to suggest a halt in the bombing in a 1965 speech in Philadelphia, President Lyndon Johnson grabbed him by the lapels and berated him. Any influence Canada now had on US foreign policy was obviously limited.

Canada and Vietnam However, Canada's role in the war was not what it seemed. Publicly, Canada wanted to appear as an objective party seeking peace. Privately, Canadians acted as spies for the CIA in Vietnam and secretly helped get American weapons and soldiers into South Vietnam, further escalating the war. Even Canadian aid was coordinated by the US Secretary of State and went only to South Vietnam, the US ally. Canadian corporations got rich from the war: Canada sold over $10 billion worth of ammunition, equipment, and raw materials like nickel to the US for the war effort. Agent Orange, the infamous and deadly herbicide, was first tested at a base in Gagetown, New Brunswick.

About 20 000 American **draft dodgers** came to Canada during the war, along with 12 000 deserters. Even when they were allowed to return to the US after the war ended, half of them stayed to become Canadian citizens. They saw Canada as a peaceful country where racial hatred was not tolerated.

Considering the extent of its involvement, Canada showed surprisingly little support for the estimated 30 000 Canadians who volunteered for the Vietnam War. They were there unofficially, since Canada had not officially joined the war, and when they returned home, they were ignored. They are still trying to build a memorial in Ottawa. A monument in Windsor is the only one that names the estimated 400 Canadians who died in Vietnam.

Heritage Minute

In an era marked by touchy Canada-US relations, Jackie Robinson stood out. In 1946, he was the American that Montrealers loved. That year, Robinson played for a minor league affiliate of the Brooklyn Dodgers—the Montreal Royals. On April 18, he stepped onto a field in New Jersey in a Royals uniform. He drove in four runs with four hits and stole two bases. Montreal went wild. The 1946 season was so successful that Robinson was asked to play in the major leagues. But he never forgot the inspiration he received in Canada.

Figure 10–19 Marcel Roy, a veteran of the Vietnam War, salutes as students from Laurier Macdonald High School hold a banner during Remembrance Day ceremonies in Montreal.

CONCLUSION

Canada grew as a nation in the 20 years after World War II. It played a more decisive role in international affairs, both in the Commonwealth and in the United Nations. Canada's new role as peacekeeper suited it well. Yet it also had to come to terms with the difficult realities of this period. It became more dependent on trade with the US, and faced more competition as Europe recovered from the war. However, Canada was now a fully independent nation. In the Suez Crisis, for example, Canada proved it could make the right decision, even at the risk of angering Britain and France.

CHAPTER ACTIVITIES

■ Check Your Understanding

1. How did the Cold War and the build-up of nuclear weapons change Canada's defence policies and strategies? Create a time line of key agreements and events.

2. Summarize the events that pushed Canada into a peacekeeping role at the United Nations.

■ Develop Your Thinking

3. Peacekeeping was a role that Canada pursued under Lester Pearson. Using the information in the chapter, develop an argument that supports or refutes the idea that Canada is suited to peacekeeping.

4. The Commonwealth never became the force for progress that many Canadians had hoped it would. Using examples, explain how Commonwealth members could help each other. Address issues such as racism, development, language rights, peace, democracy, and human rights. Was the United Nations a better solution? Why or why not?

■ Express Yourself

5. Write a short piece of fiction (a sketch or short story) about life after a nuclear war. Assume that the super powers are crippled and that radioactive fallout is having unpredictable effects on the environment. Research the details of a nuclear aftermath to make your fiction believable.

6. In this chapter, you learned that *Sputnik I* caused Canadian governments to put more money into education, so that students would have more scientific and technical skills. Do you agree that the primary focus of education should be to teach scientific and technical skills? Explain in an essay whether you think this is a worthy goal.

Apply Your Learning

7. Research one of Canada's peacekeeping missions from this period. Prepare a short report on the problem, the objectives of the mission, and the outcome. Was the mission a success? Provide a logical argument that supports your opinion.

8. Find out the differences between nuclear technology that produces a bomb and nuclear technology that generates power. Prepare a short report on how Canada and other nuclear powers try to avoid selling nuclear technologies and materials to forces that might use them to produce bombs.

Extend Your Learning Using the Internet

9. Use archival and current Internet sources to chart and analyse Canada's role in NATO from the 1950s to the present time. Develop and present an argument to convince your classmates that NATO has been either a positive or a negative force for Canadian security.

10. What were the short- and long-term effects for Canada of one of the defensive or destructive technologies developed during the Cold War? Create a cause-and-effect chart to demonstrate these effects on one Canadian company or one sector of the Canadian economy.

Unit 4
Changing Times
1967–1983

Social issues became important and controversial during the 1970s. Not all Canadians had benefited equally from the prosperity and opportunities of the 1950s and 1960s. Many disadvantaged groups clamoured and worked for change.

Pierre Trudeau was prime minister for almost all of this period. Many Canadians saw him as a prime minister who was willing to spearhead change. His last and most important political act was to bring the Canadian Constitution back from Britain. Trudeau hoped it would strengthen national unity. But Quebec had become so alienated from the rest of Canada that Trudeau's policies seemed barely relevant. And his concerns about social justice were severely tested by tough economic times.

Canada also developed new approaches to immigration, environment, and foreign ownership. Cultural industries were protected, and Canada participated in international ventures such as the space program. And Canada's aboriginal peoples became an organized force whose political voice could no longer be ignored.

Prime Ministers	Dates of Office
Lester Pearson	1963–1968
Pierre Trudeau	1968–1979
Joe Clark	1979–1980
Pierre Trudeau	1980–1984

Anticipation Guide

In this unit, you will:

- explore Canada's social conflicts of the late 1960s
- find out about the Just Society
- learn how new immigration policies changed the Canadian population
- explore why multiculturalism became a distinctive Canadian characteristic
- learn how women's lives changed during this time
- explore why Quebec wanted out of Confederation
- summarize Quebec's efforts to protect the French language
- learn about the global economy's impact on Canada
- analyse how the economic recession affected Canada's social justice
- explore the beginnings of western discontent
- examine Canada's efforts to be independent from US defence policies
- look at how Canada protects its cultural industries
- learn how aboriginal Canadians continued to recover their culture and land

11
Living in Trudeau's Canada

Focus Questions

Demographic Patterns
What were Trudeau's goals with respect to multiculturalism? What were the actual effects on Canadian people and on immigration policies?

Canadian Identity
What problems did the Canadian arts, entertainment, and media industries confront during this period? What steps did the government take to protect them?

Social and Political Movements
How did the women's movement advance in the 1960s and 1970s?

How did the political status of the Native peoples change during this period?

During the decades immediately following World War II, Canadians worried about the arms race between the Communist and non-Communist nations, as well as other important international issues. However, many Canadians were also becoming dissatisfied with their status at home. Canadians who were neither English nor French were beginning to be more vocal. These Canadians felt excluded by the English–French language and cultural debates. Their understanding of Canada was multicultural, not bicultural. Canadian women were also becoming dissatisfied with their role in society. More women entered politics, and began to work for changes in women's legal, social, and economic status. The Native peoples, facing the threat of cultural extinction, began to restore to public life a cultural voice of their own.

The coming of age of the baby boomers was a major factor for social change during this period. Many boomers pinned their political hopes on the charismatic Pierre Trudeau as the prime minister who would usher in social reform. Trudeau, for his part, believed that the Charter of Rights and Freedoms would help to create the kind of social equality that could answer the sense of injustice that many Canadians felt.

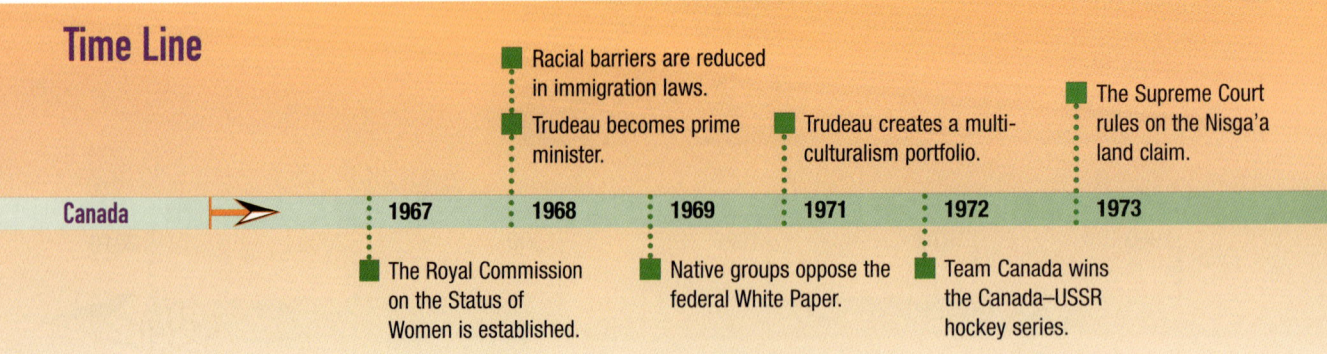

Perspectives

This photograph appeared in Canadian newspapers when Pauline McGibbon was appointed Ontario's new lieutenant-governor in 1974. It was the first time a woman had been so honoured in Canada. The caption explained that McGibbon is making a sandwich for her husband, Donald. What does this convey about the media's view of women? Would a prominent woman pose for such a photo today? Step into the picture as a photographer or reporter of today. Describe the directions you would give to Donald and Pauline McGibbon. What directions might they give you?

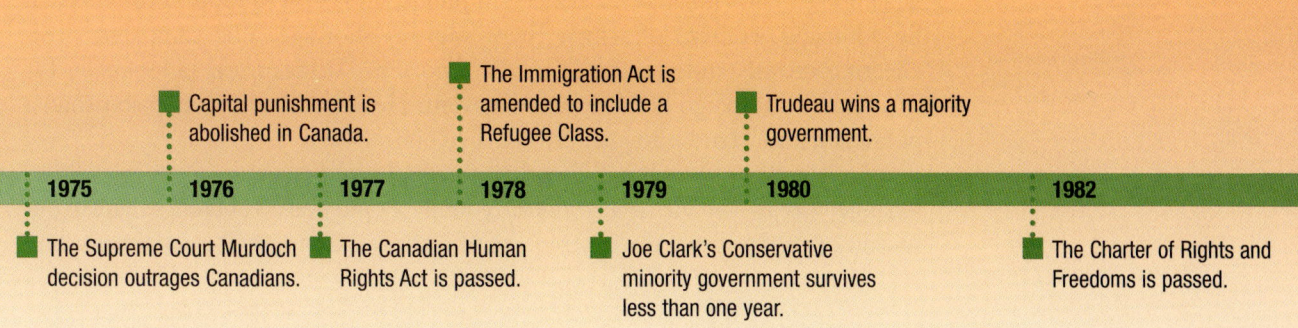

| 1975 | 1976 | 1977 | 1978 | 1979 | 1980 | 1982 |

- Capital punishment is abolished in Canada. (1976)
- The Immigration Act is amended to include a Refugee Class. (1978)
- Trudeau wins a majority government. (1980)
- The Supreme Court Murdoch decision outrages Canadians. (1975)
- The Canadian Human Rights Act is passed. (1977)
- Joe Clark's Conservative minority government survives less than one year. (1979)
- The Charter of Rights and Freedoms is passed. (1982)

PIERRE TRUDEAU AND THE "JUST SOCIETY"

Pierre Elliott Trudeau was born into wealth and privilege in 1919, but from an early age he fought for social justice in Quebec. As a university student, he spoke out against conscription during WW II. Later, in 1949, he supported mine workers in the town of Asbestos in their strike against the Quebec government. For years he campaigned against Duplessis's Union Nationale, insisting that Quebec's political **elites** must change.

In the 1960s, Trudeau criticized former Canadian governments for accepting US nuclear weapons and for giving the provinces too much power. Pearson's Liberals needed strong representatives in Quebec, however, and Trudeau was asked to join the Liberal Party. In 1965, he became a Liberal Party member. In the same year, Trudeau was elected MP for Mount Royal in Montreal. A fierce opponent of the separatist movement, he had decided that the best way to change the political system was to work within the governing federal party.

As justice minister in 1967, Trudeau introduced radical changes in sensitive legal areas. Canada's divorce laws, he said, were "highly unsatisfactory and indeed produce some very evil results." He liberalized these laws, adding physical and mental cruelty, as well as adultery, as reasonable grounds for divorce. Next Trudeau reformed the Criminal Code in the areas of abortion and prostitution, and he decriminalized homosexuality. Conservative Canadians disagreed with these **initiatives**, but Trudeau responded that "The state has no place in the bedrooms of the nation." The phrase reflected the times, and many Canadians welcomed Trudeau's candour as long overdue. While justice minister, Trudeau also revealed his committed federalism: Canada's federal government must maintain central authority over the provinces.

In December 1967, Pearson announced his retirement and chose Trudeau as his successor. Trudeau ran for the Liberal leadership, and won. Shortly after being sworn in as Canada's fifteenth prime minister, he called a general election for June 25, 1968.

Trudeaumania

In the 1968 election campaign, Trudeau presented Canadians with a very different kind of politician. He was in his 40s—young, compared to previous prime ministers. He was witty, charismatic, and spontaneous. Here was a politician who drove a sports car, and who wore cloaks, stylish hats, sandals, and a rose in his lapel. He slid down banisters, danced in public, and allowed himself to be kissed by admiring women, of which there was no shortage. His campaign drew cheering crowds and swarms of media reporters. Trudeau was tailor-made for TV, and his campaign became a media event. He seemed more a pop star than a politician, and "Trudeaumania" swept the country.

Trudeau's popularity tied directly into social undercurrents of the late 1960s. Change was in the air. Everywhere, young people were rebelling against old social norms. Expo 67, the centrepiece of Canada's Centennial celebrations, had

Up Close

1. As you read the next few pages, make jot notes of the kinds of things that made Trudeau popular and respected, both before and after he became prime minister.

Figure 11–1 Left, Trudeau hops a banister to escape reporters in 1968. Right, the Trudeaus at a Canadian music festival in 1971.

filled Canadians, young and old, with national pride and had encouraged them to look outward—to a new, brighter, and different kind of future. Even for older Canadians who rejected the radicalism of 1960s "youth culture," Trudeau seemed just the person to guide Canada into the next century. In Quebec, however, many young people saw Trudeau differently.

On the eve of the 1968 federal election, Trudeau sat in a VIP box watching Montreal's traditional St. Jean Baptiste Day Parade. Then violence erupted, and mounted police surged into the crowd as molotov cocktails exploded and sirens wailed. In the reviewing stand, federal VIPs scattered to avoid being pelted by angry protesters. Not Trudeau, who refused to move and brushed aside bodyguards. After the parade, Trudeau stood up and shrugged calmly. Trudeau's courage was broadcast live across the country and earned him respect across Canada. It was a public relations coup. The next day, Canadians went to the polls. Trudeau's Liberals won a majority government with 154 seats, representing 45.5 percent of the popular vote. The Conservatives won 72 seats, and the New Democratic Party 23. It was Canada's first majority government in a decade.

For many people, Trudeau had become a symbol not only of the new 1960s idealism, but of the new permissiveness as well. His status as a "swinging single" raised eyebrows and obsessed the international media. He was photographed with many women, some of them famous, such as Barbra Streisand. Then, in 1971, he stunned the country by secretly marrying Margaret Sinclair, who was 30 years younger. At first, the marriage was a kind of national fairy tale, but then it became tempestuous. As the media watched their every move, the Trudeaus separated in 1977 and divorced in 1984.

The Just Society

Canadians were eager to see how Trudeau would go about meeting their expectations. As prime minister, he faced many challenges as the 1960s drew to a close. Trudeau promoted what he called the "Just Society," which would strike a balance between individual **liberty** and **social justice**. Trudeau also worked to create a federal system in which all provinces were equal. In this way, he hoped that all Canadians would consider Canada their homeland as much as the province in which they lived.

"Either one nation with two languages," said Trudeau, "or, ultimately, two separate nations."

To promote this vision in Quebec, Trudeau introduced the Official Languages Act in 1969. It guaranteed francophones across the country the right to their language, and guaranteed that public servants would provide services in both English and French. Other policy initiatives included protecting the rights of minorities and creating opportunities for development in disadvantaged regions of the country.

Figure 11–2 The annual Caribana festival has become one of Toronto's major public events, and reflects its multicultural status.

The Importance of Multiculturalism

In 1971, Trudeau proclaimed "a policy of **multiculturalism** within a bilingual framework." He challenged Canadians to accept **cultural pluralism**, encouraging everyone to participate fully and equally in Canadian society. His multicultural policy was meant to allow ethnic groups to preserve their cultural heritage. It recognized what many people in urban English-speaking Canada saw as a fact of life: Canadian society included peoples from many different countries and backgrounds. In 1972, Trudeau appointed a cabinet minister for multiculturalism. Four provinces with large immigrant populations, including Ontario, initiated their own multicultural policies and programs.

Primary Source

The Cultural Freedom of All Canadians

Figure 11–3 Canada's Year of the Dragon stamp, issued in 2000

Trudeau introduced the government policy on multiculturalism in the House of Commons on October 8, 1971. As with the Official Languages Act, it was based on recommendations that had been made by the 1969 Report of the Royal Commission on Bilingualism and Biculturalism. The following is an excerpt from Trudeau's speech.

> [T]here cannot be one cultural policy for Canadians of British and French origin, another for the original peoples and yet another for all others. For although there are two official languages, there is no official culture, nor does any ethnic group take precedence over any other. No citizen or group of citizens is other than Canadian, and all should be treated fairly.
>
> The Royal Commission was guided by the belief that adherence to one's ethnic group is influenced not so much by one's origin or mother tongue as by one's sense of belonging to the group and by what the Commission calls the group's 'collective will to exist.' The Government shares this belief.
>
> The individual's freedom would be hampered if he were locked for life within a particular cultural compartment by the accident of birth or language. It is vital, therefore, that every Canadian, whatever his ethnic origin, be given a chance to learn at least one of the two official languages in which his country conducts its official business and its politics.
>
> A policy of multiculturalism within a bilingual framework commends itself to the Government as the most suitable means of assuring the cultural freedom of Canadians. Such a policy should help to break down discriminatory attitudes and cultural jealousies. National unity, if it is to mean anything in the deeply personal sense, must be founded on confidence in one's own individual identity; out of this can grow respect for that of others and a willingness to share ideas, attitudes and assumptions. A vigorous policy of multiculturalism will help create this initial confidence. It can form the base of a society which is based on fair play for all.
>
> In conclusion, I wish to emphasize the view of the Government that a policy of multiculturalism within a bilingual framework is basically the conscious support of individual freedom of choice. We are free to be ourselves. But this cannot be left to chance. It must be fostered and pursued actively. If freedom of choice is in danger for some ethnic group, it is in danger for us all. It is the policy of this Government to eliminate any such danger and to 'safeguard' this freedom.

Activity

1. Create a government announcement for the release of the Year of the Dragon stamp. Which Canadian community does the stamp honour? Refer to Trudeau's statement for ideas to include in your announcement.

The policy of multiculturalism did not solve all the tensions associated with Canada's increasingly diverse population. Many Canadians opposed multiculturalism on the grounds that it would splinter the Canadian identity. Also, non-European immigrants who entered Canada in the following decades were more concerned with overcoming racial prejudice and discrimination than with talking about cultural heritage. Trudeau's policy was based on his vision of a "Just Society," but the question remained: How could the government support a diversity of cultures and also foster Canadian identity?

Changing Immigration Patterns

As you have learned in earlier chapters, Canada's economic development depended on immigration. Even so, successive waves of immigrants had often been treated with hostility by Canadians and their governments. After World War II, immigrants had helped meet the demand for labourers and skilled professionals. But the unfamiliar customs and languages of some immigrants still made many Canadians uncomfortable. They accused immigrants of taking jobs away from people who were born in Canada. In the 1960s, many Canadians continued to express the view that if immigrants could not put aside their cultural traditions and integrate themselves into the ways of Canada, then they should go back to their countries of origin.

In the late 1960s more people were questioning this attitude. They argued that Canada should not follow the **melting pot** model of the United States, which encouraged immigrants to think of themselves first and foremost as Americans. Many Canadians preferred the idea of a **cultural mosaic**. This would allow different peoples from different places to come together, creating a new Canadian society while maintaining their cultural heritage. Trudeau's policy of multiculturalism reflected this view and reshaped Canada's immigration policies. As the government passed legislation to end racial discrimination within Canada, it also moved to eliminate similar biases in immigration policy.

In the late 1960s, a point system was introduced to help determine which immigrants would be accepted. Under this more colour-blind system, applicants were given points according to criteria such as age, education, ability to speak English or French, and the current demand for any specific job skills the applicant possessed. Those who received enough points were allowed to immigrate.

Immigration Population

Place of Birth	Period of Immigration		
	Before 1961	1961–1970	1971–1980
United States	45 050	50 200	74 015
Central and South America	6 370	17 410	67 470
Caribbean and Bermuda	8 390	45 270	96 025
United Kingdom	265 580	168 140	132 950
Other Northern and Western Europe	284 205	90 465	59 850
Eastern Europe	175 430	40 855	32 280
Southern Europe	228 145	244 380	131 620
Africa	4 945	25 685	58 150
West-central Asia and the Middle East	4 975	15 165	30 980
Eastern Asia	20 555	38 865	104 940
Southeast Asia	2 485	14 040	111 700
Southern Asia	4 565	28 875	80 755
Oceania and Other	4 250	9 240	15 420
Totals	1 054 945	788 590	996 155

Figure 11–4 Describe how this table reflects changes to Canada's immigration policy in the 1960s and 1970s.

By 1971, non-European immigrants outnumbered immigrants from Europe for the first time in Canada's history. (See Figure 11–4.) Before the reforms, many of these people would have been rejected.

A later review of immigration rules led to the 1975 Green Paper on Immigration Policy. The Green Paper's recommendations helped to form a new Immigration Act in 1978, which spelled out the goals of Canada's immigration policy. These goals included non-discrimination, family reunion, and government assistance to help newcomers adapt to Canadian society. The Act also created a **refugee** class as part of the regular immigration system. Before this, refugees had been dealt with only through special, temporary provisions.

Opening immigration to applicants from many countries did more than just increase the diversity of the population and enrich the cultural mosaic. Changes to immigration policy were also a response to Canada's economic needs. In the 1970s, Canada's birth rate and the size of Canadian families began to decline. Increased immigration offered a way for the federal government to sustain Canada's population and encourage economic growth.

Up Close

2. Write an explanation of the difference between the terms "melting pot" and "cultural mosaic." Express your ideas verbally to a partner.

CULTURE AND COUNTERCULTURE

In the 1960s and 1970s, the postwar "baby boom" generation was coming of age. Many members of this generation became part of the "counterculture," and rebelled against the earlier generation's values and traditions. Fashions flaunted a new attitude: young men wore long hair and young women wore miniskirts and jeans. Peace signs and flowers were everywhere. The philosophy of "free love" advocated sex outside of marriage, an idea that had been completely unacceptable up to that time.

Across the country, small alternative newspapers sprang up and were distributed at coffee houses from Victoria to St. John's. Popular music became a vital medium for expressing counterculture values and attitudes. Protest songs filled radio airwaves, with US artists such as Bob Dylan, British artists such as the Beatles and the Rolling Stones, and Canadian artists such as Buffy Sainte-Marie, Neil Young, Leonard Cohen, and Joni Mitchell. Their songs often had powerful political messages. Many older Canadians felt that the values they had lived by were under attack.

Indeed, the counterculture did reject the conformity of the postwar era. It envisioned a world different from the 1950s ideal of a life-long corporate job and a house in the suburbs. Social and political issues—such as the US **civil rights**

Figure 11–5 Colourful clothes, long hair, face-painting, and a relaxed, fun-loving attitude characterized the youth of the 1960s.

THE TRUDEAU TIME CAPSULE TRUNK

Open Up a Time Capsule

In Canada, youth counterculture and the Trudeau era went hand in hand. For many Canadians, it was a time to celebrate, rebel, and demonstrate. Fashion, music, and politics fused together, and the hippie era was in its heyday. Today, if you opened a trunk containing artifacts from the late 1960s you might find ...

Trudeau fans Trudeau's youthful leadership reflected other social changes. This is artist Gordon Raynor's *Trudeau Bag*, which he created while trying to track down a vacationing Trudeau on the Spanish Island of Ibiza.

Peace medallions Almost as popular as flashing the peace sign, the peace symbol was made into jewellery, belt buckles, buttons, and badges—among other things. Most of the protest was directed at US involvement in the war in Vietnam.

Clothing statements Women of all ages wore the miniskirt, and they had to sit very carefully. No one seemed to mind, and women viewed it as a statement of their new freedom. Other popular looks were fringes, bell bottoms, and tie-dyed anything. Buttons were a favourite accessory. All of a sudden it was hip to broadcast your opinions in public.

Lava lamp No one really knows what lava lamps are supposed to do, but they were a hit in the '60s. Many hours were spent watching colourful blobs in motion.

Beads galore Probably more popular than the peace medallion, beads were everywhere—as jewellery, clothing, accessories, and home furnishings. Lots of people made their own.

Sit-ins, love-ins, and sleep-ins John Lennon and Yoko Ono stayed in bed at Montreal's Queen Elizabeth Hotel for the cause of world peace. And they even visited Trudeau.

Rock Music was the mainstay of the '60s. Psychedelic music, art, and fashion symbolized freedom of thought. It was an era of drug experimentation—and that kind of imagery found its way into popular poster art.

Glasses for the masses Musicians such as Bruce Cockburn, Janis Joplin, and John Lennon popularized "granny glasses."

Hippie havens Yorkville in Toronto, Carnaby Street in London, England, and the Haight-Ashbury district of San Francisco became the capitals of the counterculture.

Flower power Daisies became the flower icon of the '60s after US students placed them in police rifles during the days of student unrest.

Living in Trudeau's Canada

Heritage Minute

Canada celebrated its Centennial with Expo 67, a world's fair held in Montreal. Nations from around the world built extraordinary pavilions, which were visited by more than 50 million people. A huge success, the exhibition raised Canada's global profile and united Canadians in national pride.

movement and the international nuclear arms race—topped the agenda. By the mid-1960s, counterculture protests also focused on US involvement in the **Vietnam War**. The fight for equality by women, Native peoples, and immigrants were also popular causes. In Quebec, Expo 67 and the increasing sense of Canadian nationalism pushed many young people into the separatist movement—in their view, the Canadian government was an oppressor.

Counterculture activism often centred on the rights of the individual versus the rights of the state. University campuses were hotbeds of protest in which students often pitted their demands for greater equality and individual freedom against more traditional views of institutional and government power. Canadian society seemed to be increasingly dominated by the angry voices of the young, proclaiming their ideals and their vision of the future.

Anne Cools Joined a Sit-in "Sit-ins" became a form of protest on college campuses in the 1960s and 1970s. In February 1969, for example, several Black students staged a sit-in at Sir George Williams University in Montreal. They alleged that one of the professors had been racist in grading the assignments of Trinidadian students. Anne Cools, who would become a senator in 1984, was one of the students who protested. After several days, the protesters destroyed the computer centre. The event came to symbolize the frustrations of Black youth in Canada at the lack of opportunities open to them.

Many Black Canadians had been optimistic when Pierre Trudeau became prime minister, but they felt that change was happening too slowly. Education was perceived as the only means of upward mobility, and the students felt that **systemic** racism was blocking their avenue to advancement. The university finally investigated the professor and cleared him of any wrongdoing, but many people were dissatisfied with both the process and the outcome.

Stirrings of Environmental Awareness

Before World War II, the major focus of public environmental concern had been on preserving the beauty of natural spaces. Governments had responded by creating national and provincial parks. After WW II, many of these parks were expanded to provide areas for recreational purposes. During the 1960s, public concern about the dangers of air and water pollution, hazardous wastes, and pesticides increased. People began to see that stronger protection of the environment was necessary for the survival of many plant and animal species—including human beings. As environmental activism grew, groups such as Pollution Probe formed across the country. These helped spur governments into taking environmental preservation and protection far more seriously.

Up Close

3. Why did groups such as Pollution Probe and Greenpeace form? What are their main objectives?

Citizenship and Heritage: Canadian Identity

Flashpoint

Eight Games that Gripped the Nation

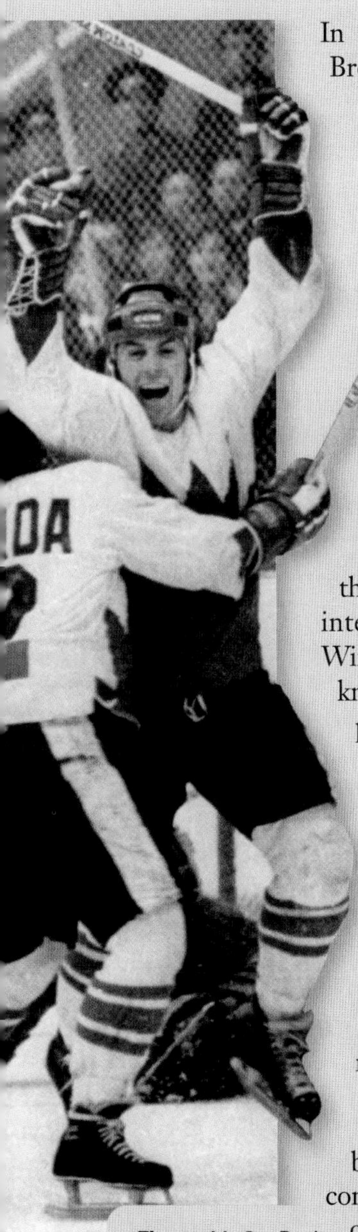

In 1999, the Canadian Press and Broadcast News voted the 1972 Team Canada "Canada's sports team of the century."

It's easy to see why. Hockey is more than Canada's favourite sport—it forms a big part of our national identity. Canada's national teams, however, had always been composed of amateur players, to comply with international rules. Since the 1950s, Canada often lost in international series and at the Winter Olympics. Still, Canadians knew in their hearts that its top players, the pros in the NHL, could beat any team in the world.

With the 1972 Canada-USSR hockey series, the world was ready to call our bluff. The NHL's top players formed Team Canada and faced off against the powerful Soviet team. There would be no excuses. The Cold War was still on, and many Canadians saw the issue as bigger than hockey—it was a contest between democracy and communism. The series opener was a blow to Canada's confidence: the Soviets won, 7-3. But Team Canada won Game 2 in Toronto, 4-1, and tied the third game, in Winnipeg, 4-4. At Game 4, in Vancouver, Team Canada lost, 5-3. The crowd turned ugly, jeering and booing the Canadian players.

"We're trying our best," said an upset Phil Esposito. "I can't believe people are booing us."

Before moving on to play in Moscow, Team Canada spent a week in Stockholm practising on the larger European ice surface. The European press criticized Team Canada's style of hockey, calling it rough and ungentlemanly. Back home, Canadians recognized Team Canada's grit and determination as defining qualities of the Canadian game. In Moscow's Luzhniki Arena, a group of 2700 Canadians displayed a noisy, militant spirit as Game 5 unfolded, but the Soviets won, 5-4. The three remarkable hockey games that followed roused the Canadian population and united the nation.

In Game 6, Paul Henderson scored three straight goals to win the game. In Game 7 of the series, Henderson scored with 2:06 left to play, leading the Canadians to yet another victory. It seemed nothing short of a miracle. The last game took place on September 28, 1972. The series was tied 3-3 and Canada's national pride was at stake. The game was so important that, in schools across the country, students were led to gymnasiums to witness the outcome on TV. With the score tied and time running out, Canadians held their breath. Foster Hewitt, the legendary broadcaster, called the play-by-play: "The puck comes out to Henderson. He shoots! He scores! Paul Henderson has scored for Canada!" Team Canada had won the series. It was a moment many Canadians would never forget.

Figure 11–6 Paul Henderson scores the winning goal in the Canada-USSR hockey series.

What Do You Think?

1. Different peoples and regions of Canada often bitterly disagree with each other, yet during this hockey series differences were put aside. Why do you think that national unity seemed spontaneous in this instance, when it is so difficult to achieve on other issues?

Living in Trudeau's Canada

Figure 11–7 On July 13, 1985, French government agents sank Greenpeace's *Rainbow Warrior* in Aukland, New Zealand, killing a Greenpeace photographer. Greenpeace was leading a protest against French nuclear testing in the Pacific.

Federal and provincial governments established ministries or departments of the environment and passed legislation for protection of the environment. The Ontario government became a world leader in acting to protect endangered species of plants and animals. In 1973, the federal government created the Environmental Assessment and Review Program, which required that proposed development projects undergo an environmental impact assessment (EIA) to determine how they would affect the surrounding environment. Public involvement played—and still plays—a central role in these assessments. In some cases, an EIA meant that a proposed project had to be relocated, modified, or altogether cancelled.

One of the most prominent environmental activist groups in the world was born in Canada during this period. In 1971, the United States carried out nuclear tests beneath the island of Amchitka, off the west coast of Alaska. Many people feared the tests could trigger a major earthquake, while others were concerned about the impact on wildlife, including endangered sea otters. A group in Vancouver formed Greenpeace to protest the nuclear testing and chartered a fishing vessel to take their protest directly to the site of the tests. The US Coast Guard stopped the ship, and the nuclear tests took place. Greenpeace, however, had invited members of the media to join the ship's crew. Their protest—a small group of activists against the mighty US military—made headlines around the world. Since then, Greenpeace has often used media attention to heighten public awareness of environmental issues. Since the 1970s, Greenpeace has been active in protests against nuclear testing in the South Pacific, commercial whale hunting, and the Canadian seal hunt. Their methods have often been controversial, but Greenpeace now owns its own fleet of ships and has become global, with offices in more than 30 countries.

Up Close

4. Begin a chart of Canadian artists who have become famous partly because of government support. Start with the people named in this section, and add to it from your own knowledge. Use headings such as Writers, Singers, Actors, and so on.

Arts and Culture

By the 1960s, Canadians had become concerned about the increasing US influence on Canadian culture. The growing sense of Canadian nationalism in the Trudeau government led to a range of policies aimed at protecting and promoting Canada's cultural identity. Under the Broadcasting Act of 1968, the Canadian Radio-Television Commission (CRTC) was established to regulate and supervise the broadcasting system in Canada. In 1976, CRTC jurisdiction was expanded to include telecommunications, and its name was changed to the Canadian Radio-Television and Telecommunications Commission. All Canadian broadcasters must apply for licences from the CRTC, which also has the power to amend, review, and revoke licences.

Communities: Canadian Identity

Images

Miyuke Tanobe: A Meeting of Cultures

"I often ask myself where I get this insatiable interest in the daily lives of people," says Miyuke Tanobe, one of Quebec's most popular painters. "This ebb and flow of daily life is my passion, and what my painting is all about."

While living in her native Japan, Tanobe had received letters from a Canadian friend who described the sights and sounds of his Montreal neighbourhood. Curious to see these scenes for herself, Tanobe came to Montreal in 1971. She spent all her spare time exploring the streets and observing the people she'd heard so much about. For her, the neighbourhood became "not only a place to live, but a constant source of discovery and inspiration—the corner grocery stores, spiral staircases, overloaded clotheslines, and the people, whose warmth can be felt in the streets." Tanobe's ability to convey this warmth in her paintings is part of what makes them so appealing.

Before coming to Canada, Tanobe studied at the Tokyo School of Fine Arts and later at the École Nationale des Beaux Arts in Paris, France. She works in a style known as Nihonga, which makes use of Chinese and Indian techniques that were further developed in Japan. To make her own paints, Tanobe grinds special stones to create a powder. She then adds water and a glue made of fish bones and antlers. The paint is applied in many layers, a long process that requires much patience.

"Finishing a painting that was difficult for me is one of the great pleasures," says Tanobe. "I paint to earn a living, but no money can buy me what I feel when I've finished something good. All the energy, the thinking, frustration—all comes back as satisfaction. The paintings I like now are the ones that gave me the greatest problems in the making."

Tanobe eventually married the friend who had written to her about his Montreal neighbourhood,

Figure 11–8 Tanobe's *Mont-Royal Avenue*

and the two moved to Saint-Antoine-sur-le-Richelieu, a town in rural Quebec. Here, Tanobe paints the townspeople and their festivities, illustrating their strong links to local traditions. She also makes trips to other parts of the province, sketching the people and surrounding countryside. Painting the daily life of people had long been an artistic tradition in Japan. Tanobe has combined this tradition with her experiences to create vibrant canvases that capture a unique perspective on life in *la belle province*.

What Do You Think?

1. Do you think that the people painted by Tanobe thought that their daily surroundings and activities were interesting? Or might they see them as "humdrum" and "routine"? Try to see your own neighbourhood with entirely fresh eyes, and describe or illustrate what you see.

Living in Trudeau's Canada

CRTC regulations forced television and radio stations to broadcast a specific quota of **Canadian content**. In 1970, the CRTC required that a minimum of 30 percent of radio programming had to be Canadian content. To qualify, a recording had to meet two of the following four criteria: the song is composed by a Canadian; the lyrics are written by a Canadian; the song is performed by a Canadian; the song is recorded in Canada. Many commercial broadcasters protested that their audiences wanted to listen to popular US recordings, but they had to comply. These regulations allowed many Canadian performers, such as Anne Murray, to achieve a level of exposure that might not otherwise have been possible. Some of these performers went on to become international stars.

The government also provided financial incentives to encourage the growth of Canadian culture. Special income tax deductions were introduced to increase investment in Canadian movies. Changes to tax laws on advertising revenue discouraged US magazines such as *Time* and *Newsweek* from publishing Canadian editions. *Maclean's* took advantage of this policy and went from a monthly to a weekly newsmagazine in 1976. The Canada Council was more generously funded by the Trudeau government, and awarded subsidies and grants to a large group of artists and arts organizations involved in the visual arts, music, literature, film, dance, and theatre. The council's financial assistance enabled many Canadian artists to practise and develop their talents in Canada. To encourage a Canadian feature film industry, the Canadian Film Development Corporation was established in 1967. The organization was renamed Telefilm Canada in 1984.

During the Trudeau years, many Canadian artists rose to international prominence. In 1969, acclaimed Quebec actress Geneviève Bujold was nominated for an Oscar for her portrayal of Anne Boleyn in *Anne of the Thousand Days*. Ballerinas Karen Kain and Evelyn Hart achieved world-class status as artists. Canadian authors such as Margaret Atwood, Margaret Laurence, and Mordecai Richler grew in popularity. Acadian writer Antonine Maillet and Quebec writer Anne Hebert were hailed in France as major French-language novelists. Montreal jazz pianist and composer Oscar Peterson, an international success since the 1950s, released recordings which paired him with jazz legends such as Ella Fitzgerald and Count Basie.

Figure 11–9 Ballerina Karen Kain was one of many Canadians who achieved world-class status as artists during this period.

THE WOMEN'S MOVEMENT

In the first half of the twentieth century, women had won significant battles for equality, but progress was slow. In the late 1960s, a new feminism spread throughout Europe, the US, and Canada. The publication of *The Feminine Mystique* by US writer Betty Friedan and *The Female Eunuch* by Australian

Germaine Greer had a profound impact on the way many women viewed their role in society. These books, which showed how women had been systematically denied opportunities open to men, became instant bestsellers. In the late 1960s, two events shone the spotlight on the Canadian women's movement: the Irene Murdoch case and the Royal Commission on the Status of Women.

Irene Murdoch Went to Court Irene Murdoch married an Alberta farmer in 1943. For 25 years she worked hard with him running the farm—money from her parents helped them begin their life together. For months at a time, she ran the farm by herself while her husband was away. In 1968, her husband wanted to sell the farm and make a new start, but Irene disagreed. Her husband put the farm up for sale anyway.

The Murdochs began divorce proceedings, and Irene expected a share of the money from the sale of the farm, in recognition of her years of hard work. The court decision awarded the farm to her husband, which meant he could keep all the money from its sale. Irene received $200 a month. She appealed the divorce settlement all the way to the Supreme Court. In 1975, the Supreme Court awarded her husband the ranch, the buildings, the house, the furniture, even her clothes and car. Only one of the all-male Supreme Court justices, Bora Laskin, supported Irene's claim to a share of the farm.

Figure 11–10 Germaine Greer's bestselling *The Female Eunuch* caused many Canadian women to rethink their traditional roles.

Divorce still made Canadians uncomfortable in the late 1960s, but many felt that Irene Murdoch had been let down by the Supreme Court. Women across Canada were shocked, and the case focused public attention on the legal inequities women faced. It seemed little had changed since 1929, when the Supreme Court had ruled that "women were not persons," a ruling later overturned by the Privy Council in England.

The Royal Commission on the Status of Women

Irene Murdoch's long-fought battle eventually made a difference. Although the federal government was responsible for determining grounds for divorce, provincial governments decided on child custody and property settlements. In 1975, Ontario passed legislation that recognized a woman's right to a share of property in divorce settlements. Other provinces soon followed, resulting in Family Reform Acts that recognized the right of women to a share of the family property.

Living in Trudeau's Canada

Figure 11–11 Editorial staff of *Chatelaine*, 1972. Traditionally a homemakers' magazine, *Chatelaine* switched its emphasis to women's issues in the 1970s.

The Murdoch case was a lightning rod for women's groups across the country. Since the mid-1960s, they had been demanding improvements to women's position in society. In 1967, Prime Minister Pearson had instituted a Royal Commission on the Status of Women. It was chaired by Florence Bird, the first woman ever to head a Royal Commission. Bird, an Ottawa journalist, and six other commissioners began public hearings in 1968, visiting 14 cities across Canada, including some in the Far North. The Commission received over 460 briefs and 2000 letters, heard over 800 witnesses, and cost $3 million. The final report made 167 recommendations.

The Royal Commission was either ignored or ridiculed when it began. But the public hearings became media events that drew national attention on issues related to equality: equal pay for work of equal value, maternity leave, birth control and abortion, pensions, discrimination against women under the Indian Act, and the "glass ceiling" that prevented professional women from reaching the top ranks in corporate Canada.

The Royal Commission on the Status of Women presented its report in 1970. The recommendations included

- expanding pensions to include housewives
- granting maternity leave of up to 18 weeks
- prohibiting discrimination based on gender or marital status
- making a wife responsible for supporting her husband, just as the husband was responsible for supporting his wife
- providing a guaranteed annual income to the head of all one-parent families with dependent children
- appointing more women judges and senators
- making birth control information widely available to everyone (made legal in 1969, this information was usually provided to married women only)
- amending the Criminal Code to permit abortion on request up to 12 weeks into term

Trudeau generally supported the principles of the Report, and created a **junior cabinet position** responsible for the Status of Women. Some critics questioned how committed the government was in responding to the Royal Commission Report. In frustration, 30 separate women's groups joined together in 1971 to create the National Action Committee on the Status of Women (NAC). Their purpose was to pursue equality and social justice for women, primarily through pressuring the federal government to make changes to improve the status and rights of women. The NAC has grown dramatically since it first began, and is today the largest feminist organization in the country, including over 700 women's groups.

Up Close

5. For each of these people, write a sentence describing their role in the changing status of women in Canada: Irene Murdoch, Florence Bird, Betty Friedan, Germaine Greer, Prime Minister Pearson, Prime Minister Trudeau.

Women in Politics and the Workplace

In the 1970s, women started to become much more visible in politics. Between 1917 and 1970, only 67 women had been elected in federal and provincial elections, compared to 6778 men. Also first elected to the House in 1972 was Jeanne Sauvé, whose distinguished career would later include Cabinet portfolios in science and technology, the environment, and communications. She would go on to become the first female Speaker of the House of Commons and the first female governor general of Canada.

Women also made significant strides in provincial politics. By 1974, there were 14 female provincial MLAs or MPs, with BC leading the entire country with six. Ontario had three; Alberta two and Quebec, New Brunswick, and Prince Edward Island each had one.

Figure 11–12 Rosemary Brown congratulates Ed Broadbent after he defeated her in the 1975 NDP national leadership race.

In 1972, Rosemary Brown became the first Black woman elected in British Columbia. She ran unsuccessfully for the leadership of the NDP in 1975. Brown had come to Canada from Jamaica to attend Montreal's McGill University in the 1950s. In Canada, she encountered an atmosphere that was not as racially tolerant as she had expected. Nevertheless, Brown used her experiences as a basis for exploring the inequities of Canadian society. She pursued a Master's degree in social work, and became an activist in the areas of poverty, sexual discrimination, and protection of the environment. She called running for the NDP leadership the result of dreaming the seemingly impossible—"a Black Canadian being a national political leader."

When Alexa McDonough became leader of the Nova Scotia NDP in 1980, she was one of the first women to lead a provincial party. She won the NDP federal leadership in 1995, taking over from Audrey McLaughlin, who had been the first woman to lead a federal political party in 1989. Other significant milestones include the 1974 appointment of Pauline McGibbon as lieutenant-governor of Ontario, the first female lieutenant-governor in the country. Bertha Wilson became the first female Supreme Court justice in 1982.

In the workplace, women were pursuing jobs traditionally held by men. In 1974, Pauline Jewett became the first female president of a co-ed university in Canada, Simon Fraser University in BC. Shirley Carr was elected executive vice-president of the Canadian Labour Congress (CLC) and eventually became its first female president. In 1975, the first ten policewomen began training with the Ontario Provincial Police. Acceptance of women in these careers was slow to come, but the courage and perseverance of a few women forged the way for many to follow.

Women who did establish careers in predominantly male professions were often paid less than the men. The 1977 Canadian Human Rights Act specifically prohibited discrimination on the basis of gender and extended the concept of "equal pay for work of equal value" to include any jobs requiring comparable

Data File

In 1970, there were five women in the House of Commons: Albanie Morin, Monique Bégin, Jeanne Sauvé, Flora MacDonald, Grace MacInnis. All but two were Liberals from Quebec.

Up Close

6. Choose five "firsts" for women that you have read about in this section. Describe them and name the woman who accomplished each.

skills and level of education. It was hoped this Act would close the wage gap between men and women, but that has not happened yet. The Human Rights Act led to the establishment of the Canadian Human Rights Commission and the Human Rights Tribunal Panel. These bodies were created to promote equal opportunity, including pay equity and equal access to services, and to provide Canadians the opportunity to file grievances if they believe they have suffered discrimination.

THE NATIVE PEOPLES

> **Data File**
>
> In 1969, the last residential school for Native children was closed.

In 1969, the goals of the "Just Society" would clash with those of the Native peoples. One reason was the new ability of First Nations to form effective political lobby groups. Although the Pearson government had established an inquiry into aboriginal affairs in 1964—marking the first time First Nations would participate in an inquiry about their own society and culture—their needs were still largely ignored. Government still expected the Native peoples to completely assimilate into Canadian life. By contrast, Native communities were concerned with defining their unique status as a people, and with securing rights to the land they once controlled.

Between 1968 and 1969, the Trudeau government met with Native leaders, including representatives from the National Indian Brotherhood, a lobby group formed in 1968. The NIB was made up of treaty and status Indians who had once been members of the National Indian Council (see Chapter 8). Representatives from both sides discussed the possibility of revising the Indian Act yet again. On this occasion, however, Native leaders made it clear that the priority was recognition of their special rights and settlement of their land claims.

The White Paper

> **Data File**
>
> Since 1927, the Indian Act had made it illegal for the Native peoples to form political organizations. They did anyway, and were often jailed by the RCMP for their initiatives.

The Native peoples were disappointed when the federal government released its White Paper in 1969. The views expressed in the White Paper reflected Trudeau's personal philosophy of the importance of individual rights over collective rights. The proposal was simple. The government would "enable the Indian people to be free—free to develop Indian culture in an environment of legal, social and economic equality with other Canadians."

The government proposed to repeal the Indian Act and amend the British North America (BNA) Act to end the legal distinction between the Native peoples and other Canadians. Aboriginal peoples would take control of the reserves, but aboriginal rights would not be recognized—and all signed treaties would be terminated. In compensation, the government promised to pay $50 million over five years. By cancelling the Indian Act and treaties, aboriginal peoples would be treated as individuals, not communities. In losing their special status, they would also lose compensation for the surrender of ancestral lands.

Historical Inquiry: Recording/Organizing Information

Historian at Work

Identifying Your Sources of Information

When you write essays and reports, it is important to identify your sources of information. A basic guide to correct style for different types of sources follows. Refer to a style guide for more detailed information when necessary.

Figure 11–13 Correctly identifying your sources gives your reader confidence in the facts you provide.

Bibliography

A bibliography lists all the sources you used for information. Here are some examples of correct style:

- **Book (one author)**

  Include the author's name, the full title of the book, the place of publication, the publisher, and the date of publication.

  Wilson, Ken. *Outstanding Canadian Prime Ministers*. Vancouver: Maple Leaf Books, 1998.

- **Magazine article (two authors)**

  If the article is longer than one page, write a plus sign after the first page number.

  Aubin, Michel and Ken Li. "A Look at Canada's Defence Spending." *The Journal of Canadian Politics* Oct. 1999: 12+

- **Reference book**

  Where no author is listed, start with the title of the book.

  Encyclopedia of Canadian Wildlife 3rd ed. 1996. "Muskrat."

- **Web site**

  Include the date you accessed the information and enclose the web address in angle brackets.

  "Quebec Language Laws." *The Online Political Forum*. 11 Apr. 2000 <www.polforum.ca>

Citations

Citations identify the source of specific ideas and quotes in a report or essay. Three different types of citations are shown below:

- **In-text citations**

  Put the author's name and the page number(s) in brackets at the end of a sentence that contains information from a source. Readers can use the bibliography to find out more about the source.

  Surveys showed that most people did not agree with the prime minister's decision (Winters 127).

- **Footnotes**

  Put a small, raised number at the end of the sentence. At the bottom of the page, write the number and information about the source. Put the page number last.

  An investigation revealed that toxic substances were present in the water.[1]

  [1]Michael Murphy, *Ontario's Waterways* (Scarborough, ON: Naturalist Publications, 1997) 186.

- **Endnotes**

  Prepare endnotes in the same way as footnotes, but list all the sources in order on a page at the end of the document.

What Do You Think?

1. Why is it important to acknowledge the sources you use for information?

Figure 11–14 Harold Cardinal, president of the Alberta Indian Association, urges Trudeau (bottom left) to settle treaties.

The government was forced to withdraw the White Paper in 1971 because it was so unpopular. Almost all Native peoples joined together in hostile opposition. The NIB condemned the White Paper in these remarks:

> We view this as a policy designed to divest us of our aboriginal, residential and statutory rights. If we accept this policy, and in the process lose our rights and our lands, we become willing partners in cultural genocide. This we cannot do.

Following the release of the White Paper, the NIB grew in stature as a lobby group, and helped to shape Native policy on education, health care, and economic development. It produced a policy paper in 1972 that recommended aboriginal control of education for Native youth. In 1982, the NIB became the Assembly of First Nations (AFN) to better reflect the diverse communities of Native peoples in Canada. Its leaders have included George Erasmus and Ovide Mercredi. Today, the AFN is made up of chiefs from approximately 630 First Nations in Canada.

Jeannette Corbière-Lavell Went to Court One of the most difficult issues facing Native peoples in the 1970s stemmed from the consequences of marrying a non-Native person. This issue is illustrated by the story of Jeannette Corbière-Lavell. Born on the Wikwemikong Reserve on Manitoulin Island in Ontario, Jeannette was a member of the Nishnawbe people. Fluent in both English and Ojibway, she eventually moved to Toronto to work as an executive secretary.

In 1970, Jeannette married David Lavell. Soon afterwards, she received a notice from the Department of Indian Affairs and Northern Development, informing her that she was no longer an Indian according to the Indian Act. Section 12(1)(b) of the Indian Act stated that Native women who married non-

Up Close

7. Create a time line that spans 1968 to 1987, showing events that relate to the changing political status of Native Canadians.

Natives lost their Indian status, as did any children they might have. In contrast, the Indian Act allowed Native men who married non-Natives to keep their status. Their children, including children from a previous marriage, were also allowed to keep their status. Jeannette demanded that the government change the Indian Act to end this discrimination against Native women.

The issue involved the question of individual versus collective rights. Jeannette and other women who had lost their Indian status under the Indian Act wanted recognition, while registered Native peoples insisted on protecting their ethnic autonomy by evicting Native women living with white spouses. They argued that this was necessary to protect First Nations communities from gradually losing their culture through assimilation.

Women's groups across Canada supported Jeannette's case. The Native Council of Canada, a group representing non-status Indians and Métis, also supported her. The NIB, however, did not. In 1971, Jeannette lost her case in County Court, but won after appealing her case to the Federal Court of Appeal. In 1973, the Supreme Court ruled against her, saying that the Canadian Bill of Rights did not apply to her situation. It wasn't until 1985 that the Indian Act was amended to guarantee the status of a Native woman who married outside her culture.

Jeannette Corbière-Lavell became a founding member of the Ontario Native Women's Association and served as vice-president of the Native Women's Association of Canada. In 1987, the Ontario Native Women's Association established the Jeannette Corbière-Lavell Award, to be presented to a Native woman who demonstrated the same perseverance shown by Jeannette during her 14-year battle for justice.

Figure 11–15 Jeannette Corbière-Lavell and her husband express joy after winning a landmark court challenge of the section of the Indian Act that deprived a Native woman of her Indian status if she married a non-Native.

Land Claims and Clashes with Industry

Nineteen seventy-three ushered in a key event in the history of aboriginal land claims disputes. The date marked a victory for the Nisga'a, one of the Native peoples of British Columbia's Northwest Coast. As you learned in Chapter 1, the Nisga'a had never signed a treaty with their provincial government. They began fighting for title to their land in 1907. During the Trudeau years, the legal battle of the Nisga'a reached the Supreme Court. In 1973, the court rejected the Nisga'a claim, but it acknowledged the idea of aboriginal title. This paved the way for later successful land claims.

Land claims became a focus of attention for Inuit and Cree when, on April 30, 1971, Quebec Premier Robert Bourassa announced that the James Bay Project would start immediately. The $5.8 billion hydroelectric project, which was to be built on Native land, was announced without any Native consultation and did not address compensation. The Inuit immediately organized themselves into an association, the Inuit Tapirisat of Canada, coordinated by Tagek Curley and Meeha Wilson.

Figure 11–16 Quebec planned to expand the James Bay Project in the 1990s. By 1996, Cree Grand Chief Matthew Coon Come had attracted supporters such as Robert Kennedy, Jr. to the Native campaign against the project.

The association's objective was to "gain political and economic control and to preserve the culture, identity, and way of life of the Inuit, and to help them find their role in a changing society." And they met with some immediate successes. Classroom instruction in **Inuktitut** increased. Cooperation with the Grand Council of Cree provided a stronger voice in pushing for outstanding land claims settlements. Media coverage of the James Bay Project grabbed the public's attention, and the Quebec government was forced to negotiate. The James Bay and Northern Quebec Agreement was signed in 1975. It was the first modern aboriginal land-claims settlement to include financial compensation and control of natural resources, but it did not guarantee Native rights. The environmental impact of the agreement has not been positive for the Inuit and Cree. More than 10 000 square kilometres of land now lie under water, and massive, negative environmental impact is expected to be long-term.

A 1974 government inquiry into the proposed Mackenzie Valley Pipeline took a very different approach in dealing with Native communities. The proposed pipeline would have carried natural gas from the Arctic to Alberta and threatened to disrupt the aboriginal communities of the North. When Justice Thomas Berger was appointed to chair the inquiry, he consulted with Native groups directly and interviewed thousands of people in their communities across the North. As a result of Berger's efforts to keep the media informed, many Canadians learned for the first time about the complex problems of northern development. At one of the hearings, a witness summed up the perspective of the Native peoples:

Up Close

8. Reread this witness's comment, and recall Nellie McClung's Mock Parliament (see Flashpoint, page 41). Write a similar scenario related to the Natives' situation and your own community.

> I wonder how people in Toronto would react if the people of Old Crow went down to Toronto and said, 'Well, look, we are going to knock down all those skyscrapers and high rises, blast a few holes to make lakes for muskrat trapping, and you people are just going to have to move out and stop driving cars and move into cabins.'

In 1977, the Berger Inquiry issued its report. It recommended that the government should wait ten years, and deal with Native land claims first. It also opposed the idea of construction in the northern Yukon, which could upset the delicate ecological balance. To the surprise of many, the government abandoned the project. You will read more about this issue in Chapter 13.

TRUDEAU'S LAST TERM

As the 1970s progressed, Trudeau's popularity plummeted. He came to be seen by many Canadians as arrogant and condescending. He was blamed for Canada's ongoing economic problems, especially in western Canada. You will learn more about this in Chapter 13. The election of many non-Liberal provincial governments seemed to express Canadians' discontent with the federal Liberals. On the night of May 22, 1979, sixteen years of Liberal government came to an end with the election of Joe Clark and the Conservative Party. Joe Clark had been the Conservative Party leader since 1976. He was far less flamboyant than Trudeau, and Canadians joked about "Joe Who?". But Clark's party won a minority with 136 seats, compared to 114 for the Liberals, and 26 for the NDP.

Inexperience and a few miscalculated political moves led to the fall of the Conservative government in the House of Commons. On December 13, 1979, finance minister John Crosbie's budget was defeated in a vote of 139 to 133. After only seven months in power, the government had to call another election. Remarkably, Trudeau regained his energy and appeal with voters, and was returned to office in 1980 with another majority government.

Figure 11–17 Trudeau lost popularity with voters but Joe Clark's minority government lasted only a few months.

The Charter of Rights and Freedoms

In his last term, Trudeau returned to his vision of the "Just Society" with renewed purpose. In 1982, the government passed the Charter of Rights and Freedoms, which protected the rights of individual Canadians. The Charter enshrined rights for women, aboriginal peoples, and, in Section 15 (1), it guaranteed "equality without discrimination based on race, national or ethnic origin, colour, religion, sex, age or mental or physical disability." Women campaigned hard for the inclusion of Section 28, which ensured that "the rights and freedoms referred to in [the Charter] are guaranteed equally to male and female persons." Aboriginal peoples pushed for protection of previous aboriginal rights and freedoms in Section 25, particularly with respect to land claims.

Justice Thomas Berger noted that the Charter did not resolve "the great questions of human rights and fundamental freedoms. In a sense these are never resolved. They will continue to be the subject of inquiry, debate and controversy. But the Charter will offer minorities a place to stand, ground to defend and the means for others to come to their aid." Trudeau wanted the Charter of Rights and Freedoms to be entrenched as part of the Canadian Constitution, and he wanted that constitution to be patriated from Britain. In the next chapter, you will learn how these goals were achieved and of consequences that would threaten the very survival of Canada.

CONCLUSION

Many groups of Canadians, including women, the Native peoples, and Canadians of many cultures experienced gains in their social, legal, and political opportunities during this period. Nationalism was affirmed. Canadian culture was increasingly protected, and the environment began to be seen as an important public concern. But could all issues in Canadian life be solved by social or legal changes? Another way of asking the question is this: Was legal equality a solution to everybody's problems? Would the Charter of Rights and Freedoms address all the important issues? In the next chapter you will find out how Trudeau's approach to Canada's needs fared in Quebec.

CHAPTER ACTIVITIES

Check Your Understanding

1. Create a definition of a "Just Society" that you think Pierre Trudeau would agree with.
2. Create a chart comparing Pierre Trudeau's behaviour to traditional Canadian expectations for politicians. Did Trudeau better represent the lifestyle of the 1960s? Why or why not?
3. List ways in which Trudeau tried to make Canadian society more inclusive for all of its members.

Develop Your Thinking

4. In the late 1960s, the government introduced a "point system" to regulate immigration. Referring to each category, explain why this system met the goals of Canadian immigration.
5. Did Trudeau's reforms meet everyone's needs? Was anyone left out? Discuss.
6. This text, like any other source, is written from a perspective, or bias. For example, the actions of government and special interest groups are presented in a positive or negative light. Do you agree with the perspective of the text? Why or why not?

Express Yourself

7. Prepare arguments to debate one of the following issues with classmates:
   - "Trudeau's multicultural policy weakened the Canadian identity."

- "The Canadian content regulations of the Trudeau era were unfair because they forced broadcasters to play songs and programs that the Canadian public did not want."
- "The Canadian government has effectively responded to the social demands of women since the Irene Murdoch Case."

8. Write a protest poem or song that accurately captures the counterculture view of a key event of the 1960s.

9. Create a poster advertising an event sponsored by a special interest group active during this period, for example, Greenpeace, the National Action Committee on the Status of Women, or the Assembly of First Nations.

10. Research the issues of the 1980 election and write a campaign speech for either Clark or Trudeau, outlining their past efforts and future promises.

Apply Your Learning

11. Music lyrics often express the feelings of a generation. Choose two protest songs, one from the late 1960s and one from today. Compare the values expressed in each. Does the difference in lyrics reflect a change in society? How?

12. Research Greenpeace activities during the 1970s and 1980s. To what degree did their use of media attention succeed in raising awareness and changing environmental policy?

13. After reading this chapter, you have a good understanding of many issues that developed in Canada during this period:
    - multiculturalism
    - environmental issues
    - the role of women
    - Native issues

    What is happening in Canadian society today with respect to these issues? Use evidence to support your answers.

Extend Your Learning Using the Internet

14. During the Trudeau years, Canadians lived through, and often struggled with, many cultural and social changes. Research media and personal accounts of those years, and formulate questions on change and continuity as these forces affected people's lives. Identify any biases you should consider as you evaluate the viewpoints of different people and different media.

15. Was "Trudeaumania" a creation of the mass media? Research newspaper Internet archives on the phenomenon and create interview questions. Then interview two people who were eyewitnesses to that period of Canadian history and write a report of your findings.

12
The Question of Quebec

Focus Questions

Economic and Political Structures
Why did many Quebecers begin to see separation from Canada as the only effective solution to the problems they faced?

French–English Relations
Why did the Parti Québécois enact legislation requiring the use of French in the workplace and on commercial signs?

Social and Political Movements
What solution to Quebec's problems did Lévesque's new Parti Québécois offer, as contrasted to the solution offered by Trudeau's federalism?

Canada's International Status and Foreign Policy
What difference did repatriating the Constitution make to Canadians outside Quebec? What difference did it make within Quebec?

Following the Quiet Revolution, francophones in Quebec became increasingly dissatisfied with Confederation. Trudeau responded with a vision for a bilingual Canada in which English and French would be equal. But how relevant was bilingualism to Quebec's concerns? The growth of the violent Front de Liberation de Québec and the democratic separatist Parti Québécois illustrated the widening gap between English Canada. The FLQ's violent approach was quickly discredited in Quebec. But René Lévesque's Parti Québécois (PQ) gained a large following and became the new provincial government in 1976, defeating the federalist Union Nationale. Both the Union Nationale and the PQ introduced legislation to protect French and limit the use of English.

Meanwhile, the PQ had promised a referendum in Quebec on sovereignty-association (a form of separation). The federalists won by a very slight margin. This victory gave Trudeau his chance to try for a renewed federalism. He now hoped that by developing a Canadian constitution, most Quebecers would renew their commitment to federalism. The other nine provinces eventually sided with Trudeau's plan, but he could not get Quebec to agree. Finally, the other nine provinces agreed with Quebec. Canada had a new constitution, written by Canadians. But because Quebec did not sign, Canada still had a national unity problem.

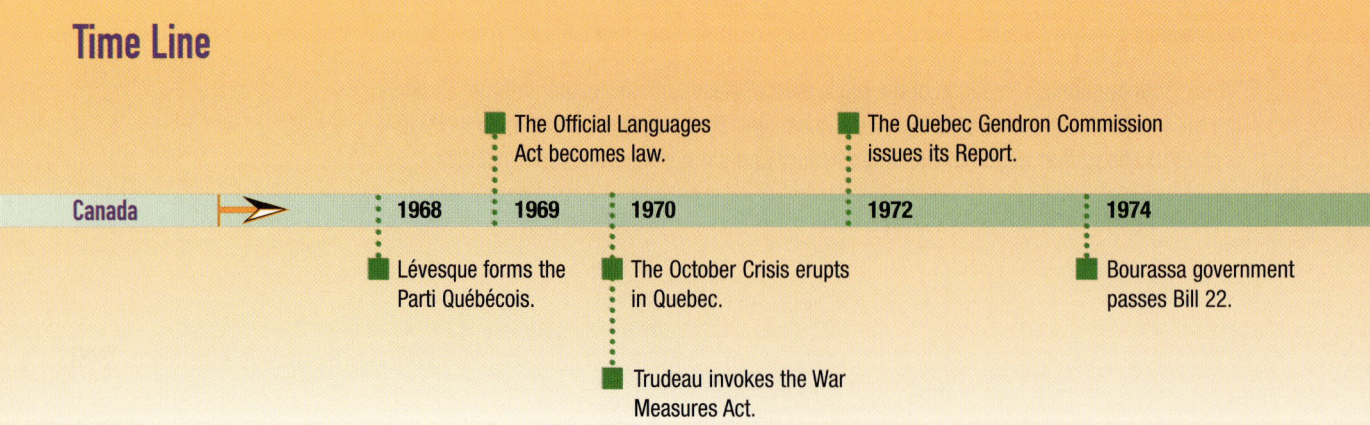

Time Line

Canada

- 1968 — Lévesque forms the Parti Québécois.
- 1969 — The Official Languages Act becomes law.
- 1970 — The October Crisis erupts in Quebec. Trudeau invokes the War Measures Act.
- 1972 — The Quebec Gendron Commission issues its Report.
- 1974 — Bourassa government passes Bill 22.

Perspectives

The 1976 provincial "sweep" by the Parti Québécois was celebrated with great fanfare by this group of Montrealers on November 15, the night of the election triumph. Why would the expression *maîtres chez nous* be especially appropriate on this evening—for these celebrants? Canadian newspapers described the event as an "upset" victory over the Liberals. What might a Liberal supporter be thinking as this crowd passed by?

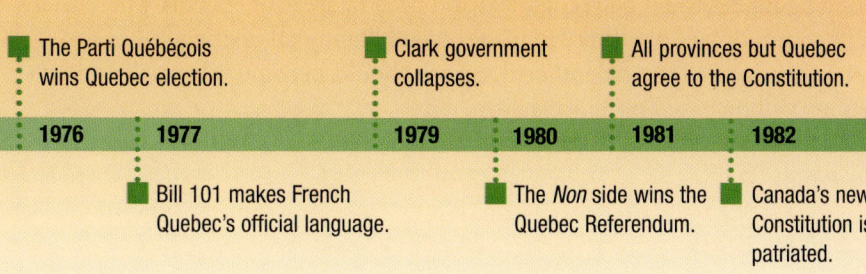

- 1976 — The Parti Québécois wins Quebec election.
- 1977 — Bill 101 makes French Quebec's official language.
- 1979 — Clark government collapses.
- 1980 — The *Non* side wins the Quebec Referendum.
- 1981 — All provinces but Quebec agree to the Constitution.
- 1982 — Canada's new Constitution is patriated.

COMPETING VISIONS OF CANADA

By the late 1960s, many Quebecers had become completely frustrated with Canada's federal system. English continued to be the dominant language in the worlds of Quebec business and finance. Quebec's leaders were trying to correct the imbalance, but the rate of change was too slow for many. The Quiet Revolution had raised the hopes of young people in Quebec, and many more were now going to college or university. But then they found that the top management and corporate jobs, for which they were qualified, just were not available to francophones. For these and other dissatisfied people, separation from Canada seemed the best way to make the French-speaking majority of Quebec *maîtres chez nous* ("masters of our own house").

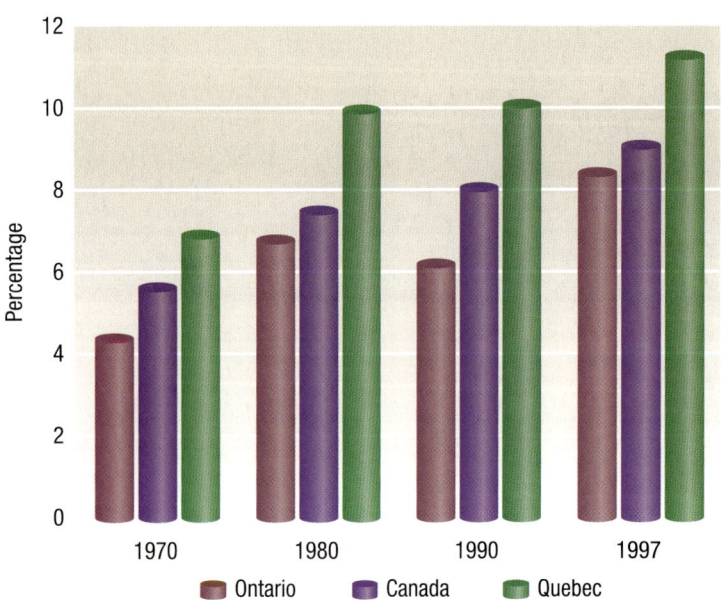

Figure 12–1 Percentage of people unemployed in Quebec compared with Ontario and Canada overall

Trudeau's Solution: The Official Languages Act

As you learned in Chapter 11, the Official Languages Act of 1969 was meant to ease growing tensions over French-English language rights. The Act would give both languages equal status throughout Canada. Prime Minister Trudeau described it as "a reflection of the nature of this country as a whole, and of a conscious choice we are making about our future." He proposed that having two official languages would not only resolve political problems, it would serve as the basis for a better, richer society. "We want to live in a country in which French Canadians can choose to live among English Canadians and English Canadians can choose to live among French Canadians without abandoning their cultural heritage," he said. And he dismissed Quebec separatists as "prisoners of past injustice, blind to the possibilities of the future."

The Official Languages Act had four main components:

- English and French are the official languages of Canada and either language can be used in parliament, federal courts, and federal government offices.
- Both languages should be recognized and used in areas of Canada where there are large minorities of either language, called "bilingual districts."
- Certain sections of the federal civil service should become bilingual, and promotions will be based on bilingualism.
- All schools in Ottawa, a bilingual district, will offer French and English instruction.

The Act had an immediate impact, and a mixed reception. Many Canadians shared Trudeau's vision. An increasing number of English-speaking parents across the country, for example, enrolled their children in French-immersion programs. In western Canada, however, many people questioned the expense of retraining career civil servants to become bilingual. Many other disgruntled English-speaking Canadians felt that French was being forced on them. Quebec nationalists were unimpressed. A bilingual Canada did not mean that Quebec's position in the federation would improve.

Trudeau was also dissatisfied with the Act—it did not constitutionally guarantee language and individual rights. This was his ultimate goal. To do that, Trudeau would have to patriate the Constitution (the BNA Act) from Britain, where it rested on a shelf in a government office. Patriation would make it a Canadian document, negotiated and signed by all ten provinces. This would take Trudeau 13 years to achieve. In 1969, however, urgent problems were threatening Canadian unity, and another charismatic leader was offering Quebec a different vision—independence.

Figure 12–2 Trudeau thought Quebec separatists were merely "prisoners of past injustice." How do you think they might respond?

The Rise of René Lévesque

In 1968, a major development shook Quebec politics. Under the leadership of René Lévesque, a segment of the separatist movement formed a provincial party, the Parti Québécois (PQ). Its purpose was to resolve Quebec's historic and economic grievances by creating the conditions for an independent Quebec. Through the policy of **sovereignty-association**, the PQ envisioned an independent Quebec that would cooperate economically with the rest of Canada. Quebec had always negotiated different arrangements with the federal government from those accepted by other provinces, but the changes that separatists proposed would require the breakup of Canada. By the end of the 1960s, two of the most charismatic leaders in Canadian history—Trudeau and Lévesque—were leading forces that promised either to unite the country or tear it in two.

René Lévesque had been familiar to Quebecers since the 1950s as a television commentator on Radio Canada's "Point de Mire." He served as a minister in Jean Lesage's provincial Liberal government from 1960 onwards. Lesage himself did not support separatism, but by 1963 Lévesque was publicly supporting the cause. He called the Royal Commission on Bilingualism and Biculturalism irrelevant, remarking that "there are two distinct cultures and it is impossible to fuse the two into one." In 1967, Lévesque issued "Option Quebec," a Liberal party policy paper promoting separatist aims. The party defeated it at their October 1967 convention, and Lévesque quit. In November, he formed the Mouvement Souveraineté-Association (MSA) in a Montreal monastery. In 1968, Lévesque's new Parti Québécois had absorbed the Rassemblement pour l'indépendence nationale (RIN), the most important of the early independence groups that had formed just months after the 1960 election.

Up Close

1. Summarize in point form René Lévesque's rise to power in Quebec.

Figure 12–3 Lévesque had many years' experience as a journalist before he went into politics. Here he is interviewing soldiers in Korea.

Lévesque's new party confronted anglophone Canada with a new reality. The independence movement had a vibrant, astute leader who wished to take Quebec out of Confederation through democratic means. Lévesque—like many Quebec politicians, including Trudeau—had a background in journalism. He could communicate clearly and concisely. And his years as a politician and media personality meant that he was a household name. He was a force that even Trudeau had to reckon with. The intellectual, yet emotional Lévesque and the passionately federalist Pierre Trudeau soon dominated the debate over Quebec.

The FLQ and the October Crisis

Lévesque faced a challenge in Quebec. His democratic option was far too slow for some young people who wanted to free Quebec from Canadian and British domination and make it an independent state. In the 1960s, a number of radical groups around the world were using terrorism as a way to force social change. A wave of kidnappings and bombings spread to Germany, France, Britain, and the US. Terrorism hit Canada through Quebec. A small, radical group, the Front de Libération du Québec (FLQ), sought to liberate Quebec through violence. Letter bombs exploded in mailboxes, which at the time carried the insignia of the British crown. A statue of General Wolfe, hero of the British Conquest, was destroyed. Prominent English businesses were targeted. Many Quebecers, frustrated by the lack of significant change in their situation, were sympathetic to the FLQ's goals, if not its methods. Large FLQ rallies were held in many communities.

On October 5, 1970, the FLQ kidnapped James Cross, British trade commissioner to Canada. This was the first in a series of events that became known as the "October Crisis." In return for Cross's release, the FLQ made a series of demands, one of which was that the FLQ Manifesto be broadcast by the media. Many Quebecers were sympathetic to the manifesto because it included many grievances that they shared. What many Quebecers did not know at the time was that the FLQ had amassed weapons and explosives, and that several FLQ members were in prison serving sentences for robbery, manslaughter, murder, and other crimes. The FLQ called these members "political prisoners."

The FLQ then kidnapped Quebec labour minister Pierre Laporte on October 10, 1970, as he played ball with his children on his front lawn. Premier Robert Bourassa, alarmed by the threat to law and order, immediately called on Trudeau to send in the Canadian Army. Trudeau hesitated to do so. On October 12, however, armed troops were summoned into Ottawa to protect potential targets, such as cabinet ministers and federal buildings. By October 15, the Canadian Army was sent into Quebec City and Montreal to protect politicians

Data File

In 1999, Canada's journalists and broadcasters chose Lévesque as the third most newsworthy Canadian of the twentieth century.

and government buildings, and to reinforce police already straining to control the situation. Finally, at 3 p.m., October 16, the Cabinet invoked the War Measures Act, declaring that a state of "apprehended insurrection" existed in Quebec. The next day, the FLQ sent a grisly message to Ottawa: Laporte's body was found in the trunk of an abandoned car. Over the next three months, the War Measures Act remained in effect. But Trudeau refused to negotiate with the FLQ, describing them as "criminals and thugs" (see Flashpoint, pages 316–317).

Trudeau's imposition of the War Measures Act, and his refusal to negotiate with the FLQ, raised his government's popularity to a new high. Support for Trudeau's use of the War Measures Act did not mean that most Quebecers were happy with their lot. Rather, it indicated strongly that both English-speaking and French-speaking Canadians rejected violent conflict as a means of resolving the Quebec question. The October Crisis led to a new era of democratic negotiations around language and sovereignty issues. Lévesque and the Parti Québécois would benefit significantly from these changes.

Data File

From 1970 to 1973, the PQ's share of the popular vote grew from 23 percent to 30 percent. The number of seats it held in Quebec's National Assembly, however, fell from 7 seats to 6.

THE PARTI QUÉBÉCOIS: A DEMOCRATIC OPTION

The separatist Parti Québécois quietly grew in popularity in the years following the October Crisis. But this wasn't clear to most Canadians. In Canada's electoral system, seats are decided on the basis of which party candidate wins the largest number of votes in each riding—not on the party's percentage of the overall vote. In the 1973 Quebec election, the PQ won 30 percent of the vote, but only 6 seats, as opposed to the Liberals' 102 seats. Though disappointed, Lévesque reminded his followers that "This is a defeat that feels like a victory."

Figure 12–4 René Lévesque addresses his supporters after leading the PQ to victory in the 1976 Quebec election.

The Question of Quebec

Flashpoint
The War Measures Act

Figure 12–5 Troops swarmed Montreal streets during the October Crisis. Pierre Trudeau was unapologetic about the War Measures Act but many Quebecers felt it was extreme.

The War Measures Act gave the government and police extraordinary powers. Anyone suspected of belonging to—or even sympathizing with—the FLQ could be arrested and jailed. This was a profound violation of individual rights that would never be tolerated in peacetime. Thus, Trudeau had delayed using these strong-arm tactics as long as possible. Bourassa, however, had requested these powers: terrorist acts and threats, he said, had created a state of emergency in Quebec.

Once Cabinet invoked the War Measures Act on October 16, 1970, Trudeau did not back down. When a reporter asked him whether this was too extreme, Trudeau responded harshly. "There's a lot of bleeding hearts around who just don't like to see people with helmets and guns," he said. "All I can say is go on and bleed, but it is more important to

Communities: French–English Relations

keep law and order in the society than to be worried about weak-kneed people who don't like the looks of an army." The reporter pressed further. How far would Trudeau go? "Just watch me," Trudeau responded. In a televised address that night, Trudeau told the nation:

> This government is not acting out of fear. It is acting to prevent fear from spreading ... It is acting to make clear to kidnappers and revolutionaries and assassins that in this country laws are made and changed by the elected representatives of all Canadians—not by a handful of self-selected dictators.

Cabinet had immediately viewed a list of 70 suspects in the Laporte murder, and ordered several names dropped on the grounds that they were unlikely to be involved. Despite this, police raids swept across Quebec just hours after the Act was invoked. By the time the raids were over, 465 persons had been arrested and detained. Over the next few months, police actions in Quebec were criticized by many groups and people across Canada as being too extreme a violation of civil liberties.

Fifty-nine days after his abduction, James Cross was rescued by police from an FLQ cell. His three kidnappers, their lawyer, a policeman, and James Cross crowded into a car owned by one of the kidnappers. Police cars and motorcycles escorted them to the former site of Expo '67. There the kidnappers were granted safe passage on a plane to Cuba. Two days later, Cross returned to his wife in London, England, declining Trudeau's invitation to dinner. Four of the terrorists and three additional family members later left Canada and lived in exile in Cuba for a number of years before finally choosing to return and face the Canadian justice system.

The crisis passed, and the federal government did not give in to terrorist demands, as a number of worried Quebec leaders had advised. The Trudeau government's popularity soared—to the highest approval rating that any Canadian government has ever achieved. Eighty-seven percent of Canadians, both English and French, approved the government's action. Even Claude Ryan, the staunch Quebec nationalist editor of *Le Devoir*, initially welcomed the troops, noting that "the police forces which have been kept on full alert are on the point of exhaustion."

But the War Measures Act has remained an extremely controversial issue. It has raised many questions that go beyond the FLQ. Did the War Measures Act give the police too much power and unfairly suspend the civil liberties of innocent people? Most of the 465 arrested and detained were never formally charged. Did the federal government overreact to what now appears to have been an isolated and disorganized terrorist group? Was the Act invoked as much to support the goals of politicians, such as Bourassa and Trudeau, as to protect society?

Trudeau biographer George Radwanski has written that Trudeau was right to invoke the Act: "The Trudeau government's **draconian** intervention violated for a period of weeks the right of 465 individuals to physical freedom, but it safeguarded the right of those individuals and Quebec's entire population to continue living in a democratically governed violence free society." In contrast, Normand Caron, a Parti Québécois member, told *Maclean's* in 1971 that Trudeau "... indulged in demagoguery on television and tried to terrify people ... He used a sledge hammer to kill a fly when he brought in the War Measures Act."

What Do You Think?

1. If you were Trudeau, would you have declared the War Measures Act? Use evidence from this account and do your own research to develop a detailed response. Remember, you have no information later than October 16, 1970, on which to base your decision.

2. Is historian Radwanski right? Should collective rights take precedence over individual rights during a crisis? Develop a logical argument for your point of view. Refer to the Historian at Work on developing an argument (page 275) for ideas.

3. Could the War Measures Act be declared today? Why or why not?

The Question of Quebec

In the provincial election of November 15, 1976, Lévesque's optimism was confirmed. The PQ not only increased its percentage of the popular vote to 41 percent, it won the election. It formed the new government, with 71 seats, as opposed to 26 for the Liberals, 11 for the Union Nationale, and 2 for others. Many Canadians were stunned by the PQ victory and wondered if the breakup of Canada could be far behind.

During the election campaign, Lévesque had promised not to interpret an election victory as an endorsement for independence. Many Quebecers wanted to use separation as a threat to bargain with Ottawa, but they did not necessarily want to separate. At the same time, however, the PQ had promised to hold a referendum on sovereignty-association within its first term. They also intended to use their political power to enforce the use of the French language in Quebec.

LEGISLATING TO PROTECT FRENCH

Shortly after his victory in 1976, Lévesque introduced Bill 101. The bill sent shock waves across both English and French Canada. Many people accused Lévesque's pro-separatist government of adopting a radical new stance by restricting English and protecting French. But Bill 101 was simply pursuing policies that had been developing in Quebec for years. It was a far cry from the FLQ's 1963 communiqué on language:

Heritage Minute

Louis Riel (1844–1885) fought for the protection of both English- and French-language rights in Manitoba. Riel, a Métis, was born in the Red River Colony of present-day Manitoba. Like Quebecers, the Métis saw their way of life threatened by the arrival of English settlers (in the early nineteenth century). Riel became their leader. In 1885, he and his followers clashed with the Canadian government during the Northwest Rebellion. He was later arrested and hanged for treason.

> Our suicide-commandos have as their principal mission the complete destruction ... of the colonial language which holds us in contempt ... all commercial establishments and enterprises ... which do not use French as the first language and which advertise in the colonial language.

As you will see in the following discussion, many people in Quebec, not only nationalists and separatists, felt the French language needed legislative support if Quebec were to preserve its heritage and traditions.

Bill 85 and the Gendron Commission

In 1968, the provincial Union Nationale government in Quebec had introduced Bill 85 to protect the use of the French language in Quebec society. Two factors were contributing to this situation: a declining birth rate among francophones and more non-francophone immigration into Quebec. These changes—a lower birth rate and higher levels of multicultural immigration—were occurring across Canada. But in English-speaking Canada, they did not threaten the use of the English language. In Quebec, however, non-francophone immigrants tended to send their children to English-language schools. This added to Quebecers' concern about the French language. The Union Nationale's Bill 85 never became law but it caused much controversy. The Gendron Commission was appointed to study the situation. Even before the Commission began its work, a language riot broke out in Montreal. The riot demonstrated how serious the problem was.

Up Close

2. In your own words, describe how the language situation in Quebec affected school children and their parents.

Two Languages Clashed at St. Leonard School St. Leonard was a bilingual school in a section of Montreal with a largely Italian immigrant population. In 1968, it was to be converted into a unilingual French school, starting with Grade 1 and moving up one grade each year. The St. Leonard's Parents' Association opposed the move, defending the right of parents to choose the language of instruction for their child's education.

It so happened that Raymond Lemieux, spokesperson for the Mouvement pour l'Intégration Scolaire (MIS), an organization that promoted unilingual French schools, lived on the same street as Robert Beale, president of the St. Leonard's Parents' Association. And both groups led protests. The English-only advocates went to Ottawa to plead for federal intervention, while the French-only supporters marched on the Quebec legislature to demand passage of Bill 85. Supporters of parental choice also protested by putting their children in English-language schools held in local basements. Tensions mounted, and riots broke out in the streets.

The Union Nationale government responded to the crisis, rushing through legislation that restricted English-language schooling. But anglophones believed the legislation went too far, and francophones believed it did not go far enough. Everyone blamed the government, and the Union Nationale lost the 1970 election.

Figure 12–6 Demonstrators during the conflict at St. Leonard's School. Why do you think parents took the language of instruction so seriously?

The Gendron Commission issued its findings in 1972. It found that English dominated in Quebec's workplaces and that many inequalities resulted. Francophones earned less than anglophones, held less important positions, benefited little from being bilingual, and often worked only in English. The Commission concluded that French would not survive in North America without a "maximum of opportunity and protection throughout Quebec." It recommended that the government declare French the official language of Quebec and establish French as the language of the workplace. The third recommendation was that signs must be regulated, and written in French.

Bill 22 and the Mandatory Use of French

In 1974, the Liberal government of Robert Bourassa responded to the Gendron recommendations by passing Bill 22. Bill 22 made French Quebec's official language of public administration and restricted English-language schooling. Parents who wanted to enroll their children in English-language schools had to pass an English-proficiency test. The reason for this controversial restriction was that 90 percent of immigrant parents who had a choice sent their children to English-language schools. Bill 22 also encouraged the use of French in the workplace by stating that contracts with the Quebec government might depend on *francisation* (adopting French).

Bill 22, sponsored by a pro-federalist Quebec government, attempted to protect French within a federal Canada. Just as with the Union Nationale's Bill 85, English-speakers and immigrants felt that Bill 22 went too far but Quebec nationalists believed that it did not go far enough. For instance, the Bill's workplace provisions could not be legally enforced. Trudeau was asked to intervene, but he responded that, while he did not like Bill 22, he could not disallow a law simply because it was "foolish or unjust."

Although 500 000 English Quebecers signed the protest petition, an equal number did not. Many believed Bill 22 was long overdue. In any event, Bill 22 had little impact on school enrollment. Just prior to Bill 22, 16 percent of pre-college students were enrolled in English-language schools. Three years later, the percentage had increased slightly, not decreased. But perhaps the most significant change from 1970 was that the debate over Bill 22, while angry and shrill, remained democratic.

Figure 12–7 This Quebec sign was not acceptable under Bill 101. The sign used English on one side and French on the other, with the same size of lettering.

Bill 101: Legislation That Meant Business

In 1977, the Parti Québécois passed Bill 101, which strengthened Bill 22 by adding more regulations. It defined a number of "fundamental language rights." Agencies were created to ensure that everyone complied with the bill. The charter stated that all children must be taught in French. There were some exceptions for English-speaking minority parents, but these were narrowly defined. A child could be educated in English only if

- a parent had been educated at an English school in Quebec
- a parent had been educated in English outside Quebec, but was living in Quebec before August, 1977
- the child's older siblings were attending English schools.

If a parent had been educated in English in any other province, territory, or country, the child had to attend a French school.

Bill 101 stated that all products had to be labelled in French. If the label was accompanied by a translation, the translation could not be in print larger than the French. The names of firms had to be in French, but the firm could add a name in another language. Under Bill 101, French became the official language of the workplace. All communication for employees had to be in French. The right of workers to carry on their activities in French, and for consumers to be served in French, was guaranteed. All government acts, bills, and regulations were to be passed in French, although an English version would be prepared.

Bill 101's French-only legislation was seriously enforced. In one incident, a shipment of Dunkin' Donuts was discovered to have English-only packaging. The entire shipment was burned. Disobeying the act was punishable by a fine of $25 to $500 for an individual and $50 to $1000 for a corporate body. A business that ignored Bill 101 was liable to a fine of $100 to $2000 a day.

Many of these measures appeared tyrannical to Quebec's anglophones and to Canadians outside Quebec. But the Parti Québécois was committed to leaving the Canadian federal system, and was not especially concerned with their views.

Up Close

3. List the bills that affected the use of French and English in Quebec, and summarize their main points.

Reaction to Bill 101 Claude Ryan, then editor of *Le Devoir*, described Bill 101 as "rigid, dogmatic, and authoritarian" and a violation of individual rights. Indeed, many people left Quebec in the six months following the Bill's passage in 1977—up to 50 000, compared to 33 000 for the same period in 1976 and 28 000 in 1975. Royal Bank President W. Earle McLaughlin told a Quebecers' business group, in English, that if the bank's head office was not allowed to function in English, it would move. In February 1977, the Royal Bank announced it was transferring 100 head office jobs to Toronto. The Sun Life Insurance Company had already announced its intention to transfer to Toronto. Many other businesses moved their head offices to Toronto as well. But not all anglophones reacted negatively. Positive Action, an anglophone group, believed in Quebec's future, and called on "Quebecers to stay and work with us for the realization of this future."

The impact of Bill 101 on education has been dramatic. In 1971-72, 85 percent of immigrants were enrolled in English-language schools. That fell to 80 percent in 1976-77, 36 percent in 1986-87, and 21 percent in 1994-95. In Montreal, 90 percent of anglophone students had attended English schools in 1972. In 1994-95, 79 percent were attending French schools. In 1983, some provisions around education and bilingual signs

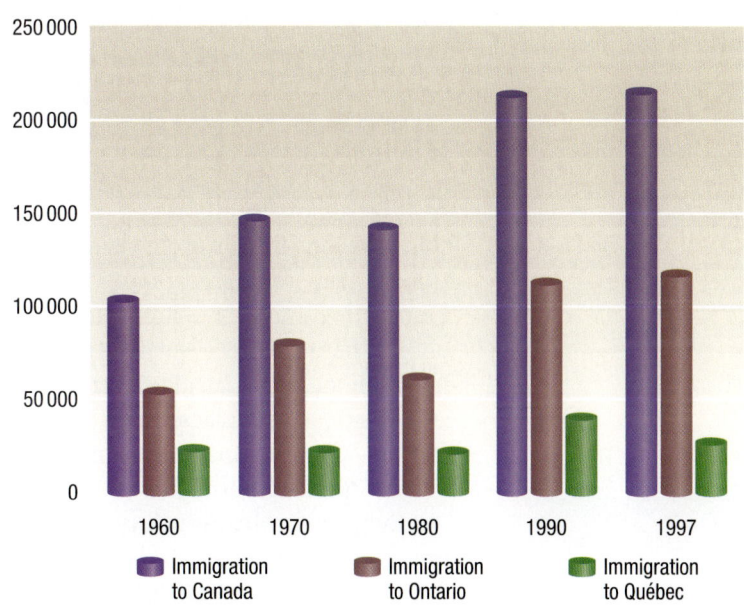

Figure 12–8 Immigration to Quebec compared with immigration to Ontario and all of Canada

were relaxed, but only in stores specializing in products typical of a "foreign country or ethnic group." This exemption to Bill 101 regulations did not apply to English-speaking Canadians.

Legal Challenges to Bill 101 Because many people saw Bill 101 as an assault on individual rights, the Bill faced many legal challenges. On July 26, 1984, the Supreme Court upheld a Quebec Court of Appeal decision that **struck down** the "Quebec clause" of Bill 101, which required at least one parent to have had primary education in English within Quebec in order for the child to attend an English-language school. In 1988, the Supreme Court also struck down the section of Bill 101 that required signs to be only in French. It did allow the Quebec government to require that French have greater visibility than English.

In 1999, a Quebec Superior Court judge ruled that the requirement that French be predominant on commercial signs was unconstitutional, but the Quebec government announced that it would appeal the ruling. The case concerned an antique store owned by Gwen Simpson and Wally Hoffman in Knowlton, Quebec. The sign broke the law because it had English on one side and French on the other, but the letters were the same size. Six other trials are pending over the sign laws. Also in 1999, the Quebec Equality Party—an English-rights group—filed a complaint with UNESCO, arguing that the government regulations on access to English-language schools were based on discrimination. Canada, however, has not signed the UNESCO convention because education is a provincial responsibility.

> **Up Close**
>
> 4. Identify each of the following and for each, write a sentence that clearly expresses their perspective on Bill 101: Claude Ryan, W. Earle McLaughlin, Positve Action, Gwen Simpson and Wally Hoffman, the Quebec Equality Party.

LANGUAGE POLITICS AND FRANCOPHONES OUTSIDE QUEBEC

In 1972, almost 1 million French Canadians—20 percent of the total—lived outside Quebec. They were considered *les autres*, because in Quebec and English Canada they were largely invisible. As protection of the French language within Quebec became increasingly associated with sovereignty, non-Quebec francophones began to feel isolated. One-third of New Brunswick's population was francophone, but Canada's French-speaking communities were generally small and scattered. In places such as Maillardville, BC; St. Boniface, Manitoba; Earlton, Ontario; and Cheticamp, Nova Scotia, it was a struggle to preserve a French-speaking heritage.

Support for the French language outside Quebec was often at the legal minimum. Francophones could communicate with the federal government in French, yet they would have to purchase a postage stamp from a unilingual employee at the post office. They could listen to the CBC in French, but only on an FM station. In Vancouver libraries in the early 1970s, French books were shelved in the "foreign languages" section. In Manitoba in 1916, the government

> **Up Close**
>
> 5. Explain the meaning of and significance of the terms "les autres" and "le drainage."

had revoked the 1870 guarantee of French-language education for francophones. It was not restored until 1970. By 1977, less than 6 percent of Manitoba's population spoke French. By 1991, the figure had decreased to 4.4 percent. Francophones outside of Quebec sometimes call this problem *le drainage*. Originally an Acadian term, the phrase describes the slow, relentless anglicization of francophone communities.

Surrounded by the English majority, the cultural survival of isolated francophone communities had depended on the special rights Quebec acquired for the French language over the century. Quebec separation would place these communities at risk. "In many ways we're just another ethnic group here, though we have a special status conferred on us nationally," Manitoba's health minister, Larry Desjardins, admitted in 1977. "If Quebec separates, it could really damage us here … it could be the end of special rights for francophones." Desjardins was one of only two francophone cabinet ministers in Manitoba.

When René Lévesque and the PQ spoke on behalf of French Canadians, they meant those living in Quebec. The fact that there were different francophone viewpoints outside Quebec was overlooked. Indeed, some francophones outside Quebec found themselves the targets of hostility because of Quebec's French-only laws, even though their own small communities were struggling simply to keep French alive.

This situation further undermined bilingualism as a solution to national unity issues.

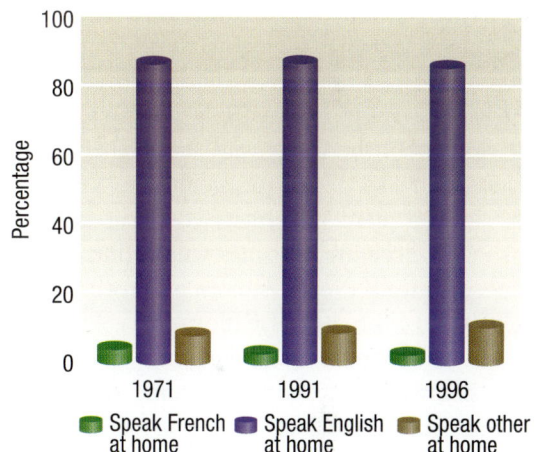

Figure 12–9 Between 1971 and 1991, the use of French declined among people living outside Quebec.

THE CONSTITUTION VERSUS THE REFERENDUM

René Lévesque was determined to follow up his 1977 electoral victory by introducing a referendum on sovereignty-association for Quebec. He hoped to resolve age-old conflicts by simply taking Quebec out of Canada. Trudeau, however, believed that the federal government could deal more effectively with language and other rights issues if Canada had control of its own Constitution. He was committed to do just that. Only one of these two strategies could prevail.

Gearing Up for the Referendum

In November 1979, the Parti Québécois published a White Paper, "Quebec/Canada: A New Deal." It cited past grievances and outlined plans for implementing sovereignty–association. Sovereignty-association, as the name implies, would include an ongoing association with Canada. The Paper proposed

Historian at Work
Internet Research that Gets Results

The Internet is the largest source of information in human history. It is cheap and easy to set up a **web site**, so a vast variety of information and opinions is available. For the researcher, this creates advantages and disadvantages. Compare the Internet to national TV news, for example. In TV news, a group of media professionals decides what the top stories are, prepares them, checks facts for accuracy, and broadcasts them. The facts you hear are probably accurate, but bias will be introduced as well. (See Historian at Work in Chapter 14 for an explanation of bias.)

The Internet is also a medium, but it is not controlled—or edited—by any single group of professionals. There are no set standards. As a result, you must make the decisions about where you will go on the Internet. You must consider your own biases and those of your source. Some sites will be relevant to your research, but most will not. To make Internet research pay off, you need certain skills. The questions below will help you develop those skills.

How should I deal with source bias on the Internet? Source bias is the same on the Internet as in any other medium. For example, in early 2000, a search on "English language rights" + "Quebec" turned up ten sites. Most offered personal opinions. But one site, sponsored by the CBC, featured many resources, including links to court judgements, political parties, and lobby groups. An experienced researcher would use this site first because of its range of views and resources. Other Internet sites should be sought whenever a needed fact or perspective is missing.

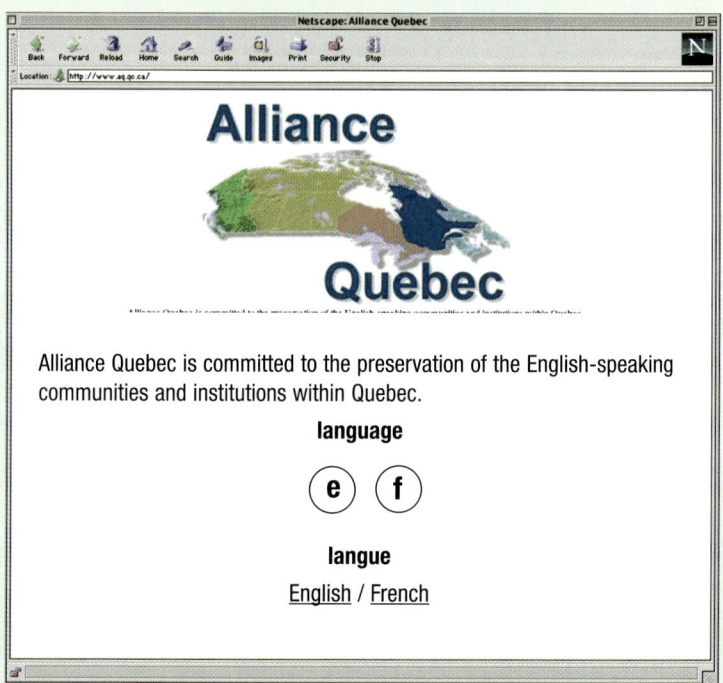

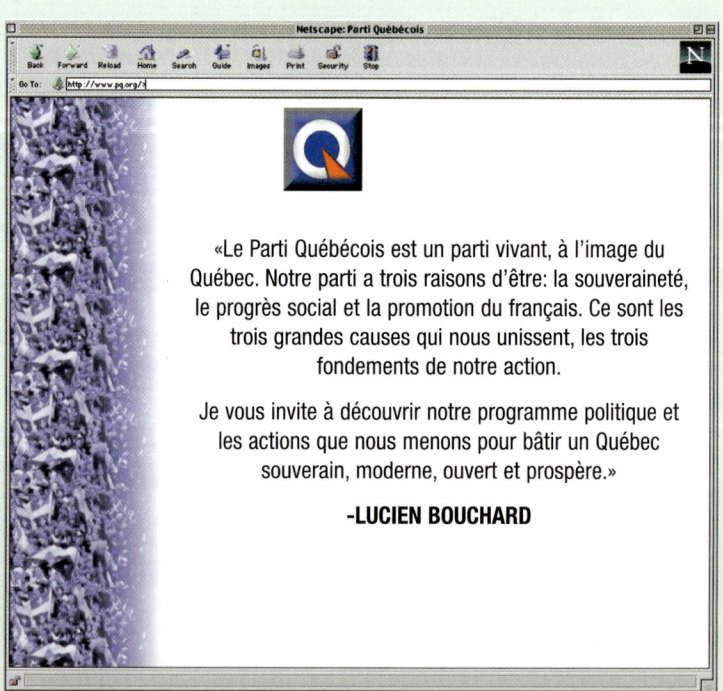

Historical Inquiry: Research

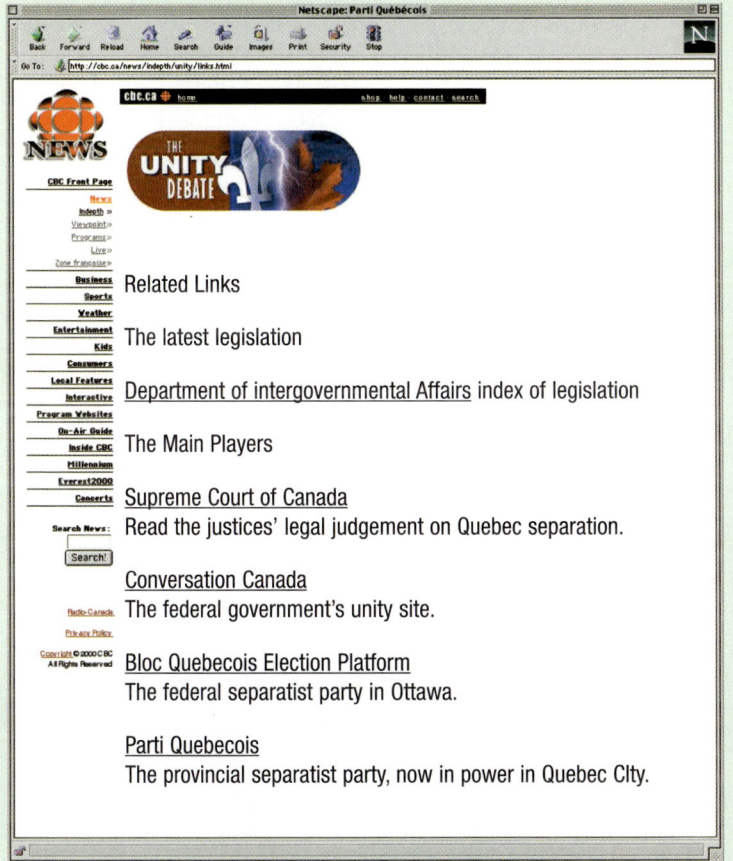

Figure 12–10 This web site and the ones on the previous page provide information on language issues in Quebec. Based on your reading in this chapter, what point of view might you expect to find at each site?

What guidelines do I need for using Internet search engines? **Search engines** are essential to find web site addresses. But vague, general search words will turn up thousands of sites. Most search engines offer information on how to construct an effective **search string**. Use these guidelines to avoid wasting time. Internet search tips can also be found at such sites as: <http://www.windweaver.com/searchguide.htm> which is a guide to search engines or at <http://home.sprintmail.com/~debflanagan/main.html> which has an online tutorial.

What other Internet research tools can help me? Tools supplied by browser software—such as Netscape and Explorer—can save you time. For example, sites that you will want to return to can be "bookmarked" by using the "bookmark" command on your browser. This saves the site address so that you can return to the site easily. Also, the command "Search/Find in page (or frame)" will find an exact reference in a long document. If you do not have regular access to the Internet, print out the relevant information.

How can I evaluate a web site's credibility? As with any other medium, when in doubt, doubt. Also remember the acronym **CARS**. **C**redibility: Who are the authors? What makes them credible? **A**ccuracy: Is the information up-to-date and comprehensive? **R**easonableness: Does the information sound fair and balanced? **S**upport: Are sources or corroboration provided?

What Do You Think?

Find an account of a controversial national or international issue in a daily newspaper. Go to the web sites of groups on different sides of the issue and read what they say. Then answer the following questions:

1. Did you learn facts from the newspaper account that you did not learn from your Internet search? What facts? Why do you think the newspaper provided that information?

2. Did you learn facts from the Internet sites that you did not learn from the newspaper account? What facts? Why do you think the newspaper did not provide that information?

3. Go to the CBC's national unity site at <cbc.ca/news/indepth/unity/links.html> and follow unity-related links that are new to you. If you can, view Real Time Video, participate in a discussion group, or e-mail a question. What did you learn starting from the CBC site that you did not find in this textbook? What types of information can the Internet provide that a textbook cannot? Why is the Internet suitable for this type of information?

4. Some analysts believe that the Internet will completely change the way people obtain information. Based on your own experience, do you feel this is true? Why or why not?

The Question of Quebec

four Quebec-Canada agencies, with responsibility for areas such as currency and justice. Quebec, however, would have sole power to make laws, levy taxes, and grant citizenship. In 1980, Claude Ryan, now leader of the Quebec Liberal Party, proposed an alternative vision. In his report, "A New Canadian Federation," Ryan highlighted the achievements of the Canadian federation and its advantages for Quebec. But he demanded changes in Canada's structure.

The PQ timed the Referendum very carefully. After losing the 1979 federal election to Conservative Joe Clark, Trudeau announced that he was retiring. For Lévesque, this was ideal—his most formidable federalist opponent would be out of the picture. But the PQ could not have foreseen what happened next. Clark's minority government collapsed before the year was out, and the Liberals convinced Trudeau to run again. Newly energized, Trudeau won another majority government in the 1980 federal election and soon plunged into campaigning on the *Non* side of the Referendum. May 20, 1980 was set as the date. *Oui* and *Non* committees were struck, led by Lévesque and Ryan respectively. Quebec law dictated that these committees must be run by Quebecers only, and within Quebec.

These rules were simple but the Referendum question was not. The question was very carefully drafted, possibly to obtain the highest possible *Oui* vote. It did not ask voters for a mandate to separate from Canada, but only for a mandate to negotiate a "proposed agreement between Quebec and Canada."

Up Close

6. Reread the referendum question carefully. Identify two assumptions made by the authors of the referendum question.

> The Government of Quebec has made its proposal to negotiate a new agreement with the rest of Canada, based on the equality of nations;
> - this agreement would enable Quebec to acquire the exclusive power to make its laws, levy its taxes and establish relations abroad—in other words, sovereignty—and at the same time, to maintain with Canada an economic association including a common currency;
> - no change in political status resulting from these negotiations will be effected without approval from the people through another referendum;
> - on these terms, do you give the Government of Quebec the mandate to negotiate the proposed agreement between Quebec and Canada?

Winners and Losers in the Campaign

René Lévesque understood media deadlines, and he planned his events carefully around them. He was front-page news wherever he spoke. His *Oui* allies were also eloquent and sure of their material. In contrast, Ryan tended to give hesitant, negative speeches on his own schedule. The media, consequently, ignored him.

After the first week, it seemed obvious that the *Oui* side would win. Federalists in Ottawa were dismayed. They knew that Ryan was floundering with the *Non* campaign, but he rejected their advice. Ignoring Lévesque's protests about federal interference, Trudeau ally Jean Chrétien organized federal politicians to visit Quebec and urge people to vote *Non*. Private citizens in other provinces also got involved: 800 000 signatures were gathered for a "We Love You, Quebec" petition.

Two other events turned the tide towards the *Non* side. First, Parti Québécois cabinet minister Lise Payette called women who supported the *Non* side *Yvettes* (Quebec slang for "dumb housewives"). Women across Quebec were enraged by Payette's assumption that they could not intelligently support a view other than the PQ's. Promptly, 12 000 self-described *Yvettes* organized a massive rally against sovereignty-association. Second, Trudeau made three key speeches in Quebec, which are considered by many as his finest ever.

When all the votes were counted, the *Non* side had won, with 59.4 percent of the vote. Voter turnout had been extremely high, at 82 percent, and emotions across Canada were extreme. In defeat, Lévesque accused the Non side of using unfair scare tactics. His dream, and that of the majority of francophone voters, had been shattered. Obviously crushed, he told his audience, many of them weeping openly, not to give up: "Let us accept defeat ... but not let go, never lose sight of such legitimate, universal objectives as equality. It will come."

Trudeau knew well that separatism in Quebec was far from dead. He warned English Canada not to forget the Quebec issue: "We will not agree to you interpreting a 'no' vote as an indication that everything is fine and can remain as it was before. We want change and we are willing to lay our seats in the House on the line to have change." The change that mattered most to Trudeau was the new Constitution, and the *Non* vote had given him both the need and the opportunity to pursue it.

Up Close

7. Identify three events that helped the *Non* side win the referendum.

Figures 12–11 and **12–12** Lévesque (left) ran the *Oui* campaign, and Claude Ryan (right) ran the *Non* campaign during the Referendum.

THE NEW CONSTITUTION

During the Quebec Referendum, Trudeau had promised a new constitution. This was a big political risk because several governments had tried and failed. But he had many reasons for wanting a constitution that Canada had control of and he gambled that the *Non* vote for Quebec separation would provide the needed push.

Britain had long wanted its Dominions to be as independent as possible, but finding the right formula for Canada wasn't proving to be easy. Canada had been trying to reach an agreement on its constitution since the Balfour Report in 1926. In 1964, all ten provinces had briefly agreed to the Fulton-Favreau formula. But when Daniel Johnson became Union Nationale premier of Quebec in 1966, he withdrew Quebec's support. After decades of trying to create an **amending formula** for the BNA Act, Canada still had no agreement. Our constitution continued to be an act of Britain's parliament. For Trudeau, this lingering symbol of British control was unacceptable for modern-day Canada. It also sent the wrong message to francophones in Quebec.

Trudeau renewed his efforts to find an amending formula when he was first elected. By 1971, the ten premiers briefly reached an agreement—the Victoria Charter—at a conference in Victoria. But Quebec nationalists, especially Claude Ryan, criticized Quebec premier Robert Bourassa for not gaining additional powers for Quebec on language and social policies. When Trudeau refused to budge on these points, Bourassa withdrew Quebec's support.

Data File

In the 1980 Quebec Referendum, 60 percent of francophone Quebecers voted Yes, while 91 percent of anglophone Quebecers voted No.

Figure 12–13 Trudeau smiles as Queen Elizabeth II signs the Constitution Act, 1982. She was said to be uncomfortable with the Act. Why might that be? Does the picture support that view?

Would the Provinces Support Trudeau?

Sensing that agreement between premiers might at last be possible, Ontario's Conservative premier, William Davis, called for a constitutional conference as "the beginning of a solution." Trudeau called a First Ministers meeting for September. Davis, however, had been wrong. Eight of the ten premiers—called the "Gang of Eight"—opposed Trudeau's Constitution. Only Ontario and New Brunswick were in favour.

Undaunted, Trudeau decided to proceed without the provinces' support. On October 24, 1980, he forced closure on the debate on the Constitution in the House of Commons. Emotions ran high. Liberal MP Ron Irwin crossed the floor and screamed at Opposition Leader Joe Clark, who opposed Trudeau's plan. Another MP rushed towards Clark and had to be physically restrained. Feelings boiled over outside the House of Commons as well. Several provinces launched court challenges against Trudeau's decision to act **unilaterally**. *Globe and Mail* publisher Roy Megarry called Trudeau's patriation plans "the scheme of a tyrant."

Up Close

8. Why did the publisher of the *Globe and Mail* call Trudeau's plan to bring home the Constitution "the scheme of a tyrant"?

Was Trudeau's Plan Legal?

Trudeau was walking on treacherous legal ground. Could he legally patriate Canada's Constitution without the provinces' agreement? The question had to be taken to the Supreme Court. It was announced that the Court would rule on the issue on September 28, 1981. "People waited all night to get in. It was jammed," recalled Colin Irving, Quebec's lead lawyer. Given the case's historic importance, television cameras were allowed to record the proceedings in the Supreme Court

Figure 12–14 Camera crews outside the Supreme Court on September 28, 1981. It was an historic moment for Canada.

The Question of Quebec **329**

for the first time. But new technology brought mixed results. One Supreme Court justice accidentally kicked a cable, disconnecting the sound at the most important point. This left the Court—and the country—unable to hear. Jean Chrétien, then federal justice minister, wrote later, "The voice of Chief Justice Laskin wasn't the only thing that wasn't clear; the majority judgement itself seemed rather ambiguous."

The Supreme Court had been asked to rule on four separate issues, two of which were momentous. In a 7-2 decision, the Court decided that Ottawa had the legal power to ask Britain to amend the Constitution, even without the provinces' consent. However, in a 6-3 decision, the Court also found that an unwritten constitutional "convention" required a "substantial measure of provincial consent." It did not define what "substantial" meant. Thus, the Court ruled, Trudeau's plan was "unconstitutional in the conventional sense." It was clear, however, that Trudeau would have to get at least a majority of the provinces on side to go ahead with patriation. It was time for the First Ministers to negotiate again, only now the atmosphere was far from friendly.

Up Close

9. The Supreme Court was asked to decide if Trudeau could legally bring home the Constitution without the consent of the provinces. Summarize the Court's answer.

The Final, Kitchen-Table Discussions

In November 1981, the First Ministers met in Ottawa. After four days of intense bargaining, they had made little progress towards an accord. Flippantly, Trudeau suggested that a national referendum might resolve the issue, but only Lévesque agreed. On November 4, key federal cabinet ministers met at 24 Sussex to discuss negotiable issues. Jean Chrétien was appointed to bring the premiers together.

Figure 12–15 When the deal was finally struck, Canada had a new constitution. Why do you think the national and provincial leaders in this photo are looking rather serious? Shouldn't they be happy?

Chrétien met with the attorneys general of Saskatchewan and Ontario in a kitchen and worked out a compromise. Later that night, seven members of the "Gang of Eight" (minus Quebec) got together in Saskatchewan Premier Alan Blakeney's suite to deal. At 1:30 a.m., Newfoundland Premier Brian Peckford wrote the text. At 2:00 a.m., Ontario Premier Bill Davis was awakened to get his agreement.

By the morning of November 5, 1981, nine premiers and the federal government had worked out a compromise accord under which the federal government accepted the provinces' amending formula. The provinces in return agreed to **entrench** the Charter of Rights and Freedoms in the Constitution, but with limitations on its power. One compromise that the federal government agreed to was to leave explicit mention of womens' rights out of the Charter, as the provinces wanted. Trudeau knew full well that women's groups would never let this pass—and Canadian women did not. Aboriginal representatives also fought the agreement, and lobbied in London. For the first time in Canada's history, aboriginal rights were entrenched in the Constitution.

When René Lévesque woke up on the morning of November 5, 1981, he discovered that a deal had been struck while he slept. Worse, the other premiers had removed Quebec's historic veto power. He was, of course, furious, and refused to sign. In Quebec, the incident became known as the "night of the long knives," and many Quebecers saw it as yet another federal betrayal of Quebec. Trudeau, who had stayed on in politics primarily to patriate the Constitution, was not surprised that Quebec would not sign. Besides, the Supreme Court had indicated that most (not necessarily all) provinces should agree. From his federalist perspective, no province—not even Quebec—should have special status.

Figure 12–16 Neither aboriginal peoples nor women were willing to be left out of the constitution.

The Question of Quebec 331

Primary Source

Political Cartoons Not Just for Laughs

For better or worse, politicians have a great deal of power in society because they make and enforce laws. Poking fun at them is one of the freedoms of a democratic society. The most politically significant source of fun is the political cartoon. But a political cartoon must have a serious side. To be effective, it must represent politicians and issues that people care about—otherwise people wouldn't get the joke. It is this "seriously funny" side of political cartoons that interests the historian. Political cartoons are a good indication of which politicians and which issues people felt strongly about in any given period.

Political cartoons are given a degree of **licence** that would be unacceptable or misleading in print news accounts. They have an edge. Politicians' personal characteristics and physical features, for example, are grossly exaggerated. Their political positions are simplified and made to seem ridiculous. But there has to be an element of truth to the distortion, or the cartoon will fall flat. No one knows whether a given policy will bring good or bad results, or have any impact at all. Cartoons heighten that sense of uncertainty or impending disaster. By poking fun at what looks like folly, cartoonists can shed new light on questions and issues.

Study these three political cartoons, drawn at the time of the constitutional debate, and answer the following questions:

Figure 12–17

1. In Figure 12–17, what point is the cartoonist trying to make? Does the account of the constitutional debate in the text support the cartoonist's view? Why or why not?
2. In Figure 12–18, the cartoonist illustrates a common proverb. Which one? What is the cartoonist trying to say about the constitutional debate?
3. You might recognize two figures from the photos in the text. Which ones? Do you see any significance in the comments attributed to them?
4. What groups who later became important in the constitutional process are not represented here?

Perspectives

Pierre Trudeau toasts Alberta Premier Peter Lougheed at the close of an oil pricing deal between the Federal government and the government of Alberta. While the event looks like a happy one, this was in fact the conclusion to a long-fought battle between the governments, and one that would further alienate Alberta from the decision-making in Ottawa. Oil was at stake, along with Alberta's right to charge what it wanted for this precious commodity. Neither side would be entirely satisfied with the deal. A poll conducted in 1981—the same year this photograph was taken—showed that 49 percent of Albertans supported separation from Canada. Look closely at the expressions on Lougheed's and Trudeau's faces. What are they saying?

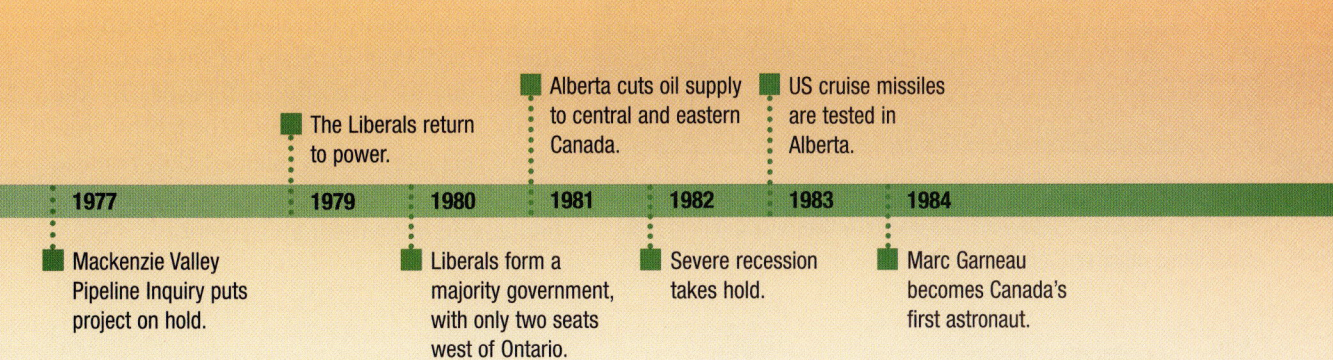

- 1977 — Mackenzie Valley Pipeline Inquiry puts project on hold.
- 1979 — The Liberals return to power.
- 1980 — Liberals form a majority government, with only two seats west of Ontario.
- 1981 — Alberta cuts oil supply to central and eastern Canada.
- 1982 — Severe recession takes hold.
- 1983 — US cruise missiles are tested in Alberta.
- 1984 — Marc Garneau becomes Canada's first astronaut.

WORLD ECONOMIC CHANGE AND CANADA

After World War II, Canada enjoyed the greatest economic boom in its history, with only a mild recession from 1958 to 1962. Between 1960 and 1967, foreign demand for Canadian goods grew tremendously. Canada's exports doubled, from $7 billion to $14.6 billion. This was partly because world markets needed its commodities. Europe was still rebuilding after World War II, and other countries in the developed and developing world were expanding and modernizing. Because of Canada's strong economic growth, the unemployment rate was low: 4.1 percent in 1967 (see Figure 14–3).

Canada's living standards were rising as well, for a number of reasons. By world standards, Canada was a vast country geographically, but with a very small population. As a result, Canada had a small national market, and many rich resources had gone untapped. Large postwar immigration, however, had increased the demand for consumer goods and services within Canada. It had also swelled Canada's labour force, which in turn kept the wheels of industrial expansion turning.

Another major factor in Canada was that members of the baby boom generation were growing up. They were entering the labour force in larger and larger numbers. As you read in Chapter 11, they were also reshaping Canadian politics. Trudeau's appeal to younger voters helped him win office in 1969.

The market for consumer goods and services within Canada changed as well to meet the demands and buying power of teenagers and young adults. For example, in 1950, about 230 000 people born in Canada turned 16. By 1970, that number increased to about 435 000. More businesses that produced goods and services aimed at teenagers could succeed, which meant that more jobs were available at those businesses. In 1973, London's prestigious business magazine, *The Economist*, rated Canada the best country in the world in which to live.

As rosy as the picture seemed, however, the world economy had slowly been changing after World War II. Many of these changes turned out to be costly to Canada. By the 1970s, these changes began to be felt by ordinary Canadians. Many blamed the Trudeau government for unwelcome changes, such as higher unemployment and inflation.

Figure 13–1 The West Edmonton Mall symbolized the prosperity of Alberta in the early 1980s. Alberta's economy was strong during this time, while much of Canada suffered.

Stagflation: A Disturbing Economic Pattern

In his first term, Trudeau was confronted by an urgent economic problem. The economy was changing in unpredictable ways. Like most Canadians, the Trudeau government expected the economy to follow a traditional pattern that had existed after the Great Depression.

The traditional business cycle has two main phases. During a period of prosperity, Canada would be selling its products at high prices in world markets. Because the economy was growing, jobs would be plentiful. Most Canadians would be making money and buying new goods and services. Because demand was high, prices would increase. Economists call this rise in prices "inflation." Governments that had to worry about inflation did not have to worry about high unemployment. Usually, unemployment rates would be low.

In the second phase, world demand for Canadian products would drop. The economy would then shift into a recession, or slow down. Because Canadian businesses could not sell their goods and services, they would lower prices. Thus, inflation would be non-existent, or very low. Businesses would also lay off workers and not hire new staff. High unemployment rates would result. As a result, governments that had to deal with high unemployment did not have to worry about inflation. They could focus on trying to stimulate the economy to create jobs.

In the 1970s, however, it became clear that something was changing in the economy. By the 1980s, a disturbing new word began to appear in the media: "stagflation." Formed from the words "**stagnation**" and "inflation," it described a situation in which high levels of unemployment and high inflation occurred together. Even though the economy was not growing (stagnation)—which led to unemployment—prices for goods and services continued to rise. The federal government was not sure how to deal with this new situation.

> **Up Close**
>
> 1. Describe the two main phases of the business cycle. Focus on what happens to prices and employment in each phase.

ECONOMIC CHOICES WITH A PRICE TAG

Most nations in the Western world were dealing with the problem of stagflation, even though no one was sure quite what it was. The Canadian government, however, had additional problems to consider:

- **Canada is a nation of wide disparities**. Unemployment and inflation did not affect all Canadians equally. The extent that Canadians were hurt depended on the region in which they lived, their age, their gender, and the ability of their union or professional association to bargain collectively. Many Canadians saw these situations as very unfair.
- **Canada's economy has historically been tied to the United States**. The US, Canada's closest neighbour and largest trading partner, is the world's most powerful economy. The Canadian government has always had to cope with the decisions of the US government. But the US government was not accountable

for the effect of its decisions and policies on Canada. Many Canadians wanted to reduce Canada's dependence on the United States.

- **Canada's economy has historically been based on exporting resource commodities (lumber, oil, wheat, fish).** When world prices for these commodities fell, Canadians lost jobs. Many Canadians believed that Canada should try to become less dependent on resource-based industries and diversify the economy.

If these distinctly Canadian issues were not dealt with, Trudeau's dream of a Just Society would fall flat. Equal opportunity would simply mean equal lack of opportunity.

> **Up Close**
>
> 2 What were Canada's additional economic problems? State these in your own words.

Unemployment in Canada by Region					
	1970	1975	1980	1985	1990
Canada	5.7	6.9	7.5	10.5	8.1
Newfoundland	7.3	14.0	13.2	20.8	17.0
Prince Edward Island	n.a.	8.0	10.8	13.4	14.9
Nova Scotia	5.3	7.7	9.7	13.6	10.5
New Brunswick	6.3	9.8	11.1	15.2	12.1
Quebec	7.0	8.1	9.9	11.9	10.2
Ontario	4.4	6.3	6.9	8.1	6.3
Manitoba	5.3	4.5	5.5	8.2	7.6
Saskatchewan	4.2	2.9	4.4	8.2	7.0
Alberta	5.1	4.1	3.8	10.1	7.0
British Columbia	7.7	8.5	6.8	14.2	8.4

Figure 13–2 Unemployment rates varied widely in Canada's regions between 1970 and 1985. Which regions appeared to be disadvantaged?

Social Spending and Inflation

In **indexing** social benefits and taxes, Trudeau was following the philosophy of John Maynard Keynes, a British economist (1883–1946). Keynes believed that governments must play a role in managing the economy. You first read about Keynes in Chapter 5.

According to Keynes's theories, governments could stimulate the economy during a recession by a combination of spending money on programs and cutting taxes and lowering interest rates. During recessions, unemployment would be high, and these measures would free up money. This would encourage businesses to expand and consumers to spend. In turn, this would create jobs. During an economic recovery—when employment would be high and inflation would become a threat—Keynes's theory called for governments to cut spending, increase taxes, and raise interest rates. Because government spending and the money supply would be restricted, inflation would be kept in check.

Keynes's economic theories had evolved during the Great Depression and had been adopted by most industrialized nations after World War II. They were

Historical Inquiry: Analysing/Evaluating Information

Primary Source

Disparity and Economic Priorities

Figure 13–3 Trudeau explained clearly in his book *Mémoires Politiques* why he made the decisions that he did.

During his campaign in 1968, Pierre Elliott Trudeau told Canadians that the federal government was not Santa Claus. He warned them not to expect social programs to provide an endless supply of "free stuff." But when Trudeau tried to cut back on social spending, his popularity started to fizzle. Saying that there was no Santa would have political consequences.

In 1969, Trudeau froze defence spending for three years, and increased spending on health and welfare. In these excerpts from his book, *Mémoires Politiques*, published in 1993, Trudeau described the reasons for his government's economic decisions, and their consequences.

… Against the invisible hand of Adam Smith, there has to be a visible hand of politicians whose objective is to have the kind of society that is caring and humane.

I worked to put this view of social justice into effect throughout my years in office. Regional policy, including the creation of the Department of Regional Economic Expansion in 1968 … aimed at equalizing opportunity in a territorial or geographic context; social policy tried to equalize opportunities for individual Canadians.

To maintain the effectiveness of the welfare state, we protected the social safety net and the real incomes of Canadians against inflation by indexing both benefits and tax brackets. We also extended Canada's welfare state in three distinct areas: unemployment insurance, family policy, and easing poverty among the aged.

The Trudeau government, in other words, decided that the best way to deal with the economic situation was to continue trying to create equal economic opportunities across Canada's regions. It continued and expanded the funding of social programs that had been introduced by the Pearson government. Canadians saw these programs as something that defined Canada and its sense of social justice and purpose.

What Do You Think?

1. Analyse the excerpt from Trudeau's book in terms of its bias and credibility. Is this information useful? What factors point to its usefulness? Why might this account be biased?

2. In a paragraph, comment on Trudeau's management of the economy from the standpoint of an economist who believes in little or no government intervention in the economy.

The Economy, the West, and the US

> **Up Close**
>
> 3. Summarize Keynes's economic theory in point form.

intended to make certain that the business cycle would never again plunge into the hardships of another depression. But Keynes's theories had never been applied during a period of stagflation—when both unemployment and inflation rates were high.

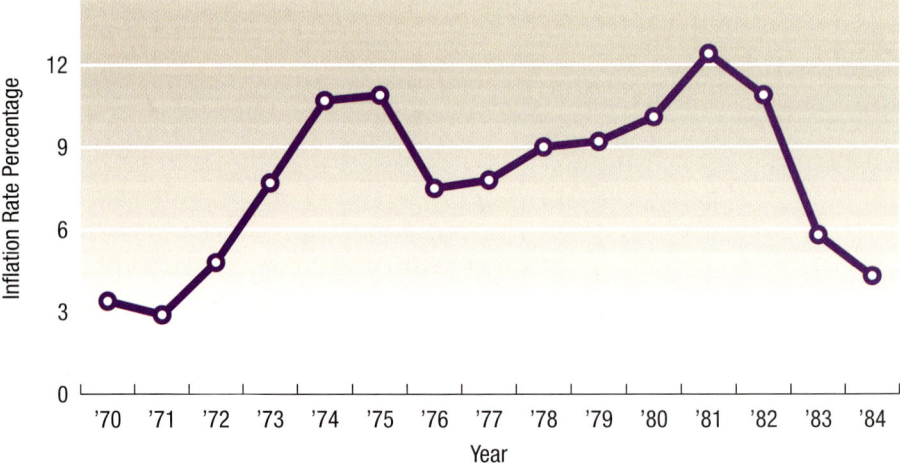

Figure 13–4 How did inflation affect Canadians on low or fixed incomes?

Managing or Mismanaging the Economy?

At the start of the 1970s, Canadians were optimistic that the federal government could solve social and economic problems, especially social inequity. However, many of these problems remained, even though the government collected and spent larger and larger amounts of money. In fact, the federal government ended up with growing annual **deficits**, which meant that the **national debt** kept rising.

Trudeau came under increasing attack for the way his government was managing the economy. Many Canadians became alarmed as federal spending continued to outstrip federal revenues. Canadian author and historian Peter C. Newman later condemned Trudeau for mismanaging the economy:

> **During his sixteen years in power, Trudeau turned the nearly balanced books he had inherited into a $38.5 billion deficit and increased the national debt by 1200 percent, from $17 billion to more than $200 billion.**

In 1978, even the **auditor general** had warned that the government was losing control of its spending. To get an idea of why people were so alarmed about the national debt, it helps to look at it as a per capita (per head) figure. In 1940, each Canadian's share of the national debt was calculated to be $288. By the end of the war, it was $936, mainly because of war expenses. That fell to $677 by 1960. During the 1960s, the national debt started to increase again. During the Trudeau years, it grew deeper. In 1984, when Brian Mulroney was elected prime minister, the per capita figure had climbed to $6436. You will read more about the consequences of deficits and the national debt in Chapter 14.

> **Up Close**
>
> 4. Create a graph to plot the fluctuation in the national debt expressed as a per capita figure. Begin in 1940 and end in 1984.

CANADA DURING THE OIL CRISIS

In 1972 Trudeau was hit by an unexpected challenge from outside Canada. In the years following World War II, oil had sold for relatively low prices. Because oil was an essential fuel and resource for industrialized economies, demand for it was centred in the industrialized world. Multinational oil companies also played oil-producing nations against one another to keep prices low. As the world's economy became more interconnected, big changes started to take place. Many developing countries began slowly to industrialize. They too needed oil. The world demand for oil began to increase.

In 1960, five countries that exported large amounts of oil—Iran, Iraq, Kuwait, Saudi Arabia, and Venezuela—had formed the Organization of Petroleum Exporting Countries (OPEC). Although these countries were quite poor and undeveloped, together they had a more powerful bargaining position. In 1972, they realized that world demand for oil was exceeding supply.

By late 1973, the OPEC nations presented a united front on oil prices. Within months, oil prices increased from approximately $3 a barrel to $12 a barrel. The increase hit industrialized nations very hard, but Canada more than most. A number of reasons accounted for this. Canada had a high standard of living, a cold climate, and a population that was used to cheap energy. Few Canadians took energy conservation seriously in the early 1970s. Transporting products to ports and markets across Canada also meant covering enormous distances, and this business fact of life became very expensive. As a Canadian truckers' slogan said at the time, "If you've got it, a truck brought it."

Up Close

5. What is OPEC? Why was it formed? What did it do in the early 1970s?

Figure 13–5 Some Canadians vented their frustrations at the new power of oil-producing nations by ridiculing Arab customs and dress. How many Canadians would know that these nations were poor by Western standards and wanted to develop their economies?

With the oil crisis, prices in Canada increased rapidly and inflation soared. At the same time, the oil crisis led to higher unemployment. Money was leaving Canada, not circulating and creating jobs. Businesses were cutting back on staff to reduce costs. In other words, the country was facing stagflation—high inflation combined with high unemployment.

Conflicts over Rising Oil Prices

Up Close

6. Describe the conflict between the western provinces and Trudeau in a cartoon. State the view of each side in a dialogue bubble.

The oil crisis that began in 1973 hit Canada in another way as well, by creating a western threat to national unity. Western Canada, particularly Alberta, had vast supplies of oil and gas. Western producers stood to make much larger profits by selling their oil at the world price. Before the oil crisis, eastern Canada had imported oil from the OPEC countries. It was cheaper than importing it from the West. The oil crisis turned the tables.

Trudeau responded to the crisis by doing two things. He protected all Canadians from rising prices by subsidizing oil imports, and he refused to allow Canadian producers to charge the full world price. Western Canadians were outraged, and so were the largely US-controlled multinational oil companies operating in Alberta and Saskatchewan.

The government also launched campaigns to raise public awareness of the need to conserve energy. It funded and promoted research into alternative energy sources—such as solar energy. Federal and provincial governments also funded programs to help homeowners insulate their homes. Canada's environmental movement was growing at the same time, and it welcomed these government initiatives.

Figure 13–6 The crisis in oil prices made energy conservation a concern for all Canadians. This building uses solar heating panels.

At the time of the oil crisis, the Trudeau government set a goal of making Canada self-sufficient in energy. This would include encouraging more oil-and-gas exploration, increasing conservation, and developing alternative sources of supply. These sources included extracting petroleum from the Athabaska Tar Sands of northern Alberta. For Trudeau, this would mean cooperating with the Alberta government, which was already angry over oil pricing.

Trudeau liked to do things his own way, but in 1972 he had a minority government. The New Democratic Party, led by David Lewis, held the balance of power. The NDP was committed to maintaining the welfare state, to energy self-sufficiency, and to creating a state-owned oil company. Trudeau, who had once considered joining the NDP himself, went ahead with these strategies. But the idea of a state-owned oil company rubbed salt into the wounds of the multinational oil companies and many people in the West.

For two years, the Liberal government survived by accommodating the NDP, but on May 9, 1974, they were defeated in the House of Commons. An election was called for July 8. It was all part of Trudeau's plan. He could sense a victory.

> **Data File**
>
> In the years before the oil crisis of 1973, Alberta crude oil sold for six times the price of crude oil from Iran.

Wage-and-Price Controls

In the 1974 election, as oil prices and inflation continued to rise, economic issues dominated the campaign. Trudeau faced off against Progressive Conservative leader Robert Stanfield, for the third time. Early on, Stanfield advocated dusting off a strategy from World War II. First, there would be a freeze on wages and prices, followed by wage-and-price controls. Trudeau quickly realized that Stanfield had made a tactical error: most Canadians strongly opposed Stanfield's idea. Trudeau sniped at wage-and-price controls at every opportunity.

"The price of energy looks as though it's going to go through the roof. How are you going to control that?" he challenged Stanfield. "How are you going to freeze the price that is being set in the Middle East by the OPEC cartel? You can't just say 'Zap! You're frozen and we're not going to pay more for your oil.'"

Trudeau's attacks on Stanfield's proposed controls paid off at the polls. The Liberals won, with a majority government. A little more than a year later, however, Trudeau did an about-face. On October 13, 1975, he announced mandatory wage-and-price controls. It was the heaviest program of economic restraints since World War II. Canadians were stunned.

Later, Trudeau would claim that 1975 presented "entirely different sets of circumstances" from 1974. By 1975, he said, it was becoming clear that OPEC was not the only cause of inflation. Canadians were becoming victims of "inflation psychology." For example, inflation was 10.9 percent in 1975, but Canadians were negotiating wage increases of 15 to 20 percent. Their efforts to stay ahead of inflation were creating even higher inflation. Trudeau felt that wage-and-price controls would force Canadians to realize that they could not expect to make gains in their living standards without also producing more goods and services.

Figure 13–7 As leader of the Conservatives, Robert Stanfield ran against Trudeau in 1968, 1972, and 1974. He lost every time. Stanfield was widely respected, but in the age of television he seemed to be from a bygone era—especially running against the media-friendly Trudeau.

The Economy, the West, and the US **345**

> **Up Close**
>
> 7. Create a diagram to illustrate the connections between existing inflation, wage demands, and more inflation.

Canadians were in no mood to listen. The program hit working Canadians where it hurt, in their pocketbooks. Wages and salaries could increase only by 10 percent for 1976, 8 percent for 1977, and 6 percent for 1978. The government created the Anti-Inflation Board (AIB), which would roll back any wage settlements that exceeded the guidelines. Unions were enraged by Trudeau's wage controls because they applied only to unionized workers. Farmers, fishers, small businesses, and non-unionized employees were exempt.

Labour and Management Fight Controls

Labour leaders had found the early 1970s very difficult, and saw Trudeau's controls as an assault on labour rights. Businesses, hit by rising oil prices, pressured labour leaders to keep wage increases down, or face layoffs. Still, workers demanded higher wages in order to keep up with inflation. Conflicts erupted all over the country, and strikes became common occurrences.

Many of these were **wildcat strikes**, which were illegal in every province except Saskatchewan. In fact, one-third of all strikes in the 1970s were wildcats, including 59 at General Motors branch plants alone. In 1975, Toronto teachers went on strike for two months, until the Ontario government legislated them back to work and imposed **binding arbitration**. Air traffic controllers and postal workers also went on strike during this period.

The unions' usual strategy was to negotiate as if the AIB did not exist, forcing it to roll back the agreement. This saved a union's reputation with its members by shifting the blame onto the government. The busiest year for the AIB was 1976, when a large number of unions defied the government controls with large wage increases. The AIB promptly rolled them back. Resentment against the government and its Anti-Inflation Board grew across Canada. On October 14, 1976, 1 million workers from coast to coast staged a massive one-day strike to protest the controls.

Management was no happier than labour, because the AIB also controlled price increases. Prices could rise, but only when production costs increased. To justify a price increase, businesses had to follow strict regulations and fill out masses of forms. These then had to be approved by the growing number of federal employees working for the AIB. From business's point of view, the federal price con-

Figure 13–8 During the mid-1970s, postal workers were some of the most visible strikers.

trols themselves increased prices by adding administrative costs. Also, a number of important items were exempted from AIB control, which added to a growing sense of unfairness.

Outcome of Wage-and-Price Controls

While wage-and-price controls were the lightning rod for protest, they were only one part of the government's anti-inflation program. The government also tightened the money supply (monetary policy) and curbed the growth of government spending (fiscal policy). After the first year, the economy started to slow down, which reduced both profits and wage increases. That in turn reduced inflation, which dipped to 7.5 percent in 1976 from 10.8 percent in 1975. Some economists said that this was only because of declining food prices, rather than the controls imposed by the government. Other economists argued that wage-and-price controls were working. They were putting the brakes on inflation psychology, as intended.

Economists still debate whether Trudeau's anti-inflation program was too extreme, and whether or not it was effective. In 1978, however, the controls ended, and inflation rose again. In 1981–1982, the economy fell into a major recession—partly triggered by another international oil crisis. You will look more closely at these events later in this chapter.

Data File
In 1867, the federal government employed 2200 people, one for every 1590 people in Canada. By 1995, federal employees numbered 252 100, or one for every 113 people in Canada.

US INVESTMENT AND CANADIAN INDEPENDENCE

During the 1960s, Canadians became more nationalistic and more concerned about growing US control of the Canadian economy. In 1940, Americans had invested $2 billion in Canadian businesses. By 1968, US investment amounted to approximately $19 billion, more than 80 percent of all foreign investment in Canada in that year.

US investment had a long history in Canada, and it had advantages and disadvantages. It brought in the money needed to develop resources and industry. Development, in turn, created jobs, including skilled technical and management jobs. Some research suggests that Canadians have enjoyed a higher standard of living as a direct result of US investment.

On the other hand, increasing US investment had meant that Canada was in danger of becoming a branch-plant economy. Decisions affecting the jobs of thousands of Canadians were—and are—made at US head offices. It also often meant that important

Heritage Minute

In 1957, Nat Taylor, a theatre owner in Ottawa, had a familiar problem on his hands. Two giant US blockbusters had just been released and he wanted to show both films. Taylor had already subdivided his theatre, so he ran both *Witness for the Prosecution* and *Bridge on the River Kwai*. People loved it, and "cineplex" was born. In 1979, Taylor's vision made the Guinness Book of World Records with the 18-screen Cineplex in the Toronto Eaton Centre.

Figure 13–9 In the 1970s, Prime Minister Trudeau welcomed US President Richard Nixon to Ottawa (at right) and also travelled to Havana to meet with Cuban President Fidel Castro (above). Anti-communist Nixon and Castro were arch enemies. Would Trudeau really be able to avoid taking sides?

research and development were conducted outside Canada and that Canadian management teams had limited power and restricted career opportunities—unless they moved to the US head office.

Perhaps the most troubling problem with increasing US investment was the question of Canadian sovereignty. In Chapter 11, you learned of the steps the Trudeau government took to protect Canada's cultural industries from US domination. More disturbing still, to many Canadians, was the mounting influence of US foreign policy on Canada. In one of the most dramatic examples, the US government tried to stop US subsidiaries in Canada from selling to Cuba. Canada, however, had friendly relations with Cuba, including trade and foreign aid. This infuriated the US government. It also led many Canadians to question US attempts to dictate Canada's foreign policy.

Foreign Investment Review Agency

In 1968, a government report pointed out that Canada had no comprehensive policy on foreign investment. The Watkins Report noted that "No other country … seems prepared to tolerate so high a degree of foreign ownership as exists in Canada." Then, in 1971, US President Richard Nixon suddenly imposed a 10 percent surcharge on all goods entering the US. The "Nixon shock" left many nations, including Canada, scrambling. It also spurred the Canadian government to study foreign investment more closely.

In 1972, the Gray Report examined the costs and benefits of foreign investment, and reported that the costs to Canada were greater than the benefits. One year later, the federal government created the Foreign Investment Review Agency (FIRA) to screen foreign investment. It would block any foreign takeovers of Canadian businesses or any foreign investment that was considered not to be "of significant benefit" to Canada.

The FIRA angered many Canadian businesses. They saw it as yet another Trudeau move to impose government control on the economy. The US government saw it as bluntly hostile. Between 1974 and 1978, 778 requests by foreigners were approved by FIRA, and 224 rejected. Nonetheless, the level of US ownership of Canadian businesses remained relatively unchanged.

In 1971, Trudeau had also established the Canada Development Corporation (CDC) as a hedge against foreign control. Its purpose was to purchase foreign-controlled businesses in Canada or businesses that were operating in sectors largely dominated by foreign businesses. The fate of two businesses was especially troubling because they had been pioneers in Canadian aviation: de Havilland and Canadair.

In 1974, the CDC bought de Havilland from a British company and in 1976 it bought Canadair from a US company. The CDC hoped eventually to **privatize** these companies, but realities of the world economy intervened. Research costs for new aircraft are very high, and few all-Canadian companies could afford to build them.

8. Summarize the steps that led to the creation of FIRA.

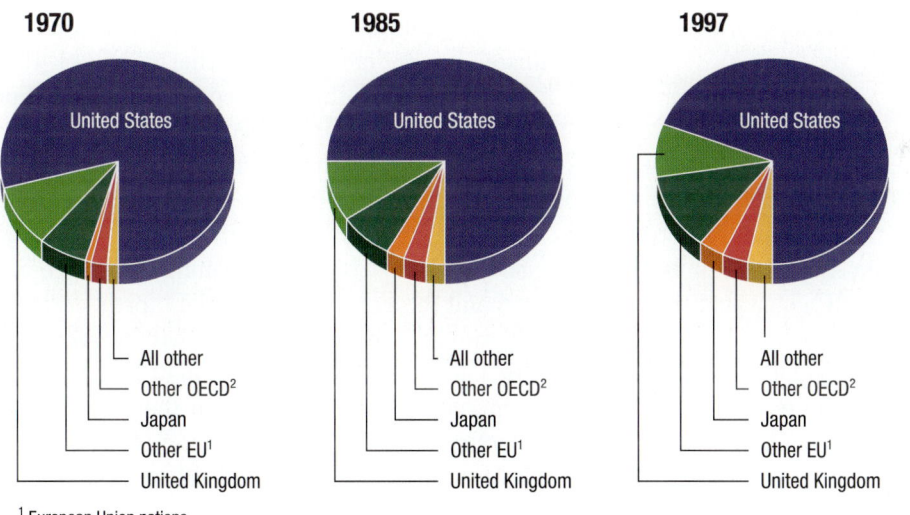

[1] European Union nations
[2] Organization for Economic Cooperation and Development nations

Figure 13–10 Foreign investment in Canada is not limited to the US, as these pie charts illustrate. What happened to other foreign investment in Canada from 1973 through 1997? Based on your observations, what would you predict about future foreign investment?

Petro-Canada: A Window on the Oil Industry

Nowhere was the power of US investment stronger than in Canada's oil-and-gas industry. The Liberal government, encouraged by the NDP, thought that Canada could have more control of oil and gas resources if it created a **nationalized** company. This, they believed, would allow government to act on energy issues and help Canada become self-sufficient in energy. On December 6, 1973, Trudeau told the House of Commons that the CDC was going to purchase a number of oil companies to give Canadians a "window on the oil industry."

Two years later, in 1975, the Petro-Canada Act created Petro-Canada as a Crown corporation. Its purpose was to promote exploration and development of new oil and gas resources and to research and develop new energy sources. At

Flashpoint
Oil and Water in the Arctic

In 1968, the largest North American bed of oil and gas ever discovered was found below the waters of Alaska's Prudhoe Bay. But the multinational oil companies behind the discovery had a problem. How could they get the oil to the US mainland? Spending more than $43 million, they built the US ship *SS Manhattan*, a massive supertanker-icebreaker.

On September 14, 1968, the *Manhattan* set off to cut through the ice-bound Northwest Passage. Travelling from the east, it arrived at Point Barrow, Alaska, on September 21. The US media followed the dramatic voyage day by day. It was seen as a triumph of American technology and daring.

In Canada, the *Manhattan* was another story. Canada claimed sovereignty over the Northwest Passage, but the US disagreed: These were international waters, over which Canada had no control. Canadians were infuriated. A Canadian Coast Guard icebreaker escorted the *Manhattan* in 1969, and again in 1970, as evidence of Canada's control of the Arctic seas.

The *Manhattan* voyages showed that oil might be transported by supertankers, but environmentalists raised concerns about oil spills and pollution. In 1970, the Canadian government passed the Arctic Water Pollution Prevention Act. Far-reaching and controversial, it proclaimed Canada's right to control shipping within a 100-nautical-mile (182 kilometres) zone around the Arctic Archipelago.

After more studies, the oil companies proposed that a pipeline be built through the Mackenzie Valley delta from Alaska to Alberta. It would be a multibillion-dollar megaproject. In 1972, Trudeau welcomed the pipeline idea. It would spur the development of Canada's North. Environmentalists and most northern aboriginal people disagreed.

Under mounting pressure from the NDP, Minister of Indian and Northern Affairs Jean Chrétien launched the Mackenzie Valley Pipeline Inquiry in 1974. He appointed BC Supreme Court Justice Thomas Berger to be head Commissioner. Between 1974 and 1977, Berger crisscrossed the North, hearing from more than 1000 witnesses. Berger made a point of listening to aboriginal leaders and the people living in the North.

It quickly became clear that northerners opposed any development that might damage their environment. Many depended on the migration of the Porcupine caribou herd for food. Tens of thousands of these animals migrated about 1000 kilome-

Change and Continuity: Technological Impact

tres to and from the calving grounds on the Arctic coast each year. The pipeline would certainly disrupt that. Besides, the pipeline would have to be built on permafrost, and no one knew if this would damage the environment.

First Nations peoples also wanted outstanding land claims settled before any development could proceed. Richard Neryson, of Fort McPherson, told the Inquiry: "To the Indian people, our land really is our life. Without our land we could no longer exist as a people."

Jim Antoine, now Premier of the Northwest Territories, was a Fort Simpson band chief at the time. He told the Inquiry, "The way I see it, if this pipeline goes ahead, it's just going to destroy a lot of people."

Many people believed that Berger would listen politely and then give the oil companies the go-ahead. But after three years, he issued a report that was stunning for its time. No project should proceed until Native land claims were settled. No pipeline should be built across the northern Yukon. A ten-year moratorium should be imposed on any development, while detailed environmental studies were done.

Berger's supporters were skeptical the federal government would agree. They feared that few southern Canadians cared about the North, as long as they had their gas and oil.

Then the unexpected happened. Berger met with Pierre Trudeau and urged him to visit the North. He described the Porcupine caribou herd, saying, "I confess the sight of this magnificent aggregation of animals helped me to make up my mind to recommend that no pipeline be built along the coastal plain." Trudeau took Berger's advice, and he and his sons witnessed the caribou migration. Later, as Berger had suspected, the pipeline proposal died.

The Berger Commission marked a watershed in Canadian history. Many non-aboriginal Canadians became deeply aware of the needs and hopes of the northern First Nations peoples for the first time. "We possess a terrible self-centredness, even arrogance, as a people," Berger said, speaking about his fellow non-aboriginal Canadians. Yet Berger probably did more to change that view than any other non-aboriginal Canadian before him.

Activities

1. Write a paragraph from the point of view of a Northerner who is a member of an aboriginal group, arguing against the pipeline. Present logical arguments and consider long-term and short-term consequences to your region. (Remember that here, and in Activity 2 below, you have no information later than 1977.)

2. Write a paragraph from the point of view of an oil company executive, arguing for the pipeline. Present logical arguments and draw on the information you learned in this chapter about the international oil situation during the 1970s.

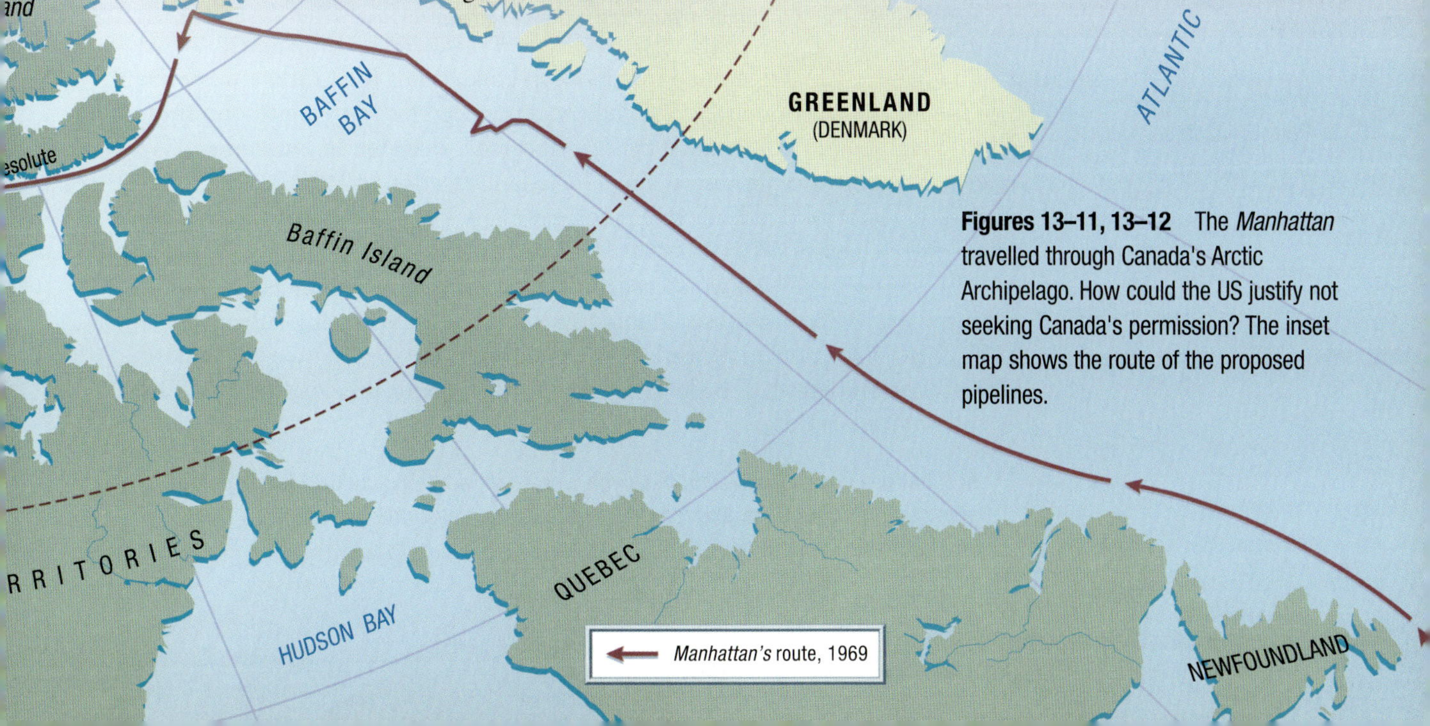

Figures 13–11, 13–12 The *Manhattan* travelled through Canada's Arctic Archipelago. How could the US justify not seeking Canada's permission? The inset map shows the route of the proposed pipelines.

← *Manhattan's* route, 1969

Figure 13–13 In the mid- to late-1980s, Petro-Canada shared in the discovery of oil fields off the coast of Newfoundland. Today it is operator of the Terra Nova project, another example of how Petro-Canada has benefited regions across Canada.

first, Petro-Canada ruffled feathers in Alberta, Canada's "oil patch." Many westerners felt it would benefit central Canada at the West's expense. Stable oil prices were essential for the manufacturing industry and oil refineries in central Canada.

In the following years, Petro-Canada learned to work with the large multinational oil companies as it pursued exploration, development, and research. In the long run, prices for Alberta oil reached world levels, and Petro-Canada was viewed more favourably. In the 1980s and 1990s, it continued to grow. Petro-Canada became a partner in major oil, gas, and energy projects across Canada.

CANADA VERSUS ALBERTA: WESTERN ALIENATION

Western Canada had become increasingly alienated from the federal government during the Trudeau decade of the 1970s. In a 1979 speech, Stan Roberts, president of the Canada West Foundation, summed up the feelings of many westerners:

> Sometimes the West's frustration and rage is misconstrued as anti-Quebec in nature. It is not. It is, in most cases, envy of Quebec's political prowess combined with the West's own impotence on the national scene.

In Chapter 12, you learned that Conservative leader Joe Clark, a westerner, won the federal election in 1979. Trudeau announced his retirement soon thereafter. When Clark's government was unexpectedly defeated in December 1979, Trudeau was convinced to run again. The federal election of 1980 was a stunning comeback victory—Trudeau won another majority. In western Canada, few people were cheering.

If westerners had ever wondered about their power in Ottawa, election night February 18, 1980, put those doubts to rest. Even before many Albertans had voted, CBC news anchor Knowlton Nash announced: "It's all over. A majority Liberal government has been re-elected." A Toronto stockbroker who had recently moved to Calgary told the *Toronto Star*:

> In Toronto, it never occurred to me, even when my (federal) candidate lost, that my vote didn't matter. Here, and it's a strange feeling, I've come to accept it's irrelevant whether I vote at all.

Data File

Petro-Canada stopped being a Crown Corporation in 1990. By 1999, it had become the twenty-fourth largest company in Canada.

He had good cause to think so. In the 1980 federal election, the Liberals won only 2 seats west of Ontario, both in Manitoba. However, the "eastern" government of Pierre Trudeau now faced a powerful Alberta government, which had been led by Peter Lougheed since 1971.

Many Albertans were still angry about Petro-Canada when the federal government introduced the National Energy Program (NEP) in October 1980. The NEP aimed to increase Canadian ownership of the oil industry from roughly 25 percent, in 1980, to 50 percent, in 1990. Under this program, Petro-Canada was permitted to take over foreign firms and acquire 25 percent ownership in foreign and offshore oil leases held by multinational corporations. Canadian firms would also receive preferential exploration grants.

Western Canada, and particularly Peter Lougheed, loudly criticized the NEP because they saw it as a federal raid on provincial resource revenues.

Alberta Cuts Oil Supplies

Under the NEP, Ottawa intended to increase its share of oil revenues from 10 to at least 24 percent. It would reduce the oil industry's take from 45 percent to 33 percent, and Alberta's take from 45 percent to 43 percent. Ottawa also wanted to encourage exploration in the Arctic, where it claimed jurisdiction.

In 1981, Lougheed responded to the NEP. He announced that Alberta would cut back oil supplies to refineries in Ontario and Quebec. On March 1, 1981, he followed through, with cutbacks of 100 000 barrels of oil a day. Lougheed threatened to increase this to 180 000 barrels a day, if Ottawa did not agree to terms on energy pricing and taxation. Bumper stickers began to appear on Alberta cars, suggesting that people in the East should "freeze in the dark."

Lougheed had made his point. Trudeau signed an oil agreement in September 1981. This reduced the feeling of alienation in western Canada, and gave Alberta more say in setting oil prices and its share of revenues. It also helped reduce the 1981 federal deficit. Canada, however, was facing a severe recession in 1981-1982. Many Canadians accused Trudeau of abandoning his policy of low oil prices, even though Canadians were paying considerably less than the world price. Once again Trudeau's popularity plummeted, and once again he was accused of mismanaging the economy.

Up Close

9. Create a time line of events surrounding the NEP. Start with its creation in 1980.

Figure 13–14 This 1915 cartoon, from the *Grain Growers Guide*, says a great deal about how prairie wheat farmers viewed central Canada at the time. Describe how you could update the cartoon to capture western resentments over oil.

The Economy, the West, and the US **353**

Images

Terry Fox: Cancer Will Be Beaten

The 1980s opened with an event that riveted Canadians and would make a young man from British Columbia a hero. Terry Fox was not a gifted athlete, but he was persistent. In Grade 8, he rated 19th out of 19 basketball players and was allowed only one minute on the court. By sheer determination, he improved his performance so much that in 1976 he won a place on the junior varsity basketball team at Simon Fraser University, where he studied kinesiology.

One morning in March 1977, he woke up unable to stand on his right leg. Athletes get used to painful damage. But he learned that he had a malignant tumour. Doctors offered the eighteen-year-old one chance at life: they could amputate his leg six inches above the knee, for a 50 to 70 percent chance of survival.

The night before the amputation, Terry's coach visited him and brought an article about an amputee who ran in the New York City Marathon. That night, Terry, who never gave up on his dreams, shifted his goals away from basketball; he dreamed about running across Canada.

As Terry recovered over the next 16 months, he planned the marathon run that would raise money for cancer research. Encouraged by his friends Rick Hansen and Doug Alward, Terry started on a running program two years after his operation. For 15 months Terry trained. Sometimes his stump was raw and bleeding; once the artificial leg snapped and he had to hitchhike home, carrying the foot. But by the time he embarked on his Marathon of Hope, he could run nearly 40 kilometres per day.

Figure 13–15 Terry Fox (1958–1981)

Citizenship and Heritage: Individual Canadians

Many were skeptical that Terry could run 8000 km across Canada, let alone raise his target of $1 million for research. However, he did attract some corporate support. On April 12, 1980, he dipped his artificial leg into the icy harbour at St. John's, Newfoundland, and set off to run a marathon distance each day, starting at 4:30 a.m. Doug drove the van behind him as he ran through six provinces, averaging 42 km per day, battling high winds, bitter cold, freezing rain, blistering heat, and humidity.

Terry had little official support in the early stages of the run, but ordinary Canadians began to gather to watch. Writer Leslie Scrivener describes the scene: "They wept as he ran by, fists clenched, eyes focussed on the road ahead, his awkward double step and hop sounding down the highway, the set of his jaw, unflinching, without compromise." Well-wishers began to meet him on the road and press money into his hand as he passed.

The fund received a big boost when Isadore Sharp, President of the Four Seasons Hotel, pledged $10 000 and challenged 999 Canadian corporations to follow suit. Endorsements began to tumble along and by the time Terry reached Toronto, Darryl Sittler, the popular captain of the Toronto Maple Leafs, ran with him to Nathan Phillips Square for a huge rally. The two guys with a van and an unshakeable dream were winning, or so it seemed.

Terry ploughed through Ontario, sure he was beating the disease—so sure that he missed some medical checkups during his run. But by September 1, 1980, at 5373 km, just east of Thunder Bay, he had to recognize that the growing, blunt pain in his chest was more than just a cold symptom. Once he had run past the people shouting "You can make it all the way!" he stopped, and asked Doug to drive him to a hospital. Doctors in Thunder Bay told him the devastating news: Cancer had spread to his lungs. His parents met him in Thunder Bay and he flew home for treatment.

Honours poured in as Terry battled cancer once again. Sharp committed himself to organize the Marathon of Hope, the fund-raising run that would be held every year in Terry's name. CTV organized a star telethon that raised $10 million. Ontario and BC each gave a million. Terry himself was made a Companion of the Order of Canada, the country's highest civilian honour. He was also voted the Lou Marsh award for outstanding athletic achievement, and nominated to the Sports Hall of Fame. But the benefits of the $24.17 million ($1 for every Canadian) that Terry's journey raised for research would belong to others. On June 28, 1981, he died, surrounded by his family, a month short of his twenty-third birthday. Today, the Terry Fox Run is held in 50 countries. In 1999, more than 1 million people participated and raised close to $18 million for cancer research.

What Do You Think?

1. Terry Fox believed that determination can make dreams come true. To what extent was he right?

2. Do you think that Terry's marathon helped change Canadians' perceptions about cancer, and about who gets cancer? If so, how? For your answer, interview some Canadians who remember the Marathon of Hope and the time before and after it.

3. Do Canadian medical scientists make significant contributions to cancer research? Research this topic through the Canadian Cancer Society or books on medicine in Canada and participate in a class discussion on the topic.

Figure 13–16
A stamp created in honour of Terry Fox's Marathon of Hope

FOREIGN POLICY AND THE US

During his 16 years in power, Trudeau created the NEP and the FIRA to shape an economic policy that would strengthen Canadian interests. Out of necessity, both focused on US influence. With nationalism a growing fact of political life in Canada, Trudeau also felt the need to devise a political policy towards the US.

In a 1972 policy paper, "Canada-US Relations: Options for the Future," the government proposed three options. Canada could 1) maintain its current relationship with the US, 2) integrate more closely with the US, or 3) reduce its "vulnerability" to US actions by developing closer economic and political ties with other countries. Trudeau favoured the "Third Option," and said: "It's a very simple strategy of creating other channels of interest than the automatic, easy, north–south, Canada–US ones in which we are always the smaller and minor partner."

Canada had already recognized communist China in 1970. With the policy in place, Canada actively pursued trading relations with more countries in the Pacific Rim, Latin America, and the European Economic Community (now the European Community). In Trudeau's view, the Third Option recognized global realities, in particular the rising power of Asian and European economies. In practice, it had little success in changing Canada's trading patterns. The US remained far and away Canada's largest trading partner.

Figure 13–17 Pierre and Margaret Trudeau in China. Trudeau recognized the new power of the Asian economies.

Defence Compromises

After World War II, Canada became closely tied to US defence policy. During the Cold War, many Canadians were concerned that international tensions could erupt into full-scale nuclear war. They wanted Canada to play a role in reducing hostilities and bringing the nuclear arms race to an end. Trudeau agreed with this, and during his early years as prime minister he transformed Canada's nuclear role.

Between 1970 and 1972, nuclear missiles were removed from Canada's NATO ground forces in Europe. Within NORAD, the Canadian Bomarc missile sites were dismantled in 1971. In May 1978, Trudeau made a major speech to the UN Special Session on Disarmament in which he described Canada's policy of removing all nuclear weapons from its territory. He recommended a "strategy of suffocation," in which the nuclear arms race could be halted by withdrawing support for technological research. Talk of peace sounded good at the UN, and it won Trudeau fans—such as counterculture heroes Yoko Ono and John Lennon.

Trudeau, however, did not follow through. Canada's connection with NATO and NORAD continued during his terms of office. In 1981, the NORAD agreement with the US was extended for another five years. NORAD had also changed its name, to North American "Aerospace" Defence. Many Canadians feared that Canada was tying itself to US President Ronald Reagan's "Star Wars" project. Even more protests greeted the US request that Canada formally allow unarmed cruise missiles to be tested in Canadian air space.

In 1983, Trudeau signed a five-year agreement for the tests to take place in northern Alberta. In addition, his government provided a US branch plant, Litton Systems (Canada), with a $26 million start-up grant to develop a navigational guidance system for the cruise missile. It was hard for many Canadians to see how this followed his proclaimed "strategy of suffocation." With the growing anti-nuclear movement in Canada, the cruise missile tests led to massive demonstrations across the country.

Trudeau, however, considered himself a realist, not a pacifist. He stressed that Canada must fulfill its commitments to NATO. In an open letter published in many Canadian newspapers on May 10, 1983, Trudeau gave his critics food for thought:

> It is hardly fair to rely on the Americans to protect the West but to refuse to lend them a hand when the going gets rough. In that sense, the anti-Americanism of some Canadians verges on hypocrisy. They're eager to take refuge under the American umbrella but don't want to help hold it.

Figure 13–18 Anti-cruise-missile protesters in 1983

Canada in Space

Canada wanted to be less tied to the United States, but Canadians were also excited by the US space program. They wanted Canada involved. The only affordable option was for Canada to become an important player in a program largely directed and financed by the US. In 1983, the Canadian Astronaut Program was established. The following year, Marc Garneau became Canada's first astronaut when he orbited the Earth as part of the *Challenger* space shuttle team. On board, he carried out a set of experiments in space sciences, space technology, and life sciences, on behalf of Canada.

Up Close

10. Summarize the changes in Canada's defence policy from the early 1970s to 1983.

The Economy, the West, and the US

Figure 13–19 Marc Garneau became Canada's first astronaut in October 1984, when he participated in a flight of the US space shuttle *Challenger*. In 1992, Dr. Roberta Bondar became Canada's second astronaut when she conducted experiments aboard the US space shuttle *Discovery*. Bondar conducted more than 43 experiments on behalf of 13 countries.

The Canadarm led the way in space robotics While Canadian astronauts attracted the most attention, Canada's other technological developments in space research were also important. During the 1960s and 1970s, Canada became a world leader in communications satellites. But probably the best-known achievement in Canada's aerospace industry was the Canadarm. This robotic space arm was built in 1975 by Spar Aerospace and the National Research Council and used on over 45 NASA space missions. Officially known as the "Shuttle Remote Manipulator System," the Canadarm allows astronauts to remove satellites from the shuttle's cargo bay and launch them into space—or catch them and stow them in the cargo bay.

First used on the space shuttle *Columbia* in 1981, the Canadarm became a symbol of Canada's contribution to the space program. It also established Canada as a world leader in space robotics. Five Canadarms were built between 1981 and 1993. Four are still in use, but the fifth was destroyed when *Challenger* exploded in 1986.

In 1999, Spar sold the Canadarm to MacDonald Dettwiler and Associates Ltd. of Richmond, BC, a Canadian-owned subsidiary of the US-based Orbital Sciences Corp. Spar wanted to concentrate on aviation services. MacDonald Dettwiler president Daniel Friedmann insisted that the Canadarm will remain Canadian. "We're a totally Canadian company. We employ all our people in Canada, we pay taxes in Canada, we invest all our profits in Canada," he told the press.

Figure 13–20 The Canadarm is seen above the African coast at work aboard space shuttle *Challenger*.

Historical Inquiry: Analysing Information

Historian at Work

Applying Insights to New Situations

Figure 13–21 Preston and Sandra Manning (right) with Alberta treasurer Stockwell Day and his wife (left).

In Chapter 15, you will read how western discontent persisted during the 1990s and led to the creation of the Reform Party. But Reform's ideas were not all new. A similar movement, the United Farmers parties, developed after World War I. What can we learn from their history that would help us understand the Reform Party (1987-2000) and predict developments within the Canadian Alliance, formed in February 2000?

At the end of World War I, angry farmers opposed conscription and high import tariffs. Their provincial United Farmers parties governed Alberta, Manitoba, and Ontario (see Chapter 4). Their federal Progressive Party won 65 seats in 1921, becoming the second largest party. These parties encouraged members to shape party policy. Progressives even refused to form the official Opposition because they believed that members should answer only to their constituents.

The Progressives argued a lot. They were unable to get Mackenzie King's minority government to pass their legislation, much of which addressed the economic concerns of farmers. By 1930, only 12 Progressives were elected. Many members defected to the Liberals or the Conservatives.

The Reform Party had similar roots. In 1980, Trudeau's Liberal government won only one seat west of Ontario. But western Canadians who voted Conservative found the party uninterested in the West. In 1987, Preston Manning founded the Reform Party to advocate policies and reforms favoured by westerners, especially **grassroots** government—government that listens to the people.

In 1993, 54 Reform MPs were elected, all from western Canada. In 1997, with 60 MPs, the party became the Official Opposition. But Reform had little support east of Manitoba and could never form a national government. Therefore, Manning tried to unite Reform with the Conservatives. Many Reformers were angry because they believed that Manning had abandoned the grassroots. However, Manning persuaded enough Reformers and Conservatives to form the Canadian Alliance in February 2000.

Applying historical insights gained from one situation to a new situation is all about paying attention to the "lessons of history." Here are the steps:

- **Step 1** State what happened in the first situation.
- **Step 2** Look at the people in the first situation. Who were they? What was their agenda?
- **Step 3** Examine the conflict in the first situation.
- **Step 4** Examine the result in the first situation.
- **Step 5** Take the information you have gathered in Steps 1–4, compare it with the information you have about the new situation.

What Do You Think?

1. Using Steps 1–5, apply insights gained from the situation of the United Farmers to the situation of the Reform Party and the Canadian Alliance. Summarize your insights in a few sentences.

The Economy, the West, and the US

CONCLUSION

Many Canadians felt that Trudeau had mismanaged the economy. They blamed him for huge debts for social programs and for a huge increase in bureaucracy. However, to avoid these outcomes, Trudeau would have had to back away from the pursuit of social equality, something in which most Canadians said they believed. With so many issues coming to the fore, the Trudeau government had to achieve a balancing act. For example, the federal government restricted the influence of foreign ownership on the oil industry. But it also established a Canadian space program that piggybacked on the American program, because an independent Canadian space program was not economically possible. As the global economy gained more influence in Canada, this balancing act—involving competing issues and interests—would become much more challenging.

CHAPTER ACTIVITIES

Check Your Understanding

1. The 1970s were a turbulent time for the economy. Some causes were worldwide, and others were unique to Canada. Draw a Venn diagram (two overlapping circles). In one circle list the economic forces of the world economy that affected Canada. In the other list the forces created within Canada. Where the circles overlap, list forces that belong under both lists.

2. List and explain three decisions the Trudeau government made for the purpose of increasing Canada's control over its own economy.

3. Why was Alberta unhappy with Trudeau's policies? What impact did Alberta's unhappiness have?

Develop Your Thinking

4. Trudeau allowed his government to go into deficit and debt in order to maintain a commitment to social programs. Recently, several governments in Canada have reduced social spending, eliminated their yearly deficit, and reduced their debt. Discuss the advantages and disadvantages of reducing social spending to eliminate debt. In your answer, consider the long term as well as the short term.

5. Politicians are often blamed for saying one thing and doing another. Give two examples of situations where Trudeau did this. Research and provide more recent examples of the same thing. Using logical reasoning based on political facts, explain why you think politicians do this. What impact does it have on the voters and on the political process?

Express Yourself

6. Write a paragraph expressing the likely views of each of the following persons about Trudeau's social spending:
   - an elderly widow who spent her life caring for family members and has no pension
   - a divorced working father of two who faces higher taxes
   - a Maritime business owner who has received government money to buy up-to-date equipment and employ seven people
   - an Ontario business owner who currently employs 15 people and worries about staying competitive with American firms operating in low tax zones.

7. Working with a partner or alone, create a dialogue between Peter Lougheed and Pierre Trudeau. Express Alberta's grievances and Trudeau's reasons for his decisions. Perform your skit in front of the class.

Apply Your Learning

8. Compare and contrast the separatist movement in Quebec with western alienation. Be sure to review the causes, development, and effect of the views and feelings of the supporters of these movements. What is their present-day status? Use a chart if needed.

9. Trudeau's remark that living next door to the United States is like sleeping with an elephant assumes a certain level of anti-Americanism among Canadians. Do you think that level exists today? Why or why not? Provide examples to support your opinion.

Extend Your Learning Using the Internet

10. Create a mind map showing the causes and effects of Prime Minister Trudeau's wage and price controls. Take into consideration Canadian regional differences, labour conditions, trade relationships with the US, social spending, and inflation. Use mind map and financial indicators web sites to help you complete this activity.

11. Western alienation has become a major factor in Canadian federal politics. Trace the evolution of Western political parties from the early years of the century and debate the effect of such parties on Canadian unity and identity.

Unit 5
Into a New Century
1984–1999

In 1984, Canada's Conservative government took the country in new directions. In a matter of years, it opened Canada for business, cut social spending, and signed a free trade deal with the US. In the "new economy," thousands of old jobs disappeared, but Canadians adapted. Canadian artists—writers, actors, singers, and directors—became international stars. At the same time, a flood of multicultural immigration enriched Canada's growing cities, expanding what it meant to be "Canadian."

Tensions erupted in Canada's regions, and new federal parties emerged. In 1995, Quebec came within a few thousand votes of separation. In the 1990s, Native peoples won major victories in their quest for self-government. And women advanced to Canada's highest political offices.

On the world stage, old political systems—as well as the Berlin Wall—were torn down. Canada took part in many UN missions to bring peace to regions ravaged by racial conflicts and famine. It led international campaigns to protect the environment and human rights. In a new era marked by war and inequality, Canada's foreign policy maintained a commitment to peace and cooperation.

Prime Ministers	Dates of Office
John Turner	1984
Brian Mulroney	1984–1993
Kim Campbell	1993
Jean Chrétien	1993–

Anticipation Guide

In this unit, you will:

- compare Canadian work-life at the beginning and end of the twentieth century
- identify how industrialists contributed to the Canadian economy
- explore how the "baby boom" changed Canadian society
- investigate the relationship between English Canada and Quebec
- analyse how communications technology changed life for Canadians
- evaluate Canada's efforts to promote human rights
- explore how the end of the Cold War affected Canada's foreign policy
- investigate how the governor general reflected Canadian identity
- summarize the positive and negative effects of closer Canada–US trade
- evaluate Canada's campaign against landmines
- explore government policies geared towards promoting Canadian culture

1950　1960　1970　1980　1990　2000　2010

14

1984: A New Direction

Focus Questions

Changing Role of Government
How did the election of the Mulroney Conservative government signal a major change for Canada and Canadians?

Economic Conditions and Structures
What challenges has Canada faced in providing all its citizens with a decent standard of living?

Demographic Patterns
How does Canada's policy of multiculturalism affect Canadian society?

Canadian Identity
How does the government support and encourage Canadian arts and culture to promote a common Canadian identity? How successful are they?

The 1984 election of Brian Mulroney's Progressive Conservative government marked the start of a new era for Canada. It was an era of gains and setbacks, depending on who you were. Women capitalized on the progress they had made in the 1960s and 1970s, and broke new barriers in education and in the workplace. The Native peoples also made strides in their quest for self-determination and self-government. They lobbied for amendments to the Indian Act and saw some of their key constitutional rights recognized by the Supreme Court in 1990.

But there were new economic forces at work that would have a negative impact on the social fabric. Under Brian Mulroney, Canada would be "open for business" in a way that it had not been before. Closer ties with the US, fewer restrictions on trade, and a greater emphasis on productivity would result in the loss of jobs. Poverty and homelessness would become much more visible. Canadian artists would start to question whether Canadian culture was being protected or neglected.

Yet despite the anxiety, the mid-1980s and the 1990s were exciting years for Canada. It was the beginning of the high-speed, high-tech society that has become our world.

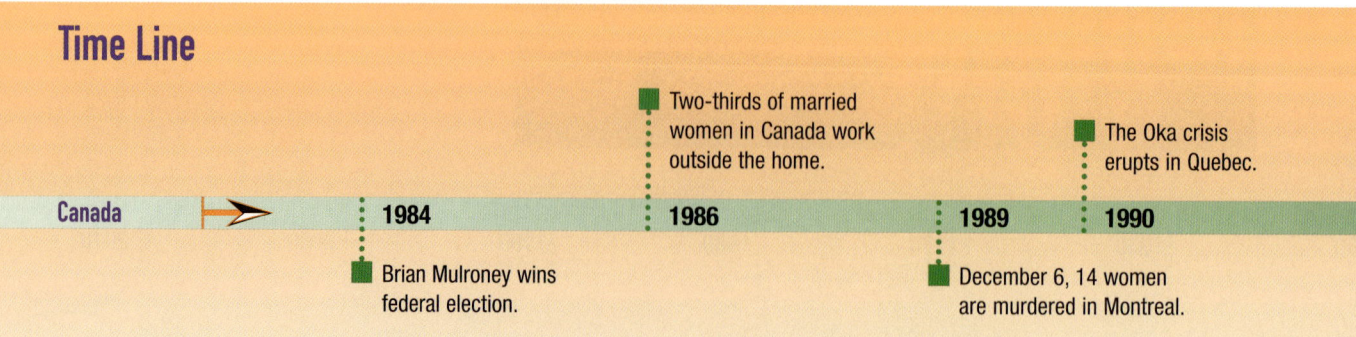

Time Line

Canada	1984	1986	1989	1990
	Brian Mulroney wins federal election.	Two-thirds of married women in Canada work outside the home.	December 6, 14 women are murdered in Montreal.	The Oka crisis erupts in Quebec.

Perspectives

This photograph originally accompanied a survey published by *Maclean's*. It found most Canadians to be optimistic about their futures in the new economy. Survey responses were split, however, when it came to the growing gap between the "haves" and the "have nots." Half of those polled favoured government intervention to help the disadvantaged. Why would editors select a photo that is so bleak if most Canadians were optimistic about the future? What does the image say about who is benefiting from the new economy? Where does the man sitting on the street fit in? Was this man a part of the survey? Whose voice is being heard?

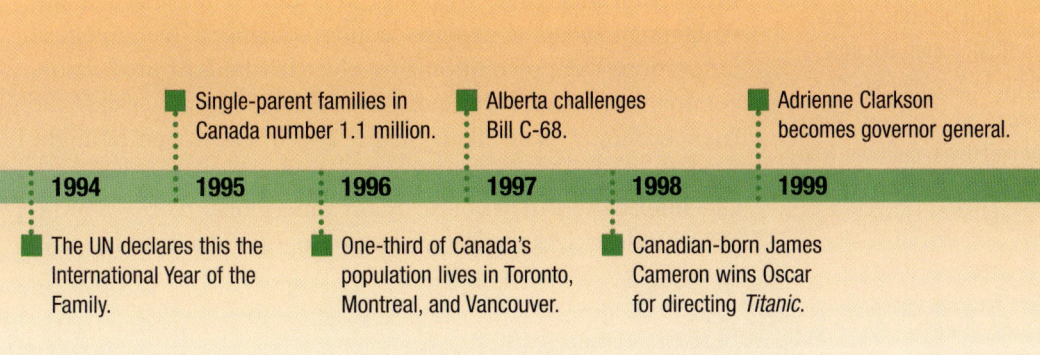

- 1994 — The UN declares this the International Year of the Family.
- 1995 — Single-parent families in Canada number 1.1 million.
- 1996 — One-third of Canada's population lives in Toronto, Montreal, and Vancouver.
- 1997 — Alberta challenges Bill C-68.
- 1998 — Canadian-born James Cameron wins Oscar for directing *Titanic*.
- 1999 — Adrienne Clarkson becomes governor general.

A NEW PRIME MINISTER

If there were any doubts that Canada's long love affair with the Liberals was coming to an end, the 1984 federal election put them to rest. Under Brian Mulroney, the Progressive Conservatives swept into power, claiming 211 of the 282 seats in the House of Commons. It was the largest number of seats a Canadian government had ever won, and it marked the beginning of a new political and economic era in Canada.

Who was Brian Mulroney? Like Trudeau, he was from Quebec. Unlike Trudeau, however, he was not born into the wealthy **elite**. Mulroney's parents were Irish immigrants. His father was an electrician in the pulp and paper town of Baie-Comeau, and had ambitions for his son. Mulroney was drawn to politics. In 1956, at the age of 17, he worked for John Diefenbaker's successful campaign to become leader of the Progressive Conservative party. He later served as a student advisor on Quebec when Diefenbaker became prime minister. By 1964, as a lawyer for one of Montreal's most well-known law firms, he specialized in labour negotiations for corporate clients. After gaining a high public profile in Quebec, Mulroney ran for the leadership of the Progressive Conservative Party in 1976, losing to Joe Clark.

Shortly after this defeat, Mulroney became president of the Iron Ore Company of Canada. Six years later, he closed down the company's operations in Schefferville, Quebec, because they were no longer profitable. Schefferville became a ghost town, but Mulroney's political career survived and flourished. In the same year, he again ran for the Progressive Conservative leadership. This time, he won. During the 1984 federal election campaign, Mulroney promised to reduce government intervention in the economy and to forge closer trading ties with the United States. In his first official speech as Canada's eighteenth prime minister, Mulroney travelled to New York, where he told an audience of top US business leaders: "Canada is open for business." True to his campaign promises, Mulroney was sending a message. The days of strong government intervention in the economy—and of protectionist trading policies with the US—were coming to an end.

The New Economy

Brian Mulroney came to power at a time when Canada was struggling to adapt to massive economic changes. Technological innovations were revolutionizing older methods of production, communication, and transportation. Something now called the "new economy" was taking shape, and it was driven by high-level technology and the high-speed communication of ideas and information. It was also based on a global world-view, as goods and services could now be produced and assembled any-

Up Close

1. Use a Venn diagram to record two similarities and two differences between Pierre Trudeau and Brian Mulroney.

Heritage Minute

In the 1960s, Canadian communications expert Marshall McLuhan coined the phrase the "global village." It soon became an international catchword and McLuhan became a famous media prophet. To this day, his predictions about the impact of communications technology on our perceptions, cultures, and sense of history influence thinkers and policy makers around the globe.

Figure 14–1 Prime Minister Brian Mulroney (left), US President Ronald Reagan, his wife Nancy, and Mila Mulroney meet in Washington on April 27, 1988. Never had a Canadian prime minister and a US president been so close.

where in the world and delivered to their destinations in record time. As the world became a global economy, international competition for trade, investment—and jobs—was fierce. For Canada, one of the most export-dependent nations in the world, the stakes were high.

It was inevitable that high technology would lead to automation and that computers and robotic devices would reduce the need for human labour. Economists and popular science fiction writers had been predicting this for decades. But when automation combined with increased international business competition, the impact on Canadian workers was severe. In the 1980s and early 1990s, tens of thousands of Canadians—skilled and unskilled—lost their jobs in traditional manufacturing industries, such as automaking and textiles, and in management positions across the country. In some cases, entire trades simply disappeared. In corporate Canada, there was a push to increase productivity, cut costs, and increase profits. This was achieved in several ways. As in the case of Schefferville, businesses sometimes closed old plants, mines, and mills that were not making money. Businesses also restructured and downsized, which meant that thousands of employees were let go and replaced by part-time and contract

Up Close

2. Name three distinguishing features of the new economy. List three ways it affected Canadian businesses, and three ways it affected Canadian workers.

1984: A New Direction

Figure 14–2 This newspaper worker does the crosswords while a robotic taxi delivers newsprint to the printing press. It's 1990. How many people would have been employed in this workplace 30 years earlier?

workers. These workers could be hired as needed and were usually paid less and offered no job benefits. This was a tremendous cost-cutting advantage for employers, but it was fought by unions and workers.

During the postwar boom and the Trudeau years, labour and union negotiations had led Canadian workers to expect that they could work at a job for a lifetime, or at least have some job security. But in the 1980s and 1990s, enormous layoffs in government and industry—and continuing high unemployment—left unions and labour with little bargaining power. In the new global economy, businesses could always open up plants and offices in other countries, rather than pay wages demanded by Canadian workers. By the mid-1990s, the average Canadian family had seen its income decline because wages had not kept up with the cost of living. You will look at some of the social consequences of this trend in the next section of this chapter.

As painful as these changes were, Canadians did adapt to the new economy. By 1984, Canada's economy was much more diversified than it had been after World War II. More than 60 percent of working Canadians were employed in the service industries. However, often these jobs provided little career growth

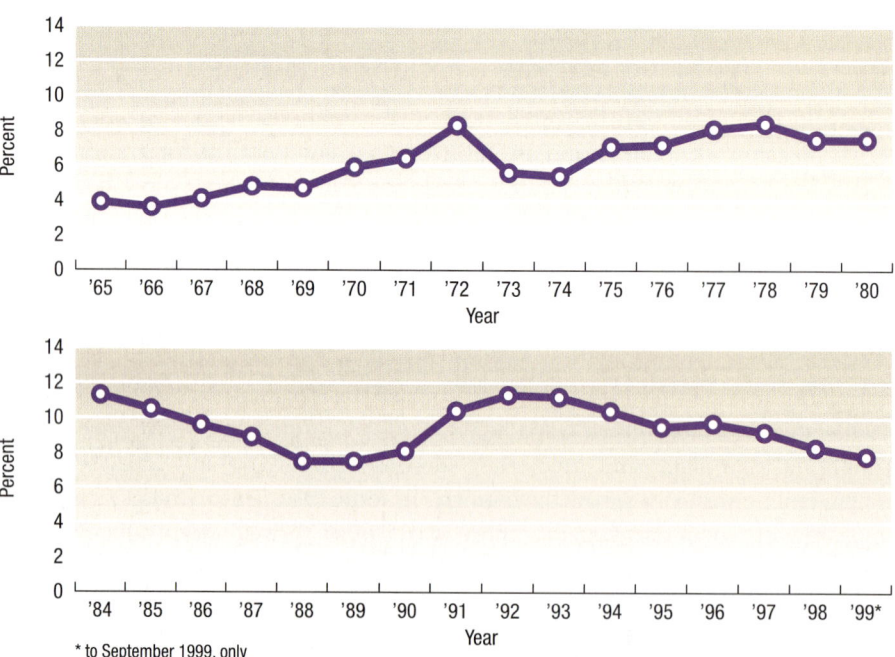

* to September 1999, only

Figure 14–3 Canada's unemployment rates in the years 1965–1980 and 1984–1999

and paid poorly—for example, food services, retail, and so on. Many Canadians who had lost their full-time jobs had to take two or three part-time jobs in the service industries to maintain their standard of living.

But as Canadian businesses and entrepreneurs met the challenges of the new economy, new employment opportunities opened up. What was becoming clear was that the new workplace was unfamiliar to the average Canadian. New, well-paying jobs demanded workers who had a broad educational background and who were highly skilled, people who could work as team members, be flexible, and take part in creative decision making.

Just as there were many stories of suffering for average workers in Canada during this period, there were also spectacular success stories. One example is Frank Stronach, who immigrated to Ontario from Austria in 1954. In 1957, he founded a small tool-and-die company and gradually expanded into manufacturing automotive components. As head of Magna International Inc., Stronach took advantage of emerging global opportunities and opened plants and offices in countries around the world. In 1984, Magna's sales topped $1 billion for the first time. By 1998, sales had mushroomed to $9 billion, and Magna had become one of the largest producers of automotive parts in the world. Headquartered in Aurora, Ontario, Magna now employs more than 54 000 workers in almost 200 manufacturing and research-and-development facilities in North America, Asia, Europe, and South America.

Up Close

3. Give three reasons for Magna International's success in the new economy.

Figure 14–4 This highly automated weld line for GM truck frames is at Magna's Formet plant in St. Thomas, Ontario. Compare this work environment to the one on the right, which shows Frank Stronach working in his first company in 1957.

1984: A New Direction

The new economy created an atmosphere that demanded research, innovation, and creative approaches. Nothing could be taken for granted. With Magna, for example, that meant focusing on a specific market and creating products that could compete anywhere in the world. In this way, many small and large Canadian businesses adapted and grew. In Chapter 16, you will learn how a number of Canadian businesses became world leaders in such areas as automobile manufacturing and high-tech transportation as the global economy took shape in the last years of the twentieth century.

Changing Families

In Chapter 8, you learned how Canada changed dramatically after World War II. These social changes had taken deep root in Brian Mulroney's Canada. Youth culture had flourished and now appealed to a broad cross section of Canadians. Clothing and music, which were once identified only with teenagers, had become the mainstay of many young adults. And women had capitalized on opportunities created by the women's movement of the 1960s. They were staying in school longer, staying single longer, and building careers. By 1986, almost two-thirds of married women were employed in the labour force. In 1967, only one-third of married women had worked outside the home.

Changing Size, Changing Structure
In fact, the very structure of Canadian families was changing in the last decades of the twentieth century. Today, because Canadians tend to be flexible in what they consider to be a "family," Statistics Canada uses two broad definitions. Parents with children—whether married, unmarried, or single—are defined as a census family. An economic family is defined as a group of two or more people who live in the same dwelling and are related to each other by blood, marriage, common-law relationship, or adoption.

The size of the Canadian family had been shrinking steadily since the 1970s. By the mid-1980s, the average number of children per family had dropped to 1.8. This was below replacement level, the number of births required to maintain Canada's population. A number of factors contributed to the trend towards smaller families. With access to birth control, couples could plan the number of children they wanted. Couples were also more concerned with providing for their children. It seemed financially safer to have fewer children when the cost of living was so high.

The number of single-parent families also started to grow as more unmarried women were having babies and the divorce rate was increasing. Between 1981 and 1995, the number of single-parent families rose from 712 000 to 1.1 million. Women with children made up the vast majority of these families—and they were often poor. Family poverty became an urgent issue, and it could not be separated from other changes happening in Canada. Continuing high unemployment, a decline in the buying power of average wages, and business restructuring contributed to family poverty throughout the 1980s and 1990s. Single mothers under the age of 25 were at the greatest risk of being poor. They were especially vulnerable if the birth of their child interrupted their education—

Data File

Between 1971 and 1994, the average marrying age for women rose from age 22 to age 30. The average marrying age for men rose from 25 to 32.

Up Close

4. List all the reasons you can find to explain the fall in the average number of children per family.

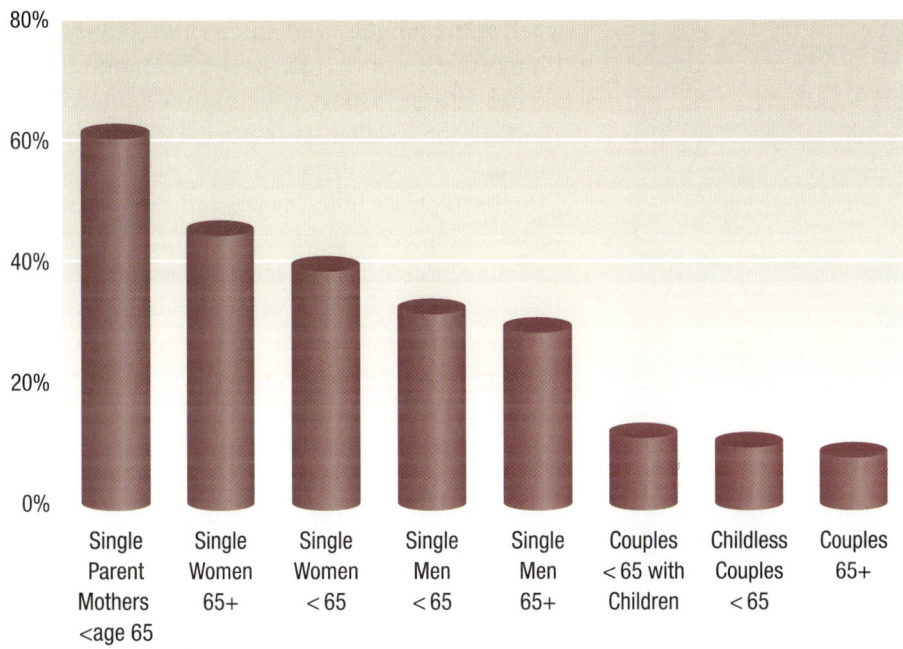

Figure 14–5 Poverty rates by family types in Canada, 1996

a critical factor in job success. Finally, Canada's "no fault" divorce law, passed in 1985, had the effect of lowering the incomes of divorced and separated women, who usually had to support children. The problem was not the divorce law, but the historic inequality of women's wages. At the end of the century, a woman was still earning approximately 70 cents for every dollar earned by a man.

Poverty was increasingly visible on the streets of Canada's cities by the end of the century. In the early 1980s, Canada had only a few food banks. They were organized by volunteers as a response to what they believed was a short-term crisis: the high cost of urban housing had left many families with little or no income for basic necessities. But the crisis didn't go away. During the 1990s, the number of people relying on food banks doubled. The largest group of users—40 percent—were children.

As the century drew to a close, homelessness had become a visible fact of life in Canadian cities, large and small. Sometimes the homeless made headlines: when a homeless man or woman died of exposure, or

Figure 14–6 Volunteers at an Ottawa food bank stock the shelves.

1984: A New Direction

Figure 14–7 What is the message of this poster?

when entire families were forced into shelters after losing their homes. Between 1992 and 1998, shelter use in Toronto, for example, more than doubled for families. It increased 80 percent for youth.

Sociologists John Hagan and Bill McCarthy, who completed a study in Vancouver and Toronto, found that homeless youth came from all classes. There were common causes, however. Most homeless youth came from families affected by chronic unemployment, parental drug and alcohol abuse, and physical violence.

Canada is not the only wealthy nation facing a crisis of homelessness. The problem has increased around the world. In a 1998 report on industrialized nations, UNICEF (United Nations Children's Fund) reported: "While it might be tempting to assume that homelessness is tied to a specific catastrophic event such as war or famine, today it is a stark reality in some of the world's wealthiest countries."

Demographic Trends

A snapshot of Canadian life in the early 1900s would be very different from one taken in the late 1990s. In order to appreciate just how much change the pictures would show, a look at **demographic trends** and patterns is helpful. One of the most pronounced changes had to do with where Canadians chose to live. At the beginning of the twentieth century, fewer than 40 percent of Canadians lived in urban areas. But by the end of World War II, as Canada became increasingly industrialized, almost 60 percent of Canada's population lived in urban areas. By the time of the 1996 census, the urban trend had continued, and more than 75 percent of Canada's population lived in urban areas.

Canada had not only become urban, a few Canadian cities were now home to a larger share of the total population. In 1996, almost a third of Canada's population lived in Canada's three largest **census metropolitan areas** (urban areas with a population of more than 100 000 people) alone: Toronto, Montreal, and Vancouver. In other words, cities were defining Canadian life. In Vancouver and Toronto, for example, some of Canada's finest agricultural land was swallowed up by metropolitan expansion, and social services were strained to the limit to accommodate the growing number of people. In Toronto, with a population of more than 4 million people, there were even calls for the city to become a province. This position was extreme, but many people felt that the city's needs were being overlooked by both the provincial and federal governments.

There were also regional changes in terms of population growth. Since 1986, BC's population had boomed, with the fastest growth rate of any province or territory. This was consistent with another trend: population growth was occurring in the West and in Ontario, but slowing in Quebec and declining in the Atlantic provinces. In 1951, Alberta and British Columbia accounted for only 15 percent of Canada's population. By 1996, that had increased to 22 percent. In the same 45-year period, Ontario's population increased from 33 percent to 37 percent of the Canadian total. In the Atlantic provinces, it fell from 12 percent to 8 percent, with Newfoundland experiencing the greatest population loss. The Atlantic figures underline the suffering of the thousands of people forced to migrate to other provinces in search of employment after the collapse of resource-based industries, especially mining and fishing. Another demographic trend revealed that Canada's population was rapidly aging. Census figures in 1986, 1991, and 1996 showed the number of elderly persons making up a larger and larger proportion of the population than younger people.

Up Close

5. Choose a visual way (for example, a graph) to show some aspect of the regional population figures given here.

Boom, Bust, Echo Demographics was such a hot topic among Canadians that the 1996 book *Boom, Bust and Echo* became an instant bestseller. Written by Canadian authors David Foot and Daniel Stoffman—who are economists and demographers—the book studies demographic trends and their impact on government and the economy. It describes three groups: the Baby Boom, born from 1947 to 1966; the Baby Bust (or "X" generation), born from 1967 to 1979, and the Baby Boom Echo, born from 1980 to 1995.

The Baby Boom generation is by far the largest segment of Canada's population, with roughly 10 million people. To understand Canada in the 1980s and 1990s, you need to understand this group. For example, people tend to become more politically conservative as they age, which may help explain Brian Mulroney's landslide victory in 1984.

The aging population has also had a major impact on Canada's cherished social programs. Canada's health care has had to adjust to demands for more chronic care facilities, geriatric medicine, even plastic surgery. Canada's pension program has also been under pressure. As the Baby Boom generation retires, more and more people will be drawing on pension benefits. Canada's pension system, however, will be funded by fewer and fewer people of working age. In the late 1990s, this became a major issue for Canadians and the federal government.

The Baby Bust generation is smaller than the Baby Boom generation, accounting for 5.5 million Canadians. As a result, it has had a less significant demographic impact on Canadian life. But the Baby Boom Echo generation is larger—6.9 million strong—and is coming of age in the new millennium. What distinguishes this generation is that they have

Figure 14–8 These students are part of the Baby Boom Echo group.

1984: A New Direction

Data File

In 1995, the Canadian Institute of Actuaries (CIA) reported that retired Canadians in 1992 accounted for 19 percent of the working-age population. They paid $9 billion in taxes, but consumed $54.4 billion in public funds, including pensions and health care.

Up Close

6. How did Mulroney change Canada's immigration policy, and why?

grown up in the age of digital communication and the Internet, much as the Baby Boom generation was the first generation to grow up in the age of television. As a group, the Echo generation is characterized by its technological and political awareness.

All of these demographic patterns raise questions that will have a continuing impact on government policies and structures. For example, should the House of Commons and the Senate be restructured to better represent Canada's population distribution? How should Canada's social programs be adjusted in the face of an aging population? By studying these demographic trends, it becomes clear that Canadian society has been moving in new directions. Not only are Canadians becoming more urban, different age groups are placing new demands and expectations on a changing Canada.

Multicultural Realities

Since Canada's birth rate and the size of Canadian families had been declining since the 1970s, the federal government turned again to immigration to sustain Canada's growth. As had been the case at the beginning of the century, economics was also a factor. By the early 1980s, Canada was looking for wealthy business people and entrepreneurs to invest their money and to create employment opportunities. Immigration was also seen as a way to create ties to emerging markets around the globe. In a speech at the Multiculturalism Business Conference, held in Toronto in 1986, Brain Mulroney noted that: "Canadians who have cultural links to other parts of the globe, who have business contacts elsewhere, are of utmost importance to our trade and investment strategy."

Under Mulroney, federal immigration policy was revamped to admit more people who could fill this role. Independent immigrants—the category in which entrepreneurs are admitted—rose from 4 percent of new arrivals in 1984 to 26 percent of new arrivals in 1988. Economics had clearly become of strategic importance to immigration policy.

In recent history, the greatest percentage of new immigrants who came to Canada were from Asia. According to the 1996 census, Chinese and South Asians were the top two immigrant groups entering Canada, followed by Blacks—from Africa or the Caribbean. Three-quarters of the immigrant population in the 1990s were members of a **visible minority** group. Seven out of ten non-White immigrants to Canada settled in Toronto, Vancouver, or Montreal. These large metropolitan centres provided assistance and integration services and better economic opportunities. Vancouver, for example, was favoured by many Asian immigrants because it is located on the Pacific Rim. Today, there are firmly established Chinese, Japanese, and Sikh communities in Vancouver and surrounding suburbs.

Immigrating to a new country—where the language and culture are not your own—is not an easy process. In early 1999, *The Toronto Star* commissioned a survey to find out how recent visible minority immigrants felt they were being treated in the city. Ninety-four percent stated that they felt accepted. However, more than two-thirds of those polled felt they had been discriminated against on certain occasions. Many said it was difficult to find work, even with the highest qualifications. Not speaking English was seen as the greatest drawback. Many new immigrants soon realized that Canada was not the "promised land," at least not for the first generation. As families develop roots and a sense of community, as children go to school and learn English, new Canadians become more hopeful and optimistic about their future in Canada.

Emigration—moving from Canada in search of opportunity—is another factor affecting population. It has become important to Canada not only to attract new Canadians, but also to keep others from leaving. Again, the motivation is economic. Throughout the 1990s, a "brain drain" occurred, as doctors, nurses, law graduates, and computer programmers moved to the US and other countries to earn more money. Although there was controversy about the extent of the brain drain, the Canadian government was worried. To counteract a loss of a third of the graduating class of nurses each year, for example, Newfoundland decided to give $3000 to each nurse educated in the province who agreed not to leave.

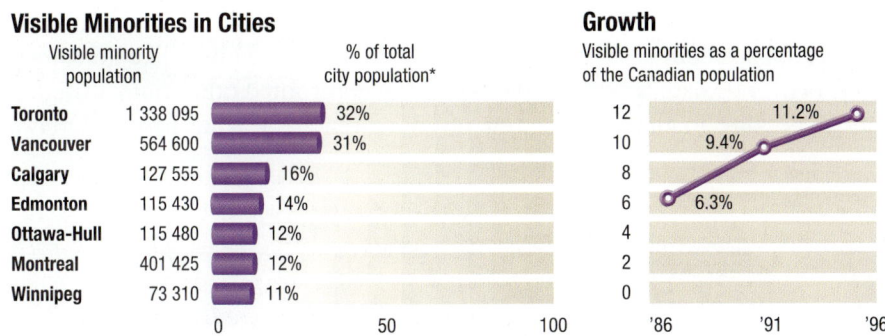

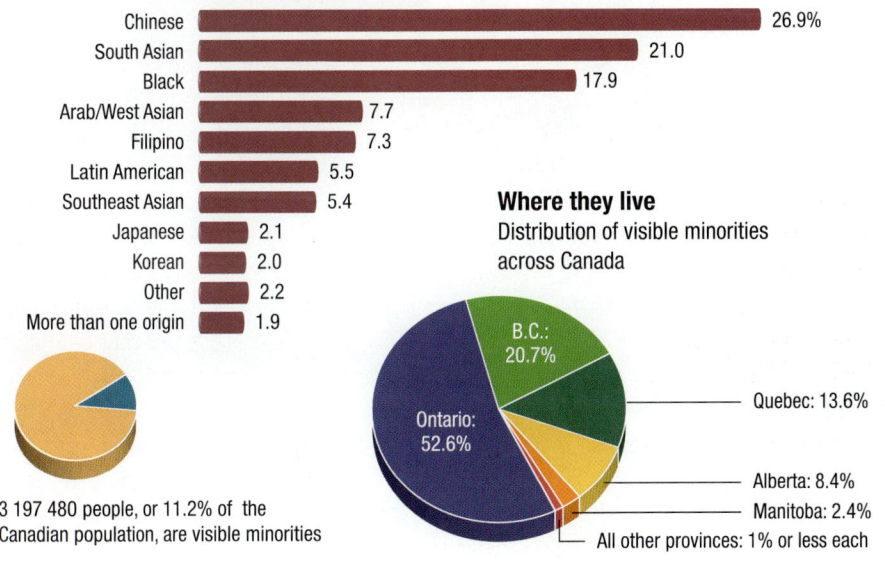

Up Close

7. State one conclusion you can draw from the information in each of these five graphs.

Figure 14–9 Visible Minorities in Canada, 1996

1984: A New Direction

Images
Adrienne Clarkson: Canadian Trailblazer

Adrienne Clarkson arrived in Ottawa for the first time when she was three years old. It was 1942, and the Japanese invasion of Hong Kong had shattered her family's life. Her father, William Poy, had been a successful businessperson, but had lost everything because of the war. The family came to Canada seeking refuge and a chance to start a new life. But Canada did not welcome Chinese immigrants in 1942, regardless of circumstances.

Fifty-seven years later, again in Ottawa, Adrienne Clarkson is giving a speech. "We did not arrive as part of a regular immigration procedure," she says. "There was no such thing for a Chinese family at that time in Canadian history." The date is October 7, 1999, and Clarkson is speaking in the tradition-steeped surroundings of the Senate Chamber. She is not, however, submitting a grievance to a royal commission into the treatment of immigrants. Nor is she bitter. She is giving her first speech as Canada's twenty-sixth governor general. It is the first time that a refugee, and only the second time that a woman, has ever been appointed to the highest, most symbolic public office in the nation. And because her life mirrors a half-century of growth and change in Canada's history, most Canadians applauded Clarkson's appointment.

During her early years in Ottawa, a city that she described as "small and white—like most of Canada," Clarkson confronted other rigid attitudes. She grew up in a French-speaking part of Ottawa

Figure 14–10 Adrienne Clarkson and crew at the CBC

Citizenship and Heritage: Canadian Identity

and tried to go to a French school at the age of five. As a Protestant, however, it was not possible for her to receive French-language education in Ottawa. "In my lifetime, this has changed to such a radical degree that I don't even need to comment on it," Clarkson said in her speech. "But that early sense of something being impossible ... put steel into me." Years later, Clarkson had so mastered French that she did postgraduate studies at the Sorbonne, the leading university in France.

Back in Canada in the 1960s and 1970s, Clarkson pursued another dream: to work in television. It was the most exciting field imaginable during that era. At this time, women and visible minorities were almost completely absent from the television screens of the nation. Clarkson did not let this stop her. By the 1970s, she had become a familiar face in most Canadian homes and was widely respected as a hard-hitting CBC journalist in award-winning current affairs shows such as "Take Thirty" and "the fifth estate." Her impact as a media role model for women and immigrants in Canada is impossible to measure. Another first for Adrienne Clarkson is that she is the first television personality ever to become Governor General of Canada.

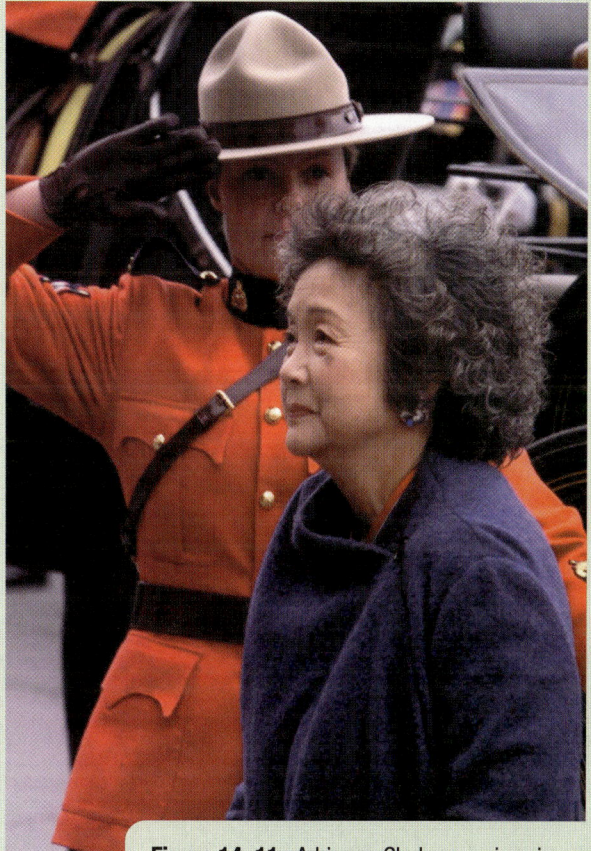

Figure 14–11 Adrienne Clarkson arrives in Ottawa in October 1999 to become governor general. This photograph shows two symbols that represent Canada. What are they? How have they changed to reflect Canadian values at the end of the twentieth century?

> I believe that my parents, like so many other immigrants, dreamed their children into being as Canadians ... Luckily, all of us came to a land where the aboriginal peoples have always dreamed life into being.
>
> It is customary to talk about how hard immigrants work and how ambitious they are, but those of us who have lived that process know that it is mainly the dream that counts. I'm not talking here of fantasy. I am talking of the true dream that is caught in the web of the past as it meets the wind of the future. All of us have this, even if we do not express it. This is what gives a nation, such as ours, its resonance, its depth, and its strength.
>
> —Governor General Adrienne Clarkson,
> October 7, 1999

During her first public speech, Clarkson communicated an intense sense of devotion to Canada and its promise. She spoke of the Inuit quality of *isuma*, which is defined as an intelligence that includes the knowledge of one's responsibility towards society. And she described Canada as a society that is "forgiving" and "inclusive."

What Do You Think?

1. How has Adrienne Clarkson's personal time line mirrored some of the important social and political developments in Canadian society from the 1940s to the present day?

2. Clarkson, an immigrant, referred many times in her first speech as governor general to the aboriginal peoples of Canada (two examples are provided on this page). Suggest a few reasons why she might do this.

ERA OF THE CHARTER

As you learned in Chapter 12, Pierre Trudeau's Liberal government **patriated** the Constitution in 1982, without Quebec's consent. Quebec and other provinces had battled Trudeau's constitutional efforts for many years, usually on the grounds that the federal government was trying to grab more power for itself at their expense. The Constitution Act of 1982 showed many signs of the compromises that the federal and provincial governments had had to make along the way.

The Canadian Charter of Rights and Freedoms was at the heart of the Constitution. Many Canadians saw it as the most important aspect of this new legislation, and the majority of Canadians strongly supported it. The new Charter gave individual Canadians and groups of Canadians more legal power in the event that their rights were violated. The Charter, in fact, was created as a form of rights protection.

Once the Act was passed, it soon became clear that the courts in Canada would have a much broader role to play in Canadian society. Canada's highest court, the Supreme Court of Canada, saw its role and powers increase tremendously in the era of the Charter. It now had an increased ability—and responsibility—to **strike down** provincial and federal laws that violated the Charter rights of Canadian citizens and groups.

Changing Legal Values

Up Close

8. As you read to page 380, note examples of controversial rulings of the Supreme Court. Choose one you feel strongly about and prepare to argue your case.

Laws are created to reflect social values and to help a society function. Over time, Canadian laws have had to adapt to the shifting values of Canadian society. This does not mean that everyone's values are the same, or that change occurs universally. On some issues, Canadians stand together. On other issues, they remain divided. Since the Constitution Act of 1982, Canada's laws have had to respect the Charter of Rights and Freedoms. Often this has led to laws and Supreme Court rulings that clash with the values of a large segment of the population.

Debating the Death Penalty

Capital punishment—or the death penalty—has been banned in Canada since 1976. This ban would seem to respect Section 12 of the Canadian Charter of Rights and Freedoms, which states that "Everyone has the right not to be subjected to any cruel and unusual treatment or punishment." In fact, only three democracies in the world today still impose capital punishment—the United States, the Philippines, and Japan.

In 1987, the issue of capital punishment was put to a free vote in the House of Commons. Members of parliament voted 148-127 in favour of continuing the ban. Yet a majority of Canadians, almost 75 percent, supported a return to the death penalty at that time.

Many Canadians felt that parliament should have represented their views. In 1997, however, federal Minister of Justice and Attorney General Anne McLellan responded to the Canadian Police Association's call to reinstate the

Political Structures: Changing Role of Government

Foundations

A Court with Too Much Power?

As Canada's highest court, the Supreme Court of Canada is the court of last appeal. It is composed of a chief justice and eight other justices. All of these justices are appointed according to a formula that is meant to provide fair regional representation. The Court not only hears appeals, it will also hear cases where an important principle of law or of public concern is involved. Every case is heard by an odd number of judges, so that there can be a majority decision. In constitutional cases, this has meant that the Court can strike down provincial and federal laws that are, in the Court's opinion, unconstitutional.

In the years since the Charter was enshrined in the Constitution, the Supreme Court has exercised its new powers in many cases. Many of its decisions have had major political consequences and have provoked public outcries. It has not been easy for the Court to balance the rights and freedoms of Canada's citizens—even those accused of heinous crimes—with society's right to protect itself through its laws.

Some of the controversial decisions that the Supreme Court has made include

- a 1994 decision to allow "extreme drunkenness" as a defence for sexual assault (the decision said the Charter protected people from criminal conviction when they were unaware of their actions)
- a 1995 decision to dismiss murder charges against two men because they had been denied their right to a speedy trial by serious Crown errors
- a 1995 decision that struck down the federal law prohibiting tobacco advertising.

Critics suggest that the Supreme Court has become too powerful. They say that appointed justices have no right to overrule laws that have been passed by elected governments: in other words, the Supreme Court has become antidemocratic. Supporters of the Charter and of the Supreme Court argue that this process is truly democratic, that it is needed to

Figure 14–12 Beverley McLachlin became Chief Justice of the Supreme Court of Canada in December 1999. She is the first woman to ever hold this position. McLachlin had served on the Court for ten years and has a reputation for dissent.

uphold all of our rights and freedoms. They argue that one purpose of the Charter is, in fact, to check the powers of governments. Many supporters understand the concerns of the Court's critics, but they see the Charter as being in a state of process. As society's views change, they argue, the Court will listen to public reactions and try to better reflect the mood of the country.

What Do You Think?

1. Do you agree or disagree that the Supreme Court has become too powerful? Build an argument to reflect your viewpoint, and include one claim and at least one reason. Review the Historian at Work on building an effective argument (page 275) before you begin.

1984: A New Direction

Figure 14–13 What happens if a country has the death penalty and convicts an innocent person of murder? David Milgaard, seen in prison in 1991, was convicted of murder in 1969. It was only the unrelenting efforts of his mother, Joyce, seen here appealing to Prime Minister Brian Mulroney in 1991, that led to a review of his case. Finally, in 1999, Milgaard was entirely cleared of the conviction through the use of DNA evidence. During the same period two other Canadians were wrongfully convicted of murder: Donald Marshall and Guy Paul Morin.

death penalty by stating: "It is not the intention of the government of Canada to reinstate the death penalty."

Medical Debates Abortion is another issue that divides Canadians, even though the Charter seems to provide a clear direction. Before 1988, abortion was illegal in Canada. A woman could obtain a legal abortion only with the permission of a hospital abortion committee, and if her life or health were threatened by the pregnancy. In 1988, the Supreme Court declared sections of the Criminal Code dealing with abortion to be unconstitutional. The Court interpreted the Charter as guaranteeing a woman's right to control her body. While many Canadians support a woman's right to have an abortion, it remains a controversial issue. The province of Prince Edward Island, for example, has refused to provide abortion services, even in the wake of the Supreme Court decision.

During the 1990s, other issues emerged in light of the Charter. One was the medicinal use of marijuana for people living with terminal and chronic illnesses. Under the Narcotics Control Act, possessing, trafficking, and growing marijuana are all criminal offences. Jim Wakeford, a man living with AIDS, started using the drug in 1996. He reported that marijuana was the only substance that controlled his nausea and gave him an appetite. In 1997, he asked the federal government for access to legal marijuana. He also asked the courts to help. His lawyer argued that forbidding Wakeford to use marijuana violated his right to life, liberty, and security of the person, which are guaranteed under the Charter. In May 1999, Wakeford won the right to use marijuana as a medical treatment to relieve his symptoms.

Free Expression The Charter has been used by hate groups to justify racism and other forms of hatred. These appeals have been mostly unsuccessful and are not supported by the majority of Canadians. A hate group is an organization that advocates violence against, or unreasonable hostility towards, persons or organizations identified by their race, religion, national origin, sexual orientation, or gender. Before the Internet, hate groups tended to be isolated. Today an explosion of websites has allowed these groups to spread propaganda and recruit members inexpensively and anonymously. The government has responded by criminalizing forms of hate literature and introducing tougher sentences for acts of violence that are motivated by hatred against an identifiable group. These laws have met with mixed success in the courts and have split public opinion.

Figure 14–14 Ernst Zundel (left) faces a protester in Ottawa.

Hate laws were tested in Canada in 1982 with the case of Jim Keegstra. The mayor of Eckville, a small Alberta town, Keegstra worked as a history and social studies teacher. In classes, he taught that the Holocaust was a fraud and that Jews were responsible for economic depressions, anarchy, and war. The province of Alberta charged Keegstra with "wilfully promoting hatred against an identifiable group." He was found guilty and fined $5000. Keegstra appealed this decision to the Supreme Court of Canada, saying the charge violated his Charter right to freedom of expression. He also suggested that the law was unconstitutional because he had to prove the validity of the statements he had made. He argued that, in a sense, he was presumed guilty before his trial had begun. In 1990, and again in 1996, the Supreme Court ruled that the Criminal Code provision against promoting hatred—although technically an infringement of rights guaranteed by the Charter—was reasonable.

In 1988, Ernst Zundel, a German immigrant who lives in Canada, was convicted of "spreading false news" about the Holocaust. That conviction, however, was overturned by the Supreme Court in 1992, when it held that the conviction was unconstitutional. Zundel, in other words, had a right to express his views freely. This decision angered many Canadians, in particular, Jewish organizations. In the 1990s, Zundel started a website that advocated theories similar to those of Keegstra. The "Zundelsite," as it came to be known, offered a forum for those who deny the Holocaust to publish and promote their ideas. It was maintained in California in an attempt to get around Canadian hate laws. In response to complaints about the site, the Canadian Human Rights Tribunal agreed to hear the case to determine whether material denying the Holocaust can be regulated on the Internet. For the first time in Canada, the Internet was on trial. The case against Zundel alleges that information found on the Zundelsite exposed persons of the Jewish faith to hatred. Section 13 (1) of the Human Rights Act states that it is illegal to send telephone messages that could cause hatred or contempt of an identifiable group.

Up Close

9. Make a chart to show comparisons between the Keegstra case and the Zundel case.

Flashpoint
The Montreal Massacre

It was just before 5 p.m. on December 6, 1989, when a deranged gunman entered Montreal's École Polytechnique armed with a semi-automatic rifle, ammunition, and a collection of knives. In Room 303, he ordered male engineering students to leave and forced female students to one side of the room. "You're all a bunch of feminists," he shouted as he raised his rifle, "and I hate feminists." One woman tried to reason with him, but the man opened fire, killing six and wounding four. Within half-an-hour, in the corridors, the cafeteria, and in other classrooms, he had shot twenty-seven students, killing fourteen—all of them women. Then he killed himself.

The "Montreal Massacre," the worst mass murder in Canada's history, stirred an outpouring of grief and rage across the country. In the House of Commons, Prime Minister Brian Mulroney asked: "Why such violence in a society that considers itself civilized and compassionate?" And although the assailant left a suicide note describing his personal anguish, many Canadians viewed the tragedy as more than an isolated act of violence. The Montreal Massacre became a catalyst for a federal review of gun legislation, and it forced Canadians to take the issue of violence against women seriously.

Figure 14–15 A procession of hearses carries the bodies of the slain students through Montreal's solemn streets on December 11, 1989.

> So now our daughters are truly frightened and it makes their mothers furious that they are frightened. They survived all the childhood dangers, they were careful as we trained them to be, they worked hard. Anything was possible and our daughters proved it. And now they are more scared than when they were little girls.
>
> –journalist and author Stevie Cameron, on the aftermath of the Montreal Massacre

In 1995, after many angry debates and delays in parliament, the Firearms Act (Bill C-68) was passed by the newly elected Liberal government. The legislation will become law in stages and make gun ownership much more difficult, prohibiting ordinary citizens from owning certain weapons altogether. Under Bill C-68, Canada's estimated 3 million gun owners must obtain licences by 2001. All rifles and pistols must be registered by 2003. Any gun owner "knowingly neglecting to register a firearm" can be imprisoned for ten years. Registration is intended to encourage citizens to store their guns safely and to help police trace gun ownership during investigations.

Families of the Montreal Massacre victims lobbied for Bill C-68, which was also supported by groups like the Canadian Association of Chiefs of Police and the Canadian Bar Association. When one politician challenged the new law, calling it a "bureaucratic nightmare," the mother of one slain student retorted: "Look me in the eye … We won't let you touch our gun laws." Many law-abiding gun owners, however, protested the severe restrictions of the new law and the powers it gave police to search private homes. The real issue, they said, is violent crime, not possession of firearms.

In 1997, Alberta challenged Bill C-68 on constitutional grounds. It argued that private property is a provincial responsibility and that Bill C-68 would set a precedent for federal intrusion into provincial areas. The Alberta Court of Appeal disagreed. In a 3-2 decision, it ruled that Bill C-68 was constitutional. Chief Justice Catherine Fraser stressed the importance of "individual responsibility and accountability for one's firearms." Gun ownership is a privilege, she wrote, not a right.

Furthermore, wrote Chief Justice Fraser, "this case is not about whether gun control is good or bad. Nor is it about whether Parliament could or should do more to achieve a cooperative solution with the Provinces or Aboriginal peoples on this issue … the question comes down to this. Is this firearms law one which the federal government has the power to enact under the Canadian Constitution? In my view … the answer to this question is yes."

The Montreal Massacre also led to the White Ribbon Campaign. Started in Canada by Michael Kaufman and Ron Sluser in 1991, the campaign asked men to wear a white ribbon from December 1

Figure 14–16 A woman clutches flowers as she watches a procession of family and friends after a memorial service held on December 6, 1999. It was the tenth anniversary of the Montreal Massacre.

to December 6, in memory of the slain women and to end violence against women. In 1997, the campaign went global, with ribbons distributed in the United States, Russia, South Africa, Australia, and New Zealand. The federal government also proclaimed December 6 Canada's National Day of Remembrance and Action on Violence Against Women. Every year on that day, in candlelight vigils across the country, thousands of Canadians remember and honour the victims of the Montreal Massacre.

What Do You Think?

1. The Firearms Act (Bill C-68) came about because of powerful social and political forces. In your opinion, which factor was most influential? Give evidence for your answer.

2. Can tougher licensing and regulation requirements prevent tragedies such as the Montreal Massacre? Build an argument for your point of view.

3. Does the Firearms Act help to define us as Canadians? Does it distinguish Canada from the US? Explain your point of view with evidence.

Charter Impact on the Native Peoples

In Chapter 11, you learned that, starting in the 1960s, Canada's Native leaders and groups began to organize more effectively. They pressured the Canadian government to recognize existing Native and treaty rights. Their efforts paid off when these rights were enshrined in the Constitution Act, 1982. The Native peoples now had the constitutional right to have their rights defined and established in Canada's courts.

One of the first breakthroughs came in 1985, when the federal government amended the Indian Act, ending more than 100 years of discrimination. Under the old Indian Act, women had received their Indian status through their husband. If a woman's husband was a status Indian, so was she. If he was not, then she and her children would lose their status. The first woman to have her status reinstated was Mary Two-Axe Early, who had fought the Act since 1968. She had lost her status when she married a non-Indian.

Figure 14–17 This Mohawk mother fled from the Kanesatake reserve during the Oka crisis of 1990. Food and medical supplies could not get past the barricades set up by Mohawk warriors. Why would she flee from the reserve when the warriors were taking a position to protect Mohawk land rights?

> The existing aboriginal and treaty rights of the aboriginal peoples of Canada are hereby recognized and affirmed.
>
> –Section 35.1, The Constitution Act, 1982

In 1988, the Indian Act was amended again. Now First Nations could collect property taxes when leasing out portions of land on their reserves. First Nations had long objected to the original wording of the Indian Act, which stated the lands were "surrendered" to the federal government. This implied that the First Nations were conquered peoples. The change in wording was considered to be especially important for future negotiations. Public opinion at the time showed that most Canadians supported the Native peoples and their issues, including the idea of **self-government**. Self-government was seen as a basic democratic right of self-determination. That support declined, however, whenever it was perceived that Native peoples were receiving "special" privileges.

While the relationship between the government and the Native peoples had been improving, many questions remained. The Supreme Court of Canada ruled in 1990 that Native peoples have the constitutional right to fish for food and for social and ceremonial purposes. In July of the same year, however, a land dispute between the Quebec municipality of Oka and the nearby Mohawk reserve of Kanesatake flared into a national crisis. Members of the Mohawk Warriors Society set up road barricades to prevent a golf course from expanding onto what they considered to be their land. After a Quebec provincial police officer was

Up Close

10. In the role of a Native leader in the 1960s, write a "wish list" of changes you would like to see the government include in the Constitution.

killed during a raid on the barricade, the Canadian Armed Forces were called in. The tense, sometimes violent, standoff lasted 78 days. It ended only when the warriors voluntarily withdrew the barricades.

Canadian and international media descended on Oka. For weeks and weeks, television broadcasted live news from the barricade and within the reserve. The issues of Native land claims, treaty rights, and the inherent right to self-government grabbed public attention. Just days before the Oka crisis ended, the federal government announced a new plan to improve Canada's relationship with its Native peoples. The Royal Commission on Aboriginal Peoples, set up in 1991, was composed of a seven-member panel. The four Native and three non-Native commissioners focused on one overriding question: "What are the foundations of a fair and honourable relationship between the Aboriginal and non-Aboriginal people of Canada?" There would be no easy answers.

In the next two chapters, you will look at how the Native quest for justice and self-government affected the course of Canadian history later in the 1990s, and how it redrew the map of Canada.

ARTS AND CULTURE

As you have already learned, the new Mulroney government wanted closer economic ties with the United States. In Chapter 16, you will look closely at the Canada–US Free Trade Agreement, which took effect in 1989. Negotiations for this agreement provoked an outburst of debates and demonstrations across the country. After all, concerns about US dominance had shaped Confederation and had run throughout Canada's history. And no issue was more explosive than Canadian culture, because of its vital role in creating a sense of Canadian identity.

Many government agencies and institutions—such as the CBC, the National Film Board, and the Canada Council—had already been established to promote and support Canadian culture. For decades, governments had felt that without some form of protection, Canada would be swamped by US culture. Tariffs and Canadian-content regulations restricted the flow of US books and magazines, movies, recordings, and television programs into Canada. These measures were one way to ensure that Canadians would have access to print, film, and television media, as well as recorded music that was created by Canadians, in Canada.

In the new economy of the 1980s and 1990s, however, protectionism could be a stumbling block to international trade. There was pressure to treat culture like any other industry, one that should compete in the global economy without government intervention. The Mulroney government continued to protect Canadian culture, but it had to walk a fine line.

For example, in 1987, the federal government introduced a bill to limit US control of the distribution of independent and foreign films in Canada. Hollywood executives, and President Ronald Reagan—a former Hollywood star—lobbied against the legislation, and it died. Today, about 80 percent of the

Up Close

11. Before reading the section on arts and culture, brainstorm lists of Canadian recording artists, actors, films, television programs, and authors that you can identify.

Data File

It has been estimated that Canadians watch an average of 3 hours of television a day, or 21 hours a week.

total rental revenues (the fees theatres pay to distributors) for films shown in Canada still flows into the US.

Canadians in the Movie Business One thing was certain, however. By this time, government programs had launched the careers of many Canadian artists. Canadian filmmakers achieved a new level of international prominence. In 1986, for example, Quebec filmmaker Denys Arcand's *Decline of the American Empire* won major awards around the world, including a 1987 Academy Award nomination for best foreign film. In the same period, Canadians David Cronenberg, Patricia Rozema, and Atom Egoyan became successful international filmmakers. One thing they had in common was financial support from provincial and federal film agencies at the beginning of their careers. Without it, they would have had to leave Canada.

Many filmmakers did leave Canada to find work. Canadian director Norman Jewison moved to Hollywood in the early 1960s after working as a director at the CBC. There he became a major director and producer, but he returned to Canada in the late 1970s. In 1986, he set up the Canadian Centre for Advanced Film Studies to help train young Canadian filmmakers. Another Canadian director and producer, Ivan Reitman, made his early films in Canada with support from government programs in the 1960s and 1970s. In the 1980s, he moved to Hollywood and directed some of Hollywood's biggest hits. His 1984 film *Ghostbusters* broke box office records. And in 1997, Canadian-born James Cameron directed *Titanic*, the biggest Hollywood blockbuster of all time.

Figure 14–18 Faces of Canada? Canadians starred in and directed some of the biggest movie hits of the 1980s and 1990s: Jim Carrey, left, in *The Mask*; Mike Myers, as Austin Powers; and David Cronenberg's *The Fly*

In the 1980s and 1990s, Canadian actors also made a huge impact in Hollywood, particularly in comedy. Hollywood's leading comic stars in the 1990s—John Candy, Martin Short, Catherine O'Hara, Dan Aykroyd, Rick Moranis, Mike Myers, and Jim Carrey—were all Canadians. Yet some of Canada's finest talent was still leaving the country and, in a sense, contributing to the ongoing dominance of US film and television.

Figure 14–19 André Alexis

Writers Win and Lose Canadian literature also reached new levels in the 1980s and 1990s. Well-known Canadian authors such as Margaret Atwood and Michael Ondaatje were recognized as among the most important writers in the world. They helped pave the way for a new generation of Canadian writers, who explored themes that reflected Canada's changing society and connections to its past. In the 1990s, Anne Michaels published her first novel, *Fugitive Pieces*. It focused on the impact of the Holocaust—and its memories—on the lives of two men, and it was soon translated into many languages and read around the world. Another young Canadian writer, André Alexis, also published his first novel, *Childhood*. It drew on Alexis's experience as a child who immigrated to Canada from Trinidad to grow up in small-town Ontario and then Ottawa. Alexis has been called a "spokesperson for the Canadian quest to articulate identity."

Again, however, the new economy was threatening government programs that had helped writers establish themselves in Canada. Mergers in the magazine and book publishing industries forced many of Canada's small magazines and publishing houses out of business. Many larger Canadian publishers were bought out by larger American or European publishers. Small Canadian bookstores, which had helped to create a market for Canadian literature since the late 1960s, were also threatened. As larger bookstores became popular, many of the small bookstores could not compete and went out of business. As a result of these economic forces, it was becoming more difficult for new Canadian authors to find publishers.

The CRTC Calls the Shots One of the most important bodies for promoting Canadian culture has been the Canadian Radio-television and Telecommunications Commission (CRTC). Because it regulates the licensing of Canada's television and radio broadcasters, the CRTC has had a major impact on television and film production in Canada. In the 1990s, the appearance of specialty channels on cable television rapidly expanded viewing choices for Canadians. The CRTC responded by maintaining the Canadian-content rules for television it had established in 1972. Generally, this meant that at least 60 percent of television programming had to be Canadian. There were fewer viewers for Canada's main television networks—the CBC, CTV, and Global—because

Data File

At the end of the 1990s, foreign films and products accounted for

- 45 percent of book sales in Canada
- 81 percent of English-language consumer magazine sales at newsstands, and 63 percent of magazine circulation revenue
- 79 percent (over $910 million) of the retail sale of music tapes, CDs, concerts, merchandise, and sheet music
- 94 to 97 percent of Canadian movie screen time.

Figure 14–20 This film crew is shooting at the University of Toronto's downtown campus. The campus has served as a location for everything from Harvard University to Jack the Ripper's Victorian London.

viewers now had so many other choices. But the emergence of specialty channels, and the need to satisfy Canadian-content regulations, contributed to an increase in television and film production in Canada.

Various funding bodies have continued to support Canadian film and television production. By 1999, it had become a $2-billion industry. But at least $700 million of that was in foreign, primarily US, productions. American producers were eager to shoot in Canada. Canada had highly skilled crews, a rich choice of locations, and a dollar worth much less than the US dollar. In the 1990s, there was a battle between Vancouver and Toronto for the title of "Hollywood North."

The CRTC had also played a key role in helping to establish a Canadian recording industry. In 1970, it imposed a 30 percent Canadian-content regulation on Canada's radio broadcasters. This meant that a minimum of 30 percent of radio programming had to be considered Canadian. To qualify as Canadian content, a recording had to meet two of the following four criteria: the song is composed by a Canadian; the lyrics are written by a Canadian; the song is performed by a Canadian; the song is recorded in Canada. Many commercial broadcasters protested this requirement, but they had to comply or lose their licence. In 1998, the CRTC increased the Canadian-content minimum to 35 percent.

Canada's recording industry also took root in the last decades of the century. In the early 1970s, recording artists such as Anne Murray benefited from the increased airplay on Canadian radio stations and went on to become international stars. By the late 1990s, Canada had produced some of the most popular recording artists of the era, superstars like Shania Twain, Alanis Morissette, Bryan Adams, and Celine Dion.

The emergence of the digital age and the Internet in the 1990s created many changes in Canadian culture. The CBC, for example, launched a major website in an effort to stay at the leading edge of technology and to link its resources to people across Canada. And the CRTC faced a problem in the late 1990s when

Figure 14–21 Alanis Morissette

it considered trying to regulate the Internet. The Internet didn't fit into the old patterns. Any individual with access to a computer terminal and a modem can become a broadcaster. Who needs a licence? And how could the CRTC regulate the Internet without infringing on the Charter right of free speech? In 1999, the CRTC ruled that it had no basis to regulate the Internet.

As the twenty-first century begins, digital technology is revolutionizing communications and all forms of culture. One example of an artist who has pioneered in new technology is Buffy Sainte-Marie, a Cree artist and singer who first became popular in the 1960s. Since the mid-1960s, she has used computer technology to record her music and to create digital art. Backed by her success as a songwriter, artist, and recording star, Sainte-Marie went on to establish the Cradleboard Teaching Project. Over the years, Cradleboard evolved as part of her mission to raise public awareness of Native issues and to facilitate linkages and communication between Native communities. One way Cradleboard achieves this is through on-line Internet sessions that link Native students and non-Native students. "Cradleboard is not about technology," says Sainte-Marie. "Cradleboard is about helping children through cross-cultural communication—whatever means they have to get to know each other."

Figure 14–22 A digitalized self-portrait by Buffy Sainte-Marie

Historian at Work

Media Bias: Who Determines the Issues?

You live in an era that has been dubbed the "information age." News about the world bombards you through a variety of media: print media (books, newspapers, and magazines); visual and broadcast media (films, television, and radio); and digital media (CD-ROMs, the Internet). While it is relatively easy simply to consume this information, the bigger challenge is to interpret it. To analyse and assess any form of information requires that you ask key questions: Who created the story? Whose viewpoint is being presented—and for what purpose?

All media stories are biased to some degree, even though the bias often is not deliberate. In fact, everyone has biases because everyone is influenced by personal factors such as background, heritage, education, political persuasion, and so forth. Bias can creep into news reports in ways that are hard to detect. Sometimes the witnesses used, the experts cited, or even the photographs chosen to accompany a story can create a biased world view. It is always up to you, the consumer, to filter the information accordingly. Use this checklist to examine different elements of the story for bias.

Bias Checklist

- **Bias through placement of story**
  Where the story appears in the newspaper or the newscast can influence your perception of the events. Stories that appear first are generally considered to be more important.

- **Bias through headline**
  Headlines are the most read section of the newspaper. Headlines summarize a news story but they are also used as a "hook." For example, they may convey excitement where none actually exists. Or they may express approval or condemnation, thereby encouraging the consumer to view the event in the same way.

- **Bias through selection and omission**
  News editors make decisions about running stories under daily deadline pressures. Still, the stories they choose to run or to omit can indicate a bias. Within a story, some details may be ignored and others may be included. This form of inclusion and omission can also slant the story in a certain direction. Bias by omission is very difficult to detect unless you can compare different stories about the same event.

Figure 14–23 News editors and copywriters work under the constant pressure of deadlines. The need to select, highlight, or even omit some stories can create bias.

Historical Inquiry: Analysing/Evaluating Information

- **Bias through tone and language**

  Mainstream journalists are taught to write objectively when reporting news and to strive for a balanced tone. That means that their reports should be based on facts, not on exaggeration or emotional manipulation. Yet news reports that don't appeal to the emotions are unlikely to sell newspapers or draw listeners and viewers. Another requirement for a "balanced tone" is to tell both sides of a story or incident. But sometimes this too can lead to bias. For example, if a racist group bombs an immigrant's home, should the reporter seek comments from racist groups on why the action was taken?

- **Bias through photos and camera angles**

  Pictures can flatter or embarrass people, and photos that are chosen to accompany a story can achieve either result. The same is true of camera angles used on television. Because people absorb images so quickly, they have a more immediate impact than texts. For this reason, images that are chosen for key events, such as an election campaign, can affect the way future events will unfold.

- **Bias through labels and titles**

  News writers and editors often use labels and titles to describe people, places, and events in a kind of shorthand. "Convicted bank robber," "health professional" and "environmental activist," for example, are all labels and, to some degree, biased.

- **Bias through statistics and crowd counts**

  Numbers can be manipulated to make an event seem more spectacular and, therefore, more newsworthy. For example, the story might describe "100 people injured in plane crash" rather than "only minor injuries in plane crash." Both versions are possibly true, but the way the information is presented will affect your interpretation of the event.

- **Bias through source**

  Is the information supplied by a reporter, an eyewitness, a police officer, a company representative, or an elected government official? Each of these people may have a particular bias. Ask yourself: is this information really news? Or is it public relations?

  If poll results are presented, consider the size of the sample group and who commissioned the poll. Was it a pressure group, a political party, a labour union, a business, or an environmental group? Check to see how the questions were phrased. Were they "leading"—that is, did they provoke certain responses—or were they open-ended? An example of a leading question is: "Do you agree with the majority of religious leaders that capital punishment is cruel and unusual punishment and should therefore be banned?" An example of an open-ended question is: "Should Canada reinstate the death penalty?"

Activities

1. Compare a story on an inside page of a regular newspaper and a tabloid. Use your bias checklist to rate them for bias.

2. In a three-column organizer compare the front page of Canada's national newspapers—*The Globe and Mail* and the *National Post*—for the same day. In the first column list articles common to both. In the second column, list only those articles found in *The Globe*. In the last column list only those articles in the *Post*. Summarize your findings using your checklist.

3. Collect images from newspapers and magazines over a week. Use the images to construct a "split-frame" collage. On the left side, include examples of pictures that are meant to flatter. On the right side, include examples that are meant to embarrass. Give your collage a title.

4. Write a series of headlines that magnify ordinary events in your life so that they are presented as great deeds. Present your headlines to the class along with a more accurate description of the event.

CONCLUSION

After 1984, Canada's government changed gears under Prime Minister Brian Mulroney. Canada's social fabric was pulled in different directions. The new economy changed how people worked, and what they expected of work. Some people prospered, but poverty became more widespread in Canada's growing cities. The Mulroney government responded to global economics and reshaped multicultural immigration, which changed Canadian society. The Charter of Rights and Freedoms led to court cases that challenged Canadian values. During this time of change, Canadian artists achieved international fame, but they worked in the presence of growing influence from the US.

Mulroney inherited the new Constitution from Trudeau, which had alienated Quebec. In many of Canada's regions, resentment towards the federal government reached new levels. In the next chapter, you will look at how "unfinished business" almost pulled Canada apart.

CHAPTER ACTIVITIES

■ Check Your Understanding

1. The 1980s and 1990s were times of dynamic change. Create a chart using the headings listed below to summarize the major changes that occurred in Canada during this time period. For each heading, list one important change.
   - Government and politics
   - The economy
   - Family structure
   - Demographics
   - Cultural identity
   - The law
   - The Native peoples

2. How did the economic developments of the 1980s and 1990s affect the lives of ordinary Canadians? List at least five examples of the impact of the "new economy" on Canadians.

■ Develop Your Thinking

3. From the list you generated in activity 1, select what you believe to be the five most significant changes faced by Canadians. Rank them in order from the most significant to the least significant. In your list, include reasons for your choices.

4. Using information from Chapters 1 and 2, create a chart to compare aspects of Canadian life at the turn of the century and at the end of it. Your chart should include the headings that follow, as well as one topic of your choice:

- Immigration policies
- The cultural make-up of Canada
- Canada's relationship with the US
- The economy
- Demographics
- The role of women

Express Yourself

5. You are a newspaper reporter sent to cover the crisis unfolding at Oka. Write an article about the standoff, drawing on a variety of viewpoints. Include "interviews" with at least three of the following:
   - a municipal leader from Oka
   - a Mohawk leader from Kanesatake
   - a Quebec provincial police spokesperson
   - a federal government leader
   - an international observer

   To avoid bias in your presentations of different viewpoints, reread the Historian at Work on media bias on pages 390 to 391.

Apply Your Learning

6. a) Create and conduct a survey of your fellow students on the success of Canada's cultural industries. Your questions should reveal whether students have knowledge of Canadian artists, companies, and products, and whether they support them (by viewing their shows, buying their music, and so on). Include several industries in your survey—for example, film and television, music, newspaper and magazine publishing, book publishing, and Internet design. When analysing the results of your survey, look for:
   - different results for males and females, or for people in different age groups
   - trends (for example, many people recognize one artist or company)
   - confirmation (the results confirm your predictions)
   - surprises (the results do not confirm your predictions)

   b) Using the results of your survey, write a summary paragraph on whether or not attempts at protecting cultural industries are necessary and useful.

Extend Your Learning Using the Internet

7. Poverty and homelessness continue to be serious problems in Canada and in other industrialized countries. Visit the UNICEF website and other sites that deal with these problems. Prepare and present an oral report on one of the factors that contributes to poverty and homelessness in Canada.

8. Create a chronological chart on the short- and long-term effects of the economic policies of Canadian prime ministers during the twentieth century. Use selected websites to help you understand and explain the financial and economic indicators involved.

15
Unfinished Business

Focus Questions

French-English Relations
How has the relationship between Quebec and the rest of Canada changed as a result of events in the 1980s and 1990s?

Social and Political Movements
What progress have Native peoples made since 1980 in their efforts to gain recognition and rights?

What political events and changes led to the formation of the Reform Party? What are its strengths and weaknesses?

Changing Role of Government
What difficulties do governments face in trying to resolve problems of diminishing natural resources?

In the final years of the twentieth century, Canada faced new issues and old ones. Many of these—constitutional reform, national unity, Native land claims, and environmental management—had challenged Canada throughout its history. In the climate of political turmoil, some traditional federal parties suffered huge defeats. New, more regional, federal parties appeared suddenly and made dramatic gains. Canada seemed to be splitting into regions.

In Canada, and around the world, a new political attitude stressed economic issues at the expense of social spending. In part, this was fuelled by fears that government spending had grown too high. Most governments in Canada responded by cutting back in areas such as health care, education, employment insurance, and welfare. The results of this shift changed Canada's political life and social fabric.

The federal and provincial governments also tried to amend the Constitution in a way that would satisfy Quebec's and other provinces' demands. In two national efforts, Canadians could not agree on a satisfactory formula. However, legal recognition of the dignity and land claims of aboriginal peoples led to major new developments. A new territory, Nunavut, was created, and for the first time Canada had an Inuit-led government. While Canada closed out the century with advancements in areas such as Native land claims and environmental management, many tensions and conflicts remained unresolved.

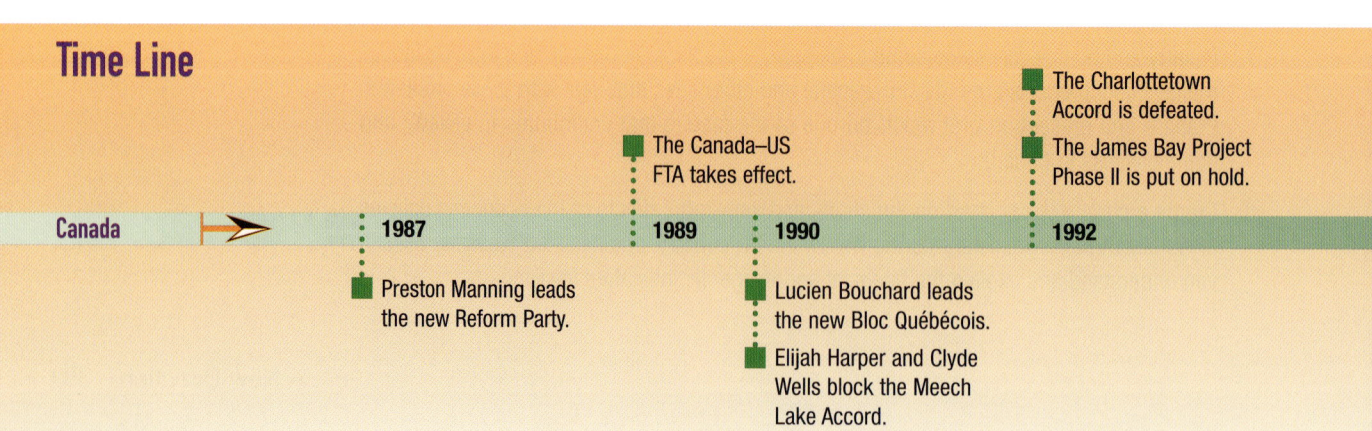

Time Line

Canada — 1987 — 1989 — 1990 — 1992

- 1987: Preston Manning leads the new Reform Party.
- 1989: The Canada–US FTA takes effect.
- 1990: Lucien Bouchard leads the new Bloc Québécois.
- 1990: Elijah Harper and Clyde Wells block the Meech Lake Accord.
- 1992: The Charlottetown Accord is defeated.
- 1992: The James Bay Project Phase II is put on hold.

Perspectives

In August 1998, in New Aiyansh, BC, Nisga'a children marched alongside elders, who were riding in a traditional longboat. Within hours, a treaty was signed that recognized Nisga'a self-government and title to a vast tract of BC land. The Nisga'a had been fighting their legal battle for 100 years. Step into the picture. Describe conversations the children might be having among themselves, or with the elders. Imagine you are standing on the roadside, watching. Describe what you would be saying and doing. Imagine there are people protesting the Nisga'a victory. Describe their conversations, slogans, posters, and so on.

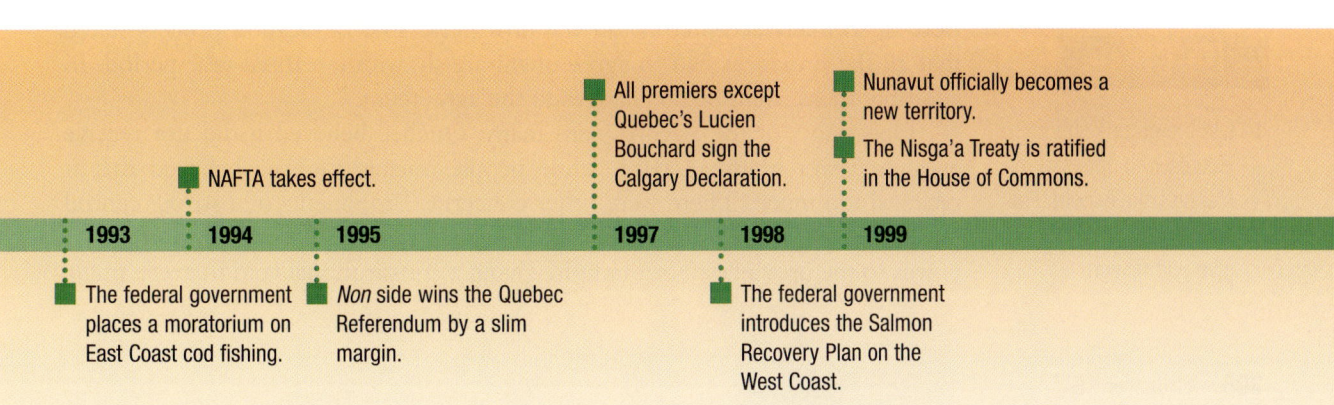

- 1993 — The federal government places a moratorium on East Coast cod fishing.
- 1994 — NAFTA takes effect.
- 1995 — *Non* side wins the Quebec Referendum by a slim margin.
- 1997 — All premiers except Quebec's Lucien Bouchard sign the Calgary Declaration.
- 1998 — The federal government introduces the Salmon Recovery Plan on the West Coast.
- 1999 — Nunavut officially becomes a new territory. The Nisga'a Treaty is ratified in the House of Commons.

FEDERALISM UNDER FIRE

In Chapter 12, you read about Pierre Trudeau's attempts to patriate the Canadian Constitution, and how Quebec rejected the process of constitutional reform proposed by the other provinces. Historically, Quebec had always had the right to veto constitutional amendments. Now it feared that the other provinces, by a majority vote, would be able to change the Constitution without considering its interests.

When Brian Mulroney and the Progressive Conservative Party came to power in 1984, they promised to reform the Constitution in a way that would satisfy Quebec. Their goal was to make the country whole. This would not be easy. Quebec's premier, Robert Bourassa, insisted that Quebec must have the power to protect its cultural makeup. He made it very clear Quebec would accept the Constitution only under certain conditions. In particular, it would have to be recognized as a "distinct society."

The Meech Lake Accord

On April 30, 1987, Mulroney called the premiers together at Meech Lake, a secluded resort in the Gatineau Hills, north of Ottawa. Here the leaders would try to find a solution that would satisfy Quebec while addressing the concerns of the other provinces. After an all-night meeting, the premiers reached an agreement in principle. It included these key points:

Figure 15–1 Brian Mulroney greeted provincial premiers at Meech Lake in 1987. It appeared as if a solution to the delicate power balance between the federal government and the provinces was finally in sight.

- recognition of Quebec as a "distinct society"
- increased powers to Quebec over areas of immigration and appointments to the Supreme Court
- restrictions to the federal government's spending power
- a veto to all provinces on constitutional changes

This was only a plan, however. For the agreement to pass, it had to be **ratified**, or formally accepted by all the provinces. The ratification process stated that all the provinces had to agree unanimously within a three-year period. In addition, there could be no changes to the agreement.

Opponents of the Accord were many. Quebec believed it did not receive enough power in the Accord, while people outside Quebec believed that it received too much. There were other concerns. Proponents of a strong central government—leaders such as Trudeau—argued that the Accord gave too much power to the provinces. For example, giving a constitutional veto to every single

Up Close

1. List the groups and individuals who opposed the Meech Lake Accord. For each group or person, give one reason.

province meant that a tiny province such as PEI could overrule the rest of Canada on any constitutional issue. Aboriginal leaders feared western governments would block their call for self-government. And some women's groups believed the Accord did not address their needs. Many Canadians questioned the process as a whole. They felt that the deal had been made behind closed doors. By 1990, polls showed that the majority of Canadians opposed it.

The "No" That Made History

As the June 23, 1990 deadline for ratification approached, support for Meech Lake was fading. Even so, as final debate was set to take place in Manitoba's legislature in June, eight provinces had already agreed. Then something unexpected happened. Procedure demanded that all members of the Manitoba Legislative Assembly must agree to bring the Accord forward for debate. Elijah Harper, a Cree member, said "No." He repeated that "no" eight times over the next several days. For Harper, the Accord had failed to recognize the Native peoples as an equal partner. As a result of Harper's refusal, the Accord could not be ratified in time. Because of this, Clyde Wells, Newfoundland's premier, did not bring the Accord forward for debate. The Meech Lake Accord was dead.

Reactions to the Failed Meech Lake Accord

In Ottawa, Lucien Bouchard, a top cabinet minister, had quit the Conservative Party in disgust in May 1990. He felt "humiliated" by the Accord's problems and betrayed by Mulroney, once a close friend. Bouchard formed the Bloc Québécois, which was composed of a number of Quebec nationalist MPs. It became an official federal party in 1991, and its primary goal was to achieve Quebec independence.

After the Accord failed, many Quebecers felt betrayed and rejected by the federal system. Premier Robert Bourassa announced that Quebec would not be involved in any more constitutional talks. He launched the Belanger-Campeau Commission to study future options for the province. It concluded that Quebec could either negotiate with Canada for a new federal partnership, or separate.

The Mulroney government launched its own commission, the Citizens' Forum on Canada's Future. Led by journalist Keith Spicer, it was meant to reassure Canadians that their input was important to government plans for Canada's future. But Canadians were furious with the government. Mulroney had admitted in an interview that he had been "rolling the dice" on Canada's

Data File

In 1993, Elijah Harper was the first and only registered Native person to have been elected to the Manitoba legislature.

> The Meech Lake Accord sputtered and died. It had gone up like a rocket, and it came down like a stick.
>
> —Will Ferguson, commentator

Figure 15–2 Elijah Harper greets supporters on the steps of the Manitoba Legislature in Winnipeg on June 22, 1990. He had just successfully blocked the Meech Lake Accord.

future. The tight deadline for ratification, he said, was a gamble to force the premiers into agreeing. Canadians came out in droves to tell Spicer they were fed up with Canada's politicians. They demanded that ordinary Canadians be included in policymaking. Their message was loud and clear: No more backroom deals.

Figure 15–3 In 1991, Keith Spicer (left) listens to separatist students in Montreal.

The Charlottetown Accord

The federal government learned some lessons from Meech Lake. In 1991, it asked Joe Clark, a former prime minister, to consult with Canadians across the country. Clark's committee listened to the people and eventually published *Shaping Canada's Future Together*, which proposed ideas for constitutional change. Assured they understood what Canadians wanted, the premiers met in Charlottetown, Prince Edward Island, in August 1992. This time they were joined by aboriginal leaders, but Quebec's Robert Bourassa was noticeably absent. The conference's participants unanimously passed the Charlottetown Accord, which included the following proposals

- recognition of the inherent right of aboriginal self-government
- recognition of Quebec's distinct society
- a Canada clause defining the character of Canadian society (specifically multiculturalism, universal health care programs, equality for provinces and the sexes)
- an elected Senate
- a veto for all provinces over constitutional changes
- increased provincial powers
- agreement to readjust representation in the House of Commons to better reflect representation by population (Quebec's guarantee of at least 25 percent of the seats was left untouched.)

Up Close

2. Using a Venn diagram, show at least two similarities and two differences between the Meech Lake Accord and the Charlottetown Accord.

The First Ministers agreed to hold two referenda to ratify the agreement: one in Quebec, and the other in all of Canada. On October 26, 1992, the question was put to the people of Canada:

Do you agree that the Constitution of Canada should be renewed on the basis of the agreement reached on August 28, 1992?

Different Time, Different Place, Same Result As with Meech Lake, the Charlottetown Accord had many critics and failed for a number of reasons. Some people were angered by guarantees made to Quebec. For example, in every province except Quebec, the number of seats in the House of Commons would be decided by population. Quebec was guaranteed 25 percent of the seats, regardless of its population. There were other questions: What exactly did aboriginal self-government mean? Should the Senate be reformed? Should it be abolished? How would gender equality issues be addressed? In the end, 54 percent of Canadians outside of Quebec, and 56 percent inside Quebec, rejected the Accord. In all, six provinces including Quebec refused to ratify the Accord.

Political Fallout: The Rise of Regional Politics

The failure of the two Accords shook Canadian politics to its core. Whoever you were, wherever you lived, it seemed Canada was being redefined. Canadians lost confidence in their leaders. By 1993, Brian Mulroney had become the most unpopular prime minister in Canadian history. In February, he announced he would resign.

The Conservative Party chose Kim Campbell as its new leader and, on June 25, 1993, she became Canada's first woman prime minister. She was quickly welcomed by Canadians and the media as a fresh, new face. During the 1993 federal election campaign, however, her connection to Mulroney dogged her at every turn.

The 1993 election revealed deep splits in Canada. Under Campbell, the Conservatives were wiped out. She lost her own seat and the Conservatives won only two seats—they no longer even qualified as an official party. The New Democratic Party won only six seats. The Liberals, under Jean Chrétien, surged to power, winning 177 seats and a majority government.

The big story, however, emerged on the other side of the House. The Bloc Québécois all but swept Quebec, with 54 seats. The Reform Party, a western-based

Figure 15–4 Prime Minister Kim Campbell campaigns in Pickering, Ontario in September 1993. Campbell campaigned tirelessly, but suffered a humiliating defeat. She was prime minister for only four months. As one commentator said, it was "her summer job."

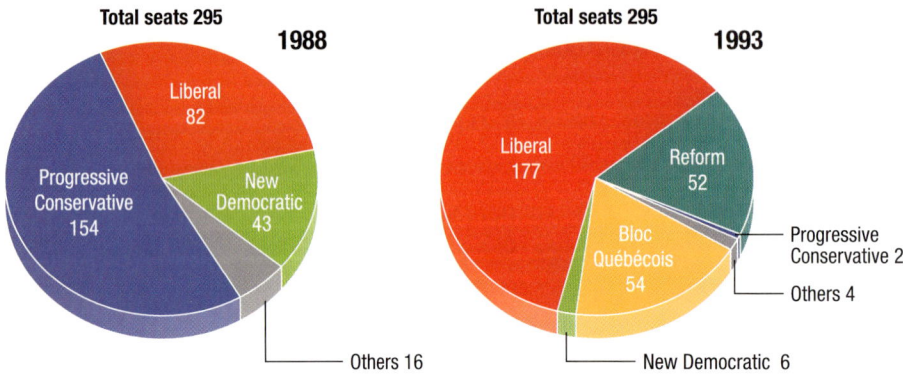

Figure 15–5 The federal election results of 1988 and 1993

and western-supported party, won 52 seats. By a margin of two seats, the Bloc formed Canada's official Opposition. Many Canadians did not welcome this outcome. They worried that the Opposition's sole purpose was to break up the country.

The new opposition mix was explosive. Both new federal parties, the Bloc and the Reform, were regionally based and represented local issues. (You will read more about Reform later in this chapter.) And while the Bloc's mandate was to increase Quebec's special powers, Reform's goal was to make sure this did not happen.

In a 1991 speech in Saskatoon, Reform leader Preston Manning had said, "If you want a revised definition of Canada … that is essentially a reaction to Quebec's latest demands, then look to the federal PCs, Liberals, or NDP because that is their starting point." It looked as if Canada was in for four years of regional wrangling.

Up Close

3. As you read about the 1995 Quebec Referendum, note the key players. Chart information about each name, under headings such as: Position; Demands; Promises; Concerns; Other Information. Also choose a way to indicate which side they were on—"Yes" or "No."

The 1995 Quebec Referendum

In the 1994 Quebec election, the Parti Québécois (PQ), led by Jacques Parizeau, swept into power. Like the federal Bloc, the PQ was committed to Quebec separation. Part of its mandate was to hold a referendum. The PQ drafted the Referendum question (see Figure 15–6) and set the Referendum date for October 30, 1995.

Premier Jacques Parizeau was the lead spokesperson for the "Oui" side. He told Quebecers that **sovereignty** was the best solution to a bad relationship with Canada. According to the separatists, Quebec could only reach its full potential through independence. In the event of a successful Yes vote, the PQ promised a new constitution, more jobs, better schools, better protection for the environment, and less bureaucracy. Quebecers who worried about the economic impact of separation were promised that Quebec would remain tied to Canada. They would still have Canadian citizenship, use Canadian money, and carry a Canadian passport. Parizeau also said that Quebec would be allowed to remain in the North American Free Trade Agreement. However, no one knew if Parizeau's claims were true.

Daniel Johnson, leader of the Quebec Liberal Party, headed the *Non* side—the side that wanted to keep Quebec within Canada. To challenge the separatists, Johnson and other federalists raised doubts about the wording of the Referendum question. They complained it was so unclear that people would not understand what they were voting for. Indeed, some polls indicated that more than half of Quebecers believed they could vote *Oui* to sovereignty, but still keep most of the benefits of being part of Canada. Next, Johnson warned that a close vote would be disastrous for Quebec's economic and political life. Johnson and other federalists also questioned whether the Quebec government should be focusing on sovereignty when the economy was weak and unemployment was high.

In Ottawa, Prime Minister Chrétien insisted that he and the federal Liberals would stay out of a "provincial" issue. As the campaign wore on, however, Chrétien came under fire for trying to stay neutral. In a Quebec by-election, Liberal Lucienne Robillard was elected. She was widely respected in Quebec, and Chrétien appointed her Minister of Labour and Responsible for the Referendum. Recognizing the growing potential for a separation victory, Chrétien became directly involved. In the weeks before the Referendum, he, cabinet minister Brian Tobin, and Conservative leader Jean Charest became key players in the *Non* campaign.

Two unexpected voices had also boosted the federalist forces. US President Bill Clinton broke his country's traditional diplomatic silence on Quebec separation. "Canada has stood for all of us as a model of how people of different cultures can live and work together in peace, prosperity, and respect," he told the House of Commons. Later, he toasted Canada, "Long Live Canada—Vive le Canada." Perhaps more significantly, some US trade experts suggested that an independent Quebec would not automatically be part of NAFTA.

The other voice was that of Ovide Mercredi, Grand Chief of the Assembly of First Nations, who raised concerns about how Native peoples might be treated in a sovereign Quebec. The federalist camp made this a lightning rod for their anti-separation argument. Mercredi promised that the Cree population of Quebec would vote *Non*. If the *Oui* side won,

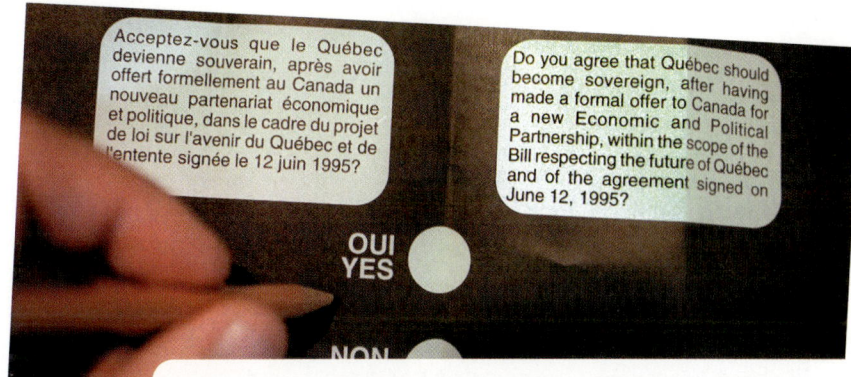

Figure 15–6 In October 1995, Quebecers were faced with another referendum. As you can see, the question did not ask for outright separation. It proposed negotiating a new relationship with Canada. If, after one year, Quebec and Canada could not reach an agreement, then Quebec would declare itself an independent country.

Figure 15–7 The separatists assured voters that a sovereign Quebec would have close economic ties with Canada, including using the Canadian currency. Do you agree that an independent Quebec should be allowed to use the Canadian dollar?

Unfinished Business

Figure 15–8 Lucien Bouchard (left) and Jacques Parizeau (right) in Quebec City on October 2, 1995. Days later, Bouchard took over the *Oui* campaign.

he said, it would lead to further talks about aboriginal peoples' future in Quebec. "If Canada is divisible," he warned, "so is Quebec." Mercredi's point was that Quebec could be **partitioned**, since aboriginal peoples could claim their own territories.

In the last weeks of the Referendum campaign, the *Oui* campaign was stumbling under leader Jacques Parizeau. Lucien Bouchard, a hero in Quebec, was convinced to take over. Support for the *Oui* side soared. Canadians became nervous, fearing the federalist side lacked emotion. With only days to go, the *Oui* side seemed sure to win. Then, on October 27, 1995, 140 000 Canadians rallied in Montreal to show Quebecers how much people across the country cared. (See this chapter's Flashpoint, pages 404–405.)

On Referendum day, October 30, 1995, almost 5 million Quebecers—93 percent of eligible voters—cast their ballots. It would be one of the longest nights in Canadian history. Not until 96 percent of the polls had reported was the outcome announced. On CBC Television, returns were illuminated on a huge map. It looked as though the whole province was voting *Oui*. But as poll results came in late from Montreal, the *Non* side edged ahead. In the end, the *Non* side won, but barely. The official result: 50.6 percent against separating, 49.4 percent in favour of it.

The country breathed a collective sigh—or gasp—of relief. With such a slight margin of victory, federalists in Quebec and across Canada could not claim a true victory.

Figure 15–9 Lucienne Robillard was expected to help win women's support for the *Non* side.

Constitutional Efforts Continue

As Chrétien had promised during the Referendum campaign, the House of Commons passed a resolution recognizing Quebec as a distinct society within Canada. In 1997, the Canadian premiers, except Quebec's Lucien Bouchard (who left federal politics and replaced Jacques Parizeau as leader of the PQ), signed the Calgary Declaration. It was meant to provide a framework for constitutional reform, with seven statements of principle. The Declaration recognizes equality of provinces and Canadians, Quebec as a distinct society, and Canada's diversity in terms of aboriginal peoples, the two founding nations, and multiculturalism. Unlike Meech Lake and Charlottetown, the Declaration was ratified by all provincial legislatures—again, all but Quebec. In the twenty-first century, it could provide a starting point for the reform of the Canadian federation.

> Whatever you do, adhere to the Union. We are a great country and shall become one of the greatest in the universe if we preserve it; we shall sink into insignificance and adversity if we suffer it to be broken."
>
> –John A. Macdonald, Canada's first prime minister

THE NATIVE PEOPLES' PUSH FOR JUSTICE

Earlier you read that Elijah Harper blocked the Meech Lake Accord and that the Cree of Quebec voted *Non* in the 1995 Quebec Referendum. Even so, the Native peoples sympathized with the sovereignty movement because they were making similar demands. They wanted self-government and the power to protect their languages and cultures. They were angry because the Quebec and Canadian governments had not included them in constitutional discussions or recognized their right to self-determination and self-government. In his book, *No Ordinary Hero*, Elijah Harper made this clear:

> **Aboriginal people are not against the right of Quebec to their own distinct society. Quebec is a distinct society ... So are the aboriginal people ... In referring to the 'two founding nations,' the architects of the [Meech Lake] Accord neglected to acknowledge the equally legitimate place of aboriginal people within the Canadian federation.**

The Native peoples had been fighting for their rights ever since Europeans first arrived in North America. With the Constitution Act of 1982, "existing aboriginal and treaty rights" had finally been recognized. By the 1990s, the aboriginal rights movement was more powerful than ever. Aboriginal issues made headlines, and the majority of Canadians supported Native demands for self-government and fair treatment. As you read in Chapter 14, sometimes land-claim disputes could turn violent, as at Oka. More often, they were pursued through legal and political channels.

Up Close

4. Where is the phrase "two founding nations" used? To what does the phrase refer? Why did Elijah Harper object to this phrase?

Flashpoint
The Montreal Rally

On October 27, 1995, Canadians from all walks of life descended on Montreal's Place du Canada in the "Crusade for Canada." This event marked one of the most important turning points in the 1995 Quebec Referendum. Companies and organizations from across Canada provided buses; Air Canada and Canadian Airlines offered "unity fares" of $99 from anywhere in Canada; and VIA Rail added more trains and cars to their routes to Montreal.

It was one of Canada's largest political rallies. Canadians with the maple leaf painted on their faces sang anthems, held hands, cheered, and waved flags in a monumental show of support for Quebec and Canada. A woman who emigrated from England in 1954 expressed a common sentiment among the demonstrators when she said, "I want Canada to stay together—forever. This country is the best thing that ever happened to me. We're one country, one country."

But the most impassioned plea came from Prime Minister Jean Chrétien. With polls showing that the *Oui* side had gained momentum, Chrétien's appeals became emotional.

Two days before the rally, Chrétien had made one of the most impassioned appeals in his career—to Quebecers who had not made up their minds on how to vote in the Referendum. On the day of the rally, the prime minister said: "Today is not the day for speeches. It is your day, the citizens of Quebec and the citizens of the rest of Canada who have come to Montreal to hold out their hand for the survival of this great country. When I see you all, coming from all provinces of Canada and all parts of Quebec, I have never felt as proud as I feel today to be a Quebecer and a Canadian."

Following Chrétien's remarks, the crowd responded with "Ca-na-da! Ca-na-da!" over and over again.

When the crowd broke into "O Canada," the singing echoed around the office towers. Separatists dismissed the gathering as a "federalist love-in" and "too little, too late." At a smaller *Oui* rally, Lucien

Figure 15–10 Canadians from across the country travelled to Montreal to show Quebecers how much they cared.

Bouchard asked, "Where was the outpouring of love a few years ago when Quebec was asking for distinct society recognition? They say they love us now—out of fear." Bouchard charged that the rally was not spontaneous, but a political operation that could backfire.

The front page of Quebec's newspaper *Le Devoir* quoted snippets of "touristy" conversations overheard at the rally, meant to show how unconcerned people really were about national unity. Although English-language papers estimated the crowd at between 130 000 and 150 000 people, many French-language papers reported the rally as a non-event that attracted as few as 30 000 people.

Despite the *Oui* side's cynicism towards the rally's sincerity, many Canadians believed that it did sway undecided voters and affected the final outcome.

What Do You Think?

1. If you were on the *Oui* side, how would you have reacted to the rally? Why?
2. Do you think Quebec should separate? Why or why not? Have a class debate.
3. Prime Minister Chrétien stayed out of the Referendum campaign at the beginning because it was a provincial matter. Should federal politicians and business leaders have a role to play in any future Quebec referendum? Explain your answer.

Prime Minister Chrétien's Televised Appeal to Quebec

The end of Canada would be nothing less than the end of a dream. The end of a country that has made us the envy of the world. Canada is not just any country. It is unique. It is the best country in the world …

My friends, we are facing a decisive moment in the history of our country…

As a proud Quebecer and a proud Canadian, I am convinced that a strong Quebec in a united Canada remains the best solution for all of us. I ask those Quebecers who have not yet made their decision to ask themselves these questions when they vote on Monday:

Do you really think that you and your family would have a better quality of life and a brighter future in a separate Quebec?

Do you really think that the French language and culture in North America would be better protected in a separate Quebec?…

Are you really ready to tell the world—the whole world—that people of different languages, different cultures, different backgrounds cannot live together in harmony?

Do you really think that ties of friendship and understanding ... ties of mutual trust and respect can be broken without harm or rancour?

Have you found one reason, one good reason, to destroy Canada?…

In a few days, all the shouting will be over. And at that moment, you will be alone to make your decision. At that moment I urge you, my fellow Quebecers, to listen to your heart—and to your head.

I am confident that Quebec and Canada will emerge strong and united.

Land Claims: From Delgamuukw to Nunavut

In 1997, the Supreme Court of Canada made a landmark decision on "existing aboriginal and treaty rights." In the case known as "Delgamuukw," the Court agreed that some of the early treaties made with the Native peoples were valid, and that they were entitled to their ancestral lands. For the first time, Native oral and tribal recollections were accepted as evidence in a court of law. The decision was profoundly important because it gave the Native peoples a way to prove their claims. It could mean that the map of Canada will be redrawn once the courts have heard all of the land claims still being negotiated.

As you learned in Chapters 1 and 11, the Nisga'a had been claiming a large section of land in the Nass River Valley in northwestern British Columbia since 1907. In August 1998, they reached an agreement with the province of BC and the federal government. It was the first treaty ever signed between Native peoples and the province of BC. According to the terms, the Nisga'a would receive $200 million and 1930 square kilometres of land in the Lower Nass Valley. As well, the Nisga'a would own the resources on their lands and make their own laws, which must be consistent with the Charter or Rights and Freedoms and the Criminal Code.

Figure 15–11 Members of the Gitxsan band celebrate the Supreme Court's Delgamuukw decision during a press conference in Vancouver in December 1997.

Many people in the Native communities saw the Nisga'a treaty as a triumph, but many people in BC and Ottawa were not enthusiastic. In Ottawa, the Reform Party attacked the treaty. They said it gave the Nisga'a "special status," not equality, and a "basket of benefits and rights solely on the basis of Nisga'a heritage."

Other critics complained that non-Natives in the Nass River Valley had never been consulted. Indeed, non-Natives in the area are affected by decisions of the new Nisga'a government. Yet they have no voting rights. The Reform Party made a last-ditch effort to stop the treaty by proposing 471 amendments to the bill. It then forced a non-stop, 43-hour vote in the House of Commons in Ottawa. Nonetheless, the Nisga'a land claim was ratified in December 1999.

Many in the Native communities point to Nunavut as a high point in the process towards Native self-government. The Inuit in the Northwest Territories proposed the creation of Nunavut in 1976, and the idea quickly gathered support among the voters in the Northwest Territories. In 1993, the

Images

Susan Aglukark: Singing with Purpose

Figure 15–12 Susan Aglukark also works to prevent drug and alcohol abuse in aboriginal communities.

For Susan Aglukark, musical success came quickly. By 1995, she had hit songs, two Juno awards, and had performed for the Queen and two prime ministers. She was called "an international star" by *The New York Times*. It was the kind of success she had never dreamed of.

Born in Churchill, Manitoba, Aglukark's family lived in several locations across the Northwest Territories before settling in Arviat, a small community on Hudson Bay. She attended high school in Yellowknife, then moved to Ottawa. Fluent in Inuktitut and English, she worked as a government translator and later with the Inuit Tapirisat (Brotherhood) of Canada.

Her big break came in 1991, when CBC Radio included her in a compilation of eastern Arctic performers and writers. In 1993, she became the first Inuk performer to sign with a major label, EMI. Before the year ended, *Maclean's* named her one of "Canada's 100 Leaders to Watch For."

To understand why many people see Aglukark as a role model, you need only listen to her songs. Her lyrics contain a combination of traditional Inuit folklore, events from the history of her people, and messages of personal empowerment. She is inspired not only by personal challenges, but by those the Inuit people have faced. In her song "E186," for example, many Canadians learned about a 1930s government policy that required Inuit to wear "dog tags" for identification.

"I don't like making political statements, but I feel that these are stories that need to be heard," says Aglukark. "I wanted to write from a different perspective, giving back dignity to the unsung heroes of past generations."

Aglukark's diverse audience includes people of different ages, backgrounds, and musical tastes. It is "part of the beauty of being a Canadian artist—people here are just more open to performers from different cultures," she says. "My ultimate message is to learn to be yourself," Aglukark explains. "It's a constant fight, an everyday process. If by example I can relay this simple message, that would be great."

What Do You Think?

1. Do you believe that a song like Susan Aglukark's "E186" tells a story that most Canadians want to hear? In your own words, write a paragraph that either supports or opposes this thesis: "Songs that bring past injustices to light make Canada a better country."

2. With a partner, create a list of historic incidents from this or other chapters that could form the basis for a song. Select the incident that you think more people need to be aware of. Using "E186" or a similar song as a model, create your own lyrics to tell this story from history.

Historian at Work

Oral Evidence: Hearing is Believing

Figure 15–13 This Mi'kmaq boy takes part in a demonstration over Native fishing rights in New Brunswick in 1999. How will recognition of oral histories affect these demands?

Oral history is inherited history, but is it "legal" history?

Native North America—or "Turtle Island," as it was known before European settlement—survives in memory today as a group of tales and legends inherited by the descendants of the Native peoples who lived so long ago. The First Nations of British Columbia argue that this oral history is substantial enough to determine their traditional tribal territories.

To win their land claim, the Gitxsan-Wet'suwet'en Tribal Council had to prove that more than 3000 years ago, near Hazelton, BC, their ancestors occupied Temlazam, a large Nisga'a settlement of 10 000 people. Nisga'a stories and songs are the record of relations between the Gitxsan and Wet'suwet'en tribes, and the history of their occupancy of the land.

In 1997, the Supreme Court of Canada agreed. It accepted oral and tribal recollections as evidence in the Delgamuukw case. This means that the stories and recollections of Native peoples, which have generally been considered "fables" by non-Natives, are now acceptable as evidence in Canadian courts.

What do we mean by historical evidence?

Evidence is used to answer key questions: How do we know if something is true? How, why, when, and where did it happen?

Historical Inquiry: Analysing Information

Most historians think of evidence in terms of written documents. Checking documents for bias, and supporting facts through more than one source, has been the standard method of reaching conclusions about the past. Of course, historians reporting on more recent events can also interview people, and in this way use eyewitness information, a kind of oral evidence.

Historians have traditionally been reluctant, however, to accept as fact the histories of **preliterate** peoples. Preliterate cultures, such as the First Nations, do not rely on written language. So their histories are not to be found in documents and books. They are sometimes called "living histories," because they are handed down orally from generation to generation. As a result, these histories have been considered impossible to verify.

How do we view the past?

Classed as "myths" and "legends," oral histories and tribal songs have been seen as bearing little relationship to historical truth.

Written knowledge of the past is sketchy at best, and often is based on limited sources. As one historian has observed, history is "a dim candle over a dark abyss." It is only possible to see a very limited picture of what life might have been like for a privileged few. Are the oral histories of Native peoples any less valid?

How did courts view oral evidence?

Before the Delgamuukw ruling, Canadian courts were suspicious of oral evidence. The trial judge in the Supreme Court of British Columbia rejected the Nisga'a claim because he considered the oral evidence unreliable and unverifiable.

The Supreme Court of Canada disagreed. It was unanimous in declaring that with oral history the "laws of evidence must be adapted in order that this type of evidence can be accommodated and placed on an equal footing with the types of historical evidence that courts are familiar with." This has generally been taken to mean that oral evidence should be given wider consideration by the courts. The ruling may make it easier in the future for Native peoples to claim secure titles to lands.

How do courts deal with conflicting claims?

If the Delgamuukw ruling makes land claims easier, it may also create problems. Most of the land in British Columbia is not covered by treaty. It is also subject to overlapping claims by different First Nations groups.

Land-claims negotiators, and eventually the courts, will have to decide between competing stories, songs, and legends. Such disputes will probably be settled through a combination of oral, **anthropological**, and **archaeological** evidence. Ultimately, conflicting oral histories will have the same problems as documentary evidence. The "truth" will still be difficult to find.

What Do You Think?

1. The Delgamuukw decision has implications beyond land claims. Make a mind map of ways in which the First Nations of Canada may be affected by the acceptance of their legends, stories, and songs as historical evidence.

2. How does the reporting of the Montreal Rally on pages 404 to 405 show the difficulty of reconstructing the "truth" by relying on evidence from the news media? For example, it is noted that *Le Devoir* reported "touristy" conversations. Since a great deal of historical information on the rally will be based on oral evidence, how would you select people to interview in order to give a balanced view of the event? Consult the Historian at Work about media bias on pages 390 to 391 for more ideas.

3. The Charter of Rights and Freedoms guarantees "equality without discrimination based on race, [or] national and ethnic origin." Analyse the rulings of the Supreme Court of British Columbia and the Supreme Court of Canada on oral evidence. With which ruling do you agree? Keeping the Charter in mind, justify your choice in a written paragraph.

> **Up Close**
>
> 5. Write a newspaper headline that might have appeared on April 1, 1999, to announce the creation of Nunavut.

federal government passed the Nunavut Land Claims Agreement and the Nunavut Act. On April 1, 1999, Nunavut became Canada's third territory as Paul Okalik, its first premier, opened the legislative assembly. It was the first Inuit-led government in Canadian history, and the first time Canada's map had been redrawn in 50 years.

Figure 15–14 Nunavut Premier Paul Okalik displays a replica of the Canadian coin that celebrates the creation of Nunavut as a new territory on April 1, 1999.

The Cree Protested the James Bay Project, Phase II Native activists had greater political success in the 1980s and 1990s because they could link their issues to environmental concerns. As you learned in Chapter 11, the James Bay Project in northern Quebec had had a devastating impact on the Native peoples and their way of life. It flooded 11 500 square kilometres of land—and higher water levels led to mercury contamination in fish. As the Quebec government started work on Phase II in 1989, the Cree organized an international protest.

Phase II of the James Bay Project would flood 30 000 square kilometres of land and cost $63 billion to build. Cree protesters, under the leadership of Cree Grand Chief Matthew Coon Come, canoed into New York harbour in 1990. Their actions attracted widespread US media attention to the threat that Phase II posed to Native lands and to the environment. Important US environmentalists joined the Cree cause. In 1992, the New York Power Authority, the project's major customer, cancelled its contract with Hydro Quebec. Without customers in the large US market, Phase II of the James Bay project was put on hold, with an uncertain future.

> **Up Close**
>
> 6. Why was the Cree's protest against the James Bay Project more successful in the US than in Canada?

CANADA'S ENVIRONMENTAL ISSUES

By the 1990s, Canada was facing many environmental crises. Once, Canada's fish, fresh water, forests, and minerals had been considered limitless natural resources. Now these resources were damaged and depleted, and governments at the provincial and federal levels knew they had to act. In addition, Canadians had to figure out ways to preserve the country's resources over the long term so that the industries that depended on them could survive.

Fishery Woes from Coast to Coast

In 1497, John Cabot, one of the first explorers of Canada, had described the waters off the coast of Newfoundland as "swarming with fish, which can be taken not only with net, but in baskets let down with a stone." By 1993, the East Coast cod fishery had collapsed. Nets were cast and came up empty. In an attempt to salvage the East Coast fisheries, the federal government imposed a **moratorium**. It will remain in place until the cod stocks come back—if they can.

Fish are considered a renewable resource, that is, a resource that can replace itself over time. However, the cod stocks are so endangered that the fish may not be able to mature and spawn in sufficient numbers to support commercial fishing. For the many people thrown out of work by the moratorium, the future remains terribly uncertain. A way of life that goes back centuries may be coming to an end, and entire communities are becoming ghost towns.

As with cod on the East Coast, salmon stocks on the West Coast are in danger. In 1998, the federal government introduced the Salmon Recovery Plan, which changed the way the Pacific fisheries operate. After consulting with Native leaders, environmental groups, and scientists, the government divided the fisheries into two zones: Red and Yellow. The Red zones are areas most likely to contain endangered species. The policy here is "no mortality," which means a ban on all fishing. In the Yellow zones, fishing is not restricted, but no endangered species—such as Coho salmon—may be caught. **Conservation** is the top priority. Time will tell whether these steps will allow the fish stocks to recover enough to support the salmon industry. One thing is certain, the livelihoods of thousands of Canadian fishers and their communities are at stake.

Many factors have contributed to the fisheries crises in Canada. Perhaps the leading cause is that **exploitation rates** have been too high. According to

Figure 15–15 At a 1993 protest in Halifax, a fisherman holds a poster of better times.

Unfinished Business

Heritage Minute

In 1978, researchers at Waterloo University in Ontario designed a water pump based on a pump used by local Mennonite farmers. Today, the Waterloo pump is used throughout the developing world. More than three quarters of the 3 billion people living in the developing world lack access to clean drinking water. Because it is inexpensive and easy to repair, the Waterloo pump is helping to improve that situation.

fishery management experts, catching 16 percent of the available stock each year would allow the fish to replenish their numbers. Unfortunately, levels had soared to between 35 and 45 percent. Other major factors have included government mismanagement, overestimation of the fish stocks, changes in the climate, and air and water pollution. Overfishing by foreign fleets and modern trawlers, which can scoop enormous quantities of fish in deep-sea nets, has also been blamed.

On the East Coast, Canada has had tense confrontations with Portugal and Spain over the issue of overfishing. In 1995, a Canadian Fisheries patrol boat fired shots and seized a Spanish trawler on the Grand Banks. In the furor that followed, the **European Union** threatened to retaliate with trade sanctions against Canada. In the end, a compromise was reached that allowed Canada to enforce fishing quotas in the international waters off its coasts.

On the West Coast, the federal and BC governments have struggled to reach agreements with the state governments of Alaska and Washington. Because salmon migrate through US and Canadian waters, agreements must be reached if the stocks are to be conserved. In 1996, talks collapsed and overfishing continued.

Fresh Water: Commodity or Public Trust?

Canada contains 20 percent of the world's fresh water, so Canadians have tended to take it for granted. The average Canadian uses 326 litres of water a day, second only to the US, where the average is 425 litres a day. Compare that to 200 litres a day in Sweden and France, and 25 litres a day in India.

Less than half of Canada's fresh water, however, is renewable. The rest is frozen in icecaps and glaciers. And as Canada industrialized and became more urban, more and more water became polluted by sewage and industrial wastes. As the 1990s drew to a close, it was clear to Canadians and their governments that the freshwater supply needed to be conserved and protected.

During the 1980s and 1990s, Canada's economy became more closely tied to the US through agreements such as the Canada–US Free Trade Agreement and NAFTA. With these closer ties, some businesses argued that Canada's fresh water could—and should—be treated like any other commodity. In other words, it should be a trade item, such as lumber, oil, gas, minerals, and so on.

Figure 15–16 Residents of Moncton, NB, had to use bottled water when their water supply became unfit for consumption in July 1997.

Some businesses proposed large-scale diversion of Canadian water into the US, such as from the Great Lakes. The Canadian government and many provincial governments, however, created policies to ban bulk-water exports. Nonetheless, in 1998, a California company sued the BC government for blocking a bulk-water plan that would have diverted BC water into California. Maude Barlow, chairperson of the independent citizens' group, the Council of Canadians, said, "It is wrong—environmentally, economically and morally—to engage in the large-scale trade of water … Water is a public trust; it belongs to the people." Water raises many emotional conflicts that will have to be resolved in the years ahead.

Canada's Forest Industry

Another area of great environmental concern is Canada's forests. Almost half of Canada's land mass is covered by forests, and the forest industry employs approximately 830 000 people. Canada is the world's largest exporter of wood and paper products. Its forests also support other industries, such as recreation and tourism, which represent hundreds of thousands of jobs and billions of dollars in revenues. With ten percent of the world's forest resources found in Canada, management of these resources has global consequences.

Canada relies on international markets to sell its forest products. In the 1980s and 1990s, many of those markets, especially in Europe, were demanding changes in Canada's forest industry for environmental reasons. Canadian forest companies adapted to these demands by changing some of their practices. For example, they reduced the amount of clear-cutting and used more selective logging. These changes came about as a result of increasing confrontations between the forestry industry and environmental groups.

Figure 15–17 Canada's forests have become a global issue, as this 1996 photo from London, England, demonstrates.

Clayoquot Sound, 2600 square kilometres of **old-growth forest** on the west coast of Vancouver Island, was the site of many protests. Beginning in the 1960s and 1970s, trees were being harvested through large-scale clear-cutting. Clear-cutting almost completely removes the trees and thus alters the area's **ecosystem**. Aboriginal leaders protested that Clayoquot Sound had special meaning to the original Northwest Coast peoples. They and other concerned groups organized opposition in the early 1980s. In a province where one person in five is employed in the forestry industry, the protests became explosive. In 1985, government injunctions halted logging in the area while aboriginal land claims went before the courts. In the end, however, the logging resumed.

Figure 15–18 Are environmental issues really just a question of businesses versus environmentalists?

In 1993, the BC government announced that most of the old-growth forests were to be clear-cut, while other environmentally sensitive areas were to be preserved. A massive protest was staged to block the logging operations, and more than 900 protesters were arrested, including NDP MP Svend Robinson.

The Canadian Environmental Protection Act

Under pressure at home and abroad, Canada's governments have acted to protect the environment. But they have had to balance the demands of industry and of environmentalists. Often this has been viewed as a conflict, the battle of "big business versus conservation." But as the moratoriums on fishing demonstrate, no one benefits when natural resources are nearly extinguished. This realization has encouraged environmentalists and business leaders to work cooperatively to sustain both the environment and the industries it supports.

In 1988, the federal government passed the Canadian Environmental Protection Act (CEPA). In the preamble, the Act stated that "It is hereby declared that the protection of the environment is essential to the well-being of Canada." The CEPA was updated in 1999 and $100 million in funding was announced. While the Act will continue to be amended, its main goals are to prevent pollution and to protect the environment and the health of Canadians. The key elements of the CEPA are to

- prevent pollution
- monitor and manage toxic substances
- involve the public, including the right to sue for environmental damage
- regulate biotechnology
- create a body of enforcement officers who can issue on-the-spot orders to stop environmental violations
- emphasize information-gathering

Up Close

7. Describe three ways in which the Canadian government has shown its concern to protect Canada's resources and environment.

WINDS OF CHANGE IN CANADIAN POLITICS

Brian Mulroney kept his promise to open Canada for business. In his first term as prime minister, he negotiated the Canada–US Free Trade Agreement (FTA). As Laurier did in 1911, Mulroney called an election based on the fact that he had a free trade deal with the US. Unlike Laurier, Mulroney was re-elected, even though the federal Liberals had declared that the FTA would destroy Canada. In 1989, the FTA went into effect. Down came tariff walls that had protected Canadian businesses since the time of Macdonald's National Policy.

Economic Structures: Economic Conditions

Foundations

Dealing with Debt and Deficit

Did you know that you owe about $20 000 dollars right now? You did not borrow the money—the federal government did, on your behalf. Each year, through taxes and investments, the government raises money, or "revenues." This is used to run the government and fund social programs. If the government spends less than it raises, it has money left over, or a **surplus**. If the government spends more than it raises, it has a **deficit**. In this case, it has to borrow money, and pay it back with interest. The **national debt** is the accumulation of all annual deficits. The $20 000 figure represents each Canadian's share of the national debt.

Between 1950 and 1974, the national debt grew slowly. These were the postwar years, and the economy boomed. But when the economy took a turn for the worse, the government began incurring larger deficits. This continued throughout the 1980s and 1990s. From 1975 to 1995, the national debt mushroomed from $20 billion to more than $545 billion.

Different economic theories either play up or play down the debt issue. The prevailing theory says that government borrowed too much in order to fund social programs. Future generations could be crippled by paying back the national debt. To give you an idea of what this means, in 1991 the government spent $0.35 of every dollar taken in just to pay the interest on the national debt. This was more than it spent on health care and welfare. The federal government cited these problems as the main reason for reducing social spending in the 1990s.

Critics of this theory say that increased interest rates caused the debt to explode, not social spending. They accuse governments of cutting back spending to satisfy business demands for higher profits and lower taxes. These critics, however, have had little impact on government policies. In considering the debate over the debt, it is important to remember that Canada's wealth has also grown. In March 2000, Statistics Canada estimated that if Canada's **net wealth** were divided equally among all Canadians, you would be worth $96 800.

Figure 15–19

Federal Government Dept (millions of dollars)

Date	Net Federal Debt
1945	11 298
1955	11 263
1965	15 504
1975	19 276
1985	199 092
1995	545 672

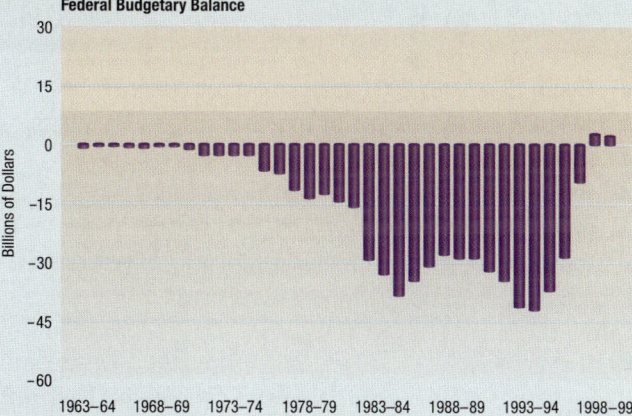

Figure 15–20 Federal budgetary balance

What Do You Think?

1. Which of the following two statements do you agree with?
   - Canada needs to maintain its social programs at all costs. They are what make us Canadian.
   - Canada should cut programs to pay off its debt to ensure a healthy economy.

   Explain your choice with specific examples.

In his second term, Mulroney negotiated the North American Free Trade Agreement (NAFTA). This broadened the FTA to include Mexico. In the 1993 federal election, Liberal leader Jean Chrétien promised to re-examine NAFTA. Yet shortly after he became prime minister, Chrétien ratified NAFTA with almost no changes. Times had changed. As you read in Chapter 14, the world economy had become more global and Canada was adopting policies to be competitive. The Trudeau era—a time of expanding social programs and of protecting Canadian culture and industry—was over.

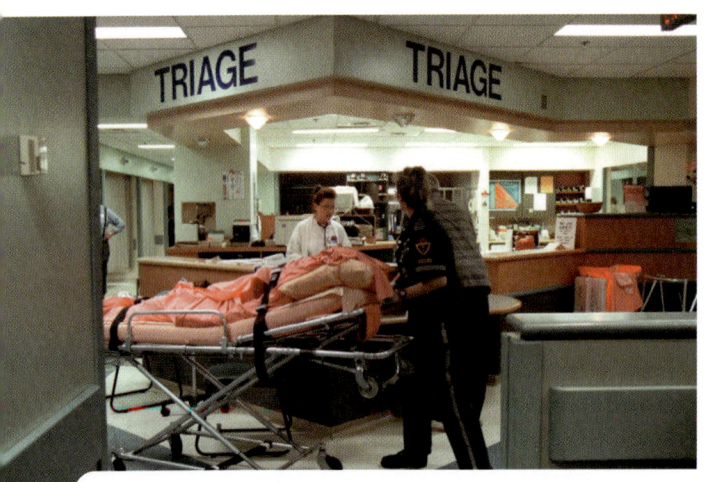

Figure 15–21 By 2000, governments had drastically cut back on health-care spending to balance their budgets. Many hospitals were closed. In January 2000, an 18-year-old man in Toronto died in an ambulance after he was turned away from an overcrowded emergency room and sent to another. Crises like these are putting governments under the gun as Canadians continue to demand top quality health care for all.

Tackling the National Debt

Social programs—such as health care, employment insurance, and the pension plan—have become a part of the Canadian identity. By the 1980s, however, they were becoming increasingly expensive. Even though taxes reached record levels, governments from the mid-1970s until the 1990s spent more money than they raised. Year after year they borrowed the difference, and Canada fell deeply into debt.

Though not the first government to raise the debt and deficit as an issue, the Mulroney government sounded alarm bells. In 1986, Mulroney said of the national debt, "Our determination to reduce it or eradicate it is, and will be, unyielding and successful." His government quickly set out to cut funding to social programs, but the public backlash was intense. As unemployment stayed high and the economy stumbled along, the government's will to cut funding softened. Annual deficits reached unprecedented levels.

After the Conservative defeat in 1993, the national debt stayed at the forefront of political and public debate. The new Opposition, the Reform Party, demanded action—fast. It wanted to make deep cuts to social spending and pay down the debt. Only by bringing down the debt and stimulating the economy through tax reductions, they said, could the social safety net be preserved for the future. Opponents argued that Reform's approach was too aggressive and extreme. Such deep cuts to social programs would place the burden of the debt on the backs of the poor.

The Liberal government took a different approach. It cut back **transfer payments** to the provinces, but not taxes. The cutbacks deeply affected funding for health care, education, and regional development. Unlike Mulroney, however, Chrétien managed to do this without losing popular support. By 1999, the government had reduced spending on federal programs to the lowest level in 50 years. And the 1998-99 federal budget ran a surplus for the second time in a row. Again, this hadn't been seen in almost 50 years. In 2000, Liberal finance minister

Paul Martin claimed the deficit had been "buried" completely as he announced an expected government surplus of almost $100 billion over the next five years.

The Rise of Neo-Conservatism

The move towards debt-and-deficit reduction in the 1980s and 1990s signalled a shift in public attitudes. It reflected a growing neo-conservative movement, which focused on economic and business issues rather than on social spending. The feeling was that a social safety net was possible only in a healthy, robust economy. The path that Canadian governments had been pursuing since the 1960s and 1970s, neo-conservatives argued, was jeopardizing Canada's long-term economic health.

This shift played itself out at the provincial level, as well as influencing federal politics. Governments such as Ralph Klein's Progressive Conservatives in Alberta and Mike Harris's PCs in Ontario put together back-to-back majority governments. They kept high levels of public support, even after incredibly unpopular cuts to education and health budgets. They argued that these steps were necessary if long-term spending goals were to be achieved. In both provinces, personal income taxes were reduced at the same time. Even provincial NDP leaders—including Roy Romanow in Saskatchewan and Bob Rae in Ontario—made fiscal decisions that ran against socialist ideals, which angered and baffled their supporters.

Up Close

8. What is meant by Canada's "social safety net"? Give two examples.

Preston Manning and the Reform Party

The Reform Party was founded in Winnipeg in October 1987 as an alternative for the western provinces. It has been led by Albertan Preston Manning from its inception. Under Manning, Reform has become a leading voice of the neo-conservative movement and has gradually gained national recognition. The party's platform stressed tax relief, debt repayment, democratic accountability, equality, criminal justice reform, and Senate reform. All of these issues brought the party tremendous support in the West, where alienation from central Canada had reached a peak during the Trudeau years.

In its first federal election in 1988, Reform ran 72 candidates. It won two percent of the national vote, but no seats. In 1993, the federal Progressive Conservatives were wiped out, and the Reform Party surged in the popular vote. It won 19 percent of the national vote and 52 seats in the House of Commons. In 1997, the Reform Party won 60 seats—all of them in the West—and formed the official Opposition.

Despite the growing popularity of the Reform Party, support was far from universal. Many Canadians take pride in having a tolerant, compassionate society and are proud of the country's cultural diversity and social safety net. During its first terms in office, Reform challenged many of these cultural and social ideals. Many people felt that programs directed at cultural, gender, and economic equality would be abolished under a Reform government. For this reason, the

Up Close

9. Create a mind map to summarize what you know about the Reform Party.

Unfinished Business **417**

Figure 15–22 Preston Manning takes part in a radio talk show in Vancouver in 1996 (left). In the photo at right, he talks to a reporter at the United Alternative convention in Ottawa in January 2000. In trying to make the Reform Party a national force, Manning has relied on media coverage. He has also tried to polish the image of the party—and of himself. What changes can you see in Manning's appearance in these two pictures?

party's platform has been seen by some Canadians as being intolerant.

Political ideology tends to swing like a pendulum, so it is difficult to predict how much neo-conservative ideas and parties will continue to grow in Canada. At present, conservative-minded people in Canada can vote for the Reform Party or the Progressive Conservatives. The results of the 1997 federal election revealed the effects of this "vote-splitting." Many people suggest that neither party will ever be able to capture enough seats to form the federal government. As a result, a strong movement towards uniting these two parties has emerged.

Senate Reform

The Canadian Parliament is composed of the Queen (represented by the governor general), the House of Commons, and the Senate. The Senate is seen as the "chamber of sober second thought." Its main function is to provide a check on decisions that are passed through the House of Commons. Senators are appointed by the governor general on the recommendation of the prime minister. Often, the Senate has forced necessary changes on controversial legislation.

Because Senators are appointed, however, the Senate has been called "**patronage** heaven." In other words, the government in power can use Senate appointments as a way to repay people for political favours. A few Senators have had poor attendance records and seemed to be completely unaccountable. Many people have questioned the effectiveness of the Senate for this reason. Its lack of regional balance has also been criticized (see Figure 15–23). Preston Manning has said that the Senate "represents the worst of partisan, political patronage … Although Senators frequently say that they will take on regional interests, when push comes to shove, they invariably vote along party lines." As a result, some people are calling for Senate reform, even for all-out abolition. For some Canadians, it has come to symbolize everything that is wrong with the federal political system.

The Reform Party is the most vocal opponent of the current Senate and supports the creation of a "Triple E" Senate, which means Equal, Elected, and Effective. Under this format, the Senate would have an equal number of members from each province, regardless of population. The people of

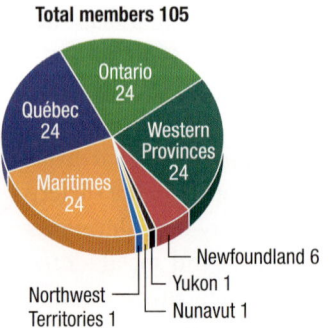

Figure 15–23 Regional division of Senate representation

each province would elect Senators, much as they do Members of Parliament. By having equal and elected representation, critics argue, Senators would be more effective in their duties and responsibilities to Canadians.

Elections Reform

Changes to the way Canada runs its elections are also on the horizon. These changes are seen as necessary to ensure fairness for all campaigning parties and to strengthen the electoral system. In October 1999, the federal government unveiled Bill C-2, which was meant to update and revise the Canada Elections Act. Some of the proposed changes included:

- *Limiting "third-party" advertising and spending* A third party is a person or group other than a candidate or registered party. The limit on third-party advertising and spending is intended to help level the playing field for all campaigning parties.
- *Increasing financial reporting by parties and candidates* All parties and candidates must account for their campaign spending. Increasing their accountability is meant to prevent parties from accepting bribes from interest groups or using campaign funds for other purposes.
- *New rules on election advertising and opinion surveys* There would be a ban on all advertising and releasing of new opinion polls on the day before and the day of the election. To assist voters in determining the validity of poll results, all opinion surveys would have to provide detailed information on how the survey was conducted. Finally, because of the growing importance of the Internet in communications, all advertising on it would fall under the new bill.

Up Close

10. Read carefully the examples of proposed changes to elections in Bill C-2. Rewrite each one in your own words.

CONCLUSION

Canada faces a key question at the beginning of this new century: How can it shape effective national strategies in an age of regional politics and global economics? At the end of the twentieth century, provinces and regions disagreed on the Constitution, the federal structure, and the importance of social policy versus the national debt. A key change also occurred. Through much of the twentieth century, Canadians had tended to view the environment—the air, the forests, the land, the lakes and seas—as an unlimited, indestructible bounty. But the collapse of the fisheries and increased pollution forced Canadians to realize that the environment is fragile. In the new century, the forest industry and the freshwater supply are likely to spark more conflicts and debates. Canada faces a key challenge: it must shape an effective national environmental strategy that takes into account the interests of all of Canada's regions and citizens.

Perhaps the greatest challenge that Canada faced in the final decades of the last century was globalization. This affected every aspect of Canadian life. In the next chapter, you will look at how Canada dealt with these new global forces.

CHAPTER ACTIVITIES

■ Check Your Understanding

1. In a paragraph, explain how the failed constitutional talks affected Canada. In particular, discuss the impact that the failures of the Meech Lake and Charlottetown Accords had on the following: regional, provincial, and federal politics; Native peoples; the province of Quebec; and the rest of Canada.

2. Summarize the environmental crises facing Canada in the last decades of the twentieth century. Discuss the problems, and the underlying reasons for why they were occurring.

■ Develop Your Thinking

3. Think about what might have occurred if Quebec had voted for sovereignty on October 30, 1995. Describe changes that could have resulted from such a decision. Consider the economy, trade, language, the military, Native peoples, borders, debt, currency and passports, education, and so on.

4. Using information from the above exercise, create a list of benefits and drawbacks to Quebec separation. For a more varied list, work in small groups. Each member can write from a different point of view: for example, as a separatist, a federalist, an anglophone inside Quebec, or a francophone living outside of Quebec.

■ Express Yourself

5. a) Working in small groups, prepare for a "national televised debate" on the state of Canada at the end of the twentieth century. Each group member can assume a different identity from the following list (or create your own):
   - Jean Chrétien
   - Lucien Bouchard
   - Jacques Parizeau
   - Lucienne Robillard
   - Ovide Mercredi
   - Elijah Harper
   - Brian Mulroney
   - Preston Manning
   - a fisher
   - a Clayoquot logger

   b) Before the "televised debate" prepare opinion statements for the following agenda items. Be prepared to take questions from the "audience":
   - the economy
   - debt and deficits
   - social spending
   - the environment
   - the Senate
   - constitutional reform
   - Native self-government
   - Quebec separation

Apply Your Learning

6. Create your own oral history. Prepare a 2–5 minute speech that tells your family history. It could be about a family adventure or myth, or about your family's journey to Canada. You may use metaphors, symbols, and so on, but your story must be rooted in the real experience of your family. An oral history is meant to be spoken, so memorize your story before presenting it to the class.

7. Research other Native land claims, focusing on a single province or territory. Read accounts from different perspectives and consider consequences of the claim, not just for the Native peoples, but on the entire province or area. Then decide: Will you grant, modify, or deny the claim? Submit your decision in written format, clearly outlining your reasons. If you grant the claim, also submit a redrawn map of the area in question.

Extend Your Learning Using the Internet

8. With the creation of Nunavut and the Nisga'a treaty, some of Canada's Native peoples gained greater autonomy. Using SchoolNet and other web links, communicate by email with students at high schools in these parts of Canada. Interview the students on how this autonomy has changed their outlook for the future.

9. Review Canadian government attitudes and policies on natural resources throughout the century. What lessons of history have led to current government policies? Develop your own Internet search strategy, and write a report on your findings. Include a bibliography in which you identify all your sources.

16
Global Forces

Focus Questions

Canada's Participation in War, Peace, and Security
What role did Canada's armed forces play in world affairs in the last decade of the century? How successful were they in their goals?

Canada's International Status and Foreign Policy
How has Canada been a world leader in the area of human rights?

External Forces Shaping Canada's Policies
Which groups have supported the North American Free Trade Agreement? Which groups have opposed it? Why?

Scientific and Technological Impact
How has rapidly developing technology in the area of communications affected the global economy?

As the twentieth century entered its final two decades, huge changes began to occur. All at once, the old systems were collapsing and giving way to new ones. Politically, governments in the East and West began to share the same concerns. Economies expanded globally as countries built trade alliances. The world was becoming the "global village" that Marshall McLuhan, the Canadian media visionary, had predicted in 1962.

Perhaps changes were happening too quickly, often at the cost of the world's natural resources. As people began to feel more responsibility for Earth and each other, human rights became an important issue. Many were appalled that their governments had made economic deals with countries that had a history of human rights violations.

In this chapter you will read how Canada, as part of this new global village, often took a leadership role in trade agreements and in **economic sanctions** against authoritarian regimes. Canada sent peacekeepers to war-torn countries, provided aid to starving regions, and led the campaign against land mines. As a citizen of the twenty-first century, you will not only witness Canada's changing role in the global village, you will inherit the world created by these new forces. What changes will you make to your world?

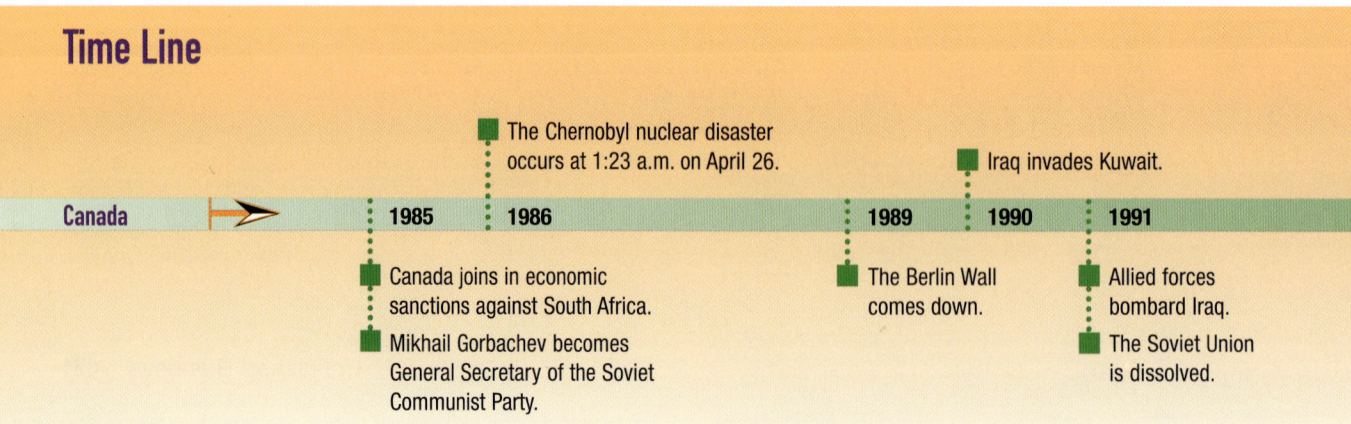

Time Line

Canada

1985 — Canada joins in economic sanctions against South Africa.
Mikhail Gorbachev becomes General Secretary of the Soviet Communist Party.

1986 — The Chernobyl nuclear disaster occurs at 1:23 a.m. on April 26.

1989 — The Berlin Wall comes down.

1990 — Iraq invades Kuwait.

1991 — Allied forces bombard Iraq.
The Soviet Union is dissolved.

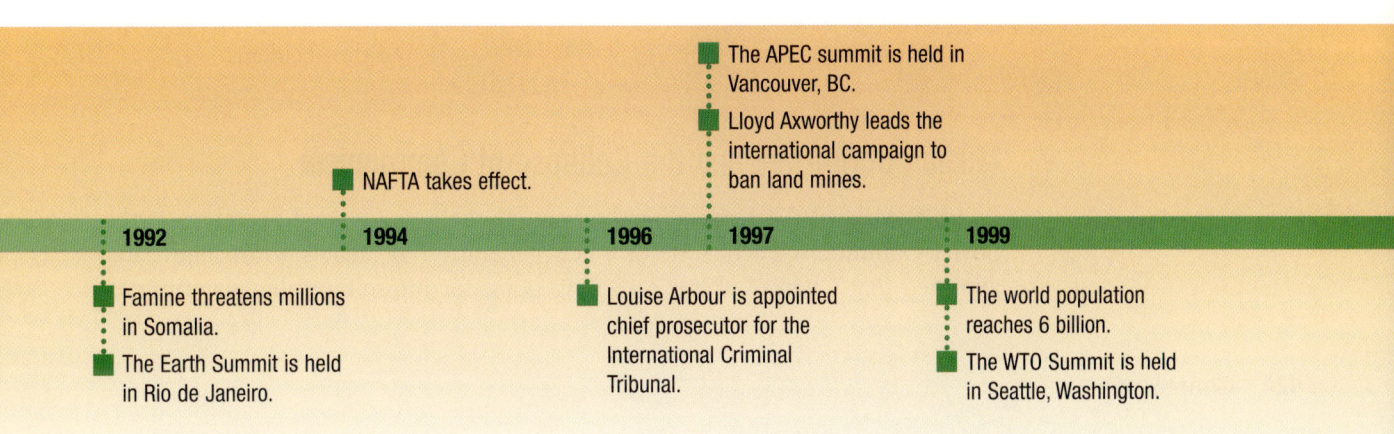

Perspectives

On November 9, 1989, the Berlin Wall, which had divided East and West Berlin for 28 years, came down. The event foreshadowed the fall of Soviet control in Central and Eastern Europe, and the end of the Cold War. What message does this photograph convey? If you were one of the East German soldiers in the middle of the photo, what might your thoughts be? Why?

1992	1994	1996	1997	1999
Famine threatens millions in Somalia.	NAFTA takes effect.	Louise Arbour is appointed chief prosecutor for the International Criminal Tribunal.	The APEC summit is held in Vancouver, BC.	The world population reaches 6 billion.
The Earth Summit is held in Rio de Janeiro.			Lloyd Axworthy leads the international campaign to ban land mines.	The WTO Summit is held in Seattle, Washington.

A TURNING POINT: THE CHERNOBYL NUCLEAR ACCIDENT

Before April 26, 1986, few people in the West had heard of Chernobyl, a city 120 kilometres north of Kiev, the capital of Ukraine. At 1:23 a.m. on that day, scientists at the Chernobyl nuclear power plant were running a safety test. Thirty seconds into the test, steam production went out of control at the reactor's core. Something had gone terribly wrong. The world awoke to an official report: a "minor" incident had occurred, but the problem was isolated and contained.

This piece of **misinformation** might have gone unchallenged only a few years before. In the new global village, photos taken by US spy satellites showed that the heavy metal cap on one of the reactors had blown off. The accident had released eight tonnes of fuel containing plutonium, other radioactive materials, and untold amounts of poisonous gases. The explosion had produced 200 times as much radiation as the atomic bombs dropped on Hiroshima and Nagasaki combined.

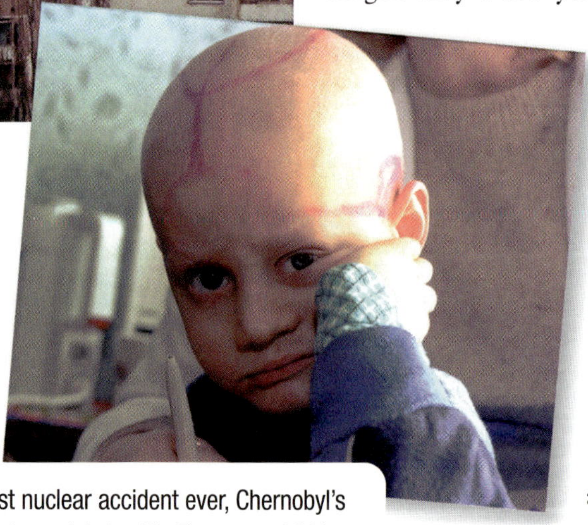

As the cloud of gases rode the winds, monitoring devices as far away as Great Britain registered increased radiation. In Norway, radiation levels were so high they could be measured in the soil. In the Chernobyl area, 31 people died instantly. To this day, cancer rates in the area continue to soar above normal. After days of denial, the Soviets at last admitted the full scope of the accident.

Figure 16–1 Chernobyl's main reactor is shown encased in steel and concrete following the accident.

Figure 16–2 The worst nuclear accident ever, Chernobyl's fallout continues to affect people's health. Five-year-old Alec Zhloba battles leukemia. The lines on her head show where she has had surgery.

> Good evening, comrades. All of you know that there has been an incredible misfortune—the accident at the Chernobyl nuclear plant. It has painfully affected the Soviet people, and shocked the international community. For the first time, we confront the real force of nuclear energy, out of control.
>
> –Mikhail Gorbachev, 1986

Mikhail Gorbachev and the Collapse of Communism

In 1985, Mikhail Gorbachev had been made the new General Secretary of the Soviet Communist Party. One of a new generation of Soviets, Gorbachev later admitted that Chernobyl was a turning point for himself and his government.

Faced with such a major crisis, it was obvious the Soviet Union was in trouble. Gorbachev knew that the prolonged standoff with the West was costing Russia billions of dollars a year. The arms race demanded huge sums from the yearly budget, as did the competitive space program. If Gorbachev wanted to give internal policies a chance to work, he had to reduce these external pressures. To reinvigorate the Soviet state, he pursued two political initiatives: **glasnost** and **perestroika**.

"Glasnost" means open dialogue. After years of fear and silence, Russians could openly criticize the government and its policies.

"Perestroika" means restructuring. There was a movement away from state socialism towards a free-market economy. State subsidies on food and consumer goods were removed. Gorbachev hoped these policies would take the burden off the government, while encouraging initiative among individual citizens. Instead, prices soared, and people stood in long lines to buy even the most basic foods.

Figure 16–3 Food shortages and high prices caused people to shop illegally on the black market, where food was sold at prices lower than at state-run stores.

The Collapse of the Berlin Wall

Gorbachev's policies affected other countries in Eastern Europe. Since August 1961, the German city of Berlin had been divided into two cities by a high wall. Built to stop people from leaving communist East Germany, the Wall stood for 28 years as a grim symbol of the gulf between East and West, communism and democracy. Its barbed wire, barricades, and guards separated families, friends, and cultures. During those years, more than 5000 people attempted to escape East Berlin. Many were shot. People tried tunnelling under the wall, and catapulting over it. One family built a small hot air balloon and floated over! When the Berlin Wall came down in 1989, the whole world saw that the Soviet empire was collapsing.

Encouraged by Gorbachev's new policies, Hungary opened its borders to Austria in September 1989. Thousands of East Germans fled through Austria to West Germany. The momentum continued into October. At protest rallies, thousands chanted "The Wall must go. We are the People." As the world watched, they clashed with troops and riot police.

Figure 16–4 West Germans greet East German soldiers as the Wall comes down.

Global Forces

Finally, on the evening of November 9, 1989, the border between East and West Germany opened, and the Wall came down. Millions around the world watched on television and cheered as Germans popped champagne while dancing and hammering at the Wall in a joyous celebration of freedom.

Free Elections in the Soviet Union

At home, Gorbachev extended his reforms and moved towards free elections. For the first time since 1917, parties other than the Communist Party could run for office. But when free elections were called in 1989, many Communist Party officials resisted being voted out of office. Gorbachev's reforms had ended Soviet power, but he could rightfully claim that "the world had become a safer place." In 1987, he and US President Ronald Reagan had signed an anti-missile treaty, thus reducing stockpiles of nuclear weapons.

In only four tumultuous years, the political winds from Chernobyl had blown away the Cold War. The world had been changed into a freer, perhaps more uncertain, planet.

Figure 16–5 Canada's UN peacekeepers serve refreshments before leaving Haiti in November 1997.

WAR AND PEACEKEEPING

In Chapter 10, you learned that Canada played a large role in the founding of the United Nations (UN). Following WW II, the United Nations had a major responsibility for peacekeeping. It identified threats to peace, imposed economic sanctions against countries that threatened world peace, and mobilized its peacekeeping forces. This role continued following the collapse of the Soviet Union, but with some differences.

The New Role of the United Nations

Between 1948 and 1987, the UN set up 13 peacekeeping missions. Between 1988 and 1992, it established 14 missions—more in those four years alone than in the previous forty. This new pace can be attributed to the breakdown of the Soviet empire. With the Soviet threat removed, the West, backed by the military superiority of the US, was freer to impose its will on regions around the world. The North Atlantic Treaty Organization (NATO) and the UN assumed the role of policing the world. As a member of NATO, Canada was swept along in this new role.

The nature of the peacekeeping mission changed significantly as well. As the Soviet empire collapsed, deep-seated feelings of ethnic nationalism emerged in **satellite countries**. These feelings had been long suppressed under communism.

Change and Continuity: Foreign Policy

Flashpoint

Canada Helps to Usher in a New Dawn

[There] can be no peace unless there is freedom wherever discrimination exists because of race or colour.

With these words in 1952, John Diefenbaker ignited Canada's first parliamentary debate on South Africa. Nine years later, South Africa was forced out of the Commonwealth in a process spearheaded by Diefenbaker.

In 1948, South Africa's ruling National Party had implemented a policy of apartheid (a Dutch word meaning "apartness"). White South Africans controlled the government, and apartheid imposed complete separation between the Black majority and the White minority. Black people could not live next to, walk on the same beaches, or even swim in the same water as Whites. They had to carry pass books, which dictated where they could travel and work. While the White population prospered, Blacks lived in poverty.

Apartheid sparked strikes, boycotts, and eventually violent riots. The African National Congress (ANC), with Nelson Mandela as leader, formed to fight apartheid. But ANC leaders, including Mandela, were imprisoned, or fled to other countries.

On March 21, 1960, more than 5000 Black men and women protested against the pass books in the township of Sharpeville. Police opened fire, killing 69. The government declared a state of emergency, banning anti-apartheid organizations. The Sharpeville massacre, however, drew worldwide attention. After Sharpeville, thousands more died fighting apartheid. On June 16, 1976, two Black students were killed in Soweto when troops shot into a crowd of students who were protesting the compulsory learning of the Afrikaans language. More protests followed. After 12 months, 575 people were dead.

In response to the situation, Canada imposed economic sanctions against South Africa in 1985. Canada became a leader in the international anti-apartheid movement, chairing the Commonwealth Committee of Foreign Affairs on South Africa. At the UN, Canada contributed the Canadian Anti-Apartheid Register, which contained the names of Canadian organizations, governments, firms, and individuals that opposed apartheid. It was meant to encourage other countries to involve their citizens in worldwide protests

In 1990, Mandela was finally released, after 27 years behind bars. It was the beginning of a "new dawn." In 1991, South African president F. W. de Klerk repealed the apartheid laws. In 1993, he and Mandela were awarded the Nobel Peace Prize. Finally, in 1994, South Africa held its first multiracial elections. The ANC was elected, and Nelson Mandela became president of South Africa.

Figure 16–6 The poverty and protests in Soweto township alarmed people around the world.

Activity

1. With a partner, research what has happened in South Africa since 1994. Consider the economy, politics, culture, and society. Have there been improvements? Are there problems? Present your findings in a report to the class.

The disputes that erupted were caused by differences in religion or ethnicity. Interfering in these types of disputes put the international community in an extremely difficult position. There was no simple "right and wrong"—just differences. There was also the question of sovereignty. Since these disputes were between factions inside an independent state, rather than between two independent states, did the UN have the right to intervene? If it did, how could the UN remain neutral? How could it respect national sovereignty?

In response to these questions, UN Secretary General Boutros Boutros-Ghali published his "Agenda for Peace" in 1992. This document redefined the UN's peacekeeping roles. It outlined four primary roles:

- *Preventive diplomacy* UN diplomats attempt to mediate disagreements before they escalate into violent conflicts.
- *Peacekeeping* Non-partisan troops carry out and enforce the terms of an agreement. Such activities may include the return of refugees to their homes or the removal of weapons. This role is closest to the vision that Canadian Prime Minister Lester Pearson originally had for UN peacekeepers.
- *Peacemaking* UN forces participate in a conflict without the consent of all the parties involved. Peacemakers then are placed in positions in which they must take sides and use force to impose a solution. This step is usually taken when the world perceives that the conflict is resulting in a humanitarian crisis.
- *Peacebuilding* The UN helps countries rebuild after a conflict ends. This aid can include things such as providing economic assistance or supplying UN observers to monitor elections.

Up Close

1. As you read the next section, find an example of each of the four peacekeeping roles identified on this page. Explain why each example fits the definition.

The United Nations in Action

In the 1990s, Canada was involved in many UN missions. Four of these missions—to the Persian Gulf, the Balkans, and the African nations of Somalia and Rwanda—helped to define Canada's role in peacemaking.

Figure 16–7 Captured Iraqi soldiers are transported away from Kuwait in February 1991.

The Persian Gulf region in the Middle East has had a long history of tension and conflicts. These involved deep religious convictions and territorial wars among Middle Eastern nations. On August 1, 1990, Iraq invaded Kuwait, a country it had once controlled. The UN saw this as an act of aggression against a smaller neighbouring state and immediately went to Kuwait's defence. Within days many nations, led by the US, imposed harsh economic sanctions against Iraq. In addition, the UN established a massive international military coalition, which included Canadian forces.

However, Iraq's leader, Saddam Hussein, refused to withdraw. Allied forces attacked Iraq from the air, using high-tech cruise missiles. They followed up with a ground war that lasted only 100 hours. When US President George Bush ordered a ceasefire, an estimated 120 000 Iraqi soldiers were dead, and Iraq lay in ruins. It was the end of the Gulf War, and Iraq's once thriving economy was shattered. Economic sanctions against Iraq have continued, causing suffering among civilians. But Hussein refused to comply with the ceasefire conditions and hostilities continued in the region.

Figure 16–8 New states of the former Yugoslavia

In the Gulf situation, the UN stepped in to defend an independent state from an aggressor. This was peacemaking. With the disintegration of the **Balkan States**, the UN faced a much more delicate situation. Yugoslavia had been created by the Allies at the end of WW I. It brought together a number of territories with very different ethnicities, languages, and religions (see Figure 16–8). In 1990, free elections brought an end to communist rule in Slovenia, Croatia, Bosnia-Herzegovinia, and Macedonia. But that was not the case in Serbia and Montenegro. The Yugoslav federation began to unravel as individual regions and ethnic groups called for independence. Intense rivalries and ethnic tensions erupted into a bitter civil war.

In June 1991, both Croatia and Slovenia declared themselves independent states. Serbia tried to prevent the separations, but was unsuccessful. The two new sovereign states organized armies, and all sides dug in. Fighting intensified, spilling over into Bosnia-Herzegovina. Serbian forces attempted to eliminate all Muslims and Croats from the Serbian communities within these areas. This strategy is known as **ethnic cleansing**, and it meant the mass movement of people and mass murders. The world was shocked by discoveries of mass graves, sometimes holding hundreds of bodies of the young and old—men, women, and children.

Up Close

2. Give some specific reasons why the UN considered the upheaval in the Balkan States a "delicate situation."

A Crisis Unfolds The European community was at a loss for what to do. With the end of the Cold War, the newly independent countries of the former Soviet Union were struggling and in need of aid. Fearing that political instability would

Global Forces

Figure 16–9 The horror of ethnic cleansing: One of the largest graves, with 274 bodies of massacred Bosnian Muslims, was found in Bosnia. Families attempt to identify the remains of loved ones.

spread, European nations at first opposed independence for the various regions in Yugoslavia.

When the fighting intensified, the UN stepped in and tried to ship relief supplies to Sarajevo. This city, once the proud capital of Yugoslavia and host of the 1984 Winter Olympics, had been under a lengthy siege. Its population was desperate for help. UN peacekeeping forces were sent to Bosnia to keep the Sarajevo airport open for civilian relief shipments. Canadian Major-General Lewis Mackenzie, who led the mission, was frustrated by the lack of support. He was outspoken in his criticism of the UN efforts, calling them "madness."

To bring an end to the atrocities, the UN imposed harsh economic sanctions against Serbia. Ceasefires were negotiated and then ignored. Eventually, Yugoslavia (Serbia) was expelled from the UN. NATO finally implemented military action. In December 1996, the warring parties signed the Dayton Accord, designed to end Europe's bloodiest conflict since WW II. The treaty terms included

- the creation of a Bosnian state with two parts: a Croat-Muslim Federation and a Serbian Republic
- the appointment of Canadian Louise Arbour to lead the UN's International Criminal Tribunal
- freedom of movement for all peoples
- enforcement of the Accord by a NATO-led ground force.

Canadians were proud to see a Canadian woman appointed to the UN post. Arbour had already distinguished herself as a long-time member of the Ontario Court of Appeal and as a trial judge for the High Court of Justice for the Supreme Court of Ontario. In addition, she had published many articles on criminal law, human rights, civil liberties, and gender issues. As chief prosecutor for the International Criminal Tribunal, Arbour had the authority to prosecute a number of offences, including violations of the customs of war, genocide, and crimes against humanity.

Slobodan Milosevic and the Kosovo Crisis In 1998, new hostilities broke out in the Balkans. This time, the conflict took place inside Serbian territory in the province of Kosovo. Kosovo was 90 percent ethnic Albanian and was considered an autonomous province. It was self-sufficient and thriving. It had its own schools, taxes, and social services. But the territory held great significance for both Serbs and Kosovars. For the Serbs, it was "the cradle" of their civilization. For Kosovars, it was their ancestral home.

Up Close

3. Create a character map to show everything you know about Louise Arbour.

In 1989, Serbian leader Slobodan Milosevic took away Kosovo's independence. He gave all government jobs to the Serbian minority, closed schools, curtailed language rights, and sent in Serbian security forces to patrol the area. In response, a civilian army called the "Kosovo Liberation Army" (KLA) formed to fight the Serbian forces. The conflict intensified throughout the 1990s, when the world took notice of masses of civilians fleeing the region. These refugees told stories of atrocities—mass rapes and slaughters. Satellite photos of what appeared to be freshly dug mass graves supported their allegations. The Serbs were, once again, engaged in ethnic cleansing.

Intense negotiations began, but they proved futile. Milosevic seemed to be using the negotiations to gain time for his troops to complete their mission in Kosovo. Meanwhile, approximately 300 000 refugees poured into neighbouring Albania and Macedonia. They set up temporary camps, putting tremendous pressure on their host countries. At one point, these regions closed their borders—Kosovars were not welcome. This stranded thousands of people in "no man's land." They had no means of escape and no hope of going home.

Milosovic refused to stop his military advance into Kosovo or the assault on refugees. In response, NATO unleashed a bombing campaign that pounded Serbian forces for 78 days. It was the second time since the end of the Cold War that Western forces, including Canadians, were involved in an aggressive military campaign. An agreement was finally reached, reinstating Kosovo as an autonomous province. However, this fell short of the Kosovars' desire for independence. The agreement also established a 48000-strong NATO force to supervise the removal of Serbian forces, the return of the refugees, and the creation of a massive rebuilding project.

This situation illustrates the difficulty the UN faced in such a conflict. Its goal was to stop the atrocities of an invading force and to restore order. It could be neither pro-Kosovar nor anti-Serbian. When the Kosovars returned to their homes, they had a renewed hatred for the Serbs. Later, Kosovars attacked the Serbian minority in Kosovo. The UN forces now had to protect the Serbs. The Kosovars reacted by accusing the UN forces of being pro-Serbian. This feeling boiled over into KLA attacks on French UN forces.

Figure 16–10 UN War Crimes Tribunal Chief Louise Arbour (centre) tours a mass grave site in Bosnia in 1998.

Global Forces

Figure 16–11 Leaving a makeshift refugee camp, an elderly Kosovar woman struggles to board a bus; others wait their turn.

Canada in Kosovo Canada played a significant role in the Kosovo crisis. CF-18 jets flew missions to "delay, isolate, neutralize, or destroy" Serbia's military potential. Canada also lent military personnel to help with air surveillance. Prime Minister Jean Chrétien led efforts to bring Russia, a dissenting voice in the UN, on side. Russian support was important for diplomatic efforts in Kosovo to be successful. Canada also accepted more than 5600 Kosovo refugees. Temporary shelters were set up, and Kosovars who wanted to stay in Canada after the war were welcomed. Most returned home. In all, Canada contributed approximately $500 million to this effort.

Canada's involvement caused a furor among Serb Canadians. They felt that Canada was endorsing the killing of Serbs in the Balkans. Serb Canadians staged mass marches and demonstrations throughout the air campaign. As with the UN peacekeepers, Canada, with its diverse ethnic populations, was caught between opposing sides.

Peacemaking Questioned

Many people around the world questioned the UN's aggressive campaigns in Iraq and Kosovo. These actions had been undertaken with good intentions, but had they gone too far? The new role of peacemaker was looking very much like warmaker. With an expanding UN membership—and many more differing viewpoints—the UN itself remains divided on these questions. As a result, the member states have to walk a very fine line to meet their goals. This division has led to some embarrassing failures for UN forces in the past decade. These failures have called into question the effectiveness of the UN efforts.

> We deserve better. Countries don't give their troops to the UN in trust to be killed trying to implement a really lousy ceasefire agreement arranged by a bunch of diplomats and politicians. That's what is happening in Yugoslavia.
>
> –Canadian Major-General Lewis Mackenzie on the efforts of the United Nations in Bosnia

Canada in Somalia In 1992, famine threatened millions of people in Somalia. The United Nations Operation in Somalia (UNOSOM) was established to provide a secure environment for humanitarian relief operations and to monitor the March 1992 ceasefire agreement between warring parties. But with no clear government in place and the country near anarchy, food supplies were looted by warring factions. When the ceasefire failed, the UN forces were caught between the opposing parties. The UN forces were too small to stop the fighting, and the country slipped deeper into chaos.

The Somalia situation became increasingly dangerous for UN forces. In 1993, UNOSOM II was given the authority to use force, but continued to have a humanitarian mandate. For US voters, Somalia was becoming reminiscent of Vietnam. When 18 American soldiers were killed, US public support began to deteriorate. By 1995, the mission came to an end as a bitter, humiliating experience for the UN. It had failed to curb the activities of Somali warlords, and its forces had suffered increasing attacks.

The experience was humiliating for Canada as well. Canada and Fiji are the only two countries that have participated in virtually every UN peacekeeping mission. Canadians are proud of that history. When the US asked for assistance in Somalia, Canada sent the Canadian Airborne Regiment, an elite combat unit with no experience in peacekeeping. A renegade group of this regiment, calling itself "the Rebels," became involved in the torture and killing of four Somali civilians. News coverage and photographs of the execution of two young Somalis horrified Canadians. One was shot in the back and one was brutally tortured for three hours before being killed. These images conflicted with the image of "Canada the Good." Canada, through a long and painful inquiry, reflected on its peacekeeping role.

Up Close

4. Describe the situation and analyse the failure of Canada's peacekeeping mission in Somalia.

Rwanda: Another UN Failure The UN peacekeeping mission to Rwanda in 1994-1996 was another horrifying failure. Between April and July of 1994, the UN failed to control a tribal conflict between Rwanda's majority Hutus and minority Tutsis. The situation escalated into a humanitarian disaster. Between 500 000 to 800 000 people, mostly Tutsis, were killed in what can only be called genocide. The UN force was simply too small and too ill-equipped to deal with the scale of the killings. Politics and the demands of the Rwandan government, not military assessment, had dictated the size of the UN force.

Figure 16–12 During the Somalia Inquiry, a man looks at evidence that Captain Clayton Matchee, a Canadian peacekeeper, pointed a gun at Shidane Arone, a 16-year-old Somali boy who was tortured and killed.

The Future of Peacekeeping

The failures in Somalia and Rwanda exposed the UN's difficulty in adapting to the realities of its new role. New circumstances required a new approach. Analysts have suggested that if the UN is to continue entering hostile situations, it must have both the military means and the ability to make decisions that will protect its peacekeeping forces and achieve its objectives. The failure to give this support has resulted in frustration, fear, and anger and may have led to reckless and indefensible acts.

Robert Fowler, Canada's ambassador to the United Nations, addressed the Security Council in New York on December 12, 1995. He outlined the problems created when peacemakers are not given the resources and decision-making authority they need to carry out their missions:

> We should have learned this in the early days in Mogadishu [the capital of Somalia], when UN troops were unable to move beyond the airport while anarchy raged outside their perimeter. Surely we should have also learned from the tragic lessons of the creation of "safe areas" in Bosnia, which we knew we could not keep safe with the forces the Security Council and Member States were prepared to make available. Indeed, we should have learned from our tragic experience of Rwanda in April 1994, when an under-manned, ill-equipped mission was unable to deter civil unrest, let alone to confront genocide.

ENVIRONMENTALISM: A GLOBAL CONCERN

The breakup of the Soviet Union not only affected foreign policies around the globe, it created a new sense of urgency about issues that affected the whole world. The incident at Chernobyl dramatically illustrated how the actions and policies of one country could affect the environment and safety of its neighbours. Offers to provide assistance for the victims of Chernobyl came from all over the world. Even Cuba, a country that is often isolated in international affairs, offered to treat some of the victims. Canadians also responded compassionately to Chernobyl victims. In 1996, for example, Canadian families invited a group of children affected by the disaster to spend the summer with them to help them clear their systems of radiation. The crisis not only united people globally in a humanitarian effort, it united countries in their call for global awareness of environmental issues.

By the 1990s, environmental issues were receiving more attention than ever before. The world's population had doubled from 3-billion to 6-billion people between 1950 and 1999. (The world's population is predicted to reach 9.4 billion by 2050.) Countries around the world were introducing pollutants into the environment and using natural resources at a rate that could not be sustained. Many scientists claimed we had reached a critical point—if we did not act immediately to reverse these trends, it would be too late. Other scientists disputed this doomsday scenario. The two sides did agree that the changes occurring in our environment potentially could threaten human life. Scientists and the media focused on three issues: deforestation (particularly in regard to the world's rain forests), **global warming**, and the deterioration of the ozone layer.

Up Close

5. Create a chart similar to the one on page 435, focusing on issues and solutions. Include the three already listed, and add other possible solutions. Also add other issues and solutions of your own choosing.

Top Environmental Issues in the 1990s			
Issue	**Status**	**Causes**	**Some Solutions**
Deforestation	Consumption of forest products more than doubles in the last three decades of the twentieth century.	Forests are overharvested to meet demand for forest products, or to clear land for raising livestock.	Government investment in forests, the forest sector, and forest-dependent communities
Global Warming	Environment Canada notes a long-term trend of global warming. The ten warmest years since 1880 all occur in the 1980s or 1990s.	Greenhouse gases are emitted by cars and trucks as well as the oil and gas industry—from refineries, gas plants, and pipelines.	Tougher emissions standards for motor vehicles The BC-based Ballard Power Systems Inc. invents a power cell for the electric car.
Ozone layer deterioration	In early 1993, ozone levels in the atmosphere reach a record low. Ozone concentrations fall by 15% from the pre-1980 average.	Ozone-depleting substances containing chlorofluorocarbons (CFCs) and hydrochlorofluoro-carbons (HCFCs) are used in refrigeration and in aerosols.	Canada agrees to a 50% reduction to 1986 levels of CFCs by 1995, and a phase-out of all ozone-harmful materials by 2005.

Figure 16–13

The Rio Conference

In June 1992, the world came together in Rio de Janeiro, Brazil, to discuss global environmental issues. The event was the UN Conference on Environment and Development or, as it later became known, the "Earth Summit." UN organizers, led by Canadian Maurice Strong, created a conference of unprecedented size and prestige. It involved 178 nations, more than 100 heads of state, more than 1500 non-governmental agencies, and some 7000 journalists.

This massive gathering also represented a turning point for many activists. It was a display of international cooperation never seen before on the environmental front. The Earth Summit issued an unprecedented direction, which called for global commitment to **sustainable development** (economic growth that meets human needs while protecting nature's ability to renew itself).

Figure 16–14 Environmental activists at the Rio Earth Summit in 1992 make their point.

HUMAN RIGHTS: CANADA'S POLICY ABROAD

Canada is seen around the world as a nation that supports human rights. Its role in international peacekeeping has secured this reputation. Canada has been applauded for its leadership in banning and clearing land mines around the world, and its introduction of the Ottawa Process. (See page 449.) In 1997, Foreign Affairs Minister Lloyd Axworthy explained it this way: "The protection and promotion of human rights is a primary Canadian value and a key goal of our domestic and foreign policy." Canada's human rights approach is known as **effective influence**. It is based on the conviction that the best way to influence other governments is through dialogue and engagement, not through a policy of isolation. In a 1997 speech, Foreign Affairs Minister Lloyd Axworthy said:

> Where Canada has made a niche for itself, and perhaps the most distinctive feature of our human rights policy, is in supporting change from within. We believe that the impulse towards democracy is inevitable, but at the same time we are realistic about the governments we are dealing with. We do not expect these governments to become sudden converts to the cause of democracy. But they will yield gradually—because they have no other choice—to pressure for change within their own society.

Canada Challenges China

Up Close

6. Write your own definition of the phrase "effective influence." Describe how Canada applied this policy while dealing with China.

The Canadian government used effective influence when dealing with China in the wake of the 1989 massacre at Tiananmen Square. When university students held a large pro-democracy demonstration in Beijing's Tiananmen Square, the Chinese government called on the military to put it down. Hundreds, perhaps thousands, of unarmed students were killed in a scene that shocked the world. Thousands more protesters were imprisoned. Canada expressed its outrage at such human rights abuses by imposing a limited range of economic sanctions.

This event encouraged Canada to think about how to deal with governments that actively oppress their own people. Some analysts suggested that economic sanctions were appropriate, citing their success in overturning apartheid in South Africa (see Flashpoint, page 427). Others claimed that economic sanctions were ineffective in creating lasting political change and called for more aggressive actions. They pointed to Vietnam, North Korea, and Cuba—all of which have been hit with sanctions for more than three decades, yet have shown little change in human rights policies. This also seems to be the case in China, whose human rights policies are still criticized in the international community.

Still, Canada pursued its strategy of effective influence. When China imposed severe penalties on three political dissidents in December 1998, Canada joined the international condemnation. They felt these actions were particularly inappropriate because China had just signed the International Covenant on Civil and Political Rights. To exert positive influence, Canada agreed to co-host a joint symposium on human rights in China in July 1999. China's involvement in the

Figure 16–15 In 1989, a lone man stands in front of a fleet of army tanks in Tiananmen Square. Although no one knows who he is, he came to symbolize courage in the face of oppression.

symposium, especially as co-host, was seen as "progress in mutual efforts to explore and develop initiatives aimed at greater understanding and further implementation of international human rights standards." Canada and China also agreed to work together on several projects aimed at improving human rights. These included revising criminal law to better reflect the rights of the accused, protecting women's rights, training judges and prosecutors, and supporting the development of a legal aid system.

Canada Hosts a Human Rights Criminal

Canada's policies towards human rights abusers were questioned in 1997. That year, Vancouver hosted the Asia-Pacific Economic Cooperation (APEC) Summit. Indonesian President Suharto was scheduled to attend. The UN, however, had condemned Suharto for "grave" rights violations in the occupied island of East Timor. Indonesia invaded the former Portuguese colony in 1975. Canadian MP Svend Robinson called for the government to deny Suharto entry into the country. According to Canada's Immigration Act, any senior official of a foreign country that has engaged in gross human rights violations, war crimes, or crimes against humanity, as defined by Canadian criminal law, will be barred from Canada. Controversy erupted.

The government refused Robinson's request, stating that "President Suharto is a guest of Canada at the APEC Summit and … he will be given the proper courtesy that any guest of Canada is afforded." In response, Robinson declared, "I think it's shameful and embarrassing that Canada is rolling out the red carpet for a war criminal." Demonstrations against Suharto flared up in Vancouver and the RCMP used pepper spray to curb protesting students. Many Canadians began to question how seriously Canada took human rights.

Images
Amnesty International

> ...recognition of the inherent dignity and of the equal and inalienable rights of all members of the human family is the foundation of freedom, justice and peace in the world.
>
> —General Assembly Resolution 217 A (III), December 10, 1948

In 1961, a group of students in Portugal were arrested and jailed for raising a toast to freedom in a restaurant. British Lawyer Peter Benenson read about the incident and responded by launching a one-year campaign, "Appeal for Amnesty 1961," in a local newspaper.

The Appeal for Amnesty encouraged people to write letters to government officials in countries with **prisoners of conscience**, calling for their release. Prisoners of conscience are people who have been imprisoned for peaceful expressions of their beliefs, politics, race, religion, colour, or national origin—such as the students in Portugal. The campaign grew quickly and spread to other countries, including Canada. By the end of 1961, Amnesty International was formed.

Amnesty International is founded on the principle that "people have fundamental rights that transcend national, cultural, religious, and ideological

Figure 16–16 Amnesty International works to expose human rights abuses around the world.

boundaries." Its mandate is based on the United Nations Universal Declaration of Human Rights. The organization works to ensure fair and prompt trials for all prisoners, to end torture and executions, and to secure the release of prisoners of conscience. Each year, members worldwide join forces to campaign on human rights issues. They lobby governments for change, and draw public awareness to human rights abuses. Amnesty International also educates people on human rights issues. It encourages youth and students to become involved so that they may become "active explorers of the world around them, rather than passive recipients of human rights knowledge."

Amnesty's work was recognized when it received the Nobel Peace Prize in 1977. Today, it has more than 1 million members, subscribers, and regular donors in more than 160 countries and territories. Its members include professors, youth, students, musicians, and artists. During the mid-1980s, musicians organized concerts and world tours to support Amnesty's work, and donated all the profits to Amnesty's cause.

Amnesty in Canada

In 1986, The Canadian branch of Amnesty International played a leading role in opposing the campaign to reinstate the death penalty in Canada. Beginning in 1986, AI members lobbied MPs with letters, telegrams, and phone calls. They also wrote letters to newspapers and magazines, spoke out in public debates, organized marches, and distributed pamphlets and buttons. On June 30, 1987, the motion to reinstate the death penalty was defeated in the House of Commons by a vote of 148-127. Canadian AI members were jubilant at their ability to affect change at home.

AI's presence in Canada continues to grow, in part because of successes such as its work against the death penalty. More than 100 community action groups are active across the country. Amnesty in Canada has also focused on involving Canadian youth. Today, more than 5000 young Canadians are involved in AI youth groups that operate out of high schools, colleges, and universities from coast-to-coast.

Sometimes people who have been released through Amnesty's involvement take up the organization's cause. One such individual is Dr. Omar Del Pozo Marrero, leader of a non-violent opposition group in Cuba, who was imprisoned for opposing the Cuban government. He was often held in punishment cells and denied medical attention for his ulcers, and heart and kidney problems.

After his release in 1998, Del Pozo was forced into exile in Canada, where he spoke out on behalf of the political prisoners left behind. He told Amnesty:

> I owe my freedom to the enormous amount of work many good and humane people have done to get me released ... I am greatly indebted to people like you and I considered it my duty to help you with your efforts in favour of freedom and peace for those who suffer persecution and imprisonment.

Activities

1. Individually or with a partner, research one of the following:
   - a prisoner of conscience
   - an existing oppressive regime
   - human rights abuses in Canada or other parts of the world

   Display your findings as a poster to educate people about your topic.

2. In a two-column chart, list reasons that support and oppose Amnesty International's 1986 campaign against the death penalty in Canada. Consider what you read earlier in this chapter about the UN's need to respect national sovereignty in the Balkans. You may also want to review the Images feature on John Humphrey and the UN Universal Declaration of Human Rights in Chapter 10. Based on the reasons you list, create a poster that expresses your point of view.

Figure 16–17 What is this cartoonist saying about trade agreements?

Heritage Minute

In 1922, 15-year-old Joseph-Armand Bombardier surprised his family with a primitive-looking invention—the world's first snowmobile. With these humble beginnings in Valcourt, Quebec, Bombardier's inventive genius flourished. Today, the Bombardier company operates in eight countries on two continents. It builds everything from snowmobiles, to jet aircraft, to high-speed trains. It has become a great Canadian success story in the global economy.

THE GLOBAL ECONOMY

With the globalization of national economies, many areas of the world are working under the notion that bigger is better. Many countries have formed regional **trade blocs** to promote freer trade among member nations. As well as lifting trade barriers, some trade arrangements even share a common currency, as in the case of 11 European Union (EU) nations. The North American Free Trade Agreement (NAFTA) is a trade bloc that involves Canada, the US, and Mexico. Trade blocs are formed by agreements between two or more nations. Their purpose is to give members access to more resources, bigger markets, and more economic opportunities. For these reasons, countries have tried to expand globally.

With a global economy comes the need for organizations that will resolve disputes and ensure fair trade. Organizations such as the G7(8) meet annually to discuss such issues as the world's economy, trade, relations with developing nations, terrorism, and arms control.

Many people, however, oppose globalization. In the late 1990s, the Organization for Economic Cooperation and Development (OECD) drafted the Multilateral Agreement on Investment (MAI). It sparked protests around the world. Because the MAI was secretly negotiated, many non-OECD nations had not been consulted. These nations were pressured to support the MAI. Critics also saw the MAI as a threat to national sovereignty. The MAI's intent was to allow global investment to flow unimpeded and to prevent any restrictions on foreign investors. In Canada, this meant that many protected and regulated areas would be completely open to foreign investors. Areas such as culture, labour, and environmental standards would be "open for business." Many critics said that the MAI could allow multinational businesses to play one country off against another, causing nations to abandon environmental standards in order to compete for investment.

In the wake of the outcry, the OECD ceased negotiations on the MAI. The failure of the MAI was an indicator of things to come. In December 1999, the World Trade Organization (WTO) met in Seattle, Washington, to set the agenda for a new round of global trade talks, entitled the "Millenium Round." This WTO Summit proved to be a disaster from start to finish. No agenda was set. Thousands of people from Canada, the US, and around the world descended on Seattle. They represented every kind of interest group, and protested against what they perceived to be "differing world visions." The groups held protests against the effects of globalization on such areas as child labour, declining labour and environmental standards, poverty, and human rights abuses. Many felt that globalization was simply capitalism at its greediest. The protests turned into riots as police used tear gas and pepper spray to control the crowds.

The protests against globalization suggest that leaders of industries and nations can no longer independently make agreements that affect the lives of their citizens. The protests made it clear that all negotiations must be open to public input.

Up Close

7. Write six questions that could be answered using the information on pages 440 to 443. Exchange questions with partner, complete them, then evaluate each other's work.

Figure 16–18 WTO protesters clashed with riot police in Seattle in 1999. To many, globalization represented the excessive greed of capitalism—sacrificing human rights, national sovereignty, and the environment for the profit of a powerful few.

International Trade Agreements and Organizations

Name	Mandate	Pros and Cons
NAFTA **North American Free Trade Agreement** Formed in 1994 between Canada, the US, and Mexico	To gradually eliminate tariffs on goods and services traded among Canada, the US, and Mexico	**Pro:** The agreement is beneficial to the Canadian economy, and it is necessary for Canada to compete globally. **Con:** Canadian industries will not be able to compete on an equal footing with those in the US. As well, Canada will lose jobs as businesses move to Mexico, where labour is cheaper.
OECD **Organization for Economic Cooperation and Development** Formed in 1961 with 29 member nations	To enhance the investment and aid opportunities of its member nations	**Pro:** The organization improves the flow of investment between its members. **Con:** Because it is an independent and unelected organization, there are no checks and balances on its activities.
ASEAN **Association of Southeast Asian Nations** Formed in 1967 with 5 member nations. Membership has since doubled.	To accelerate economic growth, social progress, and cultural development; to promote regional peace and stability	**Pro:** Any political association, even if primarily economic, will help to stabilize the region. **Con:** The association lacks a commitment to human rights; two of its members, Cambodia and Indonesia, are known to have a record of human rights violations.
G7 (8) **Group of 7 (8)** Formed in 1975 of the 6 most powerful industrialized democratic nations; with the induction of Canada in 1976 the group became known as the G7; with the induction of Russia in 1999, the G8 was created.	To deal with major economic issues facing the world (international trade, relations with developing nations, employment, terrorism, environment, arms control, human rights) Summits held annually	**Pro:** The group provides a political basis for cooperation between member nations. **Con:** The group represents the interests of the developed world almost exclusively.

Name	Mandate	Pros and Cons
APEC **Asia-Pacific Economic Cooperation** Formed in 1989 by 12 Pacific Rim economies, including Canada. Membership has grown to 21.	To improve conditions for doing business in the Asia-Pacific region, with a long-term objective of a formal free-trade agreement among its members	**Pro:** The organization provides a basis for political and economic engagement in the region. **Con:** Differing political views in the region—especially in the area of human rights—are often overlooked by members.
EU **European Union** Formed in 1993 by 12 European nations Now has 15 member nations	To create "a Europe without frontiers" that shares a common currency, financial policies, and military force; to promote open immigration between members The EURO, a common currency for 11 EU members, was introduced in January 1999 and will replace national currencies by 2002.	**Pro:** An economic and political union helps to distribute wealth and opportunity throughout the continent and provides a foundation for conflict resolution. **Con:** Centralization of authority and a common currency threaten national identity and sovereignty.
WTO **World Trade Organization** Formed in 1995, replacing the General Agreement on Tariffs and Trade (GATT)	To ensure fair competition, a stable and predictable trade environment, non-discrimination among member nations, and to dispute settlements	**Pro:** It represents a first step towards a true global economy. **Con:** It represents the most extreme form of free enterprise.
G20 **Group of 20** Formed in 1999 by G7 countries Represents 19 countries, the EU presidency, the International Monetary Fund, and the World Bank	To promote international financial stability by studying and reviewing policy issues among developed and developing nations	**Pro:** It is the most inclusive international economic group to date that links the developed and developing worlds. **Con:** It is open to the same criticisms as other trade organizations, such as the OECD and WTO.

Figure 16–19

Foundations

From the Auto Pact to NAFTA

In Chapter 14, you read that the Progressive Conservative government under Brian Mulroney negotiated the Canada–US Free Trade Agreement (FTA). This was a controversial deal and was bitterly opposed by many groups. The issue dominated the 1988 federal election campaign. Despite the controversy, Mulroney won a second term in office. In January 1989, the FTA took effect, and Mulroney delivered on his promise that Canada was "open for business."

The Auto Pact

The issue of free trade has long been debated in Canada. During the 1911 federal election, Sir Wilfrid Laurier campaigned on the idea of free trade. Unlike Mulroney, Laurier lost the election. He was defeated by Conservative Robert Borden, who promised "no … trade with the Yankees." But in 1964 Canada was forced to reopen this issue. Automobile assembly plants in Ontario were struggling. They were limited to producing four or five models of automobiles for the Canadian market only. Because of the small market, the cost of producing a car was high. Tariffs on US-made automobiles made them too expensive for most Canadians. Further, with many Canadian plants using US parts, there was an imbalance in trade.

The Canada–US Automotive Products Trade Agreement (or the Auto Pact) was signed in January 1965. It guaranteed freer trade between the two countries in auto parts and automobiles. To protect Canadian interests, the government demanded that American-based auto manufactures assemble one automobile in Canada for every new automobile they sold in Canada. Otherwise, Canada would impose tariffs on imported US-assembled autos.

After the signing of the Auto Pact, the Canadian auto industry expanded and enjoyed much higher profits. In 1996, the top three Canadian exporters were auto manufacturers—General Motors, Chrysler, and the Ford Motor Company—generating collective export sales of $42.2 billion. Little wonder that the Auto Pact has been billed as Canada's greatest achievement in trade negotiations.

The Canada–US Free Trade Agreement

Although the Auto Pact was not a free trade agreement in the truest sense, it still demonstrated how a well-managed trade agreement could benefit the Canadian economy. But when Mulroney proposed freer trade with the US, many Canadians battled against it. Opposing forces—nationalists, pensioners, unions, church groups, and women's groups—suggested that free trade would benefit only big business. They contended that many Canadian jobs would be lost because Canadian industries would be unable to compete with their larger American counterparts.

Free trade was supported by many large and small businesses, financial institutions, and consumers' groups. They argued that it was needed to counteract the growing movement in the US towards protectionism, meaning that the US government was imposing tariffs and other trade barriers to protect US industries from foreign competition.

For Canada, American protectionism would be disastrous. The US is by far its largest trading partner, supplying about 70 percent of its imports and buying about 80 percent of its exports. Free trade was seen as a way to increase foreign investment in Canada, which would translate into more jobs for Canadians. And free trade would eliminate tariffs, resulting in lower prices for US goods and services.

Despite controversies, the FTA was signed. Some of the key elements of the agreement included an elimination of tariffs, a dispute-settlement mechanism, and a reduction of investment restrictions.

Economic Structures: Conditions and Structures

North American Free Trade Agreement (NAFTA)

Under the North American Free Trade Agreement (NAFTA), which came into effect in 1994, the trading agreement between Canada and the US was expanded to include Mexico. Like the FTA, NAFTA had many critics. Bob White, president of the Canadian Labour Congress, said: "The inclusion of Mexico in the FTA would further increase pressure upon Canadians to accept lower wages ... lower environmental standards and ... even more cuts to public and social services."

Many economists say it is almost impossible to accurately assess the overall impact of NAFTA on the Canadian economy. Preliminary surveys indicate it has not hurt wages or jobs. In one study, companies cited free trade agreements as the leading factor in spurring global expansion. In another study, about 50 percent of companies surveyed said their workforce has grown, and 39 percent said it has remained the same. A 1995 study by the US-based Economic Strategy Institute found that exports to the US were about $14 billion higher than they would have been without a free trade agreement. Statistics can, however, be interpreted differently by different people. While some people see the numbers as proof of success, others see them as a sign that Canada has become too dependent on the US and foreign investment.

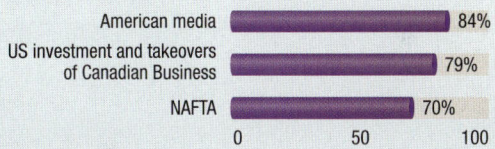

Figure 16–20 Canadian responses to this 1999 survey show widespread concern about US influence.

What Do You Think?

1. Write an essay agreeing or disagreeing with Canada's global expansion. Are we better off today? Have we sacrificed our natural resources and cultural identity for the sake of expanding globally? Use specific evidence to support your stance.

Figure 16–21 Chrysler's minivan plant in Windsor used the most up-to-date technology in the 1980s and 1990s.

Global Forces **445**

THE FORCE OF TECHNOLOGY IN GLOBALIZATION

Technology is perhaps the most powerful force in the movement towards globalization. People all over the world are now connected by telephone, television, the Internet, and electronic mail. Information travels instantaneously. Technology has ushered in the "Information Age."

As the influence of information technology has grown, people around the world have become connected in a new way, and governments have little power over information. For example, the Internet was perhaps one reason why the MAI faltered. A blitz of challenges and protests circulated on the Internet got more information out faster, and to more people, than could ever have happened through traditional media. Loss of government control has tremendous implications throughout the world, especially in closed societies such as China. It is almost certain that massive changes will occur as these countries struggle to adapt to these new realities.

> Bring me a select group of 30 hackers, and within 90 days I'll bring this country to its knees.
>
> –Jim Settle, retired director of the FBI Computer Crimes Division

Because people have become so reliant on information, having immediate access to it is crucial. Computers are at the heart of information and communication. Some have suggested that in the very near future, wars will not depend on hardware, such as planes and bombs, as much as on the control of information. In the recent past, military might was determined by access to nuclear weapons. Increasingly, these weapons are not the only factor. In information warfare, the playing field is levelled because almost any country can put together a team of hackers—experts who can crack open computer files and codes.

Just how far-fetched is that scenario? During the Kosovo conflict, a supersecret US group in the Pentagon launched a "cyber attack" as part of the military effort. It corrupted electronic communications, planted false radar targets in Yugoslavia's air defence system, and knocked out a power grid by dropping electrically charged strips of graphite in power transformers. Some sources said that if this group had been given more high-level support, the conflict would have ended a month earlier.

If technology has the potential to redefine global military powers, it has already had a tremendous effect on the global economy. This influence will become greater and greater (see Figure 16–22). It used to be said that whenever the US sneezed, Canada caught a cold. In other words, the US economy had a great impact on Canada. Although this is still true today, as the US is Canada's biggest trading partner, the circle of influence has widened. In the last years of the 1990s, Canada was exposed to the "Asian flu" as Asian stock markets tumbled. Asia's economic problems affected the whole world.

Top 10 Countries in E-Commerce				
	1998		2002*
U.S.	$37.4	U.S.	$409.0
Japan	$2.0	Germany	$62.8
Germany	$1.7	U.K.	$47.6
U.K.	$1.4	Japan	$28.8
Canada	$1.4	France	$28.5
Australia	$1.4	Canada	$19.9
France	$0.4	Italy	$18.1
Italy	$0.4	Netherlands	$12.6
Netherlands	$0.4	Sweden	$8.7
Sweden	$0.3	Spain	$8.0

* Predicted

Figure 16–22 "E-commerce" refers to business transactions conducted over the Internet. The amounts are in US$ billions.

Historical Inquiry: Investigating Historical Topics

Historian at Work

Altering History in a Digital Age

Altering historical records is not new. In Chapter 3, you learned how Reg Heath was sent back to the trenches of WW I for a third time. Convinced he would not survive, Heath had his photograph taken and sent it back to Canada. His wife then took it to a studio and had it "inserted" into a family portrait. At the very least, Heath wanted his children to know they had a father.

Heath's motive was completely personal. But photographs can be manipulated for sinister purposes. When Josef Stalin assumed absolute control of the Soviet Union in the late 1920s, he wanted to ensure his role in the history of the new state. Stalin knew that he had played a minor role when the communists had come to power in 1917. If he was in group photographs of the time at all, he was in the background. Stalin ordered new photos that showed him to be the 1917 communist leader Lenin's right-hand man. Stalin destroyed the originals, and only the altered photographs remained. Much later, a keen-eyed researcher discovered the photos had been doctored.

Today, computer-imaging technology can alter historical records and look amazingly authentic, especially with film. The process begins with old footage of a real event. Next, the film is scanned into a computer. It is now possible to put something immediately before and after the individual frames that will change the story. In other words, you can change "what happened."

Examine Figure 16–23, a still from the 1994 movie *Forrest Gump*. Here, former US President John Kennedy and Tom Hanks, the actor playing Forrest Gump, appear to be in the same scene. In the movie, they even appear to interact. However, Forrest Gump is a fictional character, and Tom Hanks was only a boy when Kennedy was assassinated in 1963. The image

Figure 16–23 Forrest Gump appears to be trailing the late US President John Kennedy.

and the scene look like genuine primary sources, yet they are complete fakes.

That historical records can be altered with such precision raises serious issues. Now a real person can be shown giving a real speech and, in the next frame, he or she can be shown having a conversation that never took place. Historians rely on many different primary sources, including photographs and news footage—so this new technology imposes the need for great vigilance. Viewers also need to be able to tell the difference between history and entertainment. In Chapter 8, you learned that historical films can be biased if a producer or director wants to make a point, regardless of facts. Today, computer imaging can distort the historical record in a more entertaining—and exasperating—way.

What Do You Think?

1. With a partner, discuss the impact of computer-imaging techniques on historical records. How might historians determine if a photograph or film footage is an accurate record? Share your opinions with the class.

2. Some businesses use computer imaging to sell their goods using "dead celebrities" as spokespersons. Company executives say that a dead celebrity will never do something to embarrass the company. As a class, discuss whether this use of historical figures is ethical.

Global influences continue to expand. Every inhabited continent has its own stock markets, and these have opened up to world investors. Some people argue that foreign investment will lead to "economic colonialism" as developed, hi-tech countries expand their influence. Others point out that Asia is rapidly becoming "wired." Taiwan, Hong Kong, and Singapore are actually exceeding Western growth in **cyberspace**. Already, more than 43 percent of the world's on-line population is non-English-speaking. And it is estimated that there will be a billion Internet users by 2003, more than 70 percent of them living outside North America.

Of particular importance to the global economy are countries such as India and China. Both have massive populations, but because of national politics have exerted limited economic influence in the past. In 1999 more than half a million Indian households had computers, 40 percent of them connected to the Internet. India could become a giant market with unprecedented power. Already a new economic class has been born, as more countries hire India's well-trained computer professionals. The surge in wealth for young Indians not only affects local economics, it challenges social structures. Changes in China could be even more dramatic. The Chinese government's decision to allow on-line trading not only opens up China to world influences, it directly challenges communist ideology. This not only has huge political, social, and economic implications for China, but for the world as a whole.

Data File

According to the *Computer Industry Almanac*, use of the Internet will skyrocket, with e-commerce revenues reaching $1.3 trillion by 2003.

SHAPING POLICIES IN THE GLOBAL VILLAGE

Globalization has raised new questions as countries struggle to come to grips with new circumstances and new roles on the global stage. Canada struggles with these issues as well. What role will we play? What will be our guiding principles?

Canada's Lloyd Axworthy has offered a vision in response to these questions. His approach recognizes the hardships that people endured in a rapidly changing world: people displaced by conflict, civil wars, and ethnic violence. The safety and security of one nation increasingly affects all other nations. And pollution and infectious diseases have become increasing global threats. Because of these new realities, Axworthy insists that people need to be at the very heart of world policies. He refers to this as "human security."

"Human security" emphasizes that policies must be created to ensure people's safety from violent and non-violent threats. This is a radical shift from traditional concerns, as it focuses on people rather than on territory and government political power. Human security has become central to the international campaign against land mines, spearheaded by Axworthy and Canada. (See next page.) It is also at the heart of the International Criminal Court, which investigates and punishes war crimes and crimes against humanity. Can this approach shape international policies around the globe?

Up Close

8. Describe Canada's role in organizing international action against the use of land mines.

Change and Continuity: Foreign Policy

Primary Source

The Ottawa Process: The Land Mines Campaign

Canada has led the international campaign to rid the world of land mines. In 1996, Minister of Foreign Affairs Lloyd Axworthy challenged world leaders to come to Ottawa to sign a convention totally banning land mines. In 1997, they came. The historic event was the result of the "Ottawa Process," which Axworthy describes below.

In December 1997, 123 countries signed a convention to eliminate the use, production, stockpiling and transfer of anti-personnel mines—more signatories than even the most optimistic supporters had envisaged at the start of the process. The ban represented a new norm in international disarmament. It was a major step towards ending the humanitarian crisis caused by these weapons of slow-motion mass destruction. And it was backed up by commitments of close to half a billion dollars US from the international community [including $100 million from Canada over the next five years]…

Attention is now focused on the next phase: ratification, universalization and full implementation of the Convention. A central element of implementation is mine action: the urgent need to clear land of mines so that people can return to their homes and their livelihoods, and the crucial long-term issue of ensuring the rehabilitation of mine victims …

The Ottawa Process emerged from the seismic shifts of world affairs since the fall of the Berlin Wall. It is only the first example of an emerging international response to these changes and the longer-term trends that underlie them …

As the Cold War standoff is replaced by a multitude of intra-state conflicts, international decision makers deal with issues that directly affect people's daily lives. It is in response to these developments that a "human security" approach has emerged, one which formulates

Figure 16–24 Princess Diana campaigned vigorously against land mines.

security goals primarily in terms of human, rather than state, needs. The land mines campaign shows how a problem viewed through a human security lens can be resolved through the principles of humanitarian law. The lives and limbs of the millions of civilians take precedence over military and national security interests …

What was unusual about the Ottawa Process was that governments and civil society worked directly together as members of a team, with remarkable success. The process was open to all—NGOs [non-government organizations], governments, the Red Cross, even individuals—and hostage to none. The coalition was setting the international agenda and exerting international leadership in the face of lack of enthusiasm or even outright hostility on the part of some larger powers …

I believe [the Ottawa Process] is a positive indicator of a new type of diplomacy suited to a new era … The democratization of international relations is a reality, one to be applauded rather than resisted.

What Do You Think?

1. Should Ottawa be spending significant money and time on removing and banning land mines? Would the money be better spent on domestic problems, such as poverty? Explain your answer in a paragraph.

CONCLUSION

In the last two decades of the twentieth century, global forces transformed Canada and the world. A nuclear disaster in Chernobyl in 1986 released clouds of radiation and set off a chain reaction of international changes. Three years later, the Berlin Wall fell and Germany was reunified. In 1991, the Soviet Union broke apart, and the Cold War came to an end. Some historians proclaimed it was the "end of history." Yet historic conflicts flared up. Between 1988 and 1992, the United Nations launched more peacekeeping missions than it had in the previous four decades. From Somalia and Rwanda, to Iraq, to the former Yugoslavia, Canada played a critical role in peacekeeping and peacemaking. Through its diplomats and foreign policy, Canada led international campaigns against apartheid in South Africa and against land mines.

Other walls also fell. Advances in communications technology linked people, organizations, and businesses instantaneously. Nations formed massive new trade blocs and organizations. Canada became part of NAFTA and pursued broader trade links around the world. Some trade agreements were made with governments that abused human rights—such as Suharto's government in Indonesia. Canada committed itself to tougher environmental standards, and struggled to achieve them.

At the start of the twenty-first century, Canada's role as a major, developed country is undisputed. Its commitment to peace and justice at home and abroad has brought Canada international recognition and respect. As Canada adapts to the competitive global economy, these values and traditions will continue to be challenged.

CHAPTER ACTIVITIES

■ Check Your Understanding

1. In your own words, explain how Marshall McLuhan's prediction that the world would become a "global village" came true during the 1980s and 1990s. In your response, identify two world events that helped McLuhan's prediction become a reality.

2. Summarize Canada's role in international affairs in the 1980s and 1990s. Create a chart to illustrate its successes and failures in this arena.

■ Develop Your Thinking

3. Choose one event from this chapter that you feel had the greatest impact—either positive or negative—on world affairs. Create a five-point argument to support your choice. Discuss

or debate your choice in class. Refer to the Historian at Work on building an argument, on page 275, for ideas.

4. Compare the changes that occurred at the beginning and the end of the twentieth century. (Refer to Chapters 1 and 2.) Which period, do you feel, experienced the greatest amount of change? Why? Create a comparison chart using the following as headings:
   - technology and communication
   - economic and environmental concerns
   - foreign policy
   - war, peace, and security

Express Yourself

5. Imagine that you work for the CBC current affairs program, "the fifth estate." It is 1999, and you have been asked to produce a ten-years-later report on the fall of the Berlin Wall. Your job is to assess its overall impact on Germany and on world affairs. Look for positive and negative outcomes, and use diverse sources in your research. Consider using one of the following formats for your presentation:
   - a live newscast from your classroom
   - a videotaped story
   - interviews with class members, who have been given roles to play
   - a Powerpoint presentation (or a similar computer program)
   - a visual retrospective, using video, still images, collage, and so on

6. Write a newspaper editorial expressing your opinion of economic globalization. Be sure to fully explain your position and to use examples, statistics, and anecdotes. Remember, the purpose of your editorial is to convince readers of your opinion.

Apply Your Learning

7. Get in touch with a member of the Canadian Forces and interview this person about Canada's changing role in international security. What do they think about modern peacekeeping and peacemaking missions? Have they been actively involved in peacekeeping? What insights can they offer ordinary Canadians on the roles and responsibilities of international peacekeepers? For help on creating other questions, refer to the Historian at Work feature on conducting an interview, on page 113.

Extend Your Learning Using the Internet

8. Media bias can affect perspectives on an event. Use archival and current Internet sources to research viewpoints on the Chernobyl nuclear accident. Brainstorm questions to be answered, and create a graphic organizer to collect and communicate your findings.

9. Trace the evolution of Canada's peacekeeping role in the United Nations. Include Canadian government and United Nations' reports in your investigation. Write a brief essay drawing conclusions about Canada's past role and predicting its future role.

Global Forces **451**

17

What History Teaches

As you read this chapter, think about the following questions:

What connections can you see?
Think about the connections among leaders, events, eras, and issues in the twentieth century.

What continuity do you see?
Think about the events and issues that seem to run like a thread throughout the century.

What comparisons can you make?
Think of both differences and similarities in leaders, issues, and conflicts.

When Sir Wilfrid Laurier claimed that the twentieth century belonged to Canada, did he envision internal harmony, prosperity, a growing role for Canada on the world stage? Certainly, he could have never predicted how much Canada would change. How could he have predicted feminism, globalization, computer technology, or the extent to which American influences would dominate Canadian culture? If history examines the forces of change, then history has become more important than ever at the beginning of the twenty-first century.

Canada has witnessed unparalleled technological and scientific advancements. These in turn have been the source of many social advances. The makeup of our population has changed. So have our attitudes, values, roles, and occupations.

To search for meanings and relationships—for "cause and effect" among so much change—makes each one of us a student of history. If we can understand what has happened to us, we might be able to anticipate what will happen next. By recognizing patterns in history, we locate lessons that we can use in the future.

Of course, many of the challenges that Canada faced when Laurier was prime minister are still being faced today. Perhaps this means that history is a story without an ending. In this chapter, you will have the opportunity to evaluate where history has taken Canada so far.

Perspectives

The statue of Sir Wilfrid Laurier, who led Canada into the twentieth century, towers over Jean Chrétien, who took the nation into the twenty-first century. What symbols of Canada are evident in this photograph? Imagine a conversation between Laurier and Chrétien occurring at this moment. What is Laurier telling Chrétien? What is Chrétien telling Laurier?

BOOKENDS TO THE CENTURY: WILFRID LAURIER AND JEAN CHRÉTIEN

Canada started and ended the twentieth century with a French-speaking, Liberal prime minister from Quebec: Sir Wilfrid Laurier, elected in 1896, and Jean Chrétien, elected in 1993. Both replaced highly unpopular Conservative governments, and then went on to complete many of the initiatives started by the governments they replaced. Laurier continued John A. Macdonald's National Dream by furthering expansion into the West. Chrétien continued the Goods and Services Tax (GST) and the free trade agreement (NAFTA) that had been established by Brian Mulroney's Conservatives.

Figure 17-1 On February 15, 1965, the old Canadian flag came down. It was replaced by the new maple leaf flag that we know today.

French-English Relations

In 1900, even more so than now, Canada was a divided country. Provincial governments clashed with the federal government, East with West, French with English, and Catholics with Protestants.

During Canada's involvement in the Boer War in South Africa (1899–1902), it became obvious to Quebecers that English Canadians considered themselves more English than Canadian. Increasingly, during the two world wars, French Canada's primary concern became the recognition of its non-British heritage. Quebecers wanted a French voice. They wanted to protect their language and culture. This concern grew, and *la survivance* (survival) became the rallying cry.

In 1963, the federal government, under Lester Pearson, tried to appease the Quiet Revolution by setting up a Royal Commission on Bilingualism and Biculturalism. Pearson legislated a new flag that wasn't British. And he offered Quebec more representation in the federal cabinet.

But Pearson's measures came late, and the last half of the century is emblazoned with famous images of French and English conflict: Charles de Gaulle's call to separatism—*Vive Le Québec Libre!* (1967) was followed by Pierre Trudeau's invoking of the War Measures Act to deal with the FLQ crisis (1970).

After 1987, Quebec separatists were not the only dissenting voice in the French-English debate. The Reform Party, born in Alberta and supported mainly by western provinces, emerged to challenge the federal government's handling of this issue. Preston Manning, the party's leader, believed that the concessions given to Quebec were unfair. The Reform Party wanted all provinces to have equal powers regardless of their cultural makeup.

As the century drew to a close, Jean Chrétien faced two separatist parties, the Bloc Québécois at the federal level and the Parti Québécois in Quebec. In 1995, voters in the second Quebec referendum chose to stay within Canada, but the federal side won by less than 1 percent. As the twenty-first century began, it seemed that Quebec was connected to Canada by a very thin thread.

With both the Reform Party and the Bloc Québécois representing regional concerns in the House of Commons, the unity question continues to be a major issue in the new millennium.

Flash Back

I didn't realize what I was getting into when I got that phone call from my father in 1964. I was just doing my father a favour, not participating in history.

—Joan Donovan

Joan Donovan stitched prototypes of the proposed flags overnight for her father Ken Donovan, when he received an urgent request from Prime Minister Lester Pearson to have the prototypes ready the next morning.

When all the referendums and debates are over, what will Canada look like at the end of this centuries-long struggle between French and English?

From Colony to Nation

Canada entered the twentieth century as a British colony. Much of the century would be spent developing independence from Britain. In 1900, Canada flew the British flag as its own, and was automatically at war whenever Britain declared war. During the 1930s, Prime Minister Mackenzie King resolutely pushed Canada toward autonomy. And during World War II, Canada first earned international recognition as an independent nation.

In 1923, Canada signed its first international treaty, the Halibut Treaty with the United States. Eight years later, in 1931, the Statute of Westminster defined a new British Commonwealth of autonomous nations, replacing the old Empire.

Figure 17-2 Showing their true colours, people celebrate Canada Day on July 1 at a street corner in Hamilton, Ontario.

Vincent Massey took up residence in Washington, DC, in 1926 as Canada's new Minister to the United States. This seemed to complete the journey to full independence. But even though the Supreme Court of Canada replaced the Judicial Committee of the British Privy Council in 1949, official independence did not come until 1982, when Prime Minister Pierre Trudeau repatriated Canada's constitution.

What official ties does Canada still have with the British Empire?

American Influence

As Canada slowly achieved independence from Britain, it grew more dependent upon the United States. In 1900, Canadian relations with the United States were conducted by the Colonial Office of the British Government. Only during the 1920s did Canada gain a more independent role in these dealings. New technologies promoted a strong bond between the two countries. American pop culture, beamed across the border through radio, was irresistible to Canadians. Canada's youth listened and danced to the same music, watched the same films, and read the same magazines as young people in the United States. With improved roads and automobiles, Canadians also began to visit the US more often.

During World War II, the two nations collaborated to help Britain defend Europe against Hitler. Prior to American involvement in 1941, many Americans who wanted to fight came north to sign up in the Canadian forces. Many young Americans served as pilots in the RCAF as North America became the "arsenal for democracy." In the postwar years, military cooperation continued through mutual participation in the United Nations and the North Atlantic Treaty Organization (NATO). Canada and the US also developed the North American Aerospace Defence Command (NORAD).

In the postwar years, the hunger for American pop culture intensified. Televisions appeared in most Canadian homes. Outside of North America, Americans and Canadians became almost indistinguishable. Many Canadians became fearful of losing their Canadian identity, but Canada–US relations continued to get stronger with an increase in economic reliance. Trade agreements signed in the 1980s and 1990s may have completed the move towards a US-dominated Canada.

Figure 17-3 The pull from the south continues today. Leading Hollywood stars such as Mike Myers (shown above) and Jim Carrey are Canadians who have made their name in the powerful US movie industry.

Canada shifted its economic dependence from one world power to another. Has it become a colony of the United States instead of a colony of Britain?

WHAT IS "CANADIAN"?

You have heard the phrase "two founding nations" several times this year. You are also aware that many Canadians are not members of the two founding nations—Britain and France.

The First Canadians

During the first half of the twentieth century, the Canadian government tried to force the first Canadians—Native peoples—to give up their rights and cultures. Following lengthy treaty negotiations, the Native peoples were no longer in charge of their own land, and were moved onto reserves where they could be "protected" from White interference. A Canadian government policy of assimilation moved Native children from their families and placed them in residential schools. Here the children could not speak their first language or observe any of their original customs. The government also prevented First Nations from forming any political organizations.

Despite these injustices, the Native peoples stayed loyal to Canada in both world wars. One in three aboriginal men enlisted during WW I. In WW II, about 6000 Native Canadians enlisted, despite discrimination in both the air force and the navy.

In the early 1960s, the Native peoples began to organize politically. The National Indian Council was formed in 1964, followed by the National Indian Brotherhood in 1968. Out of these groups came the Assembly of First Nations in 1982.

In 1969 the Trudeau government, with Jean Chrétien as its Minister of Indian Affairs, prepared a White Paper on Indian policy. It proposed to overturn the Indian Act, eliminate reserves, and transfer responsibility for Native affairs to the provinces. This move would integrate the Native population into "mainstream Canada." However, the Native peoples wanted self-government and a say in their own future. At least the Indian Act, as flawed as it was, recognized the special constitutional status of Canada's First Nations. Native elders, helped by the newly formed National Indian Brotherhood, succeeded in having the White Paper withdrawn. But Trudeau, who believed in a strong central government, refused to negotiate on the issues of self-government and outstanding land claims.

In 1973, another major event took place. The Supreme Court upheld the Nisga'a title to their land claim in British Columbia. This opened the door for more land claims, and strengthened the movement towards self-government. In the late 1990s, the territory of Nunavut was established, and the Nisga'a land claim was settled.

Figure 17-4 The promise of a new Canada: Young Shanice Peal, in traditional dress, celebrates the settlement of the Nisga'a treaty.

Can Canada continue as a united country if it consists of many self-governing nations? Or can nationhood mean "related independences"?

Canada's Immigrants

The building of Canada as a nation has depended on immigrants: first the British and French, then other Western Europeans, then people from other parts of the world. Early non-British settlers, such as the Chinese and Sikhs, were not considered desirable by the European community. To restrict the flow of Chinese immigrants, the government imposed a head tax that rose from $50 in 1885, to $100 in 1900, and then $500 by 1903. In 1914, the ship the *Komagata Maru*, which brought 400 Punjabis, mostly Sikhs, was forced back to India amidst cries of "White Canada forever" and "Rule Britannia."

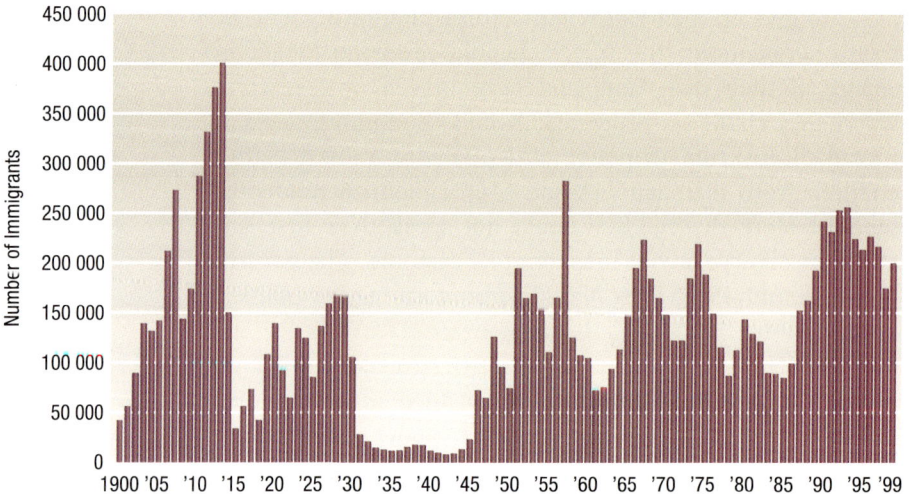

Figure 17–5 Immigration: Historical Perspectives, 1900-1999

Rhetoric versus Reality With its diverse population, Canada was the first country in the world to adopt official multiculturalism. It is the only constitutional multicultural state, meaning that the Charter of Rights and Freedoms guarantees fundamental rights to each Canadian, regardless of place of birth. Canada encourages the vision of "ethnocultural diversity, not cultural assimilation." Today, Prime Minister Jean Chrétien calls this vision "The Canadian Way."

Laurier was actually one of the first people to describe this vision of Canada as a multicultural reality. When he travelled to England and saw its impressive cathedral architecture, he said: "It is the image of a nation I would like to see Canada become ... I want the marble to remain marble, the granite to remain granite, the oak to remain oak, and on all these elements, I would build a nation great among the nations of the world."

But government rhetoric is one thing, and the reality of living in a multicultural society is another. It was not until 1991, for example, that a Sikh RCMP officer won the right to wear a turban and keep his beard. Research suggests that many White Canadians are uncomfortable when immigrants continue to speak their own language, wear their traditional dress, and practise their "un-

Figure 17-6 Constable Baltej Singh Dhillon, a Sikh, was the first RCMP graduate to wear a turban and keep his beard.

Canadian" ways. Journalist Diane Francis greeted the RCMP dress code decision with these remarks: "To me, allowing a mounted policeman to wear a turban is equivalent to letting someone change the words of our anthem or fly our flag with a *fleur de lis* or stars and stripes in the corner."

Do You Have Canadian Experience? According to Citizenship and Immigration Canada, recent immigrants had higher levels of education than the Canadian-born population. One-third of adult immigrants in 1998 had a university degree. Despite their skills and education, when they arrived in Canada they were often unable to find the jobs they were trained to do. Many immigrants, faced with "no Canadian experience, no work," had to start from the bottom, get retrained, or find menial work.

To help ensure representation of certain groups of Canadians, the Employment Equity Act of 1986 was introduced in the workplace. It required that hiring practices must reflect the wider community, which meant hiring more visible minorities, along with Native Canadians, women, and people with disabilities.

Flash Back

Our vision is of a diverse and cohesive society. A global society that is home to all the world's cultures. A multicultural society. A society that serves as an example to the world of how different people can live, learn and work together successfully, in a climate of acceptance, respect and understanding.

– Elinor Caplan, Minister of Citizenship and Immigration, December 10, 1999

Multicultural Challenges With a declining birth rate and an aging population, Canada needs immigrants to sustain its population. In the year 2000, immigration levels were set at about 1 percent of the population per year, or about 200 000 to 225 000 each year. As well, the proportion of skilled newcomers was increased. The government also planned to continue providing a safe home for refugees fleeing persecution.

With the emergence of a knowledge-based economy, entry-level jobs are disappearing for immigrants, and there is a stronger emphasis on communications skills. According to Elinor Caplan, globalization is "weakening the level of attachment that people feel for countries and national governments ... As international markets become more fluid, we will need to look at non-traditional ways to bind newcomers more closely to their communities and to Canada."

Who is a "real Canadian"? Who isn't? How do new Canadians develop a sense of belonging?

Figure 17-7 The future of Canada

THE WOMEN'S MOVEMENT

Women in Canada entered the twentieth century with few legal rights. Besides not having the right to vote, they had no legal authority over their children, and they could not own property without their husband's consent. At that time, women were not protected from exploitation and abuse.

Lady Aberdeen, wife of the governor general, founded the National Council of Women of Canada (NCWC) in 1893, which worked to improve the status of women, children, and society through education and advocacy. Most women's groups were comprised of older, well-educated, and employed middle-class women of Western European descent.

The Wartime Elections Act of 1917 extended the right to vote to all women in the armed forces, and to women who were related to military men. A year later, all Canadian women over the age of 21 received the right to vote. And in 1919, women gained the right to hold a seat in the House of Commons.

In the years following World War I, a new spirit was awakened. Young women began to smoke and drink in public. They wore short skirts, bobbed their hair, and danced the scandalous Charleston. Women played more competitive sports, and even participated in the Olympics. The famous Edmonton Grads, a women's basketball team, beat everyone in sight, including men's teams! The Miss Canada pageant, held for the first time in the 1920s, was the epitome of impropriety as it publicly paraded young women in bathing suits. Throughout the 1920s, women such as Emily Murphy and Nellie McClung fought for women's legal rights. In 1929, with the NCWC playing a crucial role, women finally were declared "persons."

The Second Wave of Feminism

In the 1960s, the women's movement experienced a rebirth. Women began to question the homemaking role to which they had been confined following WW II. By the mid-1960s, Canadian feminists were demanding an equal role for women in all areas of public life. Prime Minister Lester Pearson responded by appointing a Royal Commission on the Status of Women in 1967.

The 1960s also ushered in the sexual revolution, which had a huge impact on women. Better contraception allowed Canadians to plan the size of their families, and women could pursue more options outside the home. In 1969, abortion became legal, although access was limited. Two decades later, in 1988, the government declared the abortion law unconstitutional, and the practice was decriminalized. The abortion issue is controversial, and debate surrounding it continues.

Flash Back

On Monday, Dec. 17, I polled my first vote! I have never... felt any particular interest in politics. Perhaps this was because a woman could take only a theoretical interest anyhow ... And now that women have, or are soon to have, the vote I do not at all expect a new heaven or a new earth as the result. I hope and believe that certain reforms will be brought appreciably near by the women's vote. But I suspect that matters will jog on in pretty much the same way for a good while yet ...

– Lucy Maud Montgomery diary entry, December 19, 1917

Today's Women's Issues

Women's rights were finally guaranteed in the Canadian Human Rights Act of 1978, and the Charter of Rights and Freedoms of 1982. In 1986, the Employment Equity Act required that businesses "go beyond voluntary efforts at fairness and intentionally hire and promote" women, visible minorities, Native people, and people with disabilities. This move has helped women move increasingly into professions that were previously dominated by men.

Women have made tremendous progress in the past century. By the early 1990s, there were more female than male undergraduates at Canada's universities. Almost 42 percent of graduate students were female. In 1996, women led about 33 percent of Canadian companies. In the 1993 federal election, 53 women were elected to the 295-seat House of Commons—the highest number in Canada's history. By the close of the century, the second female governor general, Adrienne Clarkson, was chosen. Her appointment, as both a female and an immigrant, truly symbolized the new Canada as it moved into the twenty-first century.

Figure 17-8 Today, women can choose their own profession. Canada's second female astronaut, Julie Payette, can attest to this fact.

Data File

Women now make up 45% of the Canadian labour force, compared with 36% in 1975. The number of women who are self-employed has increased 172% since 1975. Women now make up 30% of all self-employed people in Canada.

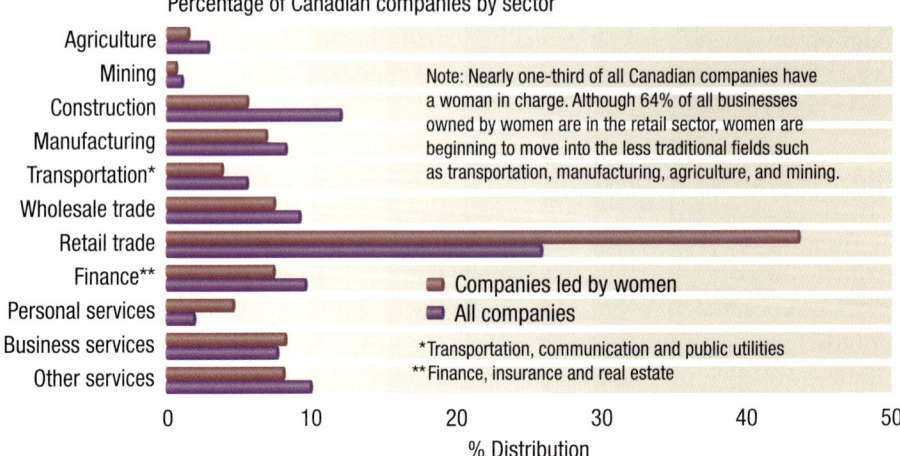

Figure 17-9 Percentage of Companies Led by Women in Selected Sectors, 1996

However, studies show that the wage gap between men and women has persisted, and statistics suggest that 40 percent of women in the workplace still experience some form of sexual harassment.

What do you think could be the next most important achievement for women in Canada?

TECHNOLOGY AND PROGRESS

At the beginning of the twentieth century, the average person lived in a small world compared to the global world you inhabit. Few people worked or travelled far from their birthplace, and usually there was little need for a formal education. But in the twentieth century, distances shrank. New populations and ideas grew. With the first successful flight in 1903 by the Wright brothers, and the introduction of mass-produced cars in 1908 by Henry Ford, society had increased mobility. Regional perspectives became national, national perspectives became international, and international perspectives became global.

The Impact of the Computer Of all recent innovations, computer technology has had the greatest impact. It has reduced the need for human labour and shortened the time it takes to perform tasks. Computers have revolutionized the workplace. Computers have also had surprising effects on work and social behaviours. While older technologies gave people the ability to roam further from their homes, many people are using the new technologies to avoid doing so. With a trend towards "telecommuting," many people now work at home. And more and more people are shopping from home. Increasingly, people are even socializing on the

Internet. Some people wonder if this is creating a kind of social isolation. Others insist that the Internet has opened channels of communication that bridge cultural, geographical, sexual, and age barriers. What is next?

When we look back at the people and technologies of 1900, it is easy to feel superior. How could they not know about these things? How could they justify their beliefs? But we should keep in mind that this is the fate of every generation—our own included.

> Which of today's technologies, beliefs, and values might the people of 2100 consider primitive and absurd? Why?

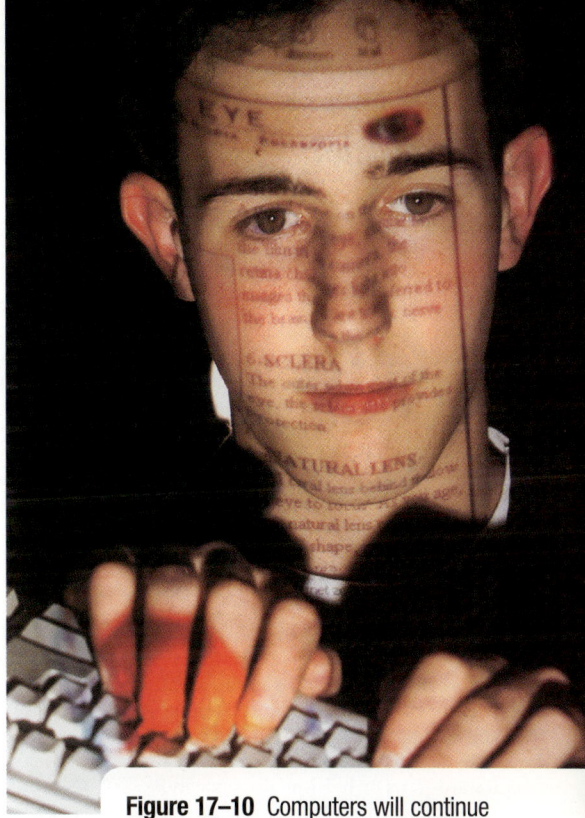

Figure 17–10 Computers will continue to have a profound impact on the future.

LOOK BACK

1. a) Reread the Flashpoint features and other pivotal events presented throughout the textbook. Working alone or in a small group, develop three or four criteria for determining what makes an event pivotal. For example, you might consider the extent to which it changed Canada at the time, or the impact it still has on Canadians today. Using your criteria, pick the most important event in Canada's twentieth-century history.

   b) Present your choice to the class using one of the following styles:
   - written essay
   - oral presentation
   - Powerpoint presentation
   - web page

2. a) The Order of Canada is our country's highest honour. It is awarded twice a year to recognize the lifetime achievement of people who have made a difference—whether locally, nationally, or internationally. Create a list of criteria to determine when and how an individual truly made a difference. For example, you might consider the impact the individual had on the lives of ordinary Canadians, and/or the impact he or she had in a specific area (culture, sports, business, and so on).

   b) Using your criteria, begin by rereading the Images features in the textbook. Then select an individual to nominate for the Order of Canada. (You may pick a Canadian individual from any part of the book.) Present your nomination in the form of an essay or oral presentation, focusing on how the individual made a difference to Canada and Canadians.

Data File

At IBM Canada, 20% of employees telecommute (work at home).

According to a survey conducted by Ekos Research, 55% of 3500 Canadian respondents want to telecommute, 43% would switch companies to telecommute, and 33% would choose telecommuting over a raise.

GLOSSARY

acceptable losses a wartime strategy that calculates the number of lives, including civilian lives, that may be sacrificed to achieve objectives

affiliate an organization associated with another

Afrikaner a South African descendant of seventeenth-century Dutch settlers

Allies during WW I, the countries that fought the Central powers, primarily Britain and the nations of the British Empire, (including Canada,) France, Russia, and later the US; during WW II, the countries that fought the Axis powers

amalgamate to combine many things into one unified whole

amending formula an authorized way to change the Constitution of Canada

anthropological relating to the scientific study of the origins and physical, social, and cultural development of human beings

anti-Semitism hostility or prejudice towards Jews or Judaism; discrimination against Jews

appeasement a policy of granting concessions to potential enemies to maintain peace

appointed an office filled by political assignment rather than by election

archaeological the study of the physical remains of past human cultures

armistice a temporary ceasefire; a truce

Aryan the Nazi idealized race, a Caucasian gentile, especially of the Nordic type

assimilate to absorb into the dominant, or majority, culture

auditor general the person responsible for examining the financial accounts of government departments and agencies

autonomy self-government, or the right of self-government

Axis the nations that fought the Allies during WW II; Germany, Italy, and Japan

Balkan States territories and countries that include Albania, Bulgaria, continental Greece, southeast Romania, European Turkey, and the territories organized as Yugoslavia in 1918

bias a preference or inclination that prevents impartial, or fair, judgment

billet lodging for troops

binding arbitration a decision by an impartial referee that is imposed on labour and management to end a lockout or strike

blitzkrieg German for "lightning war"; a swift, sudden military offensive

bloc a group of nations united for common action

branch plant a business operation owned by a parent business that makes all major decisions

buffer zone a neutral area between two hostile states that serves to prevent conflict

bunker an underground defensive position with gun emplacements above

Canadian content television and radio programming that is determined to be Canadian according to criteria established by government regulations

capital money and material resources used to create wealth

capitalist one who invests capital in business; especially someone who has a financial interest in an important enterprise, and great wealth

census metropolitan area an urban area with a population of more the 100 000 people

Centennial year 1967, the year of Canada's hundredth birthday

chlorine gas a poisonous yellowish gas used as a chemical weapon during WW I, also known as "mustard gas."

chronology the arrangement of events in time

cipher a system in which letters or numbers are organized to create a secret code; the key to such a system

civil rights movement a US political movement in the 1950s and 1960s to secure equal treatment for minority groups, especially Black Americans

collective bargaining negotiation between union representatives and employers to determine wages, hours, and working conditions

collective security secured defence for a group of countries

communism an economic system characterized by state ownership of property and the organization of labour for the common good

communistic inclined towards communism, or state control of the means of production and distribution

concentration camp a German-run camp during WW II where prisoners of war, enemy aliens, and political prisoners were detained and confined, typically under harsh conditions (see also "extermination camps")

conscription compulsory military service

conservation controlled use of a resource with the intention to preserve it

containment a policy keeping the expansion of a hostile power or ideology in check

controlling interest ownership of enough shares in a company to influence company policy

convoy a group of ships that travelled together, especially during WW II, for protection, especially from German submarines, or U-boats

corvette a fast, lightly armed warship, especially effective in antisubmarine operations

credit an arrangement for deferred payment of a loan or purchase

creeping barrage a WW I trench-warfare strategy in which heavy gunfire was shot just in front of advancing troops

cultural mosaic a society or nation composed of many distinct cultural and ethnic groups, such as Canada

cultural pluralism the condition in which different cultures can coexist within one nation

cyberspace the electronic or digital space created by computer networks and the Internet

decentralize to distribute political power among regions or provinces

decree an order with the force of law

deficit the amount by which an amount of money falls short of the required amount; a shortage

deflation a persistent decrease in consumer prices or a persistent increase in the purchasing power of money

democracy government by the people, exercised either directly or through elected representatives

demographic trends patterns that emerge in the study of the characteristics of human populations

depression a prolonged period of economic decline, characterized by decreasing production and business activity and high unemployment

dictatorship absolute control or power; a state or government under this kind of rule

diktat a harsh settlement imposed on a defeated party

direct investment money that is invested in a company or project rather than in shares or bonds of the company

division during WW I, a military unit of 20 000 soldiers, composed of several brigades

dominion one of the self-governing nations of the British Commonwealth,

draconian exceedingly harsh or severe

draft dodger a US citizen who came to Canada to avoid or protest being conscripted into the US military during the Vietnam War (1964–1973)

dust bowl a region left arid by drought and dust storms, as in the Prairies during the 1930s
duty a government tax generally imposed on imports
economic sanctions trade and economic actions taken against a country to force it to change a policy
economic stagnation a period when the economy does not grow
ecosystem an ecological community interacting with its environment
effective influence foreign policy that relies on engagement and dialogue to influence other, oppressive governments
elite a group or class of persons enjoying superior social, economic, or intellectual status
enfranchisement the right to vote
entrench to protect rights by placing them within the Constitution
equalization grants federal financial grants extended to less prosperous regions of Canada
era a period of time characterized by a certain circumstances, events, or people
espionage the practice of using spies to obtain secret information
ethnic cleansing the removal of an ethnic group from a society, by expulsion and/or mass murder
European Union a political and economic union of European countries
evidence things or testimony that help to form a conclusion or judgment
expeditionary force a military unit sent out with a definite objective
exploitation rate the amount of a resource extracted compared to the total amount available
expropriate to seize property for public use and benefit
extermination camp German-run camp during WW II where Jews, Gypsies, homosexuals, the disabled, and other groups were held and then starved or worked to death, gassed, or executed
eyewitness account first-person evidence
fallout (nuclear) the radioactive debris that falls after a nuclear explosion or accident
fascism a government marked by a totalitarian dictator, socioeconomic controls, suppression of the opposition, and usually a policy of aggressive nationalism and racism
field hospital a mobile hospital that is set up near the front line of a war
financial downturn a period when the economy slows down, with higher unemployment
flapper a woman in the 1920s who disregarded conventional codes of dress and behaviour

front the most forward line of a combat force
genocide the systematic, planned extermination of an entire national, racial, political, or ethnic group
ghettos an area of a city in which Jews were required to live
glasnost a Russian word that means "open dialogue"
global warming an increase in the world's temperature because of higher levels of carbon dioxide and other greenhouse gases
grassroots people at the local level rather than at the political centre
gross national product the total value of all goods and services produced within a country over a specified period of time
hate group an organization that advocates hostility or violence towards persons or groups based on their race, religion, ethnic origin, sexual orientation, or gender
head tax a tax imposed on new immigrants to a country, often to stop certain groups from immigrating
historical account a narrative or record of past events and experiences
historical narrative the story of past times and events as told through the lived experiences of people; their impact on the past, present, and future
Holocaust the mass slaughter of European Jews, Gypsies, and others by the Nazis during World War II
imperial conference a meeting of nations of the British Empire
imperial policy the policy of extending a powerful nation's authority over other nations through territorial acquisition or economic and political power
index to adjust wages, taxes, pension, and social benefits to take a rising cost of living into account
indictment a formal accusation of wrongdoing
inflation a persistent increase in the price of consumer goods or a persistent decrease in the purchasing power of money
insular isolated, cut off
Inuktitut the language of the Inuit, especially those of the eastern Canadian Arctic
inventory the quantity of goods in stock and available for sale
Iron Curtain the military, ideological, and political barrier between Western Europe and the Soviet controlled countries of Eastern Europe during the Cold War (1945–1990)
isolationism national policy of abstaining from political or economic relations with other countries
junior cabinet position a minister chosen by the prime minister to oversee an area of government policy but not with the full resources or a full department as with a senior cabinet minister
left-wing the liberal or radical faction of a group
liberty free from restriction or control
licence permission to break normal rules of speech or behaviour
marginalize to force to the outside, or margins, of a society
mark the German unit of currency
Marshall Plan a massive US-led aid program to help Western Europe and Japan rebuild after WW II
melting pot a place where immigrants of different cultures or races form an integrated society, as in the US
middle power a moderately powerful country that can act as a negotiator between more powerful nations
misinformation information meant to mislead
missile gap the advantage one nuclear power has over another in the number of nuclear weapons stockpiled or the technology to deliver nuclear warheads
monopoly exclusive control over the production and distribution of a good or service
moratorium suspension of an activity
most-favoured-nation a trade category by which a nation extends preferred trading policies to another nation
multiculturalism government policies and programs meant to preserve varied cultural identities
national debt the amount of money the Canadian government owes to creditors; the accumulation of annual deficits
nationalization ownership by the state or nation
nationalize to change from private to government ownership and control
net wealth the value of all Canada's tangible assets minus its net foreign debt
neutrality laws a series of US laws passed between 1935 and 1937 that forbade US trade with any nations at war
no man's land the dangerous area between the trenches during WW I
nuclear holocaust the feared destruction of all life on Earth by a nuclear war
old-growth forest a mature forest with a complex ecosystem, including wildlife and plants
overproduction producing too much of a good or service
pacifist one who believes in settling disputes peacefully
partition to divide a country into separate states
patriate to bring full governing authority back to Canada from Britain
patronage the power to appoint people to political positions

peg to fix at a certain level or within a certain range

per capita income *per capita* is Latin for "by heads"; the total income of a country or province divided by its population

perestroika a Russian word that means "restructuring"

philanthropic organization an organization formed to provide charitable assistance

pillbox a low-roofed gun emplacement

plebiscite a direct vote in which the entire electorate votes on a proposal

polarize to split into opposing principles or positions with no point of agreement

potlatch ceremony among some aboriginal peoples of the Northwest Coast at which the host distributes gifts according to each guest's rank or status

pragmatist someone who believes that the meaning of an idea lies in its practical consequences

preliterate a culture with no written language

press baron a person who owns and controls a large number of newspapers

primary sources direct historical evidence, such as artifacts and original documents

prisoner of conscience a person imprisoned for peaceful expression of their social, political, or religious beliefs

privatize to change from government to private ownership and control

production capacity the amount of goods a manufacturer can produce with existing facilities

progressive taxation a system whereby the tax rate increases with the amount of income a person earns

proliferate to increase or spread at a rapid rate

protectionism economic policies that protect domestic industries by imposing tariffs and duties on foreign goods and services

public ownership something owned and administered by a government for the public

railway rolling stock railway engines and cars

ratify to confirm or formally approve

ration to restrict the distribution of certain scarce goods

recession a time of economic slowdown

reciprocity a cooperative exchange of trade privileges between nations

Red Ensign the flag of Canada until 1965

referenda direct, public votes on proposed policies or laws

refugee a person fleeing war or persecution in one country and seeking refuge in another

regional disparity the unequal distribution of economic prosperity among Canada's regions

reliability when applied to evidence, that which is trustworthy and appropriate

residential school a boarding school run by a religious order or government to educate and assimilate aboriginal children (in Canada, 1830s–1950s)

rumrunner an alcohol smuggler during Prohibition in the 1920s and 1930s

run (on money) the sustained selling of a nation's currency in international currency markets

rust a fungal disease of grain crops

satellite (state, country) a state or country dominated by another, more powerful country

search engine a computer software program used to search the World Wide Web for web sites and web pages

search string a string of letters, characters, and words that are entered into a search engine to find information on the World Wide Web

secondary sources indirect historical evidence, such as textbooks and newspaper editorials

sedition conduct or language which incites rebellion against the authority of the state

self-government political self-determination, or autonomy

show trial a staged trial that violates legal procedure, meant to frighten the public and strengthen government control

social justice a concept that a society must be organized to allow equal opportunity for all members

solidarity unity of interests, opinions, or purpose

sovereignty independence from external control, self-government

sovereignty-association a proposed economic and political association between a sovereign Quebec and the remaining provinces and territories of Canada

SS (Nazis) abbreviation for the German word *Schutzstaffel*; an elite quasi-military unit of the Nazi Party

stagnation (economy) a period marked by lack of growth in production and living standards

staple goods major items of trade in steady demand; such a basic food items

status a federally registered member of an Indian band

strike down to rule that a law is unconstitutional

suburban municipality a city that springs up on the outskirts of large cities

subversive intended to overthrow or undercut authority

superpower a world power or influential nation, especially the nuclear powers of the US and USSR during the Cold War

surplus the amount of money that exceeds the required amount

sustainable development economic growth that meets human needs while protecting nature's ability to renew itself

systemic something that runs through or pervades an entire system or society

tariff a duty or tax imposed by a government on imports and/or exports

Third Reich *Reich* is German for "empire"; Germany between 1933–1945, under the rule of Hitler

time line a line marked out evenly in years (or other units of time) to record events

title the legal right to the control of land

totalitarianism government in which political authority exercises absolute control over all aspects of life

trade bloc a group of nations or regions that are linked to promote trade and investment

transfer payments money and tax credits that the federal government annually disperses to the provinces and territories for social programs

trench warfare war conducted from a permanent battle front of dug-out trenches

tsar a male emperor who ruled Russia (until the revolution of 1917)

U-boat a submarine of the German Navy

underconsumption when consumers buy less than they can afford or have consumed in the past

unilateral of or relating to only one side of a negotiation

Union Jack the flag of the United Kingdom, or Britain

validity when applied to evidence, that which can be defended and supported

Victoria Cross Britain's highest award for heroism in war

victory bonds government bonds sold to civilians in order to finance the war effort

Vietnam War the war between Communist North Vietnam and South Vietnam (1954–1975) in which US military forces were involved from 1964–1973

visible minority a population whose physical appearance is different from the majority

web site a group of data files (web pages) located at one address on the World Wide Web

wildcat strike an illegal strike, held before a contract expires and without the union's approval

INDEX

A
Abbott, Sir John, 7
Aberhart, William "Bible Bill", 138
aboriginal people. see Native peoples
abortion, 286, 300, 380, 461
advertising, 10, 104, 105, 106
African National Congress (ANC), 427
Aglukark, Susan, 407
agriculture, 21-22, 94, 103, 122, 129-130
Ahern, Thomas, 21
Air Canada, 211
Aird Commission, 112
Aitken, Max (Lord Beaverbrook), 22, 63, 78
Alaska Boundary Dispute, 33, 36, 194
Alberta, 194
 and Firearms Act, 383
 oil industry, 210, 215, 344, 352-353
 western alienation, 352-353, 359
Alberta Wheat Pool, 94
Alward, Doug, 354
Amalgamated Association of Street Railway Employees, 25
Amnesty International, 438-439
Annan, Kofi, 203
Anne of Green Gables (book), 42
anti-apartheid movement, 427
Anti-Inflation Board (AIB), 346
anti-Semitism 158, 160-161, 162, 175
Antoine, Jim, 351
appeasement, 167
Arab–Israeli War, 276
Arbour, Louise, 430
Arcand, Denys, 386
Arctic Water Pollution Prevention Act, 350
arts, 45-46, 296-298, 385-389
 literature, 42, 44, 144, 387
 music, 143, 388-389
 painting, 45-46, 78-79, 106, 297
 theatre, 45-46
 war art, 78-79
Aryan race, 158
Asbestos Strike, 217, 245, 286
Asia-Pacific Economic Cooperation (APEC) Summit 437
Assembly of First Nations (AFN), 304, 401, 457
Athabaska Tar Sands, 344
atomic bomb. see nuclear weapons
Atomic Energy of Canada Ltd., 267
Attlee, Clement, 262
Atwood, Margaret, 298, 387
Auschwitz, 201
automobiles, 105, 128, 219
Automotive Products Trade Agreement (Auto Pact), 444
autonomy, 150-153
Avro Arrow, 244, 265, 270, 271

Axis forces, 191
Axworthy, Lloyd, 436, 448, 449

B
Baby Boom, 218, 291, 338, 373, 374
Baby Boom Echo, 373, 374
Baby Bust, 373
Bailey, Ace, 144
Baldwin, F. W., 21
Balfour Report, 152, 328
Balkan States, 429
Ball, James, 110
Barlow, Maude, 413
basketball, 48, 111
Battle of the Atlantic, 177
Battle of Britain, 177
Battle of Dieppe, 180-181, 194
Battle of the Somme, 72-73
Battle of Vimy Ridge, 73, 74-75, 76
Battle of Ypres (second), 72
Battle of Ypres (third), 73
beaver, 34
Beaverbrook, Lord (Max Aitken), 22
Beck, Adam, 20
Belanger-Campeau Commission, 397
Bell, Alexander Graham, 21
Benenson, Peter, 438
Bennett, R. B. 22, 124, 125, 126, 127, 132, 133-134, 137, 143, 164
Berger Commission, 351
Berger, Thomas, 306, 307, 350-351
Berlin Wall, 259, 425, 449
Best, Carrie, 229
bias, 11, 390-391, 409
bibliography, 303
"Big Five", 273
Bill 22, 320
Bill 85, 318, 319
Bill 101, 318, 320, 321, 322
Bill C-2, 419
Bill C-68, 382-383
bilingualism, 8, 247, 289, 312-313, 318-323, 454, 455
Bird, Florence, 300
Bird, Will R., 64-65
Birkenau, 201
birth control, 370, 461
birth rate, 374, 460
Bishop, Billy, 71
Black Canadians
 immigrants, 97, 98
 in politics, 301
 in World War I, 57-58
 in World War II, 186
Black, George, 14
Black, Martha Purdy, 14
Black Tuesday, 120, 121, 122
Blair, Frederick, 163
Blakeney, Alan, 331
the Blitz, 179
blitzkrieg, 168
Bloc Québécois, 397, 399, 400, 455
Boer War, 31, 454
Bolshevik Revolution, 155

BOMARC anti-aircraft missile, 270, 272
Boom Bust and Echo (book), 373
Borden, Robert, 20, 32, 37, 54, 59, 61, 66, 69, 80, 87, 88, 95, 444
Bouchard, Lucien, 397, 402, 403, 404
Bourassa, Henri, 31, 32, 37, 56, 93
Bourassa, Robert, 305, 314, 316, 317, 320, 328, 396, 397, 398
Boutros-Ghali, Boutros, 428
Bowell, Mackenzie, 7, 237
British Columbia, 7
 in the Great Depression, 136
 immigration, 14, 16
 native land claims, 18, 305, 406, 408, 457
British Commonwealth, 125, 152, 153, 278, 427, 455
British Commonwealth Air Training Plan (BCATP), 177
British Empire, 30-32
British immigrants, 16-17
British North America (BNA) Act, 6, 240, 241, 302, 313, 328
Broadcasting Act, 296
Broadfoot, Barry, 133
Bronfman, Samuel, 95
Brown, Rosemary, 301
Burns, Tommy, 48
Bush, George, 429
business cycle, 123, 339, 342
Busy Man's Magazine (Maclean's) (magazine), 42
Byng, Julian, 73, 74, 91

C
Cabot, John, 411
Calgary Declaration, 403
Calgary Stampede, 12, 48
Cameron, Stevie, 382
Campbell, Kim, 399
Canada Council, 223, 298, 385
Canada Development Corporation, (CDC), 348
Canada Elections Act, 419
Canada, Foundations for the Future (book), 11
"Canada the Good", 433
Canada–U.S. relations, 446
 cultural, 111-112, 141-142, 221-222, 296, 385, 456
 economic, 36, 121, 153, 339, 347-348, 349, 356, 385, 412, 444, 456
 political, 33, 151, 278, 356
Canada West Foundation, 351
Canadair, 349
Canadarm, 358
Canada's 100 Days, 76-77
Canadian Airborne Regiment, 433
Canadian Alliance, 359
Canadian Anti-Apartheid Register, 427
Canadian Astronaut program, 357
Canadian Bill of Rights, 244, 305
Canadian Broadcasting Corporation (CBC), 141, 221-222, 385, 387, 388, 407

Canadian Centre for Advanced Film Studies, 386
Canadian Charter of Rights and Freedoms, 244, 274, 307, 331, 378, 380, 381, 384, 389, 406, 458, 461
Canadian Citizenship Act, 218, 266
The Canadian Courier, 22
Canadian Environmental Protection Act, 414
Canadian Expeditionary Force, 56, 72
Canadian Film Development Corporation (Telefilm Canada), 298
Canadian Human Rights Act, 301, 302, 381, 461
Canadian Human Rights Commission, 302
Canadian Human Rights Tribunal, 302, 381
Canadian Japanese Association, 58
Canadian Labour Congress (CLC), 216, 301, 445
Canadian Labour Union, 25
Canadian Manufacturers' Association, 16
Canadian National Railway, 92, 98, 111, 126
Canadian Pacific Railway, 7, 98, 136, 210
Canadian Peace Congress, 273
Canadian Radio Broadcasting Commission, 112, 141
Canadian Radio-television Telecommunications Commission (CRTC), 223, 296, 387-389
Canadian Rodeo Hall of Fame, 48
Canadian Suffrage Association, 38
Canadian War Records Office, 78
Canadian War Museum, 78
Canadian Women's Press Club, 39
CANDU nuclear reactor, 267
capital punishment, 378
Carr, Emily, 45, 107, 108-109
Carr, Shirley, 301
Carson, Rachel, 221
Catherwood, Ethel, 110
Central Region, 37, 102, 129
Challenger (space shuttle), 357, 358
Chamberlain, Neville, 167, 168
Chanak, 150
Charest, Jean, 401
Charlesworth, Hector, 106
Charlottetown Accord, 398, 403
Chatelaine (magazine), 143
Chernobyl, 424, 434
children's allowance, 169
China, 164, 279, 356, 436, 446, 448
Chinese Canadians
 immigrants, 12-13, 98, 458
Chinese Immigration Act, 13
Chrétien, Jean, 327, 330, 331, 350, 399, 401, 404, 416, 432, 454, 457, 458
Churchill, Winston, 167, 179, 181, 258

467

Cité Libre (magazine), 246
Citizens' Committee of 1000, 86, 87, 91
Citizens' Forum on Canada's Future, 397
Citizenship and Immigration Canada, 459
Clarion (The Negro Citizen) (newspaper), 229
Clark, Joe, 307, 326, 329, 352, 366, 398
Clarkson, Adrienne, 376, 461
Claxton, Brian Brooke, 263
Clayoquot Sound, 413
Clergue, Francis, 20
Clinton, Bill, 401
cod stocks, 411
Cohen, Leonard, 291
Cold War, 260-266, 269, 273, 278, 295, 426, 429, 431, 449
collectives, 155
Columbia (space shuttle), 358
Committee for Industrial Organizations (CIO), 138, 140
Commonwealth Committee of Foreign Affairs on South Africa, 427
Communism, 155, 165, 187, 258, 259, 266, 272, 279, 424, 426
Communist Party of Canada (CPC), 187
concentration camps, 162, 198-199, 201
Confederation, 6, 7, 93, 236-237
Conference on Environment and Development, 435
Congress of Canadian Women, 228
conscription, 32, 61, 69-70, 92, 184, 286
constitution, 6, 403
  patriation of, 313, 323, 328-331, 378, 396, 456
Constitution Act, 378, 384, 403
consumer society, 104, 128, 210, 218-220, 338
Cools, Anne, 294
Coon Come, Matthew, 410
Co-operative Commonwealth Federation (CCF) (New Democratic Party), 87, 136, 140, 169, 216, 238, 240, 241, 241
Corbière-Laval, Jeannette, 304
Council of Canadians, 413
counterculture, 291, 294
Cree, 306, 401, 403, 410
Criminal Code, 87, 286, 300, 380, 406
Cronenberg, David, 386
Crosbie, John, 307
Cross, James, 314, 317
Crusade for Canada, 404-405
Cuban Missile Crisis, 263, 272, 279
culture, 42, 44-48, 106-111, 385-389
  Canadian-content regulations, 298, 387-388
  Canadian identity, 222, 290, 296, 298, 398
  literature, 42, 44, 144, 387
  magazines, 143
  movies, 112, 142-143, 225, 386-387
  painting, 45-46, 106, 107
  pluralism, 288
  radio, 105-106, 111-112, 141-142, 298, 388
  sports, 46-47, 110-111, 144
  television, 221-222, 374, 377
  theatre, 45-46
  US influence, 111-112, 141-142, 221-222, 296, 385, 456
  war art, 78-79
Curley, Tagek, 305
Curzon, Lord, 151
Cyr, Louis, 48

D
Dafoe, Allan, 145
Dandurand, Raoul, 152
Davis, William, 329, 331
D-Day, 192, 193, 194
de Coubertin, Pierre, 111
de Gaulle, Charles, 253, 454
de Klerk, F. W., 427
de la Roche, Mazo, 107, 144
death rate, 24
deficit, 125, 415, 416
Del Pozo Marrero, Omar, 439
Delgamuukw, 406, 408, 409
democracy, 165, 258
demographic trends, 372-274, 374
Denison, Flora Macdonald, 40, 61
Department of Labour, 25
Department of Reconstruction, 210, 211
depression, in business cycle, 123
Depression. see Great Depression
Desjardins, Larry, 323
DEW Line (Distant Early Warning), 264, 265, 268
Diefenbaker, John, 230, 243-245, 247, 248, 250, 263, 264, 266, 270, 271, 272, 278, 366, 427
Dionne Quintuplets, 145
Dirty Thirties. see Great Depression
disarmament, 356
Distant Early Warning Line. see DEW Line
divorce, 286, 370, 371
Dominion Land Act, 18
Dominion of Canada, 6, 30
Dominion Women's Enfranchisement Association, 39
Dorion, Noel, 230
Douglas, C. H., 138
Douglas, T. C. (Tommy), 241
Doukhobors, 23, 62
Drapeau, Jean, 253
Drury, E. C., 93
Dulles, Foster, 260
Dunkirk, 176
Duplessis, Maurice, 140, 141, 217, 228, 240, 245, 246, 286
the Dust Bowl, 129

E
Earth Summit, 435
Eastern Region
  in the Great Depression, 129, 135
  Maritime coal mining, 91-92
  Maritime fishing industry, 215, 411-412, 414
Eaton, T., Company Limited, 105, 216, 220
economic disparity, 18, 22, 24, 246
economic policies, 8-9, 24, 347, 348, 356
economic sanctions, 427, 429
Economic Strategy Institute, 445
Economist (magazine), 338
Edmonton Commercial Graduates, 111, 144, 460
Edwards, Henrietta Muir, 101
Egoyan, Atom, 386
Einstein, Albert, 196
Elizabeth II, Queen, 253
emigration, 375
Employment Equity Act, 459
Environmental Assessment and Review Program, 296
environmental protection, 294, 296, 344, 350, 411, 414, 434, 435
Erasmus, George, 304
Ethiopia, 164
ethnic cleansing, 429
European Union, 440
Expo 67, 252, 253, 286, 294
export trade, 122, 125, 126, 153, 220, 244, 338, 340, 413
extermination camps, 198

F
Fairclough, Ellen, 244
Family Reform Acts, 299
family structure, 370, 374
fascism, 156, 165, 174, 266
federal-provincial cooperation, 241, 398
federalism, 286, 396, 401
Fédération national St-Jean-baptiste, 40
Ferdinand, Franz, 54
Ferguson, Howard, 93
Fessenden, Reginald, 21
Fielding, S. S., 36
"Final Solution", 198, 200
Firearms Act. see Bill C-68
first nations. see Native peoples
fisheries, 411-412, 414
flag debate, 250
Flavelle, Joseph, 66
FLQ (Front de Libération du Québec), 247, 314-315, 316-317, 318, 454
FLQ Manifesto, 314
food banks, 371
Foot, David, 373
Foreign Investment Review Agency (FIRA), 348-349, 356
foreign policy, 274
forestry, 413
Fowler, Robert, 434
Fox, Terry, 354
free trade, 8, 36-37, 90, 385, 412, 414
Free Trade Agreement (FTA), 385, 412, 414, 444
freight rates, 102, 103
French Canadians
  discrimination, 247
  in the Dominion, 30-32
  outside Quebec, 322-323
  in World War I, 56-57, 61
  in World War II, 185
fresh water, 412, 413
Front de Libération du Québec. see FLQ
Fulton-Favreau formula, 328

G
G7(8), 440
"Gang of Eight", 329, 331
Garneau, Marc, 357
Gendron Commission, 318, 319, 320
George VI, King, 167, 185
Gérin-Lajoie, Marie, 40
German Canadians, 60
Gitxan-Wet'suwet'en Tribal Council, 408
Gladstone, James, 230
glasnost, 425
global economy, 366, 367, 370, 385, 440, 446
global warming, 434
Globe and Mail (newspaper), 329
Good and Services Tax (GST), 454
Gorbachev, 424, 425, 426
Göring, Hermann, 202
Gouzenko affair, 260, 262
Grand Council of Cree, 306
Grand Trunk Railway, 20
Gray Report, 348
Great Depression, 118-147
  causes, 120-124
  the end, 155, 339
  government response, 124-135
  regional impact, 128-130
  relief, 131-132
Great Lakes, 413
Great Purge, 156
Green Paper on Immigration Policy, 291
Greenpeace, 296
Greenway, Thomas, 8
Grierson, John, 143
gross national product, 9, 188
Groulx, Lionel-Adolphe, 92, 93
Group of Seven, 45, 106, 107
Gulf War, 429

H
Hagan, John, 372
Haig, Douglas, 72-73, 76
Hanlan, Ned, 47
The Happy Gang, 142
Harkness, Douglas, 272
Harper, Elijah, 397, 403
Harris, Mike, 417
Hart, Evelyn, 298
head tax, 12, 458
health care, 169, 241, 242, 243, 244, 398
Hebert, Anne, 298
Henderson, Paul, 295
Henry, Martha, 223
Hepburn, 138, 140, 145
Hewitt, Foster, 110, 142, 226, 295
"Hill 70", 73, 76
Himmler, Heinrich, 198
Hind, Cora, 39
Hirohito, Emperor, 198
Hiroshima, 197, 198
Hitler, Adolf, 158, 159, 162, 164, 168, 169, 174, 179, 195, 200, 202, 456
Ho Chi Minh, 279
hockey, 47, 110, 295
Hockey Hall of Fame, 144
Holocaust, 162, 198-201, 203, 381
the homeless, 371
Howe, C. D., 210, 211, 238

Hughes, Sam, 56, 66
human rights, 273, 436, 437
human security, 448, 449
Humphrey, John, 277
Hunter-Hoodless, Adelaide, 38
Hussein, Saddam, 429
Hutt, William, 223
hydrogen bomb. see nuclear weapons

I
Ignatieff, Michael, 11
immigration, 9-18, 97-98
    advertising for immigrants, 10
    assimilation, 26, 97
    closed policy, 10
    head tax, 12
    home children, 16
    immigrants' rights, 101, 294
    and labour, 24-25, 97-98, 374
    and Native peoples, 17-18
    post-WWII, 218-219, 290, 338
    regional, 9, 13, 14, 16, 97, 161, 215, 246, 318
Immigration Act, 87, 97, 291, 437
Imperial Conference, 125, 151, 152
Imperial Munitions Board, 66, 67
imperial policy, 150
imperialism, 30, 90
In Flanders Fields (poem), 55
Income War Tax, 67
Indian Act, 17, 230, 300, 302, 305, 384, 457
Industrial Standards Act, 138
industrialization
    in Canada, 20-21, 37, 92, 93, 338, 372, 412
    in the Soviet Union, 155, 156
inflation, 68, 123, 188, 220, 338, 339, 340
information age, 390
information technology, 370, 388, 446
Intercontinental Ballistic Missiles (ICBMs), 270
International Covenant on Civil and Political Rights, 436
International Criminal Tribunal, 203, 430, 448
International Military Tribunal (IMT), 202
International Workers of the World, 25
Internet, 324-325, 370, 381, 389, 446, 461
Inuit, 306, 406, 410
Inuit Tapirisat of Canada, 305, 407
Iraq, 429
Iron Curtain, 258
Irwin, Ron, 329
isolationism, 263

J
Jackson, Robert, 202
Jalna (book), 107
James Bay Project, 305, 306, 410
Japan, 164, 180
Japanese Canadians, 98
    in World War I, 58
    in World War II, 186, 189-190
Jewett, Pauline, 301

Jewish Canadians
    immigrants, 10, 12, 98
    refugees, 161, 163, 218
"the Jewish problem", 162
Jewison, Norman, 386
John Paul II, Pope, 274
Johns-Manville strike, 217
Johnson, Daniel, 253, 328, 400-401
Johnson, Lyndon, 279
Johnson, Pauline (Tekahionwake), 44
"Just Society", 286, 288, 290, 302, 307, 340

K
Kanesatake, 384
Keegstra, Jim, 201, 381
Kennedy, John F., 228, 245, 263, 268, 272, 447
Kenney, Mart, 143
Keynes, John Maynard, 125, 340, 342
King, William Lyon Mackenzie, 25, 87, 88, 89, 90, 92, 93, 102, 124, 125, 135, 136, 140, 143, 150, 151, 152, 160, 162, 164, 168, 174, 175, 184, 238, 239, 240, 241, 250, 262, 273, 359, 455
Klee Wyck (book), 109
Klein, Ralph, 417
Klondike Gold Rush, 9, 14, 17, 194
Komagata Maru (ship), 15, 458
Kosovo, 202-203, 278, 430, 431, 432, 446
Krushchev, Nikita, 260, 272
Ku Klux Klan, 98
Kuwait, 429

L
labour movement, 24-25, 216-217, 346
lacrosse, 47
L'Action Francaise, 92
L'Alliance laurentienne (Parti Québécois), 223
LaMarsh, Judy, 228, 241
land mines, 436, 448, 449
language rights, 312, 318-323
Lapointe, Ernest, 168
Laporte, Pierre, 314-315, 317
Laskin, Bora, 299
Laurence, Margaret, 298
Laurier, Sir Wilfrid, 7, 8, 17, 18, 19, 30, 31, 32, 33, 56, 69, 88, 239, 414, 444, 454, 458
Lavallée, Calixa, 35
Leacock, Stephen, 11, 44, 95, 107
League of Indians, 100
League of Nations, 152, 164
Le Devoir (newspaper), 32, 217, 317, 321, 328, 404
Leduc, Ozias, 45
Lenin, Vladimir, 155, 187, 447
Lesage, Jean, 246, 247, 313
Levesque, Henri, 222
Lévesque, René, 249, 253, 313, 314, 315, 318, 323, 326, 327, 330, 331
Lewis, David, 344
Loft, F. O., 100
Lombardo, Guy, 143
Longboat, Tom, 47

Lougheed, Peter, 353
Luftwaffe, 164, 177
Lusitania (ship), 71
Lyon, Georges, 48

M
McCarthy, Bill, 372
McCarthy, Joseph, 266
McClung, Nellie, 40, 42, 43, 61, 100, 101, 461
McCrae, John, 55
McCurdy, J. A. D., 21
Macdonald, Sir John A., 6-7, 19, 98, 236, 244, 414, 454
McDonough, Alexa, 301
McFall, Patrick J. "Paddy", 6, 7
McGibbon, Pauline, 301
McGill University, 32
MacKenzie, Lewis, 430, 432
Mackenzie Valley Pipeline, 306, 350-351
McKinley, William, 36
McKinney, Louise, 40, 101
McLachlin, Beverley, 379
McLaughlin, Audrey, 301
McLaughlin, Sam, 105
McLaughlin, W. Earle, 321
Maclean's (magazine), 42, 143, 239, 298, 317, 407
McLellan, Anne, 378
Magna International Inc., 369
Maillet, Antonine, 298
Mandela, Nelson, 427
Manhattan Project, 196
Manitoba, 7, 8
Manitoba Act, 8
The Manitoba Free Press (newspaper), 19, 39, 43
Manitoba Independent Labour Party, 169
Manitoba Legislative Assembly, 397
Manitoba Rebellion, 31
Manitoba Schools Question, 8, 31
Manning, Preston, 359, 400, 417, 418, 455
maple leaf, 34
Maple Leaf Gardens, 142, 144
Marathon of Hope, 354-355
March on Rome, 156
Marchand, Jean, 217, 248
Marconi, Guglielmo, 21, 97
Maritime Rights movement, 91, 92
Marsh, Leonard, 241
Marsh Report, 241
Marshall Plan, 259
Martin, Paul, 417
Massey-Harris, 21, 102
Massey-Levesque Commission, 222
Massey, Vincent, 222, 456
maternity leave, 300
maximum work week 135
Mayer, Louis B., 112
mechanization, 102, 103
media, 42, 104, 112, 143, 390
medicare. see health care
Meech Lake Accord, 396, 403
Megarry, Roy, 329
Meighen, Arthur, 87, 88-89, 90, 100, 101
Mein Kampf (book), 158, 162
Mercredi, Ovide, 304, 401, 402
middle power, 274, 276

migration patterns, 19, 373
military power, Canadian, 33, 175, 263
Military Service Act, 69, 88, 89
Military Voters Act, 69
Milosevic, Slobodan, 203, 430, 431
Mock Parliament, 43
Mohawk Warriors, 384
Molotov–Ribbentrop Treaty, 168, 175, 179
Mont Blanc (ship), 71
Montgomery, Lucy Maud, 42, 461
Montreal Massacre, 382-383
Montreal Rally, 404-405
moratorium on fishing, 411, 414
Morenz, Howie, 144
Morrice, James Wilson, 45
Morton, Desmond, 275
Mountbatten, Lord Louis, 181
Mouvement pour l'Intégration Scolaire (MIS), 319
Mouvement Souveraineté-Association (MSA) (Parti Québécois), 249, 313
movies, 112, 142-143, 225, 298, 386
Mowat, Farley, 223
Mulroney, Brian, 342, 359, 366, 370, 373, 374, 382, 385, 396, 397, 399, 414, 416, 444, 454
multiculturalism, 9, 288, 290, 374, 398, 458, 460
Multilateral Agreement on Investment (MAI), 440-441, 446
Munich agreement, 167-168
Murdoch, Irene, 299, 300
Murphy, Emily, 39, 10, 461
Murray, Anne, 298, 388
Mussolini, Benito, 156, 157, 164

N
Nagasaki, 197, 198
Naismith, Dr. James, 48, 111
Narcotics Control Act, 380
NASA, 268, 269, 271
Nasser, Gamel Abdel, 276
National Action Committee on the Status of Women (NAC), 300
National Aeronautics and Space Administration. see NASA
National Council of Women of Canada, 38, 101, 460
national debt, 342, 415, 416
National Energy Program (NEP), 353, 356
National Film Board of Canada, 143, 226, 385
National Gallery, 108
National Hockey League, 47, 110
National Indian Brotherhood (NIB) (Assembly of First Nations), 302, 304, 305, 457
National Indian Council, 231, 302, 457
National Library of Canada, 222
National Party, 427
National Policy, 6, 8, 414
National Research Council, 358
National Socialist German Workers Party (the Nazi party), 158
nationalization, 136

Index   **469**

Native Council of Canada, 305
Native peoples, 17-18, 98-100, 230-231, 294, 331, 389
  assimilation, 17, 26, 98-100, 230, 302, 457
  Charter impact, 384
  discrimination, 384, 457
  and immigrants, 17-18
  Inuit, 306, 406, 410
  Inuktitut, 306
  land claims, 18, 230, 302, 305, 306, 351, 385, 403, 406, 408, 410, 457
  reserves, 18, 230, 302
  residential schools, 17, 98-100, 231, 457
  self-government, 99, 384, 385, 396, 397, 398, 399, 403, 406
  status, 100, 302, 305, 384
  Treaty 8, 17
  treaty rights, 99, 384, 385. 403
  in World War I, 57
  in World War II, 184
Native Women's Association of Canada, 305
NATO (North Atlantic Treaty Organization), 263-264, 272, 356, 357, 426, 431, 456
Naval Service Act, 32
Nazism, 158, 174, 182, 198
neo-conservatism, 417
neutrality laws, 154
New Deal, 132, 134-135, 136, 154
New Democratic Party, 87, 216
the new economy, 366, 368, 385
New York Times (newspaper), 86, 407
Newfoundland, 236-237, 239
Newman, Peter C., 342
Newsweek (magazine), 298
Nielsen, Dorise, 187
Nisga'a First Nation, 18, 305, 406, 408, 457
Nixon, Richard, 348
No Ordinary Hero (book), 403
NORAD, 265, 270, 356, 357, 456
North American Aerospace Defence Agreement. see NORAD
North American Air Defence Agreement. see NORAD
North American Free Trade Agreement (NAFTA), 400, 412, 416, 440, 445
North American Indian Brotherhood, 230
North Atlantic Treaty Organization. see NATO
North Region, 103-104, 244, 406
Northwest Territories, 406
Nova Scotia, 7
nuclear energy, 267, 424
nuclear-test ban, 273
nuclear weapons, 196, 267, 269, 270, 271, 272, 356, 357, 426
Nunavut, 406, 410, 457
Nuremberg trial, 199, 202-203

O
O Canada, 35, 253
October Crisis, 314-315, 318
Official Languages Act, 248, 288, 289, 312
oil,
  in Alberta, 210, 215
  world crisis, 343-344
Oka, 384-385, 403
Okalik, Paul, 410
Oliver, Frank, 17
Oliver, John, 94
On to Ottawa Trek, 137
One Big Union, 86, 87
Ontario Native Women's Association, 305
OPEC, 343, 344, 345
Operation Overlord, 190
Oppenheimer, J. Robert, 197
"Option Quebec," 313
Organization for Economic Cooperation and Development (OECD), 440, 441
Organization of Petroleum Exporting Countries. see OPEC
Oshawa Strike, 138, 140
Ottawa Process, 436, 449

P
Pacific Rim, 356, 374
Pacific Scandal, 6
Padlock Law, 142
Palliser Triangle, 129
Panama Canal, 36, 94
Parent Report on Education, 246
Paris Peace Conference, 77, 156
Parizeau, Jacques, 400, 402, 403
Parlby, Irene, 101
Parti Québécois, 223, 249, 313, 315, 320, 400
Patterson, Tom, 223
Pattullo, Thomas, 136
Payette, Lise, 327
peacebuilding, 428
peacekeeping, 278, 426, 428, 433-434
peacemaking, 428, 432
Pearson, Lester B., 230, 241, 245, 248, 250, 252, 253, 272, 274, 276, 279, 286, 454, 461
Peckford, Brian, 331
Peden, William J. "Torchy", 144
Pelletier, Gerard, 217, 246, 248
pensions, 135, 169, 240, 241, 300
per capita income, 9, 210
perestroika, 425
Persian Gulf, 429
Peterson, Oscar, 298
Petro Canada, 349, 352, 353
"Phoney War", 176
Pickford, Mary (Gladys Smith), 112
Plaunt, Alan, 141
Political Equality League, 40, 43, 100
pollution, 221, 350, 412, 414, 448
Pollution Probe, 294
poverty, 22, 24, 370, 371
Prairies
  agriculture, 21-22, 103, 122
  in the Great Depression, 112, 129-130
  political movements, 93-94
  settlement, 9, 18
Pratt, E. J., 144
preventive diplomacy, 428
Princip, Gavrillo, 54
Progressive Party, 90, 91, 93, 359
progressive taxation, 135
prohibition, 38-39, 90, 93, 95-96
prostitution, 286
protectionism, 90, 102, 153, 385, 444
Prudhoe Bay, 350

Q
Quebec, 310-334
  bilingualism, 8, 247, 289, 312-313, 318-323
  culture, 222-223, 247, 396, 454
  distinct society, 246, 396, 398, 403
  French–English relationships, 174, 454
  and immigration, 97, 161, 246, 318, 396
  nationalism, 92, 93
  referendum (1980), 326, 328
  referendum (1995), 400, 402, 403, 404
  separatism, 92, 223, 247, 294, 313, 318, 327, 400
  sovereignty association, 248, 313, 318, 323, 400, 401
  veto power, 331, 396
Quiet Revolution, 246, 247, 250, 312, 454

R
racism, 188-190, 290, 294, and Freedoms, 244, 274, 307, 331, 378, 380, 381
radio, 105-106, 111-112, 141-142, 388
Radio League, 141
Radwanski, George, 317
Rae, Bob, 417
railways, 7, 9, 12, 19-20, 92, 98, 111, 126, 136, 210
rationing, 71, 188
Reagan, Ronald, 357, 385, 426
recession, 88, 123, 220, 244, 338, 339
reciprocity, 36-37
Reform Party, 359, 399, 400, 406, 416, 417, 455
refugees, 161, 163, 218-219, 291, 460
Regina Manifesto, 136, 140, 240
Regina Riot, 137
regional differences, 18, 91, 135, 246, 248, 339, 373, 399
Reid, Escott, 263
Reid, Kate, 223
Reitman, Ivan, 386
relief, 126, 131-132, 240
relief camps, 127, 133, 137
Relief Project Workers' Union, 137
Remembrance Day (Armistice Day), 55, 77
Riddell, W. A., 164
riding the rails, 132
Riel, Louis, 8, 31
RIN (Rassemblement pour l'Independence Nationale), 247, 253, 313
Rio Conference, 435
Roaring Twenties, 84-115, 120
Roberts, Stan, 352
Robillard, Lucienne, 401
Robinson, Svend, 414, 437
Roblin, Rodmond, 43
Romanow, Roy, 417

Roosevelt, Franklin Delano, 134, 153, 154, 196
Roosevelt, Teddy, 36
Rosenfeld, Bobbie, 111
Routhier, Adolphe-Basile, 35
Royal Air Force (RAF), 177
Royal Canadian Air Force (RCAF), 178, 264, 456
Royal Canadian Mounted Police (RCMP), 34
The Royal Canadians, 143
Royal Commission on Aboriginal Peoples, 385
Royal Commission on Bilingualism and Biculturalism, 247, 289, 313, 454
Royal Commission on the Status of Women, 299, 300, 461
Royal North-West Mounted Police (Royal Canadian Mounted Police), 34, 87
Rozema, Patricia, 386
Russia, 155
Rwanda, 433
Ryan, Claude, 317, 321, 326, 328

S
Sainte-Marie, Buffy, 291, 389
Salmon Recovery Plan, 411
sanctions. see economic sanctions
Sarajevo, 430
Saskatchewan, 129-130, 194, 215
Saskatchewan Rebellion, 31
satellites, 269, 358
Saunders, Charles E., 21
Scott, Duncan Campbell, 100
Seagram, 96
Senate, 398, 399, 417, 418
Sennett, Mack (Michael Sinnott), 112
Selassie, Haile, 164
separate school system, 8
separatist movement. see Quebec
Serbs, 430
Service, Robert, 42
settlement,
  Dominion Land Act, 18
  of the prairies, 9, 18
Shadbolt, Jack, 223
Shaping Canada's Future Together (book), 398
Sharpeville, 427
Shaw Festival, 223
Shearer, Norma, 143
Sifton, Clifford, 8, 10, 17, 22, 37, 194
Sikhs, 14-16, 458
Silcox, Claris, 161
Silent Spring (book), 221
Six War Years (book), 186, 190
Smallwood, Joey, 237, 250
Smoot-Hawley Tariff, 122, 125
Social Credit party, 136, 138
social justice, 288
social programs, 238, 239, 240, 241, 341, 416
Somalia, 432-433
The Song My Paddle Sings (poem), 44
Sorenson, Mark, 161
soup kitchens, 132, 154
Soviet Union, 155, 179, 258, 260, 264, 268, 269, 271, 272, 279, 425, 426, 429, 434, 447

Soweto, 427
space, Canadian involvement, 269, 357
space race, 268-269
Spar Aerospace, 358
Spicer, Keith, 397-398
sports, 46-47, 110-111, 144
Sports Hall of Fame, 355
Sputnik I, 268, 271
Spry, Graham, 141
SS Manhattan (ship), 350
SS St. Louis (ship), 160-161
"stagflation", 339, 344
Stalin, Joseph, 155, 156, 175, 179, 196, 259, 447
standard of living, 338, 369
Stanfield, Robert, 345
Stanley, Lord, 47
Statute of Westminster, 152-153, 278, 455
St. Laurent, Louis, 210, 238, 258
St. Lawrence Seaway, 212, 213
St. Leonard School, 319
stock market crash. see also Black Tuesday, 120, 121, 127
Stockholm Appeal, 273
Stoffman, Daniel, 373
Stowe-Gullen, Augusta, 39
Stratford festival, 223
strikes, 25, 86-87, 216-217, 346
Stronach, Frank, 369
Strong, Maurice, 435
Suez Crisis, 276, 278
Suharto, 437
Sunshine Sketches of a Little Town (book), 107
Supreme Court of Canada, 379, 409, 456

T
Tanobe, Miyuke, 297
tariffs, 9, 37, 90, 91, 102, 122, 124, 126, 129, 153, 385, 414, 444
Taschereau, Louis-Alexandre, 93
technology, 214, 221, 265, 269, 357-358, 366, 367, 370, 388, 446, 456, 461
Tekahionwake (Pauline Johnson), 44
telecommunications, 370
Telefilm Canada, 298
Telestat Canada, 269
television, 221-222, 374, 377
temperance movements, 38, 39, 94, 95
Ten Lost Years (book), 133
Third Reich, 166
Thompson, Sir John, 7
Thomson, Tom, 106
Thousand-Year Reich, 202
Three Persons, Tom, 48
Tienanmen Square, 436
Time (magazine), 174, 298
Tobin, Brian, 401
Toronto Maple Leafs, 144

Toronto Star (newspaper), 352, 374
totalitarianism, 165
Town, Harold, 223
trade union movement. see unions
Trades and Labour Congress of Canada, 25, 86
Trans-Canada Airlines (Air Canada), 211
Trans-Canada Highway, 211, 212
Trans-Canada Pipeline, 211, 238
transfer payments, 416
Treaty of Versailles, 80, 157, 159, 164, 166
Triple Alliance ("the Central Powers"), 54
Triple E Senate, 418
Triple Entente ("the Allies"), 54
Trudeau, Margaret, 287
Trudeau, Pierre Elliot, 217, 246, 248, 250, 286-287, 294, 296, 298, 300, 307, 312, 314, 317, 320, 323, 326, 327, 329, 330, 331, 338, 339, 341, 343, 345, 351, 353, 356, 357, 359, 368, 378, 396, 416, 417, 454, 456, 457
Trudeaumania, 286
Truman Doctrine, 260
Truman, Harry S., 197, 260, 262
Tupper, Sir Charles, 7

U
U-boat, 178
Ukrainian-Canadian Legion, 185
Ukrainian Canadians, 13, 244
    in World War I, 59-60
    in World War II, 185
Ukrainian National Federation (UNF), 185
unemployment, 124, 126-127, 211, 220, 338, 339, 344, 368, 370, 401, 416
unemployment insurance, 135, 169, 241
UNICEF, 372
Union Government, 69, 88
Union Nationale, 140, 318
unions, 24-25, 86-87, 216, 368
    and conscription, 69
    strikes, 25, 86-87, 216-217, 346
    suffrage for women, 25
    and World War II, 175
United Auto Workers, 138
United Farmers of Alberta, 94, 359
United Farmers of Ontario, 91, 93
United Nations (UN), 273, 276, 277, 278, 356, 426, 428, 430, 432
United Nations Educational, Scientific and Cultural Organization (UNESCO), 273, 322

United Nations Operation in Somalia (UNOSOM), 432-433
United Nations peacekeeping missions, 278, 433
Universal Declaration of Human Rights, 273-274, 277, 439
Université Laval (Université de Montréal), 32
urbanization, 91, 92, 93, 102, 372, 412

V
veto, 396, 398
Victoria Charter, 328
Victoria, Queen, 30
victory bonds, 66, 188
Vietnam, 279, 294, 433
Voice of Women (VOW), 273

W
wage-and-price controls, 345-347
Walton, Dorothy, 144
War Art Program, 78-79
war crimes trials, 202-203
War Guilt Clause, 157
War Measures Act, 59, 66, 89, 315, 316-317, 454
Warsaw Pact, 264
Wartime Elections Act, 69, 100, 460
Watkins Report, 348
Watson, Homer, 45
welfare policies. see social programs
Wells, Clyde, 397
western alienation, 352-353, 359, 417
Western Federation of Miners, 25
Western Labour Conference, 86
White, Bob, 445
White Paper, on Native rights, 302, 304, 457
White Paper, on Quebec/Canada, 323
White, William Andrew, 58
Whitehall Nuclear Research Establishment, 267
Williams, Percy, 110
Wilson, Bertha, 301
Wilson, Cairine, 102
Wilson, Meeha, 305
Wilson, Woodrow, 195
Winnipeg General Strike, 86-87, 89, 91, 169, 175
Winnipeg Trades and Labour Council, 86, 87
Winnipeg Tribune (newspaper), 86
Woman's Christian Temperance Union (WCTU), 38, 39, 94
women, 298-302, 331
    declared legal persons, 40, 101
    "firsts", 39, 40, 102, 244, 300, 301, 379
    in the Great Depression, 127-128

pay equity, 188, 228, 301, 302, 371
and political change, 38-40, 294, 301, 370, 380, 397, 460
right to vote and hold office, 25, 43, 69, 100
social behaviour, 41, 370
in work force, 37-38, 41, 227-228, 301, 370
in World War I, 67-68
in World War II, 186-188
Women's Institute, 38, 228
Wood, Henry Wise, 94
Woodsworth, J. S., 87, 136, 140, 169
World Health Organization, 273
World Trade Organization (WTO), 441
World War I, 52-83
    armistice, 77
    causes, 54
    conscientious objectors, 62
    conscription, 32, 61, 69-70, 90, 184
    financing, 66-67
    opposition, 60-61
    recruitment, 54-61
    sea and air warfare, 71
    trench warfare, 63
    women's contribution, 67-68, 69
World War II, 172,-205, 456
    atomic bomb, 196-198
    beginning, 155, 164, 175-176, 179-180
    causes, 159, 175
    end of the war, 193, 196, 198
    invasion of Normandy, 181, 192
    Japanese expansion, 180
    in the Pacific, 180, 189, 196-198
    Pearl Harbor, 180, 189
    "Phoney War", 176
    post-war effects, 258-279, 338
    propaganda, 182-183
    women's contribution, 186-188
Wray, Fay, 143

Y
Young, Neil, 291
youth culture, 226-227, 287, 370
Yugoslavia, 429, 446
the Yukon, 9, 14, 17, 306
Yukon Gold Rush, 33, 195

Z
Zündel, Ernst, 201, 381

PHOTO CREDITS

p.2 left: © Canada Post, 1961, right: Toronto Public Library; p.3 City of Toronto Archives, SC244-1033; p.5 City of Toronto Archives, SC 244-524; p.6-7 National Archives of Canada/C-7127; p.7 inset: Reproduction owned by the Corporation of the City of Kingston. Image courtesy of Bellevue House, Kingston/Parks Canada; p.9 Glenbow Archives, Calgary/971.2, C212c, 1930 pam.; p.11 Toronto Sun; p.12 Glenbow Archives, Calgary/NA-604-1; p.13 Glenbow Archives, Calgary/NA-2798-6; p.15 Vancouver Sun; p.16 City of Toronto Archives, SC244-1033; p.17 Archives of Ontario #2475 S7681; p.20 Franklin Carmichael 1890-1945 A Northern Silver Mine 1930 oil on canvas, 101.5 x 121.2 cm Gift of Mr. A.J. Latner, McMichael Canadian Art Collection 1971.9; p.23 Saskatchewan Archives Board #SPA R-B 1964(1); p.24 City of Toronto Archives, SC244-52.24; p.25 City of Toronto Archives, SC244-1033; p.29 National Archives of Canada/C-24799; p.30 Glenbow Archives, Calgary/NA-26766; p.32 National Archives of Canada/C-51799; p.33 The Eye Opener (Calgary), Jan., 1910; p.34 top left: © Canada Post, 1851. Reproduced with permission., centre: Canadian Press; p.34-35 Department of National Defence; p.35 top: Photofest, right: Photofest; p.37 National Archives of Canada/C-2616; p.38 Royal Bank Corporate Archives; p.39 National Archives of Canada/PA-128887; p.41 Archives of Ontario #S13674; p.42 Saskatchewan Archives Board #P-A369-A (originally appeared in *The Grain Growers' Guide*, Feb. 26, 1913, p.16); p.43 National Archives of Canada/C-6-1746; p.44 National Archives of Canada/PA-143139; p.45 "Neige dorée" by Ozias, Leduc (#1368), National Gallery of Canada, Ottawa.; p.46 T.P.L. T30583; p.47 T.P.L.; p.48 National Archives of Canada/PA-1479; p.49 Norma Kennedy; p.53 City of Toronto Archives, James Collection 735A; p.55 The Toronto Star Syndicate; p.56: top: John Fielding, bottom: National Archives of Canada/C-95742; p.57 top: National Archives of Canada/C-116604, bottom: National Archives of Canada/C-68913; p.58 National Archives of Canada/PA-1193; p.59 National Archives of Canada/C-931; p.60 BC Archives #PABC 54987; p.61 Canadian Press/John Hayward; p.63 left: Imperial War Museum Q3990, right: Ivor Castle/National Archives of Canada/PA-868; p.64 National Archives of Canada/PA-2162; p.66 National Archives of Canada/C-95280; p.68 left: National Archives of Canada/PA-24436, right: National Archives of Canada/PA-1315; p.70 top: City of Toronto Archives, James Collection #736, bottom: National Archives of Canada/C-95289; p.71 National Archives of Canada/PA-1654; p.75 National Archives of Canada/PA-1020; p.78 "The Second Battle at Ypres" by Richard Jack, 1916 #8179, Copyright © Canadian War Museum (C.W.M.); p.79 top left: "For What?" by F.H. Varley, 1917, #8911, Copyright © Canadian War Museum (C.W.M.); bottom right: "The Conquerors" by Eric Kennington, 1918, #8968, Copyright © Canadian War Museum (C.W.M.); p.85 Archive Photos; p.86 Public Archives of Manitoba, PAM N-12296; p.86-87 Provincial Archives of Manitoba, Collection: Foote 1696, Neg # N2762; p.89 Glenbow Archives, Calgary/NA-3055-31; p.90 National Archives of Canada/C-20051; p.92 left: Miner's Museum, Glace Bay, Nova Scotia, right: Miner's Museum, Glace Bay, Nova Scotia; p.93 Yousef Karsh/National Arhives of Canada/C-21562; p.94 Glenbow Archives, Calgary/NA-3217-2; p.95 Archives of Ontario ACC #9379S15000; p.97 Manitoba Archives, Foote Collection, N-1888; p.98 National Archives of Canada/PA-01226; p.99 City of Vancouver Archives Photo #CVA99-1496. Photographer: Stuart Thomson.; p.100 John Boyd/National Archives of Canada/C-37113; p.101 NFB/National Archives of Canada/C-54523; p.102 Christel Gerstenberg/Corbis; p.103 Photo courtesy of Ontario Ministry of Natural Resources. Provided by Canadian Bushplane Heritage Centre.; p.104 Cunard Line colour ad (ca. 1925) courtesy of the National Museum of Science and Technology Corporation, Ottawa.; p.105 Ford ad (1925) courtesy of the National Museum of Science and Technology Corporation, Ottawa.; p.106 Eaton's Radio ads (1927/29) courtesy of the National Museum of Science and Technology Corporation, Ottawa.; p.107 top: Photo by Carlo Catenazzi/Art Gallery of Ontario, bottom: Comstock/© Karsh; p.108 "Heina" by Emily Carr, ACC.#4284, National Gallery of Canada, Ottawa.; p.109 "Pic Island" c. 1924 by Lawren Harris, 1885-1970, oil on canvas, 123.3 x 153.9 cm, McMichael Canadian Art Collection, Gift of Col. R.S. McLaughlin.; p.110 National Archives of Canada/PA-150984; p.111 Canada's Sports Hall of Fame; p.112 Photofest; p.116 left: ©Canada Post, 1989, right: Glenbow Archives, Calgary/ND3-6742; p.117 top: "Maintenance Jobs in the Hangar" by Paraskeva Clark, #14085, Copyright © Canadian War Museum (C.W.M.), bottom: "Young Canadian" by Charles Comfort, 1932, watercolour on paper, 91.4 x 106.7cm. Purchased by the Sketch Committee, 1934 (34.3) Hart House Permanent Collection, University of Toronto.; p.119 Archive Photos; p.120 Wind at My Back, Sullivan Entertainment; p.122 Nelson Photo Archives; p.125 National Archives of Canada; p.126 National Archives of Canada/PA-36697; p.128 top: University of Saskatchewan Archives, bottom: National Archives of Canada/PA-145949; p.129 © Bettmann/CORBIS; p.130 Glenbow Archives; p.131 Glenbow Archives, Calgary/ND3-6742; p.132 National Archives of Canada/C-24840; p.134 © Bettmann/CORBIS; p.137 National Archives of Canada/C-24840; p.138 © Bettmann/CORBIS; p.141 National Archives of Canada/PA-005734; p.142 National Archives of Canada/PA-203126; p.144 Canadian Press; p.145 Canadian Press/Peter Power; p.149 © Bettmann/CORBIS; p.150 © Craig Lovell/CORBIS; p.151 © E.O. Hoppe/CORBIS; p.153 149 © Bettmann/CORBIS; p.154 Nelson Photo Archives; p.155 © Hulton-Deutsch Collection/CORBIS; p.156 © Bettmann/CORBIS; p.157 © Bettmann/CORBIS; p.158 © Bettmann/CORBIS; p.159 © Bettmann/CORBIS; p.161 © Hulton-Deutsch Collection/CORBIS; p.162 © CORBIS; p.163 left: National Archives of Canada/PA-107943, right: City of Toronto Archives, Globe and Mail Collection; p.164 National Archives of Canada/C-16766; p.165 Canadian Press/Gianni Foggia/Associated Press; p.166 © Bettmann/CORBIS; p.167 National Archives of Canada/PA-119013; p.168 © CORBIS; p.169 Dick Hemingway; p.173 "Maintenance Jobs in the Hangar" by Paraskeva Clark, #14085, Copyright © Canadian War Museum (C.W.M.); p.174 © Bettmann/CORBIS; p.178 "Convoy under attack" by Tom Wood, #10553, Copyright © Canadian War Museum (C.W.M.); p.182 top: National Archives of Canada/C-33442, bottom: National Archives of Canada/C-87516; p.183 top: National Archives of Canada/C-90887, bottom left: National Archives of Canada/C-91596, bottom right: National Archives of Canada/C-91539; p.184 "Dieppe Raid" by Charles Comfort, 1946, #12276, Copyright © Canadian War Museum (C.W.M.); p.185 Glenbow Archives; p.186 top: Glenbow Archives, bottom: York University Archives, Toronto Telegram Photographic Collection; p.187 Jack Long/National Archives of Canada/PA-116133; p.188 National Archives of Canada/PA-108300; p.189 top: National Archives of Canada/057250, bottom: Vancouver Public Library, Special Collections, historic photo VPL 14925; p.190 Vancouver Public Library, Special Collections, historic photo VPL 1369; p.196 Ken Bell/National Archives of Canada/PA-137919; p.197 © CORBIS; p.198 © CORBIS; p.199 © CORBIS; p.200 inset: Jessica Pegis; p.200-201 Jessica Pegis, inset: Jessica Pegis; p.202 Associated Press/INSTITUT FUER SOZIALFORSCHUNG; p.203 © Bettmann/CORBIS; p.206 left: ©Canada Post, 1965, right: Saskatchewan Archives Board, R-B2863(1); p.207 top: ©Bettmann/CORBIS, bottom: Steinbergs; p.209 Duncan Macpherson, Toronto Star Syndicate; p.210 Thomas Fisher Library, University of Toronto; p.211 National Archives of Canada/C84023; p.212 TW Image Network/© 1992 Alitek Images; p.213 Photo courtesy of Upper Canada Village, The St. Lawrence Parks Commission.; p.214 Courtesy Bell Canada Historical Collection; p.216 Courtesy of the National Democratic Party (NDP).; p.217 ACE Newsphoto/Montreal Gazette; p.219 top: Vancouver Public Library, Special Collections, VPL 25644; p.220 top: ©Nick Gunderson/CORBIS; p.222 The Montreal Gazette; p.223 Canadian Press; p.224 "Nobody Waved Goodbye" (10538) Courtesy of the National Film Board of Canada.; p.226 Willinger (FPG); p.227 top: Archive Photos, bottom: SuperStock Inc.; p.228 Photo courtesy of Ontario Black History Society; p.229 Terry McEvoy/Canadian Press; p.230 National Archives of Canada/PA-114853; p.231 John McNeill; p.235 John McNeill; p.236 Greg Locke/Stray Light Pictures; p.237 Canadian Press; p.238 Andy Donato, *Toronto Sun*; p.239 © Hulton-Deutsch Collection/CORBIS; p.240 Saskatachewan Archives Board, R-B2863(1); p.241 Canadian Press/Rick Madonik; p.242 Canadian Press; p.243 John McNeill; p.244 Canadian Press/Dave Buston; p.246 top: John McNeill, bottom: "Lazare" by Jean-Paul Lemieux, oil, 1941, Art Gallery of Ontario (2574) photo by Carlo Catenazzi; p.248 Duncan Cameron/National Archives of Canada/C-25003; p.249 Canadian Press; p.251 © Laura Dwight/CORBIS; p.252 top: National Archives of Canada/PA-151866, bottom: Helen Taylor; p.253 John McNeill; p.257 Paul Tailleter/Canadian Press; p.259 © Bettmann/CORBIS; p.262 National Archives of Canada/PA-129625; p.265 North Bay Nuggett/Canadian Press; p.266 Canadian Press/Bruno Schlumberger; p.268 John McNeill; p.270 Publicity still © 1963 Columbia Pictures. Property of National Screen Service Corp.; p.271 Canadian Press/Joe Bryska; p.273 Toronto Star Syndicate; p.274 © Bettmann/CORBIS; p.275 Photodisk/Doug Menuez; p.276 © Hulton-Deutsch Collection/CORBIS; p.277 ©Canada Post, 1998; p.278 AP/Wide World Photos; p.279 Ryan Remoire/CP Picture Archive; p.279 Canadian Press/Ryan Remiorz; p.282 left Terry Fox memorial stamp Copyright © Canada Post, 1982. Courtesy of Canada Post, The Terry Fox Foundation and the Canadian Cancer Society., right: NASA; p.283 top: Canadian Press/Warren Toda, bottom: Canadian Press; p.285 Canadian Press; p.287 left: Canadian Press/Le Droit, bottom: Canadian Press; p.288 Canadian Press/Warren Toda; p.289 ©Canada Post, 2000; p.291 The Montreal Gazette; p.292 top: Gord Rayner; p.293 poster: Vintage Magazine Company, "beads galore": ©Bettmann/Corbis, "Sit-ins": Morris Edwards/Montreal Gazette/National Archives of Canada/PA-152444, "Hippie Havens": Vintage Magazine Company; p.295 Canadian Press/Frank Lennon; p.296 © Amos Nachoum/CORBIS; p.297 Courtesy of Miyuki Tanobe; p.298 John McNeill; p.299 Canadian Press/Dave Thomson; p.300 Courtesy of *Chatelaine* ©Maclean Hunter Publishing Ltd.; p.301 Canadian Press; p.303 Dick Hemingway; p.304 Canadian Press; p.305 Canadian Press; p.306 Canadian Press/Toronto Sun-Chris Wahl; p.307 Courtesy of Blaine; p.311Gabor Szilasi; p.313 John McNeill; p.314 National Archives of Canada/C-79010; p.315 Canadian Press; p.316 Montreal Gazette/National Archives of Canada/PA-129838, inset: Canadian Press; p.319 Canadian Press; p.320 Phil Carpenter, The Montreal Gazette; p.324 top: Courtesy of Alliance Quebec., bottom: Parti Quebecois; p.325 CBC; p.327 left: Canadian Press/Doug Bell, right: National Archives of Canada/PA-141501; p.328 Canadian Press/Ron Poling; p.329 Canadian Press/Dave Buston; p.330 Canadian Press/Ron Poling; p.331 top: Canadian Press/Winnipeg Free Press, bottom: Toronto Sun; p.332 National Archives of Canada/C-139441; p.333 top: National Archives of Canada/C-140222, bottom: Toronto Sun; p.337 CP ArchivePhoto/Bob Cooper; p.338 © Robert Holmes/CORBIS; p.341 Canadian Press/Fred Chartrand; p.343 © Bettmann/CORBIS; p.344 Kennon Cooke/Valan Photos; p.345 Canadian Press; p.346 Canadian Press/Expositor; p.348 left: Canadian Press/Fred Chartrand, right: John McNeill; p.351 Glenbow Archives, Calgary/388.5 C212; p.352 Courtesy of Petro-Canada.; p.353 Glenbow Archives; p.354 Courtesy of The Terry Fox Foundation; p.356 Canadian Press/Peter Bregg; p.357 Canadian Press; p.328 top left: NASA, top right: NASA; p.358 bottom: NASA; p.359 Canadian Press/Adrian Wyld; p.362 left: ©Canada Post, 1999, right: Canadian Press; p.363 top: Canadian Press/Robert Galbraith, bottom: Buffy Sainte-Marie; p.365 Canadian Press/Frank Gunn; p.367 Canadian Press; p.368 © Jim Sugar/CORBIS; p.369 left: Courtesy of Magna International., right: Courtesy of Magna International.; p.371 Canadian Press; p.372 Courtesy of Covenant House.; p.373 Dick Hemingway; p.376 Canadian Broadcasting Corporation; p.377 Canadian Press; p.379 Canadian Press/Tom Hanson; p.380 left: Canadian Press/WFP #088PU, right: CP/Macleans #OJSC9; p.381 Canadian Press; p.382 Canadian Press; p.383 Canadian Press; p.384 Canadian Press; p.386 left: Photofest, centre: Photofest, right: Photofest; p.387 Canadian Press/Ottawa Citizen; p.388 top: Dick Hemingway, bottom: Canadian Press; p.389 Buffy Sainte-Marie; p.390 Canadian Press/Kevin Frayer; p.396 Canadian Press; p.396 Canadian Press/Ron Poling; p.397 Canadian Press/Wayne Glowacki; p.398 Canadian Press/Paul Chiasson; p.399 Canadian Press; p.401 top: Canadian Press/Ryan Remiorz, bottom: Canadian Press/Paul Chiasson; p.402 top: Canadian Press/Jacques Boissinot, bottom: John Kenney/The Montreal Gazette; p.404-405 Canadian Press/Ryan Remiorz; p.406 Canadian Press/Chuck Stoody; p.407 Canadian Press/Shaun Best; p.408 CP Archive Photo/Andrew Vaughan; p.410

Canadian Press/Chuck Stoody; p.416 Canadian Press/Rick Madonik; p.418 left: Canadian Press/Chuck Stoody, right: Canadian Press/Fred Chartrand; p.423 Canadian Press/Lionel Cironneau; p.424 top: Canadian Press/Efrem Lukatsky/Associated Press, bottom: Canadian Press/Efrem Lukasky/Associated Press; p.425 top: Liba Taylor/CORBIS, bottom: Canadian Press/Lutz Schmidt; p.426 Canadian Press/Associated Press/Daniel Morel; p.427 © David Turnley/CORBIS; p.428 Canadian Press/Hans Deryk; p.430 Canadian Press/Associated Press/Amel Emric; p.431 Canadian Press/Associated Press/Amel Emric; p.432 Canadian Press/Peter Dejong/Associated Press; p.433 Canadian Press/Tom Hanson; p.435 Antonio Riberio/Gamma/Ponopresse; p.437 Canadian Press/Jeff Widener/Associated Press; p.438 Courtesy of Michael Craig and Amnesty International; p.440 PA Graphics/Arnoldo DeAlmeida; p.441 Canadian Press/Peter Dejong/Associated Press; p.445 ©Vern Harvey Photography; p.447 Photofest; p.449 Canadian Press/Associated Press/Joao Silva; p.452-453 left to right: Manitoba Archives/Foote Collection/N-1888, Canada's Sports Hall of Fame, City of Toronto Archives/SC244-1033, John McNeill, Canadian Press/Frank Lennon, John McNeill, Canadian Press/Chuck Stoody, Canadian Press/Ottawa Citizen, Canadian Press, Canadian Press, Canadian Press/Robert Galbraith; p.454 Canadian Press/Tom Hanson; p.454 Canadian Press; p.455 Canadian Press/The Hamilton Spectator-Ernest Doroszuk; p.456 Canadian Press/American Press/Chris Pizzello; p.457 Canadian Press/Nick Procaylo; p.459 Canadian Press/Toronto Sun-Paul Henry; p.460 Canadian Press/Andrew Vaughan; p.461 Canadian Press/American Press/Scott Audette; p.463 Toronto Star.

Cover Credits (credits are by row, from left to right)
Top Row 1: Manitoba Archives, Foote Collection, N-1888; Top Row 2: Canadian Press/Frank Lennon; Top Row 3: Canadian Press/Kevin Frayer; Middle Row 1: Canadian Press; Middle Row 2: Canadian Press/Ottawa Citizen; Middle Row 3: John McNeill; Middle Row 4: Canadian Press/Robert Galbraith; Middle Row 4: John McNeill; Bottom Row 1: Canadian Press; Bottom Row 2: Canadian Press/Tom Hanson; Bottom Row 3: City of Toronto Archives, SC244-1033; Bottom Row 4: Vancouver Sun; Bottom Row 5: Canada's Sports Hall of Fame.

TEXT SOURCES

p.8 Kingwell, M. and C. Moore. *Canada Our Century*. Toronto: Doubleday Canada, 1999. page 69; pp. 10–16 Stories of the Shumiatchers, Lem Wong, Martha Black, and Bagga Singh adapted from *A Scattering of Seeds*, a book by Lindalee Tracey based on the documentary film series "A Scattering of Seeds," produced by White Pine Pictures, <www.whitepinepictures.com>; p.14 J. M. Bumstead, *The Peoples of Canada, A Post-Confederation History* (Toronto: Oxford University Press, 1992), page 114; p.19 Corbett, David C. *Canada's Immigration Policy: A Critique*. Toronto: University of Toronto Press, 1957. p.121; p.22 Bliss, Michael. "Northern Wealth: Economic life in the 20th Century." *The Beaver*, Vol. 74, no. 6 (December 1994/January 1995). page 4; p.39 J. M. Bumstead, *The Peoples of Canada, A Post-Confederation History* (Toronto: Oxford University Press, 1992), page 166; p.41 Helen K. Wright. *Nellie McClung and Women's Rights (We Built Canada)* (The Book Society of Canada, 1980), page 14; p.42 Helen K. Wright. *Nellie McClung and Women's Rights (We Built Canada)* (The Book Society of Canada, 1980), page 51; p.58 *A Scattering of Seeds: Captain of Souls*, video series by White Pine Pictures. Contact: <www.whitepinepictures.com/seeds>; p.61 *Canadians in the Global Community: War, Peace, and Security* © The CRB Foundation; p.62 Ellis, John. *Eye Deep in Hell: trench warfare in World War I*. New York: Pantheon Books, 1976. page 15; p.63 top: Mathieson, William, D. *My Grandfather's War*. Toronto: Macmillan of Canada, 1978. page 53; bottom: Aitken, Max. *Canada in Flanders*. Toronto: Hodder and Stoughton, 1916. page 16; p.64-65 Bird, Will, R. *Ghosts Have Warm Hands*. Toronto: Clarke, Irwin & Co. Ltd., 1968. pages 38–39, 81, 82, and 84; p.67 Morton, Desmond. *When Your Number's Up*. Toronto: Random House, 1993. pages 194-195; p.68 Frank Bell in *The Great War and Canadian Society*. ed. Daphne Read. Toronto: New Hogtown Press, 1979. page 189; p.74 top: Captain Ian Sinclair, *Poor Bloody Murder*, page 149; p.74 centre: Captain Walter Moorhouse, 4th Canadian Mounted Rifles, in *Poor Bloody Murder*, page 143; p.74 bottom: Bombadier James F. Johnson, 5th Canadian Mounted Rifles, *Poor Bloody Murder*, page 148; p.96 Marsh, James H. (Editor in Chief). *The Canadian Encyclopedia, Second Edition*. Edmonton: Hurtig Publishers, 1988. page 1765; p.97 <http://www.statcan.ca/english/freepub/11-516-XIE/sectiona/sectiona.htm#Immigration> select: A350. Immigrant arrivals in Canada, 1852 to 1977; p.101 Marsh, James H. (Editor in Chief). *The Canadian Encyclopedia, Second Edition*. Edmonton: Hurtig Publishers, 1988. pages 834, 2330; p.131–132 Cassidy, H. M. *Unemployment and Relief in Ontario, 1929–1932*. Toronto: J. M. Dent & Sons, 1932; p.133 Broadfoot, Barry. *Ten Lost Years 1929–1939*. Toronto: Doubleday Canada Ltd., 1973. pages 93–96; p.151 Dawson, R. MacGregor. *William Lyon Mackenzie King: a political biography*. Toronto: University of Toronto Press, 1976. page 465; p.152 top: Dawson, R. MacGregor. *William Lyon Mackenzie King: a political biography*. Toronto: University of Toronto Press, 1976. page 477; p.152 bottom: "Towards Autonomy" section, Senator Raoul Dandurand speaking in the League of Nations Assembly, 1924. In: *Saturday Night*, November 24, 1945; p.153 *Historical Statistics of Canada*, G389–400; p.176 Granatstein, J. L., and Desmond Morton. *A Nation Forged in Fire: Canadians and the Second World War*. Toronto: Lester & Orpen Dennys, 1989. page 103; p.177 Granatstein, J. L., and Desmond Morton. *A Nation Forged in Fire: Canadians and the Second World War*. Toronto: Lester & Orpen Dennys, 1989. page 75; p.180 Whitehead, William. *Dieppe 1942: Echoes of Disaster*. Toronto: Personal Library, 1979. page 127; p.186 *Six War Years 1939–1945: Memories of Canadians at Home and Abroad*, page 112; p.187 top: Dorise Nielsen, MP for N. Battleford, Sask., House of Commons, 4 May 1944; quoted in: Bruce, Jean. *Back the Attack*, Toronto: Macmillian of Canada, 1985. pages 59, 74; p.187 bottom: Dorise Nielsen, MP, *New Worlds for Women*, Toronto, 1944; quoted in: Bruce, Jean. *Back the Attack*, Toronto: Macmillian of Canada, 1985. page 112; p.190 box source: *Six War Years 1939–1945: Memories of Canadians at Home and Abroad*, page 110; p.193 Marsh, James H. (Editor in Chief). *The Canadian Encyclopedia, Second Edition*. Edmonton: Hurtig Publishers, 1988. page 2344; p.194 Marsh, James H. (Editor in Chief). *The Canadian Encyclopedia, Second Edition*. Edmonton: Hurtig Publishers, 1988. page 2344; p.197 Richard Rhodes. *The Making of the Atomic Bomb*. New York: Simon & Schuster, 1984. page 714; p.201 Jessica Pegis; p.202 Justice Robert Jackson, October 20, 1945, Nuremberg, Germany, source: <http://www.courttv.com/old/casefiles/nuremberg/legacy.html>; p.204 Christopher A. Sharpe, "Military Activity in the Second World War," Plate 47 of Donald Kerr and Deryck W. Holdworth, eds., *Hiistorical Atlas of Canada*, vol. 3 (Toronto: University of Toronto Press, 1993). page 294; p.218 Munro, Iain R. *Immigration*. Toronto: Wiley Publishers of Canada, 1978. p.62. Source: Fitzgerald. *The Cold War & Beyond*. Scarborough: Nelson, 1995. page 28; p.264 Colombo, John R., ed. *1999 The Canadian Global Almanac*. Toronto: Macmillan Canada, 1998. page 271; p.289 *House of Commons Debates: Official Report*, Vol. VIII, 1971. Ottawa: The Queen's Printer, 1971. October 8, 1971, pages 8545–6; p.290 Statistics Canada website: <http://www.statcan.ca/english/Pgdb/People/Population/demo25a.htm>; p.297 Miyuke Tanobe, quoted in a feature on her work *My floating world—Miyuke Tanobe*. NFB video; p.306 Dickason, Olive Patricia. *Canada's First Nations: A History of Founding Peoples from Earliest Times*. Toronto: McClelland & Stewart Inc., 1992. page 406; p.307 Berger, Thomas R. "The Constitution, the Charter and 'Fragile Freedoms'." *The Canadian Forum* (May 1982). page 14; p.312 Colombo, John R., ed. *1999 The Canadian Global Almanac*. Toronto: Macmillan Canada, 1998. page 201; p.316–317 Radwanski, George. *Trudeau*. Toronto: Macmillan of Canada, 1978. page 326; p.9 Bothwell, Robert, Ian Drummond, and John English. *Canada since 1945: Power, Politics, and Provincialism*. Toronto: University of Toronto Press, 1996. page 373; p.321 Colombo, John R., ed. *1999 The Canadian Global Almanac*. Toronto: Macmillan Canada, 1998. page 65; p.325 <source: http://cbc.ca/news/indepth/unity/links.html>; p.326 Bothwell, Robert, Ian Drummond, and John English. *Canada since 1945: Power, Politics, and Provincialism*. Toronto: University of Toronto Press, 1996. pages 384–385; p.340 Colombo, John R., ed. *1999 The Canadian Global Almanac*. Toronto: Macmillan Canada, 1998. page 201; p.341 Trudeau, three par. excerpt from Trudeau, Pierre Elliott. *Memoirs*. Toronto: McClelland & Stewart, 1993. pages 190–191; p.342 Colombo, John R., ed. *1999 The Canadian Global Almanac*. Toronto: Macmillan Canada, 1998. page 197; p.349 Colombo, John R., ed. *1999 The Canadian Global Almanac*. Toronto: Macmillan Canada, 1998. page 216; p.357 Trudeau, Pierre. "Hypocrisy' to protest cruise." *The Toronto Star*. 10 May 1983. page A13; p.368 Bothwell, Robert, Ian Drummond, and John English. *Canada since 1945: Power, Politics, and Provincialism*. Toronto: University of Toronto Press, 1996. page 19; p.371 National Council of Welfare. *Poverty Profile 1996*. Ottawa: Minister of Public Works and Government Services Canada, 1998. page 34; p.375 Colombo, John R., ed. *1999 The Canadian Global Almanac*. Toronto: Macmillan Canada, 1998. page 49; p.377 Governor General Adrienne Clarkson, October 7, 1999; her first public speech as Governor General, Source: the GG website; p.382 Kingwell, Mark and Moore, Christopher. *Canada Our Century*. Toronto: Doubleday Canada, 1999. page 453; p.383 Chief Justice Catherine Fraser, on Bill C-68 Source: Alberta Courts website; p.400 Colombo, John R., ed. *1999 The Canadian Global Almanac*. Toronto: Macmillan Canada, 1998. page 178; p.403 Harper, Elijah and Pauline Comeau. *No Ordinary Hero*. Vancouver: Douglas & McIntyre, 1993. page 1; p.405 Prime Minister's Web Site: <http://pm.gc.ca/>; p.415 Colombo, John R., ed. *1999 The Canadian Global Almanac*. Toronto: Macmillan Canada, 1998. page 204; p.429 Draper, Graham, Fred McFadden, Don Quinlan, and Victor Zenliski. *Twentieth Century Viewpoints: An Interpretive History*. Toronto: Oxford University Press, 1996. page 2350; p.434 Robert Fowler, Canada's ambassador to the UN, in a speech to the Security Council on 12 December 1995; p.436 Lloyd Axworthy, speech of February 5, 1997; p.439 Dr. Omar Del Pozo, leader of Cuban opposition group, to Amnesty International, p.445 Sources: G7 G8: <http://www.library.utoronto.ca/g7/what_is_g7.html> WTO: <http://www.wto.org>; p.446 Kenna, Kathleen. "NAFTA hasn't hurt wages or jobs, bank survey says." *The Toronto Star*. 4 March 1998. page A15; p.449 Lloyd Axworthy, speech given June 19, 1998; p.458 Colombo, John R., ed. *1999 The Canadian Global Almanac*. Toronto: Macmillan Canada, 1998. page 63; p.459 Elinor Caplan, Minister of Citizenship and Immigration, December 10, 1999; p.461 Montgomery, L. M. *The Selected Journals of L. M. Montgomery*. Edited by Mary Rubio and Elizabeth Waterston. Toronto: University of Toronto Press, 1987. page 234; p.462 Based on "Myths and Realities, The Economic Power of Women-Led Firms in Canada," a 1996 study conducted by Dun & Bradstreet Information Services and Bank of Montreal's Economics Department, with funding from Bank of Montreal's Institute for Small Business. Reprinted by permission of Dun & Bradstreet Information Services and Bank of Montreal.